THE VENERABLE AND ADORABLE EUCHARIST

A Study of the Lutheran Doctrine of the Lord's Supper in the 1500s

TOM G. A. HARDT

Translated by Mark DeGarmeaux

CONCORDIA PUBLISHING HOUSE • SAINT LOUIS

Respectfully dedicated to
Professor Hermann Sasse

3558 S. Jefferson Ave., St. Louis, MO 63118-3968
1-800-325-3040 • cph.org

Unless otherwise indicated, all quotations in this volume are translated from the Swedish edition.

Quotation from the Lutheran Confessions on the back cover is taken from *The Book of Concord: The Confessions of the Evangelical Lutheran Church*, edited by Theodore G. Tappert, published in 1959 by Fortress Press.

Manufactured in the United States of America

2 3 4 5 6 7 8 9 10 32 31 30 29 28 27 26 25 24

Contents

Foreword

TOM G. A. HARDT dedicated his 1971 doctoral dissertation to Professor Hermann Sasse. That dedication points to the genesis of *The Venerable and Adorable Eucharist* [*Venerabilis et Adorabilis Eucharistia*]. Later, in 1995, Hardt pointed to a specific writing by Sasse that began the journey which became this volume: "I had not reached the age of twenty-one when I wrote my first letter to Hermann Sasse, having read his *Vom Sakrament des Altars*, which raised some questions for me. I was at that time a student of history at the Royal University of Stockholm. . . . It was from Australia that the answer eventually came, an answer that in time would change not only my life, but the lives of others as well."[1] The correspondence between the two continued until Sasse's death in 1976.

Sasse has been referred to as a "lonely" or "stand-alone" Lutheran. The two-volume set of collected essays and letters of Sasse entitled *The Lonely Way* reflects the epithet that was applied to him. In the context of Confessional Lutheranism, the term describes one who professes the doctrines of Holy Scripture as set forth in the Lutheran Book of Concord and who is led for the sake of conscience to separate from a previous fellowship that has departed from a conscientious adherence to the Lutheran Confession. Sasse marked the time in 1948 when he could no longer stand with the Bavarian church in Germany and resigned his membership there. He then joined the *Evangelisch-lutherische Kirche* (*Altlutherische*), later accepting a position in Australia.

Much of Tom Hardt's life was also lived under the mantle of "lonely Lutheran." While at Sweden's Uppsala University, Hardt and other like-minded

1 Tom G. A. Hardt, "Hermann Sasse in His Letters," *Logia: A Journal of Lutheran Theology* 4, no. 4 (1995): 5. *Vom Sakrament des Altars* is a collection of Sasse's essays on the Lord's Supper that was published in 1941. It may be considered the forerunner of Sasse's *This Is My Body*. See Ronald Feuerhahn and Matthew Harrison, eds., *The Lonely Way* (St. Louis: Concordia Publishing House, 2002), 2:11. When Hardt published a popular summary of his dissertation, he entitled it *Om altarets sakrament* in honor of Sasse's *Vom Sakrament des Altars* (see below, p. vi n. 4).

Confessional Lutheran students formed a club devoted to studying Lutheran doctrine and piety. When Hardt concluded that it was impossible for him to be ordained by the Church of Sweden, the small group followed him and organized St. Martin's Evangelical Lutheran Church. Since he could not accept ordination by the Church of Sweden, Tom was ordained by the congregation, following Philip Melanchthon's conclusion in the Treatise on the Power and Primacy of the Pope that if the bishops are heretical or will not ordain pastors, the congregations would have to do it themselves.[2]

For the next forty years, Tom served as pastor of St. Martin's congregation. The congregation could not boast of much growth; it was isolated from the Church of Sweden and had no formal connection to any other church. Yet in his isolation, Hardt carried on a worldwide correspondence, serving not only those lonely Lutherans in Sweden but also faithful Confessional Lutherans the world over. Much of his correspondence was of a scholarly nature, but Hardt's weekly sermons in Swedish were read widely in Sweden and beyond and were appreciated for their faithful, Law-Gospel preaching.

Hardt was not without his detractors. He gave me a copy of his dissertation, *Venerabilis et Adorabilis Eucharistia*, apologizing that it had been sent originally to an Uppsala professor who returned it unread—with his condemnation of the book. With his tiny, insignificant congregation and lack of a well-paid academic position, Hardt was not highly regarded, but he understood this slight in the light of Jesus' dictum that "no prophet is accepted in his own country" (Luke 4:24). Yet outside Sweden, Hardt found many supporters and received praise for his theology of the Lord's Supper and his research skills.

In an essay for the fiftieth anniversary of St. Martin's Lutheran Church in Stockholm (1961–2011), Pastor Sten Rydh writes that "Tom Hardt's mentor was the great Lutheran theologian Hermann Sasse."[3] It was a mentorship carried on almost completely by mail. Hardt emphasized his debt to Sasse in a preface to the English translation of *Om Altarets Sakrament*: "The Rev. Professor Dr. Hermann Sasse, North Adelaide South Australia, had helped me from the very beginning of my career as a scholar . . . To the memory of my beloved Hermann Sasse I dedicate this book."[4] While walking on the beach of a Swedish island, Hardt made it clear to me that his interest in exploring more deeply the doctrine of the Sacrament of the Altar was because of Hermann Sasse. When Tom

2 See Robert Kolb and Timothy Wengert, eds., *Book of Concord* (Minneapolis: Fortress Press, 2000), p. 341 (Treatise 72).

3 Sten Rydh, Några tankar kring Tom Hardts teologi, Evangelisk-lutherska kyrkan i Sverige, St. Martin's Congregation. https://www.evluth.se/dokument/hardts_teologi.pdf. Accessed January 9, 2023.

4 Tom G. A. Hardt, *On the Sacrament of the Altar*, trans. Edward L. Rye (St. Catharines, Ontario: Concordia Lutheran Theological Seminary, 2007).

described feeling like a young student in the presence of a great teacher, I had a sense of what that felt like.

At various times, Dr. Hardt expressed his hope that the dissertation could be translated into English. In 1980, Hardt had his attorney draw up a legal document designating Bjarne and Erling Teigen his agents for any publication of his works in the United States. This was accomplished for a small summary of his dissertation intended for laity under the title *Om Altarets Sakrament.* While published in German translation in 1988,[5] when Hardt passed away in 1998 his dissertation had not yet been translated into English. Now, fifty years after its first publication, English readers have access to the results of Hardt's research. We are grateful to Prof. Mark DeGarmeaux for the translation.

We express our thanks also to the children of Dr. Hardt for granting permission to publish this book. The power of attorney for publishing Tom's writings ended with his death in 1998, and thus it became necessary to ask his heirs, whom I had learned to know while visiting the Hardts several times in the 1990s, to authorize publication.

The Hardt home, with four of the six children still living there, was a cordial, warm, busy household. Karin Hassler Hardt was not only an excellent hostess and homemaker but also a multilingual, with a master's degree in theology from Uppsala University. Rare is the scholar who can footnote the scholarship of his wife: Hardt cites Karin Hassler Hardt on Luther and the elevation of the Sacrament (below, p. 236 n. 6). The Hardt children were also multilingual, well-informed, and able to participate in the table talk. The evening meal with the Hardts was delightful, filled with wide-ranging discussion and family devotion that would include a Swedish hymn accompanied by one of the sons at the piano. We are most grateful to Dr. Hardt's children for making the translation and publication of this important theological research possible.

Erling T. Teigen, Professor Emeritus
Bethany Lutheran College, Mankato, Minnesota
Eastertide 2023

5 Tom G. A. Hardt, *Venerabilis et adorabilis eucharistia: Ein Studie über die Lutherische Abendmahlslehre im 16 Jh.*, trans. Susanne Diestelmann (Göttingen: Vandenhoeck & Ruprecht, 1988).

Translator's Preface

WHEN I was asked to translate Tom Hardt's dissertation on the Lord's Supper, I was curious and somewhat reluctant. I offered to make a start to see if I could do the work justice. Now, several years later, the reader may judge whether I have done so.

Deep and heartfelt thanks to Bror Erickson for proofreading the translation and giving helpful comments and suggestions.

Translation is an art as well as a skill. Word choices are not always simple. Some mistakes or misunderstandings are almost inevitable. The linguistic challenge here is that the main text is Swedish with very extensive quotations in sixteenth-century German and Latin. It is also a challenge to give an accurate translation of the philosophical and theological terminology. I hope that I have given a fair approximation to the language and the thoughts. I often give references to English translations such as American Edition of *Luther's Works* and the writings of Martin Chemnitz. These are for cross-reference and comparison; the text translations are almost always mine, though I did consult the other translations as well.

Hardt's dissertation represents extensive research of primary sources and careful analysis of secondary sources. I was privileged to work with Hardt's own copy, which contained corrections and notes that I have included or noted. Whether or not one agrees with all of Hardt's assessments, the research is valuable in giving a fuller picture of an important time in Lutheran theological history. He clearly shows how highly the Lutheran Church values the Sacrament of the Altar, the real presence of Christ in the Sacrament, the power of God's Word, and the comfort of forgiveness received in the Sacrament. It is my hope and prayer that the reader will find a greater appreciation for this blessed and comforting Sacrament through reading this work.

Mark DeGarmeaux

Introduction

HEARTY thanks are due to Professor Mark DeGarmeaux and to Concordia Publishing House for the unremitting toil of the former and the bold daring of the latter in publishing the *magnum opus* of an obscure theologian of the twentieth century whose major contribution to Lutheran theology and church life has threatened, since his death, to fall into the pit of oblivion.

As conscience dictated quitting his beloved Church of Sweden in the wake of the ordination of women in the late 1950s, and as it proved impossible for him to come into full communion with either of the two larger church bodies that emerged from the collapse of the Synodical Conference, Dr. Tom Hardt's unflinching fidelity to the Lutheran Symbols entailed poverty for his family along with ecclesial and scholarly isolation for himself. Much more than his beloved mentor and father in God, Hermann Sasse, Tom plowed his solitary furrow as the loneliest of the so-called "Lonely Lutherans." Hence his appreciation for the social life raft thrown out to him by Bjarne and Erling Teigen, uncle and nephew, in faraway Mankato, Minnesota.

Alas, Dr. Hardt's name was never mentioned as I researched, 798 miles from Stockholm, on Luther's eucharistic theology. I only heard his name during my sojourn at Westfield House, and not until I became fieldworker to the late Dr. Evanson at Redeemer, Fort Wayne, Indiana, did I gain a sense of Tom's background, context, achievement—and controversial quality. Encouraged by Dr. Evanson, I penned a letter—the old snail mail—to Dr. Hardt, receiving a reply in March 1984, the beginning of a steady stream of correspondence that only ended with his sudden death in the summer of 1998.

To begin with, we corresponded as "Dr. Hardt" with "Dr. Stephenson," but, noting that I signed one letter as simply "John," Tom invited me to address him in like terms. Almost a decade later, when I picked him up from the Toronto airport to be a major speaker at the Sasse Symposium at Concordia Lutheran Theological Seminary, St. Catharines, Ontario, I discovered the limits of Tom's "matey-ness." Having collected Gottfried Martens from another gate, German was the *lingua franca* of conversation, and Tom proved quite amenable to conversing in this tongue. However, on the way down the busy Queen Elizabeth Way, already addressing my two passengers with the plural *Ihr*, I turned to the back seat and used the *Du* form specifically for Tom. A wall of ice swiftly descended upon the inside of the vehicle, and after some silence, Tom explained that he could not possibly indulge in such verbal familiarity. Thinking quickly, I switched over to English, a move that swiftly thawed the ice. An ecumenical acquaintance told me some years ago how the late Edmund Schlink became the fastest of friends with an Orthodox bishop whom he encountered at an ecumenical dialogue. At the end of the meeting, which had been held in English, Schlink said to his valued comrade, "You may call me you."

Happily, Tom stayed in St. Catharines for a few days after the symposium ended, which gave the opportunity for him to come twice to dinner at our house and for me to take him to view Niagara Falls, an office gladly repeated for his widow, Karin, when she stopped over in St. Catharines after visiting the Teigens in Mankato a couple of years after his death. Tom explained to me how his correspondence with Hermann Sasse turned into a deep friendship across the generations, and how Sasse stayed at least once in the Hardt's Stockholm apartment. After much pressing, Tom consented to address the distinguished Herr Professor as "Hermann," but adamantly drew the line at accepting the older man's invitation to use the familiar *Du*.

Tom was an exquisitely courteous and dazzlingly learned Swede who represented a type presumably now extinct in that ancient kingdom. I recall his loyalty to his king and his love for Queen Sylvia, whom he regarded in his heart as an orthodox Lutheran. (Karin disagreed, expressing irritation over her German-born majesty's inability properly to pronounce a certain Swedish word.) One lunchtime at the Symposium, I looked across to see Tom conversing with a group of Quebecois whose English I knew to be almost nonexistent. Upon asking how they had managed to speak so easily with our Swedish guest, the brethren from *la belle Province* informed me that Dr. Hardt was fluent in French.

Hardt's scholarship, refined over long hours sitting at his own cubicle in Stockholm's Royal Library—he must have had an ample supply of what Heiko Oberman called *Sitzfleisch*—dealt the knockout blow in the running controversy (begun by Hermann Sasse?) over the nature of the consecration in the Lutheran Mass. Old habits die hard, with the result that conservative Lutherans in Europe and North America read the Formula of Concord through lenses supplied by the middle and closing periods of Lutheran Orthodoxy. The elements are set apart for sacred use by the recitation over them of the *verba testamenti*, and the Lord's body and blood are distributed *with* the consecrated elements, their presence restricted to a second or two. Already in the nineteenth century, Wilhelm Löhe, no professional scholar, suspected on the basis of his research that this was not the case, but that Luther at any rate timed the presence from the consecration, insisting that the bread *is* the body and the wine *is* the blood, a state of affairs requiring the reverent consumption of the *reliquiae*. Tom was not the only twentieth-century scholar to correct a long-standing misunderstanding of the Formula of Concord and other early Lutheran sources—Edward F. Peters, Jobst Schöne, and later Bjarne W. Teigen deserve their share of credit—but the sheer level of his scholarship towers over the rest of us who have argued the "Luther line," who are of medium height and perhaps even pygmies when stood alongside him.

Early in our friendship, Tom gave me the paperback copy of *Venerabilis et adorabilis eucharistia* that he had earlier bestowed on the lady who had been his nanny, and in due course Susanne Diestelmann's German translation landed on my bookshelves. The scholarship underlying this dissertation is of stunning quality, its author displaying a mind that could have kept up with Thomas Aquinas step by step. He reaches back into the ancient church and demonstrates a knowledge of medieval scholasticism that has perhaps been equalled by no Lutheran for centuries. Moreover, he details the contrary opinions of Melanchthon and lays out in black and white the range of opinions held by the first and second generations of Lutheran divines. If you want to know what the sixteenth-century Lutherans believed, confessed, and practiced concerning the Sacrament of the Altar as opposed to what they are said to have said, then be Concordia Publishing House's guest and *tolle, lege* ["take and read"].

Hardt's published dissertation is one of the great works of historical theology to emerge from the twentieth century, but it is devoutly to be wished that he be accorded a wider role as interlocutor of North American Lutheran theologians in the century that is now in its third decade. In the early days of our acquaintance, Tom contributed a stellar piece of Walther scholarship to the *festschrift* in honor of Robert Preus, whom he delighted to meet in person for the first time at table on the last night of our Sasse Symposium. "My dear brother, I had a most delightful time with Dr. Robert Preus; we discovered that we are fourth cousins." Hardt's symposium paper doubtless exceeded the capacities of not a few of his listeners as he drilled deep into the wells of what our Roman Catholic friends label "fundamental theology." My conscience is afflicted as I recall replacing his "gnoseology" with "epistemology," much to his displeasure; someone, please explain to me the difference. Shortly after the symposium and the death of Dr. Preus, Hardt agreed to write the Confessional Lutheran Dogmatics volume *de sacra scriptura*, a commitment rendered impossible by his own sudden death. And there are a host of untranslated papers and essays to render into English for the edification of the brethren.

Polycarp asked for an hour of prayer time before the Smyrna police force took him to the city's stadium for a martyr's death and is remembered to have spent more than twice that time "remembering all he had ever known in the catholic Church." Should I be allowed and take advantage of such a prayer opportunity when my own time to depart this world arrives, I shall certainly spend some minutes recalling with thanksgiving Tom and Karin Hardt, whose friendship I cherish and whose company we hiddenly enjoy at each celebration of the *venerabilis et adorabilis Eucharistia*.

Those who open this volume are in for a challenging read as Dr. Hardt practices scholarship at a level almost universally unknown in our Anglosphere. So I recommend preparation for this venture by digesting appropriate secondary literature, and not least by carefully studying the popular shorter version available in Swedish and English under the title *On the Sacrament of the Altar*. Having taken those baby steps, may those who undertake the intellectual marathon of covering the successive chapters of this book be vouchsafed to make their own the words of Bunyan's Pilgrim as he is about to enter the Celestial City: "Though with great difficulty I have got hither, yet do I not repent me of all the trouble I have been at to arrive where I am."

John R. Stephenson
St. Catharines, Ontario
Monday of the First Week of Lent 2023

Abbreviations

AC	Augsburg Confession.
ADB	*Allgemeine Deutsche Biographie.* Edited by Historische Kommission bei der Bayerischen Königlichen Akademie der Wissenschaften. Leipzig: Duncker & Humblot, 1875–1912. Reprinted, 1967–71.
AE	*Luther's Works*: American Edition. Volumes 1–30: Edited by Jaroslav Pelikan. St. Louis: Concordia Publishing House, 1955–76. Volumes 31–55: Edited by Helmut Lehmann. Philadelphia/Minneapolis: Muhlenberg/Fortress, 1957–86. Volumes 56–82: Edited by Christopher Boyd Brown and Benjamin T. G. Mayes. St. Louis: Concordia Publishing House, 2009–.
Ap	Apology of the Augsburg Confession.
ARG	*Archiv für Reformationsgeschichte.*
Birch	Birch, T. Bruce, ed. *The De Sacramento Altaris of William of Ockham.* Burlington, IA: Lutheran Library Board, 1930.
BS	*Die Bekenntnisschriften der evangelisch-lutherischen Kirche.* 2nd edition. Göttingen: Vandenhoeck & Ruprecht, 1952.
CCSL	*Corpus Christianorum: Series Latina.* Turnhout: Brepols, 1953–.
CR	*Corpus Reformatorum.* Volumes 1–28: *Philippi Melanthonis Opera quae supersunt omnia.* Edited by C. G. Bretschneider and H. E. Bindseil. Halle: C. A. Schwetschke, 1834–60. Volumes 29–87: *Ioannis Calvini Opera quae supersunt omnia.* Edited by W. Baum, E. Cunitz, E. Reuss. Braunschweig: C. A. Schwetschke & Sons, 1863–1900. Volumes 88–: *Huldreich Zwinglis Sämtliche Werke.* Edited by Emil Egli et al. Leipzig: Heinsius, 1905–.
CS	*Corpus Schwenckfeldianorum.* 19 volumes. Leipzig: Breitkopf & Härtel, 1907–61.
Denzinger	Heinrich Denzinger, ed. *Enchiridion symbolorum definitionum et declarationum de rebus fidei et morum.* 34th edition. Edited by Adolf Schönmetzer. Freiburg: Herder, 1967.
DWB	Jacob Grimm and Wilhelm Grimm. *Deutsches Wörterbuch.* 16 volumes in 32. Leipzig: S. Hirzel, 1854–1960.

E	*D. Martin Luthers sämmtliche Werke.* 67 volumes. Frankfurt and Erlangen: Carl Heyder, 1826–57.
Enders	Ernst Ludwig Enders, ed. *Dr. Martin Luther's Briefwechsel.* 19 volumes. Frankfurt am Main: Schriften-Niederlage des Evangel. Vereins, 1884–1932.
FC	Formula of Concord.
FC Ep	Epitome of the Formula of Concord.
FC SD	Solid Declaration of the Formula of Concord.
Friedberg	Emil Friedberg, ed. *Corpus Iuris Canonici.* 2 volumes. Leipzig: Tauchnitz, 1879. Reprint, Graz: Akademische Druck- u. Verlagsanstalt, 1959.
Jena edition of Luther's works	*Die erste [-achte] Teil aller Bücher und Schrifften des thewren/ selingen Mans Doc[tor] Mart[ini] Lutheri.* 8 volumes. Jena: Christian Rödinger, 1555–58. *Tomvs Primvs [-Qvartvs] Omnivm Opervm Reverendi Patris D. M. L.* Jena: Donatus Richtzenhain, 1564–70; Tobias Steinmann, 1600–1611.
*LTK*²	Josef Höfer and Karl Rahner, eds. *Lexikon für Theologie und Kirche.* 2nd edition. 14 volumes. Freiburg im Breisgau: Herder, 1957–68.
PG	*Patrologiae cursus completus: Series Graeca.* Edited by J.-P. Migne. 161 volumes in 167. Petit-Montrouge: Apud J. P. Migne, 1857–66.
PL	*Patrologiae cursus completus: Series Latina.* Edited by J.-P. Migne. 221 volumes in 223. Paris: Garnier Fratres, 1844–64.
RE	*Realencyklopädie für protestantische Theologie und Kirche.* 3rd edition. Leipzig, 1896–1913.
*RGG*³	*Die Religion in Geschichte und Gegenwart.* Edited by K. Galling. 7 volumes. 3rd edition. Tübingen, 1957–65.
SA	Smalcald Articles.
Sehling	Emil Sehling et al., eds. *Die evangelischen Kirchenordnungen des XVI. Jahrhunderts.* Volumes 1–5: Leipzig: O. R. Reisland, 1902–13. Volumes 6–: Tübingen: Mohr (Paul Siebeck), 1957–.
ST	Thomas Aquinas. *Summa theologica.*
StL	Johann Georg Walch, ed. *Dr. Martin Luthers sämmtliche Schriften: Neue revidirte Stereotypausgabe.* 23 volumes in 25. St. Louis: Concordia Publishing House, 1880–1910.
Triglotta	*Concordia Triglotta: The Symbolic Books of the Evangelical Lutheran Church.* St. Louis: Concordia Publishing House, 1921.
WA	*D. Martin Luthers Werke: Kritische Gesamtausgabe.* 73 volumes in 85. Weimar: H. Böhlau, 1883–.

WA Br — *D. Martin Luthers Werke: Briefwechsel*. 18 volumes. Weimar: H. Böhlau, 1930–.

WA TR — *D. Martin Luthers Werke: Tischreden*. 6 volumes. Weimar: H. Böhlau, 1912–21.

Walch — *D. Martin Luthers sowol in Deutscher als Lateinischer Sprache verfertigte und aus der letztern in die erstere übersetzte Sämmtliche Schriften*. Edited by Johann G. Walch. 24 volumes. Halle: Gebauer, 1740–53.

ZKG — *Zeitschrift für Kirchengeschichte*.

CHAPTER 1

Verum Corpus

The Identicalness of Christ's Heavenly and Eucharistic Body

IN the Christological statements of doctrine during the time of the early church, Christian theology worked out formulas that established the full and unrestricted humanity [human nature] of the God-man. In contrast to the Gnostic speculations about a "phantom" body, they placed the concept of a real man "with reasonable soul and human body," just as the Athanasian Creed asserted.[1] This statement was directed also against interpretations that occurred against an otherwise Christian background but which then attacked the concreteness of Jesus' humanity.[2] Even at the right hand of the Father, the Son must be completely and fully human. The ascension and the final exaltation do not nullify the reality of the incarnation. This idea, of the historic Jesus being proclaimed enthroned in the midst of the worlds by virtue of His Sonship with the Father, filled the believer with dread. The church father John Chrysostom speaks about this in lofty terms: "It is a great and incomprehensible miracle that our flesh is seated up there and is worshiped by angels and archangels. As often as I think about this, it is as if I were placed outside myself."[3]

1 Denzinger §§ 75–76. (*Svenska kyrkans bekännelseskrifter*, p. 49.) Completely devoted to this topic is Tertullian's writing *On the Body of Christ*, CCSL 2.871ff.

2 Compare to this [Reinhold] Seeberg, *Lehrbuch der Dogmengeschichte*, 3:273ff.; Denzinger § 146, *De incarnatione contra Appolinaristas* by Damasus; [Denzinger] §§ 357ff., *Professio fidei* of Anastasius II: "And not appearing as a phantom"; "But after the resurrection of the union of natures He never left the actual temple, nor can He leave on account of His unspeakable benevolence, but the Lord Jesus Christ Himself [is] both able to suffer and not able to suffer—able to suffer according to His humanity, not able to suffer according to His divinity"; [Denzinger] § 605, Nicene Council II, act VIII: "If anyone does not confess Christ our God as circumscribed according to His humanity, let him be anathema."

3 PG 63:46.

The same church father also stops in wonder before "heaven on earth."[4] The heavenly world is present, fully, on the Communion table of the Christian assembly. What makes heaven into heaven is not heavenly glory but the presence of the Lord, just as the focus of a royal fortress is not the splendor of the throne room but the physical presence of the king.[5] This sacramental presence builds on Jesus' words about the bread and the wine at the first Supper: "This is My body" and "This cup is the new testament in My blood" ([see] Luke 22:19f.). This presence is reiterated in all older statements of Christian doctrine, in the sense that there was never an express denial of the presence, as arises later.[6] On the other hand, the mode of the presence is the subject of various definitions and, in a certain way, the various alternatives that would rise later within these. Platonic philosophy, here as elsewhere, offered the possibility of spiritualizing such biblical concepts as were considered crass and repulsive.[7] Augustine can be listed as the best-known name in this tradition. His concept of the Sacrament is

---

4 PG 61:206.

5 Ibid.

6 The most easily accessible exposé of the early church's faith in the real presence is in Solano, *Textos eucharisticos primitivos*. Regarding what is said about the absence of an express denial of the real presence during the time of the early church, compare Sasse, op. cit., pp. 29ff. It is also the same observation that is behind Luther's words (WA 23:129.4ff. [cf. AE 37:54]):

> But it is a miracle that the fathers, as much as there is of them, never said anything at all about the Sacrament the way these Enthusiasts do. For they use no such words as "It is mere bread and wine" or "Christ's body and blood are not there." . . . Among so many fathers and so many writings there should be something negative once, as happens in other articles [of faith], but now they all are affirmatively unanimous and consistent. Our Enthusiasts, however, can say nothing at all except the negative.

Cleve (*Luthers nattvardslära*, p. 294 n. 92) misunderstands Luther when he summarizes this: "Luther underscores that all the church fathers were agreed that Christ's body and blood are present in the Supper. None of the church fathers denied this despite the fact that in many other questions they were disagreed." Luther did not express himself so simply. He pointed out that the Reformed *exegesis* in relation to that of the church fathers is an innovation and that the church fathers, who in "many other questions" clearly rejected heresy [were not "disagreed"], never *rejected* the real presence. Thereby the Reformed are without patristic support for their purely negative view. Luther does not say more than this and thereby formulates a statement that even today would be incontestable.

7 Contemporary research often allows for a Hellenistic-colored materialization of an originally nonrealistically understood Supper. The change is thought to have been inserted either in the post-biblical era, [or] with the evangelist John, with some of the Synoptics, or already in the whole biblical material. This research does not yet show to what extent the mystery religions, which never established their ideas in history, really were "realistic," and neither can it support a symbolic concept of the Supper in any older extrabiblical writing, which would be natural, if in any case some tradition of the Supper that was earlier was nonrealistic. Here compare [Albrecht] Peters, *Realpräsenz*,

"symbolic," insofar as the "sign" for him plays a decisive role, yet without thereby denying the presence, in a modern sense.[8] While Jesus' humanity, according to the principles of the history of salvation, takes its special place in the heavenly world without any change, it is made present on earth through its sign, the bread and wine of the Supper, which convey the content of the concept depicted, the Platonic Ideal. This original image [archetype], it is to be noted, is an almost independent reality in relation to the visible phenomenon.[9] It is this independence in relation to the material that makes it possible to assert that Christ's body is present in the Sacrament. Understood according to this scheme, such a "real presence" was asserted by Augustine with the whole realism of the liturgical tradition: Jesus' body and blood are received by all, regardless of faith; Judas received the true Sacrament; at the first consecration Jesus bore Himself in His hands.[10] Herein lies the tension that brings about such different interpretations of Augustine's doctrine of the Supper. Herein also lies the origin of the later Augustinian school's distinction between the heavenly and the eucharistic body of Christ. Modern deniers of the presence often cite Ratramnus of Corbia, who in the year 844 wrote his critique of the doctrine of the Supper [put forward by] his abbot, Radbertus Paschasius. He was simply supposed to have asserted such a presence "*ad modum ideae*."[11]

A different dogmatic tradition in the matter of understanding the presence worked without this philosophical structure of concept. This realistic view, however, came to use the term "change" in the face of similar complications. In and of itself, this word says no more than the simple idea that through the

pp. 170ff., with the detailed report of contemporary exegesis, as well as Sasse, "Das Abendmahl im Neuen Testament," pp. 26ff.

8 Seeberg, op. cit., 2:460: "does not exclude the real presence of Christ"; compare *LTK*[2] 1:1099, "Augustinus."

9 *LTK*[2] 3:1148, "Eucharistie": "In which the points under consideration [Platonizing designations of the elements as symbols] . . . are to be understood in an ancient-realistic sense as means of visualization, a mode of appearance of the original image"; compare also *Dictionnaire de théologie catholique* 5:1173ff., "Eucharistie d'après les pères"; *RGG*[3] 1:24f., "Abendmahl." On the question of the independence of ideas, compare Gilson [and] Böhner, *Die Geschichte der christlichen Philosophie*, p. 184: "The things thus have a double existence: a real created one and one imagined [*gedachte*] by God, in the Son, generated, eternal . . . ."

10 PL 38:303, 453.

11 Jorissen, *Die Entfaltung der Transsubstantiationslehre bis zum Beginn der Hochscholastik*, p. 5. Jorissen (pp. 4ff.) gives an overview of literature concerning the controversy between Radbertus and Ratramnus. The most recent interpretation, to which the text above is connected, is summarized: "How, according to Platonic-Neoplatonic thinking, phenomena really participate in the eternal ideal, as participated existence [*partizipierten Sein*], however, are distinct from the ideal itself, 'so also the sacramental body of Christ is a real'—as such, at the same time also really distinct—'phenomenon of the genuine reality of the ideal of the Risen One above and of His heavenly power.'"

miracle of the consecration the common earthly elements become Christ's body and blood. "Change" in this sense is found already in John Chrysostom and his Western contemporary, Ambrose. It is liturgically set in the Eastern, Gallican, and Spanish orders of Divine Service. It is accepted as ordinary use of language both in Latin and Eastern Christianity as an expression of the start of the presence, and it is repeated in this universal meaning also in Luther and in one place in the Lutheran Confessions.[12] But already early on, among some fathers an attempt was made to give the concept of change a more set significance. If the bread is Christ's body, it must rest on an occurrence like the one during Jesus' earthly lifetime, when the bread that He ate was, of course, changed into His corporeality. Another parallel, for example, is changing the water into wine at Cana. The underlying logic in this case is that two things cannot be one without the one having to suppress the other and the incoming material arising from what disappears. The thought is found already in Gregory of Nyssa[13] and above all in John of Damascus.[14] Two difficulties arise from this: it calls into question whether the bread and wine still endure in reality after the consecration; and the relation between the heavenly and eucharistic body of Christ becomes unclear, just as in the Augustinian tradition. The eucharistic body of Christ becomes a newly created body, no longer completely identical with the Lord's previously existing corporeality. This, of course, through the miracle of the change, came to include what did not belong to it previously, and thus is extended through a new, special eucharistic body. The German researcher Rudolf Rocholl gives proper attention to this in the systematic difficulty of maintaining the identity between the heavenly and eucharistic body for which theologians of almost every era strive. The mode of presence of the heavenly body threatened to call that identity into question.[15]

In the middle of the 1000s, Berengar of Tours polemicized against the realistic tradition of interpretation. The solution he offered meanwhile is no longer an Augustinian spiritualizing. For the first time, a direct denial of the presence is expressed. The basis for this denial is the conviction that if Jesus' body and blood

12 Here compare Sasse, *This Is My Body*, pp. 27ff.

13 *Orat. Catech.* 37 (PG 45:93ff.); compare *Die deutsche Thomas-Ausgabe* 30:514; Rocholl, *Die Realpräsenz*, p. 286.

14 *Orth. Fid.* 4.13 (PG 94:1135ff.); Rocholl, op. cit., p. 287. The sixteenth-century Lutheran theologian Martin Chemnitz (*Repetitio sanae doctrinae*, p. 308) dates the doctrine of transubstantiation in its oldest form to the Damascene [John of Damascus].

15 Rocholl, op. cit., pp. 286ff. Rocholl writes (op. cit., pp. 286f.): "It would be most valuable if someone would undertake to show how the Church, in conclusive doctrine of the Eucharist, endeavored to present the identity of the body of the exalted Lord and the sacramental body. . . . We will find how the identity of the heavenly and the eucharistic body, to which naturally every dogmatician wants to adhere, soon goes missing again . . ." Compare also Seeberg, op. cit., 2:330ff.

were really made present in the Sacrament, it must be a presence of the heavenly Lord, concretely understood. This concrete presence is impossible, meanwhile, for only the bread and wine on the altar exist concretely. The substance of a thing includes its visible characteristics, and since bread and wine are visibly unchanged, thus Christ's body and blood are not present.[16] When Berengar was forced by the Church to confess the traditional, realistic understanding of the presence, it comes in the form of a confession of the change of substance, the very one that he himself defined and disputed. First, the heretic Berengar had introduced the dual concepts of substance and accidence (*subiectum—id, quod in subiecto est*), and church orthodoxy took them over. From the year 1079, in his confession "*Ego Berengarius*," there was the expression "*substantialiter converti*" ["substantially changed"] regarding the miracle of the Supper.[17] The synodal authority of these [words] implied an essential point in the development. Every responsible theologian now has to occupy himself systematically with what the change of substance means.

Proceeding from Berengar's premises, some asserted that the concrete, heavenly body of Christ actually precludes the existence of the bread on the altar. Thus there is no earthly element on the altar, but only an appearance.[18] The breaking of bread, then, is a simple illusion.[19] Against these conclusions, which must be understood as offensive, the thesis is set forth that it is possible to distinguish accidence and substance so that the change of the latter leaves the former intact. Such an objection was formulated by Thomas Aquinas: the truth of the Sacrament does not allow reason to be deceived in what occurs under its jurisdiction.[20]

Thomas Aquinas then develops his form of the doctrine of transubstantiation, which was set as church doctrine in 1215, but without precisely indicating its meaning.[21] Thomas's agreement with a previous, sensorial concept of substance has consequences not only for maintaining the reality of the visible gifts but also for the definition of the nature of the invisible gifts. With Thomas, the

16 Jorissen, op. cit., pp. 6ff. This sensorial concept of substance appears again in the late-ancient philosopher Boethius.

17 Denzinger § 700.

18 Jorissen, op. cit., pp. 75ff. This depiction is found again, among others, in *Sententia Divinitatis* (1141–1147/48).

19 This opinion is expressed from *Sententia Divinitatis*: "It seems to be broken, and it is not broken. . . . Just as the form of a man appears [to be] in a mirror and nevertheless is not, and a stick seems broken in water and yet is not." Jorissen, op. cit., p. 78 n. 46. The same view is found in Guitmund of Aversa, PL 149:1434f. Compare *Die deutsche Thomas-Ausgabe* 30:427.

20 *ST*, III, qu. 77, 7: "But this cannot stand, because in this sacrament of truth, sense is not deceived concerning those things, which are proper for it to judge."

21 Jorissen, op. cit., pp. 65ff.

"how" of the Supper can be said to govern even the "what" of the Supper. Thomas shows the necessity of transubstantiation against the theory that Christ's body coexists with the host, so that it is the plain substance of Christ's body in all its physical concreteness that becomes present, distinct from accidence, quantity, and quality. One can question whether the Augustinian definition of the presence does not in fact enter in here again, in a certain way. This spiritualizing trait does not lie in actually denying the continued existence of the substance of the bread but in the assertion of the Supper "*per modum substantiae*,"[22] not a different presence "*per modum ideae*." Certainly, when Thomas contrasts the "*per modum substantiae et non per modum quantitatis*"[23] against each other, it can be thought to include little more than avoiding the aforementioned offensive, coarse form of the presence. Clarity about the design of thought is achieved, however, through a closer study of one section in Thomas that gives an almost inexhaustible presentation of his doctrine of transubstantiation in terms of its rational justification. He writes:

> But this position [namely, the coexistence of Christ's body and the substance of the bread] cannot stand: first, because this position destroys the truth of this Sacrament to which it pertains, that the true body of Christ exists in this Sacrament, which indeed is not there before the consecration. But something cannot be where it was not before except by actually changing places or by converting the other thing into itself, just as a fire starts up anew in some house either because it is brought there or because it is generated there. But it is obvious that the body of Christ does not begin to be present in this Sacrament by local movement. First, because it would follow that it would cease to be in heaven: indeed, because what is moved locally does not come to some new place unless it leaves the previous one. Second, because every body that is moved locally passes through all the places in between, which cannot be said here. Third, because it is impossible that one movement of the same body, moved locally, ends up in various places at the same time, nevertheless the body of Christ under this Sacrament begins to be in many places at the same time. And so it remains that the body of Christ cannot begin to be in this Sacrament anew except by converting the substance of the bread into [the body] itself; but what is converted into something does not remain when the conversion has taken place. Hence the conclusion in preserving the truth of this Sacrament is that the substance of the bread cannot remain after the consecration.[24]

Thomas thus begins by excluding the possibility of Christ moving locally to the Sacrament from the place in heaven where He is located after the ascension. Consequently, it would be in conflict with the doctrine of faith that Christ

22 *ST*, III, qu. 76, 1, 3.

23 Ibid.

24 *ST*, III, qu. 75, 2.

would leave the Father's right side, Christ would be compelled to pass through the intervening space, and, finally, the miracle of the Mass could not happen in more than one place at a time. Therefore, transubstantiation, the *illocal* change of substance, must occur, which does not include absurd physical consequences. It ought to be noted that Thomas's objections, cited above, build on all movement of Christ's body being physical and local, since it is a physical and local reality. Therefore, Thomas must find a plane where these laws do not apply: the illocal, nonphysical level of the substance.[25]

The ability of this substance to free its presence from any spatiality is emphasized by Thomas in the immediate context with the words "*per modum substantiae et non per modum quantitatis.*" Thomas wants to refute the objection to the real presence that Christ's body cannot be confined under the small dimensions of what is consecrated.[26] The solution then becomes that the substance is illocal: "But the actual wholeness of the substance is contained without distinction in small or large quantity; just as the whole nature of air is in a large or small [amount of] air, and the whole nature of a human being is in a large or small human being."[27] The "preposterous" idea that [even] a small portion of the gifts of the altar contains the whole body and blood of Christ is, for Thomas, actually not preposterous but rationally explicable: it belongs to the nature of the substance to be independent of the physical substrate, the material stretched out in space, through the complete freedom of the concept in contrast to the material world. When the question is put as to why Christ cannot be seen in His Sacrament, the answer given is that substances indeed are invisible: "But the substance, inasmuch [as it is] of this kind, is not visible to the physical eye,

25 Transubstantiation is justified by Thomas also purely in written form. *ST*, III, qu. 75, 2: "Second [first is the justification in the text cited above], because this position [the coexistence of Christ's body and the host] is opposed to the form for this Sacrament in which it is said, 'This is My body,' which would not be true if the substance of bread remained there; for the substance of bread is never the body of Christ; but rather this would have to be said, 'Here is My body.' " This reference to Scripture is the occasion for Thomas to judge the doctrine of the coexistence as heretical (compare Jorissen, op. cit., pp. 50f.). Yet thus it occupies only a different space. When Thomas asserts that the Words of Institution should have said, "Here is My body," about the substance of the bread being present, his axiom is that the bread cannot possibly be said to be Christ's body: "For the substance of bread is never the body of Christ." For the Reformation's critique of this postulation, see below, chapter 4.

26 *ST*, III, qu. 76, 1: "The dimension of the consecrated bread and wine is much less than the actual dimension of Christ's body." The formal consequences are not the invalidation of the real presence, but: "It cannot be, therefore, that the whole Christ is contained under this Sacrament."

27 *ST*, III, qu. 76, 1, 3.

nor is it subject to any of the senses, nor even to the imagination, but only to the intellect, whose object is 'what something is.'"[28]

Christ does not "hide" His presence in the host. The presence, as stated, is basically inaccessible to anything other than an intellectual consideration. The Christ who is visible through the popular miracle of change [popular view of transubstantiation] in the form of the Child Jesus, or the suffering man of sorrows, cannot possibly have reality for Thomas. If the eucharistic forms are thereby brought to an end, this highest manifestation of the presence has, in fact, gotten the presence to disappear. In order to make a continued presence possible in such a case, Thomas must accept that the element is changed only in respect to color and form but remains in its dimensions. The new form and color, which show Christ, are in such a case still only the "figure of the truth." This reasoning is valid only when the miracle demonstrates obvious permanence. Otherwise Thomas accepts merely an image, effected by God in the eye of the beholder, a purely subjective occurrence. Under no circumstances can it effect a real seeing of Christ in the host, for as a concrete, physical reality, He is not in the Sacrament, but in heaven.[29]

The kind of presence that applies here, according to Thomas, is not even the "*esse definitive*," which applies to the angels, but only *the relation to the space, which the substance has through its accidence.*[30] The remaining spatial accidence ("*dimensionibus alienis*") of the vanished, changed substance of the bread is the only intermediary link to space, whereby the principally illocal substance can obtain a kind of definition of place. Therefore, neither can Christ's body be said to be in the Sacrament "*mobiliter*" ["by movement"], so that the presence in the Sacrament in its essential meaning can be said to enter or cease.[31] Just as one can say that the unchangeable God ceases to be [present] in a thing through His general presence as Creator only by the thing itself ceasing to be, likewise change, and a presence that can cease, are ascribed to Christ's body only in the sense that the host perishes and thereby, in a transferred sense, the presence "ceases." Objectively no change has occurred in the heavenly existence of God or of Christ's body. They neither become present nor cease to be present in creation

28 *ST*, III, qu. 76, 7.

29 *ST*, III, qu. 76, 8.

30 *ST*, III, qu. 76, 5: "Whence it remains that the body of Christ is not in this Sacrament as in a place, but through the mode of substance, namely, in that mode by which a substance is contained by the dimensions, for the substance of Christ's body goes under the substance of bread in this Sacrament: whence as the substance of bread was not under its dimensions locally, but through the mode of substance, so neither is the substance of Christ's body . . . but the substance of Christ's body is compared to that place with half-alien dimensions."

31 *ST*, III, qu. 76, 6: "*Mobiliter*" thus has to do both with the immutability of the abstract characteristic as well as a physical change.

with respect to the host. Only a certain relationship begins or ceases: "*quaedam habitudo ejus ad sacramentum*" ["its certain relationship to the Sacrament"].[32] The presence is exclusively to relate to "*formae et spirtuales substantiae*" ["forms and spiritual substances"] and possesses no spatial definition that applies to Christ's body "according to itself."[33] Thomas's doctrine of transubstantiation, which usually is perceived as materialistic, is thus formulated in order to disallow the real presence's character of being present and instead to express it as a mere conceptual relationship. Statements about God's omnipresence and Christ's sacramental presence are of the same kind and express the [divine] Majesty's continuing theoretical, temporary connection with a physical thing, the origin and disappearing of which leave the other higher components of the relationship untouched. Without embracing the Cyrillian and later Lutheran presentation of Christ's divinized humanity,[34] Thomas still lets Christ's body in heaven take a perspective toward creation that is parallel to the divine, intangible omnipresence:

> Because that which of itself has an imperishable essence cannot have a perishable essence; but in a perishable thing, this [imperishable] thing ceases to be in it, just as God, whose essence is imperishable and incorruptible, ceases to be in any corruptible creature because the corruptible creature thus ceases to be. And in this way, since *Christ has of Himself an unfailing and incorruptible essence*, He ceases to be [present] under this Sacrament not by actually ceasing to exist, nor even through His own local movement, as is clear from what has been said, but [He ceases to be under this Sacrament] only by the fact that the forms [elements] of this Sacrament cease to be.[35]

Incorruptible existence is ascribed to Christ and His body, and this intangible can in no regard submit to any kind of attribute that belongs to creation.

While in Thomas, with each clarification, Christ's body in the Sacrament loses some of its concreteness, this is not a necessary consequence of every model of the doctrine of transubstantiation. Without applying the thoughts that let the bread become an illusion in order to ensure a real presence, other interpretations of the change of substance were able to allow that the ascended Jesus becomes concretely present on Christian altars. Bonaventure, who shares Thomas's zeal for the change of essence of the consecrated gifts and with reference to the text of the Words of Institution sharply rejects the possibility of a coexistence between

32 Ibid.

33 Ibid.

34 Compare below, chapter 2.

35 *ST*, III, qu. 76, 6. Some manuscripts omit "*of Himself* [*de se*]" in "*Christ has of Himself an unfailing and incorruptible essence.*" Compare *Die deutsche Thomas-Ausgabe* 30:109 n. 1. It ought to be noted that the physical mobility is contested only secondarily.

Christ and the elements,[36] does not have Thomas's reasoning concerning the logical necessity of transubstantiation and therefore does not teach a body of Christ deprived of accidence either.[37] The presence that Bonaventure embraces is not a presence "*modo substantiae*" or "*modo ideae*," but one that is unique, "sacramentally" miraculous,[38] somewhat limited compared to other *modi*. The full identicalness of the heavenly and eucharistic body of Christ is thereby maintained. The same way of thinking is found again in Scotus.[39]

Our current survey now approaches schools of theology and eras that are closer to our main subject, the Lutheran doctrine of the Sacrament. Just like them, their historical background is of unequivocal value in scholarly investigations. This applies especially to William of Ockham, whose whole theology and life's work face critiques that are diametrically opposed regarding their actual contents. That applies also to the topic of this chapter. In his dogmatic-historical

---

36 Compare here Thomas' identical argumentation, above, p. 7 n. 25.

37 Jorissen (op. cit., p. 53 n. 165) still asserts: "Essentially the same argumentation [namely, as in Thomas] is found in Bonaventure" with reference to Bonaventure, In IV, d. 11, p. 1 a. un. qu. 1. fund. 3. Seeberg again (op. cit., 3:525f.) differentiates the depictions made by Thomas and Bonaventure and thinks that Bonaventure asserts that Christ's body, precisely as organic and living, must possess intact quantity and accidence in the Supper (In IV d. 10, p. 1, a. un. qu. 2). — In the passage cited by Jorissen, indeed the assertion is repeated that Christ is not changed into bread and therefore should leave the Father's side according to the physical laws of motion, but instead that the bread is changed into Christ's heavenly body, whereby no local change needs to happen. This change is still not a Thomistic change of an abstract substance but [a change] into a full and complete ("*bene esse*") presence (In IV, d. 10, p. 1, a. un., qu. 2, ib., fund. 4): "Also, if quantity were not there, it would give up quantity; but giving up the absolute accidence influences the transformation according to form; therefore, the glorified body of Christ is transformed." A nonconcretely understood Christ thus would imply a humiliation of the glorified one, reasoning that is contrary to Thomas. Even if in Bonaventure local change and change of essence are the given alternatives, the nonlocal change still results in a new relationship to space. Compare *Scholion* in Bonaventure (*Opera omnia*, 4:243):

> But in his explanation of this matter elsewhere he somewhat favors Scotus. Besides the things that he says here at question 2 (d. 9, p. 1, a. un.), in d. 10 p. II, a. 1. qu. 1 he places transubstantiation in it only because Christ's body is *elsewhere* without its being changed; below in q. 6 (d. 11, p. 1, a. un.) he teaches that the phrase "the body of Christ *becomes*" [*fit*, "*comes to be (present)*"] is improper and that the proper one indeed is "*it becomes here*" [*fit hic*, "*comes to be (present) here*"].

A real making present is there, and the ideal is not used at all, which also fits with Bonaventure's greater independence from philosophy.

38 In IV, d. 10, p. 1, a. un., qu. 3. Bonaventure affirms the first of the alternatives—"whether Christ's body is on the altar according to its natural quantity, or is there abstract from quantity" (In IV, d. 10, p. 1, a. un., qu. 2)—but at the same time distances himself from a physically perceived presence.

39 Seeberg, op. cit., 3:526.

standard work, the German researcher Reinhold Seeberg asserts that Ockham teaches a completely spiritualized presence "in sharpest contrast to the actual body,"[40] and that Christ as the omnipresent one ("*ein gewisses allgegenwärtiges Etwas*" ["a certain omnipresent Something"]) was at hand in the Sacrament, without this presence being connected to the host. Therefore, Seeberg puts forward the following opinion from Ockham: "The body of Christ is present for everyone; it is itself immediately present, and by consequence that form of bread does nothing to the presence of the body, that is, the host," from which it should be clear that the bread is not significant ("*nihil facit*" ["does nothing"]) for the presence. In addition, Ockham is supposed to have taught that Christ in the Sacrament lacks quantity.[41] An essentially different meaning is found in current Roman Catholic researchers who with convincing breadth present material supporting their theses. These researchers still differ from one another in certain respects, whereby [Philotheus] Böhner and [Gabriel] Buescher represent a Franciscan tradition, characterized by an understanding of Ockham's thoughts as cohesive and thought out, while [Erwin] Iserloh presents a Thomistic critique of Ockham's reasoning, which, according to him, is unclear.[42] They are agreed about certain basic concepts. While Thomas excludes any movement of Christ's body, Ockham permits such by expanding the concept of movement. For Ockham it is not necessary that the previous locality is abandoned when something moves, for which reason Christ's body can begin to be present ("*incipit esse*") in the host without leaving the Father's right hand.[43] Furthermore, two things are able to coexist in the same place, just as at the Easter appearance to the disciples behind closed doors Christ's body really passed through these [doors]. Herewith the *logical* necessity of transubstantiation as a dogma that must still be accepted[44] falls away, since the relationship of the substance to the

40 Id., op. cit., p. 791.

41 Ibid.

42 A cursory presentation is found in Junghans, *Ockham im Lichte der neueren Forschung*, pp. 305ff.; see also Iserloh, *Gnade und Eucharistie in der philosophischen Theologie des Wilhelm von Ockham*, pp. 148ff.

43 Buescher, *Eucharistic Teaching of William Ockham*, p. 45: "Christ is truly changed, only locally and accidentally to be sure, but changed nevertheless in the proper and most strict sense of the word when He becomes present in the Eucharist. Such likewise is Ockham's conclusion." Compare Iserloh, op. cit., p. 165.

44 Junghans (op. cit., p. 317) refers generally to the dogmatizing of transubstantiation by Innocent III and the Fourth Lateran Council as responsible for theology subsequently being bound by it. Jorissen (op. cit., p. 62 n. 183) still shows that the "*determinatio ecclesiae*" was the motive for transubstantiation first coming up in Scotus, Ockham, and Biel, and that in earlier texts there are "references nowhere to the officially taught sanctioning of the doctrine of transubstantiation through the Fourth Lateran Council." Jorissen thinks that conciliar authority replaces *scriptural authority* when these later theologians "reject the stringency of the evidence of the Words of Institution (*quoad*

accidence no longer becomes the only way to define the spatial relationship of Christ's body in the Sacrament. Christ's body is not dependent on "external mediating dimensions" but has its own existence in the Sacrament. The debated continuation of Ockham's presentation, not cited above by Seeberg, reads thus: "God can preserve the body in that place where only the host is, and [He can] destroy the host; and this includes no contradiction, and by this deed the body of Christ would be present in that place immediately."[45] That the host does nothing for the presence means that Christ's body is immediately present in it, so that this [the host] is its [Christ's body's] definite position. If the host ceases, Christ's body can, without contradiction, exist in the same space that was recently occupied by the host. For Thomas this thought is unviable, since according to him Christ's body actually does not have its own spatial existence in the Sacrament.[46] On the other hand, what Seeberg means is that for Ockham, to the highest degree, the host and Christ's body would actually relate to each other. They have physical coexistence, and the presence is in no way changed into an indefinite omnipresence.

Seeberg's view that Ockham teaches a nonquantitative presence of Christ's body in the Sacrament is technically correct. Yet the difference with Thomas is clearly stated. First, Ockham denies the possibility of distinguishing substance and quantity in a material object, the principle that for Thomas made possible both the presence of the substance of Christ's body without quantity and the continuance of the substance of the host in its mere quantity.[47] Second, Ockham certainly accepts, in a sense that shall be examined more closely below, that Christ's body does not possess dimension in the Sacrament and therefore lacks

---

nos) [up to our time]." It would be even more correct to point to conciliar authority replacing the urgent *logical* necessity that came first, at least in Thomas, but fell away among the later [theologians].

45 Ockham, IV *Sent.*, qu. 4 N resp. ad 2. dubium, quoted according to Iserloh (op. cit., p. 197), which however does not respond to Seeberg, as here. To this indirect text citation, compare Junghans (op. cit., p. 361): "The Ockham texts were mostly taken from the footnotes of works by Böhner, Hochstetter, or Iserloh, since these authors had emended their Ockham texts by comparison with manuscripts."

46 Considerable lack of clarity in questions in this category is reported by Cleve (*Luthers nattvardslära*, p. 284 n. 55): "When it comes to the real presence, there is a distinction between Thomism and Nominalism. Only for Thomism is Christ's body not actually in the place where the substance of the bread is found, but Christ's body is present on the basis of natural accompaniment. Only for Nominalism is Christ's body present immediately and not on the basis of natural accompaniment." Despite the reference to Iserloh, op. cit., p. 174, Iserloh cannot be made responsible for Cleve's depiction. Cleve's "accompaniment" is a translation of the German word for concomitance, "*Mitfolge*," and Iserloh's reasoning has to do with the presence of the *quantity*, which is misunderstood by Cleve to the point that it is completely meaningless: "Christ's body is present on the basis of the natural accompaniment."

47 Iserloh, op. cit., pp. 174ff.

quantity, but at the same time he defines this mode of presence as possessing all possible realistic concreteness. Through Christ's body moving into the host, all the parts of Christ's body ("*organa*") come to occupy the same space there and are contained in the smallest part of the host. Here all the parts retain their distinct character and function, since this "*diffinitiva*"[48] presence, of course, does not include any physical abridgment of an existing "circumscribed" body under earthly conditions.[49] It is reasonably presumed, for example, that Christ's eye can exercise the function of seeing from the Sacrament. Christ's body itself would also be able to be seen, if God were not hindering this through special intervention. With that, Ockham's doctrine comes to offer the theological foundation for the visible reality of the eucharistic miracle of transformation. Iserloh writes: "As Ockham shows us, in this respect even scholarly theology has quickly trod the paths of popular piety."[50] In summary, Iserloh, who avowedly makes a Thomistic critique of Ockham, says, "Ockham thus has a rather massive idea of the definitive mode of existence of Christ's body."[51] The massiveness that is offensive from a Thomistic viewpoint lies in Ockham letting Christ's body be present as an independent subject and the consequences that flow from this. In contrast to the usual definitions of Realism as more focused on the obvious and tangible, and Nominalism as more focused on what is more vague and more speculative, a Thomistic theologian must condemn Ockham's doctrine as crass.

Iserloh meanwhile underscores very powerfully what, in his opinion, is contradictory in Ockham's doctrine. For Iserloh, Ockham's concession that Christ's body still lacks quantity in the Sacrament is evidence that his doctrine of the Eucharist is insufficiently cohesive. Iserloh's critique proceeds from never being able to say that quantity principally coincides with substance and that in the Sacrament it is *distinct* from the substance of Christ's body.[52] Meanwhile, he thereby postulates a Thomistic definition of quantity so that a likewise Thomistically understood substance of a pure spiritual kind should principally be said to be inseparably united to a dimensional quantity. With this premise it would indeed be illogical to understand the relationship as at once indissoluble and dissoluble. But Ockham thinks otherwise. For him the substance *is* material,

48 Ockham writes "*diffinitive*"; Thomas, "*definitive*." Compare Sasse, *This Is My Body*, p. 157, who points out that the usage is not identical. He would thereby intend that while Thomas limits the "*definitive*" presence to such a phenomenon as is present in a single place without therefore being "*circumscribed*," so that the thing corresponds to the dimensions of the space (*ST*, III, qu. 76, a. 5, ad 1), Ockham has "*diffinitive*" mean simultaneous existence in several places without circumscriptive attribute. Compare Iserloh, op. cit., p. 196.

49 Iserloh, op. cit., pp. 257ff.

50 Id., op. cit., p. 257, not p. 243.

51 Id., op. cit., p. 206.

52 Id., op. cit., pp. 188ff.

and "quantity" is only a statement that expresses this connection of the relationship to space, that is, that the substance-thing is circumscribed by space so that part is in the part (*pars in parte*). In the Sacrament there is no size or quantity of Christ's body *inasmuch as* Christ's body is not circumscriptively present *pars in parte*. Yet thereby a Thomistic quantity has not been loosed from Christ's body, so that a Thomistic substance enters into a quantity-less bareness and spirituality. The substance is instead present in the Sacrament so that in a supernatural way its materialness is made present in its totality in the host, "*totum in parte*" ["the whole in the part"]. The quantity is thereby "distinguished" from the substance; it is just not stated, since the materialness here does not occupy its usual spatial relationship. *Ockham's whole reasoning goes on to deny the Thomistic construction of an actually existing quantity that could "be distinguished" from the substance.* Iserloh's incorrect reasoning is expressed in his summary: "Substance and quantity must therefore, for Ockham, be seen ontologically, must be identical and inseparable from each other."[53] For Ockham again, quantity does not exist "ontologically." Iserloh comes closest to a correct presentation with a posed rhetorical question: "Does this relinquishing of quantity as absolute accidence thereby mean its evaporation into a mere idea or a mere connection perhaps to a place, whose loss of substance retains no existence?"[54] Here Iserloh has an idea of what Ockham expressed with the words that the quantity "is predicated contingently."[55] Otherwise, the significance of Ockham's definitions would be inaccessible to Iserloh.[56]

53 Iserloh, op. cit., p. 188; compare ibid.: "Dimension is an essential component or, better, an immediate given, we could say, a transcendental designation of matter or physical substance, which is inseparable from them, as these also cannot exist otherwise without quantity."

54 Ibid.

55 Ockham, "*Expositio aurea*," chapter 10, cited according to Iserloh, op. cit., p. 177.

56 The critique of Iserloh's critique that has been presented is repeated in the analyses of Ockham by Franciscan researchers Böhner and Buescher. Compare Buescher, op. cit., pp. 72ff. Böhner, "Recent Presentation of Ockham's Philosophy," p. 446 (= *Collected Articles on Ockham*, 12:142), which, against M. de Wulf, *Histoire de la Philosophie mediévale* (Louvain-Paris, 1947), 3:42, no. 382, asserts that Ockham is to have anticipated Descartes's thesis that "'dimension merges with the essence of the body' is incorrect. For actual extent has nothing to do with the 'essence' of a body or material substance, since it can be absent, as in the case of the body of Christ existing in non-quantitative manner in the Holy Eucharist." Iserloh (op. cit., pp. 188f.) finds Böhner's remark in and of itself to be correct, but it does not remove what is contradictory in Ockham's way of thinking. Junghans (op. cit., p. 308) relates to this:

> Despite Iserloh's objection, Böhner appears to me to have shown the way in which the solution to the problem is to be sought. For Ockham, quantity had not only no absolute existence, but it was also not even an absolute component of substance. It was only a description of one form of existence of the substance, namely, the circumscribed. The substance cannot be quantity

An indirect proof of consistency in Ockham's doctrine is that the scholastic tradition that joined itself to Ockham does not show any ambivalence either, in its assertion of the full identity between Christ's body in heaven and in the Eucharist.[57] [Gabriel] Biel, who can be seen as the foremost intermediary of this school's doctrinal legacy to the generation of the reformers, implements a more

> per se, but only one definite mode of appearance for the substance, namely, when it was in one place so that its totality would fill the whole place, and one of its parts, according to its extent, would fill one part of the place.

57 What Damerau (*Die Abendmahlslehre des Nominalismus insbesondere die des Gabriel Biel*) puts forth here is generally characterized by a low degree of accuracy. To Ockham *is ascribed* the presence of quantity (p. 183) under a reference to what Biel says about this (*Canonis misse expositio*, lec. 43 N and O), but the opposite is mentioned on pp. 52f. There the following critique is expressed concerning the Ockhamist Heinrich von Langenstein against his masterful exposition:

> He strikes Ockham decidedly in this, that he shows him that the true, organic Christ becomes a concept (*sensus*) in the Supper and has lost life and reality. Langenstein tries [to use] this revolutionary and abstract logical thinking that voids the theological reality in order to bring back an acknowledgment of the organic and really present Christ. That fits with his confession of faith that is filled with reality and indeed became for him the main concern in the evidence of his doctrine of the Supper.

The critique that Damerau sees Langenstein using against Ockham "though without mentioning his name" (op. cit., p. 48) consists in two theses being set against each other, of which the first is presumed by Damerau to be Langenstein's own, and the other, Ockham's spiritualistic one. In italics Damerau cites: "Nevertheless Langenstein now argues with this second one against the first." That would depend on Langenstein's thesis being the second one. The first thesis, as it presents the text cited by Damerau, is a speculative hypothesis about a form of *circumscribed* presence, all the details of which are misunderstood by Damerau. Langenstein assumes a change to Christ's heavenly location or His [presence] dressed in authority, through which Christ's body even so would be present in a circumscribed manner without a circumscribed relationship to the earthly location: "It would be restricted not into the body of Christ, but into some appropriate place or into having mere clothing, and thus it would be there dimensionally and in a circumscribed manner indeed, in a place outside itself, granted, not indeed a place that contains the forms in a circumscribed way, and that mode would be more beautiful. . . ." Damerau simply transcribes: "If the body of Christ in the Eucharist is restricted by space from the outside, then it is present in a circumscribed manner. But that cannot be understood concerning space that encloses the forms of appearance of bread and wine!" Just as little does Damerau understand the hypothesis that the target of the change [*terminus conversionis*] would be "the whole world," through which all circumscribed relationships that now exist would continue to exist intact definitively in the host. Damerau further asserts (p. 27) that the papal doctrinal commission in Avignon found fault with Ockham for the diffinitive mode of presence but not for the circumscribed; the fact is actually the opposite. Compare Pelzer ("Les 51 articles de Guillaume Occam censurés en Avignon en 1326," p. 261): "locally, which is erroneous," while only philosophical objections are directed against "*diffinitive*": "not touching the faith." Damerau's book displays similar misunderstandings very often. Furberg's critical words about Damerau (*Das Pater Noster in der Messe*, p. 189 n. 48) must therefore be granted. Furberg's judgment applies to

precise defining of terms concerning the concept of quantity, for which the attentive reader of Ockham's presentations should often look. Biel distinguishes the "quantity of mass" [*quantitas molis*] and the "discrete quantity of completion or duration" [*quantitas discretiva perfectionis aut durationis*], whereby the first is a quantity according to normal spatial conditions where the thing possesses "*partem extra partem*" ["part outside the part"], while the other is a quantity that does not possess size in a measurable sense but still has "*partes realiter distinctas*" ["genuinely distinct parts"] just as exist in the miraculous, definitive mode of presence.[58] That comes close to one of Ockham's own proposals, but [it] rejects the solution that "a quantity is there, but not there in a quantitative way."[59] Like Ockham, Biel supposes that Christ in the Sacrament can see the surroundings and that He Himself could be seen, if God did not command invisibility.[60] Biel thereby in principle affirms the possibility of the visible miracle in the

a sequel work by Damerau about Biel in the same series, but in its sharpness—"The work in question is of little value"—it applies also to the volume being discussed here.

58 Biel, op. cit., lect. 43 N and R. This distinction is not noted by Damerau, but only while giving attention to it is Damerau's proposition that Biel teaches the presence of quantity (Damerau, op. cit., p. 183) correct. Damerau defaces Biel's propositions in order to imply something overriding in Realism in relation to Ockham's supposed spiritualizing, which lacks any foundation in the texts. So it is said (Damerau, op. cit., p. 192) that Biel teaches a *mutatio deperditiva* of Christ's body, that is, that it would leave heaven at the consecration! Damerau cites (ibid., n. 113) Biel's *Canonis misse expositio*, lect. 46 R: "But it must be noted that when the body moves from the place it leaves to the place it acquires, there are two local changes: one deprived of the place that it leaves, the other the one acquired of the place that it enters," after which, by means of several points, the critical omitted passage is noted where Biel assures that "what is present is accessible anew by being locally changed according to the mode last spoken of." That is, Christ's body does *not* leave heaven according to a *mutatio deperditiva* without moving, but only according to a *mutatio acquisitiva*, so that while retaining its heavenly place it occupies a new one. Compare here Ockham's thoughts identical to this, above, p. 12, text associated with n. 45.

59 Ockham, *De sacramento altaris*, ch. 41 (Birch, p. 494).

60 Damerau (op. cit., p. 185) insists on the opposite with regard to Biel (op. cit., lect. 45 P), which is explained by Biel in the intended passage *referring to Scotus*. Lect. 45 Q thus takes Ockham's thesis ("*non assentit Ockham*"), the reasoning of which in its premises corresponds with Biel's, and gives expression to his meaning. As a rule Biel extrapolates the *last* thought repeated; compare op. cit., lect. 46 Aff., regarding the ability of Christ's body to be circumscribed in many places, at which Thomas is mentioned, letter B, and Scotus and Ockham, letter C, with a clear "*probabilior*"; lect. 46 Q, where Thomas is first cited and rejected; lect. 41 G, where Thomas's idea about the coexistence in the Sacrament is cited, and in letter H this follows: "But Scotus shows that these reasons are not effective." It is therefore natural that in Damerau, when he covers it correctly, one sometimes finds [these] formulations: "Biel affiliates himself with this second view" (op. cit., p. 227; compare pp. 48, 205, 216, 218). Damerau (op. cit., pp. 185f.) makes Biel into a Thomist, denies all real visibility, and unwittingly writes: "The body of Christ in itself only as substance—the substance in itself is of a diffinitive, that is, invisible

Sacrament, insofar as he maintains the reality of the presence itself, yet without actually expressing himself on the visible aspect of Christ's revelation. Restraint is dictated by uncertainty, for example, as to whether the visible species of the revealed Jesus is, with absolute certainty, the species of the heavenly Lord or simply concealing Him. Yet such an identification would be possible: Christ is in the Sacrament as really existing and can allow Himself to be seen there.[61] While

nature—can be seen just as little as its accidence, which likewise are present invisibly." This formulation reveals that Damerau did not understand even the main points in *Die Abendmahlslehre des Nominalismus insbesondere die des Gabriel Biel*. For himself, Damerau puts forth Biel (op. cit., lect. 45 T), where Biel discusses "whether it can be conceded that Christ is seen in the Sacrament with the physical eye in another mode, since in common the people claim that they saw Christ the Lord when they saw the Sacrament." According to the medieval use of language, "seeing God (their Creator)" in the elevation of the Mass does *not* apply here to the eucharistic miracle but to what happens "*communiter*" ["in common"]. Damerau believes that this is the only "seeing" Biel knows. When Biel here writes (op. cit., lect. 45 U): "What appears is not of itself, because a body is a substance, and no substance is seen of itself, since no substance would be seen separate from color and light," he does not fall back on a Thomistic definition of substance about the immaterial substance with a noncircumscribed existence. For Nominalism, substance is usually circumscribed; its *definitiva* existence in the Sacrament does not make it invisible either. On the other hand, in the Eucharist, God through a special act has suspended the function of the accidence of *light and color*, which are necessary for the eye to be able to perceive them: "On its own what is seen is what would be seen if it were separated from everything else, and without which nothing would be seen at all. Thus only color or light are seen because color, even if it were to be seen separated from the subject, as in the Sacrament, cannot be seen at all by the physical eye without color or light. Also color or light are the proper object of sight." The substance is not robbed of its power of spirituality but is robbed of its power of being optically observable. This cessation is by no means the *natural* result of the substance's presence, but would not have occurred "if God did not suspend the action of *natural* causes" (lect. 45 S). But this is still valid only according to the "*general* rule" ["regula *generalis*"] (lect. 45 P), which Damerau (op. cit., p. 185) believes to be absolute: "that God now once would act so that the presence of Christ in the Supper remains a mystery." Biel again acknowledges the possibility of the proposition of Alexander of Hales: "Because this regularly is true. Nevertheless by dispensation, on account of the robustness of faith, it shows itself to be either the kindling of devotion or another cause" (lect. 51 G).

61 Biel, op. cit., lect. 51 H: "From the recitation of these opinions it is sufficiently apparent that all those agree in this way that the body of Christ is indeed miraculously visible under that form, except that blessed Thomas thinks that the bread does not remain the body of Christ when the dimensions cease." But the miraculously revealed forms could be deceiving and under all circumstances lose the character of the obligatory truth of faith, for which reason one should "rather suspend his mind and be taught by God, by man, or by Scripture. Or (if no deception is obvious) conditionally adore by saying, 'If You are Christ, I adore You as Christ,' and on this not only customary but even actual condition" (op. cit., lect. 51 I). Thereby is expressed a theological acknowledgment of the possibility of a visible miracle of the Mass; in any case, a conditional adoration can be offered at the revelation of a Mass of St. Gregory. Iserloh's insistence that Nominalism in this respect treads the path of popular piety (see above, pp. 3–4,

for Thomas somehow the element must still remain in order to ensure the presence, no such demand is made by Biel. Herein lies a decisive distinction.

Luther

The discussion of the distinction between substance and quantity in the consecrated host that is taken up by Ockham is repeated in the first polemical document of the Reformation, Luther's *On the Babylonian Captivity of the Church.* It is generally acknowledged that Luther was trained within the Ockhamistic school in regard to philosophy.[62] Here he takes Ockham's side: "But from this comes that Babylonian philosophy concerning continuing quantity, distinct from substance. . . ."[63] Luther's use of Ockham's concept of substance here has consequences not only for that document's immediate question about the substance of the host but also for the view concerning Christ's body. We have reason to think that in Luther we do not find the Thomistic idea of a body of Christ that is present only "*modo substantiae*." The more precise statements that he makes about the Supper do not challenge this assumption either.

Luther's stance meets us first in a reaction with his opponent Andreas Karlstadt. In the *Dialog* that Karlstadt composed, there is an exchange:

> Victus [Defeated = Karlstadt]: "I certainly have doubts whether the body of Christ is in the bread and His blood is in the cup." Gemser [the Lutheran opponent]: "Why?" Victus: "Because they say that His natural body, which was conceived in the womb, then beaten on the cross, would be as large, wide, thick, and long in the Sacrament as when He hung on the cross." Gemser: "It is true that Christ is as large in the Sacrament as when He hung on the cross."[64]

---

text accompanying nn. 10–13) must thus be modified so that Nominalistic reasoning does not include a general credulity and simple faith in the miracle. Nominalism reserves for itself free right of examination, but after examination is willing to accept that Christ in that individual case really brought about what always was possible: the visible presence. Here again Iserloh's observation hits the mark: Nominalism coincides with popular faith's spontaneous confidence in the full identity of Christ's heavenly and eucharistic body, a "path of popular piety" that is fundamentally closed to Thomism.

62 But here compare Link, *Das Ringen Luthers um die Freiheit der Theologie von der Philosophie*, p. 192, which will not allow this fact to apply in the sense that other schools were unknown to Luther: "It is indeed very unlikely that Thomism was unknown to Luther. For at one time the official teacher of his order, Aegidius Romanus, was a Thomist, and then we know today that even Staupitz was strongly under Thomistic influence theologically."

63 WA 6:510.13f., with detailed comments in Grane, "Om Luthers anvendelse af den middelalderlige tradition," pp. 31f., but only with regard to the definition of the substance of the elements.

64 *Dialogus oder Gesprächbüchlein*, cited according to StL 20:2318.

The first one who answered Karlstadt's description from a Lutheran stance was Urbanus Rhegius. He finds nothing exaggerated in Karlstadt's description of the real presence, but opts for the philosophical training that Karlstadt still retains: "But I think you are joking when you wonder, however, how Christ who is [so] long and large may be [present] under the little form. For thirteen or fourteen years ago, you brought your understanding from your brawling theology so far that it can be argued like this, and it is dishonorable to announce it and to set a limit for the power of God."[65] Luther takes up Rhegius's criticisms when he publishes his writing *Against the Heavenly Prophets concerning Images and the Sacraments* in 1524–25. He defends and affirms medieval theology in certain points: "Here, I say, Dr. Karlstadt is not wrong, but his conscience is obviously lying concerning the pope. For he, too, is a sophist and has both learned and taught the theology of the higher schools and of the pope. Now the pope nowhere teaches . . . ."[66] Luther counts on this scholastic educational heritage being in common for him and his opponents, and his confession of the full concreteness of Christ's body must be seen with this as a background. He does not reject what Karlstadt said regarding the length and breadth of Christ's body as absurdities. Luther instead identifies himself with "preaching that *until now* it was said that Christ's natural body is as large, wide, thick, and long in the Sacrament as when He hung on the cross."[67] The offense that Karlstadt took from this shows how Karlstadt was governed by respect for reason and public opinion. "And [this] he says he cannot believe, etc. God compelled him (like Caiaphas) to speak spontaneously, whereby everyone sees that he got his opinion not from Scripture, but brought it in."[68] The rejection of the idea that "Christ's body and blood are hidden there"[69] must lead to this: that "no article of

65 *Warnung wider . . . Carlstadt*, cited according to StL 20:117. Compare [StL 20:]114: "Here Karlstadt has completely forgotten his philosophy, and the fact that several years ago he conceded to his Scotus that here he is unwilling to understand how the body of Christ may particularly be in many places." Appealing to Scotus should not have had the effect that Rhegius imagines, for Karlstadt had belonged to the Thomistic school; compare StL 20:2: "The most significant thing for him was, even according to the judgment of his friends, the Thomist." All Karlstadt's objections can in a certain sense be seen as Thomistic. The form of the presence, which the Lutherans preached following medieval popular piety and Nominalism, contains absurdities that are insurmountable to Thomism, and it is these objections that the Thomist Karlstadt offers without further citing Thomas's way out "*per modum substantiae*."

66 WA 18:190.14ff. [cf. AE 40:200].

67 WA 18:142.35ff. [cf. AE 40:153] [emphasis added]. Pedersen (*Luther som skriftfortolker*, p. 359 n. 116) perceives Karlstadt's question as "an oversimplification of the opposition's viewpoint, a false materialization." This interpretation of Luther's stance is a false spiritualization.

68 WA 18:142.38ff. [cf. AE 40:153].

69 WA 18:143.10 [cf. AE 40:153].

faith will remain."[70] Even the incarnation must be threatened: "Thus I might also say: I cannot believe that God's Son became a man and has majesty that heaven and earth do not comprehend, was enclosed in a narrow womb of a woman, and then allows Himself to be crucified. Then I would snatch away all Scripture and God's Word and interpret it from my mind, as Mani does."[71] The miraculous presence of the concrete Christ, under the lowly dimensions of what is consecrated, is seen thus not as the product of a speculative theology, but as the truth of faith, with the same content as the doctrine of the union of the omnipresent God with [Christ's] humanity and the presence in the Virgin's body. The denial of this is a continuation of Manichaeism's offense at the assumption of humanity [by Christ]. In the same document, Luther reiterates the Ockhamistic definition of movement: Christ's coming to the Sacrament does not include His withdrawing from heaven.[72]

In the sermon on *The Sacrament of Christ's Body and Blood: Against the Fanatics* (originally intended for the Easter communicants in Wittenberg in 1526), the whole apparatus of everyday miracles is explained: physical events of miraculous character, which surround people daily and which are used by Nominalism as parallels to the miraculous, hyperphysical character of the sacramental presence. From the pulpit, and later in print in German—in both cases, for laypeople—Luther depicts the duty of faith as not shying away from the miracle:

> So they say it is not proper that God should do so much of a miracle in the Sacrament, as He does nowhere else. For we believe that the one body of Christ is in a hundred thousand places, wherever bread is broken, and that *the large bones then should be hidden so that no one sees or feels them*. They consider that to be an improper thing; they make great miracles of it, but they do not see that these are plainly unhelpful thoughts. For if one would measure things this way, then one must not let any creature remain.[73]

> Also I myself would therefore have pondered . . . how such a large body might be in such a small piece of bread, yet undivided and whole in every piece.[74]

The incomprehensible presence of the concrete body of Christ in the round wafer *is* a miracle to be received in the same faith that believes many miraculous works of [everyday] existence. The words about "the large bones" were such an

70 WA 18:143.19 [cf. AE 40:153].

71 WA 18:143.24ff. [cf. AE 40:153f.].

72 WA 18:206.10f. [cf. AE 40:216]: "For we do not say that He comes from heaven or leaves His place empty."

73 WA 19:486.22ff. [cf. AE 36:338] [emphasis added].

74 WA 19:497.14ff. [cf. AE 36:345].

offense to the Melanchthon-inspired publishers of the first edition of Luther's works that they had to be omitted.[75]

A similar offense came even from Luther's most famous sacramental hymn: "Jesus Christ, Our Blessed Savior" [*Jesus Christus, unser Heiland*].[76] The second stanza says, "That we never forget He gave us His body to eat, *hidden in bread so small*, and His blood to drink in the wine."[77] The words italicized here obviously fit the miraculous tension discussed above, which flows from the full identicalness of Christ's heavenly and eucharistic body that was held by Luther. The modern edition [Weimar] of Luther's works wants to translate "small" [*kleyn*] with "least" [*wenig*],[78] but this ignores what is referred to above. The wondrous paradox is thereby dismissed with a view of evening things out. The Reformed critique took the words more seriously; they were perceived as teaching a kind of presence in which Christ's body was compressed down to the size of the host. And by doing so, the meaning of the hymn verse was misinterpreted.[79]

When Luther sometimes uses the predicate "spiritual" concerning the body of Christ, he is in no way nullifying its corporeality, but he is expressing its power and effect: "For it is a spiritual flesh and does not let itself be changed, but changes and gives the Spirit to the one who eats it."[80] Both in heaven after the

75 Compare here StL 20:737 (in this edition the variations of the older text editions are noted in the text). WA 19:481 n. 1 writes generally about this text of the first edition of the sermon from 1526: "Here several changes in a Calvinist sense have been made to the original text; compare *Zeitschr. f. Protest. u. Kirche* 19, p. 46." "Calvinist" is too strong and is not expressed in the cited document either; compare here also E 29:328.

76 Of its incorrectly alleged dependence on Hus, compare WA 35:142ff. [cf. AE 53:249].

77 WA 35:435.21ff. [cf. AE 53:249ff.].

78 WA 35:436 n. 1, 432 n. 4.

79 Compare here Bacmeister, *Christliche Anleitung wie Ern Johannis Rhuelii*, pp. 86f.: "But Mr. Rhuelius mentions our customary church hymn, which we sing during the administration of the holy Supper, 'hidden in this bread so small'; and will he thus convince us that we understand thereby a spatial confinement of the body of Christ in the bread?" Compare also Krauth, *Conservative Reformation and Its Theology*, p. 769, with the citation from Johann Adam Scherzer (*Collegium Anti-Calvinianum* [Leipzig, 1704], pp. 606, 630, 632): "In the German hymn, [in] the phrase 'hidden in the bread so small (*Verborgen in brod so klein*),' the [word] 'hidden' notes a mystical hiding—that the body of Christ is not open to the senses—not a physical one, which is local; the words 'so small' are a limitation of the *bread*, not of the body" [and] with the citation from Kromayer (*Theologia positivo-polemica*, 1:917f.): "Instance: But we confess *impanation* or local enclosure in the hymn which Luther translated from Hus's little song into the German language: '*verborgen in Brot so klein*.' But we respond: . . . The sense is: He gave us His body mystically in the little bread. '*Im kleinen Brot gab er uns seinen Leib verborgener Weise zu essen.*' "

80 WA 23:205.10f. [cf. AE 37:100]; compare [WA 23:]243.24ff., 251.21ff. [cf. AE 37:124, 129]. Compare also here below, chapter 2, where this life-giving function of Christ's body is examined more carefully. Köhler (*Zwingli und Luther*, 1:509) consequently interprets all spiritual predications of Christ's body as disruptive of its reality: "That

resurrection and ascension, in the Sacrament, and in the heart of the believer, Christ is a physical reality: "Christ's flesh, *wherever it may be*, in spiritual or physical essence, visible or invisible, is true, natural flesh, which one can grasp, can feel,* see and hear, was born of a woman, died on the cross."[81] Heavenly glory has not robbed Christ of His attribute of being an "outwardly physical [*leiblich*] thing."[82] Although the resurrection removes Christ from "passions of mortals"—to which belong, for example, the need for food—He remains "not something that lacks bones and flesh." It is as such that He exists in the pious heart, "*in spiritu*."[83] Luther rejects any attempt to allow Christ's coming by faith to happen simply "virtually" or "potentially." Even in this case He comes as true man: "Thus Christ is with us with His true body, of course, spiritually and invisibly. He does not leave us. 'I do not leave,' etc. John [14:18?].† [To say,] 'He comes through power virtually'—this is to distort Scripture by using a particularly unusual word that requires interpretation."[84]

---

is, however, finally no flesh at all." The same misunderstanding, also with reference to Köhler, in Neuser (*Die Abendmahlslehre Melanchthons*, 1:466f.): "Indeed, after he (Luther) now emphasizes 'spiritual' or 'flesh,' it is a spiritual or more material gift." Id., p. 394: "Likewise, he (Luther) in 1528 calls the body of Christ 'an immortal, spiritual flesh.' Nevertheless (!) Luther tightens it up that it (was) 'even the same that was seen and crucified.' "

81 * [Marginal note in Hardt's working copy corrects *turen* to *fulen (fühlen)*.]
WA 23:185.1ff. [cf. AE 37:89] [emphasis added].

82 WA 23:261.26ff. [cf. AE 37:136]: "For Christ's body, even if it is at the right hand of God, yet it is still a body and an outwardly corporeal thing that has bones and flesh, which no spirit has, as He Himself says in the last chapter of Luke: 'Spirit does not have flesh and bones, as you see I have' [Luke 24:39]."

83 WA 20:759.6ff. [cf. AE 30:302, though AE does not seem to follow WA here]: "Therefore, Christ is not spirit thus as the Enthusiasts dream. Although He is with us in spirit, nevertheless they do not understand because they make of Christ a spirit without flesh, blood, and bones (last chapter of Luke). Christ's flesh is no longer fleshly [carnal], but spiritual; it does not have mortal feelings, does not eat, etc., 1 Corinthians 15. The spiritual must be distinguished, not compared to flesh and blood but compared to animal, as Paul [does]. It is spiritual not because it lacks bones and flesh, but because it is not animal, as animals live on land, and they live so that they eat. They live, they reproduce, they are exposed to corrupt conditions. Christ does not have such a body. Thus we, too, will have; [there will be] no suffering of corrupt condition."

84 † [The reference may be to a Latin plainchant: *Apparuit Thomae Dominus in visu noctis, dicens ei: Ne timeas descendere in Indiam, quia* ***ego te non derelinquo****. V. A. (S) Domine, mitte me ubi vis, praeter aliunde (sic). Et dixit Dominus ad eum. — Ne timeas. V. B. (E) Domine, quovis mitte me, praeter ad Indos. Et respondens Dominus dixit. — Ne timeas.*]
WA 20:759.15ff. [cf. AE 30:302]. This view of the spiritual eating [*manducatio spiritualis*] as a presence of the bodily Christ is found only in a few cases during the Middle Ages, as, for example, in the late medieval theologian Wessel; compare Dieckhoff, *Die evangelische Abendmahlslehre im Reformationszeitalter*, pp. 285ff. Usually such a possibility was seen as a miraculous exception; compare Köhler, op. cit., 1:57, about the nun Mechthild from Waldeck who "became a partaker of this grace."

In his so-called "Great Confession," the *Confession concerning Christ's Supper*, Luther returns to the question of the content of the presence. Opponents have asserted that a necessary attribute for Christ's body would be that it could be visible; therefore, it is demonstrably not in the host. Luther answers that being visible is a "most common and changeable accidence"[85] and that "the accidental term cannot be subsumed under the substantial term."[86] One cannot say, for example: "Rachel has no veil; therefore, Rachel is not a wife."[87] His joke implies the idea that Christ is free to choose the easily changeable attribute of being visible or not being visible in His [post-Easter] appearances. Luther does not take up the Thomistic concept of the immateriality of substances and the resulting invisibility. He proceeds from a present, physical reality, which can be visible or not visible according to God's will.

Concerning the mode of presence that exists, parallel with the sacramental presence, in the miraculous passing through the gravestone and the closed doors, it says, "For since it cannot be measured or perceived where His head or feet were when He went through the stone, and yet He indeed had to go through it, yet since He thereby took up no space, the stone also gave Him no room, but the stone remains complete and firm as before, and *His body also remains as large and thick as it was before*. . . . So also thus, Christ can be and is in the bread."[88] Again, it is maintained that the sacramental presence, despite its hyperphysical nature, does not impart any other body of Christ than one that is "large and thick" and which is absolutely identical with the historic body of Christ, which is in heaven.

Just how very zealous Luther is for the concrete content of the definitive presence is clear in distinction from medieval theology's solution in regard to the ability of Christ's body to override the laws of [physical] matter. Earlier, the attribute of "being thinned out [*subtilitas*]" had been attributed to the body of the God-man. The speculation of natural philosophy espoused light as a forming cause [*causa formatrix*] for the eternal material world, and the ability to penetrate bodies, "*subtilitas*" ["being thinned out"], was attributed to the characteristics of light. Principles of the elemental world suppress manifestations of the everlasting power in the material world, but Christ's resurrection frees His body from these limitations.[89] The transcendence of Christ's body compared to [physical] matter had thus been gained through a thinning out of the corporeality to be similar to fire. Luther rejects this thought when his Reformed opponent Oecolampadius cites tenuity [being thinned out] as an alternative to the definitive mode of

85 WA 26:280.34f. [cf. AE 37:178].

86 WA 26:298.30f. [cf. AE 37:195].

87 WA 26:282.7ff. [cf. AE 37:180].

88 WA 26:328.33ff., 334.2ff., 334.20ff. [cf. AE 37:216, 220, 221] [emphasis added].

89 Compare here Rocholl, op. cit., pp. 92ff.; the presentation refers directly to Bonaventure.

presence, as well as an explanation of the miracles of the Easter appearances: "But they do not escape from me with the [idea of] tenuity [being thinned out]. It is nevertheless the same body of Christ, and the doors are also closed. And Christ did not slip through between the cracks or nail holes. He had bones and flesh, as He Himself confesses in the last chapter of Luke [24:39]."[90] That is the same thought as he just expressed: "He took up no space, so the stone also gave Him no room." Two completely intact materials confront each other without either of them changing as a result of their coexistence in the same space. Neither one yields, is dissolved, or is thinned out.[91] Christ's body, while maintaining its physical concreteness, occupies a supranatural relationship to the other material. This is the form of presence that applies also to the Sacrament of the Altar. The divine miracle rests in the complete contraposition between two quantities and [on] it not being ironed out in favor of a false harmonization.

The polemic regarding these actual concepts, which Luther's foremost opponent, Zwingli, directed against him, can give further outline to the depiction. Zwingli proceeds with this from a Thomistic thought pattern, just as Karlstadt did earlier, but Zwingli's remarks offer clarity nevertheless. By "*circumscriptive*" Luther had meant the bodily presence under earthly conditions; by "*diffinitive*," the same body's mode in passing through the gravestone and the closed doors, but also the form of the sacramental presence. Zwingli now accuses Luther of having "not correctly picked through the trash of the sophists." "*Circumscriptive*,

90 WA 26:419.25ff. [cf. AE 37:279].

91 Luther's solution is thus not to see it as analogous to Calvin's explanation, which counts on the closed doors being opened somehow. Grass (*Die Abendmahlslehre bei Luther und Calvin*, p. 264 n. 4) writes: "Here, however, the Lutheran meaning is not only closer to the text (John 20:19, 26) but also more sensible, since it has the miracle happen in the body of Christ, which indeed is itself an eschatological miracle as a resurrected body; and not, like Calvin, [having the miracle happen] to the doors and stones, thus to dead creatures, through which the miracle is miraculous." Grass's depiction lets Christ's body be subject to the miracle that Calvin ascribes to the doors, but that is how the word "eschatological" comes to be used in contrast to concrete-physical. For Luther, the essential thing is that "dead creatures" already contain countless unobserved miracles that God's wondrous governance of this world makes possible; for example, the miracle of sight does not stop at the Sacrament, especially not at His own body, and in the case of the presence the miracle consists in the real, physical body of Christ (even before the resurrection), without being changed into something else, occupying its place in the host, which is likewise intact. The "eschatological" nature of the resurrected body becomes this: that according to God's will it is invested with a general wielding of these miraculous prerogatives. Grass's presentation is based on his assessment, which, despite his efforts, he cannot abandon "without consideration": religious statements could not be compared with concrete-physical descriptions ("*eine Kritik an diesen realistischen Zügen der Auferstehungsberichte, die für uns heute unumgänglich ist*" ["a critique of these realistic traits of the resurrection accounts, which is inevitable for us today"]). As far as possible, he tries to fit Luther's statements within his own basic view.

that is, contained, limited, and compressed, he would not translate thus as bodily ([*lyplich*], *corporaliter*), but 'bodily' in a poetic way."[92] One gets an illustration of Zwingli's *deductio ad absurdum*: "But would Luther say: Before His death Christ was confined, but after death, not?"[93] Zwingli looks at the most essential content of the word *circumscriptive*: "circumscribed," "confined," that is, "limited." To preclude expressing this characteristic regarding Christ's earthly appearances, Christ's humanity should cease in other cases and produce a then-insubstantial, phantomlike Christ. Meanwhile, Luther makes use of *circumscriptive* in a different meaning, which even Zwingli's complaint about clumsy definitions presupposes. With Luther, *circumscriptive* is exactly synonymous with *leiblich* ["bodily," "physical"], that is, the simple relationship to space "part in part" [*pars in parte*], in a normal mode of regular bodies. In Zwingli's opinion, "circumscribed," the characteristic of being limited, which is implied by Luther's *circumscriptive*, still coincides with the latter, but not therefore applying equally to the *diffinitiva* mode of presence. In the way of thinking of Thomas and Zwingli, this is exclusively reserved for spiritual beings—souls and angels—a completely incorporeal existence, which is why Luther's claims of a definitive corporeality are absurd to his opponents. Zwingli's attack has the benefit of making it clear that Luther—un-Thomistically, but Nominalistically—allows for a *circumscriptive* (adjective) presence of Christ's body diffinitively (*diffinitive*, adverb).[94]

Against the background of what was explained above, the pertinent content in the formula of conciliation presented by Luther at Marburg in 1529 offers [this]: "We confess that by virtue of these words: 'This is My body; this is My

92 CR 93/2:158.

93 CR 93/2:161.

94 Nor, of course, does Zwingli share Luther's definition of "*diffinitive*." Compare above, p. 13 n. 48, where Thomas's view is presented, and Zwingli, CR 93/2:170, where Thomas's meaning is supported by Zwingli. CR 92:697 makes use of Zwingli's concept of "*circumscriptum*" even of spiritual entities, in contrast to the "*infinita*" of the divinity. Compare Köhler, op. cit., 1:480, 662f., which, however, nowhere penetrates the schools standing behind Luther and Zwingli. When Köhler (op. cit., 1:655) writes correctly, in theory: "One easily acknowledges: the contrasts between Nominalism [Luther] and Realism [Zwingli] play into this dialectic," he finds this distinction in the controversy of the predicate after the copula "*est*" (1:655 n. 3: "[Zwingli] Compare 22:105: So Luther comes with such words: a single word becomes two words—or several words when he should say: One word is used in various ways and now still remains [just] one word (whose *name* [*nomen*] is the same), but means or indicates many things, which are not one thing (but the *things* [*res*] are diverse)." This, of course, has nothing to do with the classic controversy about the *universalis* character of *res* or *nomina*! Even less does it apply to the assertion (ibid.) that "Luther abstracts the characteristic of essence from all kinds of modes of appearance." "Zwingli, on the other hand, proceeds from the reality of the single appearance or the type and sees the 'essence' [*Wesen*] in it." Besides this definition making Luther into a Realist and Zwingli into a Nominalist, the whole quotation above is misinterpreted.

blood,' the body and the blood of Christ truly, that is, according to their substance and essence, but not quantitatively or qualitatively or locally, are present and are given in the Supper."[95] We have no cause to believe, along with [Walter] Köhler and other researchers of this and similar Lutheran formulations, that the concrete reality of Christ's body and blood should thereby be evaporated into something purely spiritual. This presupposes that Luther acted as a Thomist and withdrew from the stance that he otherwise took in following Nominalism and medieval popular faith in the miracle of the Mass.[96]

In the prevalent literature about Luther's doctrine of the Supper, usually this point is touched on rather briefly and in passing. No discussion of the research exists. Paul-Wilhelm Gennrich has Luther proving the possibility of the presence through the abstraction of the concept of substance in a completely Thomistic way.[97] Ruben Josefson finds that "corporeality in a commonly accepted sense" is not valid, because Luther made the sacramental presence parallel with the presence within Christians through faith. The form of this latter, "which is not without bones and flesh," then, was not taken into consideration.[98]

---

95 According to Oecolampadius' record in Köhler, *Das Marburger Religionsgespräch*, pp. 131f. The concepts reproduced here are not thus "not locally nor circumscriptively nor diffinitively," as Köhler asserts in *Zwingli und Luther*, 1:527. It is a Thomistic, non-Nominalistic formulation.

96 Köhler, op. cit., 1:578: "Precisely this lack of quantitative and qualitative limitation separates the eating of the substantial body and blood of Christ apart from carnality and puts it into the spiritual realm." The formulation should not have in view only the manner of eating, but in its context it denotes unambiguous concreteness of the object; compare op. cit., p. 509: "It is 'an unfading, immortal, imperishable flesh.' But, in the end, that is no flesh at all." Köhler still thinks that Luther never reached final clarity on these questions (op. cit., 2:135): "But he [Luther] never completely loosed himself from the physical; otherwise he would not have constantly insisted on the *bodily* presence. 'Bodily' never means 'purely spiritual'; Luther knows no pure, spiritual body. So he remains in limbo, between the spiritual and physical, between faith and visible eating." Rather, it is Köhler himself who still wavers between the perception that Luther, as an unsystematic religious genius, always in his experience, gives definitions on concrete dogmatic points that are not thought through and the realization that finally these definitions even now coincide with traditional sacramental Realism (op. cit., 1:528): "While the reformer rested on religious experience and, urged by the rational arguments of the Zwinglians, only hesitantly descended to rational considerations, moreover he cared little about the lack of clarity arising from this"; "With—I would even say—a frightening clarity, the Catholic basis of Luther's conceptual world of the Supper becomes evident in this mirror" (p. 521).

97 Gennrich, *Die Christologie Luthers im Abendmahlsstreit 1524–1529*, p. 145: "In this way all the objections of the opponents regarding the impossibility of an existence in various places at the same time become untenable from the outset. . . . In order to make it clear, Luther only needed to recall the scholastic concepts."

98 Josefson, "Luthers [nattvardsuppfattning]," p. 343. The same reasoning in Köhler (op. cit., 1:388): "Luther's repeated reference to the presence of the true Christ *in the heart* . . . so this comparison still limps all too precariously. For no preaching can

[Albrecht] Peters touches on the problem without noting it when he comments on Luther's instruction to Melanchthon before the Colloquy of Cassel in 1534: "Whatever motion or action the bread has, the body of Christ has the same."[99] Although the Nominalist view of the self-existence of Christ's body and its ability to move can easily be identified here, Peters only finds reason to complain about the scarcity of statements in contrast to the thoroughness of Scholasticism. [Hermann] Sasse again sheds some light on the problem when he underscores that for Luther the concept of substance in the Supper will only talk about "the real true body and blood," and at the same time [he] adds that " 'substance' is not the same as '*materia*' either in the Lutheran or in the Catholic dogmaticians, though it may include the material side of a thing."[100] [101]

Through his thoroughness and unmistakable emphasis, Regin Prenter's depiction of the identity between the heavenly and eucharistic body of Christ deviates from the other scantier depictions, an example of which is given above. Concerning the thought that the sacramental gifts should be actually identical with the heavenly Christ, Prenter says,

> The error in this way of thinking is that one mainly thinks of Jesus' body and blood as a kind of "heavenly material" that is present in heaven as a substance existing beforehand and which is brought down from there to earth at Communion. [. . .] Such ideas are far from Luther's dynamic view of [Christ] being seated at the right hand of the Father and the omnipresence. *The body and blood, really present, are nothing other than the body and blood that were offered on Golgotha.* The ascended Christ is identical with the crucified [Christ]. And the miracle of the Supper is not that a heavenly substance is brought down onto earth, but that the risen and ascended [Christ] is still present precisely as the suffering and sacrificed Son of Man. *The miracle is this: that the sacrifice of Golgotha has not become the past, but is and remains eternally the present.* [. . .] If His body and blood were only present as heavenly, glorified substances, we would not really be able to partake of them. How would sinners here on earth digest heavenly substances?[102]

Prenter here, within the framework of a contemporary systematic task, makes the claim of reproducing Luther's doctrine. This, however, is turned into the

---

bring Christ *with flesh and blood* into the heart." By virtue of his particular lack of the powers of observation, Köhler here praises Zwingli (p. 389): "The 'coarse grammatical Enthusiasts' here were superiors in the power of logic. Luther's strength lay in 'faith,' in the good as well as the bad sense."

99 Albrecht Peters, *Realpräsenz*, p. 92 n. 21; [cf.] WA 38:299.

100 [The Swedish edition numbers footnotes up to 99, then restarts at 1, which this translation lists as 101, etc.]

101 Sasse, op. cit., p. 42 n. 36; compare pp. 102ff., 266f.

102 Prenter, *Skabelse og genløsning*, p. 550.

complete opposite; any identity, concrete or abstract, is denied. The character of the gifts becomes the point of comparison between Christ's body and the bread:

> It does not revolve around the identity of Jesus' body and bread and wine as substances that merely exist beforehand. Jesus' words about the bread and the wine are not magic formulas. It revolves around the identity of Jesus' body and blood, on one hand, and the distributed bread and wine, on the other, *as sacrificial gift*. That is to say: it is one and the same all-sacrificing love that in one and the same act delivers the body to be mistreated on the cross and offers the bread and the wine to the bereaved, offended, and prodigal disciples. Both the physical body and the physical bread and wine on the table, in one and the same deed of love, become "signs" of His sacrificial gift of love.[103]

In the way that one thus, in an irregular sense, speaks about the presence of Christ's body, this applies to Jesus' nonglorified body in its state of self-sacrifice. In a later depiction Prenter has completely turned to this reasoning, though maintaining a distance from Luther's actual view: "It is indeed not Jesus' physical body and blood, offered on the cross, that are present under bread and wine, but Jesus' glorified, risen body, which by death He brought into the heavenly sanctuary as a gift to God. And that means it is Jesus Christ Himself, just as the Father in heaven received Him as an atoning gift of love. This gift is invisible and *can only be present invisibly* under a visible sign." According to Prenter, it is to be a parallel to the Old Testament sacrifices, where God did not receive the physical bodies of the animals ("Should I eat the flesh of bulls" [Ps. 50:13]) but looked to the "man himself, the obedience of his heart; the sacrificial gifts were only an outwardly visible expression of that." The eating of the sacrificial flesh was therefore not a receiving, "in the strictest sense, of the same gift, which the Lord had received."[104] The occasion for Prenter now to claim the presence of the "heavenly material," so clearly rejected earlier, is that Jesus' internal gift is understood in this way: His "obedience of the heart," which only "can . . . be present invisibly." This sacrificial surrendering, by definition invisible [and] distinct from Jesus' physical body, as expressly equated with the Old Testament *bodies of animals*, is contrasted with transubstantiation, which includes "a weakening of the sense that it is Jesus' glorified body and blood that are received under the bread and the wine." With this doctrinal depiction, where neither real presence nor atonement is related to Jesus' physical body, Prenter's intention is to replicate Luther's "dynamic view." It is obvious that this depiction is incorrect. Concerning the depiction, these words can rightly be cited, which the Roman

103 Prenter, op. cit., p. 536.

104 Prenter, *Kyrkans tro* (Swedish translation), p. 158. Compare id., *Skabelse og genløsning*, p. 536: "It is love itself in which Jesus gives up rescuing His life in order to be able to remain in solidarity with the guilty race, which makes the sacrificed physical body on the cross into the 'sign' of His love, into the gift that is offered to God."

Catholic researcher Karl Rahner wrote concerning Prenter's thoughts about similar questions: "One may call the Catholic doctrine of transubstantiation the doctrine of 'the miracle of transformation' (Prenter) . . . ; it seems certain to me that it can be very Calvinistic, but not Lutheran, to make the real presence of Christ's body into an 'omnipresence' of His 'love' that is not 'limited by space.' "[105]

Besides the usual literature about Luther's doctrine of the Supper in recent years, the meaning of the concepts "substance" [and] "heavenly material," among other things, meanwhile has been investigated in a number of smaller essays occasioned by the so-called Arnoldshain Theses from 1957, a contemporary attempt to find a formulation of the doctrine of the Supper that can be approved by churches of both Lutheran and Reformed background.[106] These theses reject the "*materia coelestis*": "V. Therefore, what happens in the Supper is not described properly . . . (c) if one teaches that in the Supper a natural or supernatural material is administered."[107] The theses represent an opinion that coincides most closely with Prenter. Only Peter Brunner wants to find room, in the document he signed, for a "substantial" presence that only lacks "material" character: "There is a great distinction between the two concepts. Basically the concept of 'substance' is directly opposed to the concept of 'material' "; "Whoever says the body and blood of Christ are administered in the Supper according to the substance [*substantialiter*] is not thereby saying that a natural or supernatural material is administered in the Supper. — The formula *substantia corporis Christi* means this much: the one true body of the Lord in its identity under all modes of His existence. But this identity is also what the Arnoldshain Theses

105 Rahner, "Die Gegenwart Christi im Sakrament des Herrenmahles nach dem katholischen Bekenntnis im Gegenüber zum evangelisch-lutherischen Bekenntnis," p. 338. Prenter (*Skabelse og genløsning*, p. 550) joins Althaus's critique of the Old Lutheran doctrine of the Sacrament, but it ought to be noted that Althaus is aware that his systematic critique cannot invoke Luther ("Luthers Abendmahlslehre," pp. 34ff.; *Die christliche Wahrheit*, pp. 582ff.; compare pp. 568ff.). Gollwitzer (*Coena Domini*, p. 114) highlights this disagreement between Luther and Althaus. Prenter's writing, which is characterized by a generally "conservative" terminology but not the use of the Roman Catholic concept, easily leads the reader astray in the question of the actual content. Wisløff (*Nattverd og messe*, p. 165 n. 59) ascribes to Prenter even an exclusively substantial presence in the sense of a presence of the physical body of Christ without the presence of the person of Christ.

106 See here, among others, Grass, "Die Arnoldshainer Thesen und die lutherische Abendmahlslehre," pp. 64ff.; Peters, "Zur Kritik an den Abendmahlsthesen von Arnoldshain," pp. 182ff. (id., *Realpräsenz*, pp. 197ff.); Sasse, "Zum Ergebnis des 'Abendmahlsgesprächs der Evangelischen Kirche in Deutschland 1947–1957,' " pp. 98ff. The theses have given rise to a great many writings; see Gottfried Niemeier, ed., *Lehrgespräch über das Heilige Abendmahl: Stimmen und Studien zu den Arholdshainer Thesen* [Munich: Kaiser, 1961].

107 Quoted according to the reprint in [Hans Wenschkewitz, ed.,] *Lutherische Abendmahlslehre heute* [Göttingen: Vandenhoeck & Ruprecht, 1960], p. 5.

are interested in." The reasoning implies that some "*modus*" ["modes"] would convey a "*Sein*" [an "existence"] that is not material.[108]

The articles about the concept of substance, articles occasioned by the Arnoldshain Theses, do not at all take up discussion of the various medieval views of substance or material from Luther's hand. Mostly they confront general allegations, the intent of which is to evade a concrete perception of Christ's body. So Werner Schilling claims that Luther has a purely immaterial concept of substance. Descartes and Kant were supposed to have been the first ones to have introduced quantity into the concept of substance.[109] Heinrich Benckert takes up Brunner's thought: "Basically the concept of substance is directly opposed to the concept of material."[110] This thesis, which is cited by Benckert as applying to Luther's theology, is advanced with obvious front against—transubstantiation! Just as in Prenter, this is taken to offer a more material body of Christ *per diffinitionem*. Johannes Grünwald in the same way expounds on the adverbial definitions of the Marburg formula with, among others, three references to contemporary Thomistic literature, through which the immaterial substance is thought to be supported in Luther.[111] Ulrich Asendorf writes "Zur Frage der *materia coelestis* in der lutherischen Abendmahlslehre ['On the question of the *materia coelestis* in the Lutheran doctrine of the Lord's Supper']" and relates the term to "substantial materialization" and to the doctrine of transubstantiation connected with it. Yet Luther does not have any such view.[112] These various

108 Brunner, "Die dogmatische und kirchliche Bedeutung des Ertrages des Abendmahlsgesprächs," pp. 119f. Compare here Grass, op. cit., p. 74 n. 15: "If one poses the old question: body on the cross or heavenly body, blood poured out on the cross or heavenly blood, in the text of the theses, then he is clearly speaking of the body given into death and the blood poured out, and also not in the sense of any substances, which as such are no longer there, but as indication of what happened on the cross." Concerning Brunner's distinctions, Grass writes ("Die Arnoldshainer Thesen und die lutherische Abendmahlslehre," p. 143): "This understanding of substance and matter is quite artificial."

109 Schilling, *Christus unter Brot und Wein*, p. 28 n. 2 (= p. 32). Compare here above, pp. 14–15 n. 56, where Böhner thinks of quantity as something completely different than Schilling does.

110 Benckert, *Die Stofflichkeit des Abendmahlsgabe*, p. 10. In another context (p. 18), Benckert even says, "The concept of substance says nothing about materiality or immateriality." This insight applies, but not in Scripture. The deficiency in the writings of Schilling and Benckert was not noticed by Ahlberg (*Laurentius Petris nattvardsuppfattning*, p. 233 n. 2), but they were accepted there without critique, just as by Aalen ("Der Kampf um das Evangelium im Abendmahl," p. 96 n. 63).

111 Grünwald, "Zur Ontologie der Realpräsenz," p. 14 n. 5.

112 In Wenschkewitz, *Lutherische Abendmahlslehre heute*, p. 25. No definition of the term under discussion is given by Asendorf, who himself even writes (p. 29): "If this formula should also be used again in modern conversation, which is urgently warned against, then it would have to be made precisely clear what it would mean." — The expression

depictions are all outdone by Gerold Kühne, who sets forth the principal thesis: "The nonspatial concept of substance from the creative power of God in the sacramental act is the basis of Luther's doctrine of the Lord's Supper."[113]

An American counterpart to both the Arnoldshain Theses and the literature inspired by them makes up the compilation *Marburg Revisited* from 1966. A number of articles by prominent American theologians from Lutheran and Reformed traditions on the doctrine of the Supper (and other points of doctrine) comprises the basis for a final thesis about essential unity among the participants and their church bodies. Joseph McLelland in his contribution refers to the problem of substance: "Luther had understood substance or essence (*Wesen*) in the scholastic sense as that which makes an entity what it is—hence, there is even a divine substance. But Zwingli regarded *wesentlich* as *dinglich*—'real' in the legal sense of real property, as we speak of a 'man of substance.' "[114] McLelland does not work with any [of] [Luther's texts]. Nor does the depiction have at any point a connection to actual situations. It makes Luther into a Thomist and Zwingli into a Nominalist. So McLelland does not give any substantive contribution to the problem either.

---

as such cannot be imposed on Luther. The first time it was expressed was probably by the Gnesio-Lutheran Benedict Morgenstern in 1567 in *Widerlegung der Notel * / damit die Sacramentirer zu Dantzig / jhren Irrthumb . . . / verkleistern*, fol. #IIIb: "The other material is heavenly." In the works preparatory to the Formula of Concord, the concept of *causa materialis* is used of both the bread and Christ's body: "*Formula concordiae inter svevicas et saxonicas ecclesias*," in *Acta et scripta publica ecclesiae Wirtembergicae*, p. 453. The most coherent presentation of the later use of *materia coelestis* within Lutheranism is found in C. F. W. Walther's newly edited and commentated edition of Baier's theological compendium: *Compendium theologiae*, 3/3:501ff.

* [Corrected from the misprint *Nobel*.]

113 Kühne, "Die Substanzfrage beim Abendmahl," p. 143. Compare ibid.: "The evangelical churches (as well as the Catholic Church) are agreed that the body and blood of the Lord are present as divine substance in wine and bread (!), not in the sense of a material matter." Kühne advocates for this: that because "matter" according to modern science is a wave, any "concrete substance" is "questionable," which Luther understood and anticipated "consciously or unconsciously."

114 McLelland, "Lutheran-Reformed Debate on the Eucharist and Christology," p. 46. The famous concept of substance, specific to Zwingli, where "substance" is equated with "characteristic," is ordinary Latin use of language, occurring even in Luther; compare, for example, WA Br 3[:173].12, no. 670: "nevertheless when the whole substance would return to the prince," which describes the taking over of the Augustinian cloister's *capital* by the elector. Neither this occurrence in Luther, Zwingli, or in anyone else has connection with the topic discussed here. — The same collection (p. 61) shares Tappert, "Christology and Lord's Supper in the Perspective of History": "Despite contemporary misunderstanding and overstatement, Luther and Calvin agreed that the expression 'the body and blood of Christ' does not mean things or substances but means Christ himself.' " Tappert's words are supplied here without comment.

In conclusion, it ought to be mentioned that a German contribution, in the question at hand, differs from the researchers referenced here. Hans-Joachim Huhnke asserts: "To the actual substance of the flesh and blood, however, belongs also its *Stofflichkeit* or materiality." This dogmatic remark is correct but is not supported by any analysis of texts.[115]

The publishers of the first edition of Luther's collected writings shied away from the words "that the large bones then should be hidden" in the sermon on *The Sacrament of the Body and Blood of Christ* from 1526 and omitted them. Nevertheless, in the generation after Luther that administered the legacy from him until the completion of the *Book of Concord*, there is no controversy about the concept of substance in the Supper. "Substance" means just the same as "reality" in the ordinary sense. Nicolaus Selnecker, one of the co-authors of the Formula of Concord, writes: "So, accordingly, if we use the little words 'bodily' [*leiblich*] *realiter, essentialiter, substantialiter*, essentially (truly present) *praesentia corporali*, orally (outwardly), etc., nothing is to be maintained by them other than that the true [*Warhafftig*] Lord Christ is in the Supper."[116] Nowhere do the definitions that contrast substance and concrete existence encounter or seek to extract an abstract type of identity between the heavenly and eucharistic body of Christ.

Nowhere can Grünwald's claim be imposed upon Luther's successors: "Only according to this immateriality can the substance ever exist under the accidence that is fleeting in appearance."[117] This means that Thomistic philosophy was dead within Lutheranism and that the offense that was prompted by Luther's

115 Huhnke, "Realpräsenz und Konsekration," p. 5. But in a writing to the Supreme Ecclesiastical Council [*Oberkirchenrat*] of the Ev.-Luth. Landeskirche Mecklenburgs in Schwerin, from November 11, 1961 (published in *Informationen der Lutherische Bruderkreise Deutschlands* 21, no. 25 [January 1962]: 14ff.), Huhnke has somewhat more extensively tried to clear up the questions with a statement from the Apology of the Augsburg Confession, [Article] X. By asserting the proposition that "the genus of the Incarnate does not exclude tangibility," Huhnke wants to refute the writing by the Supreme Ecclesiastical Council from October 10, 1961, where it is said, "The question to be asked is whether you [the council] understand the '*substantialiter adesse*' ['presence substantially'] from the Apology as 'material, physical presence' [*dingliche, körperliche Gegenwart*] while it had to be understood as 'essential' [*wesentlich*]. It is generally known that the concept of *substantia*, in the metaphysics influenced by Aristotle, means both materiality in the sense of concreteness as well as consubstantiality [*Wesensgleichheit*, 'equality of essence'] and oneness of type" (id., p. 13). The exchange of letters applies to "Concerning a Proposal for Introducing a Procedure of Complaining about Doctrine [*Betrifft Antrag auf Einleitungen eines Verfahrens wegen Beanstandung der Lehre*]."

116 Selnecker, *Christliche wahrhafftige Widerlegung*, fol. GIIb; compare id., *Tractus brevis et utilis de coena domini*, p. 393: "Concerning the adverbs: truly bodily, substantially, really, etc., antiquity used these adverbs to show the very substance and nature of the body and blood of Christ to be present, offered, and received not in a sign, nor only in effect, but truly."

117 Grünwald, op. cit., p. 16.

concrete sacramental faith must take different routes in order to formulate its protest.[118] More detailed account about this will be given in what follows.

118 An odd contribution to the question about "Christ's true body" is in Bejerholm and Hornig, *Wort und Handlung*, chapter 3, "'Wahrer Leib'—Eine semantische Katechismusfrage," pp. 77ff. The task is defined by way of introduction (p. 78) as actually not theological-historical, but soon enough the authors set forth propositions that are purely dogmatic-historical. Page 86: "Surely this formulation [true body and blood] will trigger certain associations with the theologically trained. He knows, for example, that Lutheran theology excludes the thought that the elements of the Supper could be what one designates with the concept of 'earthly body.'" Page 87:

> The word "true" in the formulation of the Small Catechism's "true body and blood of Jesus Christ" belongs to the type of vague exclusionary words and leaves wide leeway for the various possibilities as to what things can be excluded by it. A theologically untrained layman, who considers the possibility of making the word "true" precisely by interchanging it with the term "natural," would immediately entangle himself in difficulties. The theologically educated person who has studied the present Luther citation in FC II 7 knows that the formulation of the catechism excludes the possibility that an "earthly" body could be meant. There the view is expressed that "Christ's body" can be present in three ways, and in this so-called doctrine of ubiquity it is clearly stated that the formulation "true body and blood of Christ" in the formulation cited by us from the catechism excludes the possibility that it could refer to the spatially defined body of Jesus Christ.

Thus an erroneous spiritualizing of Christ's body has been adopted, which is laid as the basis for sophisticated and protracted development of what "lies hidden in these texts" (op. cit., p. 106; compare p. 100: "to give expression to the views maintained in the Formula of Concord"). The texts are excused for being unclear and now are improved by means of modern "semantics" (p. 98). Since identity between Christ's actual body and His eucharistic body does not pass [the test], according to Bejerholm and Hornig the expression "true body" concerning the Supper includes an "adaptive word that serves to adapt a situation that is unclear in some sense to the normal situation" (p. 95). Objectively, this includes no more than a certain similarity through which to achieve the possibility of interpreting Luther and the Formula of Concord as teaching "the Words of Institution as a religious performative" (p. 107 n. 23), even though this in no way claims to "present a 'correct meaning' of the texts in that regard" (pp. 105f.). To aid this interpretation of Luther's and the Formula of Concord's doctrine of the Supper, which is supposed to imply that the expression "This is My body" would imply a recognition of a certain *status* for the bread without ontological implication, Ingemar Hedenius is put forward ("Performatives," in *Theoria* [1963], p. 125). The depiction that Bejerholm and Hornig produce of their topic cannot be defended with the disclaimers that are given in it from time to time. It is in *every* respect a completely incorrect interpretation that is given. Their main error is not primarily their unsuccessful attempts to discuss the material that exists, and the serious misreadings and failed attempts to handle the material that occur there (compare p. 107 n. 23), but their fundamental confidence in scientific solutions by virtue of "semantics" and "philosophy of religion," the insights of which are presumed not to have been available to earlier generations and which would give direct access to extracting the truth without making use of historical research's laborious working with the texts.

CHAPTER 2

Ad Dexteram Patris

The Attribute of Majesty of Christ's Body

THE biblical concept of God had such extraordinary loftiness that it was inherently necessary to think of the divinity not only as independent of matter but also as ruling over it at every point. Nothing can possibly separate the Creator from His work. This inseparability had to be formulated just like the [sacramental] presence, where many predications about God were available to be borrowed from philosophy and could be made more precise later.[1] In the expressions about Jesus as the eternal Son and about the exaltation of His humanity to the right hand of the Father, therefore, there was a need for the same relationship of majesty to be applied to Jesus in relation to creation. The questions about the omnipresence of Jesus' body, which are inseparably associated with the topic of this survey, belong in this larger complex: participation in the attribute of majesty.

A full and complete participation like this was represented by the Alexandrian school during the Christological controversies. Here the most prominent name is the church father Cyril of Alexandria. He builds on the conviction that the biblical texts really intend to describe such a communication of all glory to Jesus' humanity: "That He received honor, power, and dominion over all things is to be attributed to the state of the human nature."[2] The God-man implies a concrete, personal union of the divinity and the humanity, where the historical Jesus as such possesses divine power.[3] This Christian belief received its character as a creedal [symbolic, confessional] statement in the

1 Concerning the biblical idea of presence, see Lerle, *Die neutestamentliche Raumvorstellung*, which goes through various contemporary ideas about the biblical writers' dependence on a material idea of heaven.

2 PG 76:1359 C.

3 Seeberg, op. cit., 2:223: "He wants to find the redeeming power of the historical Christ in His works." Ibid.: "Cyril's style is in many ways described as 'speculative.' Yet that does not make the contrast clear, but strikes almost the opposite of reality.

Council of Ephesus, canon II: "If anyone does not confess that the Lord's flesh is life-giving because it has become the Word's own flesh, the Word, that causes all life, let him be anathema."[4] The liturgical expression for the same reality, faith in the divine man Jesus, is found in Ambrose: "Christ's flesh, which we still adore today in the mysteries [sacraments] and which, as we said above, even the apostles worshiped in the Lord Christ."[5]

Research has wanted to portray the Cyrillian tradition as extreme and fundamentally rejected by the significant Council of Chalcedon, even though it hailed Cyril and condemned his opponent Nestorius.[6] Against this paradox, Werner Elert has asserted that the meaning of Chalcedon was misinterpreted in a Nestorian direction. He finds the core of the council's resolution to be the bringing together of the two natures into one.[7] It is certain that the resolution's insistence on the continued integrity of both natures "without commingling" is mostly understood as incompatible with a real communication of divine attributes to the humanity. However, the perception of this contradiction need not always exist; the Lutheran Reformation, among other things, is an example of this. When this axiom falls, it is possible to achieve a new understanding of Chalcedon that corresponds with that of Elert and affirms his sharp critique.

Along this line, it is possible to express the omnipresence of Jesus' body, when necessary. To what degree this should be done became the subject of later controversies. This problem is still completely subject to and dependent on detailed exegesis of certain short texts. Cyrillian Christology as such, however, means an unalterable basis for any predication of the majesty of Jesus' humanity.[8]

The Antiochenes treated the Christology above with scholarly interest; Cyril takes his viewpoint in the historical appearance of Christ, like Apollinaris."

4 Denzinger § 262.

5 PL 16:794 A/D.

6 Seeberg, op. cit., 2:265: "Nothing has so strongly paralyzed the effects of Cyril in history as the Council of Chalcedon, even though it praised him and condemned Nestorius"; compare id., p. 234 n. 2, with an account of earlier literature.

7 Elert, *Der christliche Glaube*, p. 399: "For one hardly goes wrong when one explains the current popularity of this confession with the thought that it is understood in a Nestorian way." On the problem, see [Alois Grillmeier and Heinrich Bacht, eds.,] *Das Konzil von Chalkedon* [Würzburg: Echter, 1954, 1962], 1:324ff. Seeberg's judgment of the council has its counterpart in his words about Nestorius (op. cit., 2:220): "No one among the great 'heretics' of dogma-history bears this title as unjustly as Nestorius."

8 Compare here Theophylact, PG 124:1083 D; Oecumenicus, PG 118:1217, 1220, who put together the proof passages [*loci probandi*] for the patristic foundation of the Lutheran [doctrine of] omnipresence (compare *BS* 1132.40ff.) and who was controversial for his interpretation. Rocholl (op. cit., pp. 176f.) formulates a commonly held viewpoint [in which] he thinks that these passages indicate a mere "operative presence," as opposed to the view intended by Lutherans [of a presence] "in the all-embracing, so to speak poured-out elements." With the latter expression, Rocholl ascribes to the

The meaning of the personal union was understood differently by the other side of the Christological controversy, the Antiochene school. A strict distinction between the natures ruled out anything other than a dialectical, nominal unity, resting in the divine person as mutual subject for both natures.[9] This relationship underlies Augustine's idea when he writes in the first Christian dissertation on omnipresence:

> And thus, as that angelic voice testified, He shall come again just as He was seen going into heaven (Acts 1:10–11), that is, in the same form and substance of flesh, to which He indeed gave immortality and whose nature He did not take away. One must not think that according to this mode, He is spread out everywhere [throughout the universe]. For we must beware, lest we build on the divinity of the man in such a way that we take away the reality of His body. It does not follow, however, that because He is in God, thus He is everywhere, the way God is. For Scripture, which is most reliable, also says of us that in Him we live and move and have our being (Acts 17:28); yet we are not everywhere, as He is. But this man [is] in God in a different way, because also this God is in the man in a different way, in a certain particular and unique way. For one person is God and man, and both are one Christ Jesus, everywhere through the fact that He is God, but in heaven through the fact that He is man.[10]

These words of Augustine, which were repeated in various formulations during that whole time period being discussed in the present survey, proceed from the idea that it is important not to invalidate the attributes of the human nature. In order to maintain these, Christ's body may not be thought of as "spread out everywhere." The thought is carried through with the help of a parallel: just as human beings are not everywhere [simply] because according to Acts 17:28 they "live and move and have [their] being" in God who is everywhere, so Christ's body is not everywhere [simply] because it is in God who is everywhere. With these words, the union between the natures to a large degree surrenders its special character. The attributes of the natures are maintained, at the price of the unity of the person. Consequently, Augustine rejects any actual adoration of Christ's body, which is equated to a king's purple robe or diadem.

Lutherans a caricature of their actual view, as developed in the present volume. If the Lutheran position is stated more adequately, it is no longer absurd to appeal to the early church. Rocholl's procedure, viewed according to its method, implies the same approach as the current research applied to the question of Cyril's agreement with Chalcedon. By assuming that the former's Christology annuls the enduring individuality of the natures, it rules out *a priori* a congruence with Chalcedon's "preserving the property of each nature" (Denzinger § 302).

9 Compare above, pp. 35–36 n. 3!

10 PL 33:835 [Letter 187, *On the Presence of God*, ch. 10].

Adoration toward these signs of majesty is dependent simply on the fact that they are worn by the king.[11]

Cyrillian Christology continues with John of Damascus. In [the writings of] this dogmatician who was decisive for Western theology, we likewise find repeated the picture, already known earlier, of fire that conveys to iron its attribute of burning,[12] as an illustration of the communication of the attribute of majesty to Jesus' humanity. The opposite tradition, in turn, would find its home within Latin Christianity. Yet it was not undisputed within earlier Western Scholasticism, where even the adoration of Christ's body (*adoratio Christi secundum carnem*), for example, could be defended.[13] Even in the latter half of the 1100s, the majority of the influential writers are still of the opposite view.[14] Now a Christology dominates where the human nature in Jesus cannot receive divine attributes. Jesus' humanity is not a proper object for the Church's adoration. In relation to the Word that is worthy of adoration, it has the same relation as the royal robe to a king, just as Augustine taught. The foundational book of Western Scholasticism, Peter Lombard's *Sentences* (*Libri IV Sententiarum*), establishes this fact,[15] and the commentators of the subsequent centuries repeat it. Thomas writes: "And thus to adore the flesh of Christ is nothing other than to adore a robed king."[16]

In the same way, for Thomas, the relationship of Christ's body to creation did not need to have any other attributes than those that apply to created things otherwise. Where it is after the ascension is a locality that was reached by passing through the uppermost heavens without piercing them. This localization in heaven, with regard to firmly establishing His actual whereabouts, indeed does not fundamentally exclude a simultaneous relationship of Creator

11 PL 39:2200.

12 PG 94:1069 B/C. An account of the use of this image since the time of Origen is given by Chemnitz, *De duabus naturis*, pp. 114f. [cf. *Two Natures in Christ*, p. 396].

13 Landgraf, *Dogmengeschichte der Frühscholastik*, 2/2:132ff.

14 Id., op. cit., p. 148.

15 Peter Lombard's *Libri IV Sententiarum*, book 3, dist. IX, cap. *unicum*.

16 *ST*, III, 25, 2. *Die deutsche Thomas-Ausgabe* 26:403 places Thomas in this respect somewhat in opposition to Cyril but in agreement with John of Damascus. Thomas certainly calls upon this (ibid.): "But on the other hand, Damascus says this: the flesh of Christ, moreover, is adored, the Word of God being incarnate, not on account of itself, but on account of the Word of God united to it according to its hypostasis" (PG 94:1105 B), but it ought to be noted that John of Damascus is explaining *why* "the flesh of Christ, moreover, is adored," while Thomas again is explaining *in what sense* such a statement can be understood ("*potest intelligi*"); that is, he cannot accept the assertion by John of Damascus according to the way the words read. Compare to this Backes, "Die Christologie des hl. Thomas v. Aquin und die griechischen Kirchenväter," p. 316, who, regarding the adoration of Christ's humanity, writes: "But thereby Thomas has stepped into opposition with John of Damascus."

to creation and an omnipresence resulting from this. How these ideas are not mutually exclusive shall be presented later. With Thomas, the local definition is still the only one. How exclusively Thomas sets Jesus' humanity within the conditions of created things comes from the idea of passing through the dome of heaven's vault: "Although from the nature of the body it is impossible for it to be in the same space as another body, nevertheless through a miracle God is able to make it so that they are in the same space, just as He also made 'the body of Christ come forth from the closed womb of the blessed Virgin' and that 'He entered [the room], though the doors were closed,' just as blessed Gregory says."[17] When Thomas, in a section cited earlier, mentioned the absurdity of passing through a space in between, this did not apply absolutely, but just "that it cannot be said *here*," thus at the regularly repeated celebrations of the Mass.[18] God makes the miracle of coexistence possible, which Ockham later in his theology of the Supper would adduce as decisive. When this miracle [of the sacramental presence] is to begin, the divine power necessary for it proceeds not from Christ's body but directly from the divinity: "not from the special character of the body, but by the power that is nearby and performing it."[19] Not even in respect to this lowly miracle does Christ's body possess power over things.

Bonaventure states it expressly, though only in the form of theses for disputation concerning the omnipresence of Christ's body. "On the opposite side" this proposition is set forth: "Also, if Christ in the Sacrament can be in many places, suppose that there are only three places in which it is possible for Christ's body to be; therefore, it is possible for it to be everywhere; but since this is of God alone, it is impossible for it to happen to someone else." The answer to the proposal to let the body of Christ be omnipresent by reducing the world to a few points where Christ's body can be, which would still encourage the absurdity of letting such a divine attribute happen to something created, comes in "*Solutio*": "I consider through an impossibility that there are only three places; then it must be said that it is everywhere, but not the way God is, because God is everywhere on account of His immensity, and therefore He cannot be absent from anyone; but the body of Christ is everywhere on account of the paucity of places."[20] The answer will be that omnipresence as a divine attribute, a result of God's immeasurability, cannot be transferred to Jesus' humanity. But by hypothetically reducing the space of the universe, Christ's body would indeed become omnipresent by definition under the assumed suppositions, yet *not the way God is*, but on the basis of the paucity of spaces. This same "not the way God is" is also behind Bonaventure's explanation of the adoration of Christ's body,

17 *ST*, III, 57, 4, ad 2.

18 *ST*, III, 72, 2; compare above, pp. 6–7, text near n. 25.

19 *ST*, III, 57, 4, ad 2.

20 In IV, d. 10, p. 1, art. un., qu. 3.

where he refers to the images of mantle and diadem "just as Augustine says, and Master [Lombard] recites in the letter."[21]

What Bonaventure achieved theoretically concerning the omnipresence of Christ's body is found again also within the Ockhamist school.[22] In an earlier document ascribed to Ockham himself, *Centiloquium*,[23] it is assumed, by way of reasoning, that God allows the presence to enter into the entire universe, which then takes on the role of the host, or that God consecrates a host filling the whole universe; in both cases, the situation arises that Christ's body would be said to be omnipresent just the way God is ("*sicut Deus est ubique*").[23a] This does not imply a departure from Bonaventure's restrictive "not the way God is." "Omnipresence" is thought of only as diffinitive or circumscribed, never as divine. Nor does this apply to any attribute ascribed to Christ's body through the personal union of the two natures, which it is able to use. It does not touch on speculations about previously unstated Christological corollaries, but on a miraculous deed, which through God's omnipotence could begin with any created thing at all.[24]

Therefore, when [Gabriel] Biel, also on this point, develops a clearer distinction of terminology, and distinguishes between "repletive" (divine) and diffinitive presence, he is actually introducing nothing new.[25] He is only explicating the traditional demarcation vis-à-vis Cyrillian theology: "Fifth, it is conceded that the same body could *de facto* be everywhere through divine power, and thus it is not omnipresent as a characteristic of God, but it is omnipresent through its characteristic nature, so it is characteristic of God that it is impossible for there to be a place in which He would not be, and this is not communicated to any creature."[26] Divine omnipresence cannot be transferred

21 In III, d. 9, art. I, qu. 1, concl. op. 2.

22 Iserloh (op. cit., pp. 267ff.) proceeds from the idea that only an impious "Ockhamistic" intellect can offer reasoning of this hypothetical character. Also, if a certain distinction exists between Bonaventure and the Ockhamist depicted by Iserloh, so that the latter does not mean a "*paucity* of places" in the hypothesis, the logic is the same and shows that Iserloh's complaints about irreligious drought and sophistry would actually apply also to Bonaventure, known for his piety. Iserloh builds on an unproven contrast between speculative intellect and religious commitment.

23 Compare here Junghans, op. cit., pp. 67ff., 73.

23a *Centiloquium*, concl. 25, cited according to Iserloh, op. cit, p. 269; compare Seeberg, op. cit., 3:791; Loofs, *Leitfaden zum Studium der Dogmengeschichte*, p. 512; Rocholl, op. cit., p. 185.

24 This latter is asserted by Rocholl, op. cit., ibid.

25 Loofs (op. cit., p. 512) asserts this erroneously and proceeds from the idea that Ockham reckoned with a divine form of omnipresence of Christ's body. Seeberg (op. cit., 4:472 n. 1) thinks that Ockham would have taught that a divine omnipresence of Christ's body would be possible.

26 Biel, op. cit., lect. 46 H.

to any creature. But there is a significant difference between this omnipresence and what could be said "*de facto*" in a hypothetical situation.[27] The chasm between the Word and the Word's body also hinders Christ's body from being able to be adored.[28]

What is stated here about the Nominalist school's theories of the "omnipresence" of Christ's body means that all assertions about Nominalism as preparatory to the later Lutheran doctrine of the omnipresence of Christ's body must be fundamentally rejected. As shall be shown here, Luther and his successors insist on an omnipresence that is repletive and divine, not diffinitive/circumscribed and angelic/human, which is a result of the personal union and not an arbitrary act of the divine will. This is a Christological dogma and not a thesis set forth by evidence of reasoning. Whatever similarity remains between the two thought systems is limited to verbal formulations that do not at all suffice to set forth [even] a very diluted conjecture about onset and achievement, seed and fruit.[29] The connection between Nominalism and Luther on this point is a rather

27 This distinction has been noted by Damerau, op. cit., p. 190 n. 108.

28 Biel, op. cit., lect. 50 G: "Not that the human nature is the object of this adoration, but because the whole person of the Word . . . is adored. . . . And helpful for this is the comparison of a king dressed in purple and crown, likewise of coal to fire." (In this case, then, the early church's image of fire and iron is understood according to the pattern of the personal image/clothing, that is, as coexistence and not as communication.) Damerau thinks that Biel teaches the adoration of the human nature (op. cit., p. 166 n. 50) and blocks Biel's opinion: "Therefore, the human nature must not be shut off from this adoration," disregarding the idea that it retains its decisive limitation in the subsequent statement, which is quoted above ("*not that* . . ."). The act of adoration thus is actually directed to the concrete Christ but intentionally disregards His human nature ("not . . . the object"). Furthermore, Damerau (ibid., "Lect. G" [should be "H"]) adduces this: "The human nature in Christ must be adored with *latria* (*latria* is the form of adoration that is appropriate for God). . . ." Here Damerau omits the decisive "it is an act of adoration, taken broadly." This distinction goes back to what Biel (op. cit., lect. 50 E) explained concerning *latria* in the figurative sense, by connecting it to a word about this by Rabanus Maurus [compare Landgraf, op. cit., 2/2:162 n. 11: "a passage from Rabanus that has not been verified"; the modern edition of Biel* notes "PL 111:1482 seq.," which only infers an approximate agreement]. Rabanus here distinguishes "delight" [*dilectio*] toward the Redeemer from the actual adoration of the Creator: "because He created us." This former sentiment toward Christ's body is based only on the idea that "we have been redeemed through it (that is, the flesh)" and "adoration [*latria*] is used in an extended sense or broadly." (The modern edition of Biel here has a mistake: Rabanus's "we do *not* adore . . . because He created us" has become "we adore . . . ." The correct text is in Biel, *Epitome et collectorium ex Occamo circa quatuor sententiarum Libros*, book 3, d. IX, a. 1, C. Compare the same text in Bonaventure, In III, d. 9, dub. 1, u. 3.)

* [Misprint says, "modern edition of the Bible."]

29 Rettberg, "Occam und Luther, oder Vergleich ihrer Lehren vom heiligen Abendmahl," is criticized by Dieckhoff (*Die evangelische Abendmahlslehre im Reformationszeitalter*, p. 130 n. **) for having equated Nominalist and Lutheran omnipresence of Christ's

unnecessary thesis, as the Middle Ages, despite everything, offers examples of numerous other theologians whose doctrinal system allows the possibility of a real omnipresence of Christ's body. Even if no historical influence from them on Luther can be proved and is even excluded by the way in which Luther's doctrine of the omnipresence of Christ's humanity came about, the present investigation will show, at any rate, that there is a beginning of an actual identity and not just a merely theoretical one.

Among these, one must certainly not count men such as Johannes Scotus Eriugena, who at Charlemagne's court developed a Neoplatonist-colored theology, tending toward pantheism. Within the framework of this system, Christ's body is ascribed unlimited omnipresence, but at the price of all the attributes of the human nature.[30] Within an equally divergent system, Amalric of Bena put forth a teaching of the omnipresence of Christ's body by virtue of which the sacramental presence existed even before the consecration, which had only a demonstrative function.[31] Even here the pantheistic element was apparent.[32] Amalric was condemned by the Fourth Lateran Council in 1215, shortly after his death, for his tendencies that were antinomian and generally destructive to the Church.[33] Impulses of this kind, of course, are outside the bounds within which traditional Christological schools wage their battle. Hugh of St. Victor again worked within the framework of an orthodox theology and with connection to Cyrillian Christology. He acknowledges a real communication of divine attributes to Jesus' human nature. The presence in the Sacrament is said to occur

---

body. Dieckhoff underscores that Nominalism only considered it a hypothesis, whereas Luther spoke of it as a fact. But Dieckhoff himself overlooks the fact that the hypothesis, with regard to dogma, was not talking about the same type of omnipresence. Dieckhoff (ibid., p. 134) concludes, concerning the dependent relationship, that

> the Lutheran doctrine of ubiquity, and thus also the consequent Lutheran doctrine that Christ's body is in the Sacrament, is a *new* teaching, not borrowed from Scholasticism but completely foreign to scholastic doctrine, and then also is proved to be just as thoroughly groundless as a scholastic one. But now this does not exclude the idea that the scholastic development of doctrine paved the way for . . . this new doctrine of Luther's concerning the ubiquity of Christ's body.

Loofs and Seeberg (compare above, p. 40 n. 25) also proceed from the idea that Ockham taught a repletive omnipresence, while Iserloh (op. cit., p. 278) ascribed to Luther a nonrepletive omnipresence, through which, in any case on erroneous grounds, a similarity between Nominalism and Luther arises.

30 See concerning this Rocholl, op. cit., pp. 177ff.

31 Compare to this Jorissen, op. cit., pp. 23f.; *Dictionnaire de théologie catholique* 15/2:2034ff., "Ubiquisme"; *LTK*² 1:415, "Amalrik von Bena."

32 Mansi, *Sacrorum conciliorum nova collectio*, 12:809: "These, on the other hand, [say:] Everything is one, because whatever is, is God."

33 Compare Denzinger §§ 803, 808.

because of the divinity's special mode of existence: "I do not deny that the reality and essence of Christ's body is on several altars at the same time, but through this I am indicating that that mode of existence does not have what is common to other bodies by the very nature of the body, but rather what is common with a spirit, not created, but uncreated."[34] Hugh of St. Cher also stands in the same tradition.[35] Cyrillian Christology emerges likewise in the brothers Gerhoh and Arno of Reichersberg, who accuse Lombard of Nestorianism.[36] This thought system concedes, when necessary, setting forth the proposition of the omnipresence of Christ's body.[37] Meanwhile, all these later theologians' expressions, which only implied or suggested a divine omnipresence of Christ's body, were outdone by Faber Stapulensis [Jacques Lefèvre d'Étaples], who, just on the threshold of Reformation-era theology, not only takes up the problem primarily as a part of the doctrine of the Sacrament but [also], with a perspective on this narrower aspect, says, "It is greater to recognize that He is absolutely everywhere bodily."[38]

---

34 PL 175:584; see concerning this Rocholl, op. cit., pp. 180ff.; compare Seeberg, op. cit., 3:259f., who sees Hugh of St. Victor as being closer to the usual Latin Christology.

35 Rocholl, op. cit., p. 182.

36 Seeberg, op. cit., 3:263ff. Page 263: "Gerhoh, as once Cyril—whom he was not familiar with, however—his authority is Hilary—has the vivid desire to see divine life in the man Jesus."

37 Damerau (op. cit., p. 53) wants to fortify this chain of tradition with the Nominalist Heinrich of Langenstein. But the citation does not correspond with Damerau's text and merely indicates that Heinrich is a good Nominalist. Damerau, op. cit., p. 53: "In Christology, Langenstein comes very close to Luther's religious insight when in the counterargument he speaks of Christ being there already before the change takes place." Ibid., p. 35: "One could indeed take it as absolutely possible that Christ enters into a coexistence with the substance of the bread. The change does not bring the body of Christ to this place, for Christ's body was there already before the change." Heinrich meanwhile says (Damerau, op. cit., p. 35 n. 11): "It is absolutely possible that the body of Christ becomes [present] for a coexistence of the bread, for the whole substance of the bread along with the accidence, and *afterward* the substance of the bread is converted into the body of Christ; it does not come there *then* by virtue of the conversion, because it was there beforehand" (emphasis added). That is the Ockhamist proof that the body of Christ can in fact first become ("*fiat*") present *together with* the bread, that *after that* transubstantiation's annihilation of the bread can occur, and that *thus* Christ's body, even under the presumption of the reality of transubstantiation, does not need to have been made present *by virtue of this* ("*ex vi conversione*"); compare Iserloh, op. cit., pp. 159ff. This has nothing to do with either Christology or "Luther's religious insight."

38 Quoted according to Rocholl, op. cit., p. 187. Compare also *Dictionnaire de théologie catholique* 15/2:2038, "Ubiquisme": "Luther was perhaps inspired by Occam, but surely he knew the formula of Lefèvre d'Étaples [Faber Stapulensis]." This latter point cannot be proven at all. Luther used the *Epistolae Pauli* (1512) and *Quincuplex psalterium* (1509) of Faber Stapulensis (compare WA 56:xxxiv, lii), but nothing is known regarding the later John commentary that contains the quoted words. Compare Hahn, "Faber Stapulensis und Luther"; E. Thestrup Pedersen, *Luther som skriftfortolker*,

Luther's background will be rightly characterized as belonging to these and similar formulations rather than to Nominalist speculations, though Luther's viewpoint, in regard to its origin, is equally independent of both.

Luther

Concerning scholastic theology, Luther writes against Zwingli in 1531: "Many teachers have taught like this, and I also used to be a doctor like that. I thus excluded the humanity and therefore considered that I was doing the right thing when I was separating Christ's divinity and humanity from each other. The highest theologians used to do that."[39] Luther's words about himself having previously taught scholastic Christology[40] must refer to a time from his academic activity, not just instruction received passively during his studies. Therefore, there is reason to assume that Luther's own earlier works would show traces of this scholastic Christology.

[Hans] Grass has suggested that the Romans lectures of 1515–16 already include the actual communication of attributes.[41] Yet scholastic Christology is found here to be in opposition to Luther's later view. The words cited by Grass as an innovation—"the divinity is emptied and hidden in the flesh"—are of special importance in this respect. The medieval tradition of interpreting Phil. 2:7, which includes the word *exinanivit* ("He emptied Himself"), is stated this way by Thomas:

> Moreover, it beautifully says: He emptied [Himself]. For empty is contrasted with full. The divine nature, however, is full enough; because all perfection of goodness is there. . . . The human nature, however, and the soul are not full, but capable of fullness, because it became like a *tabula rasa.* And therefore the human nature is empty. Therefore, it says: He emptied [Himself], because He assumed the human nature. Therefore, first, he touches on the assumption of the human nature, saying: Taking on the form of a servant. For man, by his creation, is a servant of God, and the human nature is the form of a servant.[42]

Thomas says here that the incarnation itself constitutes an emptying, through which the complete takes on the nature of the incomplete. The finite creation cannot be assumed by the infinite Creator without an incompleteness

pp. 305ff. — On the other hand, the words of Faber Stapulensis were known to later Lutheranism and cited by Jacob Andreae, *De maiestate hominis Christi*, pp. IIIIf.

39 WA 33:155.10ff. [cf. AE 23:102].

40 For the expression "the highest theologians," compare WA 16:74.23f., where Thomas Aquinas (as the author of the canonical hours and the Mass of the Corpus Christi festival) is referred to with these words.

41 Grass, op. cit., p. 69.

42 *S. Thomae Aquinatis in omnes S. Pauli apostoli epistolas commentaria* 2:92.

or emptying in a certain way having to be ascribed to Him. There is an inescapable tension between Creator and creation. What is emptied, thus, is the un-incarnate Logos, which assumed human nature. Even the assumption [of the human nature] ("*assumpsit*") is not effected by the Logos that has become flesh and does not refer to any event in Jesus' life.[43] Emptying and incarnation thus coincide for Thomas: "The apostle calls the incarnation an emptying."[44] The expression "form of God" (*forma Dei*) in the Bible verse in question is explained in this way: *forma* is understood as the philosophical concept *forma*, and since God's *forma* is [God] Himself, the "form of God" refers to the divinity.[45] This form of God rightly applies to Christ "because He is in the form of God and knows His own nature well," in contrast to the devil and wicked men who want to make themselves into God's equals.[46] "Form of a servant" (*forma servi*) is understood as congruent with the "humanity" mentioned above.[47] The glorification of the form of a servant includes "making known His divinity": "Therefore, He gave to Him, that is, to Christ, this name, so that He was called and was God." The corollary of the personal union, the human nature's belonging to the divine person by name, is now proclaimed. In biblical phraseology, it is natural to designate a proclamation as a real event, as if the proclamation, publicly announced beforehand, was [already] a fact: "In Sacred Scripture something is said to happen when it is proclaimed. Therefore, He gave, that is, made manifest to the world what this name holds."[48]

43 Thomas's opinion is thus the opposite of what Persson (*Sacra doctrina*, p. 229 n. 46) ascribes to him: "*Exinanitio* ['emptying'] thus, according to Thomas, does not aim at anything that applies to God, but to the human nature. . . ." But at the same time, what is important is that the act that the un-incarnate Logos carries out does not mean any change of the divinity but only means a certain relation (*ST*, III, 57, 2, ad 2): "Indeed, just as *exinanitus* ['emptied'] is said not of that which would lose its fullness, but of that which takes on our smallness." The divinity as the one who performs the act of emptying thus makes the emptying into a way of speaking and not into a reality.

44 *S. Thomae [Aquinatis in omnes S. Pauli apostoli epistolas] commentaria* [2:]93.

45 Op. cit., p. 92: "It must not be understood that the form of God is one thing and God Himself is another: because in individual things and in materials the form is the same thing, and it is of the thing, especially in God."

46 Ibid.

47 Ibid.: "Indeed, man from his creation is a servant of God, and human nature is the form of a servant."

48 Op. cit., p. 94. In this context, Thomas rejects as heretical the view that the glorification should simply refer to the imparting of certain human gifts with the highest power. He maintains that it really means an impartation of the divine name. On the contrary, Thomas does not consider divine attributes to have been conveyed as gifts to Jesus' humanity. [For example,] *judicaria potestas*, that is, the real "power to judge" the living and the dead, has been given to Him only in the sense that the "original authority" remains with God: "Nevertheless, the power to judge is entrusted by God to men with respect to those who are subject to their jurisdiction. . . . For which reason, it

The same thoughts are in Luther's lectures on Romans: "So that just as He emptied Himself according to the form of God (up to the emptiness of the flesh) by being born into the world, so according to the [form] of a servant He filled Himself into the fullness of the divinity by ascending into heaven."[49] "*Forma Dei*" and "*forma servi*" here, as in Thomas, stand for divine and human nature, respectively. The emptying occurs according to the first; according to the other, the glorification that consists of this: that "the Holy Spirit through the apostles indeed defined and declared Him to be the Son of God now in power over all things."[50] The revealing of the previously hidden relationship—Jesus' humanity participating in the divine person "on account of the union of both [natures]"[51]—is described as glorification: "The humanity is filled with and drawn into the divinity."[52] In the same way, the opposite assertion includes the idea that the divine person is united with the humanity: "God is the Son of David"; the description of the very emptying: "emptied is the divinity."[53]

Identifying this with scholastic Christology can also be supported here through an argument from silence [*deductio e silentio*]. On the passage in question, Luther breaks with the tradition in the case of translating and clarifying the Greek *oristhentos*, which in its Latin form, *praedestinatus*, gave Scholasticism great difficulties.[54] Here, however, Luther indicates the break very clearly.[55] It is therefore out of the question that he would have silently passed over another much more important difference.[56]

---

pertains to Him also to have the power to judge according to His human nature" (*ST*, III, 59, 2). The participation of Jesus' humanity in the power to judge is not different from what can also be given to other men. In the same way, it says (*ST*, III, 42, 2) that the emergence of the divinity at the transfiguration on Tabor happens "to the body itself, not through an immanent and influencing type of mode, but rather through the mode of transitory passion, just as when the sky is illuminated by the sun." The divine manifestations occur thus from the outside, and Christ's body partakes of the same kind of relationship to divine glory as any other object that is illuminated by the sun.

49 WA 56:167.19ff. [cf. AE 25:147].

50 WA 56:168.10ff. [cf. AE 25:148].

51 WA 56:167.24 [cf. AE 25:147].

52 WA 56:168.3 [cf. AE 25:147].

53 WA 56:168.1 [cf. AE 25:147].

54 Compare to this *ST*, III, 24.

55 WA 56:166.18f. [cf. AE 25:147]: "I do not know if that passage has been truly and properly explained by anyone. The ancients were hindered by their peculiar manner of interpretation; more recent people, in fact, were hindered by the absence of the Spirit."

56 Nilsson (*Simul*, pp. 217ff.) cites the Luther material taken up in the text above, which meanwhile is not different from Luther's later expressions. WA 56:168.2 [cf. AE 25:147] is used in this way (op. cit., p. 226 n. 65 and p. 227) as [an] illustration of Luther's later view.

This scholastic interpretation of the emptying is also found in [Luther's] *Lectures on the Psalms* [*Dictata super Psalterium*]. It says there: "'*You lowered Him*'; through the incarnation You showed Your Son to be lowered; the same one who is of man. Thus he [Paul] goes from the human nature in Christ in the preceding verse to the divine nature in this one."[57] While in Ps. 8:4 "Son of Man" still applies to the man Jesus—"*or Son of Man*, namely, Christ, of the virgin"—it is supposed that the psalmist in v. 5 *changes* the object: "You lowered Him" applies to the divine nature. Gathering material for this exposition of the psalter accounts for the underlying scholastic Christology. It is only the preexisting Logos that can reasonably be said to empty Himself: "For it does not say 'I lowered' [someone] who was not great before."[58] Only this meeting of things of unmatched magnitude in becoming man warrants the word "emptying."

Nor is there any change in relation to Scholasticism in Luther's commentary on the Epistle to the Hebrews with its introductory section on Christology.[59] Also in the Lenten sermon from 1518, the medieval view of emptying is repeated. Luther does not actually state things clearly here, but the connection to the earlier tradition is still there. Luther also misses the opportunity to account for any divergent understanding of the concept *forma*.[60]

57 WA 3:80.8ff. [cf. AE 10:88].

58 WA 3:80.31 (gloss) [cf. AE 10:87f.]; compare WA 3:81.30ff. (scholae). Harnack (*Luthers Theologie*, 2:163) thinks that Luther here "wants it known that the words of this passage apply not to the person of Christ but to His natures." Luther does not have any concept of any such contrast between person and nature. The gloss used by Harnack—"in this verse each nature of Christ appears, and it is not properly explained concerning man" (WA 3:80.32f. [cf. AE 10:88])—contrasts in the passage *the union of the natures* that warrants the "*est minutus*" and "*homo*," that is, "man," *not* Christ, but "I explain it concerning created man" (WA 3:80.34 [cf. AE 10:88]); compare WA 3:81.24 [cf. AE 10:87]: "man here is taken collectively." Luther thus, in contrast to the adjacent statements, does not want to have the emptying apply to the *human race* but only to the *Son of Man*. Harnack's mistake is expressed in his inserted parenthesis, that Phil. 2:7 "is indeed not explained concerning man (Jesus)." — The reading of Psalm 8 which Luther postulates is in the modern Swedish Bible at Heb. 2:6ff., which should properly be applied by the reader who wants to immerse himself in Luther's way of thinking.

59 WA 57/3:7.3f. The adoration that Christ receives as incarnate is completely identical with what is always offered to the divinity; the incarnation does not broaden the adoration: "And they may adore Him, as true God, who nevertheless was adored before" (compare WA 57/3:104.11ff. [cf. AE 29:115]). Already in a marginal note to Biel's *Collectorium*, Luther expresses caution against idolatry of Christ's humanity ([Hermann Degering, ed.,] *Festgabe der Kommission zur Herausgabe der Werke M. Luthers 10. November 1933* [Weimar: Böhlaus, 1933], pp. 6f.). Link (op. cit., p. 106) underscores that Luther turns "against the adoration of the human side of the person of Christ." Link understands this as a criticism of Biel (compare op. cit., pp. 309, 313), but, on the contrary, it is support.

60 WA 1:269.1ff. [cf. AE 51:37f.].

A completely new interpretation appears in 1519, with wide-reaching consequences, in the *Sermon on Two Kinds of Righteousness*. Now *forma* no longer coincides with *natura*. Luther writes:

> The form of God here does not mean the substance of God, because Christ never emptied Himself of that, just as the form of a servant cannot mean human substance. But the form of God is wisdom, virtue, righteousness, kindness, and liberty, so that Christ the man was free, powerful, wise, subject to no one and to no vice . . . and yet He did not show pride in this form. . . . He emptied [Himself], not wishing to use these titles against us, not wishing to be dissimilar to us. Instead, He became just like one of us and took on the form of a servant (that is, He subjected Himself to all evils).[61]

Forma has been freed from its philosophical meaning and has been equated with divine attributes, which could be distinguished conceptually from the divinity and transferred to "Christ the man" [*Christus homo*], who becomes the bearer of them. His form as a servant and even the reality of the emptying is assumed to be the fact that He does not make use of these divine attributes intended for Him. The likeness of a servant again is not the human nature itself but what the human nature possesses in order to suffer in the corruptible world, since it abstained from its prerogatives.

This new explanation of the text stands in a definite parallel relationship to the main thought in this treatise by Luther: that "righteousness of God" [*iustitia Dei*] does not mean [righteousness as] God's own intrinsic attribute, but a kind of righteousness that can [also] be ascribed to man. In both cases, Luther frees himself exegetically from the scholastic demand for a meaning that can be inserted into the scheme that could make use of philosophical phraseology naturally. In both cases, Luther shows that he has learned to transfer the divinely defined predicate to the creature: "righteousness of God" [*iustitia Dei*] in men, "form of God" [*forma Dei*] in the man Jesus. This accords well with what Luther writes in 1545 about the analogies to the discovery he made:

> Immediately a different face of the entire Scripture appeared to me there. I then rushed through the Scriptures, as I remembered them, and I also gathered the analogy in other words, such as "work of God," that is, what God does in us; the "power of God," by which He makes us powerful; the "wisdom of God," by which He makes us wise; the "strength of God, salvation, the glory of God."[62]

61 WA 2:147.38ff. [cf. AE 31:301].

62 WA 54:186.9ff. [cf. AE 34:337]. That Luther deviated from the traditional exposition is noted by Hieronymus Dungersheim, who in December 1519 ascribed to Luther (WA Br 1:[582].248ff., no. 230): "But also among your other things, I nonetheless really wonder why you have wanted to turn away from the understanding and opinion of the oft-quoted Nicene Council and the holy Greek fathers, and of those also who

In the epistle sermon on Hebrews 1 for Christmas Day High Mass, in the 1522 *Church Postil*, Luther speaks about this change in his Christology:

> Thus Scripture corresponds even more fittingly to Christ than to us, and it swaddles the person [of Christ] so nicely in the [two] natures, and again distinguishes the natures, which only a few rightly understand. And I myself have often erred in these and similar passages, in that I ascribed to the natures what belongs to the person and vice versa. Thus Philippians 2; . . . indeed, this passage is dark.[63]

Essentially, the change means this: "And, finally, everything that is said of Christ's humiliation and exaltation should be ascribed to the man [human nature]; for divine nature may neither be humbled nor exalted."[64] The emptying is no longer that the divinity is dishonored by being united with an imperfect nature, but what happens with this latter nature: the emptying of the human nature's divine attributes.

The human nature's participation in the attributes of the divinity is now clarified. Luther explains that though Christ's human nature was not always entitled to perfect knowledge of all things during His earthly life, "as some make of Him an omnipotent man, mixing the two natures," still according to God's will it sometimes shared in the omniscience that resided in the human nature through the incarnation: "as God led Him and brought Him forth, He was full of grace and wisdom, so that He was able to judge and rule everything that happened to Him. Therefore, the divinity, which alone sees and knows all things, was personal and present in Him."[65] This text could be understood as a declaration of independence for Christ's human nature, directed against a scholastic monophysitism, but, on the contrary, all the attempts of Scholasticism [to use it] to elevate Jesus' humanity are outmatched on the essential points. How this is different from the Middle Ages here is not primarily that the depiction of Jesus as the perfect man is abandoned,[66] which was the meaning of Luther's words

---

did not know Greek, both Latins and others, who always were regarded as sure pillars in the Church, when you expound the apostle's passage: 'Who was in the form of God,' etc., at Philippians 2."

63 WA 10/1.1:163.10ff. [cf. AE 75:268]. WA states (ibid., n. 2): "At Luther's self-critique here, in our copy of B there is written in the margin by a sixteenth-century hand: N.B. N.B." The background for this would be the Reformed attempt to show that Luther in this passage was supposed to have retracted the doctrine of the omnipresence of Christ's body, as mentioned by the *Apologia oder verantwortung des Christlichen Concordien Buchs*, fol. 155af. [cf. *Apology*, p. 211f.]; and the comment there is completely correct, that what is referred to here is "how he perhaps before or in the papacy or even afterward, before the year [15]21, erred in the doctrine of the person of Christ."

64 WA 10/1.1:150.8f. [cf. AE 75:259].

65 WA 10/1.1:150.4ff. [cf. AE 75:259].

66 See concerning this Persson (op. cit., p. 211), which depicts Thomas, and Landgraf (op. cit., 2/2:44ff., chapter "Das Wissen der Seele Christi"). Here as elsewhere the

"mixing the two natures," but that the knowledge that Christ used "as God led Him" in exercising His prophetic office is motivated by and identified with the presence of divine omniscience in the flesh. The knowledge that Thomas and the rest of the Scholastics ascribe to Christ as a man is certainly an everlasting and perfect knowledge, but a *human* knowledge, since a divine knowledge cannot possibly be contained in a created intellect, while according to Luther, Christ's knowledge during His earthly life is, in fact, a temporary occurrence but still divine knowledge.

A Christology built in this way faces the problem of explaining how unawareness and other limitations on the divine fullness, such as suffering, could be ascribed to a human nature that still possesses divine attributes by virtue of the personal union. Just as Luther's Christology outdoes all expressions of Scholasticism, in a similar way it is systematically more difficult to reconcile a simultaneous glory and lowliness. It is thus impossible to compare, as Per Erik Persson does, Thomas's peculiar "miraculous intervention," whereby a "barrier between higher and lower layers" in Christ's human nature makes Christ's suffering possible, and Luther, who does not have "any difficulties seeing in these human events a direct expression of God's essence."[67] Thomas's problem is there for the finding in Luther, but not as a psychological one, but as Christological. The unity of the psyche, which for scholastic theology prevented a simultaneous "beatific vision" and a real suffering,[68] corresponds in Luther to the unity of the natures, which is thought to prevent the human nature from simultaneously possessing and abstaining from the divine attributes.

---

explanation means that the human nature's ability to take up divine attributes is rejected more and more. Alcuin still represents the Cyrillian view, which was simply repeated later in various theologians, such as Hugh of St. Victor (pp. 63ff.).

67 Id., p. 223 n. 27.

68 Vogelsang, *Die Anfänge von Luthers Christologie*, p. 97, presents *Dictata super Psalterium* [*Lectures on the Psalms*] as un-scholastic in this regard. Luther's words "most illustrious, nevertheless simultaneously (!) also most disturbed" are commented on (Vogelsang's writing): "The new thing is offered in the 'simultaneously,'" whereby Vogelsang himself still has to add [that Luther was] "still inhibited by the scholastic doctrine of the will—and the separation of Christ's soul." Vogelsang hereby overlooks the fact that, for example, Thomas ascribes to Christ on the cross both beatific vision as well as the highest pains (*ST*, III, 46, 6): "Christ's suffering was the greatest. . . . But the cause of His internal suffering was, first of all, indeed all the sins of the human race, for which He made satisfaction by suffering, whence He ascribes those things as to Himself, saying in the psalm: 'the words of My delights.'" *ST*, III, 46, 6 ad 4: "That suffering in Christ exceeded all suffering of any contrite person. Then, because it proceeded from greater wisdom and love, the grief of the contrite will be increased from these things." One can compare to this Vogelsang's simplified picture of the pre-Lutheran interpretations of the suffering: "pure physical pain(s)" (op. cit., p. 93). If the scholastic expressions are noted, it becomes impossible that "the beginnings of Luther's Christology" are built on the "simultaneously" above.

How even Luther here lets divine intervention make the suffering possible emerges from the Palm Sunday sermon on Phil. 2:5–12 in the *Lenten Postil* from 1525. Here again he rejects the thought that "form of God" [*forma Dei*] and "form of a servant" [*forma servi*] should be the same as "God" and "man." *Forma* is distinguished from "the divine essence and nature in Christ" and means that "it behaves in a divine way or sets itself as God." In contrast to the blasphemous pretense raised by the antichrist, the devil, and wicked men, Christ possesses sole right to consider the divine likeness to be consistent with His essence: "He also could not consider it robbery, since He certainly was [God], since He had that essence within Him, and it was innate to Him; rather, He considered it His natural, eternal possession."[69] Meanwhile, Christ does not always exercise this divine likeness of His during His earthly life. "Out of good will and grace" He took on the "form of a servant"; through a special voluntary decision He allowed a "servantlike nature," that is, the human nature, to be accompanied by the "form of a servant" and not by "divine form," "as when God hides Himself."[70] The use of these different likenesses occurs on account of the economy of salvation: sometimes the divine likeness is revealed, as with "miracles and words of healing contained in the Gospels," [and] sometimes the form of a servant.[71]

---

69 WA 17/2:240.20ff. [cf. AE 76:418]. This exegesis of "did not consider equality with God as plunder," in the question of what the verb means, coincides with Thomas's "He knew His nature well," even if the subject is understood in various ways; compare above, pp. 45–46 n. 48 and the accompanying text. Yet it would be this very meaning in the text about "emptying" in the Epistle to the Philippians that gave rise to Luther's words in 1522 (WA 10/1.1:163.17 [cf. AE 75:268]): "Although this passage is dark." Luther does not think that he has achieved definitive clarity in the question of what these words mean. In 1519 (WA 2:147.25ff. [cf. AE 31:295]), Luther had interpreted the passage "negatively," so that "not considering" became "He did not wish to be equal," an emptying that should follow in Christians to their [own] measure, but on the other hand was not to be understood "affirmatively," that Christ had the right to ascribe to Himself the form of God: "because He is equal to God, He did not consider it robbery." WA 11:76.35ff. (1523) retains this interpretation. In 1525, Luther goes back to the scholastic, affirmative interpretation, which is repeated above in the text; and in 1528 (WA 27:93.29ff., 94.2ff.) it is repeated: "Paul wanted to indicate that He was similar to God, not in a devilish way like that of an ungodly man, who considered it robbery." In 1531 (WA 34/1:182.8ff., 183.7ff.) both interpretations are offered as alternatives.

70 WA 17/2:239.22 [cf. AE 76:417].

71 WA 17/2:242.12 [cf. AE 76:419–20]. Thus, for Luther, suffering is not an attribute that is ascribed to the divinity. Persson's words apply to Luther as well as to Thomas (op. cit., p. 223 n. 27): "So Thomas places the divinity in the Golgotha event, not for the suffering on the cross, but for the miraculous occurrences in His surroundings." Compare to this WA 17/2:243.8ff. [cf. AE 76:420]: "Although He also does not thus set aside the divine form . . . for He does miracles even while suffering and on the cross, when He, as God, gave the thief paradise and in the garden when He drove back the mob with a word." Persson's contrast between Thomas and Luther, the latter of which would see in the suffering "a direct expression of God's essence," is fabricated. But it ought to be noted

This emptying is a particular, special act of Christ's will, where the effect of the divine attributes is withheld from the human nature: "Therefore, he [Paul] does not say that someone said it about Him, but He said it about Himself, just as a wise man does not formally lay aside both his wisdom and wise behavior, and yet he lays them aside in order to serve the fools who should reasonably serve him. Such a person also is manifest even in the midst of wisdom and in the form of wisdom."[72] Thus this abstaining is not a cessation, but it is done "in the midst of wisdom"; it applies to an emptying that can thus also be described as a concealing. *This expression is rejected: that incarnation and emptying should coincide:* "Through His being born of Mary, He became a natural man. But then in that same humanity He still had power to exalt Himself over all people and to serve no one."[73] So, hypothetically, the taking on of the humanity could have meant that the divinity communicated its majesty to the humanity without limitation, which would exclude the emptying. Christ's voluntary act of restraining this flow constitutes the implemented likeness of servant. Here is the identical designation as in later works: "the divinity withheld its power from us";[74] "that the divinity restrained itself and hid itself";[75] "He has not used His divine power nor shown His almighty power (= [not] let it be seen)."[76]

Thereby Luther, through a new exposition of the Bible, established the only Christology that is able to acknowledge that the omnipresence of Christ's body is possible. Before this point of doctrine is presented more specifically, it is necessary to recall that the difference between scholastic and Lutheran Christology does not include the omnipresence of the divine nature. Therefore, when Luther uses the phrase "the right hand of God is everywhere," it cannot be said that he shattered the medieval worldview, as Elert and [Hermann] Sasse assert.[77] Sasse thinks that Luther, in his view of "the right hand of God," agrees with illocal definition set forth by John of Damascus in *De fide orthodoxa* [*On the Orthodox Faith*], but that this was not accepted later within subsequent Western Scholasticism. Yet Thomas quotes approvingly: "First, therefore, it must be said, just as the Damascene says in Book 4 (*De fide Orth.*, ch. 2): 'We do not call the

---

that Persson uses the word "divine" in a Ritschl-like meaning, as *value judgment*. In this sense, of course, even Thomas would regard the suffering as "divine," because "through this, man recognizes how much God loves man" (*ST*, III, 46, 3).

72 WA 17/2:243.13ff. [cf. AE 76:420–21].

73 WA 17/2:243.30f. [cf. AE 76:421].

74 WA 45:239.39f. [cf. AE 12:126–27].

75 WA 45:239.36 [cf. AE 12:126–27].

76 WA 45:240.10f. [cf. AE 12:127].

77 Elert, *Morphologie des Luthertums*, 1:363ff. [cf. *Structure of Lutheranism*, pp. 415ff.]; Sasse, op. cit., p. 159.

right hand of the Father local. . . .' "[78] Thus the statement as such is not new, and it cannot be said to have any consequences for the worldview. The doctrine of God's omnipresence and a medieval worldview are not incompatible quantities.

While researching the omnipresence of Christ's body, one usually finds that it was first stated unequivocally in the sermon on *The Sacrament of Christ's Body and Blood* from 1526.[79] Meanwhile, the question has been put as to whether an early form of this doctrine may be found in the writing *The Adoration of the Sacrament*, though not "stated clearly."[80] People have paused at the words: "The body which you receive, the Word which you hear, is that of Him who holds the whole world in His hand and is in all places; then let that be enough for you."[81] Even with strong safeguards, this passage still cannot be interpreted in the way that was thought possible. "Then let that be enough for you" shows that it has to do with answering a question. The question is about whether the Sacrament, above and beyond Christ's body and blood, also includes the divinity and Christ's human soul through the so-called concomitance. Here, as shall be presented and explained more closely in a later chapter, Luther rejects any attempt to "conjure the divinity into the Sacrament." The divinity cannot be ascribed the limited presence that applies to the Sacrament: "It is enough for me that I know that the Word that I hear and the body that I receive are truly the Word and body of my Lord and God."[82] Scholasticism's speculations are rejected; then follows the paragraph quoted above, which should settle the matter: the divinity is omnipresent, which is answer enough to the question about His presence in the Sacrament. Therefore, this passage can be completely removed from the discussion about the date for [Luther's] first assertion of the omnipresence of Christ's humanity.

Nevertheless, there is a dogmatic-historical change here, of the same magnitude as Grass vaguely imagined. Although Luther denied a sacramental presence of the divinity, despite this he insists on a sacramental adoration of Christ's body. This is the larger framework of the question and answer that are expressed with the opinion that immediately follows regarding the thesis under discussion: "This is our opinion concerning the adoration of the Sacrament . . . thus we certainly may not forbid the body of Christ its honor."[83] That means that Christ's body no longer is worthy of adoration in an improper sense, as in Scholasticism, but that the adoration of it is motivated from its relationship to the divinity, which is the proper object of the adoration; now Christ's body

78 *ST*, III, 58, 1, ad 1.

79 The dating goes back to the article "*Ubiquität*" by Hunzinger in *RE* 20:182ff. and is, among others, in Grass, op. cit., pp. 57f.; [and] Sasse, op. cit., p. 155.

80 Grass, op. cit., p. 58.

81 WA 11:450.15f. [cf. AE 36:298].

82 WA 11:450.11ff. [cf. AE 36:297].

83 WA 11:450.17ff. [cf. AE 36:298].

itself is worthy of adoration. Cyrillian Christology emerges with complete consistency on this point.

There is still no expression of the omnipresence of Christ's body, however. Nor does it come in *Against the Heavenly Prophets* from 1525.[84] Luther is defending himself[85] here against Karlstadt's objection, based on a Thomistic definition of movement, that a sacramental presence annuls a heavenly one, and, as a parallel to the sacramental miracle, he [Luther] cites the fact that Christ, according to Eph. 1:23, fills everything with His kingdom and is "in all places" at the same time. The term "in all places" parallels the corresponding medieval use of *ubique* ["everywhere"] and simply means that the Church is "everywhere," not bound to any particular place.[86] The reasoning stops at the possibility of a simultaneous presence, and no reference is made to Christology. Above all, sitting at the "right hand of the Father" is interpreted as a "local" form of presence, though the expression later exclusively means a repletive presence: "And Christ also must not be in heaven at the right hand of the Father, since one might also say here: Behold, there is Christ."[87] This is made parallel to the presence during [Christ's] earthly life "in locations and places" and is supposed to prove the legitimacy of designating the Sacrament as a location defined by Christ, the possibility of which was fundamentally rejected by the opponents. This local interpretation of the heavenly enthronement at the Father's right hand challenges the possibility of the doctrine of the omnipresence of Christ's body. (As shall be shown later, on the other hand, not every thought of a local presence in heaven is incompatible with the omnipresence of the human nature; what is decisive here is the interpretation of the expression "at the right hand of the Father.")

On the other hand, the sermon on *The Sacrament of Christ's Body and Blood* from 1526 includes the full, repletive presence of Christ's body. Here divine omnipresence is ascribed outright to "Jesus Christ according to His humanity."[88] The dogmatic concept "at the right hand of the Father" is now equal to "around us and in us in all places,"[89] "above all creatures and within all and beyond all creatures."

84 Dieckhoff (op. cit., p. 403) dates the doctrine to this writing. Hunzinger (*RE*, loc. cit.) finds beginnings of this in this writing.

85 WA 18:206.10ff., 211.6ff. [cf. AE 40:216].

86 Compare to this how Bonaventure (In IV, d. 10, p. 1, a. un., qu. 2) sets against each other *uno loco* ["in one place"] (heaven) and *ubique* ["everywhere"] (the manifold sacramental presence). The same terminology [is] in [Joachim] Westphal, *Apologia confessionis*, p. 219; compare Mahlmann, *Das neue Dogma der lutherischen Christologie*, p. 60: "Westphal thus concedes the use of *ubique esse* ['to be everywhere'], when one is conscious of the transferred use of the phrase, that is, expresses with it only the presence of Jesus' body in carrying out the instituting celebration of the Supper."

87 WA 18:211.34f. [cf. AE 40:221].

88 WA 19:491.17 [cf. AE 36:342].

89 WA 19:491.24f. [cf. AE 36:342].

Earlier, Eph. 1:22f. had spoken about "Christ's kingdom";[90] now this applies: "one Lord of all things has everything in His hand and is present everywhere."[91] This imperceptible presence of Jesus' humanity in the world is portrayed vividly and broadly. Luther's wordiness shows that he was treading previously unused territory. Earlier mention of the "omnipresence" of Christ's kingdom had not come to anything but a terse reference to the Bible passage in question.

That a dogmatic innovation appeared in Luther's writing may be indirectly supported by citing Zwingli, who in *Amica exegesis*, from the year 1527, mentions this very sermon in order to point out to Luther his debatable innovation.[92] Yet, unwittingly, Zwingli himself establishes the idea that Luther's view of the divinity of Christ's body is older than that. While referring to Luther's writing mentioned above—*On the Adoration of the Sacrament* from 1521—he asserts that Luther is inconsistent by at once rejecting concomitance of the divinity and allowing the adoration of the Sacrament. He is unaware that Luther does not share the Christology that is the starting point for this reasoning. In his critique, Zwingli has thus touched on a difference between himself and Luther that already existed beforehand, not simply confusion in the latter.[93] This means that the criticism against the Lutherans' adoration of the Sacrament, viewed at its core, does not belong to the theology of the Sacrament. It is a part of a Christology that cannot and will not adore the body of Christ, whether within or outside the Sacrament.[94]

---

90 WA 18:206.19 [cf. AE 40:216].

91 WA 19:491.19f. [cf. AE 36:342].

92 CR 92:676.8ff. Compare CR 92:813ff., where Zwingli also develops his Christology against Luther's. He interprets Phil. 2:7 in a Thomistic way as pointing to the divinity's taking up of the human nature (CR 92:939.19f.): "[He] graciously came to help the poor, needy race of men." (Compare ibid., n. 13: "The Reformed system does not need the doctrine of the humiliation, but only the concept of the incarnation; this finds its full application, at least, in Zwingli.") The image of the glowing iron used by John of Damascus is changed into its opposite: "so it cuts, and it also burns"; that is, it is interpreted as the image of two coordinate, dissimilar attributes: "Thus in Christ Jesus also, one has actually always seen either nature's property and effect" (CR 92:924.1ff.). During the Marburg Colloquy, Zwingli cites Phil. 2:6ff. and interprets *forma* as human nature: WA 30/3:134.19ff. [cf. AE 38:47].

93 CR 92:658.6ff.: "For which reason also all ancient as well as recent theologians never allowed that the pure or bare humanity *of Christ* (indeed, they speak that way) can be adored; and if anything like that may be found, it should not be understood other than through alleosis of the more powerful, pure,* divine nature. Therefore, if the Eucharist must be adored, it is because *Christ*, God and man, is there; and the Roman pontiff or *Thomas* won with the *Parisian* theologians, and concomitance returned, which horrifies you so much." Compare to this Köhler, op. cit., 1:481.

* [Reading *pura* for the printed *puta*.]

94 CR 90:817.20ff.: "Indeed, since only God must be adored, and indeed no creature, thus, as the theologians say that not even the pure humanity *of Christ* can be adored

A further witness that comes forward is Johann Brenz, the Lutheran reformer of Swabia, who likewise refers to Luther's sermon on *The Sacrament [of Christ's Body and Blood]* when he discusses the omnipresence of Christ's body. In contrast to Zwingli, Brenz very emphatically agrees with what he found in Luther's writing.[95]

The most detailed description of the various modes of presence of Christ's body, to which even the divine omnipresence now belongs, is in the so-called *Great Confession* on the Supper [*Confession concerning Christ's Supper*] from 1528. Here the Nominalist distinction between the various modes is repeated, especially in connection with Biel,[96] but with the newfound insight as a definite departure from the older scheme.[97] — The first mode of presence is the circumscribed presence, which applies to everything material in ordinary life: "First, a thing is in a place in a circumscribed manner or locally, perceptibly, that is, when the space or the object actually moves, touches something, and is measured inside something else, just the way wine or water is in a jar."[98] The second mode of presence is the diffinitive, which has a very special character: "Second, a thing is in a place diffinitively, imperceptibly, when the thing or body is not perceptible in a place and is not measured according to the dimensions of the place. . . . The place is indeed physical and perceptible and has its mass according to length, breadth, and width. But what is inside does not have the same length or breadth. . . . We cannot perceive it nor measure it, as we measure bodies, and yet it is indeed in the place."[99] The third is the divine omnipresence:

---

without the danger of idolatry, how is it not the highest impiety to have adored the bread? What does it really matter that they say they do not adore the bread but the body of Christ? Are they not now adoring the creature?" Compare Köhler, op. cit., 1:177, who uses a similar citation from Erasmus of Rotterdam.

95 Compare to this Brecht, *Die frühe Theologie des Johannes Brenz*, p. 98 n. 2:

> Brenz himself says from where he gets the new view of the sitting at the right hand of God: "For as much as it pertains to this passage (He ascended to the heavens), Luther's splendid *Sermon on the Sacrament*, recently published, will abundantly satisfy you" (p. 860 [= *In Evangelion . . . secundum Joannem, Iohannes Brentius, Opera* 6]). Brenz appeals to Luther's *Sermon on the Sacrament* 1526, WA 19:489.24ff., and 491.17ff. [cf. AE 26:341f.]. Already in *Against the Heavenly Prophets* (WA 18:211.14ff. [cf. AE 40:220f.]), Luther had expressed these thoughts, but Brenz did not yet make use of them in the *Syngramma*.

Brecht's last point is actually incorrect, but at the same time it means support for the thesis of this volume, that Luther was unable to give Brenz any dogmatic idea earlier.

96 Seeberg, op. cit., 4/1:472.

97 This depiction is, of course, often described in the literature. A more precise critique of its use by different authors is given below, chapter 3.

98 WA 26:327.23ff. [cf. AE 37:215].

99 WA 26:327.33ff. [cf. AE 37:215].

"Third, a thing is in places repletively, supernaturally, that is, when something is totally and completely in all places at the same time. . . . This mode is attributed only to God."[100 101]

Circumscribed presence is ascribed to the body of Christ during His earthly life, during the forty days after the resurrection, and on the Last Day.[102] Diffinitive presence, which only applies to angels, demons, and the human soul, is ascribed to Christ's humanity when passing through the gravestone, as well as the closed doors on Easter evening, in the bread and wine of the Sacrament, as well as His birth from the closed womb.[103] Repletive omnipresence is ascribed to Christ's humanity by virtue of the personal union between the natures of the God-man.[104] This, the divine omnipresence of Christ's body, thus builds on the proposition: "If God is here, then you must say: Then Christ the man is also there."[105] This presence is not viewed as the final stage in a transformation of Christ's humanity, conditioned by salvation history, so that after the materiality of Christ's earthly life it is superseded by the forty-day resurrection body, which is surpassed in the deification of the ascension, after which eventually on the Last Day the state of its earthly life is revived through His visible return in the clouds of heaven. It applies instead to the reality based on the personal union, expressed concerning the incarnate Word from its conception. "Now indeed from His mother's womb Christ's humanity was higher and deeper in God and in God's presence than any angel."[106] So it is the case that "Christ was in heaven, even when He walked on earth."[107] In another context, Luther expressly rejects the thought that the ascension would mean that omnipresence applies to Christ through this event: "For He did not become a different person through His glorification, but as He was present everywhere before, so He was also afterward."[108]

Behind the thought that the states of His presence might be perceived as sequential in some way—so that either the local presence would exclude the repletive, or the repletive [would exclude] the definitive presence, either in the Sacrament or in a special place for the blessed things—would be the idea that the modes of presence meant changes in Christ's body, through which the

100 [The Swedish edition numbers footnotes up to 99, then restarts at 1, which this translation lists as 101, etc.]

101 WA 26:329.27ff. [cf. AE 37:216].

102 WA 26:335.30ff. [cf. AE 37:218].

103 WA 26:328.31ff., 336.4ff. [cf. AE 37:216, 220].

104 WA 26:336.8ff. [cf. AE 37:218].

105 WA 26:332.31f. [cf. AE 37:218].

106 WA 26:344.28ff. [cf. AE 37:232].

107 WA 26:343.36f. [cf. AE 37:232].

108 WA 23:147.31f. [cf. AE 27:66].

omnipresence would become a diffusion of matter to a physically imagined infinity. Luther himself takes up discussion of this misunderstanding:

> Here you will ... say: ... Should the humanity of Christ spread itself out and stretch like a pelt ... ? I answer ... You will not understand this according to this old dark [thinking] that accepts nothing more than the first, physical, perceptible mode, just as the Enthusiasts do, who imagine nothing other than that the divinity is of a physical, perceptible mode everywhere, as if God were some big, stretched-out thing that reaches through and beyond all creation ....[109]

Just as little as the omnipresence of the divine nature means a physical diffusion, so the omnipresence of the human nature demands nothing corresponding to that: "Yet if Christ passed through closed doors with His body, and nevertheless neither the door was expanded nor His body compressed, how, then, would the humanity be expanded here or the divinity compressed, since there is rather a different and higher mode?"[110] It is the concrete humanity of Christ that occupies the relationship of Creator to creature, without any spiritualizing. Likewise, the diffinitive—and thus the sacramental—presence occurs without the least change to Christ's true body, nor does the repletive [presence], which is "different and higher," result in any redesign of Christ's humanity.

That type of divine omnipresence is rather that created things are located in God rather than God being located in them: "that they do not quantify nor circumscribe Him, but rather, that He has them present before Him, and He quantifies and circumscribes them."[111] These words obviously connect to an expression by Augustine that was picked up from him by Scholasticism: "All things are in Him, rather than He being somewhere else."[112] This relationship of the divinity to the creation is an unfathomable attribute of the divinity, which surpasses even the knowledge of the angels: "It is beyond the nature and reason even of the angels in heaven; [it is] known and familiar only to God."[113] It coincides with God's preservation of the creation, since God works through His own essence and not through means: "He indeed does nothing except through His Word, Genesis 1, John 1, which is His power. And His power is

109 WA 26:333.26ff. [cf. AE 37:219]. Even such an insightful researcher as Rocholl (op. cit., p. 117) is misled to the expression "so to speak, poured out elements" concerning the omnipresence of Christ's body.

110 WA 26:334.2ff. [cf. AE 37:220]. Compare WA 50:[596].1ff. [cf. AE 41:110]: "For He sits now at God's right hand, no longer eats, drinks, sleeps, grieves, suffers, dies, for eternity.... Such things are temporal and transitory attributes [*idiomata*]. But the natural [attributes] remain, such as that He has body and soul, skin and hair, flesh and blood, marrow and bone, and all the members of the human nature."

111 WA 26:336.13f. [cf. AE 37:223].

112 PL 40:15; compare *ST*, I, 8, 1, ad 2. The identification is not in WA or in the literature.

113 WA 26:336.22 [cf. AE 37:223].

not a hatchet, ax, saw, or file, through which He works, but [it is] He Himself."[114] Even this thought takes on a classical definition of the divine essence. Thomas writes: "He acts immediately in all things."[115]

Likewise, the immutability of the omnipresence applies: "For the divinity is immutable in itself, cannot go from one place to another like a creature."[116] To this corresponds Thomas's "It is impossible for God to be changed in any way."[117] Christ's humanity, without any onset of physically imagined fusion, is elevated precisely to this divine omnipresence,[118] classically defined and agreeing with Scholasticism, so that now one can emphasize that things are in the God-man rather than He in them. Creation rests in Christ's body. This is the decisive new thing in Luther, not what he might take up from the Middle Ages concerning the loftiness of the divinity.

The omnipresence, thus acquired, is not the same as infinity, in a strict philosophical sense. "Yet the world in itself is not infinite or unending, as it would then follow that Christ's body is infinite and would be everywhere."[119] Christ's body is not "another infinity."[120] Rejecting this does not aim primarily to establish that Christ's body is circumscribed, but to assign it to the class of created things and creatures that are limited in this sense. Zwingli, whose attack Luther answers with these disclaimers, had directed his attack on this point and introduced the concepts *finitum-infinitum* in the latter sense.[121] Here Luther will agree with Zwingli and the tradition of thought that stands behind him, [a tradition] that knows only a single infinite, namely, the divinity. Only the divinity is omnipresent by virtue of its nature, as Thomas emphasizes: "Indeed, it is ascribed to God that He is everywhere and in all things, inasmuch as He

114 WA 23:139.17ff. [cf. AE 37:61].

115 *ST*, I, 8, 1, ad 3.

116 WA 23:141.13ff. [cf. AE 37:62].

117 *ST*, I, 9, 1.

118 WA 23:147.26ff. [cf. AE 37:66]: "Because God is immutable and also Christ is sitting at the right hand of God and does not move about." This loftiness of the divine nature is common to Luther and Thomas. The incarnation, for Luther, does not include any change of location for the divinity, which of course was in Mary's womb even before taking on the humanity; "without this presence, God would not have been able to become man and one person of divinity and humanity" (WA 23:143.3ff. [cf. AE 37:63]). Persson (op. cit., p. 208) sees Thomas as opposed to Luther by avoiding any definition that would mean a change of the divinity. Compare id., p. 223 n. 27, with the appeal to Bring and Vogelsang, which defends against a kenotic Christology. — Cleve (op. cit., p. 141; compare also id., pp. 108f., 135f.) asserts correctly that Luther, unlike Biel, does not allow for any omnipresence through God's contemplation of the eternal ideas in things. No actual difference comes from this, however.

119 WA 26:343.26ff. [cf. AE 37:232].

120 WA 26:343.24 [cf. AE 37:232].

121 Compare above, p. 25 n. 94.

cannot be circumscribed and is infinite [*inquantum est incircumscriptibilis et infinitus*]."[122] The omnipresence of Christ's body does not have its basis in this "inasmuch as He is."

Thus, since the omnipresence of Christ's body does not invalidate its given, physical character, *Christ's body, parallel with the repletive presence, can use both the circumscribed and/or diffinitive presence.* A well-formulated commentary on Luther's view, similar to what is repeated here, mainly with the support of his *Great Confession* on the Supper, is in the Apology of the Formula of Concord, written by Timotheus Kirchner, Nicolaus Selnecker, and Martin Chemnitz. It takes up for discussion a Reformed objection to the three modes of presence:

> *Christi corpus non habere repugnantes existendi modos*, that is, Christ's body does not have incompatible modes of being, we gladly confess: For the three modes according to which Christ's body can exist (as they are clarified from Luther in the *Book of Concord*) are not incompatible with each other, as they [the adversaries] imagine but do not prove. For such is said of Christ's body in a different respect and in one mode; therefore, there can be no incompatibility in it.[123]

"In a different respect" the one and same physical body of Christ thus at the first Supper has all three modes of presence: repletive, filling the universe as the body of the Creator; diffinitive, in the bread; and circumscribed, sitting at the table of the Supper. A special chapter will be dedicated to the relationship between repletive and diffinitive presence in the Sacrament. Therefore, only the relationship between the repletive presence, on the one hand, and, on the other hand, the circumscribed and diffinitive presence outside the Sacrament, respectively, will be touched on here.

Coexistence of the repletive and the circumscribed presence is granted along with the idea that Christ during His earthly life is said to be omnipresent. Since Peters[124] assumes that Luther thinks the visible coming on the Last Day invalidates the divine mode of omnipresence, and that, regarding a continued use of this mode of presence after that, he can only say that "[the] limit of what is conceivable" is reached, there appears to be no understanding in Peters that the doctrinal point is being fundamentally expanded.

Also a special, concrete presence in heaven, distinct from the omnipresence, applies to Christ's humanity. In the polemic against Karlstadt, his exegetical

122 *ST*, I, 7, 1. The theology behind the Formula of Concord also made this condition of immeasurability through the communication of attributes: Frank, *Die Theologie der Concordienformel*, 3:279f. Thus such a tradition is continued from Luther.

123 *Apologia oder verantwortung des Christlichen Concordien Buchs*, fol. 97a [cf. *Apology*, pp. 131–32].

124 Peters, op. cit., p. 162.

method is refuted that allows the spiritual eating according to John 6 to exclude the sacramental eating of Christ's body with the following *deductio ad absurdum*: "For you would make the same conclusions: Galatians 4, Christ is spiritually born in the Galatians, therefore He cannot be born physically from Mary; Christ dwells spiritually in believers, Ephesians 2, therefore He cannot dwell in Capernaum or in heaven."[125] Peters cites[126] three other quotations: among others, the famous passage from Luther's *German Mass*, concerning the pastor's elevation of Christ's body and blood in the Mass for the people to view, where it is said that faith hereby is reminded of "how Christ gave His body and blood for us, and yet daily appears before God and offers Himself for us in order to attain mercy for us."[127] In this quotation, Peters considers it possible that Luther "still" thinks of heaven as a place *despite* the "emptying of heaven" introduced by him through the doctrine of the omnipresence. This local presence in heaven is seen by Peters as an inconsistent vestige "that no longer gives the right idea." The evaluation may have limited validity, partly because Luther very rarely speaks about this special mode of presence, partly because he does not take up anything like this in his schemata of the modes of presence, since the emphasis is on the repletive presence introduced by him, which was rejected by the opponents in favor of *a local presence that nullifies a sacramental presence and makes it impossible.*

It is in contrast to this thesis of the opponents that Luther can write: "If Christ's body were just in one place in heaven (as they prattle) . . . ."[128] The absurd thing in the opponents' idea here is still the thought that [Christ] being enthroned at the right hand of the Father should express a local presence and not be an expression of majesty. Peters's formulation means that he overlooks the sense in which Luther rejects a local presence in heaven. Luther has certainly not undertaken any "emptying of heaven." His doctrine of the omnipresence of Christ's humanity shatters medieval Christology, but not the medieval worldview, especially not in the sense of the concept of heaven as the place of the saints.[129] The fact that in a certain respect the medieval worldview

125 WA Br 4:[365–66].108ff., no. 1214.

126 Peters, op. cit., p. 85 n. 91.

127 WA 19:100.1ff. [cf. AE 53:82]. The quotation in Peters is technically incorrect, since the introductory "how" is changed to "the place 'where'"; but it has actual relevance, since here the heavenly existence bears concrete features. The rest of the passages are WA 20:382.25, which, however, are not connected to the problem discussed here, and WA Br 8[:297].31f., no. 3263, which contains an unambiguous concrete statement: "but existing in one place in heaven, He is at the same time in the Sacrament."

128 WA 26:336.38f. [cf. AE 37:224].

129 How very closely the views of the omnipresence of Christ's body and the heavenly spheres are connected emerges from a line of reasoning in the Lutheran Jacob Strauss' writing from 1527, *That the True Body of Christ and His Holy Blood Are Present in the*

nevertheless disappears in Luther is a parallel event, without logical connection to the Christological innovations. This can be seen most immediately as a part of the general depreciation of the inherited philosophical-patristic doctrinal heritage, whereby only the unambiguous biblically supported material was left untouched. In his Genesis lectures,[130] Luther accepts the eight heavenly spheres as scientific theories with definite experimental provability, for which no biblical authority can be cited. The crystal heaven and the heaven of the blessed, "*coelum empyreum*," are seen as senseless theological additions to the rationally supported physical universe.[131] In the absence of any explanations about the location of the heaven of the blessed, which no longer is seen as localized within the number of the spheres, but thus in no way is denied as a reality,

---

Sacrament [*Das der war leyb Christi und seyn heiliges blut im Sacrament gegenwertig sey*], which is cited, though without analysis, by Köhler, op. cit., 1:415ff. Strauss teaches the presence of Christ's body "in all things" and at the same time asserts (Köhler, op. cit., p. 417): "Yes, if two bodies cannot be 'momentarily' in one place, then Christ also did not ascend through the great celestial bodies to the right hand of God." Page 418: "According to its nature Christ's humanity would not have gone with Him through the fire and the mighty heavens." The "according to its nature" in the last sentence does not aim to exclude but rather to insist on a communication of divine attributes. This communication is made possible through Christ's body passing through the spheres, whose "ether" was impenetrable for solid bodies; compare Olaf Pedersen, *Medeltidens världsbild*, p. 52.

130 WA 42:21f. [cf. AE 1:28]. What matters is the part that came out already during Luther's lifetime.

131 Compare Maurach, *Coelum empyreum*, p. 11, which shows how, first, the *Summa Sententiarum* takes up the *coelum empyreum* as the locally defined fortress of heaven within the Church's doctrinal view. Normative for subsequent theology was Peter Lombard's approval of it (op. cit., p. 12). But Anselm of Canterbury rejected the idea (op. cit., p. 85). In describing this doctrine being given up, Maurach completely overlooks Luther's role and the account of Lutheranism's position, given by Elert, "Wirkungen der lutherischen Abendmahlslehre in der Geschichte der Weltanschauung," pp. 746–52, 770–73, 794–98, and id., *Morphologie des Luthertums*, 1:220 n. 2, 273f., 363ff. [cf. *Structure of Lutheranism*, pp. 251 n. 24, 312, 414ff.]. Even if Elert's immediate linking of theology and worldview is not tenable, he is correct in observing that Lutherans very much promoted the freedom of astronomical research. This should be explained from two causes: it was brought about partly by the aforementioned lessening of tradition; it was accomplished partly by the polemic against the Reformed, which found a counterargument against the sacramental presence by insisting on the closed *coelum empyreum* as the location of Christ's body: "In their dreaming they have been fascinated about the *coelum empyreum* where Christ now sits, now stands, now walks about, and about the condition of His body, which cannot be a true body unless it is circumscribed in a place." This quotation from Brenz, *De maiestate*, p. 93, which Elert uses (*Morphologie des Luthertums*, 1:273 [cf. *Structure of Lutheranism*, p. 312]), ought to be observed in its double construction: the latter part, "and about the condition of His body," gives the decisive detail to the first part, "the *coelum empyreum*." First, the thought that the *coelum empyreum* hinders a sacramental presence is rejected. This is especially clear in Brenz, *De personali unione*

Luther writes: "Just as now we cannot say anything with certainty either about the heaven in which the angels and God dwell with the blessed, or about other things that will be revealed on the Last Day when we shall be clothed with different flesh."[132]

The heaven of the blessed is impossible to localize, but that does not at all mean that it is empty. The existing expressions about the special heavenly presence of Christ's body freely refer to this place of the saints. This is in no way excluded, but rather is postulated by the system that Luther describes, and through which the repletive mode of presence never becomes the essential existence [*egenexistens*] of Christ's humanity, for which either the circumscribed or diffinitive mode of presence is required. In the letter to Karlstadt cited above, a bodily presence in heaven ("*corporaliter*") is discussed, but what is understood by this, in context, is only a contrast to "*spiritualiter*" and not necessarily a circumscribed existence. The heavenly type of presence is read best in the descriptions of the bodies of the saints after the resurrection: "For the other mode (diffinitive), the way Christ's body was in the stone, will also be common to all saints in heaven, so that with their body they may pass through all created things."[133] The diffinitive mode of presence in this passage is thought to be Luther's answer to the question about the form of presence of the heavenly existence, but Luther cannot give a definite answer: "Although now we will be exactly where He is according to the first or second mode, as shown above, yet we will not be where He is in the third [mode], namely, at the right hand of God, one person with God."[134] Whatever the right answer is, the resurrection world that Christ introduced is depicted totally concretely. Already before the resurrection on the Last Day, it is a world where Christ is not alone: "God dwells with the blessed." Among those blessed ones are not only the souls of the departed but also the Old Testament figures who enjoy blessedness even in the body: Enoch and Elijah.[135]

---

duarum naturarum in Christo, fol. 14af., where Christ's presence in the outermost physical, celestial layer is accepted hypothetically:

> We are not unaware that that mundane heaven, etc., itself is not in a place, just as was said above, nevertheless that it has and contains within itself its own places that, by human eyes, are different and far distant from the places of this earth. Nor do we deny this; indeed, Christ can be in this heaven locally, wherever He wishes to reveal Himself locally and in a circumscribed manner. But is it said that now, as heavenly and earthly places differ in human eyes, that they also differ for the body of Christ, which is personally and inseparably united with the divinity?

132 WA 42:23.42f. [cf. AE 1:31].

133 WA 26:335.13f. [cf. AE 37:222].

134 WA 26:349.20ff. [cf. AE 37:235].

135 WA 42:254.1ff. [cf. AE 1:346].

Luther did not empty this glorious heaven when he judged the medieval definition as unbiblical. It is a self-explanatory part of his belief.[136]

The fact that the omnipresence of Christ's body, for its part, allows other attributes of presence does not invalidate the fact of the omnipresence. It is an inextricable part of Luther's Christology. It is therefore incorrect to think that after 1529 Luther would have more or less knowingly downplayed the teaching of the repletive presence.[137] Not only the existence of later expressions about the omnipresence[138] but, above all, its obvious place as an integral part of Lutheran Christology makes such an assertion impossible. For various reasons, of course, not every point of doctrine can occur the same number of times during every era within a larger body of the literature. This does not displace the doctrine.

136 Peters (op. cit., p. 85 n. 91) asserts, without giving a reference, that Luther rejected the image of Christ as *pantokrator*, the heavenly ruler sitting on the throne. The passages probably meant by Peters number into the twenties, which all are accounted for in Steinlein, "Luthers Anlage zur Bildhaftigkeit," pp. 14ff. They do not imply any "emptying of heaven" in favor of what Peters calls "Christ here below," Christ as an object of faith without ontological self-determination. They aim only at the depiction of the Christ imagined as *angry judge*, whose majestic attributes (rod, sword, et al.) exclude mercy. This is a question of iconographic appropriateness, not a denial of Christ's heavenly existence.

137 Sasse, op. cit., p. 160: "Thus Luther himself did not repeat in later years all that he had said about the 'ubiquity' in his controversies in the years before Marburg." Sasse often returns to the thought that the omnipresence of Christ's body would only be a hypothesis proposed by Luther, which was never considered a dogma (op. cit., pp. 182, 193, 283, 301, 308, 341f.). This idea goes back to the older Reformed polemic: compare *Apologia oder verantwortung des Christlichen Concordien Buchs*, fol. 145f. [cf. *Apology*, pp. 196–97]:

> That they assert, however, that Luther from 1528 on would have considered the ubiquity (as they call it) in none of his doctrinal writings is to report* an obvious untruth. For vol. 3 of the Jena Latin edition, on Solomon's Ecclesiastes, chapter 9, page 282 (which book was published in 1532), likewise on John 17, Jena vol. 6 (which was published in 1534), and in many other places is found the counterpoint as it can be read in the places noted.

The objection is treated in even more detail by Aegidius Hunnius in his appendix to Chemnitz, *Fundamenta . . . de vera et substantiali praesentia*, p. 120, where it is maintained concerning Luther that "concerning the majesty of the man Christ and individually of His personal omnipresence (which the enemies of the truth call 'ubiquity' through their lies), that holy man of God clearly defended the same doctrine with us and maintained it intact with complete heroic zeal without any modification or retraction to the end of his life."

* [Reading *melden* for the misprint *medlen*.]

138 Compare WA 43:580.23 [cf. AE 5:220]: "Here there is God and man: highest and lowest, infinite and finite in one person, emptying and filling everything" (*Genesis Lectures*, 1535–45); "My flesh, My blood sit at the right hand of God and rule over all things" (WA 52:45.14, *House Postil* 1544 [second sermon for Christmas on Luke 2:1–14; compare Klug translation (1996), 1:115f.; and Schulze (Columbus, OH, 1884), 1:99]).

Luther's Christology is often regarded as summarized with the term "communication of attributes." Controversies about the meaning of this were fought already during Lutheranism's early history. In the 1800s, the so-called kenotic Christology arose,[139] which ascribed to Luther the thought of an emptying of the actual divinity. Thus the classical concept of God had been broken down on a decisive point. Such a reimagined Christology could easily be fit into the theological system that was established at that time and mainly wanted to disallow Luther's theology of any ontological orientation. Unlike Scholasticism and later Lutheranism, it was supposed that Luther's intent was not to make a statement about metaphysical realities, but only to provide terms that express certain forms of divine action. This tradition, which is now dominant in modern Luther research, has recently been summarized in detail by Kjell Ove Nilsson, *Simul: Das Miteinander von Göttlichem und Menschlichem in Luthers Theologie.* Especially to gain clarity concerning the concept of the "communication of attributes," a review of Nilsson's reasoning seems to be beneficial.

Nilsson makes this general assertion: "According to Luther, one cannot ascribe any naturalistic and metaphysical content to the natures, but must define them in a dynamic, versatile, and vivid way, so that the term 'nature' actually gets the meaning 'work,' human work and divine work."[140] If this observation were correct, the present volume essentially would have misinterpreted Luther from the false premise that Luther's use of language and his world of ideas were traditional theological [language and ideas]. This misunderstanding would then rest on Luther speaking "in a seemingly correct scholastic sense." "He can do that because 'all words' [*omnia vocabula*] have received a 'new meaning' [*nova significatio*] in Christ."[141] This later formulation of Nilsson's goes back to a statement in one of Luther's Christological disputations: "Nevertheless it is certain that all words receive a new meaning in Christ, when the same thing is meant [WA 39/2:94.20 (cf. AE 73:255)]." By virtue of this, Luther would allow himself a change of meaning very adventurous to the uninitiated, whose meaning unfolded for Nilsson and the tradition on which he relies.

Nilsson also overlooked the context of the cited statement. Luther does not formulate any spiritual [*pneumatisk*] rule, through which he evades regular accountability for his writings, but a secular, scientific rule that lets each topic choose its own mode of expression regardless of the customs of everyday language. In the sentence immediately before the one under discussion, Luther says, "And universally, in every category of things and skills, usage often dictates against the rule."[142] Each topic has its own particular type of language.

139 Compare the article "Kenosis" by Loofs in *RE* 10:246ff.

140 Nilsson, op. cit., p. 186.

141 Ibid.

142 WA 39/2:94.15f. [cf. AE 73:255].

Schwenkfeld, against whom the thesis is directed, thus showed himself to be uneducated, "a man without letters, without training,"[143] when he simply mocks the statement that Christ, according to the human nature, is a created being, a "*creatura*."[144] Of course, Christ, according to this [human] nature, is not a creature in the meaning of everyday language: "a thing separate from divinity in infinite ways."[145] It is not about something that is separate from God, which is the only definition that experience can give for "creature" without the help of revelation. In a theological, Christian sense, Christ's humanity is still a created thing, "a thing inseparably joined with the divinity in the same person in indescribable ways."[146] This part of creation is not separate from the Creator. A unique fact gives a new definition of *creatura*. This means that theological language creates its own way of speaking, but like this: "not that it signifies a new or different thing, but it signifies it in a new and different way, unless you would actually want to call it a new thing."[147] This [definition] still applies to *creatura* in the meaning familiar to everyone: something that exists in time, but placed into a new and different context, "*nove et aliter*," associated with eternity. The statement that Christ is a created being is not built on [the word] "creature" having its meaning changed to its opposite or to something indefinable. It is built on the tension that the eternal one is temporal in His assumed nature.

Such changes are common in theology. For example, in the *Te Deum* it says, "You took upon Yourself to deliver man [*hominem*],"[148] though "the rule (so it seems) would dictate that this must be said: You took upon Yourself to deliver humanity or human nature."[149] It is improper, even according to the special rules of theological language, to say that Christ took on "*hominem*" ("human being") instead of *humanitatem* or *humanam naturam* ("humanity" or "human nature"). But even this may be accepted: "It is rightly taught in this case that the use of language in the Scriptures and the orthodox fathers is valid. 16. In fact, things we might not be permitted to imitate are conceded to the fathers (who are known to be orthodox)."[150] Although sometimes confusing and not always worth following, the fathers' way of speaking may be granted its right, for in principle this applies: "Therefore, heresy is in the meaning, not in the words."[151] It is important

143 WA 39/2:94.29 [cf. AE 73:256].

144 WA 39/2:94.28f. [cf. AE 73:256].

145 WA 39/2:94.19f. [cf. AE 73:255].

146 WA 39/2:94.21f. [cf. AE 73:255]. Yet the statement "Christ is a creature" ought to be used with care (WA 39/2:105.16ff. [cf. AE 73:266]).

147 WA 39/2:94.25f. [cf. AE 73:255].

148 WA 39/2:93.20 [cf. AE 73:255].

149 WA 39/2:94.1f. [cf. AE 73:255].

150 WA 39/2:94.7ff. [cf. AE 73:255].

151 WA 39/2:96.23 [cf. AE 73:259].

to look at the content and not at the form. Even the most peculiar expressions of the late Middle Ages may be excused: "They all are wise in a correct and catholic way, and they must be excused for their unusual way of speaking."[152] The reason Schwenkfeld does not get a share of the same generosity in the question of his silly critique is the fact that his obviously naive-orthodox rejection of Jesus as creature conceals a Monophysite heresy: "But Eutyches lives hidden in such heretics, who are prepared finally to deny that the Word became flesh."[153]

After clarifying the meaning of the rule overlooked by Nilsson, his individual applications of it can be investigated more closely. The new meaning of "nature," which Nilsson found actually to be "work"—that is, the opposite—hardly corresponds to the careful distinctions that Luther makes between these terms. In the polemic against Zwingli's false Christology, which makes the participation of Jesus' humanity in the divinity a mere manner of speaking, an alleosis, or one thing for another [*unus pro altero*], Luther writes in his *Great Confession* of the Supper:

> If he would likewise insist on the alleosis, that one nature is named for the other, then such applies only to the work or activity of the natures, and not to the essence of the natures. For though in the works, when one says: Christ preaches, drinks, prays, dies, [the name] "Christ" might mean the human nature, still it cannot be so in essence when one says: God is man, or man is God. Here indeed there can be no alleosis—indeed, not even synecdoche or any kind of trope. For there God must mean God, and man must mean man. Now, when I write that Christ's body is everywhere, I am dealing neither with works nor natures, but with the essence of the natures; therefore, neither alleosis nor synecdoche can invalidate that for me. For essence is essence, each one on its own, not one for the other. . . .[154]

This polemic builds on a consistent and conscious distinction between "work" and "nature." It is repeated in Luther's writing *On the Councils and the Church*[155] from 1539:

> For the human nature's attributes [*idiomata*] were left behind by Christ, such as eating, drinking, sleeping, grieving, suffering, dying, being buried, etc. For He sits now at God's right hand, no longer eats, drinks, sleeps,

152 WA 39/2:96.1f. [cf. AE 73:258].

153 WA 39/2:95.1f. [cf. AE 73:256].

154 WA 26:325.33ff [cf. AE 37:214].

155 Luther's title *On the Councils and the Church* is almost always translated as if both main words were in the plural; compare the English edition of 1847: "Martin Luther's Authority of Councils and Churches" (WA 50:507). The last word is singular, however. Compare the German excerpt from 1540: "Of the Church, what, who and where it *is* [*Von der Kirchen, Was, wer und wo sie* sey]" [WA 50:507].

[Translator's note: Hardt italicizes the ending of *Kirchen*; the dative article *der* ("the") is also the indicator of the singular here, along with the singular verb *sey* ("is").]

> grieves, suffers, dies for eternity, just as will also happen to us when we go from this life into that life. 1 Cor. 15 [:49, 53]. Such things are temporal and transitory attributes [*idiomata*], but the natural [attributes] remain, such as that He has body and soul, skin and hair, flesh and blood, marrow and bone, and all the limbs of the human nature. That is why one must say this man Christ, the flesh and blood of Mary, is the Creator of heaven and earth, has conquered death, atoned for sin, shattered hell, which are purely divine attributes [*idiomata*]. And yet these are rightly and in a Christian manner ascribed to the person, who is the flesh and blood of Mary, because there are not two persons, but one person.[156]

Here is emphasized how in this humanity of Christ all the usual activities of human life are now laid aside. All that remains are the "natural" attributes [*idiomata*], which consist in Christ *having* body and soul. It is this *dormant* human nature that, by virtue of the personal union, is ascribed attributes that belong exclusively to the divinity. So even here Luther is able to distinguish "nature" and "work." Nilsson's depiction is refuted not only through the proper understanding of Luther's "*nova significatio*" but also by Luther's direct clarification of the meaning of nature.

The biggest departure from Luther is when Nilsson ascribes to him the so-called *genus tapeinoticum*, a real emptying of the divinity itself. Nilsson, who nowhere mentions the decisive exegetical development from *exinanivit* according to Philippians 2, uses the aforementioned Luther writing as the main basis for his reasoning. He correctly cites that the divinity's *idiomata* are "that it is immortal, omnipotent, infinite, not born, does not eat, drink, sleep, stand, walk, grieve, cry."[157] At first, Nilsson correctly summarizes that the *idiomata* partly are metaphysical, partly are negations of human attributes. Then, in the meantime, it is said that Luther's definition actually is not the traditional one, but rather it means the actions that are important for the work of salvation: "Thus in reference to the divinity, first, he also does not emphasize, for example, eternity and omnipotence in a philosophical sense."[158] Since the traditional metaphysical attributes are adduced as the first thing, and among them Luther calls omnipotence the second thing, Nilsson's procedure hardly seems adequate.

156 WA 50:595.36ff. [cf. AE 41:110].

157 Nilsson, op. cit., p. 232; WA 50:587.29f. [cf. AE 41:101].

158 Ibid.

Even Nilsson's use of the terms "abstract" and "concrete" aims at presenting the teaching that the divine nature suffers. In doing this, certain mistakes are made.[159] Nilsson writes:

> Also, God does not suffer if one is speaking "of an abstract and separate divinity" [*de abstracto et de separata divinitate*]; and if one considers the man "separately," then it is just as clear that He cannot create. But that is the mistake: one should not discuss the natures "*in abstracto*," but only "*in concreto*." *In Christ* the human nature or the divine nature is never separate, "in itself," isolated, or absolute, but always only united in oneness with the other. The "separate nature" [*natura separata*] is not the object of

159 Cleve (op. cit., p. 157 n. 170) writes: "Nilsson has a tendency to transfer immediately the attributes of one nature to the other, without emphasizing strongly enough that according to Luther it is the person of Christ that is the subject of all that Christ does, according to His divine and His human nature, and that it is for the sake of the person that it can be said of Christ that this God suffered and died and that this man created the world." Cleve's critique is correct, but not proved. Cleve himself (op. cit., p. 156) still has great difficulties in following Luther's reasoning. WA 39/2:93.10ff. [cf. AE 73:254–55] says: ["Nevertheless these things are not considered in the abstract (as it is said) of the human nature. Indeed, it is not permitted to say: Christ is thirsty, a servant, dead; therefore, He is thirst, servitude, death. For which reason this also is condemned: Christ is humanity, though it may be said: Christ is divinity. 'Man' and 'humanity' are permitted to be synonyms elsewhere, likewise 'God' and 'divinity.' In divine predicates or idioms there is no such distinction between concrete and abstract."] [Cleve] renders it thus: "The communication of attributes applies only to the latter. Just because Christ is hungry, because He has died, and because He has come to serve, one may not say that Christ is hungry, dead, serving. Nor is it right to say that He is humanity, though one can say that He is divinity. There is no distinction between concrete and abstract when it has to do with the divine attributes, but rather when it has to do with the human [attributes]." Cleve here is unaware that Luther is not speaking about the concreteness of the personhood compared to the abstractness of the natures, but about the predicates as abstract or concrete, a trivial tangent in the debate. According to this, Christ is thus "thirsty" (Cleve's "hungry" should be "thirsty"!), "servant" (slave; Cleve's "came to serve"!), "dead" (Cleve's "He died"), completely concrete attributes from which do not follow abstract attributes such as the idea that Christ is "thirst" (thirst; Cleve: "is hungry"!), "servitude" (slavery; Cleve: "serving"!), "death" (death, noun; Cleve: "dead," adjective!). Armed with this misunderstanding, Cleve attacks Koopmans (*Das altkirchliche Dogma in der Reformation*, pp. 80f.) for "claiming that Luther would have denied the distinction between concrete and abstract validity of the *communicatio idiomatum*." Certainly even Koopmans (op. cit., p. 81 n. 23) refers to the passage under discussion, whose special character is not obvious to him, but his text clarifies his meaning: "that the predicates of the divine nature of Christ also apply to the human nature." Thus it is clear that Koopmans is right in his statement: the transfer of divine attributes occurs not merely concretely (in respect to the person) but also abstractly (in respect to the human nature, which, for example, becomes omnipresent). On the question of the relationship between the usual *communicatio idiomatum* and this special communication, see the paragraphs that follow in the main text.

> the *communicatio* expression, but the "concreteness, joining, and uniting" [*concretio, coniunctio, et copulatio*] of each nature.[160]

> In other words, the distinction between a *communicatio in concreto* and *in abstracto* is not to be equated with the distinction that applies between the communication of nature to person and nature to nature. For when Luther speaks of the abstract, he is thinking of an isolated, "separate" nature—therefore it is *not* in context with the *communicatio*, for the natures are *united* in the person of Christ. . . . A communication *in abstracto* is indeed a *contradictio in adiecto*. . . .[161]

This investigation is occasioned by Luther's rejection of the idea that the divinity *in abstracto* suffers or that the humanity *in abstracto* created the world. Only concretely, just as the statement about the person in which the divinity/humanity exists, can the divinity/humanity be said to suffer/to have created the world.

Nilsson knows how to change this statement that rejects the *genus tapeinoticum* into its opposite: by "abstract," Luther would mean the unincarnate divinity with respect to the common man. Luther thus would particularly devote himself to the remark that the incarnation is the premise for all talk of *communicatio idiomatum*, and emphatically disputes such an abstract, which nevertheless would be a contradiction in terms [*contradictio in adiecto*]! Nilsson's text does not give evidence for such a senseless procedure. The text's point of departure is "how He who is the Son of God can be the servant."[162] "Christ, therefore, is true God and servant—and indeed the most worthless of all sinners, just as He is also the servant."[163] What is taken under consideration is the biblical doctrine about the Lord's servant who at the same time is the arm[164] of the Lord. It is in this doctrine about the taking on of humanity, which has occurred, that the words "abstract" and "concrete" are introduced:

> Therefore, I think it is right and admirable in grammar to call certain words concrete, certain ones abstract, where the layers of disputations concerning concrete and abstract things are infinite. And I do not believe it can ever be determined, even in philosophy and created things, whether something is abstract, as: when I say whiteness, indeed I am not calling any thing or any object white. But whiteness distinguishes the object, which afterward joins and connects white from the object, indeed separately and abstractly.[165]

160 Nilsson, op. cit., p. 255.

161 Id., op. cit., p. 256.

162 WA 40/3:707.7 [forthcoming AE 63].

163 WA 40/3:707.11f. [forthcoming AE 63].

164 WA 40/3:702.15 [forthcoming AE 63].: "Remarkable, therefore, is the expression 'arm of the Lord' and 'servant.'"

165 WA 40/3:707.15ff. [forthcoming AE 63]. Walch 6:1084 translates: "As when I say *Albedo*, 'whiteness,' I am in fact calling nothing white, or an object that is white; but

"Concrete" and "abstract" are thus used for an enduring entity, where the abstract is the kind of existence that whiteness has vis-à-vis the white thing. The abstract "whiteness" corresponds to the natures, and the concrete "white thing" corresponds to the person. "So I am right to say: divinity does not suffer; humanity does not create. Here I am speaking about the abstract and about the separate divinity." The *fact* of the God-man applies here, which is rightly subject to these distinctions that are reached through a process of abstraction. Luther finds no reason to emphasize that the divinity *before* assuming humanity does not suffer and that *ordinary* people, respectively, do not create. A thought process applies here that does not occur at all in Nilsson: his un-incarnate divinity as well as ordinary human nature do not have the character of intellectual abstraction but are realities.

Luther's appeal to an already existing use of language that had occurred under divine inspiration further confirms the extent of Nilsson's misreading. Already in his marginal notes to Biel's *Collectorium*, from 1515–16, Luther had noted the words *concreta* and *abstracta*[166] for his Christological investigations, and it is probably Biel's description that he now falls back on. Biel writes: "It is said by noting of concrete things that the abstract things of the natures are not predicated of them reciprocally. Just as, moreover, the natures in Christ remain unmingled and distinct."[167] Biel talks about the distance from an abstract connection keeping the natures unchanged, that is, abstract with respect to concrete having reference to the present union of the God-man, not in a suddenly suggested hypothesis of whether it exists or not. The final words "unmingled and distinct" remind us that what Biel and Luther wanted to defend is the Council of Chalcedon's decree: "without commingling." Nilsson's understanding of *abstractum* would nullify the core statement of this Christology in favor of the mutability of the divine nature.

This is how Nilsson defends his approach: "But if Luther really had reckoned with a nominal *communicatio*, his stance toward Nestorius and Zwingli, among others, would be inexplicable."[168] This appeal may seem to coincide with what is expressly documented in the present volume. But such is not the case. How the divine attributes *still* actually apply to the humanity in an abstract sense will be shown, since the exact meaning of the communication of attributes [*communicatio idiomatum*] in Luther is presented in connection with the texts. Luther's battle over the *communicatio idiomatum* is a battle precisely about terms

---

(*albedo*) 'whiteness' isolates the object that accordingly is connected [to it] and joins the thing that is white according to the object and the separate or abstract [thing]."

166 *Festgabe*, p. 5.

167 Biel, *Epitome et collectorium ex Occamo circa quatuor sententiarum Libros*, book III, d. VII, qu. un. A.

168 Nilsson, op. cit., p. 256.

[*nomina*]: "But if I thus say God is walking there on the street, fetching water and bread, that He is eating and drinking with His mother, to me Nestorius does not confess this *statement.*"[169] "For the uneducated, crass, proud man insisted on [a literal understanding of] these *letters*, God born of Mary, and interprets 'born' according to grammar or philosophy, as though it meant that the nature had its divinity from the one who bore Him, which also the *Tripartite* says, Let him consider such *words* to be an abomination, as we and all Christians also consider them (if they are to be understood this way)."[170] Nestorius thus ignored the double relationship that exists in the person of Christ and read incorrect ideas into the verbs that have this person as the subject: "But according to his lack of judgment, he does not know what he is saying and how he is speaking, since he did not really know how to speak about such things and yet wanted to be the master in speaking."[171] Along with Nestorius denying the possibility of this linguistic construction where God is the subject of a human predicate, he *de facto* denied the unity between God and man otherwise advocated by him: "It is wrong, and he as much as actually denies the nature itself."[172] It is a battle over *words*, over a *nominal communicatio idiomatum*, which Nestorius rejects and Luther defends.

Likewise, the battle with Zwingli has to do with the very same nominal *communicatio idiomatum*. Zwingli, in his *Amica Exegesis* of 1527, as mentioned earlier, attacked Luther's sermon on *The Sacrament [of Christ's Body and Blood]* from 1526. In a chapter entitled "Concerning the exchanges [*alloeosibus*] of the two natures in Christ," he asserts that by *alleosis* he means what the Scholastics called "attributes, that is, a communication of properties [*proprietarum*]."[173] He equates this *alleosis* with *tropus*,[174] "a leap or exchange from one thing to the other,"[175] and he finds it has been used by theologians "freely concerning *Christ*, regarding the union of the two natures in Him; also *Christ* Himself used a delightful variation concerning His very self."[176] A rhetorical device is important in the expressions, for which he appeals to Plutarch, [expressions] which are made for the sake of an agreeable exchange. One thing is spoken about, but another is meant. This "agreeable exchange" in Christology means "an exchange by which, when we speak about one nature in Him, we use the words for the other [nature], as when *Christ* says, My flesh is food indeed (John 6:55). Flesh

169 WA 50:588.3ff. [cf. AE 41:101] (emphasis added).

170 WA 50:586.3ff. [cf. AE 41:98] (emphasis added).

171 WA 50:586.10ff. [cf. AE 41:98f.].

172 WA 50:591.4 [cf. AE 41:104].

173 CR 92:679.14.

174 CR 92:679.8.

175 CR 92:679.10.

176 CR 92:679.11ff.

is in Him properly of His human nature; nevertheless, through an exchange, in this passage it is used for the divine nature."[177] "I say, when what is predicated of one belongs to the other, finally, that is an alleosis or a communication or exchange of attributes."[178] Thus Zwingli meanwhile has essentially changed the meaning of the scholastic *communicatio idiomatum*, which functioned with the concrete person's right to receive the predicate of both natures, and not with rhetorical rules from the writers of antiquity.[179]

Luther refers to this in his reply in the *Great Confession* on the Supper. The essential thing in the reference is not in the subordinate problem of whether Zwingli more or less deviates from Scholasticism. The decisive thing is that Luther himself specifies his position as defending a nominal *communicatio idiomatum* against Zwingli, who denies it. Luther writes there:

> Thus one should attribute to the whole person what happens to the other part of the person for this reason: that the two are one person. That is also how all the ancient teachers speak, as well as all recent theologians, all language, and all of Scripture. But the accursed alleosis turns that right around and wants to make an exchange, and attribute to a part what is attributed to the whole person in Scripture. It makes its own tropes, to twist Scripture and to divide the person of Christ, just as he does with "is," for the sole reason that he might teach something new and even bring his foolish thoughts into the light. And indeed, since he really wants to trope, why does he not stay with the old trope, which Scripture and all teachers to this day have used here? Namely, synecdoche, like this: "Christ died according to the humanity," etc. But that would have been nothing new, and there was no fame to be sought in that; he also would not have been able to bring in a new error.[180]

Luther sees himself as the true heir of Scholasticism in the battle over the correct expressions, the nominal *communcatio idiomatum*.

But that does not give a complete account of Luther's Christology. Abundant proofs for a Christology that goes far beyond this have already been given within the framework of this volume. *They mean that, besides a nominal* communicatio idiomatum, *Luther developed a doctrinal opinion about the participation of Jesus' humanity in the divine attributes that deviates from Scholasticism.* Nilsson again allows the identification of the *communicatio idiomatum* and the participation in the attribute of majesty, which a later generation would categorize as a special subdivision under the main concept of the *communicatio idiomatum*. Nilsson polemicizes against the ambition of Lutheran orthodoxy to hold the so-called

177 CR 92:680.3ff.

178 CR 92:681.8f.

179 Compare to this *ST*, III, 16; *Die deutsche Thomas-Ausgabe* 26:436ff.; Landgraf, op. cit., 2/1:138ff.

180 WA 26:322.23ff. [cf. AE 37:211].

genus maiestaticum as a separate group of expressions, and [he] absolutely wants to consider both types identical.[181] From this, of course, follows Nilsson's desired *reciprocal* influence between the attributes, so that corresponding to the humanity's elevation to divine power is the divinity's demotion to human emptiness. *By doing this he has been able to find in Luther a nonontological concept of God, and all the rest of the theological expressions are similarly made powerless.* In his polemic against orthodoxy, Nilsson does not realize that he allows himself to be misled by the very school that he is attacking. Orthodoxy, of its own accord, introduced the participation of the attributes of majesty under the *communicatio idiomatum* but, aware of certain difficulties in the definitions, retained the existence of a special group of predicates.[182] Nilsson now accepts orthodoxy's rubric of *genus*, but with disregard for its special distinction of *species*. He thereby commits the decisive mistake, for *Luther does not use the* communicatio

---

181 Nilsson, op. cit., p. 241: "But Luther makes no distinction between different types [*genera*]; he does not express himself in such categories and does not even try to hold on to his viewpoint in any teaching method. Now if one asserts that Luther's expressions on the *genus idiomaticum* apply right away also to the *genus maiestaticum*, then there is no problem in that for *Luther's* view. A divine attribute, for example, 'creating,' which is ascribed not only to the person of the God-man but also to the human nature, does not mean for Luther, as seen from his own applications, any *new* stage in this principle. By doing this, he merely develops further what is already implicit in the thought of the *communicatio*."

182 Mahlmann, *Das neue Dogma der lutherischen Christologie*, p. 83: "Johannes Bötker, as far as I see, was the first and, up to Melanchthon's death in 1560, the only theologian who made this expression specifically of the Lutheran understanding of the personal union [scil., *communicatio realis*]." Thereby the *genus maiestaticum* had entered into the *communicatio idiomatum*. The theoretical distinction followed later. Page 229f.: "So Chemnitz in the *Repetitio* had developed for the first time the categorization of the *communicatio* into three types." When the Formula of Concord (*BS* 1045.24ff. [FC VIII 26]) appeals to WA 54:49.33ff. [cf. AE 15:293] for the *communicatio idiomatum* in the sense of the *genus maiestaticum*,* this is incorrect. Luther speaks there only about the actual assuming of the human nature into personal union with the divinity: "That God is man" (WA 54:50.22 [cf. AE 15:293], Psalm 110), about the sitting at the right hand of the Father, just as WA 40/3:709.10 [forthcoming AE 63], about Psalm 8, "You have subjected all things under His feet," precisely means the nominal (outside the reality of the concept of person, of course, even ontologically) idiomatic predications (*genus idiomaticum*); compare above, pp. 45–46 n. 48. Concerning the worthiness of adoration derived from this, compare below, pp. 246–47 n. 65. — Also the source of broadening the concept of the *communicatio idiomatum* to the *genus maiestaticum*, of course, is in Luther, along with this latter *genus* actually meaning, however, that attributes are transferred, which corresponds to the term *communicatio idiomatum*. In Luther's, unfortunately, poorly preserved letter to Franz Gross (after 1541)—WA TR 6:[67–70], no. 6600; WA 48:647ff.; Enders 14, no. 3084—there is a depiction that begins with traditional idiom-communication and ends with omnipresence of the human nature, that is, *genus maiestaticum*. If Luther in time changed his formal mode of teaching to something like this, he certainly would have provided it with safeguards against a *genus tapeinoticum*, which later Lutheran

idiomatum *as an explanation of the doctrine of Jesus' exaltation to participation in the divine.* Orthodoxy's procedure is in and of itself completely defensible; it chose to define things in a somewhat different way, but without thereby causing actual confusion. Nilsson, on the other hand, causes not a little confusion.

Nowhere in the expressions of the elevation of Jesus' humanity cited here earlier is there any reference to the *communicatio idiomatum*. Luther builds on two kinds of reasoning: partly on the relationship that the person-forming element in the God-man is the eternal Logos, which cannot possibly be changed but indeed changes the assumed humanity; partly on the Bible words that elaborate on the consequences of this view. Thus, concerning the omnipresence, this means: "Where God is, there He [Christ] must also be, or our faith is false";[183] or this is said: "And where Christ is, there is the Godhead complete and whole, as Paul says, 'In Him dwells all the fullness of the Godhead bodily' [see Col. 2:9] and John 6 [see 14:6, 9]: 'I have been with you so long, and you do not know Me, Philip? Whoever sees Me sees the Father.' "[184] Nowhere does Luther work with the thought that is ludicrous to him, the thought of a human person who would exercise a corresponding influence on the divinity and turn omnipresence into its opposite.

---

generations introduced. Such disclaimers exist also in the Cyrillian tradition: compare John of Damascus, PG 94:1012 C, 1058 C; compare *BS* 1109.49ff., 1123.39ff.

* [A misprint reads *idiomaticum.*]

183 WA 26:336.18f. [cf. AE 37:223].

184 WA 23:131.20ff. [cf. AE 37:61]. [WA and Hardt have "John 6"; AE has "John 16." However, both WA and AE note the reference should be John 14.]

CHAPTER 3

Possibile—Necessarium

Christology and Sacrament

AS already presented, the repletive and diffinitive modes of presence of Christ's body are distinct from each other: the presence expressed in Christological terms is not immediately identical with the sacramental presence. In the literature, the author of the present investigation[1] and then Ragnar Holte[2] have emphasized this, against making the different modes identical. Holte gives a brief overview of the basis for research, where Vilmos Vajta[3] consistently maintains that the modes are identical, which again is questioned by [Carl Fredrik] Wisløff.[4] Holte finds that Vajta's interpretation has its immediate origin in [Reinhold] Seeberg,[5] who in his history of dogma, while analyzing Luther's *Great Confession* of the Supper, claimed that when Luther asserts a special diffinitive form of presence, he does not render his opinion without making a hypothetical argument, suited to the premises of the opponents. The idea of the sacramental presence as coinciding with the omnipresence can be

1 Hardt, "Dette är min lekamen," pp. 47ff. (review of Sasse, *This Is My Body*).

2 Holte, "Luthersk nattvardslära i ljuset av nyare exegetik och patristik," pp. 65ff. The same interpretation as in Hardt and Holte is found also in Pieper, *Christliche Dogmatik*, 2:210 [cf. *Christian Dogmatics*, 2:190].

3 Vajta, *Die Theologie des Gottesdienstes bei Luther*, pp. 176ff.

4 Wisløff, *Nattvord og messe*, p. 155. Holte (op. cit., p. 75 n. 3) asserts that Wisløff gives a "substantively destructive critique" of Vajta's identification of the modes of presence, but Wisløff considers an evangelical tension in Luther, and Vajta only latches on to the failure to pay attention to all the material: "*All this is seen correctly*, and Vajta's whole presentation is consistently thought out from the doctrine of ubiquity. The question is just whether Vajta's view allows itself to be joined with the *fullness* that is in the present material." Wisløff therefore cannot make an outright appeal to the critique that is put forth by Hardt and Holte.

5 Seeberg, op. cit., 4/1:471.

noted, to various degrees, in [Hans] Grass,[6] Peters,[7] [Hermann] Sasse,[8] and E. Thestrup Pedersen,[9] though these researchers do not at all agree. In a larger Christological work, Theodor Mahlmann has recently asserted that the sacramental presence for Luther really is distinct from omnipresence.[10]

Seeberg's view of the modes of presence as identical builds on the thought that Luther introduced a hypothetical alternative, that is, the diffinitive presence, "in order to make it clear to the opponents according to scholastic tradition that even if one maintains the local existence of the body of Christ in heaven, His bodily presence in the Supper would still be possible"; for this opinion he [Seeberg] appeals to WA 26:329f., 336f., and 414f. [cf. AE 37:219f., 224f., 270f.].

6 Grass, op. cit., p. 234: "According to the *Great Confession* on the Supper from 1528, the diffinitive and also the repletive modes of existence of Christ's body in the Supper are consistent"; cf. id., p. 62.

7 Peters, op. cit., p. 96. Compare here id., p. 63: "Reason can understand the word 'in'—Christ in the Word, in bread and wine—only in a physical way; it only knows the presence in space and time. Faith, however, 'accepts that "in"' in this case means the same as above, outside of, through and through, and everywhere" (WA 26:341.17 [cf. AE 37:230]). This—Peters' separation here of the concrete restriction to space of the sacramental presence for an undefined "above, outside of," yes, "everywhere"—rests on the mistake of overlooking what Luther says in the cited passage about the intangibility of God's presence in *creation* (WA 26:341.1f. [cf. AE 37:229]: "That it is one person with the divinity, so it must also be higher, above, and outside of all other creatures")! By interpreting these words as a part of sacramental theology, Peters in addition prepared his later formulation (op. cit., p. 96): "Thus he has in a certain sense taken back his expression about the Lord's 'diffinitive' presence in the Sacrament."

8 Sasse, op. cit., p. 158. But Sasse feels that Luther did not dogmatize his doctrine of the omnipresence of Christ's body and in later years did not come back to it (op. cit., pp. 283, 308). Compare above, p. 43 n. 37. The interpretation of Hardt and Holte, outside of Sasse's standpoint, in a certain sense would be correct about the older Luther.

9 E. Thestrup Pedersen (*Luther som skriftfortolker*, pp. 101f.) asserts: "It was asserted that Luther himself did not find any solution to question 2 [= What is the relationship between Christ's general omnipresence and His special presence in the bread and wine of the Supper?], which naturally also applies in a purely philosophical way." Id., p. 102 n. 28: "This viewpoint can be overstretched so that 'revelation' is only considered as uncovering of a condition previously unknown to man, though Luther's central understanding of 'revelation' is that it is one with God's new deed." Compare below, n. 10.

10 Mahlmann (op. cit., p. 171 n. 144) points out that behind the identification of the modes of presence in a number of researchers there is the depiction that Luther worked with ideas that were contradictory to one another: through the doctrine of the omnipresence of Christ's body Luther is thought to have gone too far in his zeal for the sacramental presence and invalidated it. But it ought to be noted that Seeberg, Grass, and Peters, who are called upon for this, do not think that Luther was actually unsuccessful in his presentation; there is only an "apparent" lack of success (Peters, op. cit., p. 86), for the solution consists in the sacramental presence becoming the existential-subjective concretization of what has always been.

It is further asserted "that Luther himself states and admits that 'in, with, under' ... can be misunderstood, that they could really first help the opponents as an occasion to misinterpret his doctrine (WA 26:442, 447 [cf. AE 37:300, 306]). This formulation, according to the 'diffinitive,' is not formed [*gebildet*] according to the authoritative 'repletive' way of thinking."[11] Seeberg's claim of the existence of a hypothetical argument is completely correct, but this still does not mean the diffinitive presence in the *Sacrament*, but the diffinitive presence in *heaven*, understood as opposite to and excluding a repletive presence, as an accommodation to the opponents! "If Christ's body were likewise in one place in heaven (as they prattle), still all creatures may be here in front of Him and around Him, like bright, transparent air."[12] With this, Luther simply goes back to the Ockhamist definition of movement and concept of presence, where being bound to a local, heavenly presence at the Father's right hand did not exclude the sacramental presence. This, in and of itself, suffices as a possible explanation of the presence. In the same way, Aristotelian physics as making the presence possible is put forward by Luther at the Marburg Colloquy with Zwingli.[13] The doctrinal material of the past contains a rich collection of arguments for the possibility of the sacramental miracle, which Luther did not at all disdain to use—even if only secondarily. Luther's own, nonhypothetically conceived view in this case, however, is that Christ is omnipresent even in His humanity and that this explains the presence. This *explanation* does not mean, however, a simple identification. It is of importance that here the occasion for the *repletive* presence of Christ's body mainly comes to be put forward by Luther in connection with the *diffinitive* presence of the same body. Luther writes:

> For when I showed how Christ's body is everywhere, since God's right hand is everywhere, I did so for this reason ... that I might still demonstrate one way in which it is possible with God that Christ is at the same time in heaven and His body is in the Supper, and [that He] reserved to His divine wisdom and power even more ways by which He is able to do the same, because we do not know the limit or measure of His power.[14]

This explanation in the *Great Confession* on the Supper is intended to expound the earlier *That These Words [This Is My Body]* where Luther wrote:

> If Christ had never said these words "This is My body" nor placed them in the Supper, still these words "Christ sits at the right hand of God" enforce that fact that His body and blood may be in all other places, and here one does not need transubstantiation or changing of the bread into His body; it

11 Seeberg, op. cit., 4/1:471 n. 2.

12 WA 26:336.38f. [cf. AE 37:224].

13 WA 30/3:138.24.

14 WA 26:318.1ff. [cf. AE 37:207].

> can still be, just as the right hand of God must not necessarily be changed into all things, though it is there or in them.[15]

The words "when *it is possible* with God" and "then it *may* be" (= "would be able") contain the thought that the repletive presence of Christ's body also includes the *possibility* of the diffinitive presence. The sacramental presence in the form of the co-presence of the heavenly and the bodily can therefore easily commence, whereby the change of substance is not necessary, since the sacramental coexistence has a parallel ("just as") in the repletive presence [existing] in creation without this latter ceasing. Nothing in the text justifies the confusing of possibility and reality, "may be" and "is," "may" and "was."[16] Repletive presence is not diffinitive; it simply opens up the possibilities ("reserves . . . shows"). Luther's careful precision in using the modal helping verbs should not be forgotten: "How often have you heard now that these two terms, *possibile*, *necessarium*, 'may' and 'must,' are farther apart than heaven and earth?"[17] This distinction, expressed in another context, includes a formulation that is essential for this problem.

In the controversy on the Supper, Luther asserted the repletive presence of Christ's body to refute the Zwinglian insistence that "Christ's body *must* not be in the Supper,"[18] *for a simultaneous presence of Christ's body in two places is impossible*. This Zwinglian assertion and its premise are disproved through the repletive presence—of course, without appealing to the Words of Institution, which could not be used here since their literal meaning was rejected [by the Zwinglians] when they insisted on their absurd conclusions (the physical impossibility of simultaneous presence). In this dispute it is *not* necessarily the controverted, diffinitive presence that is proved, but a different one. The Zwinglians had relied on a universal impossibility as a logical main thesis in order to introduce the Supper in the middle thesis and its impossibility in the final thesis. It therefore became Luther's task to attack the universal application of the main thesis; showing it to be invalid resulted in the possibility of the miracle of the Supper.

One must maintain that theses such as "So it (= the right hand of God) is certainly also in the bread and wine on the table"[19] are introductory theses in a longer argumentation. Luther is thereby only making a Christological statement with reference to the Scripture passages about the meaning of the elevation—

15 WA 23:145.13ff. [cf. AE 37:64].

16 Metzke (*Sakrament und Metaphysik*, p. 51) transcribes WA 23:145.13 [cf. AE 37:64]: "Even if He (= Christ) had not said the words 'This is My body,' He would still be in the bread and wine with His 'body and blood' . . . ." By changing "may" [*müge*] to "would" [*wäre*], Metzke makes the repletive and sacramental presence identical.

17 WA 23:169.1ff. [cf. AE 37:79]; compare above, n. 16.

18 WA 26:317.31 [cf. AE 37:207] [emphasis added].

19 WA 23:143.32 [cf. AE 37:64].

well to note, without making use of the *communicatio idiomatum*—in order, with these as argument, to be able to proceed in a way of thinking that did not yet reach its conclusion. After this Luther asks rhetorically, "What will be here now?" and answers, "It will be from outside: . . . that His body and blood then may be there."[20] By doing this, Luther can thus proceed from the main thesis to the middle thesis and the final thesis.

Luther himself polemicizes against a naive equating of the two modes of presence. He maintains that the repletive presence "is in all places, but still at the same time is also nowhere and imperceptible, above and beyond all creatures. There is a difference between His presence and your grasping."[21] What applies here is not merely distinguishing "in itself" as opposed to "for me," through which the latter would become merely a subjective experiential assurance of what already existed. The divine presence *is* impossible to comprehend in itself: "It is not thus grasped and grabbed."[22] These and similar concepts—"grasp," "grab," "gobble," "guzzle"—have to do with the physical encounter with the sacramental eating of Christ's body, which cannot come about in its divine, repletive form of existence. Just as Luther, in the section about concomitance, will show it to be "sorcery" to reject the thought of a presence of the divinity in the Sacrament,[23] supported by the axiom about the immutable divine nature, he maintains here the repletive presence's exaltation and separation from creation, just as it clearly applies to the *un-incarnate divinity*:

> Just as I say of the right hand of God: although it is everywhere, as we may not deny, yet because it is also nowhere, as is said, you cannot truly grasp it anywhere, unless it connects itself to you to summon you to a place. *But it does that when it comes to dwell in the humanity of Christ.* Then you find it indeed; otherwise you might sort through all creatures, grab here and there, and yet never find it again, even though it is truly there at the same time. For it is not there for you.[24]

The repletive divinity could not be grasped and fetched with hands before it took on a physical existence through the incarnation in and through the circumscribed-diffinitive humanity. The miracle of the Sacrament is an exact parallel to this: since Christ's body at the ascension is swallowed up by the mist that surrounds the divinity, the tangibility is renewed through the onset of the diffinitive presence. Luther writes:

> Thus also, since Christ's humanity is at the right hand of God and now also is in all and above all things according to the manner of the divine right hand,

20 WA 23:145.13ff. [cf. AE 37:64].

21 WA 23:151.1ff. [cf. AE 37:68].

22 WA 23:151.11 [cf. AE 37:68].

23 WA 11:450.13f. [cf. AE 36:297]; compare below, chapter 6.

24 WA 23:151.17ff. [cf. AE 37:69f.] (emphasis mine).

> so you will not so gobble and guzzle Him like cabbage and soup on your table, unless He wills it. Now He has also become imperceptible, and you will not grab Him, though He is in your bread. For it happens that He connects Himself to you and summons you to a particular table through His Word.... If you eat this [bread], then you eat My body, and *otherwise not.*[25]

First, the divine will and the words of consecration create the miracle, *which otherwise is not at hand, namely, the diffinitive presence.* This is also an obvious result of the precise distinctions with which Luther is working.

As already stated, in order to strengthen his thesis, Luther would have been able to make use of other arguments also, formed within Scholasticism, which did not know the main argument he now brings forward. Therefore, *in this conflict* the doctrine of the omnipresence of Christ's body has the character of an ancillary proposition. The discussion about the Supper cannot fundamentally be carried out through this Christological controversy.[26] If Luther had made a mistake in the latter, the doctrine of the Supper would not fall, even though, conversely, the correctness of the Christological statements includes the possibility that the miracle of the Sacrament would be disputed by Zwingli.[27] This, of course, does not mean that the doctrine of the omnipresence of Christ's body *as such* should have a hypothetical character, as Ernst Sommerlath[28] and Sasse asserted.[29]

Even if the term "ancillary construction," which is used by Sommerlath, has its application in one area where Luther only wants "to show in abundance,"[30] it

---

25 WA 23:151.25ff. [cf. AE 37:69, which translates the last phrase as "nowhere else"] (emphasis mine).

26 WA 26:318.27f. [cf. AE 37:203].

27 Mahlmann (op. cit., pp. 169ff.) gives a depiction of Luther's words cited here that actually conforms to the depiction above, which supports the view that was presented in 1960 by the author of this volume and was further developed in a mimeographed licentiate [pre-PhD] dissertation in 1966. But Mahlmann, whose main subject is not Luther but the later Christological controversy, does not develop his position from the differences given here among the three modes of presence as the starting point. He cites, however (p. 173 n. 152): "Which passages of Luther's Lord's Supper writings are the most difficult to interpret, one can indeed learn already from Johannes Hülsemann's *Calixtinischer Gewissenswurm*, Leipzig, 1653, which on pages 223–63 reproduces verbatim the crucial sections and provides an astute commentary in numerous marginalia." In a presentation whose brilliant analysis undoubtedly earns Mahlmann's praise, Hülsemann explains very clearly the "threefold presence of the body" (Hülsemann, op. cit., p. 245). Calixt, Hülsemann's opponent, "repudiated sainted Luther, if he would defend the way of stating the presence of Christ's body in the Eucharist through its ubiquity" (op. cit., p. 228), which goes against Luther's true meaning (op. cit., p. 234): "The mode of ubiquity is not the only mode of presence for Christ's body."

28 Sommerlath, "Das Abendmahl bei Luther," p. 120.

29 Sasse, op. cit., p. 341.

30 WA 23:129.31f. [cf. AE 37:55].

does not at all cover the role of the doctrine within Christology, as is apparent from chapter 2, above. The words of Aegidius Hunnius could be cited against the idea of Sommerlath and Sasse: "Therefore, the conclusion is very false when they argue in this way: 'Luther thought that one should not bother to argue about the omnipresence in the Lord's Supper; therefore, he felt that one should not argue about it at all, not even in the topic [*sede*] of the appropriate article.' It is a fallacy of drawing a conclusion from something that is simply stated."[31]

Since the thesis-hypothesis in question about repletive and diffinitive presence is discussed in this connection, Seeberg's other argument can be taken up. Even this presentation—that Luther's rejection of the formula "in, with, under" should affect the diffinitive presence—is based on a misunderstanding. The background is that Luther's opponents asserted that he himself does not take the Words of Institution literally: "since we [Luther] say: The words 'This is My body' should be understood in this way: Under the bread is My body, or in the bread is My body, etc."[32]

Luther answers, "But we are not thereby making any different, new text";[33] but in order to ensure the sacramental presence, he is willing to give up the preposition-expressions, which the opponents find to show that Luther does not take the biblical "is" literally: "And where one would seek our approval even with such great force, or would show that the text 'This is My body' cannot mean what I say elsewhere: 'Christ's body is in the Supper,' then we are ready and willing to have it retracted. Then it should not be said that way, but plainly

31 Printed in Chemnitz, *Fundamenta sanae doctrinae*, p. 120 (a later appendix to Chemnitz's book); the same opinion in Wigand, ibid., p. 117: "And he did not simply dismiss it either, but with the disclaimer [*secundum quid*]: in this matter. Also here: he is speaking, however, concerning the holy Supper." It is thus important also in connection with Luther to distinguish the various loci, which are each entitled to their own logical and exegetical viability, as was the goal of Chemnitz and of Lutheran orthodoxy. Compare Mahlmann, op. cit., pp. 223f., also p. 220 n. 1 (= pp. 220–23), where full clarity is given concerning Chemnitz's mistake of ascribing to Luther a quotation from Melanchthon on this point. The mistake, which does not have *substantial* significance, was pointed out by several of the Lutheran orthodox teachers, among others, Leonhard Hutter, with a large scholarly apparatus. Ahlberg (op. cit., p. 252 n. 4) asserts that Ritschl (*Dogmengeschichte des Protestantismus*, 4:8 n. 26) would have been unable to recognize the mistake in Chemnitz's use of the quotation, which Ahlberg himself learned first through WA 48:236f., but the discovery is almost as old as the mistake. In modern literature before WA 48, it was most recently pointed out by Pieper (op. cit., 2:227 n. 183). [Although not in the English edition, the footnote reads: "In *De duabus naturis*, p. 206, Chemnitz refers to a statement by Luther in the Jena edition (8:375), according to which Luther, too, wanted to employ the disputation about general omnipresence. Hutter, in *Concordia Concors*, pp. 31ff., shows that these words are not Luther's but probably Melanchthon's. Hutter also explains to what extent Chemnitz could in good faith attribute the words to Luther" (*Two Natures in Christ*, p. 464).]

32 WA 26:264.34ff. [cf. AE 37:166].

33 WA 26:265.6f. [cf. AE 37:166].

and simply 'This is My body,' as the words stand there."[34] It is these lines that got Seeberg to believe that Luther saw in [the phrase] "in, with, under" a possibility of falsely defining his doctrine of the sacramental presence diffinitively, and not, as would be correct, repletively, and that is why he rejected these prepositions. In the same work, Luther sees "in, with, under" as useful for denying the presence, in accordance with the reasoning that was used against him, and he lets the Enthusiasts shout about whether Christ used the actual expressions of locality: "Oh, how we would gladly believe if He had said, 'This is My body.' That would be stating it plainly and clearly. But now He says 'in the bread, with the bread, under the bread,' so it does not follow that His body is there. And thus they would imagine a thousand excuses and glosses on the words 'in, with, under,' even with grander appearance."[35] "In, with, under" as a formulation[36] is only here in Luther, and then rejected, but in no way as asserting a particular form of presence in the Sacrament but as useful for denying any presence. Thus they were ready-made for the foundation of Seeberg's idea, whose place in a generally accepted standard work granted him the greatest circulation.

Vilmos Vajta, in a special monograph, went far beyond Seeberg by laying the omnipresence as a foundation for his concept of the sacramental presence in a completely different and very consistent way. In an analysis of Vajta's procedure, further worthwhile observations about Luther's opinion are made. Fundamentally, Vajta sees Luther's doctrine of the omnipresence of the divinity as an exclusive expression of faith, impossible within the framework of a natural theology based on reason without the support of revelation. For support, Vajta cites Luther's Jonah commentary from 1526: "His [people] are those who alone perceive that God is the kind of Lord who is almighty and in all places."[37] Concerning these words, it can be said first and foremost that they give dimension to what was recently said about the impossibility of understanding the distinction between omnipresence and sacramental presence as a distinction between objectively and subjectively experienced presence, "in itself" and "for me." Luther reckons that omnipresence can also be experienced subjectively as a comforting "for me," even if it can never be grasped and touched with

34 WA 26:265.12ff. [cf. AE 37:166].

35 WA 26:447.22ff. [cf. AE 37:306].

36 Separate not simultaneous use of the three prepositions in Luther is reported by Sasse (op. cit., p. 161 n. 59). For the origin of the formulation as a confession of orthodox Lutheranism against Tileman Hesshusius, compare *BS* 983 n. 2, along with the portrayal in Salig, *Vollständige Historie der Augsburgischen Confession*, 3:451ff. Since the conditions under which the expression exists in Luther are not made clear, in the literature it often meets statements such as, for example, in Andrén (*Högmässa och nattvärdsgång i reformationstidens svenska kyrkoliv*, p. 48): "as Luther expressed the matter: 'in, with, and under bread and wine.' "

37 WA 19:197.25f. [cf. AE 19:45]. Vajta, op. cit., p. 158.

hands and mouth. *Therefore, the special character of the sacramental presence can never be explained with what can be attributed also to the omnipresence.* Furthermore, Vajta's quotation is followed by a later statement [from Luther] that he does not cite: "The godless, however, do not feel and do not believe and know that God is in all places, though they likewise hear it said and in fact can repeat it."[38] In the context, Luther divides God's presence into a "natural" and a "spiritual" form: the natural presence is actually the fact that God fills everything, while the spiritual presence is found where the believers are, "who alone perceive" God's dominion through "Word, faith, Spirit, and divine service."[39] This presence, and this knowledge that constitutes it, is reserved for Christians as regenerated. It cannot be questioned that the unbelieving are by definition excluded from this Spirit-wrought knowledge of God's all-conquering presence, but this does not give any reason that the omnipresence in its natural form according to Luther could not be defined *intellectually*, even emphatically, in the very writing just invoked by Vajta: "The natural light of reason reaches so far that it regards God as good, gracious, merciful, and mild; that is a great light."[40] Here faith also comes with power to help: "For it believes the power and recognizes it."[41]

But nature is lacking in those two points that grace offers: faith that "God will be gracious not only to others but also to me,"[42] and faith in "whoever or whatever it is that is rightly called God."[43] The words "though they hear it said and can even repeat it" undoubtedly fit in this very thought pattern, which Luther developed elsewhere with the words about the philosophical knowledge of God: "One might speak of this as sniffing the existence of God without tasting it."[44] Omnipresence, for Luther, cannot be an exception to this type of

38 WA 19:197.26ff. [cf. AE 19:45].

39 WA 19:197.24 [cf. AE 19:45].

40 WA 19:206.12f. [cf. AE 19:54].

41 WA 19:206.17 [cf. AE 19:54].

42 WA 19:206.28f. [cf. AE 19:54].

43 WA 19:206.33 [cf. AE 19:55].

44 WA 46:668.33f. [cf. AE 22:152]; compare WA 21:509.6f. [cf. AE 78:4]: "For human reason and wisdom can still come so far on its own that it concludes (though weakly), that there must be a single, eternal divine being, which creates, sustains, and rules all things. Since it sees such a beautiful, excellent creation, . . . so wonderful, orderly, and certain . . . [it is] not possible that it should be made like thus or on its own. . . . And thus God must be acknowledged in creation, as St. Paul also says in Romans 1 . . . ." The word "weakly" is not in opposition to the above-cited "a great light." In the exposition of Jonah, Luther stresses *when* the great light is weakened: "Thus you see here also that these people in the ship all know about God, but they have no certain God" (WA 19:208.21ff. [cf. AE 19:56]); "For their god lets them sink in the danger and cry out in vain, so that they completely despair and do not know where they would find a god who would save them" (WA 19:208.27ff. [cf. AE 19:57]); "As long as it goes well

for him and suits him, then he is bold, even above God and all that God is; and is so stubborn and harder than any anvil ever was. But if he begins to sink and despair, then there is nothing more timid" (WA 19:208.8ff. [cf. AE 19:57]). *The strong light becomes weak in dangerous tribulation*; that is, the perceived truth cannot be maintained when man becomes *emotionally* heartsick. This cannot be understood as if in dangerous situations what would otherwise be affirmed intellectually would be disputed *intellectually*. When Luther in the *Bondage of the Will* from 1525, the year before the Jonah commentary, is thought by Cleve (op. cit., p. 227, for example) to develop the thought that "God's omnipotence cannot be understood by natural reason," this is mistaken. (This is repeated also in Lohse, *Ratio und fides*, p. 63.) This builds on Luther's reasoning in the face of the world's obviously unfair course:

> What do you think Demosthenes and Cicero thought when they did everything they could and got a reward of miserable destruction? And nevertheless this "unfairness of God" is strongly commendable and is brought into such arguments for which there is no rationale or can still be opposed to nature; it is very easily destroyed through the light of the Gospel and knowledge of grace, by which we are taught that the impious indeed flourish physically, but their soul is destroyed. (WA 18:785.11ff. [cf. AE 33:291])

It does not say here that the revelation of the immortality of the soul and punishment or reward after death strengthens natural reason's poor argument into intellectual viability. That would distort Luther's main thought. The light of the Gospel, the "knowledge of grace," does not convey intellectual arguments but *dogmas*, spirit-filled "*assertiones*": "Take away the assertions, and you have taken away Christianity. Indeed, the Holy Spirit is given from His heaven to explain Christ and to confess until death—unless dying for one's confession and assertion is not making a statement" (WA 18:603.28ff. [cf. AE 33:21]). These, the Spirit's dogmas, give strength to confess until death, which well-founded *thoughts* never offer. Luther knows that "Cicero and Plato elegantly argue about the immortality of the soul; their thoughts are very good" (WA 39/2:14.24ff. [cf. AE 38:249]), but he will argue that the man Cicero, as an affective [emotional] being, could not have been filled by the comfort of faith in God's gracious governance and omnipotence at his undeserved doom. The philosopher Cicero's "very good thoughts" were not of comfort at this moment. On the other hand, Luther does not insist that they were forfeited of strictly intellectual, objective worth. — Generally it ought to be said that the view of Luther's position toward natural theology should reflect an earlier conviction that Ockham's school, in which Luther is counted, denied the proof of God, and that Luther thus only carried out his school's traditions. The reversal that occurred in the question of Ockham (compare Junghans, op. cit., pp. 158, 219, 225, 230) also ought to come to Luther's aid. (Grane, *Contra Gabrielem*, p. 55 n. 8, criticizes [Erich] Seeberg, *Luthers Theologie*, 1:19, and Olsson, "Den naturliga gudskunskapens problem enligt den senmedeltida nominalismen," pp. 382ff., but does not explain possible consequences for Luther.) An early, correct judgment of Luther is in Arnold, *Zur Frage des Naturrechts bei Martin Luther*. And more detailed working out of this stance of Luther must bring consequences from the radical dissimilarity that is found between the young and the older Luther. *The former denies the latter's exposition of Romans 1 above*; compare WA 1:354.17f. [cf. AE 31:40], where Luther, within the framework of his doctrine of salvation from that time, promotes the thesis "Renunciation of the visible is the satisfaction that we owe to God," formulated by Bizer, "Glaube und Demut in Luthers Vorlesung über den Römerbrief," p. 68; compare Lohse, *Ratio und fides*, p. 12, about the natural knowledge of God as a self-righteous work of man, with an account of other researchers. For Luther's stance it

knowledge, the existence of which, in a different context, Luther asserted as different from revelation. *Thus it is not possible to see the assertion of omnipresence as a mere fact, as a specifically Christian characteristic.*

Another mistake Vajta makes is when he asserts concerning omnipresence that it is made understandable by the Last Day.[45] Behind this thought is the idea that only the present age, imprinted by sin, would require the sacramental concretization of the divine presence, but that sinless, restored man would always know and experience the reality that previously required the function of the elements.[46] Ontologically this touches on the same presence, just taken with varying degrees of insight. Luther again insists that finding God in things is a sin of the heathen: "You are committing idolatry."[47] Even if, for Luther, omnipresence can be experienced subjectively as comforting, it is inaccessible to the created intellect, [even] apart from the corruption of sin: "It is beyond the nature and reason even of all the angels in heaven, known and familiar only to God."[48] Not even angelic knowledge in its sinlessness is able to comprehend what can never be comprehended by creation.

The defect in Vajta's depiction becomes especially clear when, while making the distinction between the Roman and Reformed doctrines of the Sacrament, it says, "The 'local' [presence] or the 'speculative' presence form the opposite of the real presence of Christ. These characterize the theology of the Papists and the Enthusiasts, respectively."[49] *The idea that Luther would have imagined the Roman concept of the presence as "local" is incorrect.* Rather, Luther defends Scholasticism and the Roman Church on this point, against the Enthusiasts who bring forth the very allegations that Vajta puts in Luther's mouth: "For the sophists speak correctly about this when they say: There

---

ought especially to be observed that Luther consciously (WA 1:355.16ff. [cf. AE 31:42]) joins *Plato* (compare Link, op. cit., p. 225): "not only in this, that he praises Plato compared to Aristotle, but also in the substantive use of Platonic thinking." The Platonic features have, above all, been underscored by Hunzinger ("Luthers Neoplatonismus in der Psalmenvorlesung von 1513 bis 1515," p. 73): "It is the Neo-Platonic thought-world of Augustine that experiences an unexpected revival here in Luther's lectures on the Psalms." A development from Platonic rejection of the visible as intermediary insight to outright natural theology inserts itself into the development that Bizer (*Fides ex auditu*) drew up from universalistic theology of humility ("renunciation of the visible") to exclusively Christian faith in the means of grace and salvation.

45 Vajta, op. cit., p. 167: "For nothing more is secret or hidden in God's essence."

46 Vajta, op. cit., p. 161: "The captivity of man under sin is the reason God is present for us only in His incarnate Son, though He is everywhere." Page 177: "Even before bread and wine are used in the Supper, Christ is in the natural gifts by reason of His omnipresence. It is only man in his sin who cannot recognize Him."

47 WA 19:492.24 [cf. AE 36:342].

48 WA 26:336.22f. [cf. AE 37:223].

49 Vajta, op. cit., p. 170 n. 43.

are three ways of being in a place: *localiter* or circumscribed, *diffinitive*, and *repletive*."[50] "For they [the Enthusiasts] knew that we never taught this . . . that we did not think of Christ in the Sacrament locally . . . for the Papists also had never taught this . . . as we also hold and still teach . . . [the doctrine of the diffinitive presence follows]. No, God be praised, such great fools we are not, even [when we were] the holy Church under the papacy."[51] "For they [the Enthusiasts] knew very well that neither the Papists nor we had taught that. . . . But thus the Papists, yes, not the Papists but the holy Christian Church, and we with them, teach . . . that Christ's body is not there locally . . . but definitively."[52] "Therefore, the Enthusiasts are wrong, as well as the glosses in the divines, when they criticize Pope Nicolaus of pressuring Berengar into such a confession that he says he would press and tear the true body of Christ with his teeth. Would to God that all popes had dealt in such a Christian manner in all points as this pope. . . ."[53] With these latter words Luther rejects even a great part of the medieval commentators of "*Ego Berengarius*" as too *spiritualizing*. Parallel to these expressions are Luther's words about the adoration of the elevated Sacrament, which were attacked by Karlstadt: "Here, I say, Dr. Karlstadt is not wrong, but his conscience knows that he is obviously lying concerning the pope. For he is also a sophist and has both learned and taught the theology of the higher schools and of the pope. Now nowhere does the pope teach that one should say to the form of the bread: 'My God, You are gracious to me.' "[54] One must characterize Vajta's depiction of Luther's demarcation against Roman Church doctrine on the Sacrament as thoroughly misleading. Here Luther is put forward with citations from, among others, the *Great Confession* as well as his shorter *Confession of the Supper*, which are two decades apart and therefore show the consistency in Luther's view. They

50 WA 26:327.20ff. [cf. AE 37:214f.].

51 WA 54:145.7f. [cf. AE 38:301].

52 WA 54:153.17ff. [cf. AE 38:301, 293]. It is peculiar that Luther ascribes to all of Scholasticism the diffinitive presence that was foreign to Thomas Aquinas. Actually Luther let his procedure be defended, as an expression that all of Scholasticism rejected the *local* presence. In this context, Luther cited Thomas's [hymn] *Lauda Sion*: "Whether one or thousands eat; All receive the self-same meat; Nor the less for others leave" [translation by E. Caswall, *Lyra Catholica*]. WA 54:146 n. 1 comments: "The hymn 'O Lord, We Praise Thee' [*Gott sei gelobet und gebenedeiet*] is common," an incorrect reference, since Luther expressly appeals to the sequence of the Corpus Christi Mass ("Mass of the 'Holy True Body'") (WA 54:146.1f. [cf. AE 38:293]), which is *Lauda Sion*. WA's commentator was misled by the pre-Reformation origin of "O Lord, We Praise Thee" [*Gott sei gelobet und gebenedeiet*], sung in connection with *Lauda Sion*; compare WA 35:183 and Luther's own words about its use, WA 38:245.23 [cf. AE 38:206] ("at the Sacrament, yes, in *procession*").

53 WA 26:442.39ff. [cf. AE 37:300].

54 Vajta, op. cit., p. 180.

show how Luther did not at all criticize the Roman concept of the sacramental presence as "local," but rather he shows himself as partaking of the scholastic doctrinal tradition in which the voice of the holy Church is heard.

The demarcation against the Enthusiasts, as it is portrayed by Vajta, is correct insofar as they rejected the real presence in favor of a "speculative," that is, nonreal, presence. But the kind of demarcation is mischaracterized: "They [the Enthusiasts] had a Deistic view of God, the idea of a God enthroned in exalted majesty, separated from His creation. This view of God affected their Christology so that they even understood revelation in Christ falsely."[55] The basis for Vajta's view has already been noted: here, in this case, accusations were raised of having obscured the specific Christian revelation of God's omnipresence. But no support for this asserted distinction can be found in Luther.[56] Luther never charged the opponents with such an elementary error as denying God's omnipresence. Grass has collected citations from Zwingli (and Calvin) that show how Luther's opponents clearly acknowledge the omnipresence of the divinity.[57] That applies also to Karlstadt, who writes: "The question whether Christ,* according to His divinity, is here or there is a question of whether Christ is in all creatures according to His divinity. That is foolish, for God is

55 Vajta, op. cit., p. 180.

56 Possibly Vajta's idea can be deduced from the following argument of Luther not cited by him, WA 23:131.9ff. [cf. AE 37:55–56]:

> If we now ask them [the Enthusiasts] here what they call the right hand of God, where Christ sits, I expect that they will rave about . . . an imaginary heaven, where there is a golden throne and where Christ sits next to the Father in a robe and golden crown. . . . For if they did not have such childish, carnal thoughts about the right hand of God, they would certainly not let it be disputed that the body of Christ is in the Supper. . . . From these childish thoughts, then, it must further follow that they bind God Himself to a place in heaven on the same golden throne, because there is no God outside of Christ. . . . From that it will follow even further that we and all creatures also sit on the same throne of God, perhaps like lice and flies in His robe, because Paul says, Acts 17[:28], "We are of His kind, and in Him we live and move and have our being."

In this ridiculous *deductio ad absurdum*, the premise is Luther's thesis about the mode of the state of union ("no God outside of Christ"), which, if it were accepted by the opponents, would extract from them the conclusion that if Christ's body were not omnipresent, neither would God be, and also God's right hand would have repletive existence, whereby finally creation would be forced by God's presence into a locally understood heaven (the folds in God's robe). This depiction is obviously rhetorical and is not making a claim of reproducing the opponents' meaning.

57 Grass, op. cit., p. 54.

* [Translator's note: There seems to be some dittography here. I have removed the first "in all creatures," which doesn't appear in other sources.]

in hell as well as in heaven and fills all creatures."[58] It is impracticable that with Vajta the distinction is over against the Enthusiasts in regard to the attributes of the divinity ("Deistic view of God"), as if Luther's dogmatic contribution consisted of teaching the omnipresence of the divinity. Vajta overlooks the fact that the controversy applies only to the type of union between Christ's two natures. The little interest Vajta devotes to the specifically Christological question comes from the fact that he has the omnipresence of Christ's humanity begin with the ascension.[59]

An omnipresence defined in this way is considered by Vajta to be identical with the sacramental presence.[60] In this way, *faith* becomes a constitutive factor for the sacramental presence, for it is faith that discerns the presence that always exists:

> This sacramental unity is promised in the Word and received in faith. Therefore, *Word and faith* are essential prerequisites for the spiritual presence of Christ in bread and wine. When Luther emphasizes this, on the one hand he distances himself from the view that can assert the presence of Christ separate from the believing reception of the earthly elements bound

58 Karlstadt, *Dialogus oder ein gesprechbüchlein von dem grewlichen unnd abgöttischen missbrauch / des hochwirdigsten sacraments Jesu Christi* (1524), fol. AIVa; also StL 20:2318.

59 Vajta, op. cit., p. 164. It ought to be noted that the text, WA 14:28.11ff. [cf. AE 30:153], cited in ibid., n. 25, does not deal with the ascension but [with] Christ's transfiguration on Tabor. Systematically, such revelations of glory have greater weight for Luther than for Scholasticism, with its rejection of the exaltation of the humanity to divine power; compare above, pp. 45–46 n. 48, on Thomas's definition of the transfiguration. Andrén (op. cit., p. 194) sees Johan III's introduction into Sweden of the festival of Christ's transfiguration as an un-Lutheran, Romanizing innovation, centered "around the divine nature's shining through the human nature." *This definition lets Lutheran and scholastic theology trade places completely.* It applies identically to Andrén's opinion (op. cit., p. 195) about Marian days, "this pointed localizing of what is holy." The Lutheran understanding of the Ephesine *theotokos* is more drastic than the Roman, which is a natural result of Luther's Christology reproduced above. What is noteworthy in Johan III's fight for setting the Festival [of Transfiguration] on August 6 is instead *the connection to the papal calendar*, which would thereby commemorate through a festival of indulgences of the same dimension as Corpus Christi the battle of Belgrade in 1456, won by the efforts of the papal see; compare *Enciclopedia universal ilustrada europeo-americana* 63:853, s.v. "Transfiguración," but which during the Middle Ages was unable to enforce this date; compare *Enciclopedia cattolica* 12:440, s.v. "Transfigurazione"; compare also de Waal, *Die Verklärung auf Thabor in Liturgie und Kunst*, p. 298. Andrén's explanation refers to a view of the omnipresence that conforms to Vajta, according to which Luther would have produced a view directed against the Roman "localizing" and purified of physical attributes.

60 For support, Vajta (op. cit., p. 159) invokes WA 23:145.13ff. [cf. AE 37:64] ("Even if Christ had never said the words 'This is My body' . . .") with the same mistaken explanation as refuted above, p. 9, text near n. 35 [Swedish edition, p. 16].

to the Word (Rome), and on the other hand from a view that relegates faith to a heavenly gift beyond the elements (Enthusiasts).[61]

[Vajta writes:] "Therefore, the presence of Christ is a presence for the believers. God deals in earthly means, to which He adds His Word. Only faith can connect the two. . . ."[62] This presence, for faith, in Vajta['s writings] is inserted into a defined systematic context: "The hiddenness in the Sacrament means waiting for the Spirit of God, who is not bound to the external means but is given through them 'where and when it seems best to God.'"[63] Thus Luther's doctrine of the sacramental presence is transformed into its direct opposite. Luther endeavors to distinguish words of Christ that presuppose faith in order to be actualized and the kind [of words] that get results "irrespective of a believing use [of them]." To the latter belong the words of the Sacrament, and the battle for their independence from the faith of the communicants is the battle for the reality of the Sacrament in Luther's theology.

> The command words are of two kinds: some, where faith is bound to them, as in Matthew 21, about moving a mountain, and in the last chapter of Mark, concerning the signs that should follow the believers. Now if someone without faith speaks such words to the mountain, "move," and boasts that he is doing it from the command words, then it does not happen because Christ Himself binds faith to the command word. The other [kind of command words] are when faith is not bound to them, as these words

61 Vajta, op. cit., p. 187.

62 Id., p. 171. The quotation continues: "and possibly bring it about that the commanding word lets the earthly gifts become a blessing," which does not mean, however, that faith is necessary merely for a *proper* reception. Vajta lets the presence and the blessing coincide. Under appeal to Ragnar Bring's denial of a Lutheran consecration in "On the Lutheran Concept of the Sacrament," in *World Lutheranism of Today*, the context is directed against the Roman doctrine, which is presented like this: "The power of the consecration transforms the elements into the body and blood of Christ and *effects* Christ's presence. The blessing of the sacramental act can be allocated to a person, without himself being in the struggle between faith and unbelief" (ibid.). Luther's doctrine is said to be that the presence "is not a presence that man can have in his hand and can bring to God as a means of atonement." But Luther teaches this presence "in the hand" (WA 30/3:561.3, 19, 21) and does not at all refute the sacrifice of the Mass by disputing the presence being accessible by hand on the altar.

63 Vajta, op. cit., p. 173 n. 53. This latter Latin quotation from the Augsburg Confession (*BS* 58.7f. [cf. AC V 2]) is cited by Vajta according to modern, mainly Barthian practice, without regard to its context, which reads: "For through the Word and Sacraments the Holy Spirit is granted, *who effects faith* where and when it seems best to God, in those who hear the Gospel." "Where and when" thus applies to the monergistically defined awakening of faith and not at all to the character of the means of grace as Spirit-bearing instruments. These words refer even less to the sacramental presence, which is identical neither with the awakening of faith nor the Spirit, without being directed by Luther to that part of the means of grace that is designated as the sign and which is part of the irreversibility of the Gospel.

> in the Supper, "Take, eat," for here even the unworthy and unbelieving eat Christ's body, as did even Judas and many of the Corinthians.[64]

This clear view of the consecration in Luther Vajta tries to correct as an expression of a merely revelatory act, appealing to Luther's words: "Yes, we also do not say that His body comes into existence out of the bread, but we say that His body, which was made long ago and has long existed, is there when we say, 'This is My body,' for Christ does not command us to say, 'Let My body come into being' or 'Make My body,' but 'This is My body.' "[65] But these words do not say that Christ's body was present long before the consecration, but that Christ's body, which was created and came to be long ago (in the Virgin's womb), is present *when* the holy words are spoken. This formulation of Luther's is completely understandable against the double background of Scholasticism and Zwingli's attack on Luther. Vajta completely overlooks this dogmatical-historical fact. Luther here is defending himself against Zwingli's attack ("as this spirit [Zwingli] accuses us"),[66] in which he asserts that Luther revived the former papistic doctrine of the creation of Christ's body out of the bread.[67] Luther confesses here a transformation that brings Christ's body to the Sacrament while rejecting a transformation that produces Christ's body. In a different context, he shows that he is familiar with these distinctions and how one comes to teach a newly created, growing body of Christ in the Eucharist.[68] Only with these perspectives do Luther's words become understandable. Properly understood, through the statement that Christ's body "is there when we say, 'This is My body,'" they confirm that Luther even here

64 WA 26:287.34ff. [cf. AE 37:188].

65 WA 26:287.27f. [cf. AE 37:187]; Vajta, op. cit., p. 184 n. 91. The citation is more extensive in Vajta, who cites in addition WA 38:240.1ff., 248.28ff. [cf. AE 38:199], where the consecration is said to occur not through the work of men, which of course Vajta's thesis does not show.

66 WA 26:287.26f. [cf. AE 37:187].

67 CR 92:585.16ff.: Luther is supposed to be of an "opinion of the pontificates who once taught that 'Do this in remembrance of Me' (1 Cor. 11:24) ought to be referred to the body: Make My body out of, or in, the bread in remembrance of Me." The word *facere* ["do/make"] in the command to commemorate would thus for Luther mean creating Christ's body, according to Zwingli's view. Zwingli knows that this doctrine is no longer ("once") found in the Roman Church.

68 WA Br 9[:443–44].10ff., no. 3629, Supplement: "The conversion of the bread into the body of Christ, that is, the essence of the bread is transformed into the body of Christ, just as food is transformed into my flesh and blood. Now since some seem to have thought wickedly that Christ's body would actually be transformed into so much bread and wine in itself in the whole world daily that He might finally become so big and fat that heaven and earth would be too narrow for Him, so now, more glorified, His body cannot be added to nor subtracted from. Therefore, they have thought differently. . . ."

insists on his doctrine of the special, sacramental, diffinitive presence in the host by virtue of an act of consecration.

The critique by Vajta showed how definitions, applied improperly, could completely distort Luther's doctrine of the omnipresence of Christ's body and the presence in the Sacrament of the Altar. At the same time, with increasing clarity, Luther's doctrine took shape as a well-thought-through, coherent quantity. The latitude that the investigation by Vajta is allowed to assume is further motivated by a remarkable connection to the history of ideas. Certainly this attempt to interpret Luther is a modern innovation from a definite, modern, systematic position, but in certain essential parts it has a background in the expositions of Luther's doctrine by the Melanchthonian school during the 1500s. As shall be presented here, Melanchthon's doctrine of the Sacrament includes not only an actual departure from Luther but also a not-infrequent claim of being an *interpretation of Luther*. Without questioning the originality of the stream of thought that found its impact in Vajta's contribution to Luther research, one can regard it as reasonable that the ease with which he could make the claim of acknowledgment is offered by the not-insignificant influence of Melanchthonianism or Philippism on the development of Protestantism.

Melanchthon

In the year 1530, Melanchthon stated the Lutheran doctrine of the Supper on one occasion in this way: "II. Although we say that Christ's body is really present, nevertheless Luther does not say that it is present locally, as in some bundle, by being circumscribed, but in that mode by which the person of Christ or the whole Christ is present in all creatures."[69] This statement deserves to be placed as an introduction to this section about Melanchthon. *In this short thesis, Melanchthon identified himself with Luther, as well as confessing the real presence, embracing the doctrine of the omnipresence of Christ's body, and equating the sacramental and repletive presence. According to the opinion that the present volume will maintain, here is the solution of the dogmatical-historical problem that Melanchthon's doctrine of the Supper presents. The crucial point is the very equating of omnipresence and sacramental presence.* This stance has consequences later within the other loci in the doctrine of the Supper, as shall be reviewed in the following chapter and through which the interpretation presented below gains further evidence.

Connected with the thesis now presented, in a certain sense, are the statements of a similar meaning in Albert Herrlinger, who in 1879 presented the only summary monograph up to now on *Die Theologie Melanchthons*. He asserts that, for a time, Melanchthon embraced Luther's doctrine of the omnipresence of

69 CR 2:224.

Christ's body, and that this doctrine in the question of the Sacrament served as safeguard against "materialistic views."[70] This spiritualizing function in the omnipresence, according to Herrlinger, led Melanchthon finally to reject this doctrine in favor of a form of the presence defined by Christ's will, which already earlier, however, stood "immediately alongside."[71] Otto Ritschl puts forth the thesis that Melanchthon, during the latter part of his life, taught the omnipresence of Christ's human soul, that its immaterial substance made up the content of the sacramental presence,[72] since at an early stage he had misgivings about Luther's doctrine of the omnipresence of Christ's body.[73] [Helmut] Gollwitzer disputes the idea that the omnipresence of Christ's body occurs in Melanchthon's theology; after having silently ignored it, Melanchthon finally openly opposed it.[74] [Theodor] Mahlmann allows for a gradual abandonment of the omnipresence of Christ's humanity [in Melanchthon's theology].[75] — Since research waited for a long time for a special work on Melanchthon's doctrine of the Supper, in 1968 Wilhelm Neuser presented *Die Abendmahlslehre Melanchthons in ihrer geschichtlichen Entwicklung (1519–1530)*, which would be followed by a second part, covering the time up to Melanchthon's death in 1560. Neuser agrees with Gollwitzer's idea that Melanchthon never taught the omnipresence of Christ's body, but that the omnipresence of the person made possible a sacramental presence of Christ's body, the same kind [of presence] as the omnipresence.[76]

First, the Christological question ought to be examined more closely in this context. Melanchthon presents his view as coinciding with Luther in connection with the great writings on the Supper published at the end of the 1520s. At this time Melanchthon, in clear dogmatically composed opinions, gives expression to Luther's doctrine of the participation of Christ's human nature in the

70 Herrlinger, *Die Theologie Melanchthons*, p. 131.

71 Id., op. cit., pp. 139f.: "But soon Melanchthon thought that he realized that the idea of omnipresence and Luther's own thought about the presence of the body in the bread do not coincide, that the first leads as much to spiritualism as the latter leads to materialism, and it was this perception that determined for him that he should look for a different dogmatic rationale for the bodily presence, from which indeed a different modality of the same was produced."

72 Ritschl, op. cit., 4:23f.

73 Id., op. cit., p. 19.

74 Gollwitzer, op. cit., pp. 69, 92.

75 Mahlmann, op. cit., p. 184.

76 Neuser, op. cit., p. 357. Maurer (*Der junge Melanchthon zwischen Humanismus und Reformation*, 2:497ff. ["VII. Die Abendmahlsfrage"]), in the absence of precise statements, does not contribute to the actual complications here. Fraenkel ("Ten Questions concerning Melanchthon, the Fathers and the Eucharist") underscores "the 'functional' doctrine of the presence" (op. cit., p. 152) but is not relevant here either. For an overview of the literature, compare Fraenkel, op. cit., p. 146 n. 1; Ahlberg, op. cit., pp. 155ff., 233ff.

attributes of the divinity: "And since certain people argue that Christ's body cannot be in many places, they do not examine it enough. For Christ is exalted above all creatures and is present everywhere."[77] Concerning the argument of the opponents, it says,

> Again: "Christ is seated at the right hand of the Father; it is therefore necessary for Him to be in a certain place, and He cannot be in heaven and on earth at the same time." This argument is born completely from carnal thinking, because they imagine a certain place of divine majesty. Indeed, where was that majesty before the world was founded? It must not be imagined that the divinity of Christ is in a different place, where the humanity is not. What is this other than to divide Christ?[78]

These words from 1529—which furthermore, in fact, bear Luther's attestation "This pleases me"—unambiguously teach that the human and the divine accompany each other in Christ. The opposite would dissolve ("*separare*") the personal union. "Now there was no reason to tear Christ apart, so that according to His divinity He is with us [and] according to His humanity He is not with us."[79] Luther's ridicule of the opponents' idea of the local enthronement at the Father's right hand is repeated in Melanchthon: "They themselves depict Christ thus, sitting in some definite place, just as Homer depicts his Jupiter, dining among the Ethiopians."[80] "It is not at all beneficial to separate the divinity from the humanity. . . . For it is an opinion unworthy of Christians, that Christ occupied a certain part of heaven in such a way that He thus sits in it, as if locked in prison."[81] All these statements are made in connection with the question of the presence of Christ's *body*. There is no possibility that any of the theologians named above deal with a *humanitas* that does not comprehend Christ's body. Not only is it impossible to present even one theologian within the orthodox Christological tradition—where Melanchthon considered himself to have nearly obsessive concern for correctness of expression—who proceeds in this way, but even the context of the texts forbids such a separation [of the humanity and Christ's body].[82]

---

77 CR 1:949.

78 CR 1:1036.

79 CR 1:760, where it is mistakenly dated to 1525; compare Neuser, op. cit., p. 357 n. 262.

80 CR 1:974.

81 CR 1:1049.

82 Neuser, op. cit., pp. 357f.:

> Luther simply puts "body and blood" for "humanity," but Melanchthon distinguishes between the result of the doctrine of the two natures and the assertion of the Words of Institution, between [the] humanity of Christ and the body and blood. The quotation shows that Melanchthon classifies Christ's

It is this very form of the presence, through which Christ's humanity shares the divinity's majesty and closeness to creation, which *is* the sacramental presence for Melanchthon. The introductory programmatic quotation—"in that way . . . He is present in all creatures"—is the watchword for the sacramental problem during Melanchthon's lifetime and not at all, as Herrlinger thinks,[83] the last vestige of a doctrine given up afterward. The same year (1530), [Melanchthon] writes: "Meanwhile, [Bucer] concedes the idea that the body of Christ is in heaven locally, and yet is present—indeed, not locally, but in a hidden way in creatures and sacraments. Just as Luther also says, it is not necessary for Christ to be in the Sacrament locally, but He can be present in the way in which all creatures are present in Christ, in a hidden way."[84] Again Luther is understood as teaching omnipresence as the mode of the real presence, which places him in promising proximity to the mediating theologian Bucer, who takes offense at a traditional, concrete sacramental presence. In 1531, Melanchthon wants to reconcile the two Blaurer brothers with Luther on the basis of the same identification. Melanchthon writes to Thomas Blaurer:

> But I wish that you or your brother would send to our theologian [Luther] about that matter, as to why he would differ with you. He proposes that the body of Christ is somehow with the bread in this way, just as Christ is everywhere. For if He is present thus according to the communication of substances, the body is not present bodily, but Christ is present, not according to the body but according to the divinity, and this agrees with Augustine.[85]

Words of Institution with the doctrine of the personal union of the natures. The exegetical consideration completes the Christological consideration.

Neuser's lack of clarity is thus summarized in a pregnant way. He first maintains that the term "humanity" in Luther's Christology includes also the body, after which he later denied this connection in Melanchthon, since the latter lets the presence of Christ's body in the Sacrament be dependent on the Words of Institution and not on Christology. This reasoning has the unproven premise that the omnipresence of Christ's body would be incompatible with a specific, sacramental presence. The result of this presence is somewhat that Luther, whose Christology, understood correctly, cannot recognize a special sacramental presence, somewhat that Melanchthon, who was alleged to recognize a special real presence, is not regarded as being able to have a Lutheran Christology. Furthermore, Neuser overlooks the fact that Melanchthon in the same work, *for the very reason* that he shared Neuser's unproven premise, does not recognize a separate form of presence, but by virtue of the supremacy of Christology lets the Words of Institution have merely revelatory power; more about this above.

83 Herrlinger, op. cit., p. 131.

84 CR 2:316.

85 Bindseil, *Philippi Melanchthonis epistolae*, p. 85. Melanchthon's words are *quoted* here in a letter from Thomas Blaurer to his brother Ambrose. The genuineness has not been questioned the way it deserves; the words are introduced with "The words of the letter are," upon which follows the section that is mainly composed in Greek. The language guarantees that we are working with an approximate and perhaps partisan reproduction of Melanchthon's words; Melanchthon's typical choice of language could

Melanchthon found an inconsistency in Luther: talk about a special *bodily* presence does not fit well with omnipresence, which alone must prevail.[86] The Blaurer brothers now get Melanchthon's mandate—though without permission to disclose his role, "without mentioning my name"—to purge Luther's doctrine of irrelevant, localizing thoughts and unequivocally to connect the sacramental presence with the omnipresence. That is also the way the presentation was understood by Ambrose Blaurer, who kept his brother Thomas's letter, which includes Melanchthon's words cited above. Melanchthon, who was "very discreet," realized "that with the word 'bodily' Luther may have gone somewhat farther than his argument and its foundation."[87] The insight about Luther's actual meaning now justifies correcting and completing his doctrine.

How far Melanchthon informed others of his view identifying the real presence with the repletive presence emerges from Caspar Cruciger's letter to Veit Dietrich in April 1538. Cruciger, in Melanchthon's absence, opened a letter directed to him by Dietrich and, in his mentor's stead, answers his questions about the theology of the Sacrament. Cruciger puts himself under Melanchthon's authority for his expressions: "And I often talk about these things with our

---

not really have been fabricated for the Blaurer brothers' private Latin correspondence, where Luther's theology was not a topic that was embarrassing to the parties.

86 This letter has attracted various interpretations. Jacoby (*Die Liturgik der Reformatoren*, 2:104f.) finds it to be an attempt at reconciliation, presented by Melanchthon to create unity between Luther and the Blaurer brothers. Its contents would be to let the Sacrament come about through a merely potential, latent omnipresence of Christ's body, which, however, could not have been accepted by Luther. Jacoby is right in that it was a matter of a serious attempt at reconciliation, which also comes out in Thomas Blaurer's words: "[Melanchthon] thinks that we can accomplish something with Luther." On the other hand, he misunderstands the actual content in the attempt at reconciliation, which would not at all make the omnipresence merely potential, but rather, by virtue of its reality, disputes what is seen to be a false localizing of the Sacrament. Herrlinger (op. cit., pp. 140f.) disputes the reconciliatory character of the letter and thinks that Melanchthon here wants to show that it is unreasonable to let the sacramental presence be based on the omnipresence, which must nullify the special character of the Sacrament. Herrlinger puts the absurdity in the wrong place: it is not the form of the divine presence that agreed with Augustine that is unreasonable, but it is always the bodily presence [*sōmatikōs*] that Melanchthon disputes. It would be strange also to let the Reformed Blaurer brothers, as Melanchthon's anonymous envoys, put forth a critique that would *dispute* "a presence in the form being of pure Spirit" (Herrlinger, ibid.)! Mahlmann (op. cit., p. 73 n. 48) understands the lines as merely a reference to Augustine's distinctions. Here as elsewhere, Mahlmann reckons with Melanchthon being in conscious opposition to Augustine.

87 Ambrose Blaurer, April 24, 1532, in a letter to Bucer, here cited according to Köhler (op. cit., 2:294), who however does not refer to the background for Blaurer's praise of Melanchthon. Melanchthon's letter also explains the frankness with which Ambrose Blaurer in the summer of 1534 could assert against the orthodox Lutheran Schnepf (Köhler, op. cit., 2:335f.) that "'more sound Lutherans' had spoken and written very decisively"; "Just don't bother me, as recently, with the adverbs 'fleshly, bodily.'"

[Teacher]." With great insight, Cruciger defines what in time would give rise to the battle over the Sacrament in the Lutheran camp: "Good God, how much these questions of tragedies will stir us up. It is not permitted to touch on them now, nor are they set free yet from those things where they should be."[88] These dangerous points are somewhat the adoration of the Sacrament,[89] somewhat the questions about whether the presence is "local or enclosed in a place, then whether it must be claimed that the division or separation of the body and the blood must be made, or whether it is believed only in the way that Christ is truly omnipresent otherwise, present not only in *energeía* [but also] present in all things."[90] With these words, Cruciger places the diffinitive alternative whose consequence is a *mere* presence of Christ's body and blood *without* the repletive presence of the divinity (which relationship is investigated in the chapter on concomitance, below) against the Melanchthonian repletive alternative in which Christ is present in His omnipresence, which embraces *both* the divinity and humanity. It was obvious even to Melanchthon's disciples that these alternatives could not be reconciled with each other.[91]

---

88 CR 3:510.

89 The letter is referred to by Frank (op. cit., 3:25f.), who misunderstands it: "The difficulty still remaining faces on the one hand the adoration of the Sacrament, concerning which he did not believe anything, so that one has only to apply it to the divinity or to the person of Christ." Frank overlooks the fact that Cruciger disputes that "signs of reverence, when they are shown in the Eucharist," must be understood as actual *latreía*, that is, divine adoration; they are only signs of *reverence*. No discussion about which nature receives the adoration is taken up. In the same way, Melanchthon, in his answer to Dietrich five days later, discusses only the act of adoration (CR 3:514): "Since this is so, it is not necessary for the bowing to be added; or if it is added, it must not be directed toward the bread." Theologically there is no difference here, though Melanchthon refuses to distinguish between the signs of reverence and the adoration; he puts them together and therefore advises the discontinuation of the bowing [*proskynesis*], or explaining that it is not being directed toward the host (as the location of Christ's body).

90 CR 3:510.

91 Even to others a tension was noticeable. A month earlier, Melanchthon had been able to write to Dietrich (CR 3:503): "Amsdorf wrote to Luther that he was nurturing a snake in his bosom, meaning me." Four years earlier, 1534, the Saxon Chancellor Brück, in a letter to the elector, had already expressed his suspicions about Melanchthon's doctrine of the Sacrament (*ZKG* 34:98f.; compare WA Br 7[:412–13], no. 3022, Supplement). Brück cites Luther as the source. But no clearly formulated accusations are raised; Brück moderates himself this far: "[I] do not think that it would be his [Melanchthon's] intention to give the Zwinglians an opportunity in regard to the Sacrament." In 1537, Brück again cites Luther as the source in a letter to the elector. After the meeting in Kassel in 1534, the time of the first letter, Luther observed an argument with Melanchthon, "from which he asked how he was of an almost Zwinglian opinion" (Enders 11:271; compare Köhler, op. cit., 2:442f.). Melanchthon refrains from communing and refuses to connect himself with Wittenberg by not accepting an offered pay raise. Luther considers the possibility of Melanchthon's withdrawal:

The constant appeal by Melanchthon and his school to the heavenly majesty of Christ's body is built on the thesis that Christ's body has a real participation in the attributes of the divinity, formulated already in Melanchthon's Colossians commentary from 1527 in this way: "There are not certain designated gifts in Christ as in other saints, for there are distributions of graces, but the actual divine nature poured itself into the flesh with all its power and did so in order that it might dwell there bodily."[92] Just as in Luther, this in no way nullifies the particular attributes of the human nature. Divine omnipresence does not nullify any assertion of a particular form of presence in heaven. The difficulty of effecting these distinctions has, within the research, generated the proposition that Melanchthon gave up his earlier position or never embraced it. Clearly Melanchthon fosters the possibility of both by asserting in 1551:

> Nor do this and similar statements of Augustine: "Christ's body is in a definite place," conflict with these statements: "Christ is at the right hand of the Father; Christ is everywhere," because that hidden exaltation in the kingdom and priesthood is not a physical locality, and Augustine is speaking about the physical locality. Christ is one person, and indeed the ancients [say]: Christ is everywhere personally. But the declarations of the *Sententiarists* are rather cold. Since there is one person, Christ very freely, with both divine essence and human nature, lives beyond [*iuxta*] that hidden exaltation by which He is at the right hand of the Father.[93]

"So Philip would depart" (*ZKG* 34:99). Later testimony by Melanchthon (CR 9:1029f.) shows that around 1540 he feared exile regarding the adoration of the Sacrament. Nevertheless, when the break did not come about during Luther's lifetime, this is not to be attributed to a conscious compromise for both sides. No one seems to be able to determine the actual *status controversiae*. When Melanchthon is convinced that a unity exists, it is by asserting that Luther's doctrine of a special sacramental presence only constitutes a way of speaking that is less thought through: "even if people actually understand this in an unfortunate way" (CR 3:504); "I knew that Luther would write more wildly than he means" (CR 5:208). The presumed Evangelical unity is built in no small measure on the thesis about the impetuous, untheological Luther who for the sake of good intent can be excused for his exaggerations. The mistake by the Gnesio-Lutheran party after Luther's death will be to make theology from words that Luther occasionally uttered. Compare Tappert, "Christology and Lord's Supper in the Perspective of History," p. 62: "When, after Luther's death, some of his followers, like Nicholas Amsdorf and Joachim Westphal, advocated positions which were extreme extensions of Luther's most extravagant anti-Zwinglian statements, Melanchthon was charged with a betrayal of Lutheranism." Page 58: "Luther sometimes made extreme statements."

92 Stupperich, *Melanchthons Werke*, 4:246.

93 CR 7:780; compare CR 2:223 (year 1530): "With Augustine we also say that Christ, on account of the mode of His true body, is in one certain place of heaven, not indeed locally, but by the mode that properly fits with this Sacrament." ("Not locally" here seems to indicate a mode of presence that makes a sacramental presence impossible.) Melanchthon's words "they do not conflict" can go back to *Luther's* interpretation of Augustine, which Melanchthon retained in the instructions for the Colloquy at Kassel

Here Augustine's thesis *supports* the idea that Christ is in a certain place in heaven, for it does not conflict with ("*nec pugnant*") the particular character of the omnipresence ("*arcana exaltatio*") that is completely illocal ("*non est physica localitas*"). Augustine's assertion has in view only the circumscriptive form of the presence ("*de qua physica localitate Augustinus loquitur*") and was not intended to conflict with the repletive form.[94] Melanchthon reckons with the idea that the fathers meant this form of the presence when they said that Christ is omnipresent personally ("*personaliter*"), thus in the repletive mode, which applies to the divine person. On the other hand, the *Sentences* commentators do not teach this.[95] In the newly published Colossians commentary in 1559, when it says that the ascension occurred toward "a celestial place,"[96] it is not a retraction of an earlier view.[97] On the contrary, it is the result of the earlier insight. Already in connection with the words about Augustine in 1551, the statement "Christ is everywhere bodily" had been rejected: "The fathers say, however, that the nature retains its *idiomata*. Both Augustine and others say that the body of

1534 (WA 38:298 [cf. AE 61:255]: "This statement of St. Augustine will easily thus explain what Augustine [says] about the visible body, just as the words 'which you see' read; thus Augustine does not at all conflict with the clear words of Christ"; compare WA 38:303.17f. [cf. AE 61:259]).

94 Thus it has nothing to do with an "exception to the authority of Augustine" (Mahlmann, op. cit., p. 184), about "the argument in regard to Augustine (and the Swiss) that rejects the idea that special extent has to do with the body as an object of physics according to its quantity" (id., p. 73). The mistake in Mahlmann's reading comes from his way of writing (id., p. 184): "The clear statement that Jesus' existence in heaven 'is not a physical location, concerning which location Augustine is speaking,'" whereby Mahlmann lets contrasts arise where Melanchthon reports dissimilar and *therefore* not conflicting statements. Obviously Mahlmann interprets Melanchthon's words "do not conflict" as "do not refute": "Augustine's words and similar expressions: 'Christ's body is in a definite place,' do not refute these words: 'Christ is at the Father's right hand . . . .'" The correct translation is [this]: ". . . do not conflict with these words: 'Christ is at the Father's right hand.'"

95 Melanchthon is thus negatively positioned toward Lombard and the tradition going back to him, which shows his Lutheran theology. Herrlinger (op. cit., p. 184) believes that Melanchthon was referring to John of Damascus as the originator of scholastic Christology (CR 2:660). But the polemic is obviously directed toward Peter Lombard. In this context, Herrlinger presents a later retreat to the positions of Scholasticism, when here (1533) and CR 21:255 (1532) a merely verbal *communicatio idiomatum* is rejected, while this doctrine is accepted in CR 21:363 (1535). The opposite is fictitious, since Melanchthon in the earlier words rejects that the emptying should be in the actual communication of attributes (incarnation = emptying), while in the later he uses the communication of attributes for the emptying of the human nature so that the divine person becomes its subject.

96 CR 15:1271.

97 Thus in Mahlmann, op. cit., pp. 181ff., especially p. 184.

Christ is in a certain place."[98] The problem of the irrevocably enduring problem of Christ's body existing somewhere locally has been adequately formulated by an unknown hand, which added the correct explanation:

> For thus says Augustine: Christ will come again in this way, as the angelic voice testifies, just as He was seen going into heaven, that is, in the same form and substance of the flesh, to which He immediately gave immortality. One must not think that He is spread out everywhere according to this form. For we must take care not to think of the divinity of the man Christ in such a way that we take away the reality of His body.[99] [100]

Melanchthon wants to protect himself from thoughts of a locally understood omnipresence of Christ's body, just as earlier Luther also polemicized against this.[101] Just as in the earlier writing Christ's local presence in heaven is formulated in this way, and the omnipresence is demarcated from materialistic interpretations, a confession of the participation of Christ's humanity in the divinity's mode of presence through the exaltation is included in the later writing: "He says that Christ is raised, and indeed [is] at the hand of God, that is, not the way the blessed angels and men are raised, but exalted above the angels in that hidden light of God, reigning with the Father. . . ."[102] Regardless of the human nature's retention of its characteristics, the "right hand of God" means the divine presence far beyond the mode of presence of angels and resurrected bodies. So both writings are shown to have one and the same content and cannot be used as support for Melanchthon's gradual, alleged abandonment of Luther's Christology.

When Melanchthon takes up the Augustinian formulation "He is whole everywhere, but not a whole thing" [*ubique totus est, sed non totum*], this has been understood as conceding a nominal attribution of omnipresence to Christ "as man" [*qua homo*] according to the *communicatio idiomatum*, but as a denial of a real omnipresence.[103] But Melanchthon interprets this statement of Augustine in accordance with his interpretation of the aforementioned expression from Augustine. With "whole thing" [*totum*] he does not at all mean to dispute the real omnipresence of Christ's body, but the kind of "whole thing" that would include a physical, circumscribed omnipresence. He thus disputes an omnipresence *according to the mode* that applies to Christ's body as such ("*totum*")

98 CR 7:780.

99 Id.

100 [The Swedish edition numbers footnotes up to 99, then restarts at 1, which this translation lists as 101, etc.]

101 Compare above, pp. 57–58, text around nn. 108–10 [Swedish edition, p. 59].

102 CR 15:1271.

103 Ritschl, op. cit., 4:23f.: "Of decisive importance in answering this question is an expression of Augustine quoted approvingly by Melanchthon: The whole [Christ] is everywhere, but not as a whole thing [*Ubique totus est, sed non totum*]."

with disregard for the personal union ("*totus*"). Already earlier, the term "whole Christ" [*totus Christus*] had come to designate for Melanchthon the repletive presence of both natures, when he used it to describe the sacramental presence as identical with the omnipresence: "in that mode in which Christ's person or the whole Christ is present in all creatures."[104] It may seem as if an unreasonable change of an accepted expression has occurred there, which Melanchthon expressly receives through the intermediary of Scholasticism: "Thus Augustine says, and the words are cited in Lombard, book 3, distinction 22: Christ did not abandon the Father when He came so humbly, whole everywhere, complete everywhere."[105] But the expression was not perceived as unequivocally by Melanchthon's contemporaries as modern researchers want to assume from their knowledge and presuppositions. Two years after this, Melanchthon's use of "*totus—non totum*" is invoked *in favor of* the omnipresence of Christ's body by the most famous representative of this doctrine within Lutheranism, Johann Brenz. In his *De personali unione duarum naturarum [in Christo]*, he insists that Lombard's words certainly could be understood as the opponents understand them, but that they were correctly interpreted in the way that appears in Thomas and Bonaventure, among others.[106] Brenz, who in the following will be shown to be Melanchthon's most consistent follower in Christology and the doctrine of the Supper, points to what was understood within the Lutheran camp around the year 1560 as a reasonable explanation of the concept "*totus—non totum*." Modern researchers up to now have not paid attention to this alternative and thus have bound themselves to a scholastic understanding of the term and Melanchthon's use of it.

It is a fact of dogmatic history that Melanchthon turned very sharply against the Gnesio-Lutheran school's position on the statement that "Christ's body is omnipresent."[107] This situation naturally strengthened the thesis that Melanchthon and his school had a particular Christology that deviated from the rest of Lutheranism. Melanchthon's actions meanwhile must be seen here against their historical background. Christian theology up to that time had not *made use of* such a statement. It had even *rejected* a similar statement: "Antiquity rejected this proposition: Christ is everywhere bodily [*corporaliter*]." The position of the new statement thus lacked the support of tradition[108] and comes close to a purely heretical statement, the teaching of the *bodily* omnipresence. The

104 CR 2:224.

105 CR 15:1271.

106 Brenz, op. cit., pp. 12Bf. Brenz's understanding of the Scholastics is, of course, mistaken.

107 Frank, op. cit., 3:168: "declared himself most strongly against the omnipresence of the body."

108 On Melanchthon's traditionalism, compare Fraenkel, op. cit., p. 152.

[battle]front against Rome did not allow new dogmatic formulations that might be returned as accusations of heresy: "Not even the Papists ever said this, that 'the body is everywhere.'"[109] "These statements are new in Christianity from the beginning up to this time, and would be rejected among the Papists, so that they would talk about it in Paris."[110] Even when he expressly turns against the Gnesio-Lutheran zeal that produced splintering and bitterness within the Church, he still makes the following confession:

> Now among young and uneducated people I do not talk about this matter: whether the body [of Christ] is in all places; for it is scandalous thinking and speaking. Therefore, I myself keep quiet and advise many people also to keep quiet about it. But how the ancients spoke—namely, Dionysius, the Greek Canon, Nazianzen, Ambrose, Augustine, Prosper—is quite obvious in their writings. The Weimar writers [*Dichter*] even make a separation of body and blood, which no Papist, nor even Luther, did, and undoubtedly many learned men in other lands will write against it. I stay with this form, which was presented to the electors and is certainly true: that the Lord Christ is in His office [*ministerium*] substantially, in a different way than one says of wood and stone. In this office [*ministerium*] He works comfort and gives us His body and blood, makes us His members as Paul actually says: the bread is the communion of the body of Christ.[111]

These words from Melanchthon's hand from 1559, directed against the so-called Weimar Confutation, a Gnesio-Lutheran confession and polemical writing, give an excellent summary of Melanchthon's stance on the problem. Melanchthon does not *want* to speak, since this can give occasion to unspiritual ideas in the young and uneducated. But herein lies Melanchthon's adherence to the doctrine of the omnipresence of Christ's body. If what he thinks but does not say were a denial of the teaching, no improper thoughts could arise if he made a statement. The restraint touches on expressions, considered blasphemous, that the Reformed opponents would propose as [logical] consequences of the omnipresence of Christ's body: "whether He was in the sewers too."[112] Melanchthon does not want to conjure up such filthy talk, and therefore he avoids formulating in a pregnant dogmatic form a statement that, in the hands of foolish people, could do more harm than good. The content of the statement again is correct, as such. It also proceeds from the positive formulation of Christ's presence in the means of grace: "in a different way than one speaks of wood and stone." This special kind of presence is built on its effect: comfort. On the other hand, it is not distinguished the way the diffinitive presence is [distinguished] from the repletive.

109 CR 8:835.

110 CR 9:470.

111 CR 9:766.

112 Chemnitz, *De duabus naturis in Christo*, fol. 193A [cf. *Two Natures in Christ*, p. 463].

Ontologically, the same presence exists in creation and in the office [of the ministry]. This purely subjective distinction between real and operative presence Melanchthon had also worked out elsewhere: "And it is one thing that God is everywhere, and another that He dwells in the saints. The indwelling means not only that the universal presence is there, but that it is there in sanctification."[113] Significant also is the attack on the [Weimar] Confutation's denial of concomitance. Since the sacramental presence is repletive, with spiritual consolation as one special attribute, the presence must deliver the whole Christ. The assertion of the special existence of Christ's body and blood in the Sacrament must be denied as being built on the diffinitive and not on the repletive mode of the presence. So Melanchthon's position on the controversy over the verbal expression of the omnipresence of Christ's body is not a denial of the idea itself. [His position] remains constant and has the important, regulative function of freeing the Lutheran view of the sacramental presence from its inclinations that, in Melanchthon's opinion, are materialistic.

Brenz

As with Melanchthon, the doctrine of the Supper put forward by Brenz is judged very differently among researchers. The lack of clarity that is prevalent in this regard can be traced back to an inability to discern *the leading thought in the sacramental theology of Brenz: the complete identification of the sacramental presence with the repletive presence* and the disclaimer following from it against any sacramental-theological corollary that counts on an ontologically distinct special presence. *This stance is thus in agreement with Melanchthon's*, whose battle Brenz pursues, even when church politics separated them again.

The doctrinal statements of Brenz on the Supper belong to two periods of his life: before 1530 and after 1556, separated by decades of silence. The most familiar work of the first period is *Syngramma suevicum*. It has been understood in various ways by researchers. It has been interpreted [not only] as almost Reformed but also as Lutheran. Most of all, it has been understood as a logically unsuccessful attempt to prove the real presence, wanting to but not being able to do it, where a fundamental Lutheranism became, in fact, Reformed.[114]

113 CR 8:639; compare CR 7:779: "Also Augustine wrote: It must be said that God is everywhere through the presence of the divinity, but not everywhere through the grace of indwelling." CR 15:1253: "by which presence not only does God preserve their substances but also effects in them new light and motions [*motus*] that are pleasing to Him." [Compare] also CR 23:368f.; 10:825.

114 The older research mode is depicted by Dieckhoff, op. cit., p. 569; the more modern by Brecht, *Die frühe Theologie des Johannes Brenz*, p. 83 n. 5, p. 86 n. 2. Köhler (op. cit., 1:128ff.) perceives *Syngramma* as essentially Lutheran. WA 19:452ff. (1897 edition), in polemics against Köstlin through the volume's editor, the conservative researcher Wilhelm Walther (not "v. Walther," as Brecht, op. cit., p. 83 n. 5, writes, which would

Syngramma suevicum certainly does not contain the doctrine of the omnipresence of Christ's body. The document appeals to Luther's *Against the Heavenly Prophets* in the question of Christology, and in it, as presented above, Luther had not conclusively shaped his doctrine on this point.[115] *Syngramma* comes much closer, nevertheless, to a repletive presence of Christ's body, since the presence of God (the Spirit) and Christ's body are made parallel through faith, so that from the side of the subject, Christ's body is actually divinized: "Again, when the Word offers God as being present to faith, along with all His gifts, why would the Word not do the same in the body and blood of Christ, when these gifts are ours, and we are delivered by these from the jaws of death, sin, hell, and even Satan?"[116] It emphatically brings out the thought that Christ's body and blood are divine gifts and therefore could be given just as easily as God gives Himself to His believers according to His divinity; this leads consequently to statements about the majesty of the objective character of Christ's humanity.[117] Along with

refer to Johannes von Walter, author of *Luthers Theologie*) had earlier defended the existence of the Lutheran criteria of *manducatio oralis* and *manducatio indignorum* ("oral eating" and the "eating by the unworthy") in *Syngramma*, which Gollwitzer (op. cit., p. 62 n. 2) again disputes. The researchers who assert the Lutheran character of the *Syngramma* are always forced to note the proviso that Brecht formulated this way (op. cit., p. 81): "But if a man can communicate his view and his opinion through the word, 'why is it not also permitted to Christ who is God to distribute and communicate His body and blood in the Word with the included bread and wine'? One will not be able to say that the example is a happy choice." Compare Dieckhoff, op. cit., p. 615: "It is a false conclusion." Page 614f.: "Only an *ideal presence* of what is said for our *consciousness* is based on the Word as such." Meanwhile, this implies an unfair criticism of *Syngramma*. The point of comparison in the parallel between the gifts of the Sacrament and intellectual communications through sound is *the miraculous occurrence*. For a modern secular view, the latter occurrence is "natural," but *Syngramma* would assert that it is a *miracle* for two intellects to be able to communicate their thoughts in this way. In the case of the objections, therefore, *Syngramma* feels that an *intellectual* long-distance transmission is not "natural," and therefore it would not offer a similarity with a "supernatural" supplying by a body. The former is, for *Syngramma*, no less a miracle than the latter.

115 Compare Brecht, op. cit., p. 84: "In 1525, Brenz shared with Oecolampadius the opinion that Christ sits locally at the right hand of God." But Brecht does not work with an early dating of [the teaching of] the omnipresence of Christ's body in Luther and writes (p. 85): "Still he [Brenz] knew nothing about beginning with the later solution of the Christological question through the doctrine of the omnipresence, although he had already read Luther's writing *Against the Heavenly Prophets*, which contains the solution." Brecht's "although" is thus incorrect. Dieckhoff (op. cit., p. 620) underscores that an articulated doctrine of the omnipresence of the flesh is not found in *Syngramma*, "but even more clearly and obviously, the thought of the omnipresence of God's spiritual world is expressed anyway."

116 Quoted according to *Acta et scripta publica ecclesiae Wirtembergicae*, pp. 193f.

117 Luther wrote a preface for *Syngramma*, probably in the same Holy Week during which the *Sermon on the Sacrament* was given with its new doctrine of the omnipresence;

the fact that the sacramental presence is thus equated with God's gracious presence, there is no difference between what Luther calls the second and third mode. Even Luther had been able to refer to Christ's coming through the Word, but then as *parallel* to the sacramental event, and by doing so he had only shown how Christ in no way is bound to His heavenly place.[118] Brenz thereby describes *one and the same* event: "When the Word bestows God, why would the Word not do the same in the body and blood of Christ?" This statement means that the Word has the ability in the very same way to reveal and bestow Christ's human [nature] and His divine nature as well. In a letter from that same time, Brenz underscores the identity between the modes of presence: "Nor is the bread the body other than in the way the Word brings the body to us."[119] Above all, we encounter something completely unknown to Luther: attacks against the doctrine of the Roman Church on the real presence as being solid and fleshly: "I am unaware of whatever carnal imaginings the Papists imagine, about a little body being hidden under the bread or in the bread."[120] So it is possible to give a more precise context to Martin Brecht's more general judgment: "Still one must regard Brenz's solution as independent and in a certain regard distinct from Luther."[121] The distinction between the modes of presence has been nullified. The relative lack of clarity in Brenz's discussions has a meaning that was hidden to Luther.[122] It is not at all warranted to think that the difference must have been noted and

---

compare WA 19:451 [cf. AE 59:150–62]. It cannot be ruled out that *Syngramma* may have been a trigger for Luther's position; since previously Luther's own Christology already required the omnipresence of Christ's body, Brenz's way of thinking could easily have been taken up, reworked, and brought to completion. Compare here Dieckhoff, op. cit., p. 568, on *Syngramma suevicum*: "did not remain without influence on Luther's presentation of doctrine."

118 For example, WA 19:490.10 [cf. AE 36:342].

119 Brenz to Bucer, October 3, 1525, *Acta [et scripta publica ecclesiae Wirtembergicae]* 55, p. 202.

120 Brenz to the city of Reutlingen, April 13, 1527, *Acta [et scripta publica ecclesiae Wirtembergicae]*, p. 37. Compare here Dieckhoff, op. cit., p. 572, which underscores that Brenz in *Syngramma* wants to define the Lutheran doctrine against Rome as a part of the defense against the accusations of Oecolampadius.

121 [There is a marker for this footnote in the Swedish edition, but no text. The German edition has: "Brecht, op. cit."]

122 Dieckhoff (op. cit., p. 636) views *Syngramma* as too unequivocal, since he writes:

> But if one considers how precisely certain statements of the *Syngramma* are advanced—for example, the denial of an existence of Christ's body or His substance in the Sacrament separate from Christ's body in heaven, and the statement about offering the body and blood in the Supper first of all to faith—then one cannot possibly give in to the opinion [that] Luther could have overlooked or misunderstood these statements.

Where Brenz noted a real agreement with the scholastic doctrine of the diffinitive presence and thus struck even Luther, Luther heard an immediate theoretical rejection

approved by Luther, for even on the opposite side, people in good faith are led astray to incorrect conclusions about Brenz's position. Oecolampadius found that if the presence in the bread is the same kind as in the Word, there must be unity between Lutherans and the Reformed.[123]

For Brenz, God's presence is naturally powerful in the same way for both body and soul. The presence of Christ's body [*lekamen*] is logically also a presence for the body [*kroppen*]. On the other hand, within this system there is no room for a presence the distinctiveness of which would actually be its corporeality in *contrast* to an omnipresence that comprehends everything, spiritually and bodily.[124] When *Syngramma* appropriates the statement "What we eat enters the stomach, what we believe enters the mind,*"[125] this does not necessarily mean more than the traditional explanation that the visible part of the Sacrament belongs to the perishable [world], and its invisible part again is retained in and through the faith of the recipient. Brenz gives the words a different meaning. For him, the body [*kroppen*] does not encounter Christ's body [*lekamen*] in a physical sense any more than it encounters in a physical sense the Spirit, which is given in the Word in its repletive existence. The mouth does not encounter Christ's body in a diffinitive form of presence that is limited to the locality of the host, and in that way, in a technical sense, [it] would be received like other food, though without being consumed and crushed. The presence that is offered is like the divine presence participating in God's incomprehensibility, omnipresence, and perspective. Through the Word, it becomes a presence for faith, and faith becomes the means of grasping the presence. In facing Berengar's confession, which immediately elicited Luther's full support and his rejection of his scholastic critics,[126] Brenz does not know any positive ways of interpreting it. In his disapproval of Berengar's retraction, Brenz uses the contrast "stomach—mind" cited above to clarify: "For we eat the body and we drink the blood in the flesh, not as though we crush and break the body of Christ, as is in Berengar's retraction, but we handle the very bread in that it is bread—we break it, eat it,

of a crass, Capernaitic doctrine of the presence, understood in absurd, circumscribed categories. In the following text, the ambiguity will be explained in more detail.

123 Compare here Dieckhoff, op. cit., p. 645; Köhler, op. cit., 1:135f.

124 Compare Dieckhoff, op. cit., p. 633: "that from *Syngramma* what is significant and most intentional for the manner of distribution arranged by the Lord in the Supper is never grasped in the eye; nevertheless, there is no dispute about what is in it, that what is offered, the body and blood of Christ, is even established precisely in its *distinction* from the Word that makes it present for our faith, since through the Word '*This* is My body; *this* is My blood' He is placed in the signs of the bread and wine *outside of [ausserhalb] the Word*."

125 *Acta [et scripta publica ecclesiae Wirtembergicae]*, p. 188.

* [Correcting the misprint *ventrem* to *mentem*.]

126 WA 26:442.35ff. [cf. AE 37:301].

and crush it with our teeth. But we receive the body, just as we receive the Word, 'This is My body,' as someone very beautifully said that what we eat enters the stomach, what we believe enters the mind."[127] The essential thing in this text is the words "just as we receive the Word." The presence is concretized in the visible words of the Sacrament; what receives them must be the "mind" [*mens*]. Brenz expresses the unity between Christ's heavenly body and His eucharistic body as parallel with this: "The word heard from a person's mouth is one thing, while it still remains with the speaker,"[128] a comparison which in itself does not deviate from Scholasticism and Luther.[129] The difference emerges in that Brenz not only sees the point of comparison in "its unity also remaining" but also in the very term "word." "*Thus* also the one body of Christ, *through the Word* is distributed in the bread to the many who eat it."[130]

In the John commentary of 1527, with reference to Luther's *Sermon on the Sacrament* from 1526, Brenz incorporated the applied doctrine of the omnipresence, through which Christ's body by virtue of Christology always has repletive existence.[131] But again, the Roman doctrine of the Sacrament is rejected as materialistic: "For the bread is the body not because it is changed into the body, as the Papists dream, or because, by carnal imagination, some little body exists in the bread, so that human reason marvels; this was stated above. Therefore, it stands firm that it is called the body of Christ because through the bread the body is distributed to our faith."[132] The "little body" [*corpusculum*]

127 *Acta [et scripta publica ecclesiae Wirtembergicae]*, p. 188.

128 *Acta [et scripta publica ecclesiae Wirtembergicae]*, p. 195.

129 Compare WA 26:337.33ff. [cf. AE 37:225]: "I take for myself the comparison of Lorenzo Valla [Laurentius Vallensis]. A preacher is standing there and preaching; his voice is a single voice that goes out of his mouth and is made and is [present] in his mouth. Yet that same single voice that is in one place, that is, in his mouth, comes into four or five thousand or ten thousand ears in one moment"; [see] also WA 19:488.17ff. [cf. AE 36:340].

130 *Acta [et scripta publica ecclesiae Wirtembergicae]*, p. 195.

131 Brenz, *Opera* 6:860. Brecht, op. cit., p. 98: "The doctrine of the omnipresence, which one comes across here for the first time."

132 Brenz, op. cit., p. 858; compare id., p. 856: "Nor do we ask whether one usually imagines some little body in the bread. Let the wisdom of the flesh busy itself in this foolish imagining; let some Aristotle marvel at the upside-down nature of things. We consider the cause [to be] of faith, not of human reason." The polemic against Aristotle does not reject the fine points of the idea of substance, but mainly a presence not defined by faith; compare id., p. 860: "For the body is not in the bread, nor the blood in the wine so that they subsist there carnally and in an Aristotelian way, but so that they are of benefit to our faith and they themselves are dispensed." Brenz can thus invoke, for example, what is miraculous in an intellectual connection and apply this to the sacramental presence, but in this respect he builds only on the superiority of the spiritual in comparison to the material, not on the general miraculous character of creation that Luther asserts. The physical miracle is for Luther a part of the sacramental

that is miraculously made present within the concrete dimensions of the host is contrasted with the presence that is enjoyed by faith. All this does not mean in any way that Brenz doubts the literal explanation of the Words of Institution. Just as earlier in *Syngramma*,[133] Brenz refutes symbolic interpretations and strictly maintains the Lutheran "is" [*est*]. Faith is the recipient; that only means that the objective omnipresence is offered to the subjective recipient through the Word about the sacramental significance of the bread, which requires faith's listening in and receiving. The Word and the Sacrament here are completely identical not only in relation to the effect (forgiveness of sin) but also in relation to their own framework: "In this way, through the Word of Christ, which is the Gospel, they dispense remission of sins to the hearers, and through the Word of Christ in the Supper, in the spiritual banquet, they dispense the spiritual foods, which are the body and blood of Christ."[134]

---

apologetic: WA 19:487.3f. (Rörer) [cf. AE 36:338]: "If I would preach about creatures, you would see miracles in them just as in this Sacrament." WA 19:489.6ff. (printed) [cf. AE 36:340]: "Rather, you likewise find miracles in creatures, so that whoever takes a good look at a creature will not go wrong in this article." For Brenz, a different designation for this kind of miracle is available: "Sorcery" [*magia*]; compare below, chapter 5 on the consecration.

133 When Brecht (op. cit., p. 93) views Brenz's formula in the John commentary, "the Supper [is] in the bread through the Word" [*pane coena per verbum*], as a further development and accommodation to Bucer and Oecolampadius, he ignores the theoretical structure of the *Syngramma*, where this formula is the foundation stone, and this document's use of "through the Word." Likewise, Brecht erroneously writes (id., p. 94): "Similarly, there are two recipients: 'The mouth of the body receives the bread and wine; the mouth of faith receives the body and blood.' . . . It is quite unmistakable that this way of thinking is a rapprochement to the position of the Swiss. The statement of the *Syngramma*, that the body to be eaten spiritually is received physically, is not repeated." But Brenz says the very same thing in both writings. The contrast of the "mouth of the body—mouth of faith" corresponds completely with the *Syngramma*'s "stomach—mind." Brenz has not approached the Swiss; he continues to speak about a *real, repletive* presence in the *physical* bread but grasped in *the Word*, the medium, through which man's *faith* can experience the presence.

134 Brenz, op. cit., 6:860. The "Word-theology" that Brenz develops here should not immediately be equated with Luther's, as Brecht, for example, thinks (op. cit., p. 92): "Brenz now conceives of the Sacrament, just the way Luther does in the Lord's Supper writings from 1520, as an appendix [*Anhang*] to the Word." Luther is speaking of the Sacrament as the sign and seal of the Word for the forgiveness of sins; Brenz is defining the real presence. This distinction in a certain way changes *also* the effect. For both, it is the forgiveness of sins, but in different ways. For Luther, the Sacrament in its external function as sign is the invitation to receive the Gospel; for Brenz, this externality is lacking and is replaced by the very act of faith. Therefore, in Brenz one constantly encounters the expression that the soul eats and drinks the divine gifts, "*manducatio spiritualis*," in connection with the description of the Sacrament. Viewed most deeply, the difference in the doctrine of justification comes to light here, which in 1531 prompted Melanchthon and Luther to point out how Brenz embraces "Augustine's imagination" (Melanchthon); "Thus He says, 'I am the way, the truth, and the life'; He

The same distinction between the bread and Christ's body is repeated in the letter by Brenz, which otherwise is interpreted as a unique example of sacramental realism of an almost crass type. In 1529, Brenz defends the statement that even an unreasoning animal can consume the consecrated leftover host, which really is Christ's body.[135] The ease with which Brenz goes through the thoughts refers to the exceptions that essentially remove the support:

> Since a mouse has no understanding nor an immortal soul, it can neither sin nor be blessed in the bread of Jesus Christ's body; and therefore one may indeed say the mouse does not eat the body of Christ, for the believer is blessed, the unbeliever sins against it, and also it may plainly be said without offense that if the mouse eats the bread that is the body of Christ, since it is not blessed in it like believing humans, nor does it sin like unbelieving and unworthy people, one may with good reason indeed say it does not actually eat the body of Christ at all.[136]

In the foregoing, Brenz has rejected any thoughts of defiling the Sacrament on the basis that it is set outside the use. The bread is irrevocably the body of Christ, but nevertheless, since the animal lacks a human soul, it cannot eat Christ's body but only the bread, which this is. One cannot address the animal with the Word, the medium of the presence; just as creation is the place for the presence of the God-man, the Creator: "And so our Lord, the almighty God, fills the mouse with His glorious majesty, as He fills all in all. So how would it come about that the body of Christ might shy away from this place, in which the majesty of God is found?" The animal is never able to make subjective application of this. It cannot even reject it.

Toward the end of the 1550s, Brenz makes his voice heard in these things anew. He then accepts a Melanchthonian formula of the Supper, the so-called

---

does not say, 'I give you the way, the truth, and the life,' as if something set outside of Me effects such things in Me" (Luther) (WA Br 6[99].3, [101.]56f., no. 1818). Brenz, therefore, is completely consistent in being unable to imagine a definition of the presence not determined by faith; it would not serve any purpose. Melanchthon's later theology builds on the same reasoning. The Sacrament becomes the spiritual eating by the justified, not the sign of the sinners' pardon in the atonement outside of us [*extra nos*]. Compare Herrlinger, op. cit., p. 115: "It reminds one of Calvin, when—incidentally, only in his last years—Baptism is called the sacrament of rebirth, the Supper the spiritual eating and fortification of the regenerate." Id., p. 125: "The bodily presence of Christ in the Supper is a remembrance and pledge of the general gracious presence of the Lord in us, His people."

135 Brenz to Chancellor Vogler, in September 1529, printed in Hartmann and Jäger, *Johann Brenz*, 1:440; compare Fricke, op. cit., pp. 225ff.; Gollwitzer, op. cit., p. 83 n. 1, and p. 140. For the theological-historical background of the problem, compare Landgraf, op. cit., 3/2:207ff., the chapter "Die in der Frühscholastik klassischen Frage *quid sumit mus*."

136 Hartmann and Jäger, op. cit., 1:452.

Frankfurt Recess. This cannot be explained at all the way Mahlmann[137] does, as resting on lack of insight about how different he was from Melanchthon. On the contrary, Brenz acts consistently: he defends the very view of the Sacrament that roused the disapproval of the Gnesio-Lutherans but was embraced by Melanchthon. Nevertheless, the break that occurred between Brenz and Melanchthon comes quite unexpectedly. Just before this, there was an exchange of personal letters.[138] When the break comes, it happens in a way that shows that the controversy is not, in a strict sense, dogmatic. In the form of a letter from Duke Christopher of Württemberg to Melanchthon, Brenz points out to Melanchthon what he [Melanchthon] wrote in the Colossians commentary, discussed here earlier,[139] "about the bodily and physical location of Christ's body in heaven," that it can be interpreted by some as questioning the orthodox doctrine of the Sacrament: "the writing under consideration is *interpreted* for you, as if you had . . . changed your opinion on the Lord's Supper."[140] This is certainly not what Mahlmann finds here: "Brenz, however, thinks that Melanchthon's Christology on its own inevitably results in . . . changing the doctrine."[141] Brenz took the dogmatic breadth of allowing that the assertion of Christ's local presence in heaven did not have to be heretical at all. A year later, he himself writes: "I am not unaware that certain of the ancients disapproved of this expression: 'The humanity of Christ is everywhere.' Nor would I approve it myself if this word [*ubique*, 'everywhere'] means a locality."[142] When Melanchthon is criticized for his words about a "physical location," Brenz does not want to attack the actual content. He wants to get Melanchthon to express himself in such a way, lest "the new Zwinglians and Calvinists boast so much that this worthy man at the same time might agree with them in this article."[143] The controversy

137 Mahlmann, op. cit., p. 176.

138 Mahlmann (op. cit., p. 181), who works with the thought of an actual theological difference between Melanchthon and Brenz, must allow "an understanding undisturbed by any contradictions," a concession that Mahlmann nevertheless moderates with this addition: "The quoted formulations may seem anemic." This disclaimer is unjustified; it is most powerfully refuted in Brenz's touching and strictly personal letter to Melanchthon regarding his children, especially about a handicapped son; compare Pressel, *Anecdota Brentiana*, p. 489; compare Mahlmann, op. cit., p. 181 n. 199.

139 Compare above, p. 100, text accompanying n. 96.

140 Duke Christopher to Melanchthon, November 3, 1559, Pressel, op. cit., p. 462; *Urschrift von Brenz Hand*, Pressel, op. cit., p. xxvi.

141 Mahlmann, op. cit., p. 186.

142 Brenz, *De personali unione duarum naturarum in Christo*, fol. 11b.

143 Duke Christopher to the Elector of Saxony, November 3, 1559, Pressel, op. cit., p. 463. The letter is in *Urschrift von J. Andreas Hand*, Pressel, op. cit., p. xxvi, and is a part of the correspondence that began with the duke's [Brenz's] direct letter to Melanchthon. The letter to the elector was delayed in anticipation of Melanchthon's answer to the first letter.

is not dogmatic, but Brenz accuses Melanchthon of lacking the will to fight and [lacking] the image of being against heterodoxy. Brenz had personal experience with the perils of Melanchthon's way of writing, when in a case of doctrinal discipline, he had his attention drawn to Melanchthon's Colossians commentary, when Bartolomeus Hagen, the teacher accused of Calvinism, appealed to that writing for his defense.[144] But to what extent Brenz shared Melanchthon's view, despite statements otherwise, comes significantly from the fact that Hagen, for his denial of the oral eating and the eating of the impious [*manducatio oralis . . . impiorum*], even appealed to—Brenz! In their doctrine, both Melanchthon and Brenz had expressions that could be used against the real presence, when taken out of context. From the commentary on John's Epistles written by Brenz, Hagen thought that he had most definite support for the idea that the reformer of the Württemberg church shared his denial of the bodily presence. Hagen especially thought that the statement about the mouth of the body and [the mouth] of faith had [a] conclusive power, despite the outraged rebuff by Brenz at having the meaning distorted, which was obvious and clear to him. Hagen's skill in citation, which was honest and sincere, shows the necessity of strictly examining the content of matters under consideration.

Melanchthon did not feel compelled to reply. To the duke of Württemberg, in fact, he sends a reply that merely refers the question to an upcoming council.[145] In private letters immediately after that, on the other hand, he vehemently attacks the confession accepted by the synod in Stuttgart, December 29, 1559, which expressly defends the omnipresence of Christ's body.[146] With that [confession], all Melanchthon's advice about caution and regard for traditional use of language had been surrendered. In all its newly formulated recalcitrance, which was easily misunderstood and invited attack, the statement that "the man Christ indeed fills everything" is now in a synodal document, presented as the church's dogma. In the private correspondence that includes Melanchthon's criticism of the Stuttgart confession, there is a grim joke often repeated by researchers: the confession is "Hechingen* Latin," Swabian peasant-Latin.[147] Melanchthon's

---

144 This is not mentioned in Mahlmann's otherwise detailed account (op. cit., pp. 176ff.). Hagen's struggle is described in Hartmann and Jäger, op. cit., 2:372ff.

145 Melanchthon to Duke Christopher, November 28, 1559, Pressel, op. cit., p. 464.

146 *Confessio et doctrina theologorum et ministrorum Verbi Dei, in ducatu Wirtembergensi, de vera praesentia corporis et sanguinis Jesu Christi in Coena Dominica*; it says here, *Acta [et scripta publica ecclesiae Wirtembergicae]*, pp. 341f.: "Not only by His divinity, but the man Christ indeed fills all things in a heavenly way, and in a way unfathomable to human reason, by which majesty His presence in the Supper is not taken away, but confirmed."

147 * Hechingen is a small city in Swabia.
CR 9:1034f., 1036, 1041. Compare here, among others, Hartmann and Jäger, op. cit., 2:375; Ahlberg, op. cit., p. 248; Mahlmann, op. cit., p. 192.

description of the story surrounding the origin of this statement has been repeated extensively. A definite bluntness seems to prevail in Melanchthon's words, which according to common interpretation almost indicate that Melanchthon used the technical deficiencies in his former friend's education in a theological controversy with him. But the situation becomes even more peculiar if one shares the judgment by [Julius] Hartmann [and] [Karl] Jäger: "Here he [Melanchthon] applied the joke to the written confession, even though its Latin did not fall short compared to the style and expression of similar works of that time. Brenz's Latin at any rate does not deserve any such mocking."[148] Brenz had also made use of his very meticulous education and continually expressed himself in Latin.[149] The confession was likewise subscribed by the University of Tübingen and the abbots of the territory. The document does not show any linguistic peculiarities to modern researchers either.[149a] Against this background there is reason to look more closely at the actual meaning of Melanchthon's humor. He reports about a Chancellor Lamparter [Lampardus] who said that the poor Latin spoken by a rustic earl from Hechingen was "Hechingen Latin." "This earl's village, Lamparter says, is Swabian Hechingen, where the most horrid linen weavings are made. That is also where this earl's Latin is woven. That statement turned into a proverb about foolish writings. Brenz repeats that same 'weaving' about the 'everywhere,' and adds other things about the adoration."[150] The city of rough-linen weavers was the home of the earl's Latin. Now, *touching the omnipresence*,[151] Brenz, the earl's compatriot, created a similar weave, which earned him the invective mentioned that was common regarding foolish works. Brenz's confession is, very simply, "homespun"—"his own weave." *Melanchthon here is not swooping down on the linguistic awkwardness or grammatical mistakes. He is accusing Brenz of a terminological novelty, a technical neology within the theology whose skillful structure was thus displaced.* He is not speaking about the document or its Latin in general; his complaint refers only to the [term] "everywhere." "Recently the duke of Württemberg sent a decree to the elector of Saxony in which the statement 'the body is everywhere' is defended. And many abbots subscribed to it. Now these are the architects of dogmas."[152] Melanchthon is not speaking about false doctrine, about defacing the words of the Bible, and

148 Hartmann and Jäger, op. cit., 2:375.

149 Compare Beyschlag, *Versuch einer vollständigen Lebens-Beschreibung Joh. Brentii*, 2:355ff., where Brenz's linguistic education is described.

149a Dr. John Rohnström at the Royal Library in Stockholm has kindly examined the document's language, and it was not found to be of an irregular kind.

150 CR 9:1035.

151 The meaning of the words *de adoratione* are discussed in the final chapter, on the adoration of the Sacrament.

152 CR 9:1062.

he is not rescinding the repletive existence of Christ's body, which is identical with the presence of the Sacrament. He is dealing with an awkwardly managed dogmatizing plea of a provincial, limited type, whose mistake was neither heretical doctrine nor ignorance of Latin; but in fact [the mistake was] its lack of formal elegance and its unfortunate consequences for church politics. Despite the breach, strictly dogmatically there was no difference between Melanchthon and Brenz. Melanchthon's death, which occurred immediately after this, made the break irreversible in an external sense, but at the same time it meant that Brenz, along with his colleague Jacob Andreae, as leading theologians, assumed the heritage after Melanchthon to maintain the omnipresence as a guarantee against sacramental materialism. Just as Melanchthon had done earlier, now these men came to lay claim on Luther's authority for this position of theirs.

One of the first to observe that Brenz and Andreae consistently make the repletive and sacramental presence identical was the aged Duke Albert of Prussia, who asks them in a letter in 1563: "What difference is there, then, between this presence in the holy Supper and the kind [of presence] with which He is present in all other food and drink, yes, even in all creatures; and, finally, does Christ also in His Supper distribute Himself to people in a different way than in other sacraments, or does He also distribute Himself now in the whole ministry of the Word?"[153] Brenz confirms[154] the duke's conjecture and characterizes the sacramental presence as repletive but also "dispensative,"[155] that is, so constituted that only here the omnipresence lets itself be imparted in a concrete mode, which gives comfort, "and one may therefore indeed say that the body of Christ is neither in stone nor in wood, but [it is] in the bread and wine of Christ's Supper."[156] He does not give any account for any difference of Christ's

153 Duke Albert of Prussia to Brenz and Andreae, May 16, 1563, printed in Hartmann and Jäger, op. cit., 2:537ff. Already in 1560, the duke had shown interest in the controversy around the omnipresence: compare Hase, *Herzog Albrecht von Preussen und seine Hofprediger*, p. 280. At the exact time of the exchange of letters with Brenz and Andreae, he was surrounded by religious charlatans. One of them, the cabbalistic pretended "margrave of Verona," the theologian Paul Schalich, on March 27, 1563, described for the duke a nighttime visit by the Trinity, wearing a fur-trimmed robe, who in His conversation had "included much about the omnipresence and the Sacrament" (Hase, op. cit., pp. 306f.).

154 Brenz to Albert, summer of 1563, Hartmann and Jäger, op. cit., 2:540. Actually, despite the heading [on the letter] provided by Hartmann and Jäger, Andreae is also co-signer of the letter, which is mainly in the plural: "Your Princely Grace's writing . . . we have . . . received." Only when Brenz's writings are mentioned is it in the singular: "from my, Johannes Brenz's, pamphlet concerning the majesty of Christ." The letter wants to summarize this writing for the territorial leader who, burdened with duties of governing, did not read the book.

155 Hartmann and Jäger, op. cit., 2:544.

156 Id., p. 544.

presence in the other means of grace. At the handed-down gloss "*definitive*," Brenz nevertheless knew the answer. In the document *De personali unione* he had given a peculiar etymology of the word: ". . . *praesentia definitivé*. For by His Word Christ 'defines' where He wants to dispense His body and blood to be consumed. This 'defining' we call 'consecration' elsewhere. But concerning this matter, Luther [said] many things in a little book, which he titled *That These Words of Christ in the Supper, 'This Is My Body,' etc. Still Stand Firm*, and it has been explained by me abundantly elsewhere."[157] Thus Brenz is convinced that his innovative explanation of "definitive" is in agreement with Luther. The word simply means that Christ thus "defined" His presence.

Andreae

In 1565, Jacob Andreae presented a similar interpretation of Luther:

> Although sainted Luther, in explaining the threefold view of Christ's body, attributes that mode of presence to Christ's body in the Supper that is ascribed to glorified bodies, nevertheless he does not simply do so, but [he does so] in order to show, against the adversary, that there are more modes of presence elsewhere, other than the physical and carnal one about which the adversary always talks. And a little later he openly affirms that this second mode of the glorified body, whereby it is not circumscribed to any place, Christ has in common with us. By virtue of this alone—if the presence of Christ's body depended on this, it could not have been distributed to the disciples in the first Supper. The third mode remains . . . .[158]

Just like the modern Luther researcher Seeberg,[159] Andreae notes that Luther introduced a hypothesis in his reasoning, but it is put in the wrong place, so that the diffinitive mode of presence as such becomes an accommodation to the opponents' way of thinking. In reality Luther had only asserted that the repletive presence of Christ's body can be omitted without needing to deny the real presence for that reason. For Andreae the repletive mode of presence is the only one possible for the presence of the Sacrament: "The third mode remains . . . ." Andreae also reshapes Luther's distinctions elsewhere. The second mode of presence is identified with the mode of presence of the resurrected body; for that reason, the first Supper on Maundy Thursday cannot possibly have made use of it. For Luther, in the same work, the forty days after Easter are an example of

157 Brenz, *De personali unione duarum naturarum [in Christo]*, fol. F3b.

158 Andreae, *Pia, breuis et perspicua expositio controuersiae de duabus naturis in Christo, dequoque vera praesentia corporis et sanguinis eius in Eucharistia*, p. 91.

159 Compare this volume [Swedish edition, pp. 65f.]. [Translator's note: This reference is unclear and may be an incorrect page number. It may be above, pp. 78–79, text just after n. 10 (Swedish edition, p. 78).]

the first mode of presence,[160] while the second mode of presence applies to one or two events before the resurrection, perhaps at the birth *ex utero clauso*, and at the first Supper; and to two events after the resurrection:[161] passing through the gravestone as well as through the closed doors. For Luther, Christ always has access to a real, miraculous mode of presence independent of any arrangement connected to salvation history. For Andreae again, it is important partly to uphold the spiritual character of the Sacrament through the repletive mode of presence, partly in general to present the local, circumscribed mode of presence as connected with the emptying and that it is therefore laid aside now. So the resurrected body is also spiritualized. The concrete physical mode is found only "up until the resurrection, in which He set aside all weaknesses, and His body was glorified."[162] The distance from Luther is especially noticeable here, since Luther expects Christ's highest glorification under the form of the first mode of presence: on the Last Day.[163] Andreae's incorrect interpretation of Luther was immediately noticed by his Reformed opponents. The Reformed clergy had the above-cited section[164] printed in a document, with a critique that was, in substance, completely correct: "Therefore, I[acobus] A[ndreae] thus overturns what Luther affirms, that the body of Christ is present in the Supper in the mode of the glorified body."[165]

This reshaping of Luther's terminology was maintained by Andreae throughout his life. So it occurs in a document from 1580,[166] the year of the publication of the *Book of Concord*, as well as in 1584 in the defense document for the Formula of Concord, which forms a south German counterpart to the north German *Apology or Defense of the Christian Book of Concord* and which was published in Tübingen by its theologians under Andreae's leadership.[167] Here

160 WA 26:335.30ff. [cf. AE 37:222].

161 WA 26:328.31f., 336.4f. [cf. AE 37:218, 224].

162 Andreae, *Pia, breuis et perspicua expositio*, p. iv.

163 WA 26:335.32f. [cf. AE 37:222].

164 The Reformed quotation does not include the words taken up in this volume: "The third mode remains." [A list of Hardt's corrections removes the initial part of this footnote that said, "Compare above, p. 96."]

165 [Brenz,] *Elenchi paradoxorum . . . a ministris ecclesiae Bremensis*, fol. B2a.

166 Andreae, *Repetitio sanae doctrinae reverendissime in Christo Patris, D. N. D. Martini Lutheri, de persona Christi et de coena Dominica*, fol. F4bf., where after the three modes are mentioned, the third is subdivided into three parts: "*universalis*," "*gratia*," "*singularis modus praesentia corporis ipsius est . . . Quem praesentiae modum Sacramentalem appelant.*"

167 *Solida Refutatio Compilationis Cinglianae et Caluinianae*, attributed to Andreae personally, according to the British Museum and the card catalog of the Royal Library in Stockholm, but he is mentioned in the book in the third person (id., p. 336): "This our colleague and brother . . . Jacob Andreae."

the opponents discussed the assertion that "Luther had taught that the body of Christ has three modes *of being simultaneously*, which vary and differ from each other, namely, circumscribed, definitive, and repletive."[168] It is the expression [in italics] that evokes Andreae's disapproval: "For Luther, while he explains those three modes elsewhere, by no means [does he say] that the body of Christ has them *simultaneously*." The three modes of presence must not be considered simultaneous; so laying aside the circumscriptive mode was salvation-history's laying aside the servant-form: "For it says He *had* the first mode in this era, which He laid aside along with the form of a servant."[169] But this does not mean that Andreae gives up the thought that Christ even now is circumscribed in a finite and limited sense. In the contemporaneous colloquy in Mömpelgard (Montebéliard), Andreae says, "Just as in the first Supper, the body of *Christ* remained local, finite, and circumscribed when He distributed His body to His disciples in a heavenly way, so now indeed in glory it remains finite and circumscribed in the character of its substance."[170] What Andreae wants to say by this can be stated this way: circumscribed, but not in a circumscribed manner.

168 Id., p. 661.

169 Id., p. 662. Even if Luther never identified the circumscribed essence and the form of a servant [*esse circumscriptive* and *forma servi*], Tübingen theology fundamentally continues Luther's exegesis of Philippians 2. Wagner (*Ascendit ad coelos*, p. 4) came to the incorrect view that the Lutheran exegesis of this was a unique invention of Brenz: "His treatment of this subject is influenced largely by his somewhat singular understanding of the teaching of Paul in Phil. 2:6–8. According to Brenz, the expression *morphe theou* ['form of God'] in v. 6 should not be understood with respect to the divine essence, but rather with reference to the divine majesty of properties communicated to the humanity of Christ by virtue of the personal union"; compare id., p. 70. — When Brenz is to define the expressly circumscribed or local appearances of Christ after Easter and on the Last Day, he introduces the term "economy" [*oeconomia*] (Brenz, *Opera* 9:928, "*De divina maiestate*"): "For the sake of teaching, we distinguish economy in the presence from the humiliation; and when Christ, after the resurrection, and even after His ascension into heaven, appeared in a certain place, and will appear on the Last Day, we call it economy"; compare here Hoogland, *Calvin's Perspective on the Exaltation of Christ in Comparison with the Post-Reformation Doctrine of the Two States*, p. 28, with a correct remark about it.

170 *Acta colloquij Montisbellisgartensis*, p. 67. Compare Andreae, *Assertio piae et orthodoxae doctrinae*, p. 11:

> If the human nature is understood by itself and absolutely, by reason of its essence, we affirm: just as in the state of its emptying it was naturally circumscribed in one place physically, and not spread into everything in the place, so also in the glory with which other saints are also adorned, considered by itself and absolutely, it is not spread everywhere; but we simply retain the article of our faith that He is in heaven, even if heaven is not in a place but is defined as the highest blessedness by which God will be all in all.

In a certain regard, Christ is thus in the heavenly glory that also is ascribed to the saints. Wagner (op. cit., p. 58) notes Andreae's words and comments: "One may well gain the impression that certain Reformed dogmaticians, preoccupied with inexorable

These various investigations within Tübingen theology concerning the Sacrament serve to support the thesis about the sacramental presence as repletive and not definitive. This latter mode was not at Christ's disposal on Maundy Thursday night: "It *could not* be distributed, since it was not yet glorified." The fundamental challenge that follows from this, from the "*had simultaneously*," stands in blatant opposition not just to Luther but also to the north German *Apology of the Book of Concord*, authored by Chemnitz, Kirchner, and Selnecker. Their words about the "*diverso respectu*" of the three modes have already been mentioned.[171] This means that besides the continuation of the Melanchthonian tradition within Württemberg theology, we also have a continuation of Luther's view. Its foremost representative is [Martin Chemnitz].

Chemnitz

With this assertion, the present volume will consistently implement the redistribution of the roles of dogma-history that opened with the assertion that Württemberg theology is of a Melanchthonian type in the loci under discussion here. The conventional view was that Brenz continued Luther's doctrine, while Melanchthon's influence was felt through Chemnitz, who was thought to reject the repletive presence of Christ's body.[172] This view of Chemnitz as denying the human nature's omnipresence is contested only by Francis Pieper.[173] Pieper gives a comprehensive and thorough presentation that persuasively proves his conclusion that Chemnitz acknowledges the omnipresence of Christ's body.

Chemnitz rejects any attempt to reduce the real omnipresence of Christ's body to a merely nominal presence:

> It [Christ's humanity] indeed rules in and with the *logos* in all things, not absent from afar or at a distance, or through vicarious work and administration customary to kings when their authority is spread out through many and distant provinces, but it rules in the *logos*, in the same way that it [Christ's humanity] exists in the *logos*, so also insofar as it also has everything present in front of itself personally in the *logos* and is present in all things. We who consider the human nature of Christ not only in physical

---

polemic attack upon the dreaded ubiquity doctrine, sometimes failed to consider sufficiently the indisputable fact that the Lutheran antagonists in their own way also strove to do justice to the biblical witness concerning our Lord's departure for and residence in the heavenly world." These words of Wagner's must be extended to the whole of theological-historical research, which has dealt with the problems debated here without adequate distinctions.

171 Compare above, p. 40, text around n. 23 [Swedish edition, pp. 61f., Hardt's correction].

172 Dorner, *Entwicklungsgeschichte der Lehre von der Person Christi von den ältesten Zeiten bis auf die Neueste*, p. 697. Compare Seeberg, op. cit., 4/2:522f.; Ritschl, op. cit., 4:97, which is the basis for the rest of the research. Compare below, pp. 119–20 n. 178.

173 Pieper, *Christliche Dogmatik*, 2:215ff. [cf. *Christian Dogmatics*, 2:195f.].

> terms, nor only according to its essential or natural properties, but especially in the hypostatic union with the divinity, and according to that exaltation that it has above every name, having received all power and authority over everything—we simply believe this, even if we do not understand the way in which it happens.[174]

All things are present for Christ's humanity, which exists in the personal union of the Logos, and in this way it exercises its dominion over things through its omnipresence, not from a distance the way earthly kings rule over distant provinces. The concluding "we do not understand . . . the way" is an expression of humility that does not actually limit the previous statement. A few pages earlier, Chemnitz had used the same formulations about the omnipresence of the divine nature. About this it says, borrowing from Lombard: "But how it is everywhere, we do not understand."[175] What is expressed now concerning the human nature is its inaccessibility.

Chemnitz contemplates his opinion with a reference to Scripture: "And thus far we have Scripture, the guide that goes before and the light that shines the way [Ps. 119:105]; and so we follow simply and safely."[176] After this comes a clarification that in no way negates the preceding:

> What is in fact argued and sought more particularly in addition—since Christ is present in the Church with both His natures, and dwells in the individual members, and His body is in the Supper—is whether the body of Christ is also in wood and stones and fruits, in the birds of the sky, the flocks of the field, the fish of the sea, whether He wants to be sought and found there; and the vile things heard besides, the abominable thinking about manure and sewers, which cannot even be thought or said without blasphemy concerning the divine nature—it is agreed that it is everywhere. These things are usually woven in [as an addition], since we do not have a sure word and express promise concerning questions of this kind, that He wants to be sought and found there; nor do they bring any edification or consolation in the Church, but they offend the simple, they disturb the weak, and they offer the adversaries material for endless quarreling.[177]

It is not possible, as with earlier research in the commentaries on these words, to present Chemnitz as being in doubt regarding the question "whether Christ's body is present in corpses, in leaves and stone."[178] Chemnitz had

174 Chemnitz, *De duabus naturis*, p. 192 [cf. *Two Natures in Christ*, p. 463].

175 Id., p. 173 [cf. *Two Natures in Christ*, p. 424].

176 Id., p. 193 [cf. *Two Natures in Christ*, p. 463].

177 Ibid.

178 Rocholl, op. cit, p. 211; compare Wagner, op. cit., p. 78 n. 49; Hoogland, op. cit., p. 33. — Rocholl (op. cit., pp. 207ff.) wants to find in the presentation by Chemnitz only an operative omnipresence, in contrast to Luther, who was supposed to have taught a body of Christ ("absolutely") infinite in its essence. The same thought is in Frank

emphatically said that he could appeal to Scripture for the idea that "He has all things present before Him." A completely *different* question is [this]: "Since Christ is present in the Church with both His natures, . . . whether the body of Christ is also in wood and stones . . . [and whether He] wants *to be sought and found* there" (emphasis mine). So it has to do with the question of a presence that is accessible to faith. Christ's body is not to be found in creation *in this way* ("*ita*"). It cannot be sought in impure things in this way; nevertheless, this is valid: "It is agreed that the divine nature is everywhere." These words about the divine nature clearly show that the stipulations stated above in no way mean a partial revocation of the first statement formulated concerning the omnipresence of Christ's humanity being supported by Scripture. It is a matter of a specific problem in which one has to choose his words so as not to disturb the uneducated and to put material into the hands of the opponents. Under no circumstances does the Church have the task of directing the believers to seek Christ in creation. He is in the Church and in the means of grace. Naturally, this preciseness of Chemnitz is clearly reminiscent of that of *Melanchthon*, but in the question of the actual dogmatic content he joins Melanchthon on a point where Melanchthon also agrees with *Luther*.[179]

(op. cit., 3:312), who, opposed to Dorner (compare below, p. 121 n. 181), certainly defends the assent by Chemnitz to the repletive presence in the Formula of Concord, which also consistently cites abundant quotations from Chemnitz in which this type of presence is proved, but which presence is understood by Frank as in opposition to the omnipresence of Christ's body in Luther. The acknowledgment of this omnipresence of the human nature in Chemnitz is diminished by a similarly unique as well as artificial distinction between body [*corpus*] and humanity [*humanitas*], rightly criticized by Wagner (op. cit., p. 84 n. 68), whereby the former [body] is excluded from the omnipresence of the latter [humanity]. This distinction, according to Frank (p. 314), was supposed to say explicitly what the Formula of Concord means implicitly, but Frank is forced to concede (p. 393): "Only that here, indeed in Brenz as well as in Chemnitz, the human nature [*natura humana*] and the body of Christ [*corpus Christi*] are not distinguished [in] the way we consider necessary." — Rocholl and Frank get the same result from their analyses. Christ's body, according to Chemnitz, is not omnipresent, just as in Luther.

179 Wagner (op. cit., p. 76) asserts that Chemnitz would not draw conclusions from the incarnation regarding the omnipresence but only from the Scripture passages that directly express it. But in the passage under consideration (*De duabus naturis*, p. 177 [cf. *Two Natures in Christ*, p. 432], Chemnitz speaks only about the presence comprehendible in faith or the Sacrament:

> But if in addition in Scripture we would have no express word or special promise concerning the presence of Christ also according to the human nature, in the Church militant, still in this world, or if Scripture handed down that Christ was present for the Church in this world only with His divine nature, for my simplicity I would reasonably not dare nor would I wish either to establish or to receive anything else from bare arguments concerning the prerogatives of the hypostatic union. . . . Now indeed we have the express word and special promise, by a particular and definite institution, . . .

When Chemnitz presents his Christology in *Repetitio sanae doctrinae* from 1561, he invokes three great names: Cyril, John of Damascus, and Luther.[180] Their claims for a place within Lutheran Christology, thus raised by Chemnitz, he himself did not preclude by [their] disputing the omnipresence of Christ's body. The interpretations that came to this conclusion worked with incorrect suppositions so that, for example, the doctrine of the special heavenly presence of Christ's body is thought necessarily to exclude the omnipresence of the same body.[181] Therefore, there is also no opportunity to see the Christology of the Formula of Concord, which expresses the consensus of the north and south German schools, as an inconsistent conglomeration of opposite views, as the critics of the Formula of Concord have asserted ever since the contemporaneous Reformed opponent Hospinianus formulated the term "Discordant Concord" [*Concordia Discors*] about it.[182]

An opposite view, on the other hand, consists in seeing the relationship of Christology to Sacrament. Chemnitz certainly insists that there is a distinction between the special heavenly presence [the glorified body] and the sacramental presence, but, unlike the Tübingen theologians, he does not thereby reject the diffinitive form of the presence as belonging to the Sacrament. Chemnitz

---

> that in the observance of His Supper in the gathering of the Church in this world, it is celebrated according to the institution, He wills to be present with His body and blood.

The special comprehendible presence requires clear scriptural words, without which no presence in the Sacrament and in the Church can be taught. The personal union here cannot replace a lack of institution. On the other hand, Chemnitz is not disputing what can be extracted from the fact of the incarnation in the question of the general omnipresence in its inaccessibility. — Mahlmann (op. cit., p. 225) talks about the "careful critique of Brenz's Christology" by Chemnitz which includes an erroneous contrast, through which a Christology that is not completely Lutheran is ascribed to Chemnitz. The evidence that Mahlmann noted has to do with the relationship of the Sacrament to omnipresence: "The typical rationale for this real presence for Brenz, in contrast, . . . Chemnitz has omitted." It is not a Christological difference, but one that has to do with the theology of the Sacrament.

180 Chemnitz, *Repetitio sanae doctrinae*, pp. 354f. Here the three genera of the communication of attributes are developed for the first time; compare Mahlmann, op. cit., pp. 229ff.

181 This erroneous thinking is repeated in Noth (*Grundzüge der Theologie des Martin Chemnitz*, pp. 43f.), which also considers omnipresence to be incompatible with sacramental, diffinitive presence. In this way, he is forced to deny a complete Lutheran Christology in Chemnitz and allies himself with Dorner (op. cit., p. 697), who sees Chemnitz as a "diminution of Luther." Wagner (op. cit., p. 81) is typical of this uncertainty and inability of research to see the connection among the various expressions of Chemnitz: "The question may well arise: With what right does Chemnitz, who in such large measure shares in common with Brenz the basic formulations of orthodox Lutheran Christology, himself stop short of a doctrine of general ubiquity?"

182 Compare Pieper, op. cit., 2:215f. [cf. *Christian Dogmatics*, 2:171f.].

only considers the absence of the revelation of glory in the Sacrament: "And also Christ is not present for us with His body in this visible form, or in the state of glorified bodies, in the Church on earth in this life, but in heaven, from where He will return to judge in that form in which He displays Himself to be seen already by the blessed souls and spirits, just as several such appearances are described in Revelation. And in this form He will return in glory to judge."[183] Again Christ can very well show Himself ("by extraordinary dispensation") in this revelation of glory or in the form of His earthly life whenever He wants: "In addition, it is also true that Christ is not held and enclosed in heaven either in that glory or in His prior natural form in such a way that He could not, whenever He wished, also show and manifest His presence on earth in that form."[184] Such a revelation occurred for Paul on the road to Damascus ("not in the Milky Way of heaven, but in earthly life"; "not some apparition of a vision").[185] The sacramental presence is, of course, not "the kind of presence that is the manner and condition of glorified bodies,"[186] since it is invisible. But apart from this difference, it belongs to the kind of specific revelations that take place between the ascension and the Last Day. It is a miraculous form of presence that, by mustering several quotations from church fathers, is compared to His passing through the closed doors on Easter Day.[187] It does not coincide with omnipresence, which, however, makes the sacramental presence "not only possible, but even easy."[188] It occurs according to Christ's will: "wherever, whenever, and however He wishes; we make our judgment concerning this will of His from the Word."[189] So the various modes are distinct: "And I also distinguish these stages: One indeed when He dwelt on earth, another when He appears in glory in heaven, another when He is present in the Supper with the bread and wine, another in the whole Church, another that He has all creatures

183 Chemnitz, *De duabus naturis*, p. 176 [cf. *Two Natures in Christ*, p. 430]. With complete justification, Chemnitz goes back to *both* Luther and the ancient church regarding the specific heavenly presence in *Fundamenta sanae doctrinae*, p. 67: "Beside those attributes also, and according to the mode of the true body, Luther along with Augustine and the Scholastics perceives that the body of Christ even now in glory, in that circumscribed form by which He showed Himself to Paul and Stephen, by which also He will return to judge, is seen by angels and saints in heaven."

184 Chemnitz, *De duabus naturis*, p. 176 [cf. *Two Natures in Christ*, p. 430].

185 Ibid. [cf. *Two Natures in Christ*, p. 431].

186 Id., p. 178 [cf. *Two Natures in Christ*, p. 432].

187 Id., p. 181f. [cf. *Two Natures in Christ*, pp. 440ff.].

188 Id., p. 182 [cf. *Two Natures in Christ*, p. 441]. Compare p. 184 [cf. *Two Natures in Christ*, p. 442]: "This doctrine concerning the hypostatic union shows that it is not only possible but [even] easy for the Son of God to be willing and to be able to show and effect . . . that presence of His body." [Hardt notes the misprint "Daughter" for "Son" in the Latin edition.]

189 Id., p. 185 [cf. *Two Natures in Christ*, p. 444].

present in front of Himself in the *Logos*."[190] Even if the last two modes of presence might only be distinguished subjectively, the rest emerge as truly differentiated. This is underscored further by Chemnitz, since the Formula of Concord confessionalized Luther's doctrine of the three modes. And Chemnitz, in the *Apology of the Book of Concord*, must make a defense: "But [he teaches there] the definitive [mode], that Christ is there imperceptibly and supernaturally."[191] The explanation allows both the etymology of Brenz and Luther's real distinction: "which the man Himself first defined or expressed who is the Founder and Master: namely, Jesus Christ."[192] Besides borrowing this from Brenz, the scholastic definition is also given in connection to Biel. Luther was accused by the Reformed of having committed "a great crime of fraud" when he ascribed to Scholasticism the doctrine of three modes of presence for Christ's body. The *Apology [of the Book of Concord]* does not defend more specifically the consensus in the question of the repletive presence,[193] but rather the solidarity with the Middle Ages in regard to "definitive." "But these fellows should read what Gabriel [Biel] writes in book 4, distinction 10," and then Biel is cited. So the circle is closed. In the north German tradition, the heritage from Luther and Nominalism lives on.[194] Without fleshing out his expressions, which are in no way consciously formulated against the south German brethren in the faith,[195] Chemnitz and the other authors of the *Apology [of the Book of Concord]* nevertheless show that unity in Christology does not extend to the relationship between Christology and the Sacrament. How this difference makes an impact even within other loci of sacramental theology shall be shown in the following chapters.

---

190 Ibid.

191 *Apologia oder verantwortung des Christlichen Concordien Buchs*, fol. 223B [cf. *Apology*, pp. 306–7].

192 Ibid. [cf. *Apology*, pp. 306–7].

193 It ought to be noted that the *Apologia [oder verantwortung des Christlichen Concordien Buchs]* does not use the term "repletive" for the third mode of Christ's body: "this third heavenly mode (for thus he calls it) and not the repletive mode" (id., fol. 225A [cf. *Apology*, p. 308]), which term is reserved for the infinite divinity. The distinction helps to highlight that only through the personal union does Christ's body get this prerogative.

194 The Reformed attack proceeds from the *Thomistic* view, according to which only incorporeal beings possess definitive essence [*esse definitive*] (ibid., fol., 227a [cf. *Apology*, pp. 310–11]): "as if he (since he calls it the definitive mode) would have taught that Christ's body is a ghost [or 'spirit,' *Geist*]."

195 It says (id., fol. 226B [cf. *Apology*, pp. 310]), against the Reformed, that the controversy does not mainly have to do with the mode of presence, but the presence. But this statement is not formulated as a concession to the Melanchthonian-Württembergian tradition, whose particular character it does not seem to have noted. In the final chapter below, it shall be taken up more precisely how the idea of actual consensus could be created without a real basis.

CHAPTER 4

Transsubstantiatio, Unio Sacramentalis, Consubstantiatio

The Character of the Sacramental Presence

LUTHER'S stance toward transubstantiation has been evaluated very differently among researchers. The researchers could be divided into three different groups. The view of the first group is summarized with the word "theologoumenon," which in Swedish theological history was used by [Ragnar] Holte as a designation for Luther's connection to the doctrine of the transformation of substance [transubstantiation].[1] Here he joins with Jürgen Diestelmann.[2] Ernst Sommerlath could also be added to the same group: "He did not contend against transubstantiation with regard to content."[3] The view of the second group is represented by [Hermann] Sasse, for example, who has Luther take a more critical attitude toward transubstantiation: "It must be rejected because Paul speaks of the consecrated bread as being bread." But for Luther, this doctrine is not to be equated with heresies like the sacrifice of the Mass but is rather "a wrong attempt to explain the miracle of the real presence."[4] The same view is found in [Carl Fredrik] Wisløff.[5] Both these types of judgment meanwhile stand in very sharp contrast to the view of the third group. According to them, the

1 Holte, op. cit., p. 76.

2 Diestelmann, *Konsekration*, pp. 25f.

3 Sommerlath, "Das Abendmahl bei Luther," p. 117.

4 Sasse, op. cit., p. 103.

5 Wisløff, op. cit., p. 154. A large number of researchers could be added to this group who, like Cleve (op. cit., p. 229, for example), refer to the *Babylonian Captivity* without closer analysis of the problem, leaving the reader with the impression of a definite, though modified, rejection.

doctrine of transubstantiation would have been a severe heresy in Luther's eyes. Such a view is embraced by [Vilmos] Vajta. After an initial hesitancy, Luther would have found that his "belief in creation" conflicted with the transformation of the bread, after which the result was "a total break with the doctrine of transubstantiation, which for him was categorized as godless." "For it pertains to the belief in creation that God always makes use of the means created by Him when He deals with man."[6] "For Luther it is just as essential (over against Rome) to affirm that natural bread and wine are bearers of the presence of Christ, as (over against the Enthusiasts) that, after adding the Words of Institution, the elements are *no* longer 'mere bread and wine' "[7] (emphasis Vajta's). [Åke] Andrén has the same view: "The reformers strongly turned against binding Christ's presence in the Supper to the elements locally, which is critical for Communion and Mass and the doctrine of transubstantiation that emerges from that."[8]

In order to gain clarity about Luther's position on transubstantiation, it is necessary first to investigate the various attempts to establish the date of Luther's break with this doctrine and, in connection with that, to establish the significance of the change. Among the researchers, only Vajta wants to maintain the view that Luther "always wanted to regard natural bread and wine as the means of Christ's presence" after he gained knowledge of the Nominalistic critique of the dogma of transubstantiation around 1509.[9] But this reasoning is built on a misunderstanding regarding the form of the Nominalistic critique, which was of a speculative nature and was done "for the sake of argument" [*disputandi causa*] without intending an actual criticism.[10] Transubstantiation as "the determination of the Church" fundamentally builds on the authority of

---

6 Vajta, op. cit., p. 176.

7 Id., op. cit., p. 190.

8 Andrén, *Högmässa och nattvardsgång i reformationstidens svenska kyrkoliv*, p. 46. Although Vajta and Andrén are relatively alone among the researchers in regard to the sharpness of the formulations, they give expression to a view that is a part of the cultural heritage of Protestantism and is repeated in the Melanchthonian as well as in the Reformed doctrinal tradition.

9 Vajta, op. cit., p. 176.

10 Compare here Junghans, op. cit., pp. 306ff., the chapter "Bekämpfte Ockham das Transsubstantionsdogma?" especially p. 310:

> This section brought upon him the reproach of Lutterell [chancellor of Oxford University]; he [Ockham] asserted that the Church held a false doctrine in the Supper. Yet nowhere is this said. This conclusion would have been warranted if Ockham had paid homage to the axiom that God must do what was most easily understandable to reason. But that was never his conviction. God was free to choose for Himself one of several possible ways of doing something, even it was more difficult to understand. Ockham not only yielded this freedom to God, but he was also prepared to bow to a church decision, even if it went beyond biblical revelation.

the councils and therefore must have been embraced by Luther at least up until 1519, when in the Leipzig Disputation he was driven to reject the infallibility of the councils.[11] It is reasonable that his statements about the real presence before this time ought to be seen as expressing transubstantiation. On the other hand, Vajta must be supported in his well-documented view that terms such as "transformed" [*verwandelt*] and "changed" [*wandelt*] cannot be used to determine that the doctrine of transubstantiation is there, since Luther used them during his *whole* writing career.[12] For that matter, Vajta rightly asserts, there is no reason to think, like [Hans] Grass,[13] that Luther, by using the word "transform" in *The Blessed Sacrament of the Holy and True Body of Christ, and on the Brotherhoods*, would have taught transubstantiation. Sasse[14] even finds in this sermon a direct polemic against transubstantiation when it says, "Some use their skill and finesse to ponder if the bread remains when it is changed into Christ's flesh, and the wine into His blood, and how the whole Christ may be enclosed in such a small piece of bread and wine. . . . Asking that is meaningless. It is enough that you know it is a divine sign when Christ's flesh and blood are truly in them, however and wherever He lets it happen."[15] But that does not prove a rejection of transubstantiation. It has to do rather with problems that have transubstantiation as the presupposition and which are left to God's wisdom. "Where [*wo*] the bread remains" was actually the kind of scholastic problem to which at least three different solutions were given: prolonged transformation, annihilation, or cessation [*conversio productiva, annihilatio, destitio*].* These would be alternatives well-known to Luther,[16] which here he deems unnecessary subtleties. The question is not "*whether* [*ob*] the bread remains," but "*where* [*wo*]

11 About these data, compare Köstlin, *Martin Luther*, 1:265, also p. 210.

12 Vajta, op. cit., pp. 175f., with detailed evidence, p. 185 n. 93.

13 Grass, op. cit., p. 13.

14 Sasse, op. cit., pp. 100f.

15 WA 2.749.36ff. [cf. AE 35:60f.]. One can compare this pious warning against the speculative arrogance with similar words of Thomas à Kempis, *Opera Omnia*, 2:136 [cf. *Imitation of Christ*, book 4, chapter 18]:

> Let man not be a curious examiner of the Sacrament, but a humble imitator by subordinating his sense to sacred faith. The voice of the beloved [Christ]. Chapter 18. You must beware of curious and useless investigation of this most profound Sacrament, if you do not wish to be plunged into the depth of doubt. Whoever is an investigator of the majesty will be oppressed by the glory. God is able to do more than man can understand. Pious and humble inquiry of the truth is allowed, always being prepared to be taught and desiring to walk through the sound opinions of the fathers. Blessed is the simplicity, which abandons the difficult ways of the questions and proceeds on the even and firm path of God's commands.

16 * [Translator's note: Reading *destitio* instead of the misprint *desitio*.]
WA Br 9[:440].5ff., no. 3629, Appendix.

the bread remains"; transubstantiation is not doubted here, but thoughts must stop before making conclusions about that question. That the present interpretation is correct is confirmed also by the polemic that resulted from the printing of this sermon on the Sacrament. In attacks on Luther, *two* monstrances were even used as a symbol of a Bohemian utraquistic heresy,[17] and some even thought that "two geese were to be seen in the one monstrance, since Jan Hus in Bohemian [Czech] means John Goose [Joannes Ganss]."[18] But nowhere is it said that transubstantiation was denied in the writing under attack. The least hint of uncertainty in the question of this dogma would not have eluded Luther's critics, "the monstrance-interpreters and goose-gazers."[19] This contemporary understanding of the content can be said essentially to support the view that Grass was right after all, by referring to the Lord's Supper sermon of 1519 as teaching transubstantiation. The sermon took place already during the autumn of 1519, some months after the summer's doctrinally significant change in the question of the infallibility of the councils, and it is natural that here the implications from shifting the dogmatic premises were not realized immediately. (As shall be presented later, Luther already at this time, though privately, had found reason for a certain criticism of the teaching in question.)

Nor can any attack against transubstantiation be detected in *A Treatise on the New Testament, That Is, the Holy Mass,*[20] at Easter 1520, which would have been obvious if Luther broke publicly with this doctrine within a few months. The break comes first during the summer of 1520 in his writing *To the Christian Nobility of the German Nation*, where the Bohemian rejection of transubstantiation is defended: "For it is not an article of faith that bread and wine are not essentially and naturally in the Sacrament, which is a delusion of St. Thomas [Aquinas] and the pope, but it is an article of faith that the natural flesh and blood of Christ are in the natural bread and wine, so that one should tolerate opinions on both sides until they come to agree, since there is no danger whether you believe the bread is there or not. But we must tolerate many ways and words that are not harmful to the faith."[21] This dating [of Luther's change] is in the literature in [August Wilhelm] Dieckhoff, with whom it has been associated.[22] The document in question [*To the Christian Nobility*] includes a broad agreement with Aristotelian philosophy and the Roman See; it is the downfall of these that takes transubstantiation with it. But it must be maintained that even

17 Duke George of Saxony's letter of December 27, 1519, to Elector Frederick of Saxony, printed in StL 19:450; compare WA 6:81.32ff. [forthcoming in AE 71].

18 WA 6:81.35f. [forthcoming in AE 71].

19 WA 6:82.17 [forthcoming in AE 71].

20 WA 6:353ff. [cf. AE 35:75].

21 WA 6:456.34ff. [cf. AE 44:199].

22 Dieckhoff, op. cit., p. 249.

here Luther himself is not disputing transubstantiation; he is simply acknowledging the right of the Bohemians to reject it. *But by doing so, the doctrine ceased to be a binding dogma, even for Luther.*

This critique now expressed by Luther does not need to be identified with the actual breakthrough for the Reformation criticism of transubstantiation. Luther research on this point has disregarded Melanchthon's stance. Already on September 9, 1519, in his baccalaureate thesis, Melanchthon had posed the statement: "18. Therefore, not to believe in [indelible] character, transubstantiation, and the like is a fault, short of heresy."[23] On October 3, 1519, Luther expressed himself in a letter on these theses: "You have seen or now you see Philip's bold but very true positions."[24] Melanchthon was the first one to articulate the criticism, and it was not disputed by Luther, who rightly sees it as bold. That means that this letter from October 3, in a certain sense, can be seen as the background for the sermon on *The [Blessed] Sacrament* from 1519 discussed above, which was "in print" by November 29 of that year.[25] At the same time, it must be maintained that Luther did not openly express the thoughts that he had formulated a month earlier, commenting on another person's critique.

In the middle of February 1520, Melanchthon cites his earlier critique of transubstantiation[26] and expands it with a critique of Scholasticism and the papacy, which reminds one of Luther in *To the Christian Nobility*. But what matters here is that Melanchthon makes this interpolation: "Indeed, I am not at all reluctant to embrace the opinion of transubstantiation, but I would not rashly list it among the articles of faith."[27] So, despite the criticism, Melanchthon is willing for his own part to embrace transubstantiation. It is the same fundamental emancipation from teaching it as dogma that Luther maintains in *To the Christian Nobility* in the summer of that same year.

In his *Babylonian Captivity of the Church*, Luther goes a bit further, to an actual criticism of the content. Now the dogma of transubstantiation is openly considered as the Church's captivity under foreign powers, and Luther for his part also refused to believe in it. Thus he became equal to the Bohemians:[28] "Here

23 Stupperich, *Melanchthons Werke*, 1:24; "*Supplementa Melanchthoniana*," 4/1:78. Compare Herrlinger, op. cit., p. 125; Kohler, op. cit., 1:187f.; Neuser, op. cit., pp. 20ff.

24 WA Br 1[:514].33ff., no. 202.

25 WA 2:739 [cf. AE 35:45].

26 CR 1:138ff.

27 CR 1:145.

28 The development that occurred is the same process that was established by Sasse (op. cit., pp. 90ff.) regarding *sub una* ["under one kind"]: In *Explanation of Some Articles in the Sermon on the Holy Sacrament*, Luther writes: "*we* Romans—*you* Bohemians" (WA 6:80.4f. [forthcoming in AE 71]: "They are not right . . . and we also are not right"), but in the [*Babylonian*] *Captivity*: "*you* Romans" (WA 6:505.23: "*vos*

I will be a Wycliffite and a heretic with six hundred names."[29] The future tense, "I will be," shows that *from now on* Luther expects all kinds of abusive names because he rejects it. Luther depicts his development in a way that agrees with the portrayal above. He talks about three different periods. The first stage includes: "Once, when I was drinking in scholastic theology, Dr. Cardinal Cambrai [Pierre d'Ailly] gave me an occasion to think." His reading of the Nominalist d'Ailly's critique of transubstantiation, however, gave no more than just an "occasion to think," a certain intellectual stimulus, for the whole argument was made with the condition "unless the Church had determined the contrary."[30] The next stage again included: "Afterward, seeing that the Church that had determined this was certainly Thomistic, that is, Aristotelian—I was emboldened."[31] And with that, the downfall of church authority was in sight, and thereby transubstantiation as a binding dogma fell (in *To the Christian Nobility*). The third phase emerges in and with the *[Babylonian] Captivity*: "And I, being stuck between knife and victim,* nevertheless fortified my conscience in my previous opinion";[32] that is, Luther finally achieved clarity and confesses that the substance of the bread remains ("my previous opinion") and even denies the content of transubstantiation. When Seeberg dates the break with transubstantiation to this writing, he is right only if the break is understood as the positive expression of an opposing view.[33]

It is still true that Luther considers both his own view and that of the opponents as within the possible theologoumena of the same Church: "And so I permit whoever wishes to hold either opinion."[34] Even after Luther went over to the Bohemians' doctrine, he maintains the possibility of a peaceful coexistence of both views concerning the reality of the substance of the bread after the consecration. As a preamble to the description of Luther's further development, it may be appropriate here to remember that this tolerance does not mean as much broad-mindedness as it might seem when one first encounters the expression. If both statements are granted the same position within the Church, the Church has not bound itself to more than what Luther says: that Christ's body is present. Luther's doctrine thus is dogma. The opponents must give up the "*Firmiter*" decree [of the Fourth Lateran Council], on which rested the stance

---

Romani" [cf. AE 36:24]). "Notice that Luther no longer says 'we Romans' as he did half a year earlier."

29 WA 6:508.3 [cf. AE 36:28].

30 WA 6:508.11 [cf. AE 36:29].

31 WA 6:508.11f. [cf. AE 36:29].

32 WA 6:508.13f. [cf. AE 36:29].

* [Translator's note: Or "between the devil and the deep blue sea." *Inter saxum et sacrum*. AE has "after floating in a sea of doubt."]

33 Seeberg, op. cit., 4/1:399.

34 WA 6:508.27 [cf. AE 36:30].

of church law on transubstantiation, and they must grant that transformation of substance is a separate supposition. Even the adherents of transubstantiation would thereby be forced *de facto* to accept Luther's latter thesis: "Indeed, no one doubts that God can transubstantiate the bread, but they cannot show that He does so."[35] This statement—"And so I permit whoever wishes to hold either opinion"—is the result of something that, on the surface, is tolerant.

Luther offers a *biblically* based reasoning for [the idea of] the substance remaining in the host: "So meanwhile I understand it [the idea of the substance remaining in the host] to honor God's words. I will not allow human poor reasoning to do violence to them [God's words], nor will I let them be twisted to strange meanings."[36] The Bible speaks unequivocally about "bread," and this may not be denied. At the same time, Luther tempers himself with the words "so *meanwhile* I understand it thus"; this opinion, maintained "*for the meanwhile*," also gets this appendix: "Nevertheless, I permit others to follow a different opinion." There is an ambiguity here. Luther's own formulation demands taking a *definitive* stance. What is said to be biblical doctrine cannot *in the long run* tolerate its opposite, even less since Luther's tolerance actually was only seeming [tolerance].

This "*for-the-meanwhile*" tension between "I do not allow" and "I permit" in the [*Babylonian*] *Captivity* is settled in *Against Henry, King of England*, which follows it. Against Henry VIII of England who attacked the [*Babylonian*] *Captivity*, he says,

> . . . Now I change and wish my opinion to be transubstantiated, and I say: Before, I could not at all propose that you should think this way or that way about the transubstantiation; now, however, after seeing the reasons and beautiful arguments of the champion of the Sacraments, I decree that it is impious and blasphemous if anyone says that the bread is transubstantiated, but catholic and pious if one says with Paul: The bread that we break is the body of Christ. Let him be anathema who would say otherwise and would change a jot or tittle, even if it is Lord Henry, a new and extraordinary Thomist.[37]

Now transubstantiation is excluded as a possible alternative. This change in Luther's viewpoint occurs "after seeing the reasons and arguments"—thus since Henry, in order to prove his thesis, partly was forced to assume that Scripture was ambiguous, so that Paul's words about "bread" did not need to be taken literally,[38] [and] partly asserted that God could not be united with His unworthy creation, and for that reason had to annihilate the substance of bread before the

---

35 WA 10/2:206.38f. [cf. AE 61:42].

36 WA 6:512.2ff. [cf. AE 36:35].

37 WA 10/2:208.28ff. [cf. AE 61:44].

38 WA 10/2:204.17ff. [cf. AE 61:39].

onset of the real presence.[39] In that way, Scripture's authority was revoked and God's Spirit could not be poured out into the hearts of the faithful ("so that I leave unmentioned the impious justifications").[40] Transubstantiation is rejected because the arguments *for* it imply these consequences. Wisløff has pointed out that the words about the blasphemous transubstantiation are lacking in the German edition of the document in question.[41] Here it simply says, "It doesn't matter to me; let each one hold [i.e., think] what he will."[42] This view has been inserted into the scheme that is set forth here. The German document is a popular edition, without claiming to be an academic exchange of views like the Latin version. That is why it issues the attacks on transubstantiation that are conditioned by considering it from a certain angle: "having seen the reasons and arguments." As shall be touched on further in the following, throughout his life Luther remains restrained in his attacks on transubstantiation when he speaks to laypeople. Their naive faith in transformation—which, objectively speaking, is nothing other than faith in the miracle of the presence, which Luther himself embraced—demanded caution in expression. The Latin text meanwhile also recognized this latitude. [Such latitude] was shown toward the teachers of the early church, such as Ambrose, who was rightly tolerated for his view[43] in contrast to "the Thomists; it is right for them to be ensnared and harassed with their lethargic dreams, as if it were an article of faith."[44] This early church teaching of transubstantiation obviously seems undeveloped and innocuous to Luther, just like the contemporary layman's belief in the transformation. Under no condition are we faced with a rejection of the type that Vajta depicts. The "godlessness" of the doctrine consists not in any tendency toward materialism, but in its disrespect for the unequivocal letter of Scripture. Nor did Luther's "faith in creation" require that the substance of the bread remain. It is not the Renaissance man's admiration of the "creatureliness" of the bread that Luther attacks, but he simply rejects Henry's *a priori* that the substance of the bread must necessarily disappear as a consequence of the Creator's majesty compared to creation. No modern kind of "systematic requirement" can be gained from the continued existence of the substance. One speculative, fundamental claim cannot yield to another without an examination of what is the biblically revealed truth.

What Luther's positive thesis includes must be left aside until the discussion of transubstantiation is followed to its final conclusion. In *The Adoration of the Sacrament of the Holy Body of Christ* from 1523, the transformation of substance

39 WA 10/2:207.23ff. [cf. AE 61:43].

40 WA 10/2:207.40 [cf. AE 61:43].

41 Wisløff, op. cit., p. 154 n. 5.

42 WA 10/2:247.17f.

43 WA 10/2:202.20f. [cf. AE 61:37].

44 WA 10/2:203.1f. [cf. AE 61:37].

is called an "error": "Yet not much is placed on this error as long as Christ's body and blood are left there along with the Word."[45] So, despite everything, the error of transubstantiation is an expression of faith in the real presence. Yet a battle must be waged against it on the basis of Scripture:

> But since they urge it so forcefully by their own sacrilege and without Scripture, we will simply maintain, against it and despite it, that true bread and wine remain there along with the body and blood of Christ, and we will gladly be chastised as heretics before such dream-Christians and plain sophists. For the *Euangelion* [Gospel] calls the Sacrament bread. . . . If it deceives us, we will risk it. [We will risk being deceived by the Gospel.][46]

The candidness against the doctrine of transubstantiation expressed in the midst of this critique is not an acceptance of it as a possible opinion, with the assumption that it is not valid as a dogma, but it is a judgment of it as being loathsome to Scripture. This would not be worth noting if it had not come to be emphasized by the Roman Church the way it was. When controversy is indeed warranted, it should proceed in the name of the Gospel; here the word *Euangelion* ["Gospel"] is understood as the written, Christian record of revelation, which demands compliance from Christians even in regard to the meaning of a single word of admittedly small significance.

In the *Great Confession* on the Supper from 1528, it says, "Now I have learned and taught up to now that such a battle is unnecessary and that there is no great power in whether it remains bread or not. Although I hold with Wycliffe that bread remains there, again I also hold with the sophists that the body of Christ is there."[47] The expression "such a battle" is aiming here, strictly speaking, not at the doctrine of transubstantiation itself but at the dispute mentioned in the previous section about "identical predication," according to which the linguistic rule of subject and complementary predicate in "This is My body" must be totally identical. This is disputed by Luther, who nevertheless finds the controversy relatively unimportant, even though he himself holds to the continued existence of the substance. The same verb of speaking ("hold" [*halten*]) is used with this affirmation as with faith in the real presence. That is why it does not make sense to say that transubstantiation was perceived by Luther as a theologoumenon. On the contrary, this writing insists that transubstantiation must be judged positively in contrast to the denial of the real presence by the Enthusiasts. Luther proceeds from a supposed objection by the Enthusiasts: "You yourself say that the wine remains in the new Supper,"[48] that is, the basis for the reasoning is that Luther's rejection of the transformation of substance is

45 WA 11:441.19f. [cf. AE 36:287].

46 WA 11:441.24ff. [cf. AE 36:287].

47 WA 26:439.26ff. [cf. AE 37:296].

48 WA 26:461.41f. [cf. AE 37:317].

known. It says later: "It does not concern me much, for as I have confessed often enough, no quarrel would matter to me: The wine may remain there or not. It is enough for me that Christ's blood is there. It can be however God wants it to be with the wine. And before I would have pure wine with the Enthusiasts, I would rather retain pure blood with the pope."[49] *Luther knows that he is only repeating here what he said many times before: that regardless of the lack of biblical support for transubstantiation, it is still in no way loathsome to him, and least of all is it to be equated with the denial of the real presence by the Enthusiasts.* No trace is to be found of the cabbage soup theory [AE 37:69], formulated by Vajta, who considered Luther's doctrine a *via media* between Roman materialism and Enthusiast spiritualism. Therewith also falls the widespread speculation that, in connection with Luther's supposed fundamental rejection of transubstantiation, set forth a systematic principle about the coexistence of the divine and human elements within Lutheran theology.

In the Smalcald Articles of 1537, transubstantiation is rejected with reference to Scripture: "For it fits best with Scripture that the bread is and remains there."[50] Thus, in the form of a confession, it is now taught that the substance of bread remains. Four years later, in connection with the religious colloquy at Regensburg, Luther expressed himself on transubstantiation in a letter to Prince George of Anhalt on May 25, 1541. Luther says that he had been moderate on this point in order not to be confused with those who deny the real presence: "But up to this point, because it first offended Wycliffe, I did not give attention to whether it was or not."[51] The silence thus was for pedagogical reasons. Since the papal side in Regensburg wanted to insist on this doctrine, Luther meanwhile [exhorted] Prince George definitely to oppose it: "But when they want to

49 WA 26:462.1ff. [cf. AE 37:317]. At the end of 1527, Luther published *Leonhard Kaiser in Bavaria, Burned for the Sake of the Gospel*, along with a preface he himself wrote for it. Facing the fire, Kaiser is said to have answered the question about the correctness of transubstantiation: "It is not for me to debate about things. I defer that to those who are very wise. For me it is enough that I firmly remain with the words of our Savior. It may remain bread, or it may be transformed; that doesn't concern me" (WA 23:459.32ff.). These words of Kaiser, who had been a student in Wittenberg for a year and a half (WA 23:445), deserve attention, especially since Luther must have been thought to have authorized their content by his preface and careful work on the publication (compare WA 23:446f.). [For Luther's preface and accompanying letters, see AE 59:194–202]. Bugenhagen presents very similar thoughts at the disputation in Flensburg 1529 (*Acta der Disputation zu Flensburg*, fol. FVIIIbf.): "They concerned themselves with *transsubstantion* [*sic*] and taught that in the Sacrament there was no longer bread or wine, which was not necessary to teach (we also do not argue about it), but they spoke with more reason and modesty in this point on the Sacrament than our Sacrament-blasphemers."

50 WA 50:243.7ff. [cf. SA III VI 5].

51 WA Br 9[:419].13ff., no. 3622.

insist on making it into an article of faith, that is not to be tolerated at all."[52] This means that Luther [did not see] the transformation of substance as a possible opinion but [rather as] an objectionable dogma. The only thing that matters is the didactic consideration of the protest's formulation and its suitability in different situations, which clearly comes from Luther's letter, June 11 [12] the same year, to Prince George and his brother Prince John, where transubstantiation is discussed among the "impure" points of doctrine, concerning which one must preach "how they are wrong and to be discarded or avoided."[53] The kind of tolerance that is allowed, nevertheless, is of a different kind than being able to tolerate in the meantime the various disputed "opinions" of the doctrinal schools within the framework of general obedience to the institution of the Church. Luther imagines an eventual church body where transubstantiation together with certain other doctrines did not need to be expressly rejected in the beginning, whereby those who are weak in faith would be able to be led "in time" to a correct view. This action toward weak brothers according to the apostle's words "receive one who is weak in faith" presupposes, however, that since the opposition confesses the main points about original sin, justification, free will, faith and works,[54] no written or otherwise formal agreement *liberates* the rest of the parts to "everlasting tolerance,"[55] which would invalidate the arrangement's pastoral and interim character: "So if the tolerance of an everlasting harshness were advised among you, as I had touched on before, then your people who might still be weak would never become strong."[56] The actual doctrinal situation in such a church would thus be completely governed by clear Lutheran doctrine in all points, and there would be no ambiguity about who is "strong" as opposed to "weak." The strong would teach the weak, who would not have the right to make their "weakness" into "doctrine." To this religious colloquy belongs a "dinner speech" on transubstantiation in which he, as an educated medieval theologian, presents the various opinions that have arisen about this article, the rejection of what is called "worthless fiction."[57]

Besides these rejections of transubstantiation as fundamentally a theologoumenon, there are further expressions of a more positive character in Luther at this time. In a letter to the Hungarian Count Franz Réway from 1538, he says,

> Concerning the trans-elementation of the substance of the bread, there is no quarrel, for it is not dangerous to salvation if you hold that the bread

52 WA Br 9[:419].15f., no. 3622.

53 WA Br 9[:439].58, no. 3629A.

54 WA Br 9:434.

55 WA Br 9[:439].74, no. 3629A. The letter was corrected before it was sent, in another version, B.

56 WA Br 9[:442].90ff., no. 3629B.

57 WA Br 9[:444].33, no. 3629, Appendix.

> and wine remain, just as we hold. Nevertheless, just as we hold at the same time that the bread is truly the body of Christ, which we receive invisibly in the Sacrament, so also the wine truly is the blood of Christ poured out for us. But those men also seem to have invented transubstantiation so that they could teach coarsely and plainly to the uneducated that the true body of Christ and no other substance is in the Sacrament. For the substance of the bread perhaps prevented them from being able to teach that the true body of Christ is there. But it is not necessary to do away with the bread, just as you might teach that there is fire in red-hot iron. . . .[58]

Previously, transubstantiation had been perceived as a product of lofty Thomistic speculation,[59] but now it is presented as a robust and almost commendable attempt to give a simple explanation that what was once bread has become the body of Christ through the consecration. The explanation hereby introduced an unnecessary factor and, if it were removed, that would not at all invalidate the statement "that Christ's true body is there." This open posture occurs again in Luther's letter to the Venetians from 1543: "We reject the useless and sophistic disputation concerning transubstantiation, without any delay, whether anyone believes it otherwise or not."[60] After he rejected the framework of scholastic disputations, he expressed a basic indifference toward the very idea of a total transformation.[61] What these two later remarks have in common is that they occurred in letters, which in a simple and summary way intended to state Luther's doctrine of the Sacrament for distant and foreign laymen who made inquiries. Here Luther seems to be aware that for a layman's faith the expression "transubstantiation" often became synonymous with real presence, and therefore in this context it should not be attacked indiscriminately. *What conveyed the content of Christ's Words of Institution "coarsely and plainly to the uneducated" was not subjected to the criticism that is expressed on the higher level required in dogmatic polemics against the Roman theologians. This observation is confirmed in an otherwise overlooked circumstance, namely, that in his sermons, which are rich with dogmatic statements, Luther nowhere attacks the transformation of substance.* The background for this had already found its formulation in the *Babylonian Captivity*:

> Perhaps they will say that the danger of idolatry urges [the thought] that it is not truly bread and wine. This is very silly, since the laypeople never knew the subtle philosophy about substance and accidence, nor can they

58 WA Br 8[:297].38ff., no. 3263.

59 Compare above, p. 114, text around n. 153 and following [Swedish edition, pp. 107ff.].

60 WA Br 10[:331].84ff., no. 3885. The remark evoked Melanchthon's resentment and consternation; compare WA Br 10:333 n. 36.

61 Compare Gollwitzer, op. cit., p. 80: "The doctrine of transubstantiation emancipates." But Gollwitzer does not analyze the place of this viewpoint within Luther's world of thought.

> grasp it if they are taught, and the danger is the same in the accidences, which remain and which they see, as in the substance, which they do not see. For if they do not adore the accidence but the Christ hidden there, why would they adore bread, which they do not see?[62]
>
> And clearly I rejoice that the simple faith in this Sacrament remains, at least among the common people. For as they do not understand, so they do not argue about whether the accidences are there without the substance, but in simple faith they believe the body of Christ is truly contained there; the business of arguing about what contains it is deferred to people of leisure [who have nothing else to do].[63]

Here in express words this verifies [Erwin] Iserloh's view about identifying the Nominalistic doctrine of the Sacrament with popular piety.[64] Luther appeals to medieval church people's simple faith in the miracle of the Mass, and he has undivided joy at their simplicity, which could plainly understand from the distinctions of the scholars that what is seen is bread and what is not seen under the form of bread is Christ, hidden and worthy of adoration. Untroubled by useless subtleties, those who attended Mass in the Middle Ages believed in "transubstantiation," adored Jesus in the host, and thus embraced the faith in the real presence, which Luther himself had. Therefore, what Luther says within earshot of such people about the permissibility of transubstantiation falls outside the alternatives of theologoumenon or heresy. What matters is to present this in a pastorally motivated way.

There is a final statement about transubstantiation in *Against the Thirty-Two Articles of the Louvain Theologians* from 1545. Here we are met with a settlement on the very concept of theologoumenon outside Luther's central descriptions of faith. The same phenomenon will be found in a later chapter with the discussion of the validity of the private Mass. Luther writes: "I. Whatever is taught in the Church without the Word is a lie and impiety. II. If it is set up as an article of faith, it is impiety and heresy."[65] Luther's German translation [reads]: "I. Everything that one teaches in the Church (which is God's people) without God's Word is certainly untruthful and un-Christian. II. And where one presents such as an article of faith is not only un-Christian but even heretical and devilish."[66] In the German version there is an enlightening extra thesis, without a corresponding one in the Latin: "V. And where God's Word is not [present], there can be no faith, since even good works are nothing where they are not done with faith

62 WA 6:509.35ff. [cf. AE 36:31f.].

63 WA 6:510.20ff. [cf. AE 36:32].

64 Compare above, pp. 3–4, text around n. 12 [Swedish edition, p. 11].

65 WA 54:425.1ff. [cf. AE 34:354].

66 WA 54:430.20ff. [cf. AE 34:354].

in God's Word."[67] The thought in this presentation is that there is a distinction between undogmatized (I) and dogmatized (II) false doctrine, which does not coincide with the distinction that is usually made between a theologoumenon and a teaching that is not objectionable until it is taught as dogma. Only dogmatized false doctrine is actually called "heresy," but even an opinion that is simply and plainly presented "without the Word" is an *un-Christian lie*, for without God's Word there is no faith. (V) Through this situation, the Christian theologian is prevented from holding his "opinions" alongside an obligatory dogma. Where the Word does not speak, he must be silent, and whatever else he presents "is certainly untruthful and un-Christian." Article XVIII on transubstantiation is seen in light of this introductory presentation, where it says, "XVIII. The transubstantiation of the bread and wine is taught without cause, even without the Word, by mere vanity of the teacherlings."[68] "XIX. It is not necessary and there is no reason that one should believe the knaves at Louvain to teach us that bread and wine are transformed and lose their natural substance."[69] In its context, this means that transubstantiation already as an offered opinion is a judgment by a Scripture-less theologian who is thinking outside the Word and therefore without faith. Again, without faith even a materially good work is not good, and therefore transubstantiation, already as an *opinion*, becomes a "lie and impiety." These are, of course, corollaries of faith in the Word as the only criterion for piety. The alternative "theologoumenon" is fundamentally impossible. In summary, it can be said that the judgment made by Sasse and Wisløff thus seems to have the greatest support in the sources. The opinion maintained by Sommerlath, Diestelmann, and Holte presents only a certain aspect of Luther's stance and must be supplemented in order to be correct, but still it has some justification in a briefer and limited presentation, in contrast to the view formulated by Vajta and generally prevalent in Protestantism.

The real contours of this problem are depicted most easily against the background of the idea Luther wants to put in place of transubstantiation. The research, of course, had no difficulty establishing unanimously that Luther teaches an actual real presence with the continued existence of the substances of the bread and wine. One then proceeds from the problem with the transformed, as opposed to untransformed, substance of the bread and finds that, for Luther, Christ's body is present not only under the accidence of the bread but also under the form of its substance. This is correct, of course, but [it] does not elaborate Luther's expressions in their full meaning. The central question here for Luther is of a more specific nature, oriented according to the literally composed Word of Scripture.

67 WA 54:431.4ff.

68 WA 54:426.22f. [cf. AE 34:355].

69 WA 54:432.13ff. [cf. AE 34:355].

Already in the [*Babylonian*] *Captivity*, Luther's positive belief in the Sacrament is repeated. He examines what the word "this" points to in [the phrase] "This is My body." Scholasticism's answer had been that "this," of course, points to—"My body." That is based on this statement:

> From Aristotle we learn that in an affirmative proposition subject and predicate must be identical, or, to set down the monster's own words in the sixth book of his *Metaphysics*: "An affirmative proposition demands the agreement of subject and predicate," which they interpret as above. Hence, when it is said, "This is My body," the subject cannot be identical with the bread but must be identical with the body of Christ.[70]

These words of Aristotle mean that since "is" must mean only "is," the subject and predicate complement ("*praedicatum*") must be *identical*. "This" must refer to Christ's body, and Jesus' words mean: "My body is My body." Luther's challenge of this philosophically schooled exegesis leads him to a statement whose character, startling for the time, is ignored by modern researchers. Luther lets the demonstrative "this" point to the *bread* and writes: "Simply sticking to His words, I firmly believe not only that the body of Christ is in the bread but [also] that the bread is the body of Christ."[71] Those last words "*that the bread is the body of Christ*" trump scholastic theology on a decisive point. It is no longer a matter of one mode or another connecting a presence of Christ's body to the host, nor giving expression to a presence of something in something else. Luther says instead that the earthly bread actually *is* Christ's body. The parallel that is drawn is daring:

> Therefore, just as the thing is considered in [the person of] Christ, so also in the Sacrament. For it is not necessary for the human nature to be transubstantiated in order for the divinity to dwell in Him bodily, so that the divinity might be held under the accidence of the human nature. But, with each nature intact, it is right to say: "This man is God; this God is man." Even if philosophy does not grasp it, nevertheless faith does.[72]

One ought not to summarize this parallel of Luther's in such a way that just as there are two unchanged natures in Christ, so there can also be two unchanged substances in the Sacrament. Such a reading proceeds from a different Christology than Luther's and overlooks what is essential. For Luther, the decisive thing is the personal union that makes it possible for "is" to unite two dissimilar substantives ("The man is God"). That is what makes the parallel to the words of the Sacrament: "the bread is the body." This meaning of "this,"

---

70 WA 6:510.25ff. [cf. AE 36:33]. [The translation here is based on Henry Eyster Jacobs and Adolph Spaeth, *Works of Martin Luther* (Philadelphia: Holman, 1915), 2:192. NB: The note in AE gives a corrected reference for Aristotle.]

71 WA 6:511.19ff. [cf. AE 36:34].

72 WA 6:511.34ff. [cf. AE 36:35].

which points to the bread, comes from "the usage of language and common sense": "The subject, of course, indicates the bread and not the body, while He says '*Hoc est corpus meum*, This is My body,' that is, 'This bread is My body.'"[73] Thus it is natural to put together the "this" and the "bread," since the texts have Christ taking only "bread" in His hands and saying about this tangible bread: "This (that is, this bread which He had taken and broken) is My body. And Paul says: 'Is not the bread which we break the communion of the body of Christ?'" The opponents' talk about "this" [*hoc*] as a neuter having to point to the neuter "body" [*corpus*] and not to the masculine "bread" [*panis*] is rejected by pointing out that that does not extend to the Hebrew, but also by referring to common use of language that allows expressions like this. (Luther thus thinks that one can very well say: "This [*detta*, neuter] is my son," not only "This one [*denne*, masculine] is my son.") "The Holy Spirit is greater than Aristotle";[74] this implies not only an appeal to a pneumatic [spiritual] grammar, available only to those gifted by the Spirit, but an exegetical thesis of the distinction between regular biblical form of language and a narrow artificial scholarly grammar that expounds the biblical texts according to a constructed template.[75] This way of teaching language lays hands on the biblical text: "Therefore a new application of the words

73 WA 6:511.30ff. [cf. AE 36:34f.].

74 WA 6:511.26 [cf. AE 36:34].

75 Althaus (*Die Theologie Martin Luthers*, p. 324) writes about Luther's exegesis of the Supper: "Not only the text and not only the thing made up his mind." This statement gives the impression of being *intermediary* between two alternatives, but it actually only summarizes the one *alternative*: that Luther's exegesis happened by going back not only to the text but also to internal enlightenment concurrent with it, which arises from the gifts of the righteousness of faith. (No researcher could defend the thought of Luther's exposition of the Bible as completely without conscious connection to the text!) The citations by Althaus for the thesis of Luther's pneumatic non-grammatical hermeneutical principle are misinterpretations. Luther's opposition to Karlstadt: "It must all be somewhat higher than grammatical rules" (WA 18:157.23f. [cf. AE 40:167]) is a challenge, quite similar to the one above, of Karlstadt's use of classical rules of language according to the model grammarian Donatus for the benefit of New Testament grammar with its irregularities, thus an assertion of a linguistic principle. Just as in the [*Babylonian*] *Captivity*, what matters is the controversy: "Why I cannot say, 'It man' [*Das man*], and yet say, 'It is the man' [*Das ist der man*]" (WA 18:155.1f. [cf. AE 40:165]). WA 18:195.23 [cf. AE 40:205] and 18:203.3 [cf. AE 40:213], cited from Althaus (op. cit., p. 331), in no way deduce the real presence from the righteousness of faith, so that the absence of real presence would mean one's own righteousness. Real presence is not even a topic for these expositions without Karlstadt's *concept of memorial*, which is found to be similar to that of *Rome* ("as up to now timid consciences faced the Sacrament," WA 18:195.28f. [cf. AE 40:206]). False memorial is too easily combined with the real presence, that is, false righteousness is compatible systematically with a correct exegesis of the Words of Institution. Therefore, one cannot necessarily deduce here any dependence of the real presence on righteousness of faith. In Swedish literature, Althaus's argument is repeated in Ingebrand, *Olaus Petris reformatoriska åskådning*, pp. 334f.

is also absurd, that the 'bread' is taken to mean the 'form or accidence of bread,' 'wine' to mean the 'form or accidence of wine.' "[76] Everything should be taken "in the simplest meaning," "unless obvious circumstances urge that it be taken outside the usual grammar, lest the adversaries be given opportunity to elude all of Scripture."[77] Deviation from the literal meaning leads to Origen's heresy, since he degenerated into a symbolic interpretation of the creation account.[78] This simple, everyday interpretation of the words leads to the statement not heard up to that time: *that the bread is the body of Christ.*[79] It directly says of the ordinary substance that it *is* God's body. The parallel to Christology points here to a sacramental iteration of the incarnation. A divinizing of the bread seems close by, since Luther uses the picture of glowing iron: "Behold, fire and iron, two substances, are thus mixed together in red-hot iron, so that every part is iron and fire: why is it not even more possible that the glorious body of Christ is in every part of the substance of the bread?"[80]

The scholastic condemnation of these daring theses was not long in coming. In the Sorbonne's condemnation of the [*Babylonian*] *Captivity*, it says, "X. 'I *believe* firmly that the bread is the body of Christ,' says Luther. This naivete of Luther is absurd and immediately condemned."[81] What they thought

76 WA 6:509.22ff. [cf. AE 36:31].

77 WA 6:509.10ff. [cf. AE 36:30].

78 WA 6:509.13ff. [cf. AE 36:30]. Compare also WA 23:91.10ff. [cf. AE 37:31] and WA 26:406.20ff. [cf. AE 37:272], where the literal interpretation of Genesis 1 is set alongside the literal interpretation of the Words of Institution, all according to the thesis: "Whoever lies about God in one word and blasphemes, or says that it is insignificant that he has blasphemed and lied, he blasphemes against the whole God and has little regard for any blasphemy of God" (WA 23:85.1ff. [cf. AE 37:26]). The obvious basis for such statements is naturally an expressly concrete doctrine of verbal inspiration, which can be confirmed in Luther's writings by any unprejudiced reader. It ought to be noted that in the question of the creation account, Luther proceeds from the fact that it is disputed by non-Christian science and philosophy (WA 23:91.11f. [cf. AE 37:31]).

79 Dieckhoff (op. cit., p. 256) understands Luther's meaning without emphasizing its uniqueness and sees it merely as a passing phase: "The core of this view at that time is that the *bread*, ceasing to exist without its natural essence, *is* the body of Christ"; on the other hand, in the larger sacramental writings, this applies (op. cit., p. 408): "So now if there is a thought of a substantial union between bread and the body of Christ, it would be excluded by Luther as impanation or consubstantiation." (Dieckhoff uses the two latter terms to depict Luther's view, referred to above.) The same opinion is presented by Mücke, "Luthers Abendmahlslehre bis 1522 im Zusammenhang mit seiner reformatorischen Entwicklung und mit der Abendmahlslehre der Scholastik," p. 475n; Gollwitzer, op. cit., p. 40.

80 WA 6:510.5ff. [cf. AE 36:32].

81 CR 1:373.

they were seeing was a revival of the doctrine of *impanation*.[82] The absurdity is actually not the continued existence of the substance of the bread but its divinization, just as Henry VIII clearly says, "Unless perhaps Luther imagines a new person for us, so that in some way God has taken up man, so that God and man take up the bread and wine; if he believes that, then I think that among all who are not heretics he will be considered a heretic."[83] "It is unthinkable that a created substance could be mixed with the Creator's body."[84] Henry thereby rightly saw that Luther not only teaches that Christ's body is in the bread but also that the bread *is* Christ's body. In his reply to Henry's attack, Luther further develops his argumentation that builds on the parallel of incarnation/impanation. "The substance is unworthy; therefore, it cannot [be] mixed with something worthier. . . . Let us therefore conclude for the Thomistic authors that God is not man because human substance is unworthy to be joined to the worthiness of such majesty."[85] If the host and Christ's body cannot be "combined" (*misceri*), then the possibility of the incarnation is overthrown.

> And so I can say that Christ's body thus is in the Sacrament, with the bread preserved, just as fire is in the iron in the preserved substance of the iron, and God is in man with the humanity preserved; in both cases thus with combined substances, so that each one retains its own effect and proper nature, and yet [together] they constitute one particular thing [*unum aliquod*].[86]

A "single thing" [*unum*] has been created in the Sacrament, a unity of the hypostatic-union type. This unity allows the statement "The bread is the body" just as "The man is God." The doctrine of transubstantiation's intent of letting Christ's heavenly enthronement remain undisturbed by the onset of the sacramental presence seems to be replaced by a continually repeated incarnation, which displaces what is unique in the taking on of humanity and makes bread and wine into divine things. Jesus is continually impanated on the Church's altars, a statement that is "heretical and immediately condemned."[87]

---

82 For the meaning of the term during the Reformation, compare below, p. 151, text around n. 117 [Swedish edition, pp. 140f.]. The medieval term is described by Sasse, op. cit., pp. 33, 38, 57, 124; Seeberg, op. cit., 3:214f.; Rocholl, op. cit., pp. 294ff. Only Rocholl emphasizes the actual offense in the doctrine: its implication of a continuing incarnation.

83 Henry VIII, *Assertio septem sacramentorum adversus Martinum Lutherum, aedita ab invictissimo Angliae & Franciae rege, & do. Hyberniae Henrico eius nominis octavo*, p. 41.

84 Id., p. 40.

85 WA 10/2:207.36ff. [cf. AE 61:43].

86 WA 10/2:207.12ff. [cf. AE 61:42].

87 Mücke (op. cit., p. 475n) here interprets Luther as *close* to transubstantiation: "Since he teaches a reciprocal communication of the essential characteristics of the bread and the

Meanwhile, what this view of Luther includes as opposed to what it does not include, Luther himself clearly laid out in the chapter "On Identical Predication" in his *Great Confession* of the Supper [AE 37:294–303]. *Here the very same thing is developed as was said already in 1520–22.*[88] Luther acknowledges here that an "identical predication of different natures," of the type "Paul is a stone," is impossible if the word "stone" is not taken in a transferred sense. Reason then applies this rule to the Sacrament with the familiar result: either the bread or Christ's body must yield, just as it is with Rome or Wycliffe. Luther again does not acknowledge this application: "And so against all reason and keen logic I hold that two different essences may be [one essence] and may be called one essence."[89] The reason for this simultaneous acknowledgment and nonacknowledgment of the impossibility of identical predication of different natures is that the rules that usually apply can be revoked both in Scripture and in daily speech. Within theology, the identical predication of different natures is made when the three divine persons are said to make up one essence. This identical predication of different natures isn't made possible by somehow denying the unity of the divine essence or the distinction of the persons. Compared to the statement

---

body of Christ, he comes so close to transubstantiation that the substance of the bread seems to remain only as accidence to the substantizing subject of the body of Christ." The thought is that the doctrine of transubstantiation's definition of the relationship between the accidence of the bread and the substance of Christ's body would mean a *state of union* that directly contradicts the structure of this doctrine and the caveats that on the basis of the doctrine of transubstantiation were directed against Luther's "one thing" [*unum aliquod*]. *Luther does not say less than transubstantiation does, but [he] surpasses it in realism and tangibility.* The assertion that Luther's view referenced above is similar to transubstantiation is repeated also in Gollwitzer, op. cit., p. 40.

88 Compare what was cited above, p. 141 n. 79, about the assertion by earlier research of a contradiction between the early view and the great sacramental writings.

89 WA 26:439.29ff. [cf. AE 37:296]. Metzke (op. cit., p. 38) writes: "The kind of mental energy Luther uses to pursue the questions arising here (far beyond the measure needed for practical usefulness) is characteristic of what is in his *Great Confession* of 1528, a particular section with the title 'On Identical Predication.'" Metzke's "measure needed for practical usefulness" is obviously justification through faith as the normative principle for the interpretation of Scripture. Compare here WA 30/2:601.7ff. [cf. AE 38.104]:

> And if it were such a poor Sacrament that would be neither beneficial nor necessary and would give us neither grace nor help, but were only a single commandment and law of God, which He demands that we use it by its divine power, to which we are duty bound to be subject and obedient, then for the sake of the commandment alone it should drive and incite us enough not to despise it nor consider it unnecessary or lowly, but diligently to use it and highly honor it with all sincerity and faithful obedience, since nothing can be greater and more glorious than what God commands and orders through His Word.

Plain obedience to God is reason enough to keep ourselves busy with the Sacrament.

"wood is stone," the dogma of the Trinity is even "more irrational," "for indeed wood in itself does not have a unique essence as does the Deity, and again wood and stone are not as definitely and clearly distinct as the persons are."[90] The unity in God is greater than the unity of wood; the distinction of persons in the Deity is greater than the distinction between two materials. The contradiction is not solved by any component being undermined. Nevertheless, what matters here is the identical predication of different natures. That is likewise what matters concerning the natures in Christ.[91] "There we have two unions, a natural one and a personal one, which teaches us that identical predication is not against Scripture, so that two different essences are called one essence."[92] There is talk about the *communicatio idiomatum; it does not follow from this that in order to fulfill the parallel, the bread must take up a communication of attributes according to the* genus maiestaticum, *since, as already presented, Luther distinguishes what is later called the* genus idiomaticum *and the* genus maiestaticum.[93] Likewise, Scripture says, "He makes His angels into wind and flame, just as He makes His body into bread."[94] This union, with regard to the union of the effect or deed, is called "an 'union of effect' [*wirkliche einigkeit*] because the angel and his form perform one kind of work."[95] This way of speaking makes it possible for the corporeal revealed form of the incorporeal angels to be described with the word "angel," and that thus an angel is said to be "seen" and "heard," though angels, in principle, remain invisible and inaudible. Concerning this it is important: "Now, though, here clever Wycliffe and the sophists would appeal to 'identical predication,' [the idea] that two different essences cannot be one thing, nor can

90 WA 26:440.25ff. [cf. AE 37:297]. Grass (op. cit., p. 123) here criticizes Luther's example: "since there is no direct original essential distinction in the Trinity, and no 'becoming one' [*Einswerden*], but rather the divine essence is unfolded in three persons." The criticism overlooks that fact that Luther is not speaking about "union" in the Sacrament as a *process* in which two entities are united. He is thinking instead of the [united] *condition* that exists between two united entities; that is why he can properly equate "bread = body," "1 = 3," "essence = person." Grass's thoughts about how there was no unity of the triad, but indeed that an "unfolding" of the unity occurred in the Trinity, does not identify with the historically given dogma of the Trinity that Luther embraces.

91 WA 26:440.34ff. [cf. AE 37:297].

92 WA 26:441.9ff. [cf. AE 37:297].

93 Compare above, pp. 40–41, paragraph following n. 24 [Swedish edition, pp. 61f.]. Grass (op. cit., p. 123) cites this critique. Since Luther's contemporary opponents did not embrace the *genus maiestaticum*, their criticism must be seen only to mean that they are accusing Luther of expanding the *genus idiomaticum*. Since, of course, it was not thought that Luther dogmatized an indissoluble sacramental union, corresponding to the unique character of the personal union and built on the ontological concept of person, it is not a full and complete parallel to the incarnation.

94 WA 26:441.15f. [cf. AE 37:298].

95 WA 26:441.27f. [cf. AE 37:298].

one be called the other, but either the mere form without the angel must remain, as Wycliffe wants, or pure angel without the form, as the sophists want."[96] When Luther here turns *against* identical predication, this is a denial of *the scholastic proposition* that identical predication is impossible. Luther thus uses identical predication (of different natures) in both positive and negative meaning: identical predication itself is an essential possibility for him; the scholastic rules about its impossibility are rejected.

Luther gives a final illustrative example with the dove that descends on Christ in the Jordan. The Holy Spirit here enters into a "formal union" with the dove, "since the Holy Spirit wanted to reveal Himself in such a form. And here Scripture clearly says that whoever sees such a dove sees the Holy Spirit, as John 1 says, 'Upon whom you will see the Spirit descend and rest upon Him,' etc. Why, then, should one not much more also say in the Supper: 'This is My body,' though bread and body are two different essences, and shouldn't such a 'this' refer to the bread?"[97] The sum of this reasoning is that one can point to the man Jesus, the flame, or the dove, and say, "This" is God, an angel, the Spirit.

> Therefore, when one points to the bread, it is certainly right to say, "This is Christ's body," and whoever sees the bread sees the body of Christ, just as John says that he saw the Holy Spirit when he saw the dove, as is fitting. Thus it is also right to say, "Whoever grasps this bread grasps Christ's body, and whoever eats this bread eats Christ's body; whoever crushes this bread with his teeth or tongue crushes the body of Christ with his teeth or tongue."[98]

Therefore, when Luther accepts Berengar's confession ("tearing the true body of Christ with his teeth"), this is not a statement about what happens to the body of Christ in and of itself, which, of course, cannot be torn apart ("and yet it always remains true that no one sees, grasps, eats, or chews the body of Christ the way one visibly sees and chews other flesh"),[99] but [one sees, grasps, eats, or chews] the bread, which is Christ's body and which is torn apart.[100] [101]

---

96 WA 26:441.35ff. [cf. AE 37:299].

97 WA 26:442.17ff. [cf. AE 37:299f.].

98 WA 26:442.29ff. [cf. AE 37:300].

99 WA 26:442.35ff. [cf. AE 37:300].

100 [The Swedish edition numbers footnotes up to 99, then restarts at 1, which this translation lists as 101, etc.]

101 Krauth (op. cit., p. 758) writes correctly: "It is very clear that Luther is availing himself, in this line of thought, of the distinction made in the doctrine of the person of Christ. That is affirmed of the body of Christ in the *sacramental concrete* which is denied of it in the *natural abstract*. The consecrated bread is so far *sacramentally identified* with this body, of which it is the Communion, that in a *sacramental sense* that can be affirmed of this body which is not true of it in a *natural* sense. So in Christ Jesus

Luther's medieval opponents fell victim to "inopportune logic," which does not correspond to "grammar or rhetoric," concerning which, however, this applies: that "in all languages, speaking teaches this: That where two different essences come into one essence, two such essences are embraced there in one expression."[102] "For indeed it is also true that such different natures come together into one; there really is a new single essence from such joining, according to which they are rightly and truly called one essence."[103] While preserving the "different natures," a new essence arises, which embraces both components in a new "one" [*unum*].

This putting together of two essences into one is also in colloquial synecdoche:

> Such ways of speaking about different essences as one the grammarians call "synecdoche," and it is quite common not only in Scripture but also in all languages, as when I point to or hold out a sack or bag and I say, "This is a hundred gulden." The designation and little word "this" applies to the bag, but since the bag and the gulden are in a certain sense one essence, like a lump, it also applies to the gulden at the same time.[104]

---

we can say, speaking in the *personal concrete*, God bled, God died; that is, such is the personal concrete that we can 'rightly and truly' make personal affirmation in words."

102 WA 26:443.14ff. [cf. AE 37:301].

103 WA 26:443.29ff. [cf. AE 37:301]. What is cited above about the identical predication includes a stance in a scholarly controversy about "identical predication" in Luther. In "Luthers Abendmahlslehre" (p. 36), Althaus found identical predication to be Luther's own thesis, while Gollwitzer (op. cit., p. 40 n. 5) rejects Althaus's opinion: "It is noteworthy that Althaus (among other places, p. 49 [should be 36]) considers identical predication as a typical Lutheran issue." Pedersen (op. cit., p. 392 n. 219) takes this stance on the problem: "One must distance oneself from Althaus when he wants to find a typical Lutheran issue in identical predication, a particularly 'Lutheran principle'"; but "one must concede to Althaus that, *against* the logical rule being discussed [which forbids identical predication], Luther asserts that bread can be body." "Meanwhile, after having applied this, Luther asserts that his understanding of the Supper expresses only what *appears* to be a logical absurdity," that is, "Luther of course acknowledges this technical rule of logic, and it is his task in the pertinent section of *On Christ's Supper* to show that he does not violate it in his interpretation of the Words of the Supper." According to this opinion, which was presented above, *Althaus is right: identical predication is a thesis of Luther's.* Pedersen is correct, insofar as Luther affirms the scholastic prohibition against identical predication of different natures in its simplest understanding (WA 26:443.12ff. [cf. AE 37:301]: "Logic teaches correctly, bread and body, dove and Spirit, God and man are different natures"), so that the copula ["is"] cannot make them physically identical, which would make the expression meaningless, but Pedersen does not realize that in the actual Supper controversy Luther will actually allow identical predication to be used against "the pointed logic" but in accordance with "correct logic." Neuser (op. cit., p. 376 n. 363) asserts correctly that Luther teaches identical predication, but [he] cannot explain in what sense the term is rejected, with the result that artificial explanations follow; compare below, p. 148 n. 107.

104 WA 26:444.1ff. [cf. AE 37:301f.].

Luther continues by listing similar cases: a barrel of wine, a glass of water, a red-hot iron. Luther's way of thinking is that *"This is a hundred gulden" is a statement about the moneybag, not first and foremost about the contents.* By its contents the moneybag has been elevated to something other than "plain leather or pouch";[105] it has become "a gold-leather or a moneybag."[106] The psychological

---

105 WA 26:444.30 [cf. AE 37:302].

106 WA 26:444.31 [cf. AE 37:302]. Dieckhoff (op. cit., p. 407) and his follower Gollwitzer (op. cit., p. 41) are mistaken when they assert that the totality of Christ's body and the bread [considered together] is the closest object for the word "this." They probably go from WA 18:187.16f. [cf. AE 40:197]: "So it is called synecdoche, that is, when it names a whole thing and yet means only a part." Luther here seems to set this form of language in contrast to his earlier presentation of the red-hot iron ("*ferruminatio*"), and now he would offer an alternative, "where he does not like this kind of speaking" (WA 18:187.14 [cf. AE 40:197]). It is probably from this that the view arose that the earlier red-hot iron and the later synecdoche offer two *different* ways of understanding the Words of Institution; compare above, p. 141 n. 79. But what is cited about synecdoche from WA 26:444.16f. [cf. AE 37:302] gives occasion to question this contrast: "Here also belongs my analogy of red-hot iron taken from St. Augustine." Red-hot iron thus is a part of the synecdoche and not an alternative to it. Here one must take into consideration the structure of Luther's reasoning. The basis for identical predication (A = B) is the origin of the newly formed unity AB (fire-iron, blood-wine). Since AB = B, then A = B must also be true, according to Luther's thinking. The basis is expressed differently for statements "part from part" [*pars de parte*], the proposition "whole from the part" [*totum de parte*]. Since the God-man (AB) is man (B), God (A) is man (B). Since bread-flesh (AB) is flesh (B), it is right to say bread (A) is body (B). When Luther introduces synecdoche as "alternative," it is not just an earlier unused way of explaining the possibility of A = B (red-hot iron). A = B also comes into everyday language (WA 18:186.11f. [cf. AE 40:196]): "The iron that is lying there is plainly fire," but synecdoche gives the reason for the explanation of this (WA 26:444.9f. [cf. AE 37:302]: "In all this talk [synecdoche] you see how the little word 'this' points to the vessel (A = B), and yet since the drink and the vessel in a sense are one thing (AB), so indeed, at the same time, it fits the drink primarily (AB = B)." Synecdoche is thus logically arranged and includes the red-hot iron.

Gollwitzer (op. cit., pp. 39f.) writes: "But with that, either the Zwinglian alloeosis was too dangerously close, or one would have to let the union of fire and iron become a mixture and thereby—seen apart from the fact that the firm analogy to Christology would forbid that—one was on the road to transubstantiation." Gollwitzer overlooks the fact that the Zwinglian A = B is presented as a technically incorrect *phrase* without real basis in an AB; compare above, pp. 50–51, text around nn. 68ff. [Swedish edition, pp. 71f.]. But if one perceives the Christology of Luther and Zwingli as identical, Luther's application of the *communicatio idiomatum* to the doctrine of the Sacrament must be understood as undoing the real presence. Just as little are there the parallels to transubstantiation, which emphatically denies the existence of an AB and A = B in favor of the stark B = B (body is body)! What Gollwitzer further deduces about later Lutheran theologians—above all, Chemnitz, who would perpetuate the above-named tension between part from the part (red-hot iron) and whole from the part—is to bring back the mistake touched on here. When Gollwitzer writes (op. cit., p. 44): "The Lutheran theologians tried to overcome the coexistence by expanding the concept of synecdoche, and so they found room to treat the first way of explaining it as a

idea here again is that the gleam of the gold, which cannot be seen, is transferred to the visible bag, which in the eyes of the beholder is the concretization of the sought-after gold. As such it is [not only] the symbol of the wealth, but [it is] also the wealth itself, which is in the bag. No one actually thinks of the individual coins; the moneybag is the assembled unit that exercises the power of the coins. This particular function is a result of an amalgamation of gold and pouch, which, though materially intact and distinct, have now become "one essence." The real basis for the amalgamation is the physical coexistence in the same place.

"Now because such a way of speaking is common both in Scripture and in all languages, identical predication in the Supper does not hinder us at all. There is none there."[107] The rule that forbids identical predication of different natures suffers no setback from Luther's investigation. In the Supper, no such identical predication is forbidden whereby it is alleged that the substances joined by the linking verb would be identical in a physical sense, "but it is a dream of Wycliffe and the sophists, even though the two different natures of body and bread are each on their own, and even though they are distinct from each other—indeed, one is not the other—" (thereby the scholastic prohibition occurs properly within the purely physical realm where it has application) "yet where they come together and become a whole new essence, there they lose their distinction, as far as this new single essence is concerned. And as they become and are one thing, so one calls them and speaks of them as one thing." This latter [point] makes an identical predication possible according to the rules of rhetoric, which may not be denied through a formalistic restriction by rules that do not have to do with a unity described thus: "It is not necessary that one of the two should cease to exist and be annihilated, but both bread and body remain; and on account of the sacramental union it is right to say, 'This is My body,' with the little word 'this' referring to the bread."[108] When Luther finally formulates the statement "For now it is no longer plain bread in the oven, but flesh-bread or body-bread, that is, a bread that has become a sacramental essence and one thing with the body of Christ," likewise "no longer plain wine in the cellar, but blood-wine"[109]—this is not a general emphatic statement about the real presence *in* bread and wine, but conscious, linguistic neologisms to designate what the *elements* have become. These newly coined expressions correspond to the

---

subordinate form of synecdoche," he could rightly have included Luther among these theologians also.

107 WA 26:444.39ff. [cf. AE 37:303]. Neuser (op. cit., p. 376 n. 363), who proceeds from the correct view that Luther accepts identical predication, here inserts a confused "There is also nothing [to prevent] . . ."!

108 WA 26:445.7ff. [cf. AE 37:303].

109 WA 26:445.10ff. [cf. AE 37:303].

new union that came into being: the body-bread and the blood-wine, the visible things, which by virtue of Jesus' words now *are* invisible realities. The bread is not merely a form, a substance, or an accidence, under which Christ's humanity is hidden: it *is* Christ's body through "impanation,"[110] an expression described in similarity with the "incarnation," which Luther unabashedly picks up from the opposition's invective. The synecdoche of the moneybag is valid here too: there is the round white host that is the object for everyone to see and note. The invisible body of Christ is revealed not only *in* the bread but also *by* it: "Whoever sees the bread sees the body of Christ."[111] In a completely new way, the host has become the bearer of the divine predicate.

---

110 WA 26:434.39 [cf. AE 37:292].

111 WA 26:442.30f. [cf. AE 37:300]. Grass (op. cit., pp. 124f.) discusses the point above in Luther as expressing an "anti-Enthusiast interest" and "eagerness to assure the reality of the presence against that Enthusiast flightiness," which drives Luther close to transubstantiation ("so I would rather keep pure blood with the pope"). Opposed to this, according to Grass, there are "limiting" statements that distinguish the bread and Christ's body. But in that same context Luther is not writing against the contemporary Enthusiasts, but about identical predication, which the contemporary Enthusiasts, because of their insufficient training, according to Luther, *cannot* cite in their defense. It is the Middle Ages, to which even Wycliffe belonged, who had an "honest mind" and who is a worthy opponent to Luther. This accounting, on an equal, scholastic level, is directed mainly against the interpretation of identical predication, which resulted in transubstantiation! It is not the positive but the "limiting" statements through which the bread and Christ's body are differentiated that lead Luther close to Rome! Likewise, his stance *for* Berengar's confession is a stance *against* the comments of the Middle Ages on it (WA 26:442.39ff. [cf. AE 37:300]): "Therefore, the Enthusiasts are wrong, *as well as the glosses in a spiritual sense*, when they accuse Pope Nicholas of coercing Berengar to such a confession that he says that he crushes and tears the true body of Christ with his teeth." When Grass writes: "But then the strong words about eating and tearing the body of Christ yet again are immediately curtailed," he understands Luther as a balance between materialistic and spiritualistic statements about the real presence. Luther, in retrospect, is supposed to have moderated his extreme opinions about the biting of Christ's body. It is obvious that Grass does not recognize the thought structure that draws Luther's statements together. "For the sake of the sacramental union," it is correct to say that the teeth crushing the host is a crushing of Christ's body. Christ's body is Jesus' own designation for the bread. What Grass understands as moderating is not a retracting of the physical "crushing" in favor of a less crass verb, but a reminding that the verb's *object in itself* is only bread, but through sacramental *communicatio idiomatum* it is Christ's body. (The Christological parallel here would mean that the statement "crucified divinity" cannot be "limited" to a less drastic verb but indeed to the object, so that this latter must be understood through the *communicatio idiomatum.*) Grass (op. cit., pp. 125f.) has the "limitation" culminate in the words "but, insofar as, above, outside of, under, through, and again here and everywhere, are valid in this matter," faith accepts an extreme reduction of the concretion of the real presence in the balancing act "between these two extremes" (op. cit., p. 128). As already presented above (p. 78 n. 7 [Swedish edition, p. 75]), this concept still refers to omnipresence. Grass has Luther step forward with uncertain definitions, while Luther in the same work follows a carefully considered thought structure that is

The criticism that Luther faced came from various directions. The criticism of the Sorbonne and of Henry VIII has already been mentioned. [Johann] Cochlaeus finds this doctrine of Luther's to be more godless than the Swiss denial of the real presence: No one can say, "This ox is a horse." The mixing of subject and predicate is the great offense.[112] [Johann] Eck writes: "No creature, especially an unreasoning one, is worthy to be mixed with the blessed body of Christ, otherwise the Word is to take on bread-ness in union with what it takes on [*in unitatem suppositi*]. But Luther has not yet shown us in Scripture that the Word became bread."[113] Luther's Christological parallels are understood as blasphemous: the Word became bread. Likewise, Luther's deviation from the Roman doctrine of the Supper is confirmed on this important point. Luther's view of the body of Christ's self-existence could invoke the Nominalistic school; his denial of transubstantiation had been prepared by its being challenged for the sake of argument during the Middle Ages. This doctrine of his again had no support of tradition. The literal take on the "this" in the Words of Institution can even be said to imply the greater offense. Thus it is not only a controversy about the Lutheran "is" [*est*]. "This" [*hoc*] also belongs to the revealed truths for which Luther will fight.[114]

---

hidden to Grass. — The basic mistake of Grass is that in his analysis of the "sacramental union," he proceeds solely from "union" as the process of uniting two things, and not of the third thing that arises from the two. He finds that the dove is not merely a "symbol of the Holy Spirit" but also, "according to the basic principle that the Spirit is in bodily things, *the bearer of the Holy Spirit*," but for Luther the point is that the dove *is* the Spirit, so that the Spirit *is seen* descending. Certainly Grass finds (op. cit., pp. 123f.) that the two entities are "designated as one essence" as a result of "an actual unity of existence," but he overlooks the fact that for that reason the *one* is designated by the other.

112 Johann Cochlaeus, *An die Herren Schultheis und Radt zu Bern wieder yhre vermainte Reformation. Doct. Jo. Cocleus MDXXVIII*, according to Köhler, op. cit., 1:603.

113 Eck, *Enchiridion locorum communium adversus Lutherum et alios hostes ecclesiae*, fol. 234A. This critique is described by Iserloh (op. cit, p. 313) as "extrinsically schematic and formalistic." Thus Iserloh seems to lack the understanding of what Luther's doctrine really means. Eck's attack is completely natural and, from his own viewpoint, perfectly justifiable. Iserloh in his book heaps invectives upon Eck in order to construct a picture of the Reformation as misunderstood by his Roman contemporaries but now acceptable through the insights of more recent Roman research. Compare here Wisløff, op. cit., p. 48 n. 33, on the thought of "testament": "Iserloh thinks that Eck's protests against Luther's interpretation of *testamentum* are just quibbling (1950, p. 170). One must to some degree defend Eck and his comrades. Iserloh does not seem to have seen how significant the idea of *testamentum* is for understanding the Supper as forgiveness of sins." Iserloh's approach contains some modern church politics.

114 This interpretation of Luther's does *not* go back to Scholasticism. In fact, Damerau (op. cit., p. 157) writes about Biel: "The 'this' does not yet designate the present Christ, but the bread or the observable form of appearance; it is applied in indicative form and takes the place of a noun," but that does not give a complete picture of Biel's meaning.

Luther's interpretation was also criticized by those who denied the miracle of the Sacrament. The document that is regarded as introducing the Reformed proclamation of the Sacrament, the letter of Cornelis Henricxz Hoen (Honius), already turns against Luther's picture of the red-hot iron, where the iron receives the attributes of the fire.[115] Oecolampadius, in his large Lord's Supper writing *De genuina verborum Domini Hoc est corpus meum . . . expositione*, gave the same critique of Luther as the Roman Catholic Eck. Here the word "consubstantiation"[116] comes as a designation for Luther's doctrine. Oecolampadius also introduces into the controversy the words "impanated body (it may be permitted to coin a word in a new matter)."[117] The Roman doctrine is presented as more tolerable in comparison to Luther's parallels of the incarnation and the red-hot iron: "Abhorring things so absurd, they prefer to say with their pope: I change the substance into nothing, or into the very body of Christ—even if sense and the Scriptures speak against this—rather than to speak ridiculous things."[118] Clearly Oecolampadius sees that in a certain sense Rome and the Swiss reformers share a common front against Lutheranism. He also says that if the Swiss school is called Sacrament-Enthusiasts because they do not confess the bread to be Christ's body, all Papists must also be Sacrament-Enthusiasts.[119] Zwingli also confirms

In Biel, "this" is logically connected with "body," and "bread" is met only as local designation: "Whence ['this'] not only points separately to some thing, but it can point to the thing itself with all of the surroundings, by which it can be indicated through a noun. . . . 'This' therefore points to that thing understood, for which it is substituted (that is, the body of Christ), and points to the perceived bread and the forms which it connotes" (Biel, *Canonis misse expositio*, lect. 48 M). In Biel one can take and consider the different medieval attempts at solving "whether ['this'] points to the bread or its form or the body of Christ" (lect. 48 Gff.). Naturally, in some cases the interpretation is "this = bread," in Bonaventure, for example; but that did not anticipate Luther's solution at all, for at the same time "is" is changed to "becomes": "For 'is' is only this strong, that is, [to mean] it is transformed or is converted" (lect. 48 L). So the thesis "bread is body" is avoided.

115 Enders 3:344ff., no. 552; compare Köhler, op. cit., 1:66f., 105.

116 Printed in *Acta [et scripta publica ecclesiae Wirtembergicae]*, p. 61. Compare here Köhler, op. cit., 1:120, 125 n. 3. Neuser (op. cit., p. 375 n. 361) wants to find the expression "consubstant(iat)io" in this writing for the first time, *Acta [et scripta publica ecclesiae Wirtembergicae]*, p. 106.

117 *Acta [et scripta publica ecclesiae Wirtembergicae]*, p. 70. Compare Oecolampadius's letter to Zwingli, November 4, 1525, CR 95:418.15: "impanated as the crucified Christ."

118 Id., p. 66.

119 *Johann Oekolampads Antwort auf Martin Luthers Bekenntnis vom Abendmahl Christi*, printed in StL 20:1375ff.; the opinion at issue is presented in column 1376. The document is included in *Über D. Martin Luthers Buch, Bekenntnis genannt, zwei Antworten von Johannes Oekolampad und Huldrych Zwingli*. The original printing of Oecolampadius's part comprised 106 pages and Zwingli's 256; compare CR 93/2:205 n. 14. But CR 93/2 does *not* reprint Oecolampadius's part, despite the fact that it has its place in the middle of Zwingli's contribution. Oecolampadius criticizes the picture of

that Luther deviates from Rome in this respect and also sees the difference in contrast to [Johann] Brenz, who is wary of all materialism: "He [Luther] does not hold with the pope's doctrine, he does not hold with the parsons [= Brenz's *Syngramma suevicum*], for these do not hold that the bread is the body of Christ but that it is in the bread."[120]

Corresponding to this criticism coming from outside, there is a criticism from [Luther's] own camp. The one who formulates it more than others is Melanchthon. His critical statements are found mostly in letters that sometimes reproduce private conversations with Luther. These are often retold in Greek to avoid having them read by the uninitiated. From the year 1527, there is a letter [in which] Melanchthon informs Joachim Camerarius that he had a conversation with Luther in Torgau regarding his [Luther's] doctrine of the Lord's Supper and the paradox that he used about a mixing (*symmixeōs*) of the bread and the body of Christ. Luther strongly insisted on what he stated earlier, and Melanchthon did not believe he could do anything. The letter includes hints about thoughts that could not be put in print. The addressee is asked to destroy the letter.[121] From the year 1530, there is a transcript in which Melanchthon pinpoints his position and that of [Martin] Bucer on the Sacrament. Here he condemns the picture of the red-hot iron in a significant way: "We deny transubstantiation and that the body is in the bread locally. We also reject the opinion of those who say that the body is in the bread, as wine is in a jug, or as fire is contained in red-hot iron."[122] Thus, at the same time, transubstantiation, the local presence, and the red-hot iron are condemned, the latter understood as parallel to local definitions. In Melanchthon's eyes, all three modes bear materialistic features. The alternative is the *heavenly* presence: "those things that are in heaven," which are discerned "only by inscrutable faith."[123] In 1538, Melanchthon writes to Veit Dietrich, where he openly attacks the Christological parallel to the

---

the red-hot iron as inadequate to express Luther's thought: no union seems to exist. The same criticism is encountered in a case from one of Luther's adherents, the Nürnberg patrician Willibald Pirckheimer; concerning this, see Köhler, op. cit., 1:236 n. 3.

120 CR 93/2:33.13ff.

121 CR 1:290. Herrlinger (op. cit., p. 131) asserts that "according to this passage (CR 1:920), Melanchthon distinguished between some people's [Greek: *tinés*] and Luther's own doctrine," which is a mistake. *Tinés* ["some"] obviously refers to the church fathers who used the image, and from whom Luther thus is said to have taken it. It would be inconceivable that Melanchthon would have discussed with Luther an image *not* used by him [Luther] and received in reply Luther's energetic insistence on the saying. Besides, Luther certainly made use of the image. Compare otherwise, Schwarzenau, *Der Wandel im theologischen Ansatz bei Melanchthon von 1525–1535*, p. 79; Fraenkel, op. cit., p. 153 n. 20; Neuser, op. cit., p. 79. The Colloquy at Torgau is mentioned without details also by CR 1:93; 4:964.

122 CR 2:224.

123 Ibid.

miracle of the Sacrament: It is unknown even to the Roman Church, "which the Papists also wonder at." "Up to now he wrote that your man, whoever he is, who quarrels about the elevation of the symbol, is absolutely Nestorian." — "I suspect also another person wrote these things, because he makes the joining of the bread and Christ similar to that of the divine and human natures in Christ. But perhaps I am wrong."[124] Before the anonymous accusation that rejecting the elevation was Nestorian, Melanchthon suspects that this allegation counts on a divinizing of the bread. Yet he counts on a different, acceptable alternative interpretation, which would be that denying the adoration of Christ's body is Nestorianism. Put that way, the accusation is orthodox. The letter meanwhile returns to this problem. Nicolaus von Amsdorf told Luther that he was nurturing a snake (Melanchthon!) in his bosom, and this is said spitefully about Melanchthon. The reason is the very question about synecdoche and that "the bread is the body." "And yet he [Luther] is only using a synecdoche in his proposition, *the bread is the body*. Therefore, he does not want the bread to be God, does not join it except as the Sacrament, so that God is present at the altar and is adored at the altar [*arcam*]."* Therefore, according to Luther, the adoration is done "not toward the bread, but toward Christ." According to Melanchthon, Luther does not mean ill. His expression is just a way of speaking; the presence of the Sacrament is compared to the presence *at* [*ad*] the ark [of the covenant, *arken*]. This latter is obviously understood as a limitation, through which the divine mode of presence is left unshaken and a localizing of the elements is made impossible. Not bread, but Christ's body is adored in the Sacrament. When asked, Luther referred to the adoration that can occur even at Baptism, "because God had bound Himself to His signs, where He wished to be sought." Such an adoration of Baptism thus seems calming as a parallel, since it could hardly mean more than an inner adoration of the Institutor of Baptism, without being bound by any visible element. With good conscience, therefore, Melanchthon can explain the outward gestures that seem to express a cultic adoration of the Sacrament to the inquirer, Philip of Hesse, when he encountered them in the Lutheran churches.[125] But Melanchthon thinks that the proper Lutheran distinction between the bread and Christ's body was not fully understood by the congregations: "even if the people in some places understand this poorly."[126] Some thus adore the bread instead of Christ and show that they misunderstand the

124 CR 3:503.

125 * [Translator's note: The word is "*arcam*," which may refer to the ark of the covenant, but the reference here is closely connected to the altar. John Schofield, *Philip Melanchthon and the English Reformation* (London: Taylor & Francis, 2017), p. 207, translates it as "on the altar." The Latin *aram* would definitely mean "altar."]

CR 3:503: "When Macedo [Philip Melanchthon] was present recently, he spoke with me about the adoration. For he had seen this custom in our churches."

126 CR 3:503f.

statement that "the bread is the body." But, rightly understood, the elevation need not be offensive to the Reformed.

The letter of reply from Dietrich, which arrives for Melanchthon, is opened, in his absence, by [Caspar] Cruciger, who in his mentor's name gives an answer that explains the matter further.[127] The controversy around the adoration itself is downplayed. The expressions of honor toward the Eucharist need not be identified as *latreia* ["worship"], which applies to God. The controversy instead is a matter of whether the presence is local, and whether Christ's body and blood are given without the concomitance of the whole person of the God-man, or whether Christ's presence is the personal, repletive presence, "by which Christ . . . is believed to be present everywhere otherwise." Melanchthon's own answer immediately afterward continues Cruciger's exposition with a positive statement: "these things being granted, that Christ is truly present and efficacious. Surely that is enough."[128] The negative demarcation of Christ's total, actual, effective presence then follows: "I did not add the inclusion or such a conjoining by which the body is affixed or glued to the bread or mixed with it." Yet again the picture of the red-hot iron is rejected, along with the local presence. In the matter of the adoration, Melanchthon proposes a solution that, compared with Cruciger's, is technically the opposite: [the adoration] should be abolished or not directed to the bread. The adoration thus is actually *latreia* ["worship"], which, in order to avoid misunderstanding, preferably should not be made toward the Sacrament but, in any case, should not be directed toward what is visible as the local place for what is invisible. The usage of popular piety toward the Sacrament must become a false adoration of a localized Christ. There is no essential difference with Cruciger: Cruciger made the adoration into something less than worship. Melanchthon would like to have the elevation discontinued because the adoration actually is worship, or to direct it toward something other than the visible Sacrament. In both cases, the cultic worship of Christ's body and blood as carried in the priests' hands is challenged. Melanchthon avoids all Christological parallels to the Sacrament, unknown also under the papacy: "Nor do the Papists propose such a union of the bread, and it is entirely a new thing"; "I do not propose an enclosing or gluing, but a sacramental [conjoining]: that is, that Christ is truly efficacious and present in the given signs."[129] In 1541, the elevation is defended only "if the mind judges it rightly and does not adore the sign, but understands something other than the sign to be given there." Melanchthon, of course, knows that the Church, in performing the mystery, always prostrated itself in the liturgical "proskynesis," but this is important too:

127 CR 3:510; compare above, p. 98, especially n. 89 [Swedish edition, p. 93].

128 CR 3:514.

129 Ibid.

"People must be educated properly."[130] Education is required. The worship of the bread is always looming.

The attack on transubstantiation is repeated in connection with the rejection of the local presence in some lines dated to 1551. The synecdoche in the statement "the bread is the body of Christ" is understood as a mere expression whose actual meaning is "the body and blood of Christ are shown and offered with the bread and wine." The words "in the use" [*in usu*] are set in contrast to a local, physical definition of the presence. This doctrine is "enough for the conscience."[131] In a contemporaneous document, [these phrases] are set in contrast to each other: "by a physically inflexible inclusion [enclosedness] of a live thing [*rei animatae*]" and "by a voluntary presence in some definite action."[132] A constant [battle]front against materialism is maintained.

Melanchthon writes to Calvin in 1554 that some uneducated people renewed the fight over bread-worship and thereby viciously wanted to have the possibility of suppressing him. Melanchthon himself sees the dogmatic problem, among other things, from the viewpoint that proceeds from God's revelation through the Word and the Spirit for conversion and comfort. It is obviously the same viewpoint that was stated above: "It is enough for the conscience." The letter writer seems to count on agreement with the letter's recipient regarding the adoration of the Sacrament.[133] Toward the end of this life, in 1560, Melanchthon writes that for twenty years he expected to be driven into exile for his opposition to the adoration of the bread. He is aware of a real discrepancy that lasted for many years. It is not simply a matter of church custom, which may be more or less appropriate, but the doctrines underlying it.[134] The statement that "the bread is the body," which he barely conceded earlier, is considered more and more unsatisfactory in this latter part of Melanchthon's life. In connection with the controversy over the Lord's Supper in the city of Bremen, Melanchthon disputes the statement "that the bread and wine are in essence the body and blood of Christ," in favor of "the body is received with the bread," whose biblical foundation would be the Pauline "the bread is the communion of the body."[135] The Lutheran statement is portrayed as the basis for the adoration of the bread: "O Christ, You who are bread [according to the Bremens] or in this bread, have mercy on me."[136] It must be exchanged for the Pauline words: "[Paul] does not say, as Heshusius does, that the bread is the true body of Christ, but

130 CR 4:735.

131 CR 7:882.

132 CR 7:888.

133 CR 8:362

134 CR 9:1030; compare above, pp. 98–99 n. 91 [Swedish edition, p. 94].

135 CR 9:16.

136 CR 9:471.

[it] is *koinonían*, that is, that by which the union with the body of Christ comes about, which occurs in the use, and indeed not without thought, as when mice gnaw bread."[137]

Melanchthon's position documented here must be seen against the background of what was cited earlier regarding his parameters of the sacramental presence. It is, for Melanchthon, a real presence, but it has the majesty of omnipresence and is comprehensible only to the mind ("*cogitatione*"). That is why "gluing" and any other such depiction is impossible, for Christ's body, in relation to the bread, does not partake of any greater closeness than what exists in creation otherwise. Luther's reasoning again proceeds from a real, and even diffinitive, special sacramental presence and from the visible and invisible parts being identical. The difference between Melanchthon and Luther becomes not the use of "synecdoche," but the actual meaning of it. Synecdoche is, for Melanchthon, merely a union constituted by the Word without regard for any real state of union beyond omnipresence, an inaccurate way of speaking, which in the long run cannot be seriously maintained without rather severe misunderstanding and offense. When Melanchthon, in confrontation with Luther, tries to reassure himself with the thought that Luther conceded that it was valid only by synecdoche, Melanchthon hears what he himself wants to hear: a confirmation that the bread is not made red-hot by the presence of Christ's body and cannot be placed in the center for the eucharistic cultus. Luther had merely made mention again that the bread did not lose its identity as bread despite receiving the divine predication. Therefore, Melanchthon and Luther look quite differently at the sacramental adoration by the uneducated people. Luther identified himself completely with the medieval devotion toward the Savior in the host—of course, as long as there is an actual Supper and not an inappropriate broadening of the holy Meal: "And I plainly rejoice that, at least among the common people, the simple faith in this Sacrament remains."[138] Melanchthon sees the same people as having fallen into materialistic bread-worship; only the trained mind, through biblical explanation, can distinguish between the locally present Sacrament and the gifts actually conveyed through it. The "this" in the Words of Institution actually can be understood only with the help of the tempering and more objective words of Paul: "the communion of Christ's body." Melanchthon works from a systematic

137 CR 9:962. Compare here Herrlinger, op. cit., pp. 142f.; Ritschl, op. cit., 4:26 n. 106; Gollwitzer, op. cit., p. 83: "He [Melanchthon] found his view supported in 1 Cor. 10:16, where he did not understand with Luther: 'The bread is the distributed body of Christ,' but 'The bread is the *distributing* of [the] body of Christ.' An act, not a thing, is the authenticating sign, since God's revelation is completely deed, action, will; it is not that matter is delivered, but that will is testified: the sacraments are signs of God's will toward us." From this, the significance of *usus* is understood as a part of the qualifications for the sacramental presence.

138 WA 6:510.2, 510.20f. [cf. AE 36:32].

affirmation of the place of the real presence within the heritage of the Christian faith where the detailed exegesis of the Words of Institution may yield to definite, superior definitions, derived from the general clarifications about the gracious presence. It is for that reason he immediately is able to draw in Bible texts that are not connected with the Sacrament when he describes the Supper: "Remain in Me, and I in you. Also, I am in My Father, and you in Me, and I in you. And in these true consolations He makes us members for Himself, and He testifies that He will make our bodies alive. Thus the ancients testify of the Lord's Supper."[139]

Melanchthon understands Luther's words about the adoration *at* Baptism to mean only the adoration *on account* of Baptism. For Melanchthon it apparently seems absurd that someone would imagine an actual cultic act of adoration toward a local revelation of God in Baptism. In [Christ's] Baptism at the Jordan, which was foundational for all Baptisms, Luther again had rightly found an example of identical predication and a union of the visible and invisible. For Luther, the words about the dove and the bread fell within the same category, and thereby baptismal adoration falls within what is imaginable and possible for Luther.[140]

For Melanchthon, transubstantiation falls under the judgment on the materialistic view of the Sacrament. His criticism, viewed most deeply, does not aim at the doctrine of Thomism, which at one time was developed in order to satisfy only his own demand for the exaltation of spiritual things compared to the material, while the church doctrine of the real presence would actually be left unshaken. On the other hand, Melanchthon stands in opposition to the Nominalistic doctrine of the self-existence of Christ's body and transubstantiation in the sense it was added to it. This contrast is what differentiates him also from Luther.

This rejection of transubstantiation by Melanchthon is repeated most emphatically in his disciple Brenz. But his stance need not be seen as a mere reflection of Melanchthon. The confrontation with Oecolampadius and his originally composed doctrine of the Supper give Brenz sufficient impulse for criticism. In reality, he also rejects Luther's concrete faith in the Sacrament. He fights against materialism in all forms known to him: "There is no impanation here, no transubstantiation."[141] "But for the sake of comparison, like Luther with iron and fire, you who have good knowledge, take note that he made the comparison only in order to show the foolishness of papistic transubstantiation,

139 CR 9:962; compare here Herrlinger (op. cit., p. 152): "So the Words of Institution may be understood in their essential unity with John 6, and yet may be grasped in their specific significance (bodily presence)." The latter addition is uncertain.

140 Compare below, chapter 7, where this problem is investigated more closely.

141 Brenz to Adam Weiss, November 27, 1525, according to Pressel, op. cit., p. 7; compare Köhler, op. cit., 1:220.

not to prove anything further with it."[142] In that way, not only are the misinterpretations of Luther's view rejected, [but] Luther's meaning is affected also. The fact that Luther had a positive purpose with his comparison is ignored by Brenz, for whom there is no specific state of union between two materials in the Sacrament. That is why Brenz turns against any thought of a miraculous presence where Christ in a miraculous way lets His body become present in the bread: "and not for carnal imaginings in whatever way the Papists imagine some little body that is hidden under the bread or in the bread";[143] "nor do we ask whether it is customary to imagine some little body in fleshly form in the bread. The wisdom of the flesh is busy in this foolish imagination; some kind of Aristotle marvels at the upside-down nature of things. We consider the cause [to be] of faith, not of human reason. And so we only ask this, whether the body and blood of Christ are distributed in the bread and wine of the Lord's Supper and given to our faith."[144] With that, he condemned as Aristotelian and objectionable Luther's own very obvious wonder and adoration at God's ability to rule His creation with sovereignty against all the laws of nature and to let the sacramental presence occur in various places at one and the same time.

Brenz only wants faith to receive the spiritual gift, without any thought about the type of presence. Here is revealed a dissimilarity between Luther and Brenz in their views on the function of the Sacrament. For Luther, the special form of the sacramental presence, its physical externality, has the significance of the Sacrament's *function as sign*. The physical transmission of Christ's body is the sign and seal of the reality of the forgiveness of sins, applied individually to the communicant.[145] For Brenz, Christ's body is not the Sacrament's sign, designating the spiritual gift (forgiveness of sin), but the spiritual food and

142 *Die von Gemmingen an die prediger zu Strassburg (Antwort durch Johann Brenz begriffen)*, December 1525, Pressel, op. cit., p. 23. Compare Brecht, op. cit., p. 89 n. 1: "It is significant that Brenz seems to be just as unhappy as the Strassburgers with the analogy of the red-hot iron with which Luther explained the coexistence of bread and body (e.g., WA 6:510 [cf. AE 36:32]). For Brenz, as well as for the south Germans [*Oberdeutschen*], the gift of the Word was strictly separated from that of the bread."

143 "Jo. Brentii Epistola ad Reutlingenses," April 13, 1527, *Acta [et scripta publica ecclesiae Wirtembergicae]*, p. 37.

144 Brenz, "*In evangelion Iohannis*," *Opera* 6:856.

145 WA 6:518.10ff. [cf. AE 36:44]: "So also in the Mass, this promise being chief of all, He adds the memorial sign of such a great promise, His own body and His own blood in the bread and wine, just as He says, 'Do this in remembrance of Me.' Thus in Baptism He adds to the words of promise the sign of dipping in water. From these things we understand that in whatever promise of God there may be, two things are set forth, Word and sign, so that we understand that the Word is testament, the sign indeed is sacrament, as in the Mass the Word of Christ is testament, the bread and wine are sacrament."

the gift itself. Understood in this way, the Sacrament is directed to the believer who already has faith and through the Sacrament only makes use of a new way of eating spiritually, according to John 6. For Luther, the starting point is different: when the priest in the Mass elevates what has been consecrated, it is done as an act "by which we are called forth to faith in this testament."[146] The holy thing between the priest's fingers should incite and urge [people] to faith in the Gospel.[147]

Transubstantiation emerges for Brenz as the grand and flagrant crime against the spirituality of faith and the Sacrament. It is understood as a false localizing of what is holy and at the same time as an expression of the unbiblical claim of the priesthood having special power to consecrate. The criticism against this and against the prevalent definition of the meaning of the consecration precipitates words that belong to the traditional Protestant polemic against the doctrine of the transformation: "But what, I ask, is magic if this is not?" "But we are not unaware of your magic opinion and impious incantation."[148]

[Martin] Chemnitz took a position toward the doctrine of the transformation of substances in a particularly clear and conscious way. In him there is, even by modern standards, an objective historical exposition of the origin and meaning of the doctrine of transubstantiation. He shows how the doctrine of transubstantiation originally, in its pre-scholastic form, had elements of actual materialism: "Indeed, even Theophylact has traces of transubstantiation, crass enough. For he says that the bread is transformed, converted, and

146 WA 6:524.25 [cf. AE 36:54].

147 Brenz sees Christ's body as the actual gift, while the function as sign is fulfilled by the bread, which represents Christ's body (*Opera* 6:857): "so that the external man may have his external things, bread and wine; the internal indeed [may have] his internal and spiritual things, body and blood, given in the mystery"; p. 858: "so that the body in the Sacrament may have bodily [physical] signs, and faith [may have] spiritual [signs]." Compare *Syngramma suevicum*, *Acta [et scripta publica ecclesiae Wirtembergicae]*, p. 179: "For if remission of sins is our gift, why are not the body and blood gifts, through which remission happens? Now if they are gifts, it is appropriate that they are distributed also because of the gifts. But it is obvious from the preceding that they are distributed in the Word."

148 Brenz, *Apologia Confessionis Wirtenbergensis*, *Opera* 8:512. Already in 1528, Melanchthon uses the designation "it is magic" about the Roman view of the consecration (CR 1:948); he was prompted to do so by the criticism of Oecolampadius. The same formulation that is in Brenz, partly in the form of an obvious borrowing, is in Chemnitz, *Examination of the Council of Trent*, 2:224ff. [Latin, p. 300], but it applies there to the more specific problem of the *correct form* of the consecration, not as in Brenz to a contrast between the Evangelical "only receiving a new relationship" and the "words of creation," which are identified with the Roman transubstantiation. Brenz proceeds from the idea that the omnipresence of Christ's body makes a real consecration, an inclusive transformation of substance, impossible; Chemnitz in this very context rejects this doctrine [of omnipresence] as "the foundation also of Christ's body in the Supper."

trans-elemented into the body of Christ, and thus, just as Christ moved about on earth, the bread is indeed changed into His flesh, because of the nourishment [*ratione alimenti*]."[149]

The transformation was considered physical. Likewise, the Berengar controversy "about the tangibility [*sensualitate*] of the presence of Christ's body has application here."[150] Chemnitz is also aware that the doctrine of transubstantiation in its beginning offered possible interpretations that might differ greatly: "Certain people argued that the material remained when the form of the bread was gone, just as nutritional matter is under the form of the one nourished. Others argued that the form of the bread remains while the matter was gone."[151] Likewise, Chemnitz knows that Innocent III, who dogmatized transubstantiation in 1215, in no way excludes the teaching that the substance remains, as long as the real presence is still maintained: "Nevertheless, he does not condemn as anathema that different opinion [that after the consecration the true accidence of bread remains], as the Tridentines [at the Council of Trent] do, which the reader will carefully observe."[152] Only after this historic retrospective does Chemnitz undertake the purely dogmatic treatment: "It is useful to observe these things from the beginning of the dispute concerning transubstantiation and see how it progressed, but let us come to the matter itself."[153] Chemnitz immediately allows an actual transformation in the Sacrament—"this great, miraculous, and truly divine . . . change"—that consists of this: the fact that what was at first mere bread and wine after the consecration are actually Christ's body and blood.[154] "We ourselves understand the sacramental change."[155] But this is not the same as the scholastic doctrine of transubstantiation accepted by the Council of Trent, which cannot be proved biblically. At the same time, Chemnitz rejects any deeper involvement in the battle against it: "In no way do we think of the bread and the body of Christ with equal importance. And Luther always said that in this whole argument he looked more at the presence

149 Chemnitz, *Repetitio sanae doctrinae*, p. 310.

150 Id., p. 324.

151 Chemnitz, *Examination of the Council of Trent*, 2:255 [Latin, p. 312]; compare here Jorissen, op. cit., pp. 65ff., with the same remark. The patristic knowledge of Chemnitz is a result of his studies in the library that belonged to Duke Albert of Prussia, for whom Chemnitz was court astrologer before his theological career; compare *RE*, s.v. "Chemnitz."

152 Ibid.; compare Jorissen, op. cit., p. 36 n. 304: "That is also why in the following the mere symbolic understanding of the Eucharist is rejected as heretical opposition to the Lord's words. There is no mention of consubstantiation at all in this context." [Cf. Chemnitz, *Examination of the Council of Trent*, 2:255.]

153 Ibid.

154 Id., p. 313 [cf. Chemnitz, *Examination of the Council of Trent*, 2:258].

155 Id., p. 316 [cf. Chemnitz, *Examination of the Council of Trent*, 2:267].

of the body and blood of Christ in the Supper than the presence of bread and wine."[156] Chemnitz thus expressly and consciously goes back to Luther's moderation on this point. The basis for the still ongoing criticism is also identical with Luther's: holding on to the "particle 'this' in each part, denoting the bread and the cup."[157] The Lutheran "this" is powerfully maintained, not only the "is." The Christological parallel is brought to this "identical proposition," though it is also emphasized that the bread is not taken up into hypostatic union with Christ's body.[158] Nowhere do we find any more mention of the Melanchthonian fear of a specific, concrete sacramental presence or of the consequent adherence to the statement that the bread is the body. Chemnitz, through his definition of the presence, belongs at home in Luther's camp. When, in contrast to Luther, he is critical of Berengar's confession, this is not a matter of a dogmatic difference but of a dogmatical-historical difference. Chemnitz claims to be more familiar with the meaning of the formulas, which Luther treated without going into their original significance.

The last task of this chapter will be to determine where the doctrine of the so-called consubstantiation stands in relation to the Lutheran doctrine of the Supper. The word is first found in Oecolampadius,[159] who uses the word to designate Luther's doctrine. It probably went from here to Melanchthon

156 Ibid. [cf. Chemnitz, *Examination of the Council of Trent*, 2:265]. Even Brenz can occasionally allow such a tone: In *Confessio wirttenbergensis*, which was presented before the Council of Trent, it says (*Opera* 8:13f.):

> We also believe that the omnipotence of God is so great that in the Eucharist it could either annihilate the substance of bread and wine or change them into the body and blood of Christ. But it does not seem to have been handed down in a sure Word of God that God exercises this absolute omnipotence of His in the Eucharist, and it seems to have been unknown to the ancient church.

But the rest of Brenz's criticism gives the words a different background than in Chemnitz. In fact, it is a merely hypothetical assumption that corresponds to similar Reformed concessions having to do with the possibility of the real presence; compare Köhler (*Das Marburger Religionsgespräch*, p. 30): "Certainly God can have one body be in different places, but we demand proof of whether He does this in the Supper" (Zwingli); p. 57: "I am not speaking against what God is able to do" (Oecolampadius). — Again, Chemnitz can make sharp formulations: in *Examination of the Council of Trent*, 2:253 [Latin, p. 311], transubstantiation is called "one of the pillars of the pontifical realm," but it ought to be observed that Chemnitz thereby intends to express primarily Trent's own opinion: "For they expressly recite among the other reasons for transubstantiation: so that no other substance than Christ's either be adored in the Eucharist or offered to God the Father, and that the presence of the body of Christ in the Eucharist is enduring, even outside the use." Chemnitz himself nowhere develops the theory of transubstantiation as the mother of all kinds of errors.

157 Chemnitz, op. cit., p. 315 [cf. *Examination of the Council of Trent*, 2:262].

158 Id., pp. 315f.

159 Compare above, p. 127 n. 16 [Swedish edition, p. 140].

who, according to a record from 1567 by the militant Gnesio-Lutheran Benedict Morgenstern, directed it against the Lutheran party: "Therefore, their Preceptor [Melanchthon], against the doctrine of the presence of Christ's body and blood, personally said to the respectable, honorable lord Nikolaus Gallus [Hahn]: Transubstantiation and consubstantiation, that is, the changing and the commingling or tethering—one is like the other. *But he calls consubstantiation our doctrine*."[160] The expression occurs later within historic Lutheranism, starting from the generation after Luther. The quotation from Morgenstern gives the appropriate preamble to the problem: The term lacks a set definition, since it was never developed positively by any theologian. Depending on the definition one decides to give to the term, Luther can be said to have taught or not taught consubstantiation.[161]

The most detailed available presentation of Lutheranism's stance on consubstantiation is reproduced in the comprehensive systematic-theological

160 Morgenstern, *Widerlegung der Notel*, fol. FIIa (emphasis mine). The sacramental controversy of Morgenstern and his Gnesio-Lutheran colleagues is completely unknown today; it will be reported in more detail in the final chapter, on the adoration.

161 Dieckhoff, Mücke, and Gollwitzer depict Luther's earlier doctrine as consubstantiation; compare above, p. 141 n. 79 [Swedish edition, p. 131]. Neuser (op. cit., p. 375) asserts: "The lack of the term [consubstantiation] does not prove that Luther dismissed this doctrine," and he [Neuser] thereby acknowledges the fact that is pointed out by Kattenbusch ("Luthers Idee zur Konsubstantiation im Abendmahl," pp. 83ff.) that Luther himself nowhere actually uses the expression. But Ficker proceeds from the assumption of the very reality [of it] in Luther. Andrén (op. cit., pp. 46ff.) uses the term not only for Luther but also for the subsequent theology and orthodoxy of the Concordia [Book of Concord]. Andrén thereby overlooks [the] fact that these later theologians very strongly reject the word, which they connect with materialistic views; compare the presentation that follows. Grass (op. cit., p. 58) writes briefly: "Luther taught consubstantiation already in 1520." Fagerberg (op. cit., p. 202): "This theory is generally known in theology by the name consubstantiation." Other theologians take [on] [the] position of rejecting it. Vajta (op. cit., pp. 177f.) writes: "This [Luther's] belief in creation makes it impossible to think of 'consubstantiation' in the temporary union of two substantially different things in the Supper." For a meaningful use of the term in Luther's doctrine, according to Vajta it must be examined through the omnipresence. Peters (op. cit., pp. 97f.) also rejects consubstantiation: "The category of substance is lacking in the place; yet Christ's body must be brought down to the level of things of this world." Even here omnipresence was used as the corrective, and WA 26:341.17ff. [cf. AE 37:230] ("above, outside of, under, through, and again hereby and everywhere") is applied to the Sacrament contrary to the context. Sasse (op. cit., p. 102) formulates it much more modestly: Luther and Lutheranism do not embrace "the doctrine of consubstantiation in its technical sense." Sasse proceeds from the idea that such a "technical sense" exists but is never reported. Grünwald ("Zur Ontologie der Realpräsenz," p. 16) finds that Luther did not teach consubstantiation, which belongs to "the Aristotelian-scholastic system of categories," but yet he must ascertain about Luther (p. 21): "Nevertheless, he himself cannot be completely cleared of a bias in his thinking about existence, as his perpetual emphasis on '*is*' shows."

work by Charles P. Krauth, *The Conservative Reformation and Its Theology*.[162] Krauth has as his thesis that consubstantiation is a locally defined presence of the Sacrament. He begins his presentation by discussing the so-called Wittenberg Concord of 1536, and he is undoubtedly correct to do so. He cites these words:

> And nevertheless they do not believe in any transubstantiation, that is, essential or substantial transformation of bread and wine into Christ's body and blood, and do not think that Christ's body and blood are *locally*, that is, *spatially* enclosed in the bread or permanently united with it apart from receiving the Sacrament; so they concede, however, that through the sacramental union the bread is Christ's body, etc.[163]

Krauth's depiction includes a lesser, ostensibly only formal, inaccuracy, but it is significant. Krauth writes: "In the 'Wittenberg Concord' (1536), prepared and signed by Luther and the other leaders in the Church, it is said, 'We deny the doctrine of transubstantiation, as we also deny that the body and blood of Christ are locally included in the bread.' "[164] With that, the Concord's "they" has become "we," and Luther has incorrectly been made into a subject of the confession and not into one who along with the rest of the judges initially declared: "We have heard how Martin Bucer . . . and his preachers teach." It is thus not Luther who in a confessional form interconnects transubstantiation and "local inclusion," an association that never bothered him. It is Bucer who with these terms defines himself against two depictions that he considered related, and it is Melanchthon who gives Bucer's view its outward form.[165] Luther again *heard* partly a rejection of transubstantiation, partly a denial of the depiction that Zwingli maliciously fabricated about him and the Roman Church. The kind of interconnection between them was not clear to Luther. The confession is not

---

162 Krauth, *Conservative Reformation and Its Theology*, in the index (p. 834), under the rubric "*Consubstantiation* rejected by the Lutheran Church," there are abundant references, divided systematically: "1. From Confessions of Lutheran Church. 2. Lutheran Divines. 3. Roman Catholic Divines. 4. Calvinistic Divines." — In 1677, J. W. Baier presented a special disputation *De Impanatione et Consubstantione*, which is mentioned in his *Compendium Theologiae positivae secundum anni 1694*, ed. by Preuss (p. 551), and is included in *Joh. Guilielmi Bajeri, D. Disputationum Theologicarum in Academia Jenensi* as number IV and comprises 48 pages. In the edition of Baier's book expanded by Walther in 1879, on the question of consubstantiation, there are excerpts from Luther, Gerhard, and Kromayer: *Compendium theologiae*, 3:502ff.

163 *Svenska kyrkans bekännelseskrifter*, p. 611; *BS* 977.23ff. [FC SD VII 14 quotes the Wittenberg Concord.]

164 Krauth, op. cit., p. 130.

165 Köhler, op. cit., 1:455: "that Melanchthon, its author, clearly accommodated himself to Bucer."

his. He only approved it.[166] Bucer meanwhile identified the two depictions as indications of an unspiritual materialism. Aided by the Wittenberg Concord, he builds on what he thought he perceived: the idea that Luther does not teach a "local inclusion." He confesses in a letter that he wronged Luther by ascribing to him "impanation,"[167] and in his *Retractiones* he retracts the suspicion of materialism he had held against Luther.[168] He had gained this insight meanwhile long before the [Wittenberg] Concord, since in 1530 he found a formula that would help him toward longed-for unity: "Just as Luther says, it is not necessary that Christ is locally in the Sacrament, but He can be present in the way all creatures are present for Christ, in a hidden way."[169] With that, the Melanchthonian way out had been opened up: omnipresence becomes the alternative [not only] to "locally" but also to "diffinitively" [present]. This is the meaning of the Wittenberg Concord in Bucer's eyes. Thus, within the framework of a Lutheran document of official character, with Luther's signature as confirmation of its orthodoxy, the doctrine of the local presence is rejected in connection with the repudiation of transubstantiation. This would give rise to explanations that would make the [Wittenberg] Concord into a Lutheran front position against sacramental materialism, whereby the Lutheran doctrine is understood as the golden middle way between Reformed spiritualism and Roman materialism. In

166 On the problem of the character of the Wittenberg Concord, compare Köhler, op. cit., 2:453f.:

> Next, it is technically not a "concord," that is, an agreement, to which both sides confessed. Unlike Marburg, it did not deal with the articles in which the subscribers were agreed "and those which both sides believe and hold unanimously." Rather, like the chairman of a conference, with [statements such as] "we have heard," etc., the document simply gives a lecture about the opinion of the south Germans [*Oberländer*]. They thus appear as the ones drawing near to the established opinion of the Lutherans. What was rejected earlier is not said, not even implicitly, but now they have gained true insight, which the Lutherans already had. The "continual concord," which is expected "with great hope" at the conclusion of the document, is thus the annexation, or more plainly: submission under the Lutherans.

The same view is presented in Sasse, op. cit., p. 310. Bizer (*Studien zur Geschichte des Abendmahlsstreits im 16. Jahrhundert*, p. 127), however, tries to present the Concord as a theological union document of a modern type: "The work of Concord from 1536 does not rest on a mutual misunderstanding. To suppose this would mean taking the preceding work all too lightly and powerfully undervaluing Luther's diligence in this matter. It is rather a matter of a union with clearly seen differences."

167 Krauth, op. cit., p. 340; Köhler, op. cit., 2:459.

168 Krauth, op. cit., p. 774.

169 CR 2:315. Bucer's opinion here is in agreement with Melanchthon, who, since he sees the danger that Bucer, technically in agreement with Luther, misinterprets the rejection of transubstantiation and the local inclusion into indicating actual, genuine unity on the real presence; compare Köhler, op. cit., 2:221.

light of this, "local inclusion" becomes a variant of the materialistic doctrine of transubstantiation, separate from it only by maintaining the existence of the substance of the bread.

Bucer and [Wolfgang] Capito, in their attempt at reconciliation with the Swiss following the [Wittenberg] Concord, would encounter anew the Reformed criticism of Luther's doctrine of the Supper. They conveyed to Luther that the Swiss only accept the "real presence" under certain conditions: "if only this much might be avoided, lest it appear that they have relapsed into the impiety of the Papists." "Henceforth it is, venerable father, as those three [objections]: the natural union of Christ with the bread or the local inclusion; also, that Christ becomes food for the stomach and is actually touched by our flesh; finally, that the eating of the Sacrament is salutary apart from true faith."[170] Papistic impiety thus seems to consist in this: (1) a union of bread and Christ's body that was local; (2) a coarse, Capernaitic eating of Christ's body that was physically consumed; (3) and automatic salutary effect of the Sacrament simply by consuming it. This Reformed complaint is repeated later in the letter: "They [the adversaries] hear that Christ is given in the Eucharist with the bread substantially; they think of a local presence, while the bread is the body of the Lord, impanation; [and] that the unworthy eat the Lord's body, that the sacramental eating is for salvation without faith."[171] In this situation, Bucer fills his new role as "Lutheran." He delineates "Luther's" faith against "Rome's" crass un-spirituality and tries to correct all misunderstandings in the recalcitrant Swiss, who do not immediately share his faith in the excellence of the [Wittenberg] Concord and in Luther's spirituality. According to Bucer, all are actually agreed; only verbal misunderstandings obscure the full realization.[172] These corrections could now really call upon one document. Luther, in fact, appeared to have consciously distanced himself from Rome's superstitions and to have looked for the spiritual alternative. But this is a gross misunderstanding. The problem of the Sacrament's saving effect here can be left aside—the other two complaints, particularly the first one, affect Luther more than they do the Roman Church, and from the Reformed viewpoint they must indeed be maintained. Luther taught an actual, real, diffinitive presence and a state of union between the divine and the created that far outdid the Roman doctrine in concreteness. Bucer's lack of success in

170 WA Br 8[:13].21f., 23ff., no. 3128.

171 WA Br 8[:14].64ff., no. 3128.

172 Köhler, op. cit., 2:523: "[Bucer] borders on dishonesty"; "That formula is well-nigh acceptable to him, because he knows how to turn it the right way." [Heinrich] Bullinger represents a skeptical, clearly thought-out Reformed view against Bucer: "We battle against the opinion of the Roman Church, which they [the Lutherans] confess" (Köhler, id., p. 466). [Friedrich] Myconius drew the conclusion: "Bucer is a much more stiff-necked opponent against us than Luther."

Switzerland rested on the fact that he was never successful in concealing Luther's doctrine from the eyes of the sharp-sighted Reformed.

Although in this way Luther could be alleged to have rejected transubstantiation as materialistic and the local presence as a variant of it, in many cases Luther's actual view of these things was maintained during the following generation so that the local presence was rejected only *as a Reformed accusation*, a purely negative concept.[173] Joachim Westphal, who took up the controversy against Calvin, writes about one of his earlier books: "My first *Apology* [*Defense*] rejects those expressions supposedly by us, against those authors, and testifies that we do not make the connection, not a transfusion of substance, not a local inclusion, or any such thing that is not at all consistent with the correct faith."[174] All these terms consist of attacks from the Reformed; none of them is formulated as an attack from Lutheranism against Rome.

It is among these invectives that "consubstantiation" originates and is brought into Lutheranism. Nicolaus Selnecker, for example, in a defense against such attacks rejects [as follows]:

> ... All those who imagine a natural inclusion, whether it is called transubstantiation, consubstantiation, local inclusion, magic, or whatever else. For this does not have to do with a natural way, which we could grasp and comprehend with our reason, and we are not imagining any spatial place here, as if the body and blood are in the Supper, nor elsewhere, in a natural spatial way, like bread is in a basket. Such a thought is pure human imagination and wanton drivel in divine things. ... But what do our gentle,

173 In his final writing on the Sacrament, Luther touched on the attack against his presumed "local inclusion," which is understood by him as the doctrine "that Christ's body would be in the Sacrament locally, like straw in a sack" (WA 54:153.14f. [cf. AE 38:301]), from which would follow that the Lutherans think that they "gobble up [Christ] piece by piece, like wolves gobble up a sheep, and they guzzle blood like a cow guzzles water" (WA 54:145.10f. [cf. AE 38:292]). This is, for Luther, inclusion and impanation ("breadified God" [*brötern Gott*]). This idea is rejected not only for Luther's own sake but also for the sake of Rome: "For they knew very well that neither the Papists nor we had taught like that" (WA 54:153.17f. [cf. AE 38:301]). "But thus the Papists, yes, not the Papists, but the holy Christian Church and we with them" (WA 54:153.24f. [cf. AE 38:301], "for they knew very well that we had never taught nor believed such, but for their boasting in order to shame us they had gladly created the delusion before the common people as if we were such crazy, mindless, raging people" (WA 54:145.7ff. [cf. AE 38:292]). "For under the papacy one taught just as we also still hold and teach, as the true, ancient Christian Church has held for 1,500 years" (WA 54:145.16ff. [cf. AE 38:292]).

174 Westphal, *Apologia confessionis*, p. 300. A whole chapter is devoted to the problem: "*De locali inclusione*" (id., pp. 297ff.), where Westphal recalls that Bucer takes back the accusation of the local inclusion (id., p. 298).

> extremely learned Sacramentarians do? Ah, they say . . . "in" . . . refers to a spatial place.[175]

Placing transubstantiation among the forms of natural inclusion does not indicate any criticism against Rome from Selnecker's pen. The author picks up only a Reformed, untruthful ("made-up") accusation that has this almost stereotypical formulation and rejects it. Selnecker does not merely turn against any Roman or Romanizing doctrine; he protects himself against fictitious, imagined doctrines,[176] Sacramentarian invectives, which culminate in the concluding "magic." The common denominator for all the accusations, including consubstantiation, is obviously: "It refers to a spatial place."

In the *Apologia oder verantwortung des Christlichen Concordien Buchs* [*Apology of the Book of Concord*], local inclusion and union into "one essence or substance" are equated. The thought is apparently that if the bread and Christ's body coexist under the same conditions in the same location, a physical commingling of two materials must necessarily arise, an argument of emphatically fictitious character: "As he [Luther] also expressed with exact form the local inclusion or the spatial enclosure in his *Great Confession* on the Supper, so Bucer excuses Luther in this case . . . [for saying] that the body of Christ is united in one essence or substance with the bread, which Luther never even said."[177] "One essence or substance" corresponds here to the term "consubstantiation."

175 Selnecker, *Christliche warhafftige Widerlegung*, fol. EVIb. Compare here Sasse, op. cit., p. 103 n. 53, with similar quotations from Selnecker, *Vom hl. Abendmahl des Herrn* (1591), fol. E2, where the terms "inclusion," "consubstantiation," and "hiddenness" are rejected.

176 Compare here id., fol. MIIIIb, which rejects similar accusations regarding the omnipresence:

> We know of no Sacramentarian ubiquity or omnipresence. We also have never used this word nor praised it, as Brenz, of blessed memory, called this word *ubiquity* an ominous word, an abominable, horrid word. But the Sacramentarians have this bugaboo in their garden and have run after it, and it happened that there was a thief in the garden. For they made up this word on their own and falsely applied it to our churches and teachers: Luther, Schepp, Brenz, Duke George of Anhalt, etc., and many others, without reason.

It applies to the same kind of negative idea: no one teaches this doctrine. Least of all do the Sacramentarians teach some "Sacramentarian omnipresence," which only means the kind of omnipresence that the Sacramentarians say that Lutherans teach. Andrén (op. cit., pp. 247ff.) has been misled by such a negative idea into believing that "Sacramentarians," as an exception, can designate a school that *for its own part* taught the "local inclusion of Christ." But no such use of language flourished even in the Swedish countryside during the 1500s. Compare here also the Formula of Concord, *BS* 1009.20f. [cf. FC SD VII 105]: "through which we reject the Capernaitic thoughts of coarse, fleshly presence, which is attributed and forced on our churches by the Sacramentarians beyond all our public, repeated testimonies."

177 *Apologia oder verantwortung des christlichen Concordien Buchs*, fol. 286Bf. [cf. *Apology*, p. 394]. "Local inclusion" thus includes the divinization of the bread as a natural

Already in the Wittenberg Concord it says, "Nor do they think that a local inclusion occurs in the bread, or some lasting conjoining outside the use of the Sacrament [*extra usum sacramenti*]."[178] At the same time, a physical state of union is rejected, as well as the idea that a physical union must continue, according to the laws of physics, apart from the use. In 1563, two Lutheran theologians reject this very aspect of the local inclusion. Gnesio-Lutheran Erhard Sperber rejects the Philippistic accusation: "that, by virtue of the words, the body of Christ thus moved into the bread in geometric or magical inclusion, so that even outside the use it is forced to remain there."[179] The Swedish archbishop Laurentius Petri the Elder at the same time opposes the Calvinist Beurreus's accusation: "that the body of Christ is in the bread, necessarily bound by certain fetters and commingled with the same, either consubstantiated or transubstantiated, stealthily concealed."[180] Beurreus got his formulation from Bucer,[181] who thus even here is documented as the source for talk about the local presence. In Laurentius Petri, consubstantiation clearly means the kind of physical mixing described above.

As already emphasized, the problem that was discussed on the last pages of this chapter is a matter of terminology and thus fictitious. It is up to the decision of every researcher of theological history whether or not to call the doctrine of the Supper of Luther and Lutheranism "consubstantiation," depending on the definition of the term that one comes to. Historical discretion might seem to

process. That is why Chemnitz (op. cit., p. 321 [cf. *Examination of the Council of Trent*, 2:280]), while *retaining* the adoration of the Sacrament, writes: "Neither must the adoration of Christ be connected or affixed to the elements of bread and wine, nor indeed is a local inclusion contained in them." The context here is precisely that the local inclusion creates a mixture that would divinize the bread. On the other hand, Chemnitz does not dispute the adoration of Christ's body directed locally to the bread, an act that initially is said by Chemnitz to be "outside the controversy" in the conflict with the Roman Church. Chemnitz's view of the adoration, which is Lutheran and not Melanchthonian, is described in the final chapter below.

178 *BS* 977.24ff.

179 Sperber, *Christliche und notwendige verantwortung*, fol. 13a.

180 Laurentius Petri, *Responsio . . . ad scriptum Dionijsij Beurrei*, fol. 54a.

181 Compare Beurreus, *Scriptum contra dialogos*, pp. 18f.: "I openly and plainly deny that the body of Christ is in the bread and wine corporeally by a presence connected and attached to the bread and wine" (quoted according to Ahlberg, op. cit., p. 178 n. 16). Ahlberg (op. cit., p. 178) writes: "This declaration in its phraseology is closely connected to a passage in Bucer, which is quoted in its context farther on in the document." "Beurreus, as it seems, has not taken any imprint of Laurentius Petri's criticism against the doctrine of transubstantiation. Obviously Beurreus found it tactically suitable not to observe this distinction between Laurentius Petri and the Roman view, or found it so insignificant that in reality it played no role." Ahlberg does not realize how, with the terms "bodily" [and] "consubstantiated," Bucer-Beurreus actually opposed the strictly Lutheran view of the Supper, while the latter's adherents with the same words designated a fictitious doctrine of the Supper represented by no one.

urge caution in applying an expression to theologians who were not familiar with it themselves or who even rejected it. Again, the research situation can arise in which the word "consubstantiation" is seen as associated with a concrete, realistic thought of the presence, just as the word "transubstantiation" somewhat undeservedly was associated with a stalwart interpretation of the Christian holy Supper. Under such conditions, Luther's doctrine of the Supper both can and ought to be called "consubstantiation," and contesting this designation is rejected as being dictated by incorrect and spiritualizing definitions of the kind of sacramental presence in Luther.[182]

182 The extensive material that is offered by Krauth (op. cit.) shows how seventeenth-century Lutheran orthodoxy thoroughly rejected "consubstantiation." What is quoted thus from Carpzov's *Isagoge*, 1:345ff., in Krauth (op. cit., p. 767) seems to set forth that a *Melanchthonian definition of the presence* made any reasonable use of the word "consubstantiation" impossible. The express denial of the definitive presence is the background for this. Kromayer (*Theologia positivo-polemica*, 2:917f.) concedes the use of the word—"we could allow the word"—but beware of the Calvinist explanation of it: "that is, a meat pie" [*Fleischpastete*]; compare Baier, op. cit., ed. Walther, p. 503. Orthodoxy's dependence on the Melanchthonian definition of the presence will be touched on in more detail in the chapter on the adoration.

CHAPTER 5

Per Illa Verba

Consecration, Validity, and Intention

THE Christian holy Supper not only goes back to the Words of Institution, which are found recorded in the first three Gospels and in Paul, but even from ancient times* it makes use of those same words in the central part of the Divine Service. There they are often considered to effect the miraculous onset of the presence, the sanctifying or consecration of the bread and wine. Concerning the place and function of the Words of Institution in the oldest liturgies, there are indeed various opinions.[1] It is certain that there is unambiguous testimony from the 300s concerning the power of the Words of Institution to effect the presence, both in Ambrose[2] and Chrysostom.[3] Augustine is the source for the classic formulation that summarizes this view in this way: "Let the Word come and it becomes a sacrament" [*accedat verbum et fit sacramentum*].[4] Besides this, there developed the view that in time would be embraced by the Greek Orthodox Church: the eucharistic miracle is ascribed to the whole act of prayer, particularly the invocation of the Spirit, whereby the point of time for the onset of the presence is left more indefinite.[5] The Latin tradition again is the background for the present volume, and it makes the Words

1 * [Translator's note. *av ålder*; the German mistranslates this as "altars."]
Compare here Dix, *Shape of Liturgy*, pp. 178ff., 197ff., 238ff., 275ff.; Watterich, *Der Konsekrationsmoment im heiligen Abendmahl und seine Geschichte*, with the summary on pp. 241f.

2 PL 16:440.

3 PG 49:380.

4 PL 35:1840; compare *Corpus Juris Canonici, Decretum Gratiani* c. 54 C I g. 1 (Friedberg 1:379). The question about the original meaning of the Words cannot be discussed here.

5 Compare Heiler, *Urkirche und Ostkirche*, pp. 256ff.

of Institution the cause of the presence; consequently, it has the presence occur at the speaking of those words.[6]

Within Western Scholasticism there are two different solutions to the problem of the close connection of the Words of Institution to the onset of the presence. According to the general structure of both scholastic systems, Thomism came to consider the Words of Institution as the effective instrument for the occurrence of the presence, while the Franciscan school proceeded from a parallel relationship dependent on God's will: simultaneously with the recitation of the Words of Institution, God fulfills His promise to let the miracle occur.[7] But that only gives a very rough picture of the contrast in question. This is especially true of Thomas's definitions. To gain greater clarity, it is appropriate already at this stage to draw in the Reformation critique of the teachings of the medieval schools on this point.

In the Smalcald Articles, Luther writes:

> Baptism is nothing other than God's Word in the water, commanded through His institution, or, as Paul says, "a washing in the Word," as Augustine also says, "*Accedat verbum ad elementum et fit sacramentum.*" And therefore we do not hold with Thomas and the [Dominican] preaching monks who forget the Word [God's institution] and say that God has placed a spiritual power into the water, which washes away sin through the water, and not with Scotus and the barefoot monks [Franciscans] who teach that Baptism washes away sin with the assistance of the divine will, so that this washing happens only through God's will, and not through the Word and water.[8]

The section has fundamental importance in the question of the relation between Word and element, and the interpretation of Augustine's thesis, and it [this

6 A completely independent tradition within the Latin Church, with Odo of Cambrai, Petrus of Poitiers, and Innocent III in the lead, has the consecration happen anew through a blessing distinct from the Words of Institution; only the effect is announced through the Words of Institution: compare *Die deutsche Thomas-Ausgabe* 30:427f. Building on the fact that the "He blessed" in the account of the institution precedes the "and said," this view shows how the doctrine of the Supper is not necessarily ruled by the statement *lex orandi, lex credendi*. The mentioned authors are not connected to any extant liturgical tradition of the Eastern type, but to a *study of the Bible*. Therefore, there is no reason, for example, in the question of the two competing presentations—the consecration through the Words of Institution or through prayer for the Spirit—to proceed from the idea that possibly the oldest attribution in its turn is to be found in a "living" apostolic tradition. One can never with certainty reach anything other than just an exposition of the Bible that strives to find as direct a connection as possible to the Words of Institution. These Words, nevertheless, have their liturgical place and function among all the relationships considered as the ultimate authorization of the Sacrament.

7 Seeberg, op. cit., 3:510ff.

8 *BS* 449.16ff. [SA III V 1–3].

importance] is not limited only to Baptism. The immediate impression of the text on the modern reader would be that Luther is trying to find a middle way between two extremes, between "too much" and "too little," where Thomas thus lets the words carry the divine power to too high a degree. Here Peter Brunner has wanted to assert that Luther coarsened Thomas's thought.[9] Brunner's reference[10] to a passage in Thomas's *Summa* (III, q. 60, a. 5 ad 2) includes a double mistake, however, which strikes both Thomas's meaning expressed there and the kind of critique that Luther directs against Thomas's meaning formulated in a completely different place, which is controversial only in this case. The section, which Brunner came to understand as being associated with the pertinent problem here of the relationship of the Word (the consecration) to the elements, only states that the element of the sacrament does not have power "by some virtue naturally placed in it, but only from the divine institution." This thesis of Thomas, that the element lacks *naturally given* power, is the answer to the hypothetical question of whether the instituted element could be exchanged for a different one. To this Thomas would reply that it is not valid to replace one physical power with a different one, as exchanging wine for some other drink, in natural context, would be mostly harmless. The sacramental-theological problem thus does not let itself be handled without regard for the only decisive "divine institution." It is in such a context that Thomas distances himself from "a power naturally given" [*virtus naturaliter indita*].[11] On the other hand, he does not make a statement about what Brunner wants to examine.

Thus, for Thomas, it is important to underscore that God brings the sacrament about through a special, supernatural power. Of this power Thomas says, "Whence it may be compared to the absolute and perfect power of any thing, just as an instrument may be compared to the principal agent"; "but the instrumental power has to be transferred from one thing into another, that is incomplete."[12] The instrumental power thus is not the same as *God's* power in the *instrument* of the sacrament; the instrumental power is the power *which is instrumental in connection to God's own work in the sacrament*. This [instrumental] power is imperfect, not divine. This is stated clearly also in direct connection with the

9 Brunner, *Pro Ecclesia*, 1:149f. Compare Grönvik, *Die Taufe in der Theologie Martin Luthers*, p. 91, which supports Brunner: "At the hand of Brunner's presentation, it is clear that Luther's criticism in its coarse form is not going after Thomas."

10 Brunner, op. cit., p. 150 n. 35.

11 The opinion that Thomas disputes is thus the one that nowadays applies a natural philosophical approach to the nourishing characteristics of the bread and wine, and from that derives the sacramental character of these; compare to this Sasse, *This Is My Body*, p. 374 n. 30, which cites Paul Tillich in *Religiöse Verwirklichung* [Berlin: Furche, 1930] and [Wilhelm] Stählin in *Vom göttlichen Geheimnis* [Kassel: Stauda, 1936] as proponents of this view, in Schelling's natural philosophy, repeated by Sasse.

12 *ST*, III, 62, 4.

consecration of the Sacrament of the Altar: "The result is that in the formal words of this Sacrament there is a certain *created* power to make the transformation of this Sacrament, yet [it is an] instrumental [power], just as also in other sacraments, as was said above."[13] The power placed by God into the Words of Institution is, just as "in other sacraments," not His own uncreated power but a finite, created power.

At the same time, it is clear from this reasoning that there is another, uncreated, divine power for which the *created power* [*virtus creata*] is instrumental. This former power, [the uncreated power], is not found in the Words of Institution. It is the power of the Holy Spirit who alone can do "miraculous works." Thomas knows that John of Damascus, for example, teaches that only the power of the Spirit changes the bread, and he affirms this. He only adds: "Instrumental power is not excluded."[14] The created power of the words becomes an intermediary that is interposed. The background for this is Thomas's Christology. The internal effect of the Sacrament comes only from Christ as God: "But the divine power is Christ's because He is God, but not because He is man. Therefore, Christ operates the internal effect of the Sacrament not because He is man, but because He is God."[15] Christ's humanity has not received divine power and therefore cannot exercise divine effect in the Sacrament or elsewhere. The Words of Institution, which are pronounced by Christ as man, therefore have their given limitation: "For since these words are offered from the person of Christ, from His command they achieve an instrumental power from Christ, just as also the rest of His deeds or words have a saving power instrumentally, as has been said above."[16] Therefore, neither did Christ's humanity effect the miracles in the New Testament, for "no creature can do miraculous works as the chief agent; nevertheless, it can do them instrumentally, just as the hand of Christ healed the leper through His touch."[17] Also in this respect Christ's humanity is ascribed with "the power of the chief minister" ahead of the "ministers of the Church"; there is no actual difference, on this point, between Christ's human nature and common humans, who became instruments for God.

When Luther rejects Thomas's "a spiritual power is placed into the water," he would have had a completely clear picture of Thomas's doctrine. Clearly he [Luther] expressed the opposite in another place:

> We are not saying a little power remained in the water through God's touch, but the water has in itself the Father, the Son, the Holy Spirit, and the blessing through the grace of Christ. They are personally present in it,

13 *ST*, III, 78, 4

14 *ST*, III, 78, 4.

15 *ST*, III, 64, 3.

16 *ST*, III, 78, 4.

17 *ST*, III, 78, 4, ad 2.

> not like a tinge of rose in water. But we say rebirth and renewal because the Holy Spirit makes a new thing there. Also because the grace of the Trinity and the man Christ is there, and saving.[18]

A German researcher, Otto Hof, in a commentary on this text, has correctly summarized: "This definition clearly is *not* inferior to, but rather surpasses the Catholic view with its 'metaphysical connection' between Spirit and grace, and outward sign and element."[19] Luther thus in no way wants an intermediate position between two extremes. He is not satisfied with a lowly, created "tinge," but outdoes Thomas many times by putting the Trinity itself in this passage. *"Accedat verbum" means that the element submits to the Creator's own power.*[20] In the following, it shall be presented how this view of "*Accedat verbum*" fully gets its counterpart in Luther's doctrine of the consecration of the Sacrament of the Altar.

Luther's words in the Smalcald Articles clearly indicated the Nominalist-Franciscan school's teaching on the power of the Sacrament as a course of events parallel to the use of the Words of Institution. Herein lies a dissimilarity to Thomas but at the same time a similarity: the Words of Institution contain no uncreated power.[21] This makes it impossible to see Luther's theology of the consecration as equally opposed to both medieval schools. For him the

---

18 WA 45:184.23ff. [sermon on Gallus Day, October 16, 1537].

19 Hof, "Taufe und Heilswerk Christi bei Luther," p. 231. Hof's formulation is directed against Prenter, *Spiritus Creator*, pp. 254ff.

20 Fagerberg (op. cit., p. 171) has Luther directed "to the right against a realistic and to the left against a voluntaristic view of the Sacrament" and wants to find the solution in thinking of the Word as *promise*: "This passage has its midpoint in the Word, in which is expressed what God commands, promises, and effects through the water of Baptism and through the bread and wine of the holy Supper." By disempowering the sacramental formula, for Fagerberg the element loses the divine power that Luther ascribed to it. Fagerberg writes (p. 185): "The water of Baptism is designated as 'a water of God,' 'a divine, heavenly, holy, and blessed water.' . . . That sounds as if the water as such were provided with a miraculous heavenly power; but the Smalcald Articles reject such an understanding as a direct misunderstanding (SA III 5, 2). . . ." Since Fagerberg did not work out for himself the meaning of Thomas's "*virtus creata*," he has to have Luther's words about the actual heavenly power of the water lose their full value.

21 The background for this is common Christology with its distinction of divine and human nature. Cleve (op. cit., p. 96) touches on this relationship in the summary formulation: "A distinction between Biel and Luther is in fact also in the view that Biel distinguishes between the institution and the proclamation of the Sacrament, and attributes the former to God and the latter to Christ, while Luther stresses that the Words of Institution in the Bible are God's own words, which express the meaning that is embraced by Christ in heaven." Behind these words of Cleve there is room in the same work somewhat for Scholasticism's distinction of the two natures whereby Christ's human words lose any power other than proclamation, somewhat Luther's Christology where the human nature has heavenly attributes and thus has power to institute the Sacrament.

essential thing is the words of the consecration as divine, Spirit-filled creative words. A convenient starting point for presenting this view of Luther's can be taken in his *Sermon on the Sacrament* from 1526, the same writing that is the first to contain the doctrine of the omnipresence of Christ's body. Far from thereby making an actual consecration unnecessary, this sermon makes the miraculous power of the Words of Institution the cause of a specific celebration in front of the laity who are listening. The background for this detail is not only the attack by the Sacramentarians but also Luther's positive conviction that the presence means an event beyond and contrary to what is understood from the usual laws of nature. Jesus' actual body and blood take on a new relationship to the space, a miracle effected through the Spirit in the Word. The first parallel is drawn to the Spirit's work in the heart: "When we speak them [the Words of Institution] over the bread, then He is truly there, and yet it is a plain word and voice that is heard. Now, as He comes into the heart without making a hole in it, but is grasped merely through hearing the Word, so He also comes into the bread without having to make a hole in it."[22] The parallel here is in the idea that changing the heart is a much more difficult *miracle* than changing bread: "Isn't the heart much more delicate than bread?"[23] A wicked person does not become pious without a real intervention of the Spirit. The parallel is not seen in the presence being a mere subjective application of the omnipresence through faith; the sacramental presence would therefore have the same character.

The next example takes up the comparison with the miraculously effected virgin birth used earlier by John of Damascus:

> Take another example! How did His mother, Mary, become pregnant? Indeed, it is really such a great miracle when a woman becomes pregnant by a man, but God prophesied that He would be born of a virgin. How did His mother come to that? — The angel Gabriel brings the word: "Behold, you will conceive and will bear a son," etc. With these words Christ enters not only her heart but also her womb, as she hears, grasps, and believes it. No one can say differently than that the power comes through the Word. As it cannot be denied that she becomes pregnant through the Word, and no one knows how it happens, so it is also here. For as soon as Christ speaks "This is My body," then His body is there through the Word and the power of the Holy Spirit. When the Word is not there, then it is mere bread; but when the words come to it, they bring along what they say.[24]

In both cases, the Word effects a real miracle, begetting without man's cooperation with regard to the actual sacramental presence.[25]

22 WA 19:490.20ff. [cf. AE 36:341].

23 WA 19:490.13 [cf. AE 36:341].

24 WA 19:490.24ff. [cf. AE 36:341].

25 The following section, WA 19:491.17ff. [cf. AE 36:342], does not speak about the Word cooperating in the invocation of a miracle but will also cite it as a miracle: "Also, we

In his *Great Confession* on the Supper, Luther develops the doctrine of the consecration as an obvious and indispensable part of His doctrine of the Supper. He finds that Zwingli took particular offense at the consecration: "For Christ nowhere commanded that His body would come from my word, etc."[26] This false opinion is refuted by Luther, who takes up Zwingli's terminology: "*thettelwort*" and "*heisselwort*" ["action-word" and "command-word"]. The former is a word that describes an action of God and does not invoke a repetition: "as when I would beautifully speak from Genesis 1: 'Let there be sun and moon,' yet nothing comes of it."[27] *Heisselwort* is again a word that requires human action, "as in 'You shall have no other gods.'"[28] Luther has the term *thettelwort* mean that Christ brought about a miracle in the first Lord's Supper: "Indeed, just as the sun and moon stood there when He spoke in Genesis 1, 'Let there be sun and moon,' and it was not a lying word, so indeed His Word is not an epilogue, but a powerful Word that does what it says. Psalm 33: 'He spoke, and it was done,' especially because it is spoken here for the first time and should be an action-word [*thettelwort*]."[29] It ought to be noted that "action-word" here mainly retains the sense of a *description* of a divine act in *past* time.[30] Such "action-words" are creative words that brought forth the celestial bodies, and thus are completely equivalent with Jesus' creative words in the *first* Lord's Supper. Luther continues his presentation by referring to Christ's command to repeat the actions of the first Lord's Supper: "For it is all contained in the

believe that Jesus Christ according to His humanity is placed above all creatures and fills all things." Adducing this event means the *opposite* of glossing the real presence into a relationship experienced merely "for me"; through God's work, Jesus' human nature *is made* omnipresent ("was *placed*"). This exaltation is a distinct event, parallel to the onset of the real presence, even more as in neither case does any local movement occur either upward or downward.

26 WA 26:282.24f. [cf. AE 37:181].

27 WA 26:282.20ff. [cf. AE 37:180].

28 WA 26:282.17 [cf. AE 37:180].

29 WA 26:282.2ff. [cf. AE 37:181].

30 Diestelmann (*Luthers Lehre von Konsekration und actio sacramentalis*, p. 10) writes: "Luther calls the Words of consecration '*Thettelworte*' and '*Heisselworte*,' that is, '*Thettelworte*' as words that by God's power do and make what they say, and '*Heisselworte*,' which are spoken not on the basis of human intention but on the basis of divine command ('*Heissens*')." That gives an unclear picture of Luther's definitions: *thettelwort* belong to the past times and now lose the power they once exercised (WA 26:285.26f. [cf. AE 37:185]): "because the word of the deed does not effect the deed, but tells the deed." The same technical error is in Wisløff (op. cit., pp. 154f.): "The Verba are clearly viewed as '*thettelwort*,' by which the miracle of consecration takes place." Apart from this purely terminological error, Diestelmann and Wisløff give, with what is above, a completely correct picture of Luther's doctrine of the consecration.

command-word [*heisselwort*] 'Do this,' and we must not leave out the words."[31] Thus also the words "This is My body" in the Christian celebration of the Supper become creative: "but because the action-words [*thettelwort*] thus are included in the command-words [*heisselwort*] . . . through which they are spoken."[32] This is Luther's doctrine of the consecration: the pastor celebrating the Sacrament takes in his mouth God's own creating words and thus completes the miracle of the Mass. Luther attaches to this how the other sacramental formulas would remain empty formulas without a divine command to repeat them, but through the divine institution that authorizes them, they become powerful, yes, "and if there were a command-word [*heisselwort*] that I might say these action-words [*thettelwort*] 'this is wine' to the water, then you would see whether it wouldn't become wine."[33] The Creator's right to control dead matter may be transferred to humans without limitations. So-called miracles of nature also fit in the theoretical extension of the power of the consecration. Here Luther speaks off the cuff about a word "to" the element ("to the water" [*zum wasser*]) and is not burdened by a fear of being accused of magic or wizardry that would cause the Melanchthonians and Württemberg schools to shy away from such reasoning. When Cleve writes about this view of Luther: "God directs these words to the elements,"[34] it is a terse statement that, unguarded and granted without closer comparison, might indeed seem to conflict with the result of research otherwise. Still, it is urgent here to characterize Cleve's words as, in fact, completely adequate in their immediacy. Luther's own firm statements speak on this. The more precise definitions, which shall be reported in what follows, only clarify this interpretation and do not limit it.

In [Luther's writing] *The Private Mass and the Consecration of Priests*, the opinion already expressed above is repeated: that the Words of Institution do not possess the miraculous power in their own power. Also excluded is the medieval *potestas consecrationis* ["power of consecration"] as a power residing in the priest: "So also, the fact that bread and wine become Christ's body and blood is not because of our doing, speaking, or work, much less anointing or ordination, but it is because of Christ's order, command, and institution."[35] First, Christ's authorization fills the human voice's blessing with the power that produces the miracle. The possessive pronoun "My" in "This is My body" points to Christ who is present and speaks in the consecration, which is not done "in the person of the pastor or minister."[36] If Christ's command is changed in any way,

31 WA 26:287.17f. [cf. AE 37:187].

32 WA 26:284.1ff. [cf. AE 37:183].

33 WA 26:284.22ff. [cf. AE 37:183].

34 Cleve, op. cit., p. 385.

35 WA 38:240.1ff. [cf. AE 38:199].

36 WA 38:240.14f. [cf. AE 38:199].

"then it is nothing, and Christ is no longer there nor is His order."[37] Then the consecration is done in the *pastor's* name and becomes an empty act. In such a case it is no longer Christ who is heard, and it is not His instituting command, "Do this," that sounds forth. This applies to the Roman private Mass without the communion of the assembly.

For the presentation ahead, it is not unimportant to maintain that "command and order" refer to Christ's own instituting command, not to the action of Christians. If the latter violates the first, then Christ's institution has disappeared, and this annuls the validity of the consecration. That applies also concerning Baptism: "This command and institution, which does this, makes it so that the water and Word is a Baptism. Our work or action does not do it *ex opere operato*."[38] In a sermon the following year, Luther makes a careful distinction regarding these things: "We divide Baptism into three distinct parts, which are water, Word, and God's command or order. . . . Those are the parts that belong to the complete essence and correct definition of Baptism."[39] The first part, thus, is the water (the element). To this, as two distinct components, come "God's Word and command."[40] Luther requires the presence of both. Otherwise, with a trinitarian formula for blessing, one would be able to consecrate all kinds of materials according to the Roman pattern and then could say, "Indeed, God's Word and God's creation are with each other, so that one might also say from St. Augustine: *Accedit . elementum, et fit sacramentum*. Why, then, shouldn't that apply and be done also as in Baptism?"[41] By being able to trace certain acts back to "a divine order and command,"[42] just like the legitimate sacraments, however, they would have an actual effect.[43]

---

37 WA 38:240.33 [cf. AE 38:200].

38 WA 38:239.20f. [cf. AE 38:198].

39 WA 37:630.16ff. [cf. AE 57:144]. In the printed edition of 1535, not published by Luther himself, compare WA 37:627.15f. [cf. AE 57:141]: "Therefore, I am also pleased that these sermons of mine in honor of holy Baptism have been published"; compare WA 38:xliii.

40 WA 37:632.5 [cf. AE 57:146].

41 WA 37:636.20ff [cf. AE 57:150].

42 WA 37:636.34 [cf. AE 57:151].

43 Luther, here referring to the first institution, in fact only repeats what, for example, John Chrysostom and John of Damascus expounded. Chrysostom draws the parallel to creation (PG 49:380): "'This is My body,' He says. This word transforms what was placed in front. And just like that word, 'Grow and multiply and fill the earth' (Gen. 1:28), indeed it was proffered once; in that word it offers to our nature for all time for the procreation of children." That does not exclude the act of childbearing as the cause of the child; it only puts it into effect in accordance with God's original institution; compare PG 51:213: "Indeed, what causes us to have children is not marriage at all, but that Word of God that says, 'Grow and multiply and fill the earth' (Gen. 1:28).

The meaning of this three-part definition—element-word-institution—is further explained in a disputation from 1542. For the sake of context, we cite here the thesis, the following "Contra," and the respondent's answer, which Luther attaches at the end: "15. Finally, whenever the sacrament is transferred to another use outside its institution, it is not the sacrament."[44]

> X. Contra 15. Wherever the element and Word of God are, there is the sacrament. In misuse of the sacrament there is element and Word. Therefore, in misuse of the sacrament there is a sacrament. R. Macchabaeus [the respondent in the disputation was Johannes Macchabaeus]: If the major [premise] is understood correctly, it is true: Where the Word is, that is, rightly understood and apprehended by faith, and the element is received according to Christ's institution, there is the true sacrament. But the minor [premise] thus will be false. For even if the external words are in the papistic misuse of the sacrament, nevertheless they are not rightly understood. And, likewise, they cannot be apprehended by faith as they ought. . . . Luther added these words: The sacrament is the Word and the element. The devil with his magicians has the Word and the element. Therefore, he has a sacrament. This saying of Augustine must be understood correctly: Where the Word is, performed according to the institution, and where one trusts this Word, and where the element is, received according to Christ's

---

Whatever witnesses there are, they make use of marriage, but they did not at all generate children." John of Damascus writes (PG 94:1139):

> In the beginning He said, "Let the earth bring forth green grass," and to this very day, with rain falling, by divine precept it is brought forth and strengthened; it brings forth its own offspring—just as God said, "This is My body" and "This is My blood" and "Do this in remembrance of Me" and, by His omnipotent command, until He returns, it is done (as indeed it was said, until He returns)—through the invocation for this new crop with the rain coming, undoubtedly by the overshadowing power of the Holy Spirit.

It is important to note that the reference to creation/first institution does not exclude an effective intermediary for producing fruit/real presence: rain/Spirit. The consecration is not disempowered by reference to the first Supper. Luther makes use of the same parallels as these early church authors (WA 38:242.4ff. [cf. AE 38:202]):

> Thus it happens also in created things, that our doing or work effects nothing, but only God's command and order does so. As when we plow, sow, and plant, then we do our work that is commanded of us, Genesis 3. But it is not such work of ours that produces grain, but the command and order of God when He says to the earth, Genesis 1: "Let the earth bring forth grass, herbs, and all kinds of trees." . . . Also, man and wife [about procreation]. . . . It is the same here also with the sacraments: We bring water and Word together, as He commands us. But such work of ours does not make it Baptism, but Christ's command and order do.

One ought to observe that the creating Word does not result in an automatic, wild growth; agriculture applies here with its acts empowered by the creating Word, acts that produce results.

44 WA 39/2:147.29f. [cf. AE 73:290].

> institution, that is, where the element and Word of Institution are, there is the sacrament, but outside Christ's institution this saying does not pertain to us at all. For the sacraments have their power by virtue of the institution, which God wants thus and prescribed thus. Likewise, if the institution and the will of the institution did not come first, the form would be worth nothing at all, nor the element, nor the sound of the words. Some time ago, the Papists changed the institution, and they use the sacrament in some new way contrary to Christ's institution.[45]

From this it can be learned that the instituting element does not exist without the prescribed use of the element. Undistributed hosts are not elements according to the meaning of Christ's institution. Meanwhile, it is quite important that the way of thinking under review does not consider the omission of the distribution to be the origin and cause of the invalidity of the Sacrament. *The element has never been touched by any word of God.* "Word" is ambiguous. It can refer sometimes to the "sound of words," "external words," the articulation of the human voice, sometimes to the "Word according to the institution," "Word rightly understood and apprehended by faith," the content of the term. The verbal recitation of the Words of Institution does not guarantee that they are understood correctly. Recited in the Roman private Mass, they have a skewed understanding of Christ's intention; thus they are not spoken in the person of Christ and do not have any power. That the element, as such, should not be distributed afterward is only a result of the opinion that already came to be expressed in the invalid consecration and which robbed it of the character of being the powerful Word of God.[46] This means that the communion is not mainly a "stipulation" for the effect of the consecration; having or omitting the communion touches instead on the understanding of Christ's words that are to be known in the recitation of the Words of Institution. When [Carl Fredrik] Wisløff writes: "Furthermore,

45 WA 39/2:159.15f. [cf. AE 73:300–301].

46 An isolated concession of the validity of the private Mass is claimed by Wisløff (op. cit., p. 156): "Peculiarly there is a passage in [Luther's] *The Private Mass*: If Christ's body and blood do not exist in the private Mass because of the priest's misuse . . . 'then He is still there on account of those who believe rightly that they receive the Sacrament.'" Wisløff here has overlooked the context that reads (WA 38:214.28ff. [cf. AE 38:169]): "From such Masses, nothing is offered or distributed to the Christians or to the Church, so that one might be able to say that though the body and blood of Christ are not there on account of the parson, yet He is there for the sake of those who believe rightly that they receive the Sacrament." The meaning is as follows: the Roman private Mass, where no Sacrament is offered to the Church, is invalid, for the condition that validates the Roman Communion Mass is not there, despite its sacrificial character: [that condition is] the fulfillment of the command to commune; compare WA 38:266.5ff. [cf. AE 38:225]: "Therefore, I said in that book that the Papists, if they keep the order of Christ, then they truly have in the Sacrament the true and actual body and blood of Christ." The intention of the sacrifice of the Mass does not as such nullify the validity of the Roman Mass.

it is thereby granted that the recitation of the Verba does not effect any consecration in the private Mass, unless it takes place within 'the order of Christ,' to which above all belongs the communion"[47]—this is misleading in its context. Wisløff's error proceeds from the idea that for Luther the Sacrament primarily consisted of a certain outward order, and this shows up in his astonishment that Luther rejected the Reformed Supper: "In consideration of these components, it is obviously inconsistent when Luther says that the Enthusiasts 'have mere bread and wine.' "[48] Wisløff here thinks that the Reformed, in contrast to the Roman Church, perform the whole "order of Christ." Meanwhile, Luther's condemnation of the Reformed Supper, which fulfills all the outward requisites for endorsement, shows especially clearly how the correct understanding of the Word is determinative for the consecration.

In his *Letter to Those in Frankfurt am Main* from 1533, which is cited by various researchers,[49] Luther teaches that the Sacrament that is celebrated without the pastor's clear confession in the real presence offers "mere bread and wine."[50] The church in Frankfurt, theologically oriented in a middle position and taking Bucer's position in the current dogmatic controversies,[51] forfeited the true, valid Sacrament through the pastors' unwillingness to give a substantive account of the plain biblical statements. They only said "the body that Christ intends."[52] They were unwilling to go any further in answering the question of what the Sacrament gives. If a Lutheran communicant might happen to be misled into partaking in this church's communion, he is defrauded of the true Sacrament: "Now when an uneducated person hears such, then he thinks they are teaching just as we do, and they go to the Sacrament but receive plain bread and wine."[53] "But these fellows would have to be real, lofty archdemons who give me plain bread and wine and let me think it is the body and blood of Christ, and they deceive me so pathetically."[54] This deceptive procedure presupposes a Supper that is outwardly intact: the Verba are recited, the elements are distributed, and the preaching avoids denying this directly. The Lutheran communicant believes in the real presence and approaches the altar in Frankfurt to

47 Wisløff, op. cit., p. 157.

48 Id., p. 156 n. 16.

49 Grass, op. cit., p. 113; Sasse, op. cit., p. 284; Peters, op. cit., p. 102; Wisløff, op. cit., p. 156 n. 16.

50 WA 30/3:565.10.

51 WA 30/3:555: "In Luther's letter to those at Frankfurt he saw his own position on the Supper attacked—a mediating and enigmatic position that envelops the contrasts."

52 WA 30/3:561.27.

53 WA 30/3:559.7ff.

54 WA 30/3:565.9ff.

receive Christ's body and blood. Yet the presence is not there. The Sacrament is an empty game.[55]

The fundamental biblicism that allows biblical words to replace a dogmatic investigation of the meaning of the words and that annuls the Sacrament is seen by Luther as an indication of intellectual laziness of a satanic kind: "Now where there are such preachers, they are well off and have found an easy way to preach; they no longer need Scripture and study, for on every point they can say to the people: Dear people, be content, believe what Christ intends, that is enough. Who couldn't preach like that? Who wouldn't want to be his student?"[56] Behind this decision of *not* taking a position is, in the deepest sense, taking the position *for* false doctrine: "But they are unwilling to say what it is that Christ intends, for they fear that if they were to say that, the whole world would say, That's not what Christ intends, but that's what you yourself intend, and your father, the devil, along with you; and you use Christ's name as a cover for your lies in order to deceive and destroy us."[57]

---

55 This problem has to be fundamentally distinguished from the question about church fellowship with the erring. In relation to the Reformed, of course, the possibility of Communion fellowship disappears already with regard to the invalidity of the Reformed Sacrament, but this is not the only reason. Luther's rejection of Communion with the Bohemians more clearly registers the various reasons (WA Br 12[:380].14ff., no. 4304):

> Since one does not know what these or those do, it is better that they keep the Sacrament for themselves. Especially since the Hussites hold to the pope and no longer follow Hus, their fellowship in the Sacrament is to be avoided so that one does not participate in their character as well as the pope's. And since they retain the private Mass, and speak the Words secretly, no one can be sure whether they are spoken, *quia omnis homo mendax* ["because every man is a liar," Rom. 3:4].

The validity comes only secondhand; it is more important that the Bohemians are heretical and have gotten closer to the pope. Therefore, sacramental fellowship with them is fellowship with heresy. (Obviously the basis for this statement is 2 John 11: "Whoever greets him makes himself partaker in his evil deed.")

56 WA 30/3:562.14ff.

57 WA 30/3:562.9ff. Compare WA 23:67.34ff. [cf. AE 37:15], where disinclination to controversy and inclination to unity is seen as the cause for the authority of tradition, councils, and the pope: "Thus the plan is directed for the fathers: Since they thought they could have Scripture without quarrel and discord, so that they have become the reason people have completely and totally abandoned Scripture for a purely human work." The apocalyptic finale becomes a new institutionalization, parallel with the one that led to the papacy (WA 23:69.34ff. [cf. AE 37:17]): "And if the world were to stand much longer, one would again, as the ancients did, also seek human schemes on account of such discord, and again establish laws and commandments to keep the people united in faith, which will also be as successful as it was before." The demonic power needs this, through despair of the truth in regard to the Word of the Bible (WA 23:71.3f. [cf. AE 37:17]): "that we become weary of Scripture and reluctant to trust it." *The doctrinal controversy that arose around the Sacrament is the beginning*

In the *Great Confession* on the Supper, [Luther] says that "our Enthusiasts do not consecrate or bless."[58] That does not refer to a failure to recite the Words of Institution formally, but the proper use of them. The words are actually spoken, since Luther says, "It would be good . . . instead of the uncertain texts to pray even an Ave Maria, or if they actually shy away from being old or new Papists [meaning Roman Catholics or Lutherans, according to the way the Enthusiasts spoke], . . . they might therefore sing 'Christ Is Arisen' or 'Christ Went Up to Heaven,' because such hymns and words especially go against the text in the Supper."[59] Luther understands the Reformed reading of the Words of Institution as meaningless, and [he] mockingly suggests an Ave Maria or a hymn instead. This rejection is repeated in the closing section of his *Confession on the Supper*, which has the character of a spiritual testament to prevent false interpretations of the reformer's work: "For by God's grace, I recognize Satan a lot. If he can pervert and confuse God's Word and Scripture, what wouldn't he do with my writings or those of someone else?"[60] In this testament he says that the Sacrament has its full validity regardless of the priest's personal worthiness and faith, but with the stipulation: "If it would happen that they change God's Word and order and explain it differently, as the current enemies of the Sacrament do, then they indeed have plain bread and wine, for they also do not have the words and instituted order of God, but they pervert and change it with their own darkness."[61] That does not refer to a ritual event that is truncated in its outward order, but [to] the Reformed doctrine of the Sacrament that changed Christ's Words of Institution to their own understanding, even if the outward order remains. In that way the Reformed Supper loses both God's Word (the

of this final controversy (WA 23:69.23ff. [cf. AE 37:16]): "But he will not let it go, but quickly begins with the sacraments." — For Luther, it is thus necessary to be able to give an account of the content of the words of the Bible; compare WA 39/2:305.22: "We must retain the matter; whatever words we will use to say it"; WA 50:572.23ff. [cf. AE 41:83]: "But one cannot hold that one should not use more or different words, which are not in Scripture, especially in arguing, even if the heretics want to falsify the matter with blind grasping and will twist the words of Scripture."

58 WA 26:389.14 [cf. AE 37:260].

59 WA 26:389.16f. [cf. AE 37:260]. Such a blasphemous consecration with an Ave Maria is described as a reality in WA TR 4[:704] n. 28: a Pomeranian court chaplain who while drunk confessed this breach [and] was punished with death. Compare the same description WA TR 4[:704–5].21ff., no. 5185: "As also Muntzer confessed—God forgive me that I repeat the blasphemous words—that at Halle in fact he ate two hundred unconsecrated Lord Gods. And that is the best reason for us to have attacked the private Masses. Today also a public consecration is demonstrated for me; the whole church along with the priest give consent and review the words."

60 WA 26:500.23ff. [cf. AE 37:361].

61 WA 26:506.26ff. [cf. AE 37:367].

consecration) and God's order (God's authorization of the consecration).[62] This testamental delineation by Luther regarding the validity of the Sacrament is confessionalized in the Formula of Concord.[63]

A basic commentary by Luther on where this eucharistic invalidity stands in God's counsel of salvation can be drawn conclusively from *That These Words of Christ [This Is My Body]* from 1527, where it appeals to Luke 2:34—"He is set for the fall and rising of many"—and says,

> It is beneficial and good that the arrogant godless blasphemers are thus separated, that they do not partake of the holy Sacrament, for one should "not cast holiness before dogs nor pearls before swine" [Matt. 7:6]. But now the Enthusiasts believe there is plain bread and wine there, and so that is really how it is: As they believe, so they have it. And so they eat plain bread and wine and do not receive the Lord's body either spiritually or bodily. It is very good and beneficial that our good thing is not strewn among the unworthy but is kept holy and pure among the humble alone.[64]

With these words Luther is not retracting his other statements about the objectivity of the Sacrament and about the eating of Christ's body by the unworthy. Here he is indicating the overt form of unbelief that attacks what the Word proclaims, empties it of its biblical content, and thereby awkwardly enjoys only bread and wine in the Sacrament. Herein God's rejection and wrath come true: "First, it is also beneficial that arrogant, clever spirits and [human] reason are blinded and shamed."[65] What Luther had to say about the validity or invalidity thus lays claim to stating religious realities that place man face-to-face with the ultimate decision.

This view of Luther is reflected in the research only to a small degree. It is accepted as a given that the private Mass being a valid Sacrament was rejected by Luther,[66] but in the same context there is no account for how the Word of

---

62 The word "order" [*ordnung*] is understood in a similar case by Wisløff obviously as a certain arranged [ordained, *ordnat*] event; compare above, pp. 181–82, text near nn. 47–48 [Swedish edition, p. 166], not as [prescribed] ordinance [*förordning*], which is the correct translation; compare above, p. 179, text around n. 38 and on [Swedish edition, pp. 164ff.].

63 *BS* 982.11f. [cf. FC SD VII 32].

64 WA 23:255.6ff. [cf. AE 37:131–32].

65 WA 23:255.1ff. [cf. AE 37:131].

66 Wisløff (op. cit., p. 172), however, wants to inject a certain reservation: for Luther "it is not possible to get away from the thought that it really is the body and blood of God's Son that is treated this way in the Mass." Therefore, the sacrifice of the Mass becomes a very serious sacrilege of it. Peters (op. cit., p. 101) finds the same uncertainty in Luther: "In the evaluation of the private Mass, two lines of expression run alongside each other here": a definite "we do not know," and a clear negative, "a clear no." What has become for these researchers an ambivalence between two thoughts is meanwhile for Luther a single thought (WA 38:210.5ff. [cf. AE 38:163]): "Yes, I still say further, since it is

God spoken there is robbed of its effect. Wisløff's challenge of the inconsistency in Luther's rejection of the Reformed Supper is significant. But Wisløff maintains that this thought occurs in Luther, over against [Hans] Grass, who denies that Luther really intended his words as a rejection.[67] [Hermann] Sasse makes a correct but compressed presentation: the Reformed Supper is not a sacrament of Christ, "for in those words Christ Himself speaks, and the minister would not speak '*ex persona Christi*' if he did not speak the Words of Institution as Christ understood them and wanted them to be understood."[68] No more detailed investigation is offered. Peters is of the same opinion, but like Grass includes the citation that would soften the fundamental thesis about a validity "only . . . where the pastor proclaims and acts according to the institution."[69] The reasoning of [Vilmos] Vajta likewise does not concede that a problem of validity exists, since an inadmissible objectivity would thereby destroy the dialectic framework, which is why there is no opinion about the topic in his [writings]. [Åke] Andrén rejects the thought of a validity independent of faith.[70]

The idea that Luther would have asserted a sacramental validity by virtue of the recipient's faith, with the omission of the consecration as an objective guarantee of the validity, among other things, relies on the reformer's opinion concerning chaplain Besserer, who distributed an unconsecrated host during the Mass: "He dared to consider consecrated hosts and unconsecrated hosts as the same thing."[71] Already this introductory summary of the situation by Luther in a letter to Nicolaus von Amsdorf and the decisive anathema—"*Vadat ad suos Zuinglianos*" ["Let him go to his Zwinglians"]—of someone who dared to offer a yet unconsecrated host ought to remove any doubt about whether "Luther

---

uncertain whether the body and blood of Christ are in the private Mass, and certainly it is a plain work of man, then you should not believe on body and life that Christ's body and blood are there. For faith should be certain of a thing and have a sure basis." If a teaching is uncertain, that is, if it cannot be securely ascribed to the Bible, then it must be rejected, not taught as an imaginable alternative. Faith knows only God's Word as endorsement, and outside of faith there is not a neutral no-man's-land where any speculative opinions can be promoted at all. Luther does not recognize a distinction between dogma and theologoumenon; compare above, chapter 4.

67 Grass, op. cit., p. 114.

68 Sasse, op. cit., p. 372.

69 Peters, op. cit., p. 102.

70 Andrén, op. cit., p. 51.

71 WA Br 11[:259].6f., no. 4186, cited by Grass, op. cit., p. 114; Andrén, op. cit., p. 51; Wisløff, op. cit., p. 156 n. 16; Peters, op. cit., p. 104 n. 86. Wisløff and Peters, however, see as an exception what Andrén understands as a rule. Grass can be said to take a middle position.

asserted a consecration over the elements."[72] The continuation [of the citation], which is debated unnecessarily, says,

> Furthermore, he who received the unconsecrated host did not sin; his faith saved him, in that he believed that he received the true Sacrament, and he was joined to the Word of God and was not false. Just as someone is baptized who believes, even if he was playing, or if the one who baptized him had baptized him with a different liquid. But it is not necessary to dispute anything so acutely here, lest inexperienced consciences be troubled or provoked. It suffices that all things are possible to one who believes.[73]

From this, people wanted to conclude that "one who received an unconsecrated host in good faith has nevertheless received the true Sacrament."[74] The following can be cited to refute this. Luther concludes with a warning: some people's feelings could be harmed. This careful attitude seems inexplicable if the preceding opinions contained an actual confirmation of the presence in the case under debate. That seems understandable only if the communicant who acted in good faith was actually deceived about [receiving] Christ's body. What Luther actually says in his investigation, upon closer analysis, unanimously confirms this latter alternative. In contrast to the harsh judgment on the priest who was directly removed from the church, the unknowing guest at the Lord's Supper should be reassured as far as possible: "He did not sin; his faith saved him." He has committed no sin and was deprived of no blessing, despite the fact that he received plain bread. His situation accords with what Luther in very similar terms cited elsewhere regarding those who receive the Sacrament in good faith in an assembly that is aware of the pastor's Reformed false doctrine: "Indeed, where the church is informed that there is only bread, and it is granted that there are one, two, or three who believe, nevertheless they do not receive the body of Christ. Only the mouth is cheated; faith is not cheated. Faith does not sin."[75]

---

72 Andrén, ibid.

73 WA Br 11[:259].11ff., no. 4186.

74 Wisløff, ibid.

75 WA 38:187.21ff. The words are preceded by what follows here (WA 38:187.15ff.):

> I put the case that the minister is completely wicked who thinks that he offers nothing other than bread and wine. The whole church, however, believes it is body and blood, and he alone is the Epicurean. What is happening here? I reply: The mouth is deceived, faith is not deceived; and yet, if he says the words while the church is listening, the danger is for this impious priest, not for the church, which believes in the words and receives what the words say and what faith believes. Nevertheless it is so, if he does not preach publicly against the Sacrament as happens today among the Sacramentarians.

After the words of the text, Luther continues: "Moreover, if only the [individual] person is unbelieving, this takes nothing away from the Sacrament at all. For Christ placed the Sacrament in Himself, not in the person of the minister." An individual pastor's unbelief, which he harbors privately, does not harm the administration of the

The parallel to Baptism, drawn by Luther, gives further clarity. Luther uses the same expression, "All things are possible to the believer," even in the case where a person believes he is baptized but is not: "And finally I say: If someone was never baptized, but did not know otherwise or strongly believed that he was truly and indeed baptized, then such faith would still be enough for him. For as he believes, so he is before God, and all things are possible to the believer (Christ says), and one could not baptize such a person again without endangering his faith." It is confirmed here simultaneously that there is no Baptism, that faith still believes for salvation, and that the one deceived ought not to be exposed to the objective truth since his subjective relationship would not tolerate it. In a different context Luther stated that there is no Baptism in the case of baptism with a different material ("different liquid"): "If you baptize someone without water or with ashes, even though you speak the correct words, such a baptism would not forgive sin, but would be a mark of good fellowship. Behold, that was not only a sin against Baptism, but [it also] changed Baptism itself and perverted Christ's intent. Therefore, there is no Baptism there."[76] "So also if you would use something other than the designated or named material and yet you spoke . . . the correct words, that would not be a Baptism, but flitting about and despising the Sacrament, just as one who would willfully ignore the order and command (through which the material is clearly named), just as also in the Sacrament of Christ's body and blood, if the command and institution are not kept, then it is no Sacrament."[77] This and other similar rejections of the validity of Baptism with

---

Sacrament, but it is invalidated by the pastor's "public doctrine." This section gives background to WA TR 4[:703].5ff., no. 5184:

> Can a heretic offer true sacraments? The Doctor was asked about this matter and responded: Yes! If he is not known to be a heretic. But as soon as he proclaims his heresy concerning the sacraments, then he does not offer the Sacrament. The Sacramentarians, who deny Christ's body with the church, do not distribute Christ's body; thus the Anabaptists who deny Baptism do not truly baptize. But if someone does not know and falls in among the Sacramentarians and believes that he receives the true body, he receives the true Sacrament.

Grass (op. cit., p. 114) cites this section as evidence of Luther's opinion that faith can replace the consecration as the guarantee of the Sacrament, but he does not see the background of "*he does not know* and falls in among the Sacramentarians," which is formed by the introductory "if *he is not known* to be a heretic" in contrast to "he proclaims his heresy." Luther thus is speaking not about a Lutheran who unwittingly went to a Reformed Lord's Supper, but about a Lutheran who goes to a Lutheran altar where the pastor is a crypto-Zwinglian. In this latter case, "the true Sacrament" is offered and received.

76 WA 38:235.31ff. [cf. AE 38:194]. Compare here Cleve, op. cit., p. 59 n. 93.

77 WA 37:638.11ff. [cf. AE 57:152–53].

the wrong material[78] show how Luther, in the case of Besserer, imagines that the salvation that is communicated to the communicant does not go back to a truly consecrated Sacrament but to this person's subjective character of faith.

78 A joint statement delivered by Bugenhagen from 1541 declares Baptism without water to be "an empty thing" (WA Br 9[:503].28, no. 3660); compare also WA Br 3[:611].17f., no. 942, addendum: "For as faith is sufficient in Baptism, nevertheless it is necessary for me to know that I was baptized with water and not with mud or sand." Baptism with the right material but with an Arian understanding of the trinitarian formula is described thus (WA 54:159.29f. [cf. AE 38:309]): "Then you hear that even the true holy name of God does not help at all, but harms those who do not believe rightly but misuse it. Therefore, also the ancient fathers disputed whether the baptism of Arians also was a real Baptism. Thus one misfortune always follows another." (A note in the WA correcting this shows that the publisher did not understand Luther's words: "The controversy over baptism by heretics [AD 255–257] was already before the time of Arius." It does not apply to heretical baptism in general, but to baptism by such heretics who do not in fact fundamentally change the baptism formula.) Compare here WA 39/2:231.16ff. [cf. AE 73:362–63] with Luther's answer given before in a disputation: "If he thinks and teaches contrary, it is not a true baptism. Arius and the rest cannot truly baptize even if they say, 'In the name of the Father and of the Son and of the Holy Spirit.'" (Version A, however, gives an affirmative answer: "It can, when the Words of Institution are retained" [WA 39/2:230.20ff. (cf. AE 73:362)].) — Luther's words, in the case of Besserer, "he was playing or he had baptized him with a different liquid," might be cited as an objection to the thesis of the present volume, that Luther however affirms the validity of a play-baptism; compare WA 1:323.38ff.; 1:544.1ff. [cf. AE 31:105]; 6:531.20ff. [cf. AE 36:63f.]; 7:379.8ff. [cf. AE 32:49]; 38:242.32ff. [cf. AE 38:203]. Compare here Wisløff, op. cit., p. 157 n. 17; Landgraf, op. cit., 3/1:119ff., in which latter work medieval adherents of this view are mentioned. As Wisløff points out, Luther here joins himself to this older tradition. But in none of these cases does Luther intend *primarily* to make a statement on the question of the validity of the Sacrament, as he actually does when, for example, he condemns baptism with other materials. He is looking only for illustrations for the thesis that faith is the deciding factor in salvation: "And it is not necessary to think here, 'What if the priest makes a mistake,' because remission depends not on the priest but on the Word of Christ" (WA 1:543.35f. [cf. AE 31:105]); "The power of Baptism is placed in the recipient's faith or use" (WA 6:531.21f. [cf. AE 36:64]). With the scholastic material, "The Papists themselves confess" (WA 38:242.31 [cf. AE 38:203]), Luther wants to show the power of *desired Baptism* and thus *faith*: "They must confess that the one who receives the benefit of the Sacrament is the one who heartily desires it, even if it were stubbornly denied to him by the priest" (WA 7:379.30ff. [cf. AE 32:49]). For Luther the pretend-baptism of these examples are replaced with no baptism at all. It can be proved more clearly that Luther is not discussing the validity of pretend-baptism, but faith as the only means for grasping salvation. — The WA has been unable to confirm the provenance of the example: the case of the pretend-baptism performed by the boy Athanasius and approved by Bishop Alexander is found in Rufinus, *Historia ecclesiastica* (PL 21:487); Sozomenus, *Historia ecclesiastica* (PG 67:978f.). Compare below, pp. 191–92 n. 86. Luther would have known it through *Corpus Juris Canonici*, CI qu. 1, c. 58 (Friedberg 1:380). StL 10:1229 specifies Rufinus as the source, but without reference to canon law.

As further support for his thesis that "it is valid even when the minister . . . makes a mistake, perhaps in reciting the Words of Institution," [and] "the faith of the communicant wipes away the deficiency and error of the minister,"[79] Grass refers to some words from *The Private Mass and Consecration of Priests*: "If he stumbles in the words or makes a mistake or forgets whether he has spoken the words, then we are there, listening . . . ."[80] Thus Grass thinks that, in an emergency, faith validates the Sacrament that perhaps was not consecrated at all ("forgets whether he spoke the words"). Meanwhile, Luther's intent is the direct opposite and forms a front against the type of proposed solution that Grass gives as a sample. The background to Luther's argumentation is that earlier in the same writing he asserted that the validity of the private Mass is questionable even by the priests' sometimes forgetting to read the Words of Institution. With the silent reading of the Mass, this situation never needed to be revealed.[81] Luther disallows the Scholastics' proposed solution that the consecration in such a case happens "by virtue of the first intention," that is, through the priest's previously understood intent to consecrate. This solution is rejected as "wisdom of men": "Who will assure us here that it was said correctly and that the power of the first intention is so powerful?"[82] In express contrast to the view of Scholasticism and of Grass, Luther thinks that the objective act of the consecration cannot be replaced by an additional subjective act. Luther defines himself very keenly against this possibility. Nor does he know any undogmatic generosity that thinks it can ignore the question of the validity: "So also, if they take comfort that the pastor does not make a transformation, and they had adored plain bread and wine, that is not a shame to their faith, yes, rather, you say, Whoever had the guarantee that it was true."[83] To set oneself up willingly to risk committing bread-worship in the Mass is unthinkable for Luther. This whole problem is removed once and for all by reading the consecration aloud in the Lutheran Mass: "If he stumbles in the words or makes a mistake or forgets whether he has spoken the words, then we are there, listening, confirming, and are sure that they were spoken. Therefore, we cannot be deceived."[84] By reading the consecration aloud, the Lutheran congregation can thus be convinced that the Verba were not forgotten or actually garbled, and *thus* that the Sacrament is valid. The presupposition for Luther's reasoning is that in no case does faith replace the consecration. This advantage of the Lutheran Mass gives Luther impetus for the famous triumphant description of the splendor of

79 Grass, op. cit., p. 114.

80 WA 38:248.29ff. [cf. AE 38:209].

81 WA 38:214.33ff. [cf. AE 38:169f.]; the same reasoning: WA 39/2:156.13ff.

82 WA 38:215.11ff. [cf. AE 38:170].

83 WA 38:215.16ff. [cf. AE 38:170].

84 WA 38:248.30ff. [cf. AE 38:209].

the Reformation's Divine Service, which here must have its place as a positive counterweight to the many negative distinctions that have to belong to a correct picture of Luther's sacramental theology:

> For, God be praised, in our church we can show a Christian a truly Christian Mass according to the order and institution of Christ, also according to the proper intention of Christ and the Church. So our pastor, bishop, or servant, rightly and honestly and publicly called in the pastoral office, steps before the altar, consecrated beforehand however in Baptism, anointed and born as a priest of Christ, without regard for the private anointing; he sings publicly and clearly the order of Christ, once instituted in the Supper, takes the bread and wine, gives thanks, distributes it and gives it by virtue of Christ's words: "*This* is My body, *this* is My blood. Do *this*," etc., to the rest of us who are there and will receive. And we, especially those who will receive the Sacrament, kneel beside, behind, and around—man, woman, young, old, lord, servant, lady, maidservant, parents, children—as God then brings us all together, along with the true saints and the priest, sanctified through Christ's blood and anointed with the Holy Spirit and consecrated in Baptism. And in our inborn, inherited priestly honor and adornment we are there, have (as pictured in Revelation 4) our golden crowns on our heads, harps in our hands, and golden censers, and let our pastor speak the order of Christ, not for his own person, but he is the mouth for all of us, and we all speak them with him from our heart and with faith directed to the Lamb of God who is before us and in us and feeds us with His body and blood according to His order. That is our Mass, and the true Mass, which we are not lacking.[85]

That is what the true Mass and true consecration look like.

Research has dismissed the thought that Luther would promote the teaching of the necessity of the pastor's "intention." Nor does any evidence exist that Luther would have shared this high- and late-scholastic view that a malicious priest would be able, through an internal spiritual act, to invalidate a sacrament that is connected with orthodox proclamation.[86] The material presented here

85 WA 38:247.10ff. [cf. AE 38:208f.].

86 Compare Landgraf, op. cit., 3/1:119f. Chemnitz (*Examination of the Council of Trent*, 2:99ff. [Latin, pp. 256ff.]) shows how this makes all administration of the sacraments uncertain, and the only solution was finally to use trustworthy priests and ultimately to trust in the power of the Sacrament *in voto* ["in the vow"] (desired Baptism, etc.), even if the priest suppresses the necessary intent that at any rate gives what the Church gives. Chemnitz states that Augustine and Lombard, who do not share later Scholasticism's requirement of intention, nevertheless do not acknowledge a Baptism that is performed entirely in jest. Here Chemnitz writes extensively (op. cit., 2:101f. [Latin, p. 257]):

> For the institution of Baptism does not want any common washing to happen, or what might be declared as nothing but ridiculous or farcical mocking or profaning the institution by reciting the words; but it requires that the particular act be established, and indeed that act which Christ

also excludes such a possibility. Everything is dependent on the external Word and its openly proclaimed content. On the other hand, evidences for an express denial of the intention, referred to by various researchers, cannot be accepted. Grass[87] refers to the passage on the consecration discussed above "by virtue of the first intention," but that does not refer to the priest's internal disposition in reciting the Verba, which constitutes the term "intention" within sacramental theology. What comes after that, to which Grass might also be referring, actually attacks the "intention and faith of the Church," but these words mean implicit faith or the collier's faith: "What one does in the faith and intention of the Church is correct," thus the Roman defense of the private Mass as traditionally approved and prescribed by "the Church."[88] Wisløff[89] cites a section from the same text as proof of the rejection of intention,[90] but Luther here simply says that one cannot teach the validity of the private Mass, since the recitation of the Words of Institution there always remains uncertain. Some pages later, Luther actually seems to approach this thought of intention:

> Also, if a layman or listener were certain that his private parson speaks the words, how does he know for sure that he speaks them in faith? For a parson can speak the words, and then think differently. "I will speak such words by command. I don't concern myself with whether the body and blood of Christ come from them or not; others can be concerned with that." Who knows how many parsons like that there were or still are? . . . What is the private Mass here other than a shameful abomination, which blasphemously misleads the listeners?[91]

But this is not an argumentation about intention that conforms to Scholasticism. Luther is imagining a priest who consciously acts "by command" and thereby fulfills the scholastic requirement of "doing what the Church does." On the other

---

> established. And this suffices for preserving the institution. What indeed he who administers the Baptism thinks in his heart, this does not pertain to the truth or integrity of the Baptism; nor does Lombard wish this. Also the judgment of the bishops is known, concerning the act of Athanasius, who as a boy was playing on the seashore; he pretended that he was the bishop, and by the custom of the bishop, while playing, he baptized boys in the name of the Trinity. Sozomus describes this story, book 2, ch. 17, and Rufinus, in book 10, Eusebius, ch. 14.

Here Chemnitz distinguishes the "silly game" and Athanasius's pretend baptism, which in accordance with the sources obviously is perceived as the game of a pious child with serious intent (compare PG 67:979): "who once in simplicity merited receiving divine grace." The account is repeated as evidence of the early *piety* of Athanasius.

87 Grass, op. cit., p. 114 n. 2.

88 WA 38:215.30ff. [cf. AE 38:170f.].

89 Wisløff, op. cit., p. 157 n. 17.

90 WA 38:210.31ff. [cf. AE 38:164].

91 WA 38:213.30ff. [cf. AE 38:168].

hand, he is not fulfilling Luther's requirement of consecrating in accordance with an orthodox proclamation. The Mass-priest may be one of the contemporaneous enlightened Renaissance theologians, whose candid skepticism Luther then portrayed right after this:

> It is said that now some Papists are Zwinglian and even hold that there is plain bread and wine in the Sacrament, and even boast that they want to celebrate the Mass even more from now on, since worry and risk concerning the body and blood of Christ is gone. Now they are almost Epicureans, Skeptics, and Lucians, who celebrate Mass for the sake of the pay, and they are hypocrites to the pope and bishops when they almost scold the Lutherans, even swear they would let themselves be torn apart before they would believe differently than the Church does. For since they believe in no god, they think such an oath doesn't hurt them. At the same time they mock the whole Christian religion and consider us great fools who believe such strange and fantastical articles. And among them are even bishops and scholars who have used three languages.[92]

Some of the private Mass's silent clergy, outside the control of the assembly that is celebrating the Divine Service, may thus be expected to recite the Verba in a Zwinglian way and to celebrate a Zwinglian private Mass, which falls under the condemnation against both private Masses and the Reformed Supper. That the Verba are not spoken "in faith" does not refer to the priest's personal faith, which might waver, nor the absence of intention according to medieval requirement, but an actual, open acceptance of humanism that criticizes religion, along with its contempt for traditional, dogmatic Christianity. But through the silent Mass without preaching, this apostasy does not have to become known to the congregation, which in this way is defrauded of the Sacrament.[93]

92 WA 38:212.31ff. [cf. AE 38:167].

93 Such Zwinglian private Masses are mentioned also in WA 23:270.20ff. [cf. AE 37:142]. Also whether Luther sees the Reformed doctrine of the Supper as the beginning of a general denial [of it], WA 23:69.34f. [cf. AE 37:16], compare above, pp. 183–84 n. 57; and in the Reformed refusal to acknowledge the Sacrament as means of grace he recognizes the denial of the revolution to see the government as God's means in the world of the Law (WA 30/1:220.4ff.); on the eschatological stage he presents Rome giving birth to both atheism and despising the Sacrament of the Altar, compare Headley, *Luther's View of Church History*, pp. 250ff. Erasmus is the father of atheism (WA Br 6[:565–66], no. 2076), but also of Zwingli (WA TR 5[:310], no. 5670). (The same opinion about the origin of the Lord's Supper controversy is expressed by Melanchthon, CR 1:1083: "That whole tragedy concerning the Lord's Supper can be seen to have been born from him." CR 4:970: "Zwingli confessed to me that he first drank in his opinion concerning the Lord's Supper from the writings of Erasmus.") It comes from Italy "that one made mockery of faith in an Epicurean way, and children also were no longer baptized. So both Baptism, Sacrament, and Word were all gone, and no one was saved [any more]" ([Otto] Albrecht, "Luthers Arbeiten an der Übersetzung und Auslegung des Propheten Daniel in den Jahren 1530 und 1541," *ARG* 23, p. 42). Least of all does Luther present the papacy as the special guardian of the Sacrament. Even after the course of many

MELANCHTHON

Concerning Melanchthon, [Bo] Ahlberg writes: "If it is difficult to get information on Luther's view of the consecration, it is even harder when it comes to Melanchthon's view."[94] Ahlberg finds that only [Jürgen] Diestelmann gives any detailed expression on the question, with some words "about 'Melanchthon's denial of the consecration' as an apostasy from Luther's doctrine and a dogmatic-historical 'innovation' [*novum*]." This thesis of Diestelmann is rejected as too perfunctory. In the work itself, what matters is how the consecration is defined by Melanchthon: "It is not a question of the substance changing through the power of the Words, but having the action become a comfort to the soul through Christ's Words and thanksgiving."[95]

> Thus there is a kind of doctrine of consecration in Melanchthon, even if it does not fit Diestelmann's scheme. Meanwhile, the difficulties of getting a handle on it, as well as on Melanchthon's doctrine of the Supper on the whole, are unusually great. In a series of texts, one must reckon with Melanchthon representing "a foreign opinion" [*aliena sententia*]. And finally, Melanchthon's statements are so vague that they allow several different interpretations.[96]

Since Ahlberg's work came out, Neuser has carefully tried to give Melanchthon's doctrine of consecration its due acuity, but without seeing its consequences in connection with Melanchthon's doctrine of identifying the omnipresence with

---

years, he retains the memory of the blasphemous celebration of the Mass that he witnessed in Rome during his visit there (WA 38:211.32ff. [cf. AE 38:166]):

> I was in Rome (not long), celebrated many Masses there myself and also saw many Masses celebrated, which grieves me when I think about it. Then I heard, among other good things, coarse anecdotes at table, courtiers laughing and boasting how some [priests] held Masses and spoke these words over the bread and wine: You are bread; you will remain bread. You are wine; you will remain wine. And then they elevate them . . . how nicely I was deceived, when I had heard so many Masses from them.

94 Ahlberg, op. cit., p. 155.

95 Id., op. cit., 156.

96 Id., op. cit., 157. With the expression "*aliena sententia*," Ahlberg would attribute a conscious ambiguity to Melanchthon, who at times would have represented a Lutheran standpoint that he himself did not share. The meaning that Reformed authors gave to Melanchthon's January 10, 1535, letter to Camerarius (CR 2:822f.) was refuted already in 1706 by [Valentin Ernst] Löscher (*Ausführliche Historia Motuum*, 2:27), who shows that Melanchthon thereby only intends to say that after he came home to Wittenberg from a colloquy with Bucer, he was only reporting the latter's opinion; compare CR 2:823: "I have only reported Bucer's opinion here." Compare Ritschl, op. cit., 4:18 n. 75; Gollwitzer, p. 66 n. 1.

the sacramental presence.[97] In light of this presentation, Melanchthon's doctrine of the consecration actually becomes less unclear in its structure. Already in 1528, Melanchthon in this respect expresses himself clearly under the pressure of criticism from Oecolampadius. His letter includes several points that would be repeated within the Melanchthonian school's polemic and therefore are cited here in their entirety:

> In the cause of the *synaxis*, the consecration, as they call it, has actually offended me for a long time. And Oecolampadius strongly insists: Who can cause Christ to be called down from heaven? Does this happen by the merits and prayers of the priest or the people, or, as some said, by virtue of the words? Finally, I have come to this opinion: that Christ giving us His body and blood must be attributed neither to the merits or prayers of the priest or the people, nor to the power of the Words; that, indeed, is magic, just as it sounds. I like this instead: assigning the cause to the institution of Christ. For just as the sun daily rises on account of divine ordinance, so Christ's body is in the Church on account of divine ordinance, wherever the Church is. And some dispute the idea that Christ's body can be in many places; they do not prove that sufficiently. For Christ has been exalted above every creature and is present everywhere. For He says, "I am in the midst of you." I have noted these things so that, as you may be thinking

97 Neuser, op. cit., pp. 273f., pp. 363ff. Also if Neuser is right in maintaining that Melanchthon denies an effective consecration, his depiction of Melanchthon as actually of a Reformed view and agreeing with Zwingli is very skewed. Neuser (op. cit., pp. 365f.) has Zwingli and Melanchthon agreeing on the ineffectiveness of the words of consecration: "The Word is otherwise (however) not to be understood materially, but as the preached and understood Word, that is, it gives a sense and a core of the Word. . . . (That) statement goes against Luther." "The *verbum externum*—the Words of consecration are meant—do not work mechanically, but need the Holy Spirit and thus faith." This is a distortion of the intended, introductory part of the Marburg Colloquy, which is given correctly by Köhler (op. cit., 2:78ff.), and only deals with Zwingli's doctrine about preaching, which he had to defend against Melanchthon. In the intended statement ("*verbum autem non intelligitur materialiter, sed verbum praedicatum et intellectum, hoc est: mens et medulla verbi*"), Zwingli wanted to place the Word's being filled with the Spirit on the *receiver's* hearing in faith, whereby the Word as such does not become the *intermediary* of the Spirit. Whether Melanchthon approved the statement, compare here Köhler (op. cit., p. 78 n. 2), which clarifies the uncertain source material; he then only heard the distinctions that are directed against the words that are materially correct but substantively heresy, according to the prevalent Lutheran reasoning, which is referred to above, p. 179, paragraph with nn. 38–43 [Swedish edition, pp. 164ff.]. Nor do the words "Philip conceded that the Words can do nothing but signify" show any departure from Luther; compare WA 6:359.28f. [cf. AE 35:87], where Luther speaks about the words of the Sacrament as signifying: "that shows well what the words mean," through which the linguistic function of the words is described. The Words of Institution *are* not the presence but describe it: as content-filled words, the Verba, of course, have the function, directed to the external world, to explain these things. Thus Luther stands within the Aristotelian, non-Platonic tradition of philosophy of language; compare Meinhold, *Luthers Sprachphilosophie*.

> anxiously about this controversy, I might indicate to you what I myself think about these arguments, which some especially insist upon. Farewell.[98]

This letter to Bathasar Düring (Thüring) shows that the Reformed criticism is, at any rate, one of the decisive factors behind the alienation from the consecration, that what is rejected is not only an actual union between the heavenly and the earthly but also human directive through a consecrating act, that the rejected view is seen as "magical," that God's act of volition emerges to replace the creating Word, and that all this is indeed consistent with the doctrine of the omnipresence, which is identical both to the sacramental presence and the gracious presence.[99]

As an auxiliary concept, a term is sometimes offered for Melanchthon that shows that in a certain sense he still follows a medieval Nominalistic tradition: *pactum*. In 1530 he writes: "Also, the pact through which the body and blood of Christ are offered to us in the bread and wine";[100] [101] in 1538: "The sacraments are pacts that something else is present in the things received";[102] in 1551: "Because the sacramental presence is voluntary, it is holy by the pact or promise of God being present in the action."[103] This expression, with its previous history in the scholastic *pactio*,[104] has value in recalling that disempowering the Words of Institution, which Melanchthon desired, was already accomplished.[105] Both for Thomism and Nominalism, the divine, uncreated power was distinct from the Words of Institution. The difference—apart from Melanchthon, of course,

98 CR 1:949f. Also Gollwitzer (op. cit., p. 195) begins from this letter. Köhler (op. cit., 1:801) thinks that the influence of Oecolampadius on Melanchthon can be dated from the letter. Compare also Fraenkel, op. cit., p. 157 n. 36; WA 38:294ff.

99 Neuser (op. cit., p. 367) gives this summary about the text above: "First through them, the function of the Words of Institution as consecration words is denied." Although given within the framework of a different value system than Diestelmann's, this opinion coincides with his assessment, which is criticized by Ahlberg; compare above, p. 194, text around n. 94 [Swedish edition, p. 177]. Ahlberg, of course, is right to see the matter as a question of definition, but he thereby blunts his criticism against Diestelmann; compare here Nilsson, op. cit., p. 277 n. 75: "[Bo] Ahlberg gives a good but overly critical review both on the issue as well as the state of the research."

100 [The Swedish edition numbers footnotes up to 99, then restarts at 1, which this translation lists as 101, etc.]

101 CR 2:225; compare CR 2:315.

102 CR 3:514; compare Gollwitzer, op. cit., p. 72, with reference to these citations: "Here Melanchthon likes to use the term '*pactum*.'"

103 CR 7:887.

104 Compare Seeberg, op. cit., 3:511.

105 On this point Ahlberg very correctly would have criticized Diestelmann: "dogmatic-historical innovation" [*novum*]; compare above, p. 194, after n. 95 [Swedish edition, p. 177]. He lets the Middle Ages be the period when the consecration was understood in Luther's view, which is an error of dogmatic history.

not recognizing any created power of the Words—is that Melanchthon sees in the Words of Institution the foundation for the sacramental concretion of the omnipresence to comfort [the believer]. Here the Words still have an actual real power, identical with that of the Gospel:

> We consecrate, that is, we add the sacred words and the action of thanksgiving, lest the use be profane or physical, but that it might be consolation to the soul. But the sacrificing priests say that we consecrate, that is, we make a change of substance by the power of the Words. But Christ is present in His Sacrament, not because the priest makes a change there, or because there is power in the Words to change things, but because He very freely wills to be present in the ritual that He instituted, just as the Holy Spirit very freely is present in baptizing.[106]

The idea that the Words thus serve to comfort the soul does not exclude the idea that this subjective attribute has an objective component. In connection with the question of the so-called after-consecration [when more elements are brought to the altar], Melanchthon can use the term *intentio*, referring to the desired *scope* of the act of consecration:

> When there was not enough in the chalice: Must the words of the consecration be repeated? If the vessel with wine was on the altar, it is not necessary that the words of the consecration be repeated, because the direct intention is for the whole use. But if wine is brought from somewhere else, I want the whole narration of Christ to be repeated: "After Supper, He took the cup, gave thanks," etc. And the repetition is not a rejection of the earlier consecration. For indeed these words must be considered seriously by those who receive, and this whole repetition does not displease me even if the wine in the vessel was nearby.[107]

This formulation indicates that even for the one who would only see the Words of the testament as a proclamation, it is important that the proclaimed Gospel in a concrete way point out the gifts of the Supper, which are to communicate the presence. When bringing new wine to the altar, it should be consecrated anew in contrast to the case ("*non necesse*") when the wine is poured from the flagon, since the "intention" at the first consecration is seen as directed also to the content of the flagon. The emphasis lies in the benefit of hearing the Words, but an inextricably objective importance lies in the fact that faith must be certain that the current gifts of the Supper are under the promise. To

106 CR 15:1109, from 1551, printed posthumously; compare Diestelmann, op. cit., p. 51; Ahlberg, op. cit., p. 156 n. 31.

107 Melanchthon and Georg Major in a letter from 1555, here cited from Bindseil (op. cit., p. 382), which is the basis also for the citation in Jacoby (op. cit., 2:255; Ahlberg, op. cit., p. 157 n. 82). Peters (op. cit., p. 76) uses the version that is in CR 8:598. Bindseil's version, however, is based on the original and also seems more correct otherwise. There is no essential difference between the versions.

the expression "words for faith," one cannot connect a faith that is untroubled about the Institutor's will and the concrete application of the promise.[108] Also the gracious presence, which is the subjective application of the acknowledged omnipresence, knows the stipulations: faith, as well as the assembled Church. At the same time it must be granted that the systematic construction of Melanchthon's doctrine of the Supper can never make the use of an unconsecrated host in good faith into a problem that puts the validity of the Sacrament into question. In such a case, the communicant received the presence such that it is conveyed through the Word, which he still heard. There is no direct expression by Melanchthon concerning this.

Melanchthon, replacing the effective consecration, puts the foundational factor of the Sacrament on the action with regard to the action's being completed through the communion. This will be presented in the concluding section of this investigation. The more immediate consequences of the view of the relationship of Word and action by Melanchthon and the Melanchthonian school will be reviewed in all its complicated variety.

---

108 Melanchthon's words might seem to contain a contradiction: first the consecration of newly brought elements is made implicitly necessary, since it says "the repetition is not a disapproval of the previous consecration," that is, the first consecration had still "reached." In this context, the historical background ought to be mentioned: the Lutheran after-consecration was an *innovation* in relation to the Middle Ages and is in no way a "remnant of Roman Catholicism." The only form of a second consecration known in the Roman Mass is when the first one is found to be *invalid*. In this case the second is precisely "a rejection of the previous consecration"; compare here Philipp Hartmann, *Repertorium Rituum*, pp. 330ff. When Luther writes in a letter to Prince George of Anhalt in 1542 (WA Br 10[:86].18ff., no. 3762), "For, except that, when hosts or wine are to be consecrated, and more must be consecrated, we do not elevate them the second time, just as was done also in the papacy in the situation where one had to consecrate a second time," he does not say that both he and the pope's church use the after-consecration, but that in certain cases they both omit the elevation. In Luther's case, this happens with the after-consecration; under the papacy it happens at the repeated consecration when the first is considered invalid; Hartmann, op. cit., p. 330: "At the repeated consecration the elevation and genuflection are omitted." — Luther himself begins from the obvious necessity ("must be consecrated") of the after-consecration. Andrén (op. cit., p. 51 n. 18) overlooks this evidence and blames earlier research's assertion of the appearance of the after-consecration in Luther on supposed false conclusions from WA Br 11[:257–59], no. 4186, that is, the case of Besserer: "[He] thought that Luther asserted a consecration over the elements and therefore also the after-consecration." But solving this problem does not depend on this passage. It comes down to Andrén misinterpreting the case of Besserer—compare above, p. 186 n. 71—and incorrectly interconnecting the effective consecration and the after-consecration. The former can occur without the latter, just as is presented above in the text, as well as the after-consecration in Melanchthon's case being associated with a noneffective consecration.

Brenz and Andreae

Just as elsewhere, [Johann] Brenz carries out Melanchthon's thoughts. About Brenz's eucharistic tractate, [Theodor] Mahlmann writes the following:

> Brenz clearly chooses his method of proof only in order to eradicate the Roman version of the real presence, basing transubstantiation on the priest's consecration, and in order to see in its place an Evangelical understanding of consecration and real presence: "It is no secret what trifles, what babblings the vain sophists blurt out concerning the superstitious consecration and the pretentious transubstantiation of the bread and wine in the Eucharist. Before we touch on those things, we will explain the real reason for the consecration and the presence of Christ's body and blood in the Lord's Supper." So it was primarily the anti-Roman front, not anti-Swiss, that prompts Brenz to develop Christology as an essential requirement for understanding the real presence systematically for the first time.[109]

These words of Mahlmann, which do not intend to establish any similarity with Melanchthon, mean that the negative incentive as a feature in Brenz's doctrine of the Supper is found in his hatred of the role of the medieval priest in the Mass. Significantly, this attitude appears: "What, indeed, I pray, is magic if this isn't?"[110] Through the Words, only a "new relationship"[111] begins: "Moreover, we are not unaware of your magical opinion and impious incantation. For the Words that the Son of God spoke in the Supper are not Words of creation, but of dispensation, or distribution and presentation."[112] The Roman Mass is wizardry, and its consecration [is] an incantation.

On the front line against his scholastic opponent, the Dominican Domingo de Soto, Brenz now directs his criticism also against the expressions *ex pactione divina* [and] *pactum*;[113] their origin in the Middle Ages makes them unacceptable. *Pactum* in Roman theology means that something happens—even if not by virtue of the words—that is unwarranted: "for since the body and blood of Christ are always present, even before the Supper, about to be completed, is undertaken."[114] The omnipresence cannot begin or cease according to a "pact." It is well to note that this criticism is directed against a scholastic [theologian] and, in fact, does not affect Melanchthon, whose *pactum* only referred to the divine will for the subjective application of the omnipresence. Therefore, Tübingen theology also would soon be able to resume the use of the now temporarily troubled term.

---

109 Mahlmann, op. cit., p. 135.

110 Brenz, *Apologia Confessionis Wirtembergicae*, *Opera* 8:513.

111 Id., op. cit., p. 514.

112 Id., op. cit., p. 513.

113 Id., op. cit., p. 515.

114 Ibid.

Brenz, just like Melanchthon, obviously considers the divine will as foundational for the Sacrament, so that the gifts of the Supper in some way are distinct from profane bread and wine. This comes from Brenz's emphasis on the role of the first institution. In his catechism from 1555, he writes: "But the institution itself, by which Christ first ordained the Supper and commanded the Church to use it, still endures today and sanctifies the bread and wine into His body and blood, as often as we come together in His name to celebrate the Supper. . . ." From this first Supper a sanctifying power comes through the sanctifying Word:

> Thus also this Word, which the Son of God spoke concerning the bread and wine in the first Supper—"Eat; this is My body. Drink; this is My blood"—has not fallen into disuse by the passing of time but is still always efficacious in the Supper, even if it is recited not according to those letters and syllables. [. . .] When the Lord's Supper is celebrated, a new sanctifying is not done by man, but the earlier sanctifying is revealed and is transferred into that use to which Christ ordained it. For this reason, when we hear the Words of Institution of the Supper recited in the Supper, let us direct our thought to the first Supper of Christ, and let us know that every sanctifying in our present Supper is derived from that first one by divine ordinance.[115]

From "the divine ordinance" comes the power that is "efficacious." Obviously what Melanchthon expressed with "covenant" is in this reasoning, just as in the latter [Melanchthon's writings] the recitation of the Verba also means that the elements were embraced under the consecration of the first Supper.

Brenz came to be attacked for this doctrine of the consecration when it was understood as emptying the liturgical consecration of its content. The attack came from the Gnesio-Lutherans Johann Wigand and Nikolaus Gallus, and Brenz's doctrine was the object of deliberations that only through [Jacob] Andreae's intervention did not lead to a formal condemnation.[116] Brenz was now compelled to present his opinion in a defense [i.e., an apology]. It says there that the false doctrine that he wanted to combat is this: "that one must speak his syllables and letters in a magical way." Instead, what matters is "that the meaning of His words are to be presented to the Church in a proper, true Christian understanding."[117] The contrast here is between the view that the four words "This is My body," as such, still have power to change the bread over which they are uttered, and the view that the external form doesn't matter, as long as the meaning is conveyed. "Also the Papist writers themselves allow that the consecration is not hindered when one unknowingly or vaguely speaks *Hoc est Corpum*

115 Brenz, *Catechismus piae* [sic!] *et utili explicatione illustratus*, pp. 650f.

116 Salig, *Vollständige Historie der Augsburgischen Confession*, 3:114f.

117 "*Johann Brentii Probsten zu Stuttgarden Ehren-Rettung Wider die übele Nachred etlicher Sächsischen Theologorum sonderheitlich des Galli und Stoltzii Fürstl. Weymarischen Hoffpredigers / wegen der ausgegangenen Württemberg. Kirchen-Ordnung und Catechismi*," in *Acta [et scripta publica ecclesiae Wirtembergicae]*, p. 371.

meus or *Hoc est Corpus meus* [incorrect Latin forms, somewhat like 'This is My *bohdy*,' 'This is *Me* body'], or so that these words are changed in form yet the meaning remains."[118] "That also is my understanding of the Words of the Supper, namely, that one should not omit the Word of Christ's institution in the Supper, as is expressly reported there, but one should also rightly understand this use so as not to emphasize the express words and letters in a magical way, [rather] that it belongs only to the meaning and power of Christ."[119] The meaning expressed in the letters and syllables is the power that effects the Sacrament. Similar statements about the effect of the consecration are found in one of the writings that necessitated the apology, the Württemberg Church Order from 1553, where it says concerning the distribution formula that it may be used even if the Sacrament "was sufficiently consecrated earlier in the Exhortation through the Institution, and especially read afterward, and therefore one will not have much need of any more special words; yet, to remind people more during the distribution of the body of Christ, the church minister may speak to each one approximately the following words . . . ."[120] The intention of Christ's institution is present in the Verba and consecrates the Sacrament, which thereafter needs no further consecration. The proclamation again benefits from diligent repetition and motivates the distribution formula as a useful ceremony, but not a necessary one.

In defense of his contested view, Brenz had even appealed to Rome—"even the Papist writers themselves allow"—and concerning his own Lutheran critics he used the expression: "he is more Papist than some of the Papists themselves are."[121] Brenz then actually would have said only what every adept Scholastic could say: the consecration is not bound by the correct articulation of certain syllables. Thus clearly Brenz was not speaking the whole truth about himself, as is evident from the polemic against de Soto. The Gnesio-Lutheran attacks had gotten Brenz, in a certain sense, to conceal the delineations that he made earlier. Meanwhile, that does not mean that what he says now is false. Just as for Melanchthon, there is for Brenz a function for the Verba, which, without

118 Op. cit., p. 372.

119 Op. cit., p. 373.

120 Richter, [*Die evangelischen Kirchenordnungen des sechszehnten Jahrhunderts*,] 2:137. The presence of this first institution in the sense that is expressed by the Verba is overlooked by Kawerau ("Zum lutherischen Konsekrationsbegriff," p. 40), who blocks the words "through the first institution of Christ" but not the formulation "consecrated sufficiently through the institution of Christ beforehand in the Exhortation and then especially in the recitation afterward." Kawerau did not study Brenz's apology ("I do not have it at hand," id., op. cit., p. 41), but makes use of a summary in *Zeitschrift für die historische Theologie*, 30, pp. 149f. Kawerau's presentation forms the basis for the view of Brenz's doctrine of consecration in Kjöllerström, *Striden kring kalvinismen i Sverige under Erik XIV*, pp. 98, 106; Andrén, op. cit., p. 66; Ahlberg, op. cit., p. 147.

121 *Acta [et scripta publica ecclesiae Wirtembergicae]*, p. 372.

making these into powerful words that bring about the real sacramental union, still legitimize the Supper as holy and draws into the elements the special voluntary act that comes from the first Supper and is revealed in the recitation of the Words of the testament. The presence, for [our] comfort, is based on an objective word that finally again must be ascribed with power and sanctifying effect, for which reason it does not emerge with a lower claim of being filled with the Spirit than the Gospel does otherwise. The consecration has become the Gospel concerning the bread and wine. Andrén portrays it as though the consequences of the repletive and sacramental presence being identical mean that the Verba are read not "in order that these [elements] should become a sacrament, but for the sake of the communicants, in order to document Christ's institution for them,"[122] but that is impossible. This and similar expressions present an attitude that is not in the material. When Andrén further adds that "this means that after-consecrations [when more elements are brought to the altar] became unnecessary,"[123] he presumes a logic in the theologians discussed here that cannot be taken outright as obvious. Brenz's rejection of after-consecration is evidenced for the first time by Andreae's defense of his colleague at the above-mentioned Gnesio-Lutheran attack that occurred in Baden-Durlach in 1556. Andreae cites as Brenz's explanation: "because Christ Himself did not repeat them [the Verba] often, but said them once." This example of Christ invokes only that "one must always use Christ's Words of Institution at the solemn act, according to the words of Christ: the blessed cup that we bless, etc." The after-consecration thereby lacks God's command: "For the power of the Sacrament does not come here from a magical incantation of our recitation, but because it was done and commanded once by Christ."[124] That requires thus a sacramental "power" to effect the dispensing [*dispensativa*] presence; but it begins without any after-consecration being used. Again this question is addressed in a Württemberg theological report that had Brenz as author, in which the after-consecration briefly is explained to be unnecessary from a dogmatic viewpoint, but still permissible.[125] The omnipres-

122 Andrén, op. cit., p. 66.

123 Ibid.

124 Salig, *Vollständige Historie der Augsburgischen Confession*, 3:16; compare Kawerau, "Zum lutherischen Konsekrationsbegriff," p. 41. In 1557, Andreae, for his part, expresses the same opinion in *Kurtzer und einfältiger Bericht*, fol. 25Bf., according to [Edward Frederick] Peters, *[Origin and Meaning]*, p. 423.

125 *Bedencken der Würtembergischen Theologen, uber etlichen Adiaphoris circa Coenam Domini*, printed in Bidembach, *Consilia Theologica*, Dec. III, Conc. IV, p. 113, given as an answer to Duke Christofer's question to Brenz; compare Kawerau, op. cit., p. 42. Andrén's reference (op. cit., p. 67) to Kawerau as support for the assertion that Brenz in his confession on the Supper from 1559 would take a negative stance toward the after-consecration is incorrect. Kawerau does not suggest this, and neither is any such statement found in the confession.

ence is not cited in this context, which proceeds from the historical institution. Likewise, the element used at the Communion is seen as subject to Christ's sanctifying will, which was recited one time. This thesis of Brenz is maintained also in another view of the relationship of Christology to Sacrament.

Tübingen theology's *Solida Refutatio*, cited earlier, in which Andreae and his colleagues speak, again takes up the Melanchthonian term "covenant":

> But truly the covenantal presence of Christ is sacramental, by which the covenant is with us through the Words of His testament, that He would give us His body and blood in this Sacrament, just as He promised in His own words. [. . .] Those words are recited solemnly in the celebration of this Sacrament . . . not so that *by the power of the recitation, Christ's body is drawn out of heaven in a bodily and visible form like Elysian Jove,* but the Church calls to mind the *covenant*, which Christ made with His Church. . . . And this solemn recitation of the words of Christ's testament is that benediction concerning which blessed Paul wrote: "The cup of blessing that we bless, is it not the communion of the blood of Christ?" He does not say "that Christ blessed," but "*that we* bless," that is, by repeating and commending to the people and celebrating that covenantal blessing. Also in no way should it be omitted. Because indeed this covenantal presence may happen without any descent or ascent of Christ. . . .[126]

In an earlier chapter, the *Refutatio*'s agreement with Brenz is elaborated, and when Andreae and his colleagues speak here, it is done from the same viewpoint as Brenz.[127] This does not prevent taking up the word "covenant," since Brenz's criticism never intended to hit the use that Melanchthon and later Tübingen theology made of it. The consecration releases and reveals the reality of Christ's promise.

The power that effects this miracle is *the power of the Spirit*; for this [idea], they also call upon the testimony of the fathers and the Eastern liturgies.

> And what else do all the liturgies of James, Clement, Dionysius, Basil, Chrysostom have when the priest asks for the coming of the Holy Spirit, by *virtue of which powerfully and ineffably the bread* and wine become the body and blood? For this mystery is performed by the power of the same Spirit by whose power the Word was made flesh in the Virgin's womb. Which at the same time all the orthodox fathers along with the liturgies confess and teach with unanimous consent.[128]

The Tübingen theology, which in the same writing consistently promotes Melanchthon's and Brenz's doctrine of the omnipresence, professes here the liturgies of the early church and the doctrine that lets the Spirit perform the same actual work in the eucharistic gifts as in the miracle of the incarnation!

126 [Andreae,] *Solida Refutatio*, p. 323.

127 Compare above, chapter 3, after n. 105 [Swedish edition, p. 97].

128 [Andreae,] *Solida Refutatio*, p. 404.

The supposed contradiction, meanwhile, is only an apparent one. *The parallel is maintained under the consistent assertion that in neither case does the immutability of the divinity or Christ's body according to the omnipresence suffer harm.* The divinity was in the Virgin's womb even before taking on humanity; Christ's body was in the bread before the consecration. Nevertheless, a real event takes place in the Spirit's power:

> Indeed, just as the Word was not absent before, so that it first came at the proffering of the words, but what was worked in the womb of the blessed Virgin had first been done—namely, that He assumed the human nature into the unity of His person from its very substance—thus indeed Christ is not absent from the bread with His body in the mode of majesty before it is sanctified through the proffering of the words of Christ's testament, but soon through the sacramental union, when the Words of the Supper are proffered, the bread becomes the body of Christ, which was not there before, because Dr. Musculus says that the body of Christ is present right away.[129]

The sacramental union is compared here to the personal union, by which, in both cases, the state of unity has been effected by the Spirit. The closing reference to Andreas Musculus meanwhile includes the whole tension that is noted in the foregoing between the south and north German schools, and which also exists between the *Solida Refutatio* and the cited liturgies. The *Solida Refutatio* defends itself against the Reformed observation that Andreas Musculus and Martin Chemnitz teach differently than Brenz and Andreae. The Reformed showed that Musculus had used expressions such as "At the recitation or proffering of these words, '*This is My Body*,' *the body of Christ* is immediately present in the *bread*, just as when the angel was announcing, and the Spirit arriving, the Word is soon flesh in the Virgin's womb."[130] The Reformed were not incorrect here in finding the expression of a real view of the consecration in which an actual beginning of the presence is taught. The answer given by the *Solida Refutatio* does not refute the Reformed objection. Musculus's words are connected to Luther in the *Sermon on the Sacrament*: "How did His mother, Mary, become pregnant? . . . She knew no man, and her womb was entirely closed, yet she conceived in her womb a real, natural child with flesh and blood."[131] Here also in Musculus's formulation the point is not the act itself, through which the immutable divinity in the personal union takes on the humanity, but *the virgin birth in its exclusive* sense, through which the Spirit, without man's cooperation, creates "a real, natural child." This is a real unborn [child], a fruition of what was not there before. The sacramental union is drawn parallel to this in Luther: "For as soon as [Musculus: *statim*] Christ

129 Ibid.

130 Ibid.

131 WA 19:490.24ff. [cf. AE 36:341].

says, 'This is My body,' then His body is there through the Word and power of the Holy Spirit."[132] By transferring statements about the miraculous virgin birth to the incarnation in the sense of the personal union, the *Solida Refutatio* gains the authorization of Luther and the north German theologians for the view that Christ's body in relation to the bread has the divinity's immutability compared to the humanity.[133] Herein lies the contradiction that was also able to be shown earlier in this volume. Regardless of this, the south German tradition exhibits an unassailable will to assert objective consequences of the consecration while retaining the starting point.

Laurentius Petri

Laurentius Petri Nericius provides an interesting illustration of the complicated character of the Lutheran doctrine of the consecration. His doctrine on this point is presented against a background regarding the relationship of the omnipresence and sacramental presence, which is defined thus by Ahlberg, after a comprehensive and convincing review of the material: "With his defining of the essence of the Supper and the presence of Christ's body and blood, he does not proceed from thoughts about Christ's omnipresence either, but from the Words

132 WA 19:491.13f. [cf. AE 36:341].

133 A third aspect of [Christ's] taking on the humanity is used by Luther (WA 19:491.17ff. [cf. AE 36:341]); compare above, pp. 176–77 n. 25. Luther here makes [Christ's] becoming present in the Sacrament parallel to the act in which Jesus' humanity becomes omnipresent through the *genus maiestaticum*. In similarity to the virgin birth, this means an actual change, so that Jesus' body becomes present where it was not before. — [Andreae,] *Solida Refutatio*, p. 453, in a differently constituted controversy against the Reformed, can expound the real, newly created effect of the angel's words:

> For if they are understood from the words of the angel, it is very false, that the plagiarizers [*compilatores*] say: *He did not effect what was not there before.* Although before these words of Gabriel, Mary was not pregnant, but after this word of the angel, she was, since Mary said, "Let it be to me *according to your word*." Therefore, just as the angel Gabriel did not inform her about something that existed before, but what was effected through the Holy Spirit after his word, likewise, by the recitation through the Word of the Institution, the people are not instructed concerning something that existed beforehand, but adjoining these Words the Holy Spirit *powerfully* (as orthodox antiquity says) effects the mystery of the sacramental presence of Christ's body, *which was not there before.* Although just as He is located at the right hand of God to govern all creation by His universal presence, so indeed Christ, as God and man, is there beforehand in the bread and wine and does not depart from them. On account of this communicated majesty, He does not at all need either ascending or descending from heaven for the sacramental presence.

A casual Reformed note that, moreover, was technical and did not have actual weight here triggered the interpretation of the virgin birth being parallel to the Sacrament, which invalidates the explanation given above in the text.

of Institution. A Christological rationale of the doctrine of the Supper, which, not without reason, was thought to be found in Brenz, is never presumed in the case of Laurentius Petri."[134] In a commentary on Laurentius Petri's *Dialog about the Change That Occurs in the Mass* [*Dialogus om then förwandling, som medh messone skedde*] from 1542, Ahlberg develops his view of Laurentius Petri's doctrine of the consecration: "God does not bind His power . . . to certain words or signs. . . . Everything depends on the meaning, just as the Latin marginal rubric says, 'The power of the words is in the sense, not in the letter or figures.' If this were not true, . . . then that would mean that God's power would disappear with the voice or the writing, and that would not make sense."[135] Ahlberg puts forward this [thought] from the above-mentioned writing of Laurentius Petri:

> But where the meaning, the understanding, and faith remain, there God's power and work remain, so that when I hear the words sound over the bread that the pastor and the congregation have in front of them, which words say that this is the Lord's body, the voice indeed disappears and becomes nothing, but the meaning that the voice has in it remains close in my mind and takes root there with faith, with the same meaning and the effect and truth of God's power, so that the bread is indeed the Lord's body. On this basis it is good to understand how one should use the words and what office they have, that is, to acknowledge what they give [and] when and by whom the change takes place, namely, in the congregation God makes it so, at the time the words say it.[136]

Ahlberg concludes: "The Words of Institution are proclamation, a preaching. Their task is to make known that God is active in the congregation at the moment when they are heard."[137] "But the Word is not directed to the elements, nor does it bring forth a power that works on these, but it turns to the people who are gathered to celebrate this Meal."[138] Ahlberg sets the two alternatives "message" and "incantation" against each other.

Ahlberg obviously finds the final words in the section cited above—"On this basis it is good to understand what one should use the words for"—to mean a clear denial of a consecration in the power of the Words. Ahlberg imagines only "an immediate and indissoluble simultaneousness between the proclamation of

134 Ahlberg, op. cit., p. 250. This comprises Ahlberg's most important contribution to the research discussion. Compare, op. cit., p. 153: "There is a marked difference between the latter's [Vajta's] depiction of Luther's view and that of Laurentius Petri, in that the doctrine of the omnipresence, which according to Vajta is the central thought in Luther, is completely lacking in Laurentius Petri in the sections that discuss the consecration."

135 Ahlberg, op. cit., p. 109.

136 Laurentius Petri, *Dialogus om then förwandling*, fol. 29Af.

137 Ahlberg, op. cit., p. 110.

138 Id., op. cit., p. 111.

the Words and Christ's own act."[139] Meanwhile, there is reason not to see the matter so narrowly. The words immediately before this final thought are already an argument for this: "With the same meaning there is both the effect and truth of God's power." God's power in the Words is described also in the introduction: "Where the meaning, the understanding, and faith remain, there God's power and effect remain." Clarity is given in the continuation of the citation not quoted by Ahlberg: "But in no way is such a power of God bound to human voices, that is, words or forms of words, as you would say."[140] Laurentius Petri wants to assert the power of the consecration "just as much whether those words are more or fewer, as spoken in Latin, German, or Swedish."[141] What is important is the marginal rubric's "the power of the words is in the sense" as a demarcation against the "sound of the words," in this case the Latin words of consecration, which in the *Dialogue of Simon [and Theophilus]* are exclusively ascribed the power to effect the presence. When Laurentius Petri, according to this distinction, asserts that the "sense of the words" should be used to "proclaim," he does not deny the power, which he immediately afterward acknowledged in the meaning of the same words. He is only saying that God's command to repeat the words is made necessary by the presence of the hearers, not by the necessity for God to bring about the miracle through the repetition of the words. Of course, God would bring about the real presence without the recitation of the Verba. Within the valid economy of salvation, on the other hand, He must instruct people through the Word, which requires reading the Verba aloud and in the vernacular. Meanwhile, when this is done, the power of the words, the miraculous power, is really in the meaning of the words, which cannot be identified with what is in the power of the pastor in a physical sense, the articulation of his voice and the choice of words, but coincides with what is spoken by him in concept.

In two different ways it can be further confirmed how Ahlberg unjustly disputes that Laurentius Petri would teach an effective consecration. Ahlberg disputes, first, that Laurentius Petri would count on a reciting of the Words of Institution "over" bread and wine.[142] Nonetheless Ahlberg was unable to avoid including in his own material two such passages where Laurentius Petri makes

139 Id., op. cit., p. 126.

140 Laurentius Petri, *Dialogus om then förwandling*, fol. 29B.

141 Id., op. cit., fol. 28B.

142 Ahlberg, op. cit., p. 153; compare pp. 126f.

use of this expression "over bread and wine."[143] Further examples of such use of language could be obtained by a thorough reading of Laurentius Petri's works.[144]

Second, Ahlberg allies himself with Andrén and finds Laurentius Petri basically "uninterested" in what is covered by the consecration, and the question about the treatment of remaining elements, and therefore also understanding the after-consecration [when more elements are brought to the altar] as unnecessary. This attitude is seen as a consequence of the view of the consecration as only proclamation.[145] Meanwhile, in Laurentius Petri's criticism of the after-

143 The one quotation is found (op. cit., p. 110) and repeated above, p. 206, after n. 135 [Swedish edition, p. 188]: "sound over the bread." The other quotation is found twice in the form of an account in Ahlberg, once in the text in [an] abbreviated and therefore incomprehensible form, once correctly in the notes. Op. cit., p. 135, it says that the Sacramentarians do not dare to "invoke the Lord's name out of fear that the words might be thought to have a magical power." The Latin text, *Responsio . . . ad scriptum Dionijsij Beurrei*, p. 38B, however, clearly says "over these things." The "Lord's name" and the "words" that the Enthusiasts fear to use *over* these things are unequivocally the traditional Words of Institution (ibid.): "lest they be thought to attribute any power to the words in papistic custom." Op. cit., p. 302 n. 3, Ahlberg himself unflinchingly writes "over bread and wine."

144 *Responsio. . . ad scriptum Dionysij Beurrei*, fol. 37B, cites a word from Luther: "over bread and wine"; op. cit., fol. 40B, it is said in summary fashion about a great number of patristic citations, all of which very emphatically clarify the creating power of the Words of consecration, and citing them would be absurd if Laurentius Petri did not espouse the same opinion: "that the consecration of His body and blood occurs through the Words of Christ recited over bread and wine in the celebration of the Lord's Supper." — Ahlberg's attempt in this way to prove his thesis can thereby be refuted. But it could be said that the word "over" does not have such a decisive meaning as Ahlberg thinks. Rietschel (*Lehrbuch der Liturgik*, 1:546 n. 8) points out the difference between *super panem* and *super pane*, where the former expression designates the relationship of direction, and the latter a mere local determination of the relationship of the speaker to the bread. But Rietschel's rejection of even an "application" of the Verba to the bread in the latter case is a blatant exaggeration. (The form "super pan*em*" is in Chemnitz: *Repetitio sanae doctrinae*, p. 192, which there quotes Bugenhagen concerning the consecration, and in the *Examination of the Council of Trent*, 2:224 [Latin, p. 300].) Linguistically a parallel can be made with the expression "sitting over [at] the table" [*sittiandes offuer bord*] [in] Laurentius Petri, *Dialogus om then förwandling*, fol. 7A, and the corresponding German expression "*über tisch*" in Luther ("Christ . . . preached . . . over [at] the table"); [see] *DWB* 11/2:85 ("*Über*"). In the context it ought to be stated that Thomas Aquinas in his *Summa* only writes "consecration of the bread" or "words concerning the bread" but not "over the bread," from which no conclusions can be drawn about his view of the consecration.

145 Ahlberg, op. cit., p. 161, who refers to Andrén, op. cit., pp. 89f. Andrén presents the "clearly Lutheran" view of the after-consecration as unnecessary [that] is not only repeated in Laurentius Petri but also in Denmark (id., op. cit., p. 66 n. 71), where the 1568 Synod in Lund declares the after-consecration unnecessary, as does also the Synod in Stavanger. In this respect Andrén seems to overlook the fact that Denmark-Norway at this time were not at all considered to have been "clearly Lutheran," but were under the influence of the Philippist Niels Hemmingsen, who clearly tended

consecration there is a train of thought that presupposes the power of the consecration and which makes use of a complex line of reasoning, originally coming from Scholasticism, about intention, the word here taken in the sense of consecration's intended scope. There is no "indifference" in face of the problem. The expression about the after-consecration not being necessary, noted in the research but not investigated contextually, is comprised of a statement that, when there is a shortage of elements at the Supper, new ones may be brought in "under the same consecration," and that, if there is anything that is left over, it should be kept for the next Mass like ordinary bread and wine.[146] As explanation for this, Laurentius Petri elaborates as follows: "For I regard the consecration of the elements of bread and wine both proffering and having been proffered to be determined not only by the intention of the one consecrating, as certain people think, but also by the use of the communicants; indeed, the true intention cannot differ from this." This means, positively, that the pastor's intention with the consecration refers not only to what he separates for holy use by reading the Verba but [also to] what he "takes and what *will still be taken*," as Laurentius Petri formulates it in *Om någor stycker wårs Herras Jesu Christi nattward anrörandes Dialogus* from 1562, according to [Sven] Kjöllerström's dating,[147] the same year as the Latin sentences came into print. Thus the pastor consecrates basically with the thought of the coming use, for which reason the after-consecration is forestalled through "proper intention" by greater rather than narrower scope, which only includes what is visible on the altar. Seen negatively, this means that what is not used of what is consecrated was not actually consecrated either. The procedure with what is left over is explained in this way. The thought seems absolutely complete in the question of the hosts. Upon further consideration, there does not seem to be any actual obstacle in the question of the cup either, that in this case must hold both consecrated as well as unconsecrated wine, since Scholasticism already knew the possibility of such a coexistence.[148] Laurentius Petri also ought to have pointed to Scholasticism with his formulation "as they

toward the Reformed. His Philippism has its clear impact on such points. Concerning Hemmingsen, compare *Nordisk teologisk uppslagsbok* 1:1294ff., "Hemmingsen, Niels," with the list of literature.

146 In *Korth bekiennelse*, fol. 249B, quoted in Kjöllerström, op. cit., p. 113; Andrén, op. cit., p. 92 n. 36; compare Ahlberg, p. 161 n. 45.

147 Kjöllerström, op. cit., pp. 94f.

148 Compare *ST*, III, 77, 8: "The blood of Christ will cease to be under that part of the consecrated wine, but will remain under another" (by infusing a small amount of ordinary wine). Consecration through "contact," thus by mixing consecrated and unconsecrated, is thus rejected by Thomas. The same view is expressed during the 1500s by Gnesio-Lutheran theologian Johann Saliger; compare Schöne, *Um Christi sakramentale Gegenwart*, p. 21. Saliger's view was affirmed even by the Philippistic opponents. Compare also 1575's *Church Order* in Lüneburg: "For the unconsecrated must not be added to the consecrated to become consecrated, as some wish, but rather

indeed think." An actual exchange of views of the type under discussion is found in Scholasticism, and apparently Laurentius Petri made use of it in 1562.

This controversy means that Thomas [Aquinas] rejected the idea that "the priest could not consecrate an immense quantity of bread or wine, imagine all the bread that is sold in the market or all the wine that is in the cask."[149] Bonaventure again defended this thesis about the priest's connection to the coming use regarding the scope of the consecration:

> And for this reason it must be said without prejudice that the conversion does not take place by the power of the Words, unless the intention is present and the intention agrees with the institution and intention of the Church; because, as [Hugh] says, "Any sacrament is considered invalid if it is celebrated contrary to the institution." But the intention of the Church and of the Institutor is to make the change for the use of the faithful. For this reason, since the power of the words is governed according to the intent, it extends to as much material as the priest can put together, which ought to be and corresponds to being consumed by the use of the faithful.[150]

This meaning became a part of the Franciscan, Nominalistic tradition[151] and is stated over several pages, represented by a number of authors of this school, in a printed sermon by Prince George III of Anhalt, bishop of Merseburg and cathedral provost of Magdeburg, a Lutheran theologian with great knowledge of patristics and canon law.[152] This sermon again was well-known to Laurentius Petri, since his writing on the Lord's Supper mentioned above, the *Dialog* from 1562, appears to be partly a translation of George's sermon on the Sacrament.[153] That is how Laurentius Petri's argument about intention got its point of view and background. The use of the scholastic argumentation by George as well as Laurentius Petri is, of course, not congruent with that of the medieval authors; they did not intend thereby to verify the legitimacy of the Corpus Christi procession, as well as the after-consecration and the sacramental character of the elements left over after the Mass—the first being George's problem, the latter that of Laurentius Petri. On the contrary, all these theologians speak about the consecration as suited for its effect according to the intention of the Institutor

properly [*rite*] consecrated elements must be given to the people" (Sehling 6/1:660, quoted in [Edward Frederick] Peters, *[Origin and Meaning]*, p. 316).

149 *ST*, III, 74, 2.

150 Bonaventure, In IV d. X. p. II., a. 1., qu. IV.

151 Biel, *Canonis misse expositio*, lect. 35. Hf., however, allies with Thomas, which is pointed out by Damerau, op. cit., p. 212 n. 156.

152 George [III] of Anhalt, *Die Vierdte Predigt vom hochwirdigen Sacrament des Leibs und Bluts unsers Herren Jhesu Christi*, fol. 45Aff. Biel is cited as the last author (op. cit., lect. 36 [F]) and is viewed as thereby expressing the usual Franciscan opinion, but compare above, n. 151.

153 Compare below, pp. 306–7 n. 326 [Swedish edition, p. 274 n. 26].

and the actual use. Therefore, when Laurentius Petri in this context takes the position on the after-consecration and the leftover sacramental gifts, he does not use thoughts that make the consecration powerless. It is not possible here to contrast Luther's realistic view of the consecration, expressed in his obvious use of the after-consecration and dogmatically motivated carefulness concerning the leftover elements,[154] against Laurentius Petri's supposed doctrine of the consecration as mere preaching, verified in disregarding what Luther defended against. *Laurentius Petri here would be able to say for himself that he, on the contrary, surpassed the defenders of the after-consecration in concrete belief in the power of the Verba.* In *Refutatio erroris Herbesti*, for example, he cites Christ's miracle of feeding [the thousands] as parallel to this, that "it [the duration of the action] begins from the first true consecration of the elements of bread and wine through the Word, and it ends with the completed communion of all." It says here about the miracle of the feeding: "The favor of multiplying five loaves and two fish lasted until the whole multitude of those seated had been satisfied."[155] Here he would be able to show how he sees the miraculous meal as consisting of a never-diminishing power, Jesus' table prayer as well as the Words. Only the termination of the meal can stop this flow that in no way needed any renewed act of Jesus to complete the first. The difficulties that presumably are in Laurentius Petri's view of intention and consecration cannot remove this connection.

Chemnitz

Chemnitz, in his *Repetitio sanae doctrinae*, devotes a chapter to the "Recitation of the Words of Institution, which They Commonly Call the Consecration." Concerning the designation of the Words, he says,

> They commonly call it consecration; Paul calls it benediction, that term having been taking up from Mark's description, "the cup of blessing that we bless" [1 Cor. 10:16], etc. For that reason Cyril almost always calls it the mystical benediction. But by whatever term it is called, the question is this: From where and by what power does it happen that in the Lord's Supper the body and blood of Christ are present, offered, and received with the bread and wine?[156]

"Consecration," "blessing," "mystical benediction": [these] are various expressions for the same thing—the act that Paul describes with the words about the cup of blessing that is blessed. The meaning is presented in this way: the Verba

154 Compare this below, p. 254.

155 Laurentius Petri, *Refutatio erroris Herbesti*, fol. 77B.

156 Chemnitz, *Repetitio sanae doctrinae*, p. 193. Compare here *Liturgia svecanae ecclesiae catholicae et orthodoxae conformis* (Johan III's *Red Book*), fol. XXXIXB: "They commonly call it consecration; Paul calls it blessing, saying, 'The cup of blessing . . . .' Cyril almost always calls it the mystical blessing. . . ."

are not words of incantation; magic is the idea that gave rise to the report of the shepherds who mistakenly happened to change their bread into Christ's body since they had spoken the holy Words, whose meaning was even hidden to them.[157] Only in their true context and understanding do they possess their power. [Johann] Bugenhagen's words are cited: "Indeed, 'This is My body' is not our Word, but [the Word of Him] who with His own omnipotent Word created all things and made everything that He wished."[158] In the Mass, the Words are really creating words.

In his great reply to the Council of Trent, Chemnitz confirms that the council allowed various Roman interpretations of the consecration to continue despite the desire of many participants to have a dogmatic solution.[159] While considering the fathers who saw the consecration in the Verba and not in the Canon, Chemnitz emphasizes the power of the Words of Institution. They are spoken by Christ who is present: "For it is He Himself who distributes, albeit through the minister; it is He Himself who says, 'This is My body'; it is He Himself who through His own Word is efficacious, so that the bread is His body and the wine is His blood."[160] It is depicted in detail how it is the Word that sounds forth in the Sacrament that effects the miracle. "[Christ] utters these words: 'This is My body, do this,' etc., and through that Word, His own Word, He is efficacious."[161] Here as elsewhere Chemnitz works unhindered with a great array of quotations from the Christian tradition, which all unanimously and often bluntly speak about the powerful effect of the Words of the Sacrament. Use of the quotations

157 Id., op. cit., pp. 189f.; compare ibid.: "But that recitation of the institution is not done the way magicians recite their songs about Elysian Jove"; the same expression is found in Chemnitz, *Examination of the Council of Trent*, 2:224 [Latin, p. 300]; compare Brenz, *Apologia Confessionis Wirtenbergicae*, *Opera* 8:513. It ought to be observed that when Chemnitz (ibid.) rejects the idea that "the consecration consists in the silent murmuring of these four words over the bread, 'This is My body,' . . . in the syllables and letters of those four words," he thus renders his whole front against Rome in a different way than against Brenz, whose demarcations at the Gnesio-Lutheran attacks only render a part of his actual objections; compare above, p. 175, text at n. 21 [Swedish edition, pp. 183f.]. When Chemnitz (ibid.) draws the parallel concerning the consecration, "just as in the preaching of the Gospel Paul affirms that Christ Himself speaks through the mouth of the ministers," the opposite is the false idea in the previous thought: "by the power of the letters and syllables." The consecration is a *conceptual* quantity in the same way as a point of comparison, not an identification through which he would make the Verba into a mere preaching, as in Brenz.

158 Id., op. cit., p. 192.

159 Chemnitz, *Examination of the Council of Trent*, 2:225 [Latin, p. 300]: "Among these very diverse opinions, the Tridentine fathers, though asked by many, were unwilling to intervene; but simply without explanation they call it the consecration of bread and wine."

160 Id., op. cit., p. 302.

161 Ibid.

shows Chemnitz's own position. Chemnitz's solidarity with Luther is obvious. Neither in him nor in Laurentius Petri is there Melanchthonian timidity about a power of the Word over the materials.

In the *Apology of the Book of Concord*, [Chemnitz] speaks with the same fearlessness. Chrysostom's words about Christ as Consecrator are cited: "And now Christ is present there, who adorned that Table; He Himself indeed consecrates it. The Words are offered by the mouth of the priest, and they work by the power and grace of God."[162] Against the Reformed attack on the consecration, it says,

> Moreover, they say: Christ nowhere promised that when the Words of Institution are repeated that He is present there with His body and would distribute it in and with the bread. We say in response to them, however: Did Christ not command to do what He did in the first Supper? Now, He spoke the Words that we should indeed also do: for the element does not become a sacrament without the Word, as Au[gustine] says: *Accedat verbum ad elementum et fit sacramentum*; "Let the Word come to the element, then it becomes a sacrament."[163]

This defense of the consecration as a part of Christ's institution is, in content and somewhat in form, identical with Luther's words in the face of the Reformed attack on the blessing of the elements, which they abhorred:

> But if someone would say, Christ did not command these words "This is My body" to be spoken in the Supper. Answer: It is true; nowhere in the text does it say, "You should speak, This is My body," and there is no hand drawn there to point to it. . . . For it is all included in the command-word [*heisselwort*] "Do this," and we must not omit the Words. . . . We should speak these Words, "This is My body," in His person and name, by His order and command. . . .[164]

For Luther and the north German tradition there is a mutual thought of a divinely authorized act of blessing, filled with Christ's own divine power. The pastor at the altar not only takes the Creator's body between his fingers but also speaks the Creator's own Words with his lips. Neither the actual presence nor the manner of its being brought about requires theological limitations in view of the presence of the divine world in time and space, beyond the boundaries that must be drawn against misuse in conflict with the historically given institution. Obviously, the Creator's Word has the same power over the elements as over people's hearts.

---

162 *Apologia [oder verantwortung des Christlichen Concordien Buchs]*, fol. 236B [cf. *Apology*, p. 323]; compare *BS* 998.39ff. (= PG 49:380) [cf. FC SD VII 76].

163 Op. cit., fol. 236A [cf. *Apology*, p. 323].

164 WA 26:287.4ff. [cf. AE 37:187].

CHAPTER 6

Concomitantia

The Scope of the Sacramental Presence

THE biblical accounts of the institution [of the Sacrament] speak about Christ's body and blood, and older Christian tradition maintained this phraseology without more narrowly defining the relationship of the sacramental gifts to Christ's person as the God-man, His divinity, and His soul. Of course, through the Spirit the believer partook of Christ in His fullness, but that said nothing about the scope of the sacramental presence. Even Lanfranc during the eleventh century could limit himself to saying that the sacramental receiving of Christ's body and blood is just the occasion for receiving the whole Christ, by the communicant being incited through the communion to strive for eternal life, which is Christ Himself.[1]

High Scholasticism taught differently. They introduced the term "concomitance," which means that the whole person of Christ, as well as the accompanying body and blood of Christ, is offered in the consecrated forms, and not given only as the result of properly receiving the sacramental gifts. Thomas writes concerning this that indeed "from the power of the Sacrament" bread and wine are transformed exclusively into Christ's body and blood, but "by natural concomitance, however, what is in this Sacrament is really joined to it in what is called the conversion, mentioned before."[2] On the part of Christ's divinity, this resulting relationship is defensible in this way:

> Indeed, since the divinity never laid aside the assumed body, it is necessary that wherever the body of Christ is, the divinity of Christ is there, [and] that His body is concomitant. For which reason the Creed of Ephesus reads: "We are made partakers of the body and blood of Christ, not as taking common flesh, nor [the flesh] of a sanctified man and joined to the

1 PL 150:425; compare to the above *Die deutsche Thomas-Ausgabe* 30:415ff.

2 *ST*, III, 76, 1.

> Word according to the formal unity, but the truly life-giving [flesh] that actually belongs to the Word."[3]

Thus the incarnation is the basis for the divinity being included. Concomitance embraces not only [Christ's] divinity but also Christ's soul, Christ's blood in the host, and Christ's body in the cup, so that both forms give the same gifts. Meanwhile, hypothetically, a Mass celebrated during the time between Christ's death and resurrection, the holy Triduum, would not have distributed the concomitance of Christ's blood and body or Christ's soul. Likewise, concomitance embraces the quantities of Christ's body and blood.[4]

Just as presented earlier, for Thomas the presence "from the power of the Sacrament" does not mean an essential existence [*egenexistens*] of Christ's body in the host, but it designates a relationship made possible through the accidence of the bread becoming the only intermediate indicator of location for the illocal substance of Christ's body, which replaces [the substance] of the bread through the miracle of transformation [transubstantiation]. The form of presence "by natural concomitance," which is now introduced into the argumentation, however, does not have any connection to the space that is provided by the "mode of substance" of the sacramental presence and which is accomplished "from the power of the Sacrament." In fact, for that reason the doctrine of concomitance does not say more than that Christ exists as "the whole Christ" in heaven and that an indissoluble identity exists between the heavenly Christ and the eucharistic substance of Christ's body, so that the latter is in the former, even if the concepts do not coincide. As an expression of sacramental theology, as a way to answer the question of what the communicant receives beyond the substance of Christ's body, the doctrine of concomitance is, in fact, *meaningless*. Thomas's meaning can only be made understandable through this insight, when he makes the otherwise very striking statement in his *Commentary on John*: "Indeed, if the impossible were granted, that the divinity may be separated from the body of Christ, then His divinity would not be in the Sacrament."[5] Understood literally, this statement, which the German edition of Thomas's commentary cites in translation[6] without analysis, would invalidate the statement about the immutability[7] of the divinity and thereby break apart the whole of classical theology. This statement can be understood in accord with Thomas's views of the immutability of the divinity, stated elsewhere, only if one holds that the Thomistic "in the Sacrament," here and otherwise, is not a presence in the

3 *ST*, III, 76, 1, ad 1.

4 *ST*, III, 76, 4.

5 Thomas Aquinas, *In Euangelia S. Matthaei et S. Joannis commentaria, Tomus secundus*, p. 199.

6 *Die deutsche Thomas-Ausgabe* 30:418.

7 *ST*, I, 9.

usual sense of this word, as it is understood by Nominalism and by Luther, and that concomitance has the character of presence even less.

Meanwhile, one must note that Thomas answers the question about concomitance as a part of the problem of what the communicant actually receives in Communion, and that his answer, compared with an earlier solution, technically seems to indicate a broadening of the scope of the presence. Therefore, it is possible to understand concomitance as an actual statement of sacramental theology intended to communicate the same concrete information as other dogmas. This lack of clarity is not without significance to the following discussion of the doctrine of concomitance.

Ockham's view of concomitance ought to be seen in connection with his concept of presence. Christ's body is present in the Sacrament through its self-existence, and transubstantiation loses logical connection with the presence, but [it] is affirmed anyway. Transubstantiation is thought to happen partly as transubstantiation in the real sense, into Christ's body and blood, partly as transubstantiation in a broader sense, into what is united with these, which thus means a form of concomitance. This means that multiple transubstantiations occur and that concomitance is effected in distinction from the presence that is accomplished by the first, "real" transubstantiation, simply by God intending it only secondhand.[8] In reality, the presence of Christ's blood in the host is just as concrete as the presence of Christ's body in it and likewise is produced by the transformation itself. In a strict sense, Christ's blood is present in the host (or Christ's body in the cup, or Christ's soul in both forms) not *through* concomitance, but it is this presence that completes the Words of Institution that *is* concomitance. There is a further and more important distinction in the question of the scope of the presence vis-à-vis Thomas's [teaching]. [Erwin] Iserloh uses Ockham's words in *Quod libeta*: "Thus I concede that the bread is changed by the power of conversion into [Christ's] intellectual soul and the accidence, but not into the divinity, because the soul and accidence begin to be there at the pronouncement of the Words, but the divinity does not begin to be there in this way."[9]

Christ's divinity is thus not made present as a part of concomitance, which involves only His humanity in its various aspects. Iserloh adds something incomprehensible: "But on what basis the divinity becomes present, Ockham does not express himself further."[10] Iserloh here proceeds from the idea that Ockham in some way still thinks that Christ's body cannot be separate from the divinity,

8 Compare Buescher, op. cit., pp. 52ff., 155; Iserloh, op. cit., p. 171.

9 Iserloh, op. cit., p. 171 n. 91, cited as "Vat. Lat. 3075 f. 44 va." [Compare Ockham, *Quodlibetal Questions*, translated by Alfred J. Freddoso and Francis E. Kelley (1991), p. 369.]

10 Iserloh, op. cit., p. 172.

but he does not understand the restrictions being made. Ockham's way of thinking here is not amenable to Iserloh's Thomistic definitions. Ockham's opinion is presented in the words "the divinity does not begin to be there in this way." This statement contains a truism: God's immutability. When the Thomistic statements about relationship are replaced with Nominalism's self-existence, obviously the divinity is excluded from concomitance. If Thomas's statements had been adopted by Ockham unchanged, then the result would have been a localizing of the divinity.

[Gabriel] Biel, in his commentary on Ockham, expresses the train of thought more precisely: "But there is not a conversion into the divinity. Granted, it [the divinity] is most definitely there, because it does not begin to be there since it does not begin to be anywhere, but it always is everywhere."[11] The omnipresent divinity is not made present the way, for example, Christ's human soul is. Nonetheless, Biel confesses a presence of the divinity in the Sacrament through concomitance. It is pertinent here, meanwhile, that this presence occurs "through the communication of attributes."[12] In the same way that Mary's Son can be said to exist for an eternity, the divinity can be said to be in the Sacrament. The personal union makes such a statement possible. Thereby the concomitance of the divinity becomes nothing more than the assertion that Christ's body is indissolubly united with the eternal Logos, which is what Thomas intended.[13] Nonetheless, it is possible to see Biel's differentiation as directed against a Thomistic definition of concomitance.

Between Ockham and Biel, there was the Council of Constance in 1415, where concomitance was dogmatized: "It must be believed . . . [that] the whole body of Christ and His blood are truly contained just as much under the form of the bread as under the form of the wine. . . ."[14] This limiting definition is followed by the bull *Inter cunctas* from 1418, which extended the presence by concomitance to "the soul and divinity and the whole Christ";[15] this clarification is repeated in *Decretum pro armenis*[16] in 1439.

11 In IV, d. XI, art. 2, concl. I F; compare id., [*Canonis misse expositio*], lect. 40 T: "that nothing can be converted into divinity, and on account of its own necessity and immutability it is not possible for anyone to follow." Compare Damerau, op. cit., pp. 203f., 208, who, however, does not place the matter in its larger context.

12 Id., [*Canonis misse expositio*], lect. 42, Nf.

13 This opinion of Biel *de facto* also goes back to what Ockham concisely says in *De corpore Christi*, chapter 1 (Birch, pp. 162ff.) about the eucharistic body being that of the ascended Son of God. Buescher's presentation (op. cit., p. 10) seems to suggest that this is all that Ockham says positively about the presence of the divinity.

14 Denzinger § 1199.

15 [Denzinger] § 1257.

16 [Denzinger] § 698. [The Decree for the Armenians, sometimes called the bull *Exultate Deo*, was issued by the Council of Florence.]

Since the medieval background has now been reviewed, Luther's position on concomitance can be taken up. Research shows two different groups: a large group of researchers who find that Luther basically accepted the "whole Christ," though with certain limitations; and a very small group who think the opposite. [Hans] Grass can be offered as a moderate and quite nuanced representative of the first group. He thinks that up until 1521 Luther embraced the Church's dogma of concomitance, after which time he rejected the "speculation of concomitance" but without "directly denying the thing that was intended by concomitance."[17] But after 1526 even "the thing itself" was rejected: "However, the last point is valid, with a certain limitation, for even after 1526 there are expressions in which Luther concedes the 'whole [Christ] under one kind' [*totus sub una*]."[18] Luther's motivation for rejecting concomitance really would only have been the late medieval practice of Communion "under one kind," which might be defended with the idea that the cup gives nothing additional, and the attempt by the Enthusiasts to spiritualize the bodily presence in favor of a "personal," nonbodily presence of "Christ." Also, according to Grass, being bound by the Word of Scripture played a definite, albeit subordinate, role.

In the section on omnipresence, Grass thinks that the doctrine of Christ's omnipresence according to both natures must necessarily lead to a presence of the "whole Christ" in the Sacrament. He therefore finds it natural that researchers who primarily are occupied with Luther's Christology are led to view the type of presence as a personal [presence, a presence of Christ's person], while others who are occupied with Luther's exegetical argumentation come to a more exclusively "substantial" presence of only [the substance of] Christ's body and blood.[19] When Luther disputes concomitance, Grass sees this as a blatant inconsistency in relation to the doctrine of omnipresence that is advanced elsewhere: "The idiosyncratic hiatus."[20]

Peters, to a higher degree than Grass, attributes to Luther the view of the presence of the "whole Christ." The only way one can deduce a rejection of concomitance is by misunderstanding certain passages in Luther. Positive statements about the "whole Christ" are also found in the latter material. The role of omnipresence is underscored. Definite criticism is directed against researchers who would assert a presence of only Christ's body and blood: "Thus at the same time Luther also says a clear 'No' to the words of Vilmar and Rocholl."[21] [Hermann] Sasse also finds the "whole Christ" to be in the Sacrament. Here, as in Peters, the occurrence of the adoration is underscored as evidence that

17 Grass, op. cit., p. 52.

18 Id., op. cit., p. 55.

19 Id., op. cit., p. 84.

20 Ibid.

21 Peters, op. cit., p. 111.

concomitance is necessary: without the "whole Christ," no adoration toward the Sacrament would be possible.[22] There is an unrestricted espousal of the "whole Christ" in [Vilmos] Vajta, who in accord with his consistent posture of systematizing represents a much more pronounced view than the others. By adhering to the doctrine of concomitance, Luther would even have been able to accept "under one kind," according to Vajta.[23] Grass saw "under one kind" and its rejection as an opportunity to reject concomitance, while Vajta thus sees adherence to concomitance as making it possible to maintain "under one kind." Vajta's book distinguishes itself from the rest of the literature by almost exclusively adducing the real presence as the "presence of Christ." The research otherwise mainly takes a viewpoint that lies between Grass and Peters: [Carl Fredrik] Wisløff wants to emphasize the "whole Christ" "somewhat more strongly than Grass."[24] [Reinhold] Seeberg could be equated with Wisløff.[25]

The opposite view is embraced by a much smaller number of researchers today. Here belongs [Helmut] Gollwitzer, who, according to Peters, "let himself be misled into separating the external thing [*res externa*] of the body and blood from His person."[26] Ruben Josefson has supported Gollwitzer's view.[27] The idea is also in [Francis] Pieper.[28]

22 Sasse, op. cit., p. 182 n. 122.

23 Vajta, op. cit., p. 92 n. 173.

24 Wisløff, op. cit., p. 167.

25 Seeberg, op. cit., 4/1:401 n. 22, 476 n. 1. The rest of the researchers of this view are cited in Grass, op. cit., p. 47 n. 1; and Peters, op. cit., p. 105 n. 89.

26 Peters, op. cit., p. 108 n. 104; Gollwitzer, op. cit., p. 63.

27 Josefson, "Luthersk nattvardsuppfattning," pp. 388ff. Josefson's use of "Sasse" as further support is incorrect. In the cited collection, *Vom Sakrament des Altars*, published by Sasse, only Ernst Sommerlath ("Das Abendmahl bei Luther," pp. 129f.) expresses himself on the matter: "For that reason, therefore, it cannot be right to reinterpret the character of substance of the Supper's gifts as the personal [character], but conversely to understand the personal life [of Christ] in its connection to natural existence and to consider Luther's doctrine from then on in its grand connecting of both components." This is not at all an assertion of a presence of only Christ's body and blood, and Peters (op. cit., p. 112) seems to be right in citing Sommerlath as support for his theses. Nor is it of help to Wisløff when he (op. cit., p. 165 n. 59) ascribes Gollwitzer's theses to Regin Prenter. Prenter (*Skabelse og genløsning*, p. 548) on the surface seems to want to defend Sommerlath's opinion, thus the "substantial" presence in contrast to a "personal" presence, which would thus decide that the "substantial" [presence] is excluded: "Luther sets up the idea that the gift comes to us as 'substance' against the Enthusiasts' talk about remembrance, which is considered [Christ's] 'personal' [presence]." Yet what matters is that Prenter's statements, upon deeper analysis, can be viewed only as referring to the elements in their physical concretion and in their character as gifts, and that the real presence in fact in him [his writings] is reinterpreted into its opposite; compare above, pp. 27ff., paragraphs after n. 101 [Swedish edition, pp. 32f.].

28 Pieper, op. cit., 3:416 [cf. *Christian Dogmatics*, 3:356].

Now the material can be analyzed. Grass asserts that Luther still clearly confessed concomitance in 1520 and 1521 and cites from Luther: "Who has doubted that Christ is whole under each kind?" and "Indeed, I have said that the whole Christ is received in one kind."[29] The first quotation is taken from *Answer to the Notice Issued under the Seal of the Official at Stolpen* from 1520. The continuation of the quotation reads: "Who has doubted that Christ is whole under each kind, which the Bohemians have otherwise believed or said, or against which the adversary contends so insistently and assiduously concerning these crude notices with so many useless words?" This statement ought to raise doubt about whether the interpretation of Grass is correct, since the Bohemians rejected concomitance, as shall be shown in the following. The context makes it clear. Luther was accused by the opponents of teaching that Christ's indivisible body would be given "in pieces" or "in parts," thus divided and apportioned. They wanted to discredit Luther in this way, and he points the protesters to the fact that one must distinguish "the Sacrament given piecemeal from the body of Christ being given piecemeal."[30] Luther refers to the scholastic distinction: "But if he did not understand, then he should have gone to school and learned earlier what it means that the Sacrament is given in pieces and the body of Christ is given in pieces; those [ideas] are more different than up and down."[31] Thus out of maliciousness the opponents depicted Luther as asserting that Christ's body would have to be apportioned, divided "in pieces" in the Mass, while his attacked and misinterpreted writings only said that withholding the cup was an incomplete, piecemeal distribution of the Sacrament. Luther is not defending himself against the accusation of having separated Christ's body from Christ's person but against the assertion that the "body of Christ" would have been divided up. So Grass has not construed Luther's meaning correctly.

Grass's commentary on this passage is less adequate also in other respects. When Luther emphasizes the importance of his statements being interpreted in accord with current scholarly use of language, which means "distinguishing the Sacrament . . . from the body of Christ,"[32] so that statements about the external species of the Sacrament are not transferred to Christ's indivisible body, Grass imagines that this "distinction" actually annuls the real presence and puts Luther close to the Enthusiasts. The misunderstanding in Grass should be obvious. Furthermore, Grass imagines Luther in a fit of anger wanting to conceal the difficulties in his own reasoning when he concedes that the Sacrament, distributed piecemeal, gives a complete "*res sacramenti*" ["sacramental thing"]. Against this

29 Grass, op. cit., p. 49; WA 6:139.25f.; 7:609.2. [The first quotation is taken from *Antwort auf die Zettel, so unter des Officials zu Stolpen Siegel ist ausgegangen.*]

30 WA 6:151.14f. (the Latin translation of the writing).

31 WA 6:140.19ff.

32 WA 6:151.19f.; Grass, op. cit., p. 50.

can be cited, first, that Luther, as explained above, is talking about the indivisibility of Christ's body and, second, that Grass, under a hypothetical supposition that Luther really advocated the "whole Christ" in the sense of concomitance, should not have difficulty in letting it be completely logical for Luther to teach that Communion "under one kind," the incomplete Sacrament, still gives the "whole Christ." Grass's false presupposition [*a priori*] is that Luther's criticism is basically dictated from the viewpoint of religious necessity that would be satisfied by receiving the "whole Christ" "under one kind," according to which all other criticism is made impossible. In that way, he ignores Luther as bound to the institution given in Scripture. Only under this presupposition could he have ascribed intellectual lack of clarity to Luther.

The second of Grass's quotations cited above—from 1521, "I said that the whole Christ is received in one kind"—obviously relates to the same polemics as given above. It says, "I spoke about the kinds, not about the thing contained in the Sacrament. For I said that in one kind the whole Christ is received, but not the whole Sacrament, that is, not both kinds."[33] Against the backdrop of the earlier polemics, the context is without difficulty: the contrast is kind [versus] thing contained; not body of Christ [versus] whole Christ. Nor can it be supported that Luther here expressed himself on concomitance.

Grass then discusses a letter from 1522 in which Luther takes up the topic of the Bohemians' particular opinion on the question of concomitance. Grass describes Luther's stance as restrained in regard to speculations, conceding to the Bohemians the right to deny concomitance but almost embracing it *de facto* himself. The description is incorrect. Actually, Luther warns against speculations, but simply by doing so, concomitance is excluded: "Faith does not want to know more than that under the bread is Christ's body, under the wine is the blood of the living and reigning Christ. It perseveres in this simplicity, disregarding curious questions."[34] This is the answer to the question "whether only the body is under the bread by the power of the words,"[35] whereby Luther expressly places himself on the side of the Bohemians in the question of denying concomitance. The statement that got Grass to suppose that Luther stayed with the doctrine of concomitance is this: "For no one denies, I think not even the [Bohemian] Brethren themselves, that the body and blood of Christ are there and that He must be adored. This is enough to be called concomitance."[36] Grass understands this as an uncertainty in Luther, whereby he would inscribe the "whole Christ" in the Sacrament: "At least the 'He must be adored' points to

33 WA 7:609.1ff.

34 WA Br 2[:561].64ff., no. 509.

35 WA Br 2[:561].57f., no. 509.

36 WA Br 2[:560].42f., no. 509.

the presence of Christ and not merely to a presence of body and blood."[37] The Christological logic that Grass uses here, meanwhile, is not Luther's. For Luther, Christ's humanity is made partaker of the majestic attribute of the divinity and is itself worthy of adoration. The "concomitance" of which Luther says, "This is enough to be called concomitance," is the concomitance of the divine attributes in Christ's body and blood. The act of adoration in front of the consecrated forms is fulfilled thus: "For this is how faith adores: it places in front of itself only Him whose body and blood it does not doubt to be there; if those contentious ones do not wish to call it concomitance, let them call it something else."[38] This means that faith always transfers to Christ's body and blood the divinity's worthiness to be adored in that it sees these things as resting *within* the personal union. The relative pronoun "whose" does not speak about a mere possessive relationship through which the respect for the owner's property is returned to the owner, but about the physical things that share the divine person's worthiness to be adored.

Concomitance, according to its usual definition, included to some extent Christ's divinity, to some extent Christ's humanity, insofar as this does not coincide with His body and blood. In the letter in question here, this first kind of concomitance is judged with particularly negative condemnation:

> Some, in fact, would want to explore how the divinity is grasped there by concomitance; show them that they are foolishly curious and destructive with their carnal speculations into the mysteries of God. . . . For where such foolish speculations and unnecessary things have been allowed, they make people curious, and, faith being subordinated, they lead to all kinds of muck concerning infinite space, emptiness, quantity, substance, and whatever natural reason and philosophy have raved about thus far.[39]

Here speculations that make this judgment are called "unnecessary." At the same time, there is a substantive critique of the silly thoughts that triggered the speculation: that "the divinity is grasped" [*comprehendatur*] is an absurdity. This criticism again is confronted in *On the Adoration of the Sacrament of the Holy Body of Christ* from 1523, with the words "Let the clever and unbelieving sophists think about such baseless things and *conjure the divinity into the Sacrament*."[40] To conjure the divinity into the bread and wine comes close to Luther's accusatory definition of concomitance. The eternal, immutable divinity, according to Luther, can never be conjured into the Sacrament. Thus the critique he made might, in fact, not really get at a strictly Thomistic doctrine of concomitance, but Luther still regards it as needing to be addressed to the "sophists."

37 Grass, op. cit., p. 51.

38 WA Br 2[:560].39ff., no. 509.

39 WA Br 2[:560–61].44f., no. 509.

40 WA 11:450.13ff. [cf. AE 36:297].

This procedure can only be explained from the tension that existed between the inquiries of Thomistic doctrine and actual established church practices. Thomas could not really defend the adoration[41] of Christ's body, but in his writing he willingly consented to the popular piety of adoring the Savior in the host. As an explanation for this practice, the doctrine of concomitance then had to gain the appearance of localizing the divinity: the divinity is *also* in the Sacrament, *which is why* it can be adored. Despite its rejection of the concomitance of the divinity, Nominalism also had to make the same practical decision. Luther's words must be seen as directed against this inevitable conclusion. Christ's humanity "is contained" in the Sacrament, which may never be transferred to the divinity. The adoration is not based on a localizing of the divinity in the flesh, but on the latter's [the flesh's] being elevated to being worthy of adoration.

But Grass also uses *On the Adoration* in support of his thesis: "So again also here the speculation of concomitance is certainly rejected, yet here, too, there is no direct rejection of what is intended with the concomitance."[42] He relies, among other things, on a statement of Luther that in his opinion is particularly significant: "And He is not separated from His body and blood."[43] In order honestly to give his readers as complete a picture as possible of the obviously problematic lack of clarity in Luther, Grass presents the continuation of the statement with a commentary: "*But* very significantly Luther continues: '*And* when He lay dead in the grave, He was still Christ and worthy of His honor, even when there was no longer any blood in Him.' "[44] Where Luther writes "and," Grass has to write "but," since he does not see the connection between the thoughts. Prior to the statement first cited, Luther established the thesis that one "surely cannot withhold his adoration of the body and blood of Christ without sinning,"[45] that is, Christ's physical humanity, diffinitively present in the circumscriptively existing host and chalice, must receive divine honor. Luther then explains how the physical realities of Christ's body and blood rest in the personal union: "For I must indeed confess that Christ is there, if His body and blood are there. His Words do not lie to me, and He is not separated from His body and blood." The latter expression—"not separated"—gives the context of the earlier "is there": the divinity is not localized, but the divine person, by becoming man, embraces also the physical things. Luther now continues consistently with a legitimate, introductory "and": "And when He lay dead in the grave, He was still Christ and worthy of His honor." Even in the grave Christ's lifeless body is divine, for even then the personal union is maintained, so that it really was the Logos-Christ

41 Compare above, pp. 38–39, paragraph after n. 16 [Swedish edition, p. 42].

42 Grass, op. cit., p. 52.

43 WA 11:447.10f. [cf. AE 36:294].

44 Grass, op. cit., ibid.

45 WA 11:447.8f. [cf. AE 36:294].

who, in His assumed body, was buried. On the other hand, the divinity was not wrapped in the shroud and laid down together with the body in the sense of a crudely understood concomitance. Nor did adoration of Christ's body invoke this absurdity, but [it] was ensured by the personal union.

When Grass, in order to balance his basically very moderate presentation, is going to tally the passages that speak "even directly against the matter"—that is, against concomitance—he unfortunately chooses some passages in the writings against the Enthusiasts that later were shown by Peters not to indicate a denial of the "whole Christ."[46] Conceding the correctness of Peters's remarks does not mean that Luther did not directly deny concomitance in other passages. The most detailed examination of the problem is found in *A Report to a Good Friend about Both Kinds in the Sacrament at the Mandate of the Bishop of Meissen*[47] from 1528; its actual theological content escaped Grass and Peters, who talk about "a very irrelevant conclusion"[48] with regard to "Luther being carried away by the flow of his thoughts."[49] Luther here, meanwhile, makes an actual polemical attack on the very foundation of concomitance in any form, namely, what is taken for granted in the accompanying term, which lays in the expression "natural concomitance." Luther's argumentation follows a clear line and makes use of a *deductio ad absurdum*: if the given coexistence of Christ's blood with His body, of Christ's soul with His body, of Christ's divinity with His soul, of the two other divine persons with the Son leads to a corresponding "natural" coexistence in the Sacrament, then the omnipresence of the divinity in the creature and therefore coexistence with it must imply the presence of the creature in the Sacrament.

> Here now what affects concomitance is the conclusion: since Christ's body is not without blood, then it follows that His blood is not without His soul, from which it follows that His soul is not without divinity, from which it follows that in the Sacrament, even under one kind, the soul of Christ, the holy Trinity is eaten and drunk, along with His body and blood, from which it follows that a Mass-priest in an individual Mass twice offers and sells the holy Trinity, from which it follows, since the divinity is not without the creature, that heaven and earth must also be in the Sacrament. From which it follows that the devils and hell are also in the Sacrament. From which it follows that whoever eats the Sacrament (even in one kind) gobbles up the bishop of Meissen with his mandate and notice.[50]

46 Grass, op. cit., p. 53; Peters, op. cit., pp. 106f.

47 WA 26:560f. [cf. AE 61:105–53].

48 Grass, op. cit., p. 56 n. 1.

49 Peters, op. cit., p. 107.

50 WA 26:605.27ff. [cf. AE 61:147].

These concepts, which in the disputed doctrine are subordinated to circumscriptive attributes such as "in it" and the other terms such as "contained in," are definitively or repletively existing realities that evade the deductive method that builds on parallels with liquids existing in vessels or other conjoined things. The sacramental mode of presence precludes all conclusions that apply within physics. The circumscriptively present body of Christ in heaven must "contain" blood, but this does not apply to the diffinitively present body of Christ in the Sacrament. The repletively present divinity is not "contained" in Christ's body in any context. If one would interpret the personal union in this direction, then the creation, as it also coexists with the divinity and "is contained" in it, must unconditionally be drawn into the sacramental presence, from which it follows that the bishop of Meissen is received "under one kind" and "under both kinds" by his clergy who celebrate Mass. This is polemics with the claim of being an intellectually coherent critique. It has an impact on any attempt by Thomism to present its doctrine of concomitance as a meaningful, separate dogma that says anything in regard to basic tenets of Christology. Peters, as mentioned, finds only contradictions and, finally, has Luther, in the very same thought, both state and rescind his opposition to concomitance,[51] when the latter [Luther] says, "How can you measure His wisdom and power, that He has proclaimed not only His body and blood [to be] in the Sacrament so that His soul and divinity still would not be in it, though His soul and divinity cannot be without body and blood?"[52] The "concomitance" expressed in the final subordinate clause is the coexistence that applies to the whole divine-human person of Christ repletively. The presence "in the Sacrament" again is not repletive but diffinitive [presence] and embraces only the things that this form of presence would take on through the consecration. Therefore, Luther can be said to be consistent and not at all confused, as Peters thinks. This also answers the problem that Grass called "*Hiatus*" between Christological and sacramental-exegetical argumentation. Such a leap in thought need only be presumed if one mistakenly makes the repletive and diffinitive modes of presence identical.[53]

In this writing from 1528, Peters also wants to gain support indirectly for his thesis about Luther's adherence to concomitance: "In none of those [statements of Luther] does he expressly say: What meets us in the Sacrament is not the whole Christ, but only His body and, accordingly, His blood."[54] Peters thereby does violence to Luther's doctrine. Earlier the concomitant presence of the divinity had already been expressly and fundamentally excluded as a possible theorem. There still remained the possibility of a concomitant presence according to the

51 Peters, op. cit., p. 108.

52 WA 26:606.36ff. [cf. AE 61:147].

53 Compare here Mahlmann, op. cit., p. 174 n. 155.

54 Peters, op. cit., p. 107.

Council of Constance, so that each kind at least imparts both Christ's body and blood. But that cannot be sneaked into Luther's doctrinal system, even in the roundabout way suggested by Peters. Peters counts on the latitude of a theologoumenon, but this is disproved by this statement in the writing referenced: "The Words are commanded to me and will be certain enough for me."[55] There is no knowledge "outside of and beyond His Words."[56] Likewise in the question of the validity of the private Mass and transubstantiation, it is important that the concept of theologoumenon is dismissed.

Nor is what Grass asserts possible: the idea that Luther even during his later years in certain comments "concedes to the Papists the 'whole under one kind' [*totus sub una*], and only rejects the conclusion drawn from it, the 'Communion under one kind' [*communio sub una*], as strictly against Christ's institution."[57] He cites from Luther: "But let there be under one kind whatever they wish. . . . Under one kind I receive the half and corrupted command of Christ,"[58] and a similar famous expression from the Smalcald Articles.[59] Grass concludes: "It is not to be taken that he rejects the 'whole Christ under the bread' as such because he is against the Papists, but [only] insofar as it would offer the theological basis for withholding the cup."[60] The interpretation that Grass offers here ignores the fact that the above-mentioned quotation includes the simple observation that concomitance and "under one kind" are problems completely independent of each other: the one regarding the content of the Sacrament, the other regarding the rite of the Sacrament; for which reason the former can be yielded with impunity—"let it be . . . whatever they wish"—in discussing the latter. It is the same capacity for *distinctions* that leads Luther in his doctrine of the Sacrament to explain the omnipresence of Christ's body to be a proposition that, taken strictly, is not necessary for the real presence to be accomplished. That does not mean that it has lost its status as a Christological dogma that is maintained in its proper context. Grass again, along with an overwhelming share of modern Luther research, presupposes that Luther is incapable of a more meticulous form of reasoning. The same false *a priori* attitude shows up in the often-presented complaints about his outbursts of anger. Thus the way is blocked for penetrating into Luther's intellectually connected worldview, the breadth of which is ignored by constructing a narrow, emotional definition of religion.

Wisløff's material, which intends to prove a "somewhat stronger" emphasis of the role of concomitance for Luther than Grass conceded, cannot be accepted

55 WA 26:608.19f. [cf. AE 61:148].

56 WA 26:607.21f. [cf. AE 61:148].

57 Grass, op. cit., p. 55.

58 WA 39/1:24.29 [forthcoming in AE 72].

59 WA 50:242.17ff. (= *BS* 451.4ff.) [cf. SA III VI 3].

60 Grass, op. cit., p. 55.

as confirming Wisløff's thesis.[61] WA 23:87.30 [cf. AE 37:29]: "How He [*er*/it] is in the bread" is cited, but "He" [*er*/it] refers to the closest masculine noun, namely, "body" [*leib*]. WA 23:145.13 [cf. AE 37:64] does not mean Christ as the gift of the Supper but as its Institutor. WA 26:392.20 [*noch deüten odder gleichnis ist*; cf. AE 37:263, which translates a different transcription] along with several passages certainly speaks about "Christ's presence," but this must be seen in the light of Luther's view of Christology and concomitance. The person and divinity of Christ in its exclusively repletive form of existence is, of course, present in the Sacrament just as much as it was at one time in the place where Jesus was during His earthly life. Just as *Christ* was crucified when Christ's *body* was nailed to the cross, and *Christ* was buried when Christ's *body* was buried, so *Christ* is present when Christ's *body* rests on the altar, the paten, or the communicants' lips. That does not revive the concomitance that Luther disputed and that *de facto* must have been presented as a completion of the scope of the presence. The conflict of modern research on this point may in some way be said to go back to an unexamined implication of the terminology that in turn is dependent on the deficiency in a dogmatic-historical insistence on the earlier treatment of the doctrine of concomitance. Yet it must be said that challenging [the idea] that the doctrine of concomitance occurs in Luther's theology, which was asserted by such dissimilar researchers as Gollwitzer, Josefson, and Pieper, must be given preference ahead of the opinion represented by the bulk of the researchers. Although without analysis, these have correctly given Luther's view.

Melanchthon

[Albert] Herrlinger[62] already underscored Melanchthon's rallying around concomitance. Gollwitzer agrees with this, while highlighting the contrast with Luther.[63] This stance of Melanchthon's shall be analyzed more closely here and shall be placed into its larger doctrinal context.

The validity of concomitance was the subject of dogmatic discussion already in connection with the Augsburg Confession. Roman Catholic criticism against it [the Augsburg Confession] said that the doctrine of concomitance was not clearly confessed in it. It said the Lutherans' article on the Supper can be approved, "if only they believe that the whole Christ is present under each kind, so that Christ's blood is under the species of bread through concomitance no less than under the species of wine, and vice versa. Otherwise in the Eucharist Christ's body would be dead and bloodless, contrary to St. Paul, because 'Christ,

61 Wisløff, op. cit., p. 168 nn. 76–77.

62 Herrlinger, op. cit., pp. 137, 154f.

63 Gollwitzer, op. cit., pp. 158f.

rising from the dead, dies no more,' Rom. 6[:9]."[64] This criticism has to do with concomitance especially as it was expressed by the Council of Constance: Christ's body and blood must accompany each other so that a bloodless, dead body of Christ shall not be given in the Sacrament. The Apology, the writing in defense of the Augsburg Confession, gave a clear answer to this challenge: "We speak of the presence of the living Christ: for we know that death no longer has power over Him."[65] This implies nothing beyond Luther: the body that is received in the Sacrament is the living body of Christ.[66]

Concomitance in a somewhat wider sense is discussed in a contemporaneous short document from Melanchthon's hand. It says there:

> Nestorius posited two persons in Christ and the idea that it is possible for the human nature in Christ to exist without the divine. So if we were to posit only the body of Christ in the Sacrament, and we did not posit the divinity to be there, it would follow that we divide Christ by the example of Nestorius. So, we respond that the whole Christ is in the Sacrament, lest we be in any way suspected of dividing the natures or positing two persons.[67]

Now concomitance is seen as the presence of the divinity and must be affirmed, to avoid Nestorianism. Nor did Luther's opinion come very close to that [Nestorianism] either. Also for him, the divinity was present in the Sacrament in the sense that Christ's body rested in the personal union.[68]

Soon enough, however, Melanchthon would make demarcations that would lead him to a substantive conflict with Luther on this point. It is this disagreement that is predicted by [Caspar] Cruciger in 1538 in the letter to Veit Dietrich cited earlier, with the words about "questions of tragedies," about which Cruciger spoke with Melanchthon, and to which [these words] belong: "Whether that dividing or separating of the body and blood must be posited, or whether Christ and not only His energy [Greek: *energeia*] is believed to be present only in the way He is indeed otherwise believed to be everywhere, to be

64 CR 27:106 (*Confutatio*) [on AC X].

65 *BS* 248.44f. [cf. Ap X 57].

66 Herrlinger (op. cit., p. 137) places the statement in contrast to the later Lutheran dogmatics' rejection of concomitance, but thereby reads too much into the words of the Apology.

67 CR 2:226.

68 Herrlinger (op. cit., p. 154) curiously explains this text as directed against "the *Catholic* view of the Sacrament in which attention is directed only to the body of Christ, which is present through priestly consecration, and not to the personal Christ who communicates His body and blood, [and he shows] that *this* view is Nestorian." By doing this, Herrlinger attributes to parties [involved] in the dogmatic conflict views that they oppose in the same work, and a reversal of roles takes place. As shall be presented above, Melanchthon endeavored on this very point not to be affected by a Roman Catholic criticism of denying "the personal Christ." The concentration "only on the body of Christ" is found again on the Lutheran side.

present, and to be in everything."[69] That is how the alternatives that are actually dogmatically distinct are characterized: the Lutheran presence [as] diffinitive, which only embraces Christ's body and blood; or ("*aut*") the Melanchthonian, which has the whole person of Christ be repletively present in the Sacrament.

Cruciger rightly claimed to be speaking to Dietrich in Melanchthon's name; Melanchthon's subsequent letter to the latter [Dietrich] confirms this. In connection with condemning the adoration of the Sacrament and an actual union between Christ's body and the bread, even this statement is attacked: "because some now say that the body and blood are delivered separately. That is indeed an innovation, and not even the Papists like it. Error is fertile, as they say; physical conjoining begets many questions."[70] Now this is not a matter of technical adjustments to avoid accusations of Christological heresy, but clarifications that are expressly said to connect with the definition of the presence. There are clear positions within the Lutheran camp that fall under the disapproval both of Melanchthon as well as Rome, and which imply that only Christ's body and blood are distributed. Fear of a doctrinal innovation is expressed that same year in a letter to the same addressee [Dietrich]: "But to add the dividing and separating of the body and blood is absolutely an innovation and unprecedented in the whole ancient church."[71] Thus Melanchthon thinks that the early church was not familiar with any denial of concomitance. The stance is clear, even if the evidence is relatively scarce. The polemics get a final honing against the Gnesio-Lutheran camp in 1559, when Melanchthon writes against the so-called Book of Confutation: "The Weimar writers also make a separation of body and blood, which no Papist, not even Luther, would make, and undoubtedly many scholarly men in other countries will write against it."[72] Making an appeal to Luther may be seen in the light of Melanchthon's understandable ambition, despite everything, of wanting to identify himself with Luther after Luther's death.[73] The Gnesio-Lutherans, as shown above, had more right to seek this posthumous endorsement.

Melanchthon's displeasure obviously applies to the clear stipulation made in the Book of Confutation that has the following wording:

> Whereby that papistic invention is also refuted: that both [kinds] are in each; and the error of the Sacramentarians who scandalously pervert this Supper into merely a spiritual eating. For that double affirmation ["This is

69 CR 3:510.

70 CR 3:514f.

71 CR 3:536.

72 CR 9:766.

73 Compare here Hassler, "Luther och elevationen i nattvardsmässan," p. 46, where Melanchthon's invocation of Luther on the question of abolishing the elevation seems to be an inadequate presentation of the facts, coming many years after Luther's death.

> My body; This is My blood"] then quite securely provides the presence of body and blood; then the body indeed is distinctly attributed to the bread, the blood indeed is attributed to the wine. Finally, then, in no way does it harmonize with their [idea of] spiritual communion, which receives both in each.[74]

With these words, Gnesio-Lutheranism declares that it is continuing Luther's stance on the doctrine of concomitance. Gollwitzer cited words, for example, from Erasmus Sarcerius, for whom Melanchthon had little appreciation, as expressing the same clear rejection of concomitance. The distinction that Gollwitzer quite correctly makes here between Melanchthonians and Lutherans, on the other hand, cannot be accepted in its details. The Lutherans could still affirm concomitance if it was stating nothing other than what is self-evident Christologically. So, whether a writer should actually be assigned to the Melanchthonian camp depends on the kind of assent he makes to concomitance. Nor is it certain that a Melanchthonian view of the presence would make it absolutely necessary to insist that the doctrine of concomitance be defended. For Melanchthonianism, the presence only constitutes an application of the omnipresence, an application defined by the Word. Nothing prevents this definition from being viewed as applying merely to Christ's body and blood, which are the only things named in the Words of Institution.

Gollwitzer assigns [Martin] Chemnitz to the successors of Melanchthon on this point, since he does not find in Chemnitz any polemic against concomitance. But Chemnitz expresses himself in a way that clearly shows that he would only agree with the proposition that the personal union is maintained also in the Sacrament, and not that a dead body of Christ is offered in it: "Indeed, this consideration is also useful. It was known to antiquity that wherever Christ is, He is there whole and entire; that His body is not without blood, nor is His blood apart from His body."[75] This statement should be seen against the background of an axiom from Chemnitz cited before: "after the resurrection there would be no separation"; that is, Christ does not die at every consecration so that His body is emptied of blood. What is received in the Sacrament is still Christ's body and blood, each under its kind: "Durand cites from Innocent III: It is granted that under the bread the body is not without blood, nor under the wine is the blood separate from the body; nevertheless, the blood of Christ is not drunk under the bread, nor is Christ's body eaten in the wine."[76] With this quotation, Chemnitz keeps himself from broadening the scope of the presence. He thereby also shows how the Lutheran critique could go back to an older tradition before High Scholasticism.

---

74 *Illustrissimi Principis . . . Confutatio*, fol. 29b.

75 Chemnitz, *Examination of the Council of Trent*, 2:429 [Latin, p. 379].

76 Id., op. cit., pp. 379f. [Chemnitz, *Examination of the Council of Trent*, 2:429].

In Laurentius Petri there is an oft-stated example of the Lutheran doctrine of how in the Sacrament only Christ's body and blood are present and have a right to divine adoration without concomitance of the divinity. In his *Dialog* from 1562, he explains Lutheran Christology: "that whatever honor is ascribed to His divinity, the same is also ascribed to His humanity," and he defends the possibility of prayer directed only toward the humanity with the words "May Christ's body and blood preserve me."[77] With careful distinctions, propositions are developed that all indicate that the Sacrament, worthy of adoration, need not include more than Christ's humanity in order to receive divine honor: "Isn't Christ's body a divine body? Or doesn't He Himself also call His body the true heavenly bread that gives eternal life? No [mere] sign can give this life but [only] that which is divine."[78]

Gollwitzer cites from [Johann] Brenz a quotation that shows that he [Brenz] considers concomitance a false speculation.[79] Likewise, the *Solida Refutatio*, the Tübingen school's commentary on the Book of Concord, writes

77 Laurentius Petri, *Om någor stycker wårs Herras Jesu Christi nattward anrörandes*, fol. FVa.

78 Id., op. cit., fol. FIIIIb. Ahlberg, who does not notice how the preceding polemic starts from a denial of concomitance, obviously understands the participation in the divinity as simply a relationship of concomitance: "Christ's body and blood inseparably united with Christ Himself" (Ahlberg, op. cit., p. 213 [chapter heading]); "The honor that is shown to His body and blood does not therefore apply to these as disconnected things, but it applied to Christ Himself" (op. cit., p. 215); "not even to Christ's body in and of itself, but to Christ Himself, since He can never be isolated from His body and blood" (op. cit., p. 216); "This indivisibility and omnipresence of the person of Christ is what for Laurentius Petri motivates the adoration" (op. cit., p. 220). Ahlberg's phraseology shows that for him the adoration is actually intercepted by the divinity in its omnipresence. Compare here Gollwitzer, op. cit., p. 63: "[Vivifying] here can be ascribed not only to the *person* of Christ as the subject but also to the flesh of Christ—indeed, under the presupposition of its belonging to Christ, but now considered *on its own*," which is a correct depiction of Lutheran Christology. Even for Laurentius Petri, it is decisive that Christ's body is worthy of adoration precisely "in and of itself."

79 Gollwitzer, op. cit., p. 159; Brenz, *Opera* 5:1436. In *Confessio Wirtenbergica* (*Opera* 8:84), there is a technically divergent formulation: "But that which pertains first to the use of the Eucharist, even if we do not deny that the whole Christ is distributed in the bread as well as in the wine, nevertheless we teach that the use of both kinds ought to be common to the whole Church." It can be supposed immediately that the document submitted to the Council of Trent in 1552 on this point wanted to associate itself with the Apology's phraseology to avoid unnecessary accusations about a dead body of Christ in the Sacrament. But a shift in view is also conceivable: Gollwitzer's citation is from 1537–40 (*Commentary on Luke*), thus twelve to fifteen years earlier than what is stated above. No point at all against a different, a Lutheran, view can be found in the statement, for which reason this later interpretation lacks factual support. The view of Tübingen theology, referenced above in the text, almost excludes the idea that the theologian who was influential for this school would have openly confessed concomitance.

under the marginal rubric "Error concerning the concomitance of the blood of Christ in the Eucharist": "The Papists believe that the body of Christ is not received without blood on account of what they call natural concomitance, that the body is not without blood. For the mode of the presence and distribution of Christ's body and blood is not natural, but mystical, divine, and celestial. Also, this carnal thought about a bloodless body can have no place here."[80] Only a false desire to categorize things can find this viewpoint of the Tübingen theologians inconsistent with their Melanchthonian view of the presence. Identifying the sacramental presence with the repletive presence does not exclude a certain measure of distinctiveness of the type [of presence], as the presentation on the consecration already showed. The divine will had only designated Christ's body and blood as sacramental gifts, and [thus] the doctrine of concomitance would fall. That also explains how the Melanchthonian definition of the presence in a certain sense became prevalent within the Lutheran orthodoxy of subsequent centuries but concomitance remained excluded from the doctrinal system of Lutheranism.[81]

80 [Andreae,] *Solida Refutatio*, p. 631.

81 On Melanchthonianism's victory in the question of the presence, compare below, chapter 7. Examples of orthodoxy's stance on concomitance are given in Gollwitzer, op. cit., p. 159 n. 8; Sasse, op. cit., p. 182 n. 122.

CHAPTER 7

Venerabilis et Adorabilis Eucharistia

Adoration and *Extra Usum*

REGARDLESS of the various explanations as to why the Sacrament could be adored, the adoration of the body and blood of Christ in the Mass was a part of the reality of Christian life for medieval Christianity, the use of which Luther here consciously went back to.[1] Researchers generally present this adoration as being accepted by Luther.[2] Only [Åke] Andrén presents the following thought, based on his definition of presence "alongside the bread":[3] "According to Luther, both the elevation and the adoration, that is, reverence toward the elements, were allowed as long as one did not begin to adore the elements and thereby give the elements the adoration that belongs only to Christ. Luther therefore initially retained the elevation in Wittenberg but was compelled later to give it up because of the ideas connected to it."[4] Meanwhile, Luther nowhere elaborates on this distinction between the element and the body of Christ, since he never thought of the Roman doctrine and medieval use as commingling something earthly and something heavenly and therefore calling for any rejection of the kind that Andrén imagines. Against Karlstadt, who "obviously lies about the pope," he [Luther] says, on the contrary: "Now the pope nowhere teaches that one should say to the form of the bread: 'My God, be

1 Compare above, p. 136, text near n. 61 [Swedish edition, pp. 127f.].

2 Grass, op. cit., pp. 115f.; Sasse, op. cit., pp. 105ff.; Peters, op. cit., pp. 93ff.; Wisløff, op. cit., pp. 178ff. [Edward Frederick] Peters, p. 139: "With almost complete consistency, Martin Luther defends the right of Christians to adore the Sacrament of the body and blood of Christ."

3 Andrén, op. cit., p. 48.

4 Id., op. cit., p. 50.

merciful to me.'"[5] Nor was Luther's abolishing of the elevation motivated in the way that Andrén describes, which was documented in detail by Karin Hassler.[6] The "thoughts of transformation," which Andrén speaks of, correspond substantially to Luther's parameters for the real presence.

Adoration of the Sacrament can be analyzed fairly by first comparing it with other types of adoration. For Luther, adoration is appropriate even when attending the means of grace besides the Eucharist. In his Genesis commentary, Luther writes about Baptism: "Water is the veil or mediating instrument, just like the Word with which God is veiled. Our Lord God stands behind it there. . . . It is the presence or form and epiphany of God in His means."[7] Every Baptism is a parallel to [Jesus'] Baptism in the Jordan, which means that the Trinity can be adored there under the outward forms: "where the voice of the Father is heard from heaven, the flesh of the Son is seen, and the Holy Spirit in the form of a dove."[8] "Therefore, this adoration is necessary, if not through physical bowing, at least through spiritual reverence."[9] [Carl Fredrik] Wisløff,[10] in agreement with Julius Köstlin,[11] sees this adoration of God as a mere veneration, which actually overrules Luther when he equates it with the adoration of the Sacrament of the Altar and which should lead to the thought "that Luther is only demanding a similar reverence for the Sacrament as for the Word." Wisløff, who proceeds from the idea that Luther teaches an actual stalwart adoration of Christ's body and blood in the Mass, solves the problem by disallowing the Genesis commentary, from which the cited words are taken, as a reliable source. Meanwhile, this volume has already cited a parallel written record on Luther's part regarding the adoration of Baptism and eucharistic adoration—Melanchthon's conversation with Luther in 1538: "Once when I was asking about the adoration, Luther responded that adoration can be done toward Baptism because God had bound Himself to His signs [and] wished to be sought there."[12] A further oral statement by Luther about the adoration at the Jordan Baptism, the prototype of Christian Baptism, is preserved in George of Anhalt's sacramental sermon on the day of Corpus Christi 1550: "He [Luther] told me this opinion with words something like this and with hands raised [as in an oath]: If I should see the Holy Spirit in the form of a dove coming down from heaven as the holy Baptizer of Christ,

5 WA 18:190.15ff. [cf. AE 40:200].

6 Hassler, "Luther och elevationen i nattvardsmässan," pp. 36ff.

7 WA 44:685.19ff. [cf. AE 8:145] (Gen. 47:31).

8 WA 44:685.28f. [cf. AE 8:145] (Gen. 47:31).

9 WA 44:685.33f. [cf. AE 8:145] (Gen. 47:31).

10 Wisløff, op. cit., p. 179 n. 39.

11 Köstlin, *Luthers Theologie*, 2:244.

12 CR 3:503; compare above, p. 153, text near nn. 125–126. [The Swedish edition page number is incorrect].

then I would fall on my knees, lift up my hands, and say: Holy Spirit, be gracious to me, etc. Shouldn't I, then, also do that at the most worthy Sacrament, since Christ is present?"[13] For Luther, the fact that this Baptism in the Jordan is worthy of adoration is foundational for the essence of Baptism:

> He steps into this water and wishes to bless it through His own body, through the Holy Spirit in the form of a dove, and with the voice of the Father. And this happened once; it occurs always until the end of the world. There Baptism is so glorious [and] heavenly because Jesus Christ, the Holy Spirit, and the Father are present in Baptism, even though I do not see it, etc. One time with His presence He showed what He wishes us to think concerning this water, what He does in it, and what benefit comes to people who receive it.[14]

What happened once in the Jordan is thus repeated daily in Christian Baptism, where the Trinity is in the water. Adoration of Baptism, which is expressly stated in first two quotations, also fits perfectly naturally in this connection.[15]

---

13 George of Anhalt, op. cit., fol. 18B. This statement is cited in WA Br 9:420 n. 7, according to an edition from 1741, which meanwhile is the seventh of George's works; compare *RE*, s.v. "George III von Anhalt." Through Kawerau ("Ein Beitrag zur Geschichte der lutherischen Lehre von der Konsekration im 16. Jahrhundert," p. 296), research has wrongly continued to think that Johann Hachenburg would have heard this expression and was the source for it. In his book *Wider den jrrthumb der newen zwinglianer*, Hachenburg reprints, with express citation of the source (op. cit., fol. CIIIa), portions of George's sermons, among them the account of Luther's defense of invoking the Sacrament. WA Br 10:33 (commentary), in imitation of Kawerau, that is, without noting that Hachenburg to a large extent is citing George of Anhalt, ascribes it to two "lost" letters from Luther to Hachenburg, in which Luther is supposed to have expressed himself on the adoration and the elevation. In the same work there is a question about letters to *George of Anhalt*, whose whole correspondence with Luther is preserved. All the rest of the statements in the research concerning Hachenburg's role in this respect rely on the mistake of Kawerau and WA and present the same incorrect conclusion.

14 WA 37:271.32ff (R) [sermon for Septuagesima, February 1, 1534, on Baptism]. [These notes by Georg Rörer were edited for publication during Luther's lifetime. Cf. the corresponding section of the printed sermon: AE 57:162–63.]

15 WA 26:442.16ff. [cf. AE 37:299]; in the *Great Confession*, Luther draws the exegetical parallel between [Christ's] Baptism in the Jordan and the Sacrament:

> Indeed, it is immediately called a formal union, because the Holy Spirit wanted to reveal Himself in that form, and Scripture here clearly says that whoever sees such a dove sees the Holy Spirit, as John 1[:33] says, "Upon whom you will see the Spirit descend and rest upon Him," etc. Why, then, should one not much more also say in the Supper: "This is My body" . . . ?

In this central passage in Luther's theology of the Lord's Supper, the epiphany of God in the Baptism at the Jordan is ascribed the complete concretion of the Sacrament of the Altar.

So there is no need for Wisløff to disallow the reliability[16] of the Genesis commentary on this point, even less since other examples of adoration outside the Eucharist will also be cited here soon. On the other hand, another problem arises in this context. In the foregoing, it was demonstrated that Luther opposes any sacramental localizing of the divinity and defines the sacramental presence as the diffinitive existence of Christ's humanity, which is able to take on such a limited form of presence without contradiction and in distinction from the divinity. But in Baptism the discussion is about a concrete presence of the divinity, worthy of adoration, which seems to gainsay these distinctions. But in one place Luther gives formulas that show the path to an interpretation consistent with the rest of his theology. In the same sermon that was cited above, regarding the Baptism in the Jordan being repeated in Christian Baptism, Luther discusses how God revealed Himself at the Jordan through the humanity of the Son, the Spirit's appearance as a dove, and the Father's voice, which are the main points in that biblical revelation: "In the Old and New Testament there were also revelations, but not such great ones."[17] This visible miracle is achieved invisibly in Christian Baptism: "Also it is the water in which the Holy Spirit applies His fire, the Father His light and majesty, the Son His body, because they did not descend in vain."[18] This presence is thus defined as to its nature:

> This is how Christ must be depicted: the Son is He who poured out His blood for me, died, rose again, and He is here also in Baptism through His blood, death, [and] life; not that He is [to be depicted] here metaphysically, materially, but effectively and with His presence. The Father is not here as a dead picture, but with His love and light, where it said: Thus God loved Him, when He endowed Him with all His power, etc., and took death away through the blood of Christ. Likewise, the Holy Spirit [is there] with His gifts, and the person of the Son with His gifts, though they work altogether anyway. . . .[19]

This presence of divinity and humanity in Christ and of the two other persons of the Godhead is [there] not "metaphysically, materially, but effectively and with His presence." Of course, the presence is an ontological reality, but it is not differentiated as such, which would merely mean omnipresence in its majesty. The presence in Baptism is specified as a special form of presence through [the expressions] "effectively and with His presence," to the specific

16 For the authenticity of the Genesis commentary and Meinhold's critique of it in *Die Genesisvorlesung Luthers und ihre Herausgeber*, compare Pedersen, op. cit., p. 395 n. 2, concerning Meinhold, who "operates with a picture of the older Luther that is much too strongly defined by the young Luther or, more correctly, Meinhold's definition of the theology of the young Luther."

17 WA 37:271.27f. (R).

18 WA 37:272.19ff. [cf. AE 57:165].

19 WA 37:272.26ff. [cf. AE 57:164–65].

effect that proceeds from "the holy, heavenly water."[20] Systematically, this means that the mode of eucharistic presence very much stands out as distinct. No such definition of the presence remained open for this. The divinity could not be circumscribed within that physically limited location through an "effectively." The eucharistic presence thus is "metaphysically, materially," the static, hidden, accessible presence, which is handled by the priest's hands, elevated, distributed, and tasted, and which the divinity therefore must shun in order not to be robbed of its majesty. In contrast to the Sacrament of the Altar, the other manifestations of the means of grace offer the *effective* presence of the whole divinity, indeed locatable by being made known in the water and the spoken Word, completely unbound by physical means of revelation and without the imprint of actual existence on its own.

This adoration of God in His omnipresence, through which He effectively reveals Himself, is taught by Luther in general even in the letter cited earlier from 1522 regarding concomitance. Regarding 1 Cor. 14:25, where the apostle speaks about how a stranger entering the Divine Service might come to bow down in front of the believers, declaring that God is in them, Luther reminds [us]: "An unbeliever would fall on his face and adore God in the saints if he heard them preaching. And Abraham saw three angels, and adored one God. . . . Therefore, let him be free to call upon God, whether in man or outside of man, within a creature or outside a creature, 'because I fill heaven and earth,' says the Lord."[21] So this describes an adoration of the omnipresent God in His specific forms of revelation, [adoration] by kneeling or *proskynésis* before and toward a physical thing. According to the Genesis lectures, Abraham's behavior is a model: "But even if we have no custom of prostrating ourselves, nevertheless we ought to prostrate ourselves in spirit before the brothers on account of Christ dwelling in

20 WA 37:273.20. [Otto] Hof (op. cit., p. 238) gives a completely incorrect comment on these words:

> The phrase "*non metaphysice*" warns against reducing the personal and effective presence of Christ in Baptism to a real personal presence in a style of thinking that separates [them], and having Him distribute the gifts in Baptism in His "naked" personality. Rather, as the sentence says in its context, Christ is present in Baptism in such a way that He includes in Baptism His death and His resurrection, the shed blood with which He earned salvation for us, and, being present, He places His works of salvation into it.

This exposition is an overinterpretation that in Baptism intends to transfer the determinations of *mystery theology*, which otherwise are applied to the Supper by Odo Casel and Peter Brunner, whose investigations in *Pro Ecclesia* 1:150ff., will be the basis for Hof. Grönvik (op. cit., p. 190 n. 59) presents a correct criticism of Hof's view of *metaphysice*. This word is interpreted by Grönvik: "not here in the sense that He would be bound metaphysically and materially to one place (that is, either in heaven or on earth), but that He is effectively present in Baptism."

21 WA Br 2[:561].70f., no. 509.

them,"[22] which applies especially to receiving priests: "to receive ministers of the Word, just like [receiving] God in heaven."[23] "But we are more remiss and more indifferent than the holy fathers were."[24] The insufficient embers of faith have let these good practices fall away. This manifestation of God in brothers of the faith and in pastors is based on John 13:20: "He who receives you receives Me," and is limited to confessors of the true faith:

> Even if they had been enemies, he [Abraham] would not have sent them away, but would have first refreshed them according to charity, but he would not have fallen down to the ground according to brotherly love. Indeed, he knows that God lives in brothers and in allies in the faith who are true temples of God, and not in the enemies of the faith or those who do not know the true religion.[25]

Luther therefore is not afraid of physical adoration in any context. It ought to be noted that Luther does not define idol worship as local adoration, nor does he think that paganism's worship of images means that gods and images were considered identical: "Thus the Jews erected Baal. They were not so foolish; they did not adore the wood, but they said: This is the true God who led us out [of Egypt], etc., who must be present, who delights in the worship, etc. Then the prophets said: You are worshiping Satan. They said the opposite."[26] True or false adoration depends on whether God is pleased with the adoration in front of a certain outward sign. False adoration is to choose for oneself such a place of revelation without God's Word.

The uniqueness of eucharistic adoration is emphasized in the Genesis commentary with the words: "How much more fitting indeed it becomes when we believe that the true body and the true blood are present with the Word."[27] The Sacrament of the Altar is the sacrament of the presence ahead of the other means of grace.[28] Regarding adoration of [the Sacrament], Luther has expressly

22 WA 43:9.11f. (the part that came out during Luther's lifetime) [cf. AE 3:187].

23 WA 43:9.9f. [cf. AE 3:187].

24 WA 43:9.2f. [cf. AE 3:187].

25 WA 43:9.25f. [cf. AE 3:188].

26 WA 20:615.9ff. (R). Compare here WA 10/3:31.23ff. [cf. AE 51:84]: "I therefore hold that there is no one here who has that coarse, absurd understanding so as to think this crucifix is my Christ and my God, but would simply consider it a sign by which to remember the Lord Christ and His Passion."

27 WA 44:684.32f. [cf. AE 8:144]. Compare the same "so much more" that is repeated in the *Great Confession* of the Lord's Supper's transition from the identical predication in the Baptism at the Jordan to that of the Sacrament of the Altar (WA 26:442.20f. [cf. AE 37:300]): "Why should one then not much more also say in the Supper . . . ."

28 When Luther writes (WA 11:448.34f. [cf. AE 36:296]): "The Word of God, which is owed the highest honor since God is closer to us there than Christ [is] in the bread and wine," he is speaking about preaching and the Supper from the viewpoint of their

described what this is like and how it is appropriate in his writing *The Adoration of the Sacrament.* Adoration can be done in an outward and an inward way. "Outward adoration," which in the matter of form need not be distinguished from signs of reverence toward princes, is done through prostration, genuflection, or bowing, "whereby you outwardly acknowledge your God or [your] superior."[29] This outward act—which actually ought to be called "obeisance," with the thought of its use even in civic situations and because there is no prayer as such in the physical action—must be validated by an inward act, without which the Sacrament is just as dishonored as [it is] by the [obligatory] Easter Communion, Corpus Christi, the tabernacle [for reserving the Eucharist], and the Mass generally, whenever unbelievers are entitled to come to it indiscriminately. Therefore, all extra-liturgical use of the Sacrament must cease, and "one should not celebrate any Mass where there are no actual true Christians."[30]

This inward adoration is "an obeisance or bowing of the heart, so that from the bottom of your heart you show and confess yourself to be His subservient creature."[31] This adoration presupposes saving faith: "heartfelt trust and confidence of a true, living faith"[32] is a part of faith or is "faith's highest activity toward God."[33] As such, it can of course occur outside the Sacrament and without any "special gesture."[34] But this outward adoration is a natural and obvious result of the inward adoration: "Then indeed the outward bowing, bending, kneeling, and obeisance with the body follow very nicely also."[35]

This adoration in front of the Sacrament is characterized by Luther as an adiaphoron. That does not mean that Luther allows [both] advocating and rejecting the adoration to be permissible opinions within the Church. What matters unconditionally is that no one may dogmatically dispute the correctness of the adoration of the Sacrament: "But whoever believes, as he then is sufficiently shown to believe, certainly cannot refuse his obeisance to the body and blood of

different importance for faith, where the Word clearly ranks ahead. Compare the same writing (WA 11:433.18ff. [cf. AE 36:278]): "For it is indeed true that you can live and be pious and be saved without the Sacrament, but you cannot live and be pious and be saved without the Word. . . ." This appraisal of the Word as more important than the Sacrament is presented by several medieval authors; compare here Douglass, *Justification in Late Medieval Preaching*, pp. 89f.; Massa, *Die Eucharistiepredigt am Vorabend der Reformation*, p. 12.

29 WA 11:444.6f. [cf. AE 36:290].

30 WA 11:445.6f. [cf. AE 36:291].

31 WA 11:446.14ff. [cf. AE 36:293].

32 WA 11:446.23f. [cf. AE 36:293].

33 WA 11:446.17 [cf. AE 36:293].

34 WA 11:445.18 [cf. AE 36:292].

35 WA 11:446.29f. [cf. AE 36:293].

Christ without sinning."[36] But since the time is still coming when the adoration of God is the only task of Christians, what matters is that during our earthly life the adoration is done "when there is time and opportunity."[37] The apostles, for example, remained seated at the first Supper, "forgetting both adoration and obeisance,"[38] that is, both the inward and outward adoration. This rests on the idea that "the words teach you to note and consider why Christ is there, and [they] will make you forget your work and only wait for His."[39] "As soon as one hears the Gospel, the Word of God, the highest honor is shown to it, since God is nearer [to us] in it than Christ is in the bread and wine. Yet everyone forgets to bow to the same [Christ], but sits still and while listening doesn't once think about what he would do to honor the Word."[40] The alternative to the adoration is this: faith being occupied with the forgiveness of sins that is contained in the Sacrament and proclaimed by the Verba. On the other hand, Luther does not open any possibility of theoretically disputing the adoration.

In regard to the sacramental adoration, Luther divided the communicants into four groups. The first do things like the apostles at the first Supper and [simply] stick to faith in the forgiveness of sins according to the Words of the testament while omitting the adoration. "These are the most secure and best."[41] The second group consists of those who "[outwardly] practice according to this faith, and then descend to their own works and adore Christ spiritually in the Sacrament,"[42] in combination with outward gestures. The third group is those who adore without gestures.[43] The fourth group adores merely with gestures, which is to be condemned.[44] In conclusion, Luther says, "It would be better not to adore, along with the apostles, rather than to adore along with us,"[45] which is cited by Wisløff with the comment: "Thereby the criticism of the Papists' stance is complete."[46] Wisløff thinks that the full consequence of Luther's doctrine about faith—which thus in this case was not deduced by the reformer—must exclude the adoration of the Sacrament, which threatens to

36 WA 11:447.7f. [cf. AE 36:294].

37 WA 11:448.1f. [cf. AE 36:294].

38 WA 11:448.31f. [cf. AE 36:295].

39 WA 11:448.27f. [cf. AE 36:295].

40 WA 11:448.33ff. [cf. AE 36:296].

41 WA 11:449.15f. [cf. AE 36:296].

42 WA 11:449.18ff. [cf. AE 36:296].

43 WA 11:449.24 [cf. AE 36:296].

44 WA 11:449.24ff. [cf. AE 36:296].

45 WA 11:449.28 [cf. AE 36:297].

46 Wisløff, op. cit., p. 182.

become works-righteousness. But Luther himself responds to this conclusion in what follows right after [this quotation]:

> Not that adoration is wrong, but there is not so much danger there as here, since nature easily delights in its own works and lets go of God's work, for the Sacrament cannot tolerate that. *But what more should I say? Christians belong at this Sacrament and at every work of God. Where they are not present, they are not doing what is right; God grant it, whether they adore or not.*[47]

With these words Luther shows how all activities behave in the same way as the adoration: to do them requires faith, and if there is no faith, then everything is askew. So the adoration is no more risky than other activities.

Wisløff sees the adoration and its most pregnant expression, the elevation, as erratic roadblocks in Luther's view of the Sacrament. He finds that Luther unwittingly divulges his inconsistency in the structure of his writing *The Adoration of the Sacrament*. In the introduction, Luther says that both the Bohemians and Papists look at the signs of the Sacrament and forget the Word. The Papists are criticized later as being exclusively preoccupied with self-righteous adoration of the Sacrament without embracing the Gospel. But according to Wisløff, the stated criticism stays away from the Bohemians: "That is also the way it must be, for the thinking of the Bohemian Brethren—apart from its legalistic features—in reality coincides with his own: the adoration of the Sacrament is without support in Scripture."[48] Wisløff, in this respect, overlooks the fact that Luther defined the false alternatives in this way: "Those want to force people not to adore as though Christ were not there; these want to force adoration as though Christ were there in His glorious state just as in heaven."[49] This first false doctrine, the rejection of the adoration by denying the real presence, was countered in the *first part* of the writing, which is introduced with Luther's criticism of the words of the Bohemian catechism: "that Christ is not independently and naturally in the Sacrament and is not to be adored."[50] Here is the critique Wisløff desired. Furthermore, if Luther, according to Wisløff's wish, would have designated the

47 WA 11:449.29ff. [cf. AE 36:297] (emphasis mine). Compare WA Br 2[:560].30ff., no. 509: "Nevertheless, so that they do not think that rude and foolish people cannot be answered, I would say this: It is free to adore and invoke Christ under the Sacrament; indeed, one does not sin who does not adore, nor does one sin who does adore. Let this be the end of this controversy, lest you let either party be compelled and expelled; and not that someone is led either to uncircumcision or to circumcision, nor that they judge each other here. Therefore, despise controversy in this matter, and with such contempt condemn it. Where there is faith and love, there cannot be sin by either adoring or not adoring; but where there is not faith and love, no one will ever not sin either by adoring or not adoring—indeed, one will never not sin at all by living."

48 Wisløff, op. cit., p. 182.

49 WA 11:448.12ff. [cf. AE 36:295].

50 WA 11:431.5ff. [cf. AE 36:275].

adoration of the Sacrament as wrong, he would make justification through faith into a coercive principle that would separate faith from "faith's highest activity toward God,"[51] and he would have bound faith to do only what has "proof in Scripture," a thought otherwise branded by Luther as "legalistic," and finally he would have ignored those passages in Scripture that show how Christ, without having commanded it, received faith's spontaneous adoration, "such as the three kings at the manger, the blind man, and many others."[52] Luther does not criticize these biblical events apart from his insight that in these cases Christ was not "there in a glorious state as in heaven"; this relates to a view of the role of justification within theology different from what Wisløff ascribes to Luther. It will validate Christian activity by giving the gift of the Spirit, but it does not have any systematic regulative function: "But if you exercise faith beforehand in the first part, namely, in the Words, then the adoration of the Sacrament will actually take care of itself nicely, and even if it isn't done, it would not be a sin. But where the first thing, faith, is not correct nor practiced in the Word, then no one will be rightly taught to adore, even if one were to write the world full of books."[53] Using the gifts of justification or forgiveness of sins in the Sacrament as an objection against its adoration, as Wisløff claims of Luther, will be shown later to belong at home in the Melanchthonian camp, with its sharp criticism against Luther's doctrine and practice of the Sacrament.

The distinctions above, made by Luther, almost seem to mean that faith was ascribed the function of passively receiving in relation to grace, while the adoration became an active deed of devotion from created beings toward the Creator. But in some contexts Luther can make faith and adoration of the Sacrament identical: "Faith is the true adoration: that I believe it is His very flesh and blood, given and shed for me. There it remains; that is also enough; the other [thing, that is, the act of adoration] may be completely free. What matters now is to adore in spirit and truth [that is, in faith] everywhere."[54] Here it is that faith's receiving of Christ's body and blood means an acknowledgment of the divine attributes of majesty that came to be seen in the atonement. Faith's passive "sacramental" act certainly includes an element of active "sacrificial" nature. That clearly emerges already in the distinctions Luther makes regarding faith's relationship to Christ's humanity in its existence outside the Eucharist: "And if we were ever to calculate the amount and value of the blood poured out for us, we would certainly be terrified from this day on."[55] The work of salvation is embraced by recognizing the power of God's blood: "Satan wants to make the blood of Christ contemptuous

51 WA 11:446.17f. [cf. AE 36:293].

52 WA 11:447.27f. [cf. AE 36:294].

53 WA 11:449.7ff. [cf. AE 36:296].

54 WA Br 2[:629].24ff., no. 555.

55 WA 20:759.3ff. (R) (*Lectures on 1 John*, 1527) [cf. AE 30:302].

to us, but Scripture [wants to make it] most precious."[56] "Blood is of great power; it swallows up sin, hell, and judgment."[57] "The blood of Christ is more powerful, for it is not [the blood] of goats."[58] Christian faith does not stand before an animal carcass,[59] but before God's precious body and blood, which are now presented here by Christ, when in heaven He "intercedes to His Father for us and says, 'Dear Father, there You see My blood, which I have poured out for this sinner.' "[60] Cyrillian Christology thus forms a part of Luther's doctrine of atonement, through which faith means an affirmation of the divine power of Christ's humanity and in a sense can be called adoration. "Thus here God in Christ is also incarnate and does what a God should do, or does what fire does in iron; of course, one sees merely flesh and blood, . . . which then is like red-hot iron, for it is divinized."[61]

> For if you grasp My flesh, then you are not grasping mere flesh and blood, but you are eating and drinking flesh and blood, which are divinized; that is, there is the skill and power of divinity; it does not act like flesh and blood, but it has the skill and power that God has, just as I said above: sugar-water no longer [simply] moistens, but it sweetens, gives, and effects the power that sugar has. Thus here, too, this flesh does not act like flesh when you eat this flesh, so it will not strengthen your flesh; it will not give you sin, a bad conscience, nor death, like other flesh plainly does otherwise, but it will divinize you, that is, give you divine power, virtue, and strength, and take away sin, redeem you from the devil and death, and save you from all misery.[62]

56 WA 20:758.3ff. [cf. AE 30:301, though AE omits material that is in WA]. Peters (op. cit., p. 31) writes about such words that Luther does not "seem to see the blood in these words as the substance separable from the person, but as a kind of code word for the person of Christ."

57 WA 20:758.6f. [cf. AE 30:301, though AE omits material that is in WA].

58 WA 20:758.9f. [cf. AE 30:302, though AE omits material that is in WA].

59 Compare here how Biel (*Epitome et collectorium*, IV, d. 2 q. 1 F), consistent with his Christology, disempowers Jesus' bodily sufferings: "The suffering of Christ, thus, not imposed outside the body, but willed within from the emotion of the mind, was the meritorious cause of salvation and grace and all the salvific things that were instituted and given to the human race"; compare also Thomas, *ST*, III, 49, 1, ad 1, which concedes the body's cooperation, but with the essential limitations that are a part of his Christology. Compare here Prenter's interpretation of Luther, where Luther's "dynamic view" is said to equate Jesus' body with the bodies of Old Testament animals, above, pp. 28–29, text after n. 104 [Swedish edition, p. 33], and Vogelsang's description above of the relationship between Luther and Scholasticism ("pure physical pains!"), p. 50 n. 68.

60 WA 12:264.11ff. (*The Epistles of St. Peter, Preached and Explained*, 1523) [cf. AE 30:8] (1 Peter 1).

61 WA 33:191.24ff. (weekly sermons on John 6–8) [cf. AE 23:124].

62 WA 33:188.17ff. [cf. AE 23:122].

Christ's humanity, as it is made use of already through the Gospel, thus possesses the attribute of majesty, which invokes faith that knows it is standing in front of the God-man. This wakens outward response even in the nonsacramental portions of the liturgy: "Thus with these words, 'And became man' [*et homo factus est*], we should also be moved at the miracle and sing the words with long notes, as is customary in the church, for it is proper and right; here and nowhere else is all our comfort and joy against sin, death, devil, hell, and despair."[63]

> Thus what, when, and how students sing and pray in church, the common people learn to follow. . . . When they kneel and fold their hands, then the schoolmaster taps with the baton during the singing: "And became man," the common people follow suit; when they remove their hats or kneel, as often as the name Jesus Christ is mentioned, and whatever other Christian custom and gestures they practice, the common people follow suit without it being preached, as though moved by living examples.[64]

To deny adoration to the man Jesus was Lucifer's sin of pride: before the impending incarnation "he saw that the other angels would willingly adore, even though the Son of God had clothed Himself so lowly. But because of his arrogance, he [Lucifer] was unwilling to be humbled; it [seemed] too absurd to him."[65]

---

63 WA 46:627.8ff. [cf. AE 22:105].

64 WA 50:[619.9ff.] [cf. AE 41:137]; on the outward gestures of prayer, compare WA 28:74.5ff. (R) [weekly sermons on John 16–20, end of chapter 16; cf. AE 69:16].

65 WA 40/3:709.22ff. Here Luther clarifies that he considers adoration of the human nature as a part of the *communicatio idiomatum*: WA 40/3:709.13f.: "But only according to the concretion, as all the angels also adore and bend their knees to the Virgin's Son." Compare WA 39/2:106.20ff. [cf. AE 73:267]:

> Ancient theologians struggled remarkably to solve this argument about whether the humanity [of Christ] may be adored, and they established three ways in which it is permitted to adore the humanity: *dulia*, with which Peter and Paul and all the other saints are adored; *hyperdulia*, with which the Virgin Mary is adored, and they included there the humanity of Christ because it also is invoked with that *hyperdulia*; *latria*, with which Christ is adored with relation to and in His divinity. [The word] "Christ's" clearly solves this: whoever adores Christ's humanity here (because then the joining of the natures is meant) no longer adores the creature but the very Creator, because the basis [for the adoration] is in the [personal] union [of Christ].

Against Schwenkfeld's false thesis (WA 39/2:105.25ff. [cf. AE 73:266]), "No creature must be adored. Christ must be adored. Therefore, Christ is not a creature," Luther says (WA 39/2:106.1ff. [cf. AE 73:266]): "Thus Schwenkfeld argued. And it is one of his absurdities; it is a sin against the *communicatio idiomatum*. The humanity, joined with the divinity, is adored. Christ's humanity is adored; that is not wrong, because it is inseparable from the divinity, and the addition of this genitive 'Christ's' solves the argument." Luther himself confirms here that his argumentation goes beyond that of Scholasticism. The usual *communicatio idiomatum*, which lets the human nature bear the predicate "He established the stars" [*condidit stellas*] (WA 40/3:704.5), does not make this [human] nature present at the creation in Genesis 1. In this case again,

When Luther therefore speaks about faith encountering Christ's body and blood in the Mass, in a certain sense this includes a posture of adoration. Faith and adoration do not exclude each other. So the outward act of adoration will be all the more natural: "For adoration occurs intrinsically in the eating, while kneeling to receive the true body and true blood is also without dispute."[66] Remarks about the adoration of the Sacrament are few in Luther otherwise; through his basic parameters he had consigned it to piety's own decision and could be completely consistent in concentrating on that which piety is based. Against the Enthusiast spirits, the adoration is confessed spontaneously and summarily: "We honor the body and blood in the bread."[67] In *The Private Mass and the Consecration of Priests*, he describes pangs of conscience over having adored an invalidly consecrated Sacrament during his youth at the celebration of the private Mass. The presupposition of the reasoning throughout is that a properly consecrated Sacrament can be adored.[68]

One of Luther's last[69] statements on the Sacrament, in the theses against the theologians in Louvain in September 1545, includes an emphatic confession of the adoration of the Sacrament, which in the latter part of the 1500s in various contexts would come to be debated and be made a subject of controversy: "In

---

Luther lets the nature, which with the right of personhood bears the rest of the expressions, not just to be called but also to be "able to be adored." Being worthy of adoration does not, for Luther, form one of the many corollaries that could be drawn from the personhood, but it established the meaning of personhood and the anchoring of the nominal expressions within the ontological framework of the concept of person. The nature that nominally, but still rightly, *bears* the predicate of Creator *is* worthy of adoration. On this point there is a special implementation of the *communicatio idiomatum*, which however does not at all correspond to Nilsson's meaning; compare above, p. 65, text near and after n. 140 [Swedish edition, pp. 65ff.]. One ought to maintain that being worthy of adoration is not a special communicated power like omniscience, omnipotence, and omnipresence but is a "nominal" predicate. Luther here, therefore, did not categorize the *genus maiestaticum* within the *genus idiomaticum*. It deserves to be noted that, for example, David Hollaz (*Examen Theologica Acroamatica*, par. III, theol. sect. I, ch. III, Q. 59 obs. III, pp. 152f.) affirms the adoration of Christ's humanity not only from the *genus maiestaticum* (Prob. V) but also (Prob.) "IV. From the unity of person [personal union]. The whole person of Christ must be adored. John 5:22–23. The whole person is either [or both] of His natures. T[herefore], each nature of Christ must be adored. The lesser is proven: because the person is not a third thing that comes from two natures, but the two natures are the person itself." With this latter formulation, Hollaz would correctly have delineated Lutheranism's understanding of the *genus idiomaticum* compared to Scholasticism, whose view of the image of the king's diadem and purple he then rejects.

66 WA Br 9[:420].21f., no. 3622.

67 WA 18:191.22. The words "and wine" ought to be understood [cf. AE 40:201].

68 WA 38:197f. [cf. AE 38:139].

69 The first mention of the adoration and elevation is in *Dictata super Psalterium* (1513–16), WA 3:460.15f. [This gloss is not included in AE.]

the Eucharist, the venerable and adorable Sacrament, indeed and in fact the body and blood of Christ are [present] and are exhibited, and are received by the worthy as well as the unworthy."[70] The German version reads: "In the venerable Sacrament of the Altar, which should be adored with all honor, the body and blood of the Lord Jesus Christ truly are offered and received both by the worthy and unworthy."[71] But these words in all their pointedness ("should be adored with all honor") are self-explanatory against the background of what is cited above. Also faith, which is completely occupied with the forgiveness of sins, knows that it receives in the host and the wine the Savior who is worthy of adoration, and [faith] will never deny that all honor belongs to the divine Sacrament. Especially as this adoration was attacked by those who deny the miracle of the presence, that free ceremony becomes necessary on the spur of the moment, and the confession of the real presence gains for itself a desirable image in the words "venerable and adorable Eucharist." Seen concretely, the celebration of the Supper also becomes an obvious invitation to honor the Sacrament, and in its given form the Lutheran Mass never came to know any apostles who merely sit there.

Inextricably connected with the adoration is a certain controversial ceremony: the elevation. As the presence is a presence of Christ, who is worthy of adoration, for Luther, in a certain sense, two motivations for the elevation coincide: proclamation of the real presence and adoration. Wisløff[72] tries to find a contradiction here: he concedes that Luther, in his defense of the elevation, has a good intention, proclaiming the real presence, but that he has thereby made possible the adoration, which is inconsistent with the rest of his doctrine. In Luther the two ideas do not seem to conflict in this way.[73] In a conversation from

70 WA 54:426.13 [cf. AE 34:355]. WA comments on this (n. 1): "Citing this thesis, George of Anhalt intervenes in favor of the adoration of the host," which explanation obviously intends to communicate a unique phenomenon, limited to George.

71 WA 54:432.1ff. [cf. AE 34:355].

72 Wisløff, op. cit., p. 182.

73 A comprehensive account of Luther's position on the elevation and adoration is found in Meyer, "Die Elevation im deutschen Mittelalter und bei Luther," pp. 196ff.; id., *Luther und die Messe*, pp. 281ff.; compare Hassler, op. cit.; [Edward Frederick] Peters, op. cit., pp. 139ff. Meyer cites, among other things, WA TR 1:383.4ff. [no. 803]: "If I were in their [the Papists'] church for the elevation of the Sacrament, just as I would lift my hands to [greet] another person, I would adore it in reverence of the Sacrament, because the true Sacrament is present, since His substance is present." (This is an answer to the question "whether it is permitted to take part in the ceremony of the adversaries" [WA TR 1:382.32f.], where Luther allows the right to passive but not active presence. The adoration is limited by Luther to "the High Mass," but is not conceded at the "private Mass.") Compare also WA TR 5:308.15ff. [no. 5665]: "Besides, since Christ is truly present in the bread, why wouldn't it also be treated and adored with the highest reverence?" with an addition by Joachim of Anhalt: "And Prince Joachim adds: We [*Nos*] did see Luther sincerely fall prostrate and reverently adore Christ when the Sacrament was elevated." WA actually prints "We did *not* [*Non*] see," which amounts to complete

1525 with a delegate from Strasbourg, according to one account, Luther explains the elevation: "We also preserve the elevation on account of Isaiah's 'Sanctus': because it fits the elevation very well. For it tells how He is seated on the throne and reigns. And to elevate the body and blood of Christ is nothing other than to preach the Gospel."[74] The function of proclamation is clearly emphasized, but this proclamation does not stand in opposition to the Sanctus, which adores. This oral statement agrees almost verbatim with the *German Mass* from 1526:

> We will not abolish the elevation, but will retain it, since it fits well with the German Sanctus [Luther's hymn "Isaiah, Mighty Seer," based on Isaiah 6] and signifies what Christ has commanded us to remember. For just as the Sacrament is physically lifted up and yet Christ's body and blood are not seen [here] below, thus He is remembered and elevated through the word of the sermon, and He is confessed and highly honored through receiving the Sacrament, and yet everything is grasped in faith and not seen, just as Christ gave His body and blood for us and yet daily helps, shows, and offers us grace with God.[75]

The Order of the Mass is thus designed so that the German Sanctus, described by Yngve Brilioth as an expression of numinous [supernatural] holiness,[76] should

---

nonsense, given the text's emphatic defense of the adoration and that the conversation takes place with the "three princely brothers of Anhalt"; the defender of the adoration, George III of Anhalt, belonged to this group of brothers. "Not" [*Non*] must be changed to "*we*" [*nos*], and this correction is made by Meyer (op. cit., p. 207 n. 47) in conjunction with Kroker (*Luthers Tischreden in der Mathesischen Sammlung* [Leipzig: Teubner, 1903], p. 441), Grisar (*Luther* [Freiburg im Breisgau: Herder, 1911–12], 2:573), Preuss (*Luther als Kommunikant*, p. 209); cf. the same change in Diestelmann, *Konsekration*, p. 28 n. 63. Meyer has difficulties keeping his material together, since his stance toward TR is too unguarded, which is why he accepts (op. cit., p. 200 n. 21) WA TR 5:266 [no. 5589] and WA TR 5:621 [no. 6360], which has Luther sharply attack the elevation and the adoration. Here one can justly cite the cautionary words of StL about TR (StL 22:45ff.): "a mixture of different matters," "arbitrary treatment of the original in the Table Talk," "corrupt condition of the Table Talk," "false translations," "unreliable information," "absurd things," "conscious falsifications." Precisely against the background of the subsequent battle over the adoration, where Melanchthonianism carried off the final victory, offense at Luther's view on these things and thereby a need for reshaping his words might seem understandable. "We" certainly didn't become "not" inadvertently, but by the conviction that Luther could not have said such while retaining the claim of being a true reformer. Even the first passage cited here in the Table Talk is in a version with Melanchthonian inclination.

74 WA Br 3[:610].76ff., no. 942, Appendix. In this connection, there is an account recorded with no context: "Martin often said that he had experienced [the body being present]. That he saw horrible visions; often that he saw angels, so that he was compelled to halt the Mass."

75 WA 19:99.17ff. [cf. AE 53:82].

76 Brilioth, *Nattvarden i evangeliskt gudstjänstliv*, p. 182. Iserloh (*Die Eucharistie in der Darstellung des Johannes Eck*, pp. 272f.) asserts that the German Sanctus [translator's

coincide with the elevation of the host. Proclamation and adoration are not opposites here: Sanctus and elevation speak about a revelation of God, happening at the altar, that is greeted by a congregation who in the outward act sees a remembrance of Christ's heavenly sacrifice. The elevation in Luther's earlier Latin Mass is unusual,[77] where the elevation of both forms occurs only after the consecration of the chalice is concluded, when the Benedictus, the continuation of the Sanctus, is sung.[78] The order that has the elevation of the Sacrament occur while the congregation is singing connects to the medieval practice of greeting the Sacrament at the elevation in the High Mass with special songs.[79] The presence of the elevation of both forms, both in the German and in the Latin Mass, can be compared with the situation: that the elevation of the chalice at this time was not yet expressly prescribed in the Roman Mass Book[80] and on the whole was not done among Dominicans, Carthusians, and certain other orders.[81]

The adoration, which Luther shows in word and deed to be possible and proper, is directed toward the consecrated Sacrament, such as it exists during a certain time frame, resting on the altar, elevated, carried, or distributed by the pastor. During this whole act, the Sacrament rightly receives homage through hymns, kneeling, and prostrations and by the congregation lifting their hands toward it and directing their prayers to the eucharistic Savior.[82] This latitude in the question of defining the Sacrament's existence in the material world is in obvious conflict with the Melanchthonian view, which with the same force is directed against the adoration and the temporal extension of the Sacrament. In this conflict, the opposition that was already described in connection with the earlier loci manifests itself. Since the adoration presumes the temporal extension of the Sacrament, and since the following era combined both problems in dogmatic polemics, it is necessary here to investigate the question about the duration of the Sacrament and in the concluding section to let both parts run parallel.

The question of the Sacrament's perseverance in time has to do with the beginning and ending of the real presence. Scholasticism's answer was basically that the presence begins at the reading of the Words of Institution and

---

note: Luther's hymn "Isaiah, Mighty Seer"] only means that the congregation is "taught about what happened to Isaiah the prophet," an obvious misinterpretation.

77 Fendt (*Der lutherische Gottesdienst des 16. Jahrhunderts*, p. 116) writes "as up to now," which is incorrect, given the placement.

78 WA 12:212.27f. [cf. AE 53:28].

79 Jungmann, *Missarum sollemnia*, 2:262.

80 Id., op. cit., p. 252: "Even the Roman missals from 1500, 1507, and 1526 do not mention it."

81 Bonniwell, *History of the Dominican Liturgy*, p. 127 n. 7. Regarding Luther and the rejection of the elevation, compare Hassler, op. cit., which shows that the elevation was discontinued during Luther's absence and without his knowledge.

82 Compare above, pp. 248–49 n. 73, about lifting up the hands.

lasts until the forms are consumed.[83] Uncertainty remained about which syllable it was when the miracle occurred[84] and about whether the presence exists even when the host, for example, "is eaten by a mouse."[85] An older tradition conceded a miraculous cessation of the presence in such a case, while Thomas advocates its continuance.[86]

Luther's stance toward the duration of the real presence is depicted relatively uniformly. [Hans] Grass writes: "There is hardly a doubt that it is possible that Luther recognized a real presence before and after the reception, and thus an actual duration of the real presence."[87] [Hermann] Sasse in fact asserts [not only] that Luther "repeatedly confessed his ignorance as to the how of the real presence and its beginnings"[88] but also that the occurrence of the elevation and the adoration [in Luther's writings] shows that "there cannot be the slightest doubt that he never did limit the real presence to the instant of distribution and reception."[89] Wisløff supports the opinion of Grass: "The Verba are clearly viewed as '*thettelwort*' [action-words], by which the miracle of consecration occurs."[90] Peters cites Luther's words about handling Christ's body and blood "with hands, mouth, chalice, paten, corporal, and whatever else they use, when one gives and receives it in the Mass."[91] The real presence is said to begin at the reading of the Our Father before the Verba and to end with the consumption of the elements. [Jürgen] Diestelmann refers to the same material as Peters, particularly the so-called "Wolferinus case," and he advocates also the Our Father as the point of time for the miracle: "He [Luther] did this because he viewed the Our Father as eucharistic table prayer."[92] This is obviously inconsistent with Diestelmann's main thesis about the Word that acts alone. But the cause in the mentioned case is Luther's own words: "It begins from the beginning of the Lord's oration [*orationis Dominicae*],"[93] which must be explained in some way.

83 Sasse, op. cit., pp. 40f.

84 Compare Damerau, op. cit., pp. 157f.

85 Landgraf, op. cit., 3/2:207ff.

86 *ST*, 80, 3 ad 3; compare Sasse, op. cit., pp. 40f. (incorrect reference to *ST*), and p. 50 n. 49.

87 Grass, op. cit., p. 115.

88 Sasse, op. cit., p. 172. The passages that are referred to (WA 18:206.20; 18:166.10f.; 23:87.32f. [cf. AE 40:216; 40:176; 37:30]), however, speak only about not knowing the moment.

89 Id., op. cit., p. 173.

90 Wisløff, op. cit., pp. 154f. About the use of *thettelwort*, compare above, p. 177 n. 30 [Swedish edition, p. 162].

91 Peters, op. cit., p. 92; WA 38:265.8ff. [cf. AE 38:224].

92 Diestelmann, op. cit., p. 34.

93 WA Br 10[:348].27f., no. 3894.

Examination of Luther's view of the length of the real presence may appropriately begin with a letter to Karlstadt that usually is not taken note of by the research.[94] In the battle over understanding the so-called "outside the use" [*extra usum*] during the latter part of the 1500s, the letter came to play a role that is equally as important as it is unknown today. This was occasioned by Karlstadt, vis-à-vis Luther, presenting the thought that since the bread was already consumed by the apostles ("the bread is already gone"[95]) when the words "This is My body" were expressed in the first Supper, these words could absolutely only refer to Christ sitting at the table. Against this, Luther asserts that the bread was given "therefore during these words or soon after them or along with them, and not necessarily before them."[96] Karlstadt's question, "Whether Christ gave His body before He spoke the first letter of this saying: 'This is My body,'"[97] is a sophism, for either Christ distributed the bread *before*, which is impossible, or, as is reasonable, *after* the Verba, but through the coordinating construction of the participle "saying," it is certain that the Verba refer to the bread that was distributed in the Supper. If someone gives something, it does not matter if the content of the gift is stated before or after the giving:

> In fact, imagine that the bread was given either after the speech was completed or before it was begun: I ask, what does this matter? Or how does that help you? Since the participle "saying" shows that Christ the Giver said, "This is My body." Certainly, if I were to give you a hundred florins, it would not matter whether I said, "Here are 100 florins," before or after I gave them. Nevertheless, the nature of the deed and the account of the event prove that giving and speaking were done at the same time, so that at the same time He gave the bread and at the same time said, "This is My body." For this is how it usually happens in every act, that the giver at the same time gives and says or names what he is giving.[98]

After Luther refuted Karlstadt in this way, then come the statements that would later become objects of various interpretation:

> Unless perhaps you are bringing back to us that old question "concerning the moment of the consecration," where the Papists teach that Christ's body is present after the last syllable and not before. We despise these thoughts, and we do not set moments and times for God, being content

94 Since the present volume in its shorter first version was sent out as a mimeographed licentiate dissertation [a pre-doctoral degree] ("Luther's Doctrine of the Real Presence, Its Dogmatical-Historical Context and Interpretation"), in which the role of the letter was pointed out, it was mentioned by Furberg (op. cit., p. 226) and [Edward Frederick] Peters (op. cit., pp. 198f.).

95 WA Br 4[:366].138, no. 1214.

96 WA Br 4[:367].158f., no. 1214.

97 WA Br 4[:367].169f., no. 1214.

98 WA Br 4[:367].170ff., no. 1214.

> simply to believe that what truly happens is whatever God says happens or is. Nor indeed do we argue about what moment the leper was cleansed when Christ says in Matthew 8: "I am willing; let him be cleansed," but it is enough that we believe he was made clean, just as Christ had said. Thus we believe that the nobleman's son, John 4, was healed, just as Christ had said, "Go, your son lives"; [we are] not curious at what time or moment of the syllables it happened. And that Lazarus was revived, just as the word of Christ says, "Lazarus, come forth"; we leave to idle and boastful people whether he revived at the word "come" or "forth" or "Lazarus." And there are many things like that. So also here we say the bread is the body of Christ because He says, "This is My body," leaving it to other troublesome logomachists to argue about moments and syllables. For we have the command to believe the words of God to be true, but not to investigate at what moment or in what way they are true and are fulfilled.[99] [100]

The main thought for Luther is that "giving" and "naming" coincided. Through [using an argument about] what is impossible and contrary to common use of language—Luther's main rule of interpretation—it is granted that the "giving" preceded. Even in this case, however, Christ would have been able to distribute His body, for God is not bound to wait for the last syllables of the Verba to be pronounced in order to bring about the presence, as Karlstadt seems to think. Luther wonders if Karlstadt intends to resume Scholasticism's false speculations about the last syllable having to be articulated in order for the Sacrament to happen. Luther simply despised these foolish medieval thoughts.

Thus Sasse's reticence may be based on these words not cited by him. But it ought to be noted that Luther's criticism is limited to the preoccupation just with the *syllables*. On the other hand, the miracle is viewed as happening during the uttering of the various *statements*, which are cited as examples of biblical words of power, of the [same] type as the consecration. The resurrection of Lazarus occurs when Jesus' words are spoken. That is how much Luther actually knows concerning the moment for the presence, but God is not prevented from working even before the Verba, if He so wished. These words of Luther thus stand in a particularly abstract context, formed polemically against Karlstadt's unique exegesis, and they are easily misunderstood as being directed against any fixing of the time of the consecration. To understand the further handling of the problem, it is not insignificant that Luther speaks of the Words of Institution as "*oratio*" several times in the letter.[101] The word here means "statement,"[102] not "prayer." This use

99 WA Br 4[:367–68].178ff., no. 1214.

100 [The Swedish edition numbers footnotes up to 99, then restarts at 1, which this translation lists as 101, etc.]

101 WA Br 4[:365].84, [366].147, [367].169, [367].171, no. 1214.

102 Compare Deferrari and Barry, *Lexicon of St. Thomas Aquinas*, p. 778: "oratio": "(1) speech . . . (2) speech or sentence . . . (3) prayer."

of language completely corresponds to [Gabriel] Biel's. In his exposition of the Canon [of the Mass], he speaks about "this *oratio*: This is My body."[103]

In contrast to the letter above are the letters to Simon Wolferinus from 1543, well-known and used in the research. This pastor in Eisleben, with reference to the Reformation principle that the Sacrament does not exist outside its proper use, had taught that "when the action ceases, the Sacrament ceases,"[104] and therefore he mixed together leftover consecrated elements with unconsecrated: "*reliquum Sacramenti miscendo et confundendo cum vino priori*."[105] This teaching and this procedure evoke Luther's impassioned opposition—Wolferinus made Luther's declining years gloomy, [and] he is to be equated with a Zwinglian: "Perhaps you wish to hear that you are a Zwinglian, and I would believe that you are producing the follies of Zwingli"[106] and have succumbed to the philosophical error that was spread by Cratylus, the disciple of Heraclitus.[107] According to Luther, Wolferinus unjustly invoked Melanchthon for his doctrine. Luther thinks that [Melanchthon's] statement "there is no Sacrament outside the sacramental action" is directed only at the misuse of the Sacrament, contrary to its institution, and did not at all intend to have the presence cease in the elements at a certain point of time: "Dr. Philip certainly did not wish this."[108] The following shall show that in this case Luther mistook Melanchthon's stance.

The statement of Wolferinus "when the action ceases, the Sacrament ceases" is obviously built on an axiom looming behind the formulation: "When the effect ceases, the cause ceases"[109] or, rather, "When the cause ceases, the effect also ceases,"[110] even used by Luther in a theological paraphrase: "When the promises cease, faith also ceases."[111] Wolferinus thus views the presence as conditioned by the action [*actio*] as its cause. When the celebration of the Supper ceases, the Sacrament has also ceased. Luther takes up this argumentation and

103 Biel, *[Canonis misse expositio]*, lect. 48 L: "This *oratio* . . . is not received materially," "that *oratio* is transformative [*conversiva*]," "that *oratio*, which is the form of the consecration, is a true *oratio*," "those three (ideas, *opiniones*) may be found in this *oratio*, this *oratio* . . . may be operative" (cited from Alexander Halesius).

104 WA Br 10[:340].22, no. 3888.

105 WA Br 10[:340].26, no. 3888.

106 WA Br 10[:340].22f., no. 3888.

107 WA Br 10[:341].43f., no. 3888.

108 WA Br 10[:348].19, no. 3894.

109 Compare WA 39/2:131.10 [cf. AE 73:224].

110 Compare the letter of Joachim II to Bugenhagen, December 16, 1540, [*Bugenhagens Briefwechsel*,] *Baltische Studien* 38 (1888), p. 215.

[Translator's note: Hardt has these handwritten notations on this page in his working copy: "Biel, op. cit., II, 72 (Lectio XXXVIII) *alioquin essentibus verbis non esset sacramentum eucharistiae*. Cf. *Summa Theologiae* III, 78, 6; cf. also XLVIII 47 H–Z."]

111 WA 56:45.15 [cf. AE 25:39].

wants to show its absurdity: "For if that hurried cutting short of the action indeed stands, it will follow that after the words are spoken, which is the most powerful and chief action in the Sacrament, no one receives the body and blood of Christ, since the action has ceased."[112] Luther wants to see the "speaking of the words [*prolatio verborum*]" as the most powerful and most important part of the action, and when this important action is finished, then [Luther says] according to Wolferinus, the Sacrament ought to cease. Luther here goes back to [the proof of] Biel and the rest of Scholasticism that the words are not the form of the Sacrament: "Otherwise, when the words cease, there would not be a Sacrament of the Eucharist."[113] Just as Scholasticism asserted: "The Sacrament of the Eucharist indeed is something enduring [*quoddam permanens*] even before its use,"[114] Luther also wants to show that the Verba give birth to a dormant reality, instrumentally effected through the words, but dependent on them and on every other part of the action for its existence. Wolferinus's fixation on the action could give birth to "interminable questions, just as there is a dispute among the Papists whether the body and blood of Christ are present during the first, middle, or last syllables";[115] that is, Wolferinus's reasoning will lead to the presence—and not just the beginning of the presence, as during the Middle Ages—being limited to some mathematical point or other in the Mass.

Luther had already affirmed Melanchthon's statement as directed against "outside [the use], that is, against the inclusion and carrying it around" [*ad extra, id est, contra inclusionem et circumgestationem*],[116] and of course he does not instruct Wolferinus to place the elements in the tabernacle, which would be the "*inclusio*," which is "*outside [the use]*." Instead, Luther defines the sacramental action in such a way that it is extended to include the consumption of all the elements: "We therefore define the time or sacramental action in this way: that it begins from the start of the Lord's oration [*orationis dominicae*] and lasts until all have communed, have drunk from the chalice, have eaten the wafers [*particulas*], [and] the people have been dismissed and have departed from the altar."[117] Here the Sacrament is not subordinate to the action, but the action [is

112 WA Br 10[:348].16ff., no. 3894.

113 Biel, op. cit., lect. 38 B.

114 Ibid.

115 WA Br 10[:348].20ff., no. 3894.

116 WA Br 10[:348].32, no. 3894.

117 WA Br 10[:348].27ff., no. 3894.

[Translator's note: On this page, in his working copy, Hardt adds these notes: "Biel, op. cit., lect. LIII, E *unde dicendum quod prolata rite hac forma verborum: Hoc est corpus meum verum incipit esse corpus Christi sub specie panis*. For which reason it must be said that when this form of the words is offered rightly: 'This is My body,' it begins to be the body of Christ under the form of bread. (Cf. earlier '*quod verba consecrationis panis effectum suum habent priusquam proferantur verba consecrationis*

subordinate] to the Sacrament. By virtue of this, Wolferinus is now ordered no longer to mix consecrated and unconsecrated [elements]:

> For which reason you will take care, if anything is left of the Sacrament, that either some communicants or the pastor and minister himself receive it, so that not the deacon alone or another person only drinks as much as remains in the chalice, but that he gives it to others who also partook of the body, lest you be seen as bad examples of dividing the Sacrament or treating the sacramental action irreverently. This is how I perceive it; I know this is how Philip also perceives it.[118]

In this injunction to consume what is left over, there are phrases that provide additional clarity. This does not have to do with execrated elements that are excluded from offensive profanation for reasons of liturgical propriety; the text is discussing what is "*reliquum Sacramenti*," that which is left over *of the Sacrament*, Christ's body and blood. The particular arrangement that should be observed in this respect underscores this situation. Obviously [in] connection to an earlier event that occurred in Eisleben, when a deacon caused offense by having "drunk the remaining blood of Christ—if by chance there happened to be some—not out of contempt, but quite simply and with a pious attitude,"[119] Luther prescribes

---

vini.' That the words of consecrating the bread have their effect before the words of consecrating the wine are spoken.) Cf. Damerau, op. cit., p. 163."]

118 WA Br 10[:348–49].34ff., no. 3894.

119 From the letter of Vigelius [Valentin Weigel] to Justus Jonas, June 29, 1543, printed in Kawerau, "Der Streit über die *Reliquiae Sacramenti* in Eisleben 1543," p. 295. Kawerau (op. cit., p. 304) correctly sees the offense being that the deacon himself had not communed but received the leftovers just like ordinary wine. Diestelmann ("Die Behandlung der *Reliquia Sacramenti*," pp. 1f.) presumes that the offense rather was in that the leftovers, according to the custom in Eisleben, were not given to the communicants, but that the deacon "as celebrant *alone* consumed the *reliquia* of the Sacrament." Seen in context with Luther's directive described in the text above—this parallel, however, is drawn neither by Kawerau nor Diestelmann—Kawerau's interpretation becomes the only correct one. The connection is obvious: Luther correctly writes: "so that not only the *deacon*." Compare also George of Anhalt's interesting note (*Reverendissimi et illustrissimi principis . . . Conciones et scripta*, fol. 191b): "And in the customs of the Clunians, besides which in *meminibus*, book 1, ch. 49, in addition to this caution, it also says that finally the subdeacon or acolyte should drink if any of the blood of the Lord remained in the chalice after Communion, insofar as he also previously received the body of the Lord. If not, let someone else drink it up who received the body before. Also they did not want to usurp the one without the other." — From the letter of Vigelius [Weigel] (Kawerau, op. cit., p. 295), which is an official document from the superintendent responsible for the case to the superintendent in Halle, it appears that Vigelius arranged that the *reliqua* should be offered to any communicant along with the rinsing wine (ablution): "It was customary also in the churches of the Prince Elector that the chalice be very carefully rinsed with this wine." Thus, according to Vigelius, who was himself Melanchthonian on these questions, the ablution of the chalice with wine was common in electoral Saxony and so also in Wittenberg, which corresponds to the observation in the Mass Ritual of Eisenach, which was prepared

that what remains should not be received in such a way that "only the deacon or someone else drinks as much as remains," but that it is received either by "some communicants" or by "the pastor and minister himself," concerning which this

---

in 1536 by the visiting Reformed theologian Wolfgang Musculus (Kolde, *Analecta lutherana*, p. 217): "After which the minister of the altar himself will also commune, after first adoring the bread, indeed not the chalice, which he carefully drank and then he cleansed with newly poured wine, so that no blood remained." (The omitted adoration of the chalice means that in Eisleben they exactly followed the Roman Rite, where genuflection at uncovering the chalice after receiving the host was not repeated at the covering of the chalice; Hartmann, op. cit., p. 442.) On August 2, Antonius Musa writes to George of Anhalt concerning the *reliqua* in a letter (printed in Kawerau, op. cit., p. 300) how in Jena he always observed the order prescribed by Luther, and there had the Wittenberg University [in attendance] as appreciative viewers of this (1527 and 1535, when the plague drove the university out of Wittenberg); compare Diestelmann, op. cit., p. 33. In this latter case, however, the ablution is not mentioned. The ablution, usually according to the medieval view, means that what was thus consumed was not consecrated, since the ablution's addition of unconsecrated wine in such a quantity that it exceeds the *reliqua* rescinds the real presence; compare *ST*, III, 77, 8, and *Die deutsche Thomas-Ausgabe* 30:428, with references, along with above, pp. 209–10 n. 148 [Swedish edition, p. 191] (about the opposite case with the addition of a lesser amount). Luther does not speak about the ablution, but if testimony about the use of the ablution in Wittenberg should have validity along with Luther's view of the *reliqua* as Sacrament, one may accept that the *reliqua* first were consumed as Sacrament and thereafter the ablution as common wine. The ablution, used on a Lutheran basis, must continue the medieval view of its character, since otherwise the addition of the ablution would have meant an increase[d amount] of consecrated [wine] and not a means to remove the final remnants of it, that is, a complete absurdity. One ought further to consider that where a chalice for the laity was used, the amount of the *reliqua* could far exceed the insignificant amount that might be left over in the medieval Mass, and that often therefore the ablution could not become the larger amount, in which consecrated drops could disappear. Carrying out the consumption first then made the ablution valid. This very procedure is described in Eisenach: "He drank *carefully* and cleansed with *newly* poured wine." Distributing the ablution to laymen, which is prescribed by Vigelius, was medieval custom (Fortescue, *The Mass*, p. 381). — The completely new custom, inferred by the Lutheran pastor's communion *after* the communicants, can be best explained by the idea that the pastor himself could thereby effortlessly undertake the consumption of the *reliqua*. The oldest Lutheran orders, however, have the pastor commune first, according to the Roman pattern. Nyman (*Kyrkotjänarens nattvardsgång i lutherskt gustjänstliv*, pp. 55f.) does not take up this explanation for consideration but is content with the single explanation from a Danish Reformation source: "Nor let there be delay between the consecration and the distribution" (from Pontoppidan, *Collegium pastorale practicum*, Swedish translation [1766], p. 361). The fact that Johan III in his *Red Book* retained the Lutheran order with the pastor's communion last would not rest on "Swedish custom"—compare Nyman, op. cit., p. 56 n. 3, with quotation from Swedish liturgy historians—since Johan concerned himself little otherwise about national practice, but [it rests] on thereby giving a guarantee of a proper consumption of the *reliqua*, which for Johan was an essential matter; compare Andrén, op. cit., pp. 184f.

applies: "and who partook of the body."[120] The reason for this concern about the leftover content of the chalice being received by those who earlier also received the host is so that one might not "divide the Sacrament." This latter expression goes back to canon law's prescription that is mentioned in the Augsburg Confession, Article XXII, "On Both Kinds": "Also Pope Gelasius commands that the Sacrament not be divided, *Dist.* 2 on the consecration, chapter *Comperimus*,"[121] and there it is repeated in the closing sentence: "Dividing the Sacrament does not fit with the institution of Christ."[122] To receive what is left over from the chalice without being a partaker of Christ's body would thus, according to Luther, introduce the disallowed "under one kind," that is, what is left over is *Sacrament* and is received as *Sacrament*; and this undignified procedure would "treat the *sacramental* action irreverently."[123] It cannot be stated more plainly that what is left over is still consecrated by the Word of God once spoken and, in obedience to the will of God expressed therein, should be consumed.

Luther's words about the presence or the sacramental action beginning "from the start of the Lord's statement" [*orationis dominicae*] have usually been translated [as] "from the start of the Our Father." Against the background of the analysis that is given here, such a translation must be considered unreasonable. In the immediate context with these words, Luther of course explained that "speaking the words" [*prolatio verborum*] is "the most powerful and main action," which at any rate coincides with the real presence, even if all the other parts of the Mass are not covered by it. Nor did Luther anywhere in his many statements on the consecration earlier draw the Our Father into the definition either. It would also be in very sharp contrast with his whole theology about the efficacious Word. Furthermore, Luther himself composed two Mass formulas in which the Our Father is in *different* places—in the one case, *after* the Words of Institution;[124] in the other *before*, being read either from the pulpit or from the altar in the form of a paraphrase,[125] a comprehensive general prayer of the Church. Applied to such a situation, the reading "from the start of the Our Father" becomes even more unreasonable. Understood thus, Luther's words would become meaningless, but he intended them as serious theological parameters, composed against a scandalous, Zwinglian-type false doctrine. Some decades later, they would be read in a completely different way by the Gnesio-Lutheran Erhard Sperber: "Accordingly, dear Luther defines and describes the action of the Sacrament and says it begins from the Words of the Lord [*von den Worten*

120 WA Br 10[:348].

121 *BS* 85.21ff. n. 5: "Decr. Grat. p. III. De consecr. dist. 2 c. 12" [cf. AC XXII 7].

122 *BS* 86.11f. [cf. AC XXII 12].

123 WA Br 10[:349].38, no. 3894.

124 WA 12:213.4 (*Formula Missae*) [cf. AE 53:28].

125 WA 19:95.19ff. (*Deutsche Messe*) [cf. AE 53:78].

des Herrn] and lasts until all communicants have eaten and drunk."[126] *Oratio dominica* thus is translated "the Words of the Lord." This is a translation that, with reference to the circumstances, must be recommended ahead of the usual one. Of course, *oratio dominica* means "Our Father" elsewhere, even in Luther.[127] But it was already established earlier that Luther does use *oratio* in the sense of "words" [or] "statement." Other contemporaneous theologians discussed here, such as George of Anhalt[128] and Laurentius Petri,[129] do this also. The modifier "dominical" [*dominica*], "Lord's," automatically connects to the different nouns such as "Supper" and "Words." Zwingli, for example, writes: "the trope that is in the dominical words [*in verbis dominicis*]."[130] The effortless juxtaposition "*oratio dominica*" occurred under Luther's pen in the letter to Wolferinus according to the pattern of "*verba dominica*," despite the fact that it is also in a different context where *oratio* has its other meaning of "prayer." So it is possible to analyze the actual text without resorting to speculations about a "table prayer," begun in the pulpit, as the point of time for the beginning of the presence in the as-yet-unprepared sacramental gifts.

Luther would not assert what is stated above, that a host left over *after* the Mass would be Christ's body, any more than would his later Gnesio-Lutheran successors. Luther had expressly discussed *inclusio* as outside the action. In the case of Besserer, where the pastor replaced a missing consecrated host with an unconsecrated wafer,[131] the lost sacramental-bread was found again on the floor after the Mass and Besserer placed it among the unconsecrated elements, where

126 Sperber, op. cit., fol. 42A.

127 WA 12:213f. (*Formula Missae*) [cf. AE 53:28].

128 Georg, op. cit., fol. 488B: "But the consecration happened [*tunc facta est quando dixit*] when He said, 'This is My body.' For His body was truly present there, just as also in creation He used no other *oratio* ['speech'] than '*Let there be*.' For He Himself spoke and it was done, etc."

129 Laurentius Petri, "De quibusdam Articulis, ad Sacramentum coenae dominicae pertinentibus," from 1566, p. 259: "For this *oratio* ['speech'] ('This is My body') is a simple and grammatical predication."

130 CR 91:465.11; compare also Erasmus, CR 1:691: "The sign of the body and blood of the Lord." The author of the present volume, in a conversation, presented a conjecture completely different from what is above concerning the meaning of the Luther passage discussed here, which with reference to its origin came to be cited by Furberg, op. cit., p. 227. But the thesis was never intended to be presented or defended in printed form, even less since the explanation warranted above was already presented in written form in the licentiate dissertation [a pre-doctoral degree], which laid the preparatory work for the present volume. From this, Furberg (op. cit., pp. 226f.)—but in this case without reporting the source—drew the identification "*oratio dominica*" = "*verba*" as a possible thesis. Furberg's ambitious account of his conversation in this case, not without benefit, could have been replaced with a somewhat more complete reference to the literature.

131 Compare above, pp. 186ff., text after n. 70 [Swedish edition, pp. 170ff.].

the latter could not be distinguished but, together with the rest, was burned by the summoned parson. Luther writes about this: "Concerning the mingled pieces, it was good that they were burned, though by the matter itself it was not necessary that they be burned, since nothing is a sacrament outside the use, just as the water of Baptism is not Baptism outside the use. . . . But on account of the offense, the parson acted correctly by burning them."[132] If through a dogmatically objectionable procedure, despite everything, there is a situation where a validly consecrated Sacrament came "outside the use," the real presence can no longer be said to exist. On this point the action is determinative for the Sacrament, so that the lack of the use in accordance with the institution really execrates what is holy, in accordance with the view of older Scholasticism.[133] When and if such

132 WA Br 11[:259].16f., no. 4186. The same advice to burn an unconsumed piece of bread from the Lord's Supper is repeated (WA 30/2:624.13ff. [cf. AE 38:135] and WA Br 10[:462].5f., no. 3944), though without closer inquiry regarding its sacramental character; compare here Grass, op. cit., p. 119.

133 [Edward Frederick] Peters (op. cit., pp. 218f.) views Luther's action in this very case as inconsistent: "He falls into the Melanchthonian trap." This criticism must go back to the fact that Peters interprets not only Luther but also the Formula of Concord in a grossly misleading way. Peters goes so far (op. cit., p. 221) as to think: "It must be said that Luther nowhere states that what is carried in procession is not the body of Christ." This is a misunderstanding of words such as WA Br 7[:327].13f., no. 2273:

> We certainly teach that the bread and wine are the body and blood of Christ not by the minister consecrating, but thus by Christ willing it through His institution, and that they must be eaten and drunk, but not reserved in a ciborium or carried in processions. Granted, we are not concerned whether the body of Christ is in what is carried about or in the enclosed [reserved] Sacrament. The Papists may think that. This question is not necessary for us who eat and drink according to Christ's institution.

Here it is asserted that Christ's institution does not cover the Roman practice and that therefore Lutherans cannot with the certainty of faith say that the presence exists there. The absence of the Word's guarantee makes the rejection possible: "We are not concerned whether . . . it is Christ's body." It is the same judgment that applied to transubstantiation and the validity of the private Mass: without the Word it is not possible to extract theological truths. In a letter to George of Anhalt on May 25, 1541 (WA Br 9[:419].18f., no. 3622), the reservation is also expressly equated with transubstantiation's "rationalizing of philosophy and human darkness." (Andrén, op. cit., p. 49 n. 11, has the text above, WA Br 7[:327].13f., no. 2273, illustrate the thesis: "On the basis of the thought of ubiquity Luther thus considered that Christ was present everywhere but that faith could only grasp His presence in the actual action of the Lord's Supper. This does not mean thus that one could deny Christ's presence in the monstrance, but only that one lacked certainty concerning His presence.") Luther's judgment seemed to have been quite different when it had to do with a use of the Sacrament immediately connected to the Mass. In the literature a dinner conversation from 1540 is cited concerning the possibility of carrying the Sacrament to the sick (WA TR 5[:55], no. 5314 [cf. AE 54:407–8]); compare Grass, op. cit., p. 120; Diestelmann, op. cit., p. 36; for which further can be cited Luther's letter from 1539 to Joachim II of Brandenburg concerning the new Brandenburg Church Order,

happens, a profanation of Christ's institution occurs, which in no way is a part of the regular, proper administration of the Sacrament. The rule about *extra usum* has come to have the opposite meaning of what is intended. Diestelmann writes about Luther's stance on these problems: "The rule 'outside the use or the sacramental action, nothing has the character of a sacrament' was intended to express that our celebration of the Sacrament is bound to the act that Christ implemented at the institution, but it did not intend to make a statement about the presence or absence of Christ's body and blood in the consecrated elements that remain beyond the end of the celebration of the Sacrament." No proof could be cited "either for the Roman assertion that the body and blood are still present in the consecrated Sacrament even beyond the end of the holy action, nor for the Protestant assertion that the presence in the blessed elements ceases with the

---

where carrying the Sacrament to the sick is allowed (WA Br 8[:622–23], no. 3420). In connection with Diestelmann, Holte summarizes (op. cit., p. 36): "Luther expressly approved the practice of carrying to the sick the bread and wine that were consecrated in the Mass." The *usus* is said to include a further "extension of time and space." But the determinations of Diestelmann and Holte about Luther cannot be completely accepted. In the later testimony about this form of communing the sick, there are defined limitations, which could be said to mean a basic disapproval. (An early statement from 1522, WA 10/2:32.3 [cf. AE 36:257], noted by Diestelmann, op. cit., p. 36, is disregarded here.) The cited dinner conversation begins thus: "That is not how we think of it. Indeed, one must let it happen for a while. It will certainly go away, as long as they have no ciborium." The old practice is judged positively in one respect: "I am thus happy on account of several heretics who must be opposed, for there are several who only let it be a Sacrament when it is in use; whatever is left over and remains, they throw away. That is not right. We have someone consume it. One must indeed not make it so precise, [whether] four or five steps or even several hours." The letter to Joachim tolerates carrying Communion to the sick "until it can be done in a better way." The practice must not be codified in church law: "by going into print" (WA Br 8[:623].56f., no. 3420). (Nor does this custom include a regular reservation [of the host] but only that the consecration even at night should occur in the church, and the Sacrament be brought to the sick, preceded by the sacristan [*klockar*] with bell and candle in hand, "Kirchen-ordnung im churfurstenthum der marcken zu Brandenburg," in Sehling 3:77.) Obviously Luther sees any prolongation of the Mass beyond the regular Supper as less biblical, even if it does not cause the real presence to cease in the situation mentioned above. George of Anhalt recorded a saying by Luther with this understanding (George, *Die Vierdte Predigt*, fol. 41bf.): "I myself have heard this opinion from Dr. Martin that it would be the Sacrament if it is brought to the sick, and it is to be regarded as the true body of the Lord; indeed, it would please him more that one conducted it in the presence of the sick." Then a printed letter by Luther to a good friend is quoted with the same meaning (WA 38:263.33ff. [cf. AE 38:221ff.]). In none of these cases does Luther approve the forms as Sacrament in any usage that is no longer part of the eating in a broader sense. Whatever might be dropped or the bread otherwise unconsumed after the Mass, either reserved or carried in procession, lacks sacramental character and the promise of the Word: "We are not concerned whether the body of Christ is in what is carried about or in the enclosed [reserved] Sacrament."

celebration of the meal."[134] This balanced statement accords well with Luther's position. Both the rejected statements—"does not cease" as leading to Roman misuse and "ceases," which Wolferinus's misuse created—go beyond the knowledge that the account of the institution [of the Supper] warrants for Christians to have about the Sacrament.

This view of Luther, which got its foremost expression in the settlement with Wolferinus in 1543, is completely contrary to what was ascribed to Luther in the negotiations about the so-called Wittenberg Concord in 1536. Here Luther is supposed to have accepted that the remaining bread, with proper reverence, is placed back in the box of wafers. [Ernst] Bizer writes: "at which Bucer emphasized that they [Bucer and his colleagues] did not designate what is left over as Sacrament"[135] and inferred Luther's consent. Grass summarizes explicitly: "Luther must have thus held the Bucer declaration as adequate."[136] Peter Brunner likewise comments: "Luther obviously settled for this answer as satisfactory [namely, that one might put back the bread that remained with those in the box, 'but with proper reverence']."[137]

The peculiar thing in the alleged consent is not just that Luther is of a completely different viewpoint in a case somewhat later. It is strange even that the battle fought some decades later around these questions never goes back to what was supposed to have been publicly consented to here. The Melanchthonian party then came to find itself in a situation in which, for example, in Königsberg, Veit Neuber was compelled to reject Luther's letter to Wolferinus as not binding for the Church: "Alas, Luther did not know everything [and] even had to recant much."[138] When this did not happen—for example, in Danzig—Luther's letter to Wolferinus was called upon and was given a Melanchthonian interpretation.[139] Nowhere do the Melanchthonians call upon Luther's alleged consent with Bucer, which should have been well-known, based on its public nature in a very important doctrinal discussion. If these words of Luther had been made authoritative again now, there would have been an infallible way to silence the loud accusations of heresy by the Gnesio-Lutherans, which severed Communion fellowship and let the dying suffer without the comfort of the Sacrament, and which divided married couples in spiritual matters.[140]

134 Diestelmann, "Der Fall Besserer," p. 72.

135 Bizer, *Studien zur Geschichte des Abendmahlsstreits im 16. Jahrhundert*, p. 111.

136 Grass, op. cit., p. 119 n. 1.

137 Brunner, *Zur Lehre vom Gottesdienst der im Namen Jesu versammelten Gemeinde Leiturgia*, 1:242.

138 Sperber, op. cit., fol. 44a.

139 Morgenstern (op. cit., fol. BIIIaf.), who reprints one of the Melanchthon documents in this controversy (fol. Zbff.). Compare below, p. 286 n. 238 [Swedish edition, p. 257 n. 38].

140 Compare below, p. 282, after n. 212 [Swedish edition, pp. 254ff.].

The succeeding generation's silence corresponds to the particularly insignificant number of sources. The passage under discussion is in the itinerarium of the Reformed Wolfgang Musculus, but not in any of the extensive sources about the doctrinal discussions.[141] The large joint Reformed account of the trip cites, for example, a great abundance of liturgical problems in detail but does not take up the passage in question about the *reliqua sacramenti*. The Lutheran description stops without discussing the day in question. What happens here is that there is a lot of discrepancy in how these discussions are commonly described. Even in regard to the actual main point—the exposition of the word "unworthy" in the [phrase] "the eating by the unworthy"—"our two reports typically differ now."[142] A third source, a Reformed one, absolutely shows here that the discrepancy can hardly be characterized as confirmed fact. Yet it has been accepted by modern research without critique.[143] But this record can be ascribed no value as evidence.

The text shall be taken up for analysis, however, with this proviso. Viewed from history, it is reasonable that one ought to find behind it a conversation that subjectively could be understood by Musculus in the way that he himself and the research dependent on him did. Any interpretation remains uncertain, but a reasonable solution should still be worked out here. The text reads:

> Pomeranus [Johann Bugenhagen] spoke an admonition in the ear of the one speaking about these things, concerning the leftover bread and wine of the Supper, adding that in certain churches the leftover bread was mixed with profane bread as profane. So that this would not happen in their church, they pointed out that before the Supper they would count the number of people who were going to attend, so that they got the number of pieces equal to those who would attend. Bucer responded that we do not consider leftover bread as Sacrament and also that we indeed put the leftover bread back into the container, but with due reverence.

To this description, which makes up the actual whole text here, Musculus adds the following closing appendix: "Then they made mention of private Absolution before the Supper, especially necessary on account of the uneducated." This taking up of private Absolution is apparently seen by Musculus as a new point ("then"). But that did not have to be the case. According to the [lengthy] Reformed

141 On the sources, compare Bizer, op. cit., p. 96 n. 1. The words of Musculus are reprinted in Kolde (op. cit., p. 223). Kolde's book, which came out in 1883, was the first to use Musculus's description, which was preserved in the archives in Bern, apart from a rather small document from 1860; compare Kolde, op. cit., p. 216 n. 1. So not until four hundred years after Luther's birth did the actual words here become known. The two main sources are reproduced in Walch 17:2533ff. (Lutheran), 2543ff. (Reformed).

142 Bizer, op. cit., p. 105.

143 Diestelmann ("Die Behandlung der Reliquia Sacramenti") observes that the order is cited only in a source, "as far as I can currently assess it," but therefore does not treat the statement critically.

report of the trip, which is missing the actual section about the *reliqua*, Luther gives a rather long speech here that praises confession before Communion and the power of the Keys. Bucer here answers apologetically that in Strasbourg the custom previously was in fact "that no one went to the Supper unless he registered beforehand and requested instruction and comfort. But in time they had let that go. They had been unable to insist on it at that time; but from now on they would try very diligently and seriously, so that those who are entrusted with the office might be brought to proper church discipline and be instructed about general and specific points, as needed." At this pledge of introducing a strict Lutheran church discipline instead of the earlier Reformed laxity, great satisfaction breaks out among the Lutherans: "Dr. Luther, along with his people, was also satisfied with all this, [and] discussed all kinds of confusion about church discipline and true cohesiveness of the Church of God."[144] It is not necessary to see this point as a topic of conversation that came up completely coincidentally. According to Musculus's section on the *reliqua*, the Lutherans had interconnected the questions about the *reliqua* and verifying the communicants: "They pointed out that before the Supper they would *count the number of people who were going to come, so that they would take the number of pieces equal to those who were going to attend*, so that this [mixing of leftover bread among profane bread] would not happen in their church." In Wittenberg they [counted] the communicants who announced [their intent to attend], so that an equal number of wafers could be arranged, which would prevent *reliqua* remaining. Now Bucer had promised to go home to Strasbourg and count the communicants there. The Lutherans reasonably saw in this the restoration of a proper administration of the Sacrament also in the question of the elements, which depended on verifying the communicants and their number. So the satisfaction that, according to the [lengthy] report of the trip, Luther and the Lutherans felt with Bucer was expressed after assurances of better organization, not immediately after the problem was raised, as the research had [falsely] concluded from silence. This reading of the texts, which thus are brought to complement each other, gives the version of the passage in question that is the most understandable in the larger theological context.

The picture that is given of Luther's view of the Sacrament of the Altar as a dormant ontological reality thus, even in the details, seems to confirm what Sasse says in summary: "Perhaps no Catholic ever had such reverence for the miracle of the real presence as Luther did. No one could think more highly of the consecration; no one could treat the consecrated elements more reverently."[145] It is significant how Luther answers the Roman Catholic objection that the

144 Walch 17:2560.

145 Sasse, op. cit., p. 176. Compare [Edward Frederick] Peters, op. cit., p. 227: "Luther, however, is horrified at the prospect that an accident should befall the Sacrament and stresses that extreme care should be taken in handling the sacred elements."

layman's chalice may result in spilling Christ's blood. Luther here does not make obedience to Christ's command [more] feasible by explaining potential spilled wine as "outside the use" [*extra usum*]. He accepts the risk that arises but then declares the associated, unintentional profanation to be an essentially lesser evil than the Roman Church's intentional truncation of the institution:

> But behold the blindness beyond all blindness: knowingly to condemn and change God's Word, willfully to deny and prohibit Christ's order and command through the whole Church everywhere. That is not [considered by them to be] dishonor to the blood of Christ, but the highest honor of all and the most holy divine service; but perhaps somewhere a layperson spills a little drop of blood, unintentionally and perhaps with great fear and trembling (that is, with proper heartfelt remorse and reverence), that is [considered] the greatest dishonor.[146]

The fear and trembling that Luther presumes would be evoked in the upright Christian at the sight of "a little drop of the blood," accidentally spilled, he himself seems to have displayed at the celebration of the Mass. Johann Hachenburg in one of his writings described the event that he himself witnessed, when Luther, in Wittenberg in 1542, along with a parson on duty and a deacon, very reverently tried to consume "such spilled blood of Christ": "Such a shame also went to the heart of the aforementioned Dr. Martin so very much that he even sighed and said concerning it: God help [me]. His eyes also welled up." After the Mass, Luther in medieval fashion had shavings planed from a chair on which the Sacrament had been spilled and burned them along with the fabric that had the same thing happen to it.[147] For this report, which was published in print fifteen years after the event, Hachenburg calls on the doctors, teachers, students, and citizens who were present. The book, which caused great animosity among the Melanchthonians

146 WA 26:595.26ff. (*Report to a Good Friend*, 1528) [cf. AE 61:142]. Johann Hachenburg refers to these words in *Vom anbeten des Sacraments / dazu vom ubriegen / unnd niderfallen Sacrament im Abendmal des Herrn Christi*, fol. FVb. The latter part of the title of the book refers to the situation described here. Compare WA 39/1:27.18ff. [forthcoming in AE 72], noted by Grass, op. cit., p. 120 n. 1 (p. 121), with the peculiar preamble: "*On the other hand*, Luther with great freedom took a stand regarding the danger of spilling the chalice, when it applied against the Papists' Communion under one kind" (emphasis mine). Luther retracts none of his argumentation, isn't showing "freedom," but is taking a risk that had to be taken, especially as this risk was also with "under one kind," since the pastors themselves "too often drained whole chalices" (WA 39/1:27.23f. [forthcoming in AE 72]).

147 Johann Hachenburg, *Wider den jrrthumb der newen zwinglianer*, fol. Faf.; compare Kawerau, "Ein Beitrag zur Geschichte der lutherischen Lehre von der Konsekration im 16. Jahrhundert," pp. 293ff. Compare Andrén, op. cit., p. 35, which gives an account of medieval practice, and p. 63, where the similar behavior of Gnesio-Lutheran Erasmus Sarcerius is classified as "genuinely Catholic" and was presumed to distinguish Sarcerius from Luther according to the scheme that Andrén worked out on the basis of his stipulations for the Supper.

and ushered in the controversy over the adoration of the Sacrament,[148] never met any claim that this event was invented by Hachenburg. The event described by Hachenburg is later cited with approval by the leading theologians of the Formula of Concord.[149] An oral tradition has a similar event occur in Halle, where Luther celebrated the Sacrament days before his death.[150] These transcripts are not strange curiosities without connection to Luther's world of thought. They do not depict emotional reflexes in a former medieval Mass-priest, whose conservative nature holds on to the bond that his intellectual development long ago made indefensible. They are pieces of a seamless sacramental view whose structure is completely coherent, carefully thought through, and often defended.

MELANCHTHON

In the case of Wolferinus, Luther said, in summary fashion: "This is how I perceive it; I know this is how Philip also perceives it [*Sic sentio sic sentit et Philippus, hoc scio*]."[151] In connection with [Gustav] Kawerau's earlier observation on the same topic, Diestelmann comments: "But these words of Luther prove to be wrong."[152] At the same time as Luther's letter, Melanchthon issued a writing to

148 Compare below, "The Great Adoration Controversy," pp. 275–300 [Swedish edition, p. 248]. [Edward Frederick] Peters (op. cit., p. 192 n. 169) thinks that "Chronik des Johann Oldecop," published by Karl Euling (*Bibliothek des litterarischen Vereins in Stuttgart* [CXC], Tübingen, 1891), would be a further source, but Oldecop is referring to Hachenburg; compare Kawerau, op. cit., p. 293.

149 Compare below, p. 274, n. 183.

150 This story handed down in the city of Halle is recorded in Karl Anton, *Luther und die Musik*, 3rd ed. [Zwickau: Hermann, 1928]; compare Sasse, ["Zum Ergebnis des 'Abendmahlsgespräche der Evangelischen Kirche in Deutschland 1947–1957'"]; [Edward Frederick] Peters, op. cit., p. 192 n. 170. Grass (op. cit., p. 120 n. 1 [p. 121]) and Sasse (op. cit., p. 176 n. 111) cite WA TR 3[:640], no. 3824, and WA TR 5[:416], no. 5984, regarding Luther's concern for what has been consecrated. The first passage speaks about "spilling the blood" under the heading "The substance of the institution [*ordinationis*] must be considered more than the danger." The latter one also speaks about "when some *blood* from the chalice is spilled in the church," but concludes: "There the Doctor said: One must deal wisely with it, on account of the laity and rural people, but there nevertheless not . . ." (the rest is torn away). If the rest [which is missing] means, as one can assume, that only regard for uneducated laypeople's superstitious thoughts motivated care, while it really is unnecessary, it hardly seems that WA TR 5[:416], no. 5984, in its latter part would be cited as support for Luther's strictness on this point. Then it has to do with a text treated in a Melanchthonian way, where the original Lutheran version ("spilled . . . *blood*"), however, still remains in the introduction.

151 WA Br 10[:349].39, no. 3894.

152 Diestelmann, *Konsekration*, p. 45; Kawerau, "Der Streit über die *Reliquiae Sacramenti* in Eisleben," p. 307: "There is an undeniable difference here between Luther and Melanchthon"; compare [Edward Frederick] Peters, op. cit., p. 212.

Wolferinus's superintendent and in it expresses his opinion, summarized thus by Diestelmann, in contrast to Luther: "While, for Luther, consuming leftover elements belongs to the obedient implementation of the holy Supper, according to Melanchthon this is to be advised only on account of the uneducated and for the sake of reverence."[153] Melanchthon expressly states the thesis that Luther rejected: "When the use of the Sacrament ceases, the Sacrament in fact ceases."[154] The leftover elements that never came into use "are not Sacrament, because the Sacrament is the whole action." They have never been validated as Sacrament, since the "action" that constitutes the Sacrament was not completed with them. Therefore, the view is rejected that proceeds from "the words having been spoken by the consecrator, thus the body of Christ enters into the bread, so that it is compelled to remain there forever,"[155] an objection that is not spoken against Roman usage but in connection with the Wolferinus case. The words are addressed to materialistic Lutheranism, which also is affected by the closing words: "Christ must not be adored under the form of the bread." Communion thus is not a use of that presence that is brought about by the speaking of the words, through which Christ would be subject to human actions ("*cogatur*" ["compelled"]). Christ Himself has His presence at hand: "This sacramental presence is voluntary."[156] So this must be said: "Therefore, God also must not be bound to the bread and wine outside the use for which the Lord's Supper was instituted."[157] *The problem is thus solved by considering God's freedom and His intention with the Sacrament.*[158]

153 Diestelmann, op. cit., p. 47.

154 CR 7:877.

155 CR 7:876. On the question of the Brandenburg Church Order, compare above, pp. 260–61 n. 133; Melanchthon (CR 3:846) is more positive than Luther: "I am not against carrying the holy Sacrament to the sick; for such a Sacrament is arranged for the instituted use." Through Melanchthon's view of the *actio*, which is assured first through the *sumptio*, for him carrying the Sacrament to the sick is somewhat less significant than for Luther, who therein must see a real, barely legitimized God-bearing [*teofor*] procession. Compare here [Edward Frederick] Peters, op. cit., pp. 30f.

156 CR 7:877.

157 CR 7:876.

158 Compare Gollwitzer, op. cit., p. 81: "Christ remains free from the grasp of men as well as from being bound to things; but He promises, and by promising—and that means, however, in His freedom—binds Himself to the service of men and to the actions that He Himself institutes." What is cited above concerning Melanchthon's view on *extra usum*, to some degree corresponds with what was explained earlier (above, pp. 208ff., text around n. 145 and following [Swedish edition, pp. 190ff.]) about Laurentius Petri's view of consecration. Certainly there are essential differences: Laurentius Petri has a Gnesio-Lutheran concept of the presence [and] defends a real consecration and the adoration. On the other hand, he is basically Melanchthonian in his definition of the scope of the consecration: without the reception, the action is not completed and the Sacrament has not been put under the Word of promise. Christ's action does not correspond completely with the act of consecration, which occurs at the altar. The

In 1541 we encounter the formulation: "It becomes a Sacrament at the time when all the causes come together and one keeps the intention of following up its instituted goal. . . . Therefore, it is only a Sacrament when the eating is added."[159] It ought to be noted here that Melanchthon does not say that Christ's body becomes present first at the eating. It is the Sacrament that is legitimized as sacrament through the completion of the act: "The Sacrament is the whole action." Melanchthon does not intend to have the presence begin any later than what Luther means. He thinks in completely different categories: "It is the presence of the action." "Christ is present for the sake of man, not on account of the bread, just as the words are recited not on account of the bread but on account of the listener."[160] The action becomes the proper act of Christ through man's making use of the presence. The action consists, of course, also of outward requisites: Word and elements. When these "causes" *are brought together* ("*concurrunt*"), the *whole* action becomes the *proper* action under the promise of the presence. Christ Himself is the administrator of His Sacrament and does not indiscriminately bind Himself to the elements that are not distributed. Thereby Melanchthon avoids teaching an enduring *presence*. He teaches that *the Sacrament* ceases when it is not used, which is self-evident since he defines the Sacrament as an action. No elements are thereby subjected to execration, so that Christ at some point revokes His presence, understood subjectively or objectively. If Melanchthon is falsely understood here, then his definition of presence is ascribed to the static terminology that corresponds to Luther's view, in which the word "Sacrament" designates Christ's body and blood under bread and wine. Instead, one must maintain that for Melanchthon the presence is "presence of the action" and that Christ in His words of promise to His audience never promised more than what He fulfills. His Words are true when they are uttered, and of course they possess the infallibility of the Gospel. For the leftover wafers, however, there are no recipients who can see themselves as addressees of the promise, and consequently neither has any promise been uttered. The action of the Sacrament is recorded under categories of personal relationship: the truly acting Christ speaks to a listening human being. This is the meaning of *extra usum* for Melanchthon.[161]

---

portion [of the elements] that the omniscient Institutor knows will not be used is not embraced by the Word.

159 CR 4:264. Compare WA 38:191.18ff., where even Luther uses the argumentation of form concerning the Sacrament, but without Melanchthon's conclusions; compare ibid., n. 15: "For after the Verba are pronounced, it is indeed a Sacrament, because it is now in actual use [*iam in ipso usu*]."

160 Ibid.

161 By this point in time the expression had already been taken up in the Wittenberg Concord of 1536 (*BS* 977.25f.), and is therefore mentioned by Melanchthon as "Bucer's statement" (CR 3:95). Compare [Edward Frederick] Peters, op. cit., p. 55, which traces it back to Bucer as well as Zwingli.

In accord with his general moderation, Melanchthon does not act as an iconoclast on account of this view. His advice was, in the case of Wolferinus, not to be careless with *reliqua*, but it expressed a sense for liturgical decorum: not just consideration for the weak, but even reverence required that the elements be consumed. Even after Luther's death, Melanchthon advises proceeding in this way in 1555, even though in and of itself "the wine that remains could be carried from the church for domestic use."[162] Melanchthon has to position himself differently in regard to the adoration. Both his definition of presence, which gave to the presence the majesty of omnipresence, and his definition of *actio*, which has certainty of the presence begin through the reception, necessitated a stance of complete rejection [of the adoration]. It is well-known within the research that Melanchthon zealously contested the adoration, and thus *de facto* the elevation.[163] Originally Melanchthon, like many others, had defended the adoration.[164] Apart from this very early opinion, only criticism prevails in Melanchthon. [Bo] Ahlberg objects to Andrén that he is wrong to think that the elevation and adoration would be impossibilities for Melanchthon. Ahlberg's criticism is incorrect. In fact, Andrén's statement: "For him [Melanchthon] the real presence began instead in the very moment of communing, and it was therefore

162 CR 8:598. Compare how it continues: "Just as I think the bread and wine used to be placed abundantly at the altar. But because there usually is not much wine left after the Communion in the churches, there is less of an offense if it is given to those who have been to Communion, just as is done among us. Where there is not enough in the chalice, must the Words of consecration be repeated? If the vessel with wine is standing on the altar, it is not necessary that the Words of consecration be repeated, because the direct intention is for the whole use." Since the flagon also is embraced by the intention, the *reliqua* must often be fairly "abundant," and very practical difficulties arise in undertaking the consumption. Concerning the extent of the intention in this regard, compare the detailed letters of Saliger and Fredeland to the pastors of Lübeck; Starck, op. cit., pp. 420ff.; Schöne, op. cit., pp. 28f. (Meyer, *Luther und die Messe*, p. 143, mentions that at the requiem Mass during the Middle Ages the precentor [*klockaren*] could have the right to an offering of wine. It is conceivable that the alternative of presenting the leftover wine [*reliqua vini*] to the sacristan [*aedituus*] might be based on such an arrangement.)

163 Ritschl, op. cit., 4:19 n. 82; with regard to the passage from Melanchthon's later time, compare Herrlinger, op. cit., pp. 144f. The rejection of the adoration in Lutheranism began with Gabriel Didymus (Zwilling), who in 1521 contested the adoration, later with the demarcation "*extra usum*." The adoration was defended in this case by Karlstadt, who in turn later turned away from this view; compare StL 20:8; Neuser, op. cit., p. 122; Seckendorff, op. cit., 1:216. Even Occolampadius originally defended the adoration in a writing, printed in StL 20:2360ff. In his later familiar writing *De genuina verborum Domini . . . expositione*, he rejects the adoration and the real presence; compare *Acta*, pp. 41ff., especially pp. 80ff.

164 Müller, *Die Wittenberger Bewegung*, p. 47, 1521 letter from Felix Ulscenius to Capito: "Finally, the matter was referred to Philip for them regarding the adoration of the Sacrament; he asserted that he agreed with Karlstadt, indeed to believe in Christ, wherever He is"; compare Neuser, op. cit., p. 133 n. 8.

impossible to direct any adoration or reverence toward the element,"[165] is formulated quite sharply, since Melanchthon did not wish to deny the Sacrament its "reverence," but adoration was certainly excluded. (In this context one can disregard the fact that Andrén's summary of *extra usum* according to Melanchthon is not completely correct in theory. The practical judgment of an *actio* that is validated as sacramental through the reception will be exactly what Andrén says.) Melanchthon's letter, which Ahlberg[166] cites for his support, does not say at all that Melanchthon still "approved" the elevation in 1543: "And it is more correct and I would wish that the custom of elevating had been abolished everywhere without protest. Indeed, it is very true that the rite has no reason [*ratio*] for the Sacrament except in its use. Nor indeed is the body present for the sake of [Greek: *héneka*] the bread, but for the sake of the recipient."[167] For Melanchthon, the elevation occurs at a point in time when the sacramental action did not yet have its decisive validation for the individual communicant. Insofar as the elevation ought to be retained, this is motivated only in consideration of "protest." No fundamental tolerance is found "into the 1540s."[168] From the year 1538 there are clearly statements of disapproval,[169] and the dogmatic basis for this criticism extends back in time at least a decade.[170]

The *History of the Sacramental Controversy*, published by Chemnitz, Selnecker, and Kirchner, wants to cite in Melanchthon's defense—from the viewpoint friendly to the adoration—that in 1544 "Philip, on behalf of a parish pastor who did not want to allow the adoration or reverence of the Sacrament, wrote to Eustachius von Schlieben and advised that that pastor should not be tolerated in his office but should be removed."[171] But the letter reads:

> If that pastor thus forbids the adoration because he denies the true and real presence of Christ in the proper use of the Sacrament, he must be removed from governing the church. It displeases me to provoke controversies without inquiring the origins; but it displeases me more that there are dissimilarities in the churches even of these regions. In some places the elevation is retained, elsewhere it is abolished; and this happened with no

165 Andrén, op. cit., p. 50.

166 Ahlberg, op. cit., p. 236 n. 22, by way of [Bernhard] Klaus, *Veit Dietrich[: Leben und Werke* (Nürnberg: Selbstverlag des Vereins für Bayerische Kirchengeschichte, 1958)], p. 227.

167 CR 5:258.

168 Ahlberg, op. cit., ibid.

169 CR 3:488, 503, 510.

170 Compare above, "Melanchthon," pp. 93–104, and the previous paragraph [Swedish edition, pp. 89ff.].

171 *Histori des Sacramentsstreits*, p. 549; also [Edward Frederick] Peters (op. cit., p. 66) finds Melanchthon's stance in the case of Eustace von Schlieben "surprisingly enough."

common deliberation. This is how I answer briefly now. I do not object to discussing the whole case with the educated.[172]

Melanchthon's statements contain more stipulations than what the authors of the *History of the Sacramental Controversy* wanted to read. In the letter Melanchthon makes a demarcation only against pure denial of the presence. If anything like that were the cause of the elevation being omitted, the pastor could be removed, Melanchthon writes to the noble patron involved, who apparently was a supporter of the adoration. In the closing words, it is significant that he would be able to say much more about this case to theologians.

Toward the end of his life, Melanchthon expressed himself quite blatantly about his Gnesio-Lutheran opponents, whom he describes in 1558 as heathens: "Now the highest commandment is: You shall have no other gods. Also: Flee idols. . . ." "All these who otherwise write and shout so much about surplice and adiaphora are silent about this point." The Lutherans who adore the Sacrament are equal to Mohammedans and Papists in Melanchthon's eyes.[173] He demands a clear repudiation of the adoration and elevation by the Lutherans: "Our people must also make a statement concerning the elevation and adoration, whether they would retain this adoration: 'O Christ, You who are bread [according to the Bremens] or in this bread, have mercy on me.' And so if Christ is there no differently than in stone and wood, why doesn't one say the same thing of all stone and wood?"[174]

---

172 CR 8:399, there dated to 1554. Possibly it is the event described in a letter from Melanchthon to Christofer of Württemberg in 1559: "On the Baltic coast, holy men who are killed in France because they do not approve artolatry are called martyrs of the devil. In Silesia, in fact, a mild-mannered man unwilling to keep the rite of elevation and adoration of the bread had three fingers cut off from his right hand" (printed in Pressel, op. cit., p. 464). That method of punishment is the same as what Joachim of Brandenburg, defender of the adoration, considered right against Johann Musculus, since through carelessness he spilled the blood of Christ "in the very action." In 1568 Johann Musculus was [instead] reprieved with exile because of the merits of his Gnesio-Lutheran father Andreas Musculus; compare here Spieker, "Des Johannes Musculus, Pfarrers in der Lebuser Vorstadt zu Frankfurt a.d. Oder, Landesverweisung," pp. 468ff.; compare Diestelmann, "Die Behandlung der *Reliqua Sacramenti.*"

173 CR 9:626. Mention of "surplice and adiaphora" means that Melanchthon finds the sensitivity of the Gnesio-Lutherans to the smallest concession to the Roman Church according to the so-called Interim, which prescribed the reintroduction of certain older church usages, to be inconsistent with their Romanizing battle for the adoration of the Sacrament.

174 CR 9:470f. [Edward Frederick] Peters (op. cit., p. 72) writes: "When he [Melanchthon] condemns adoration, one can take for granted that he is criticizing adoration of the Sacrament reserved in the tabernacle." This is obviously incorrect, as is clear from what is above, where Melanchthon turns against the Gnesio-Lutherans. Peters shows an irrational desire to harmonize different opinions within Lutheranism on this point

Melanchthon's accusations of "artolatry" or "bread-worship" are so common in his [writings] that they tend to lose their real meaning and instead become critical expressions toward all statements that Melanchthon disapproved in the sacramental controversy. An example of this general use of the word is in Melanchthon's judgment on the confession of the Lord's Supper by [Johann] Brenz, which is said to contain a defense of artolatry.[175] But this document comprises only a confession of the real presence, along with a Christological inquiry that expresses the omnipresence of Christ's body and implies its worthiness to be adored. Not a word is said, however, about its adoration in the Sacrament.[176] As shall be presented in what follows, Brenz even rejects the adoration of the Sacrament in other writings.[177] But Melanchthon disliked Brenz's independence in the question of formalizing the doctrine of the omnipresence, and this was sufficient for the anathema of "artolatry" to apply to him.[178]

Melanchthon's ambiguous use of the word "artolatry" cannot, however, hide the fact that the adoration of the Sacrament as well as the understanding of "outside the use" were actual points of controversy between Melanchthon and Luther, as well as Luther's successors. Melanchthon actually still wanted to identify himself with the Luther who was viewed as an authority, but this could not be done without obvious difficulties.[179] A drastic illustration of Melanchthon's difficulties in emerging as Luther's successor versus Luther's disciples is in a

(op. cit., p. 357): "No reputable Lutheran theologian accused anyone involved in the controversy of teaching what was unscriptural and un-Lutheran"!

175 CR 9:1034f.

176 "Confessio et doctrina theologorum . . . in ducatu Wirttenbergensi," printed in *Acta [et scripta publica ecclesia wirtembergicae]*, pp. 340ff.

177 Compare below, "Brenz and Andreae," pp. 313–17 [Swedish edition, p. 280].

178 Ritschl, op. cit., 4:71; and Ahlberg (op. cit., p. 248) does not notice that Melanchthon wrongly criticized Brenz. Melanchthon's generalizing view of "artolatry" is noted by Löscher (*Ausführliche Historia Motuum*, 3:143): "From Melanchthon's confidential letters . . . it is more than clear, (1) that he malevolently discusses our church's doctrine of the holy Supper under the term artolatry." Löscher on the other hand scarcely realized that Melanchthon was, in fact, waging a battle on the adoration of the Sacrament against the main part of his Lutheran adversaries. Compare how Löscher, in his famous periodical *Unschuldige Nachrichten* ("Fortgesetzte Sammlung von Alten und Neuen Theologischen Sachen" [1745], pp. 931f., on George of Anhalt's sermon on the adoration of the Sacrament), only knows how to convey that: "In the sermon itself the so-called Corpus Christi festival was severely rebuked." For someone who wanted to protect his [George's] orthodox reputation, it should have been out of the question that George would have anything positive to say about the adoration of the Sacrament.

179 Compare Hassler, op. cit., p. 46: "They themselves [Melanchthon and Paul Eber] opposed all adoration of the Sacrament as blasphemous idolatry, and they rejected the elevation. Meanwhile, they could not openly confess that in this regard they differed from Luther. Consciously or unconsciously, therefore, they ascribed to Luther the same view that they themselves harbored."

statement from 1559: "Keenly the Papists and those like them contend that the body of Christ outside the reception is said to be enclosed in the forms of bread or in the bread, and they demand the adoration, just as [Joachim] Mörlin of Braunschweig said: You must not say, Mum, mum, but you must say what this is that the priest has in his hand."[180] Mörlin's words, however, are borrowed from Luther's letter to the Christians in Frankfurt am Main: "He [the communicant] does not ask what he should believe in his heart about Christ and His body, but what is offered to him in the hands. Here it is not proper to roll mush around in one's mouth and say mum, mum."[181] The clash with the heritage from Luther is obvious.

---

180 CR 9:962.

181 WA 30/3:561.2ff. Salig (*Vollständige Historie der Augsburgischen Confession*, 3:436) writes on this: "Some of the Lutherans went further than Luther and did not continue in what he had written and taught. Westphal wrote . . . again . . . [the idea] that nothing has the character of a sacrament outside the instituted use [*nihil habere rationem sacramenti extra usum institutum*]." Id., op. cit., p. 528:

> Some [obviously Löscher; compare above, p. 272 n. 178] accuse Melanchthon of calling the Lutheran doctrine an artolatry, a bread-worship. But Melanchthon was not against the correct Lutheran doctrine but against the papacy of some Lutherans who were coarse and ignorant. For I mentioned above that Dr. Mörlin shamefully twisted Dr. Luther's words and said: You must not say "mum, mum" but [state] what the pastor has in his hand. Who told Dr. Mörlin to circulate such doctrine as Lutheran that the pastor has the body and blood of Christ in his hand? Dr. Luther says: Christ's body and blood are in the Sacrament, and apart from [*außer*] the reception there is no Sacrament. And Melanchthon also taught that, and even now all honest Lutherans [teach that], whereas no Lutheran will teach that there is a Sacrament apart from [*außer*] the reception.

At the passage referred to "above," op. cit., p. 463 n. (p), Salig pointed out that Mörlin's Luther citation is not completely verbatim, but [he] ignores that the missing "but what the pastor has in his hand" in fact in Luther does not come after but immediately before "what is offered to him in his hands." (In contrast to the orthodox Löscher, the anti-orthodox Salig has no difficulties in confessing the Gnesio-Lutherans' adoration of the Sacrament, which is attributed to them as un-Lutheran!) Salig's making Melanchthon's concepts of *usus* and adoration identical with Luther's is repeated by the modern Göttingen edition of the Lutheran Confessions when, without reservation, it identifies the Formula of Concord's statement "Nothing has the character of a sacrament outside the use instituted by Christ," taken up with an appeal to Luther with Melanchthon's thesis, and accordingly cites the latter's opponents as rejecting the statement as such (*BS* 1001 n. 1; compare Ritschl, op. cit., 4:19f.). As commentary on the Formula of Concord's rejection of the statement "that the element, the visible species or form of the consecrated bread and wine, should be adored" (*BS* 1016.4 [cf. FC SD VII 126]), the edition refers to Salig's presentation with the words "examples of 'artolatry' on the Protestant side in Salig" (*BS* 1016 n. 2). (The examples in Salig connected to the presentation on Mörlin are taken from Heidelberg / Heshusius [concerning this, however, see below, pp. 283 n. 218 (Swedish edition, p. 254)]; Erfurt / Hachenburg; Hildesheim, Silesia /Eustacius von Schlieben; Frankfurt an der Oder / Andreas Musculus.) The

Likewise, Erasmus Sarcerius faced Melanchthon's displeasure when he was so ashamed when some of the consecrated wine was accidently spilled on the floor that he carefully took care of what was spilled and after the Mass burned up what it had touched.[182] But in the actions of Sarcerius, Melanchthon was encountering nothing other than Luther's own view.[183]

A similar tension exists in relation to George of Anhalt, perhaps the foremost proponent of the sacramental adoration in the whole history of Lutheranism. Melanchthon wrote a laudatory preface to George's writings in 1555, and in a preface to the seventh volume of the so-called Wittenberg edition of Luther's writings he spoke about "what honorable, exalted, widely renowned men ['Luther and Prince George'] continued ... in the same confession of Christian truth."[184] This hardly meant that Melanchthon accepted George's theology, which is illustrated by comparing it with Melanchthon's reaction when he was faced with George's concrete faith in the Sacrament, presented under another author's name, Johann Hachenburg, who has already been discussed.

Göttingen edition's critical apparatus thereby continues Melanchthon's historiography. Selnecker, Chemnitz, and Kirchner in *Histori des Sacramentsstreits* (p. 610) already knew that Mörlin's words were taken from Luther and that the examples about artolatry go back to Luther's treatment, which was understood as [setting] a pattern; see below, n. 183.

182 CR 9:848, 962.

183 Compare above, pp. 265–66, text around n. 147 [Swedish edition, p. 240]. *Historie des Sacramentsstreits* (p. 610) cites this stance in Sarcerius's defense against Melanchthon. It is assumed that Hachenburg's book *Wider den ijrrthumb der newen zwinglianer* (fol. Fbf.) laid the basis for *Historie des Sacramentsstreits*, since it reproduces the same event as the one Hachenburg depicted. Kawerau ("Ein Beitrag zur Geschichte der lutherischen Lehre von der Konsekration im 16. Jahrhundert," p. 297) presents Hachenburg as a theological "[horse and] buggy," and his books as rare and hard to get. The copy used for this volume (from the Duke August Library in Wolfenbüttel, signum 990.37 Th.) is bound together in a sixteenth-century volume, partly with Luther's most important Lord's Supper writings, compiled for practical use by Hartman Beyer in 1561, partly with one of Chemnitz's polemical writings. Placing them together seems to show that Hachenburg was considered one of the Gnesio-Lutheran defenders; compare below, p. 283 n. 217 [Swedish edition, p. 254]. (Planck, *Geschichte der Protestantischen Theologie*, 5/2:627 n. 378, shows how the compilations of Luther's Lord's Supper writings were given a confessionalized significance by Beyer's type and were presented to the Crypto-Calvinists in Saxony when Lutheranism was restored.) Kawerau (op. cit., p. 298) himself shows how Joachim Westphal and Andreas Poach, two influential Gnesio-Lutherans, thus stood behind Hachenburg. Seen also against the background of the subsequent battle over the adoration of the Sacrament, which shall be described above [in the main text], the emergence of Hachenburg becomes not as unique as Kawerau thought.

184 This is pointed out in defense of Melanchthon from a Gnesio-Lutheran standpoint in *Histori des Sacramentsstreits*, p. 547. The preface to George's writings is printed also in CR 8:542, and to the Wittenberg edition in CR 8:200 (with the erroneous information: "Volume six" [*Tomo sextu*]).

When Hachenburg, in his book *Against the Error of the New Zwinglians* [*Wider jrrthumb der newen zwinglianer*],[185] defended the adoration of the Sacrament, the extended concept of the use, and dogmatically motivated concern about the *reliqua*, he was attacked by Melanchthon with the words: "as an ass at Erfurt recently wrote about the crumbs that fall on the ground, that they are the body of Christ and should be adored."[186] Hachenburg's writing, meanwhile, to a large extent consists of excerpts from George's sermon on the adoration of the Sacrament already cited earlier. "But such proof I will now take from the fourth sermon, which the venerable-in-Christ Prince George of Anhalt, formerly bishop of Merseburg, of blessed memory, gave concerning the venerable Sacrament of the Altar. In it he gives evidence from the honorable Dr. Martin Luther's individual writings, sent both to him and also to others, as well as having spoken with him in person, that it is not wrong to honor and adore the holy Sacrament of the Altar in its use."[187] Hachenburg's relative insignificance made it possible to attack him, and the donkey's ears that could not be given to Prince and Bishop George III of Anhalt, the Reformation's socially most prominent theologian, or to Dr. Martin Luther, now are given to the preacher in Erfurt. Hachenburg's answer to this critique was given in the next book, *On the Adoration of the Sacrament* [*Vom anbeten des Sacraments*], from 1561, and on its cover page one can read the Bible passage that begins: "In Numbers 22: And the angel spoke to Balaam, 'Why have you struck the donkey?' . . ."[188]

The Great Adoration Controversy

Joachim Westphal himself, who caused Hachenburg's action,[189] already in 1558 in his *Apologia confessionis* had a whole chapter "On the Adoration of Christ in the Eucharist," where he expressly defends the adoration. He shows that he can use various ways of speaking: "adoration of the Sacrament or of the Eucharist" is, of course, the same as "adoration of Christ present in the Eucharist."[190] He

185 The book title connects to Luther's words to Wolferinus on his Zwinglianism; compare the book's own words, fol. EVa; compare id., *Vom anbeten des Sacraments*, fol. DVIIb. It ought to be noted that Hachenburg, in *Wider den jrrthumb der newen zwinglianer* (fol. BIIIbf.), anonymously attacks Melanchthon by citing CR 8:598, without exposing the source; compare above, p. 269 n. 162, and the accompanying main text [Swedish edition, p. 243].

186 CR 9:470. Compare CR 9:409; Kawerau, op. cit., p. 298; Diestelmann, *Konsekration*, p. 60; Ahlberg, op. cit., p. 146 n. 2.

187 Hachenburg, op. cit., fol. CIIIa; compare id., *Vom anbeten des Sacraments*, fol. CIIa, FVa.

188 Id., *Vom anbeten des Sacraments*, fol. AIb.

189 CR 9:167; Kawerau, op. cit., p. 298.

190 Joachim Westphal, *Apologia confessionis*, pp. 305ff.

lists the various pious customs: "bowing the head, prostrating, genuflecting, kneeling, lifting up hands, beating the chest, and similar gestures, to use as a sign of reverence."[191]

Westphal therefore also defends ringing bells during the elevation and rejects the false accusation of the Sacramentarians: "It is a malicious lie that the common people are invited to adore the bread at the sound of the bell, a lie with which the Sacramentarians everywhere burden us out of extreme hatred and vengeful enthusiasm."[192] On the contrary, what matters is that at the ringing of the bells Lutheran people "offer due honor and worship to Christ."[193] Andreas Musculus, later co-author of the Formula of Concord, fought a battle in Frankfurt on the Oder against the Melanchthonian Abdias Praetorius concerning the adoration, mentioned by Kawerau in the research.[194] The documents here at hand grant that Praetorius relied on the rule about "outside the use" [*extra usum*].[195] By electoral command, Musculus had a special ceremony

---

191 Id., op. cit., p. 308.

192 Id., op. cit., p. 331.

193 Id., op. cit., p. 333; compare p. 308: "Since Christ is true God and man, [and] He was adored in the time of His dispensation, and He Himself did not prohibit Himself from being adored, why is adoration judged to be superstitious . . . ?"

194 Kawerau, *Johann Agricola von Eisleben*, p. 326. Compare *Propositiones de vera, reali et susbstantiali praesentia*, the theses on which, among others, Christofer Cornerus [Körner], even this later co-author of the Formula of Concord, debated in front of Musculus in 1573 for his doctor of theology degree (fol. BIVa): "IX. Whether the adoration of Christ, present in the Supper, must be approved." Andreas Musculus, in his *Precationes ex veteribus orthodoxis*, put into print both classic hymns of the sacramental adoration: *Lauda Sion* and *Pange lingua* (op. cit., pp. 179f.); id., *Precandi Formulae piae et selectae*, with only *Pange lingua* (p. 92). Compare Sasse, op. cit., p. 39 n. 24, who points out that *Lauda Sion* is introduced in a confession by the clergy in Mansfeld in 1571, as well as in Lucas Lossius's *Psalmodia* of 1553; and Andrén, op. cit., p. 170 n. 24, who cites the Swedish clergy's citation of "the pious hymn *Lauda Sion Salvatorem*" from *Svenska riksdagsakter* 2, p. 556. *Pange lingua*, best known through its second verse, "Tantum ergo sacramentum veneremur cernui," was likewise translated in the following hymnbooks printed during Luther's lifetime and with his preface: *Enchiridion oder ein handbüchlein* (Nürnberg, 1525), fol. 23bf. (= version no. 5 in Meister, *Das katholische deutsche Kirchenlied*, 1:479); *Enchiridion geistlicher gesenge* (Wittenberg, 1526), fol. AVIIIbf. (not listed in Meister, possibly a new Reformation version); *Geistliche Lieder* (Leipzig, 1539), fol. 105bf. (= version no. 5 above); *Geystlike leder* (Magdeburg, 1534), fol. NVaf. (= Low German variant of no. 5, possibly Reformation); *Geystlike leder* (Magdeburg, 1543), fol. XCVIIIaf. (= same as the previous). Meister listed ten versions of *Pange lingua* known to him between the 1300s and 1610, and he knows a large number of Lutheran hymnbooks with *Pange lingua*, among them also the last one listed here. But he does not make any investigation of the congruity of the Lutheran versions with earlier known examples, as to which are now somewhat revised here. — It ought to be noted that sacramental hymns do not necessarily imply a real, ritual adoration of the Mass; compare below, pp. 298–99 n. 306, on Johann Gerhard.

195 Codex Goth. 123, fol. 425, 429 (microfilm).

introduced, which included a new form of elevation alongside the old one. It consisted of the so-called exhibition [*ostentio*], which means that immediately before the distribution the pastor exhibited the consecrated gifts to the congregation with the words, "Behold, dear Christians, this is the body of the Lord; this is the blood of the Lord. . . ."[196] The elector's decision was directed especially against Wittenberg's Melanchthonian pastor, Paul Eber, who was a denier of the adoration.[197] In his writing *On the Sacrament of the Body and Blood* [*Vom heiligen Sacrament des Leibs und Blutes*], published in 1562, Eber had systematically disputed the adoration and the elevation. Here Eber writes:

> And though one says, "I do not worship the natural bread but the Lord Christ who is present in the Sacrament," the answer is that even the heathen and idolatrous Jews thus could also have excused themselves: "I do not worship wood [and] stone, silver and gold, but God, who in this place revealed Himself to this or that patriarch or saint or in that form and saved them from dangers," which the prophets very seriously rebuke as public idolatry and call it adultery and condemn it.[198]

Eber thus understands exactly what the proponents of the adoration mean and is not contending from some misunderstanding, believing that the adoration would apply to plain bread. For him, any physically directed adoration is impossible, which is seen as contrary to John 4:24 about worshiping God "in spirit and truth."[199] [200] For Eber, these words exclude an act of adoration toward a physical object. Thus he interprets them not as having in view the internal quality, whereby an act of adoration, directed locally or illocally, is validated. The criticism that Eber expresses seems to be directed against Westphal: "But what is proposed and contended here by some is that one may and should adore the Lord Christ in the bread and wine as it is exhibited to the people in the elevation, which is why they also defend the elevation even more strongly, so that such adoration and obeisance of the Lord Christ as the one who is truly present in the

196 Salig, op. cit., 3:436; Müller, "Zur Geschichte des Gottesdienstes der Domkirche zu Berlin," pp. 458ff. This usage, which occurred only in Frankfurt an der Oder and Berlin, was abolished 1598–1600 under pressure at that time from the increasing Melanchthonianism on these points; compare here the statement of the contemporaneous Brandenburg theologians, reprinted in Müller (op. cit., pp. 526ff.), where the exhibition [*ostentionen*] is said to be outside the use [*extra usum*], and the people's gestures of adoration—"they beat their breast or lift their hands" (p. 530)—are said to be superstition.

197 Müller, op. cit., p. 457.

198 Eber, *Vom heiligen Sacrament des Leibs und Blutes*, pp. 133f.

199 Id., op. cit., p. 132.

200 [The Swedish edition numbers footnotes up to 99, then restarts at 1, which this translation lists as 101, 201, etc.]

Supper are retained among the common people."[201] "But wanting to elevate and direct invocation to the natural bread and elements, letting prayer and sighing be indulged when that bread is moved, elevated, exhibited, and set down, [as well as] beating the chest and giving similar gestures of invocation to a creature, is very dangerous."[202]

201 Id., op. cit., p. 126.

202 Id., op. cit., p. 130. Ritschl (op. cit., 4:35) states that Eber, however, clearly confesses the real presence and therefore also was considered "among strict Lutherans." Here one can point out Selnecker (*Kurtze Schrifft und Warnung*, fol. CVIIIbf.):

> On everything, several years ago Dr. Paul Eber, pastor at Wittenberg, [now] sainted, wrote a confession on the holy Supper of the Lord, which, because it is correct and clear on the substance of the holy Supper and thoroughly refutes the objection of the Sacramentarians, was issued and printed by commission of the authorities, not only in his name but then again, and especially in the unfortunate current controversy, in the name of the whole church and school of Wittenberg.

These words contain a stipulation: "because it is correct and clear on the substance of the holy Supper," whereby it is acknowledged that Eber defends the real presence and refutes its opponents. Obviously there are other aspects of the Sacrament in which Eber, according to Selnecker, the defender of the adoration, did not teach correctly; compare below, p. 302, text surrounding n. 317 [Swedish edition, pp. 271ff.]. (Ritschl himself, ibid., n. 11, indicates other similar stipulations by, among others, Wigand. In this case, however, it is hardly only about the stipulations. Compare Wigand's sharp rejection in the censure in the controversy in Danzig; Morgenstern, op. cit., fol. RIIa: "Eber's false and Zwinglian opinion"!) Meanwhile, already in the very defense of the real presence there is the discrepancy that would bring the verdict in the question of the adoration. The whole time Eber makes use of periphrastic expressions such as "true presence of the body and blood" (op. cit., p. 172), through which Christ's action, the content of the gifts, and the communicants' participation are described without ever stating that the bread is Christ's body, which was Luther's exegetical advancement [*nyvinning*]. In the same work, this statement is made about Rome (op. cit., p. 45): "For, first of all, the Papists interpret the same all too strictly, according to the letter, and thus would have it understood that this expression 'The bread is the body of Christ' is an identical predication." For the statement "the bread is the body," which is impossible to all Roman Catholic theology, is now viewed as the basis for the doctrine of transubstantiation! While Luther wasn't at all blaming scholastic theology for great faithfulness to the letter, but he rather saw the rejection of "This [bread] is My body" as disobedience to the letter of Scripture—compare above, p. 139, paragraph that includes n. 70 [Swedish edition, pp. 129ff.]—Eber says (op. cit., p. 150): "For which reason our churches do not hold with the Papists, who understand the words of Christ all too strictly according to the letter concerning an identical predication." Lutheranism now walks a middle way between literalism and symbolism (op. cit., p. 151): "Yet along with those, [we think that] they depart too far [!!] from the Lord Christ's discourse, and they want it to be understood figuratively." The consequence of that modified faithfulness to the Bible is a real presence alongside of and simultaneous with the handling of the bread. This is the same challenge to the statement "the bread is the body" that Melanchthon offered; compare above, p. 155, text after n. 134 [Swedish edition, p. 144], and which Lutheran orthodoxy during the 1600s would put into print: Hollaz (op. cit., part III, theol. sect. II, chap. V Q 7 [8], p. 588): "Answer: The sense of the words of Christ—'This is My body;

Joachim II of Brandenburg thus went against these words of Eber when he [Joachim] adorned the Brandenburg liturgy with another ceremony, the exhibition [*ostentio*].[203] Within Joachim's electoral territory, in 1563, Johann Agricola,

this is My blood'—is not 'This bread is My body; this wine is My blood,' but this is the literal sense: 'This which I offer to you, which you will receive and eat, is not only mere bread but is My body in addition . . . . " Id., p. 590: "Christ does not say, 'The bread is My body,' but 'This is My body.'" Q. 15, p. 608:

> If the eucharistic bread is not essentially changed into the body of Christ, it follows that this proposition "The bread is the body of *Christ*" is false. But this proposition is true and used by holy fathers and Luther. Therefore. Answer: The distinction between *a biblical and an ecclesiastical proposition.* The proposition "The bread is the body of Christ" is not biblical, but must be understood as ecclesiastical by reason of the sacramental union.

"The bread is the body" is thereby taken away as simply Luther's private mode of expression. *With the risk that accompanies all generalizing, it could be said that the whole distinction between Lutheran and Melanchthonian teaching on the Lord's Supper in various loci that are presented in the present volume with a mustering of a large and perhaps in a certain sense bulky scholarly apparatus is to be traced back to this purely exegetical difference. Luther's "diffinitive," his stance on the adoration, etc., builds on the idea that "this" refers precisely to the bread. Melanchthonianism's "repletive" and other stances presuppose that Jesus actually was speaking about something else, namely, His body. Thereby Melanchthonianism has latched on to the axiom of the doctrine of transubstantiation: "This is [My] body" means "body is body"; Luther's paradox, "The bread is the body of Christ," is not biblical.*

203 Eber was not the first pastor in Wittenberg who opposed the adoration. Even Bugenhagen seems to have denied the sacramental adoration. Köhler (op. cit., pp. 200f.) points out how Bugenhagen before Schwenkfeld denies the adoration of Christ's body in the bread: "They adore Christ in heaven"; compare CS 2:245ff., and likewise at the Strasbourg Colloquy: "We are not so crass to believe in adoring the flesh in the bread"; "We do not adore Christ in the bread but in His Word; we also are able to adore Him in preaching" (Kolde, op. cit., p. 75; omitted in WA Br 3[:603–12], no. 942; Beilage, [WA Br 3:612] n. 44: "Now follows the confused section: Pomeranus [Bugenhagen] on the Supper, which we omit"). The same view of a sacramental adoration that is directed to the Verba and Christ in heaven is repeated in Bugenhagen at the disputation in Flensburg 1529 (*Acta der Disputation zu Flensburg*, fol. LIb):

> I indeed, when the pastor in front of the people begins to perform the command of Christ concerning the Sacrament, as such is done among us with clear voice and intelligible words, then I bow my knees or fall to the ground or stand upright, for such things should be free, and I honor the words of Christ's command, I listen carefully, and in my heart I thank Christ, my Redeemer, that He has given us this Sacrament as He also gave us the Gospel.

Id., fol. LIIaf.: "But we have Christ in heaven to adore and to seek in heavenly things, Col[ossians] 3, and, indeed, when we receive His body and blood in this outward Sacrament." Bugenhagen makes the same repudiation of the sacramental adoration in a private conversation with the Reformed at the closing phase of the Wittenberg Concord (Walch 17:2562): "May they also not perform the elevation of the Sacrament so that one should adore it. . . . Let this then serve so that one may thank the Lord that He has given us the Sacrament, and with it such glorious promises. . . . Dr. Pommer [Bugenhagen] and his men confess that they wanted the elevation to be abolished, in

known from the earlier Antinomian Controversy, held a "victory celebration of Lutheranism over Melanchthonianism" (as mentioned earlier by Kawerau), where subsequently they were asked to maintain the doctrine of justification through faith and the adoration of the Sacrament.[204] The Pomeranian superintendent Jacob Rungius's theses "concerning the adoration of Christ, God and man, in the Sacrament of the Supper" are mentioned in the Swedish research by [Sven] Kjöllerström[205] and Andrén.[206] The existence of these theses can be cited since the general synod in Stettin in 1566, under the leadership of Rungius, takes up "the honor and adoration of the Sacrament or the Lord Christ in the Supper"[207] as one of the necessary debate topics for an Evangelical synod. Laurentius Petri's battle for the adoration of the Sacrament in Sweden is well-known.[208]

In one case the controversy about the adoration and *extra usum* gave rise to a number of books in which the disputed opinions are established in a clear

---

addition." As a further example of Bugenhagen's fight against the adoration and (especially) the elevation, compare Bergsma, *Die Reform der Messliturgie durch Johannes Bugenhagen (1485–1558)*, pp. 194, 199, 218, 224. The picture that emerges from this agrees with the conclusion that Hassler (op. cit., p. 38) reached on the elimination of the elevation in Wittenberg: "Bugenhagen is the one responsible for its elimination." Only reverence for the Word and the action as the whole, which Bugenhagen admits should have their liturgical expression, are also mentioned positively by Eber (op. cit., p. 127): "by standing upright, by uncovering the head, by folding one's hands, by bowing the head and genuflecting." It is this reverence that isn't even actual sacramental adoration that is mentioned critically by Laurentius Petri (op. cit., fol. GVbf.):

> *Christophorus*: According to the aforementioned preachers, the adoration of the Sacrament is disapproved (as you said) just like idolatry. Why, then, do they confess that their parish folk, who are present in the churches when the consecration takes place, all kneel? *Georgius*: This, they confess (as I have mentioned before), is for them to show that through prayer, which the minister is reading with a clear voice, they would prepare themselves to receive the Sacrament in a salutary way, but not that they should venerate [*wyrda*] the Lord's body and blood. *Christophorus*: Ah, but look at what you are saying when you then say (not to venerate [*wyrda*]; the Lord, etc.). I must tell you truly that such words are quite difficult for godly people, yes, intolerable to hear.

The existence of this Melanchthonian veneration [*vördnad*] at the performance of the holy institution gives details of the special character of the Lutheran eucharistic cultus: Bugenhagen and Eber allow the former and reject the latter; Laurentius Petri embraces the latter and finds the former unsatisfactory.

204 Kawerau, *Johann Agricola von Eisleben*, p. 327.

205 Kjöllerström, op. cit., p. 80 n. 12.

206 Andrén, op. cit., p. 67.

207 Balthasar, *Erste Sammlung Einiger zur Pommerischen Kirchen-Historie gehörigen Schriften*, p. 281. Rungius reprints *O sacrum convivium* by way of introduction (*Confessio Ecclesiarum Pomeraniae*, fol. A1b).

208 Compare below, pp. 306–7 n. 326 [Swedish edition, p. 273].

and unequivocal way, but which are completely unknown to modern research on sacramental theology, research which neither pays attention to these controversies, nor can it identify them when they are transferred to other places. There is the struggle concerning the *reliqua* of the Sacrament in Danzig that was started in Königsberg and spread to Thorn,* Lübeck, and Rostock. In the latter two places the struggle is known by researchers as the Saliger controversy on the moment of the consecration and is often treated as a part of the preliminary work to the Formula of Concord's statements on this point. As shall be presented here with the help of the archives, unused and unknown to modern research, this latter controversy itself refers to the long feud in Danzig.[209]

In 1560, Veit Neuber (Vitus Nuberus) was expelled from the city of Königsberg, where he had earned a reputation of being Calvinistic and had said concerning the *reliqua* of the Sacrament: "They are something else" and "They are nothing at all."[210] His Lutheran adversary Erhard Sperber, however, also had to leave the city at the same time. Both went to Danzig, where the controversy flared up anew in 1561. This led to the city council drawing up a special *Notula* or *Formula Concordiae* on July 17, 1562, which was supposed to be signed by the pastors.[211] The agreement struck thereby was completely Melanchthonian and resulted in Sperber, and those like-minded to him, leaving or being banished. Then in 1563, Sperber published a book that contains, among other things, various *acta* [minutes of the proceedings] in the controversy. At this

209 * [Translator's note: Danzig and Thorn are German names for Gdansk and Torun in present-day Poland.]

The controversy in Danzig is described in a short church history dissertation from 1900: Kötz, *Die Danziger Konkordienformel über das Heilige Abendmahl, Notel gennant, und ihre Apologia (1561–1567)*, with a later appendix: *Beiträge zur Quellenkunde der Danziger Kirchengeschichte*. Kötz treats the topic from a local-historical viewpoint and is unfamiliar with the controversy's larger dogmatical perspective; compare also Hermann Freytag, "Die Beziehungen Danzigs zu Wittenberg," *Zeitschrift des westpreussischen Geschichtsvereins* 38 (1898): 87–94. In the older literature, the topic, among others, is treated in Hartknoch, *Preussische Kirchen Historia* from 1686, which reprints important material.

210 Kötz, *Die Danziger Konkordienformel über das Heilige Abendmahl*, p. 18. Königsberg, under its aged duke (compare above, p.114, paragraph that includes n. 153 [Swedish edition, pp. 107f.]), seems to have been Gnesio-Lutheran on the question of the doctrine of the Sacrament; compare Gundermann, *Untersuchungen zum Gebetbüchlein der Herzogin Dorothea von Preussen*. The prayer book was prepared in 1534 (id., op. cit., p. 85) by commission of the duke for his wife, with the prayer at the elevation and the presentation of the elevation (op. cit., p. 45): "Page 26v: below: a Divine Service scene in a Gothic church. In front of the opened triptych a clergyman in splendid vestments, surrounded by his acolytes, elevates the host. A richly dressed and adorned lady [Dorothea] is present at the celebration of the Supper in the company of her maids."

211 This formula is reprinted in Hartknoch (op. cit., pp. 690ff.). The document held legal force even up to 1825 and was signed by every ordinand (Kötz, op. cit., p. 1; compare Freytag, op. cit., p. 91 n. 1).

time both [Johann] Wigand and [Matthias Illyricus] Flacius acted as defense for Sperber.[212] Sperber's case received its most powerful support, however, from the Gnesio-Lutheran Benedict Morgenstern, who in Thorn preached against Sperber's opponents in Danzig and challenged the citizens of the city not to receive the Sacrament from heretics or persons who were in church fellowship with heretics. The plague in 1564 was perceived as a punishment on Neuber's doctrine, and many died without receiving the Sacrament.[213] Somewhat later it was said that the Gnesio-Lutheran minority celebrated secret, separate Divine Services.[214] In 1566, Benedict Morgenstern published a book directed against the Danzig council and clergy, with a preface by the pastors in Mansfeld (Eisleben), who continued this support in the upcoming controversy. In 1567 they [the Danzig council and clergy] answered with a printed *Apologia*, known as the "Danzig Book."

The controversy has to do with the rule "Nothing has the character of the Sacrament outside the instituted use," which both parties wanted to assert, though the Melanchthonians disputed the Gnesio-Lutherans' right to it.[215] Sperber, who says that he had read Luther's collected works in both editions then available, sees Luther as authority, "sainted Luther,"[216] but he also calls upon "the beautiful book of Prince George of Anhalt,"[217] the clergy in Mansfeld, and other theologians.[218] In the question of interpreting Luther, Sperber pauses at some of

212 Freytag, op. cit., p. 92; Hartknoch, op. cit., p. 705. Flacius's writing was supposed to have come out in 1564 (Morgenstern, op. cit., fol. D2a: "Anno 1563") and to have borne the title *Vom heiligen Abendmahl wider die Verführer*. But no such writing is known in the bibliographic lists, nor is it listed in Flacius, *Omnes libelli Mathiae Fl. Illyrici, hactenus in sacramentaria controversia editi* of 1567. Wigand's censure, on the other hand, is preserved: Morgenstern, op. cit., fol. PIVaff.

213 Kötz, op. cit., p. 47; Hartknoch, op. cit., p. 705.

214 Freytag, op. cit., pp. 94f.

215 Sperberg, op. cit., fol. 14b, 206ff.

216 Id., op. cit., fol. 32a, 32b, 34b, 38a, 49b, 84b.

217 Id., op. cit., fol. 49a. The Danzig Book or *Apologia: Gründlicher Gegenbericht* (fol. CcIIb) informs us that "they [the Gnesio-Lutherans] also delivered, for Your Highness and Your Worthiness to read, the little book of Johann Hachenbergerger's [sic!] on the *reliqua*, from which they thought they had their best foundation."

218 Sperber, op. cit., fol. 71a. Among the theologians referred to, Heshusius, Mörlin, and Westphal are noted. Reference to Tileman Heshusius, however, is actually unjust. Gollwitzer (op. cit., p. 141 n. 4) cites Heshusius as a blending of Lutheran and Melanchthonian: "For the nuances possible here, T. Heshusius is typical, who has the Lutheran concept of [sacramental] union but the Melanchthonian concept of use." Proof for this observation is given not only by Gollwitzer's quotation from Heshusius, *Responsio . . . ad praeiudicium Philippi Melanchthonis* (fol. F1a), where Heshusius denies that "though in the case of a drop of wine being spilled onto the ground from the chalice of blessing, I do not say it is the blood of Christ, but I say that

the opponents' poorly understood words "about three parts of the sacraments."[219] That has to do with the third article[220] of the *Notula*, where Luther's words in the Jena edition, part 6, 300, are called upon, and where Augustine's words about "*Accedat verbum*," according to the *Notula*, received an adequate exposition. Morgenstern also pauses at this paragraph in his book:

> Second, Luther is supposed to agree with them and also hold to three essential parts. . . . Yet Luther's words and meaning, and their words and meaning, agree about as much as day and night. For the Enthusiasts count these three parts: the first are the elements; the second, the Word; the third, the use. But Luther counts the element as the first, the Word as the second, and the command and order of God as the third.[221]

This observation stirred up protests. The Danzig Book says indignantly: "Concerning this, he [Morgenstern] makes such an atrocious clamor and heaves so many futile words, as though our meaning and Luther's were as far apart from each other as heaven and earth. But let the Christian reader envision Christ in His command speaking about the reception and about nothing else."[222] In the same work Sperber, and to an even higher degree the keen-sighted dogmatician Morgenstern, had accurately nailed down the *status controversiae* and given a correct interpretation of Luther. The text invoked by the *Notula* is the Baptism

---

what is consumed is the blood of Christ," but also by the earlier opinion not cited by Gollwitzer where any form of sacramental adoration is excluded:

> Publicly I testify that I disapprove artolatry, and not only do I condemn papistic madness concerning reservation, carrying about, sacrilegious sacrifice, elevation and adoration of the bread, but it also displeases me that the bread is adored in the true use of the Sacrament in accord with the institution of the Son of God. Indeed, it is bread and remains a creature distinct from the person of the Son, who is to be invoked always and everywhere in Spirit and truth.

Compare id., op. cit., fol. E4b: "But because we neither see it with our eyes, nor can we embrace it with our arms, but we understand it only by faith, [so it is] by faith we invoke the present Christ." Heshusius was viewed by the Reformed as the typical Lutheran sacerdotalist and power-hungry dogmatician, and one who personally observed meticulous decorum around the consecrated [elements] (Salig, op. cit., 3:443ff.); despite his struggle against Melanchthon, he could thus share Melanchthon's view on one point. This detail for Heshusius is supposed to have facilitated the unique command he gave before an altar in Heidelberg to take away by force the consecrated chalice from a pastor suspected of heresy (Salig, op. cit., 3:450)! — Gollwitzer's observation is a legitimate reminder that it is improper in an individual case to categorize according to the general guidelines that are drawn here. Compare here [Edward Frederick] Peters, op. cit., p. 372, who correctly observed Heshusius's denunciation of the adoration (elevation).

219 Sperber, op. cit., fol. 18bf.

220 Hartknoch, op. cit., pp. 629f.

221 Morgenstern, op. cit., fol. Ea.

222 *Apologia[: Gründlicher Gegenbericht]*, fol. AaIVaf.

sermon that was used above in the chapter on the consecration.[223] The *Notula* made the *use* of the element the third part of the Sacrament, which is the authorization (3) of the divine Word's (2) application to the element (1). Thereby, according to the norm of Melanchthonian theology of the Sacrament, the action is a part of achieving the presence.[224]

Morgenstern does not stop here but goes through the whole Melanchthonian concept of the Supper: "It speaks about the action when one should speak about the essence or the substance."[225] "Note also next that they hide themselves under the word *action* or the act of the Supper as also in all their writings otherwise, as though action and essence or action and the body and blood of Christ should be one thing."[226] Morgenstern examines[227] the opponents' dependence on the definition of the Sacrament in various "causes" [*causae*], which is offered in connection with the Melanchthonian statement: "Thus all concurrent causes must be together,"[228] and he knows that the opponents say in protest: "'We are accused as though we would say the body and blood are not present in the Supper . . . until the Sacrament is placed on one's lips'; as though they [the Melanchthonians] never taught that the body and blood of Christ are not present

223 Compare above, p. 179 n. 39 and accompanying text [Swedish edition, p. 164]; WA 37:630.16ff. [cf. AE 57:144–45].

224 This distinction between a Lutheran and Melanchthonian definition of the third part of the Sacrament makes it possible to detect a counterfeit, which under Luther's name and without any proviso and proof was introduced in 1967 into WA Br 12 under no. 4315 [pp. 399–401], which was published at that time. [Edward Frederick] Peters (op. cit., p. 148 n. 73) submitted a protest in advance against printing the piece in question: "It is not positively identifiable as having come from the pen of Luther (. . . it will appear in Vol. 12 of Br.)." [The piece in question] has the statement ([WA Br 12:400].22ff., no. 4315): "But when it is asked what things are necessary for the essence of the sacrament, let us respond that there are three things that pertain to the sacrament: First, the element is required, which is a visible sign. Then let the entire recitation of the Words be added. Third, let the legitimate use according to Christ's institution be added." This is not a Lutheran but a typical Melanchthonian definition. Even in the rest, the text bears clear traces of Melanchthonian theology: "let the Word be added" is explained in accordance with what is above, and the terms "magic" and "superstition" are used concerning the consecration; and concerning the adoration it says ([WA Br 12:400].32ff.): "But here, by the way, the question concerning the adoration must be discussed, which some try to establish and urge by this pretext, as if [it were] a thing not necessary [an adiaphoron]." It was precisely Luther who defended the adoration as "a thing not necessary," that is, an allowed adiaphoron, and the "some" who are mentioned are Melanchthon's anonymously accusatory paraphrases of Luther's poor advisors and actually Luther himself.

225 Morgenstern, op. cit., fol. CIVb.

226 Id., op. cit., fol. DIIIb.

227 Id., op. cit., fol. EIIIaf.

228 *Apologia[: Gründlicher Gegenbericht]*, fol. FII.

until the Sacrament is placed on our lips."[229] Thereby, however, they were merely saying that they always held that Christ Himself accomplishes the sacramental action, of which communing is the indispensable, decisive part, without which the priestly consecration results in nothing. The Danzig Book also defines the *status controversiae* in this, "that he [Morgenstern] wants to make the person of the Lord Christ and His minister [*Diener*] into one individual."[230] For the Melanchthonians, what is important is one parallel event that is picked up in the formula: "When the bread is given and received, the body of Christ is given and received."[231] The Sacrament is not the consecrated thing on the altar, which is distributed and received, but the action during which Christ distributes His gifts according to His promise. In the former case, Christ made the bread into His body with the command to eat it; in the latter He promised to distribute it [His body] if one eats the bread. The difference, seen most deeply, is a difference over what the "this" is to which the institution refers.

The practical consequences of this are that what is left over in the Mass is seen by the Gnesio-Lutherans as Sacrament, by Melanchthonians as bread and wine, and that the former defend the adoration, and the latter reject it. But the Melanchthonians take a particularly moderate position in the question of liturgical procedure. They concede in the *Notula* that *reverence* demands total consumption, for which they cite the Old Testament archetypes: the Passover lamb and the manna, which also had to be consumed in one sitting: "But perhaps because of unforeseen circumstances (which, however, should be very diligently prevented) some of the consecrated bread and wine . . . are left over after the holy action is finished; those cannot and should not be henceforth regarded as the body and blood of the Lord."[232] This almost high-churchly reverence (in modern parlance) was not sufficient for militant Gnesio-Lutheranism. They didn't want the ceremony but the doctrine, and preferred to die without any Sacrament rather than receiving [it] from such pastors who promoted or at least allowed such teaching.[233] The Gnesio-Lutherans here were offended at what was said about the *reliqua in* the Mass, not *after* it, and *that thus the sacramental character of the reliqua was not taught.* Already Sperber's initial controversy with Neuber had to do with an

229 Morgenstern, op. cit., fol. DIIIb.

230 *Apologia[: Gründlicher Gegenbericht]*, fol. Za.

231 Op. cit., fol. BbIVa.

232 Hartknoch, op. cit., p. 697.

233 Morgenstern (op. cit., fol. Abff.) is very much occupied with the otherwise orthodox clergy's fellowship with the heretics in Danzig: "That you have taken to fellowship with the Sacramentarians at Danzig"; compare id., op. cit., fol. AIIb: "So that you might know and grasp how very grievously you are sinning and have sinned against [the commands to] 'depart, beware, avoid, separate,' and the like."

element "in a still ongoing action,"[234] where the opposition thought: "Thus as soon as the distribution ceases, the Sacrament also ceases."[235] The dogmatic conflict thus gives a decision regarding that moment in the Mass when the Lord's Supper guests have been communed and consecrated elements are still resting on the altar. Sperber opposes [the practice] that then "the consecrated bread and wine, which remain in the true action, are set aside, wasted, and poured out like a mere element."[236] Luther's letters to Wolferinus[237] are invoked against this, but the opponents declared them to be merely private writings.[238] Meanwhile, Sperber's distinctions here were not noted by the opponents, who therefore accused him of saying, "I teach, among other things, that even outside the proper use and institution the consecrated bread and wine are and remain a Sacrament."[239] Morgenstern also confirms that it was the intention of Sperber and his friends "to speak about what is left over during the actual and continuing action, in the act."[240] But Morgenstern laments that those like-minded to him are compelled to make statements on a situation that has to do with "what is left over after the action has ended," namely, when one *cannot* distribute the whole Sacrament by consuming the *reliqua*, "and inevitably something is left over." But the statement was intended only as advice and not doctrine. The advice was to use the elements in the next Mass. Morgenstern refers to Wigand's *Censure*, which, like Morgenstern, maintains that according to Christ's institution and command everything should be consumed, but that in the case of "inevitable necessity,"

> I hold . . . that one should keep such bread now prescribed for use or reception [there is also similar decree about the wine], and that in the next or a future administration and distribution of the holy Supper these leftover parts should also be so set out, offered, and distributed for the action according to God's Word, but thus that the Words of the testament again are recited and repeated, etc. But I hold that it is not right to say that such holy bread that is so set out for holy action and act of the Supper, thus the body and the consecrated cup thus set aside and preserved are and remain the blood of Christ. For these elements are immediately lifted outside the testament, since there is no one who receives them. Therefore, one should

234 Sperber, op. cit., fol. 39a.

235 Id., op. cit., fol. 40af.

236 Id., op. cit., fol. 40a.

237 Id., op. cit., fol. 40b.

238 Id., op. cit., fol. 43b; compare the Melanchthonians' confession about this (*Apologia[: Gründlicher Gegenbericht]*, fol. Gaf.), where the character of private writings is emphasized at the same time that the letter is interpreted as directed only against an "irritating innovation," that is, as actually not being of a dogmatic kind.

239 Sperber, op. cit., fol. 42b.

240 Morgenstern, op. cit., fol. Ha.

not bind Christ to this and should see to it that there do not continue to be questions or inquiries.[241]

Wigand himself certainly seems to give more than advice: the elements after the Mass should also be kept for sacramental use, but Wigand carefully denies that they are a Sacrament. Just like Luther, he thus concedes a cessation of presence in those cases when the eating [*sumptio*] could not occur.

The main emphasis in this controversy is on the question of the beginning and ceasing of the presence. But the adoration is also made a topic of discussion, since it is strictly rejected in the *Notula*.[242] Morgenstern here goes back to Luther's explanations of Christian freedom, which always made the eucharistic adoration possible; and thus in this context he defends chasubles, images, candles, ringing of bells, genuflecting, prostration, and whatever else belongs to the traditional Divine Service that was the framework of the ritual adoration.[243]

These controversies were kept going immediately in the battle surrounding Johann Saliger in Lübeck and Rostock. In contrast to the feud described above, which garnered attention only in writings that dealt with the details of Prussian church history, the Saliger case always received a lot of attention, and there was always room to mention it in descriptions of the Lutheran doctrine of the Lord's Supper. Generally, one relies on Julius Wiggers' "Der Saligersche Abendmahlsstreit," printed in 1848. With reference to this presentation, it is usually claimed that Saliger's removal in this controversy rested on his offensive phraseology and arrogance, but not on his adherence to Luther's explanation of the *usus* in contrast to the Melanchthonian. But Wiggers himself does not have such an attitude. In his concluding words, Wiggers depicts Saliger's doctrine as dubious and dangerous and finds that through his dismissal, Lutheranism was rescued from ending up in materialism.[244] So he considers it a dogmatic controversy. The reading of Wiggers that often shows up in modern research can usually be reduced to presenting a clear picture of Luther's doctrine on this point and, bearing in mind the connection of Saliger's case to the Lutheran Confessions, unwittingly tending to harmonize the depiction with the judgment on Saliger being in accord with Luther and thereby fit to be connected to the Lutheran Symbols. Such an interpretation of the case on the basis of Wiggers

241 Id., op. cit., fol. Rb.

242 Hartknoch, op. cit., p. 698.

243 Morgenstern, op. cit., fol. Ka.

244 Wiggers, "Der saligersche Abendmahlstreit," p. 666.

is repeated, for example, in Grass,[245] Sasse,[246] Jobst Schöne,[247] Ahlberg,[248] and [Edward Frederick] Peters.[249] On the other hand, [Helmut] Gollwitzer[250] thinks that the doctrinal question in the Saliger controversy was not answered but suppressed as being too subtle. Diestelmann also sees Saliger as a victim for his loyalty to Luther's view of *usus*, which Ahlberg finds "misplaced."[251] John Warwick Montgomery positions himself critically against the perception of the documented event by Wiggers but does not make clear on what grounds.[252] But, upon closer analysis, Wiggers's own material, regardless of his interpretations, is already completely sufficient to shatter the theory of a nondogmatic controversy caused by a contentious Gnesio-Lutheran without a factual cause.[253] To a high degree, this insight is strengthened by examining the *acta* ["records"] of the controversy around Saliger in Rostock. These were available to Wiggers but were not examined afterward. Schöne, who only dedicated a rather small monograph to Saliger's case, considers them lost.[254] Apparently, Schöne searched the records in Rostock, whose archives were partly lost during World War II. But all the documents exist in the state archives of Schwerin.[255]

Johann Saliger (Beatus), during his pastorate in Lübeck, together with his fellow pastor, Heinrich Fredeland, had come into controversy with the clergy

245 Grass, op. cit., p. 117.

246 Sasse, op. cit., p. 175.

247 Schöne, *Um Christi sakramentale Gegenwart*, pp. 58, 64ff.

248 Ahlberg, op. cit., p. 162 n. 48.

249 [Edward Frederick] Peters, op. cit., pp. 344ff.

250 Gollwitzer, op. cit., p. 141. Ahlberg (op. cit., ibid.) misinterprets Gollwitzer here.

251 Ahlberg, op. cit., ibid.

252 Montgomery, *Chytraeus on Sacrifice*, p. 15 n. 22.

253 Compare Ahlberg, op. cit., ibid.: "The whole controversy gives the impression of being one of the many distressing wars of words with which German Lutheranism was so richly endowed." This generalizing assertion builds on the thesis of the Gnesio-Lutheran party's unreasonable maliciousness and pathological quarrelsomeness, aptly summarized in Freytag's characterization (id., op. cit., p. 94) of Morgenstern: "So only one more opponent remained, Benedict Morgenstern, but all the more dangerous since he considered it right to use any means in order to fight his enemies, whom he thought he had identified as enemies of the orthodox faith." According to Freytag, these means, sanctified by the end goal, included "spiteful criticism" and "false presentation of facts." This depiction of him could be traced back to the Melanchthonian interpretation of Morgenstern's surname: "Lucifer"; compare *ADB* 22:228ff., "Morgenstern, Benedict."

254 Schöne, op. cit., unnumbered item: "to draw from direct sources, only insofar as they are still available today. Since that is not the case for older archives . . ."

255 Compare here Schröder, *Kirchen-Historie des Evangelischen Mecklenburgs*, 3:6: "On March 5 the commission was concluded, without having changed mind of Beatus [Saliger], and the *Acta* [which are still extant today in a rather large volume in the Schwerin archives] were sent to Dr. Wigand by the prince's order."

on [three points:] "the 'now' or the moment of the presence," on the after-consecration [when new elements are brought to the altar], and the *reliqua*. Wiggers reports only that both pastors were removed.[256] It is important here that the clergy in Mansfeld, in a letter to Lübeck's pastors, immediately stood behind Saliger: "pious Saliger."[257] Both in this letter,[258] as well as in Saliger's statements,[259] the controversy is seen as identical with the controversy in Danzig. Schöne discusses the Danzig Book as "a book, issued at that time and recognized as un-Lutheran in its doctrine of the Sacrament,"[260] but he is obviously unaware of what the Danzig Book was.

---

256 Wiggers (op. cit., p. 615) claims that the reconciliation took place in the presence of Chemnitz, a statement that is supposed to go back to Starck (*Lubeca Lutherano-Evangelica*, p. 253), who—contrary to Ph. J. Rehtmeyern, *Braunschweigische Kirchen-Historie*, 3:307, which rejects Chemnitz's presence with the thought that his assignment was elsewhere at that time—tries to introduce evidence of his presence through two letters (op. cit., pp. 424f.). But these contain only injunctions for Chemnitz to travel to Lübeck, not proof that the trip took place. Rehtmeyern therefore would have been right, even more as it seems unreasonable that Wigand in a later statement to the dukes of Mecklenburg, reproduced in Wiggers (op. cit., p. 633), could advise a commission of theologians to conclude the matter in Lübeck without giving an account of the viewpoint that the highly regarded Chemnitz thus must have already taken in the case. When Chemnitz actually visits the city later in 1574 to reconcile Fredeland's brother, the licensed physician Lambert Fredeland, with the clergy in the same matter, there is no reference to any earlier attempt of the same kind (Starck, op. cit., pp. 280ff.; Schöne, op. cit., pp. 19ff.), which would have been natural if Starck's assertion above were correct. Schöne (op. cit., p. 11) follows Starck but with the remark: "Unfortunately we know nothing about the negotiations by Chemnitz in Lübeck." — Schöne (op. cit., p. 32) must concede that in Lübeck, despite everything, Saliger had grounds for his fight: "not completely without basis, certain accusations arose"; compare Jannasch, *Geschichte des lutherischen Gottesdienstes in Lübeck*, p. 79: "The ministerium, by the way, seems to have been on the losing side of the dispute." In this context it is impossible to analyze more closely the various documents from Lübeck, which Schöne (op. cit., pp. 32ff.) goes through. Against the background of the Danzig Book, however, there are more and different possible interpretations than Schöne had reason to suppose.

257 The letter is reprinted in full in Starck, op. cit., pp. 426ff.

258 Starck, op. cit., p. 427: "But now such a paper [*Zeitung*] comes to us, which we indeed highly fear, for we are informed from several places not only that a shameful and vexing schism has arisen among the ministerium in Lübeck concerning the best use of the consecrated and unconsecrated wine in the distribution of the Supper, . . . but also that from now on, the Danzig Book, which previously was recognized as suspect and Sacramentarian, is publicly praised and defended."

259 Starck, op. cit., p. 423: "As far as I [Saliger] am concerned, I know that he [Stampius] was devoted to the Danzig Sacramentarians. For in our first colloquy he said that he found no error in the Danzig Book; moreover, in the second colloquy he said that he neither would nor could disapprove the Danzig Book, except that it was first condemned and disapproved by the whole ministerium."

260 Schöne, op. cit., p. 27.

The position in the Danzig Book is not irrelevant to the controversy in Rostock, where Saliger went after Lübeck. Since Wiggers did not make frequent mention of it in his account, the research never became familiar with it. References to this controversy in the same work are legion, and apparently a large part of the material of the argumentation is taken from the books that were authored during the struggle in Danzig. Saliger refers to Wigand's censure in this controversy,[261] calls on Morgenstern,[262] says that those in Lübeck praised the Danzig Book and its view of the Verba,[263] draws parallels between Danzig and Rostock,[264] and finds that pastors in Rostock would have accepted the Danzig Book: "Master Bartholdus also said that the Danzig Book was worth being written in golden letters. Dr. Lukas said he could not disapprove the Danzig Book";[265] yes, Neuber himself called upon it in Rostock.[266] When Saliger, for example, writes: "About the moment, which is about the 'now' in the consecration, or when [*weil*] and at what time and under which syllable the body and blood of Christ are there, one should indeed not ask in jest; as soon as [*so baldt*] the Lord Christ's words are spoken and sound forth, simple faith accepts such clear, bright words of Christ, believes . . . ,"[267] this is a verbatim quotation from Wigand's censure in the Danzig case, printed by Morgenstern.[268]

Saliger's opponents build on the formal-logical argumentation about the form of the Sacrament, which is not completed without the eating: "The form of the Supper grants it to be a thing. The form of the Supper is the total action. Therefore, the whole action grants it to be a thing."[269] Faced with this statement by Valentinus Schacht, Saliger answers, "Lord Master, Paul says no one should capture us through empty philosophy" [see Col. 2:8].[270] The Sacrament cannot be explained by virtue of categories applied from the outside. Saliger thinks this form of argument was derived from Danzig.[271] The connection between Danzig and Rostock also comes out in another way. In the discussions, Saliger's

261 *Religionssachen: Handlung zwischen den theologen und Predigern zu Rostock und Herrn J. Saliger* (microfilm), fol. 27b, 58a, 92a, 99b, 134a.

262 Id., fol. 49a, 58a, 92a, 261b.

263 Id., fol. 59b, 81a.

264 Id., fol. 80a, 89b.

265 Id., fol. 81b.

266 Id., fol. 81a; compare the same information in Sperber, op. cit., fol. 74b. Further statements from Danzig: fol. 90a, 92b, 94a.

267 Id., fol. 257b.

268 Morgenstern, op. cit., fol. QIVbf.

269 *Religionssachen: Handlung*, fol. 53a.

270 Ibid.

271 Id., fol. 84b; compare fol. 80a: "But that the preachers at Rostock in this controversy operate in the same way as the Danzigers toward Christ's Supper."

main opponent, Simon Pauli, called on a quotation from [David] Chytraeus's Matthew commentary, which in turn contains a quotation from Melanchthon. Pauli says about this: "What am I saying different from my lord and teacher, Dr. David [Chytraeus]?"[272] These very words had appeared in the Danzig Book, when they had the third part of the Sacrament be just the action.[273]

Also according to Wiggers's account, it is apparent that the Rostock theologians maintain a Melanchthonian view. At the beginning of December 1568, Saliger was asked by Valentin Schacht "for the sake of learning . . . what he held concerning what is left over of the consecrated elements."[274] Then Schacht asked about the presence before the use, since he himself maintained that "the use must be added first." The actual doctrinal controversy broke out during Christmas 1568. On January 9, 1569, Rostock's pastors accused Saliger of teaching a presence "before the use, distribution, and reception."[275] On January 23, Saliger invoked as support for his cause the elevation retained by Luther.[276] On January 24, the clergy rejected the doctrine ascribed to them by Saliger: that the Sacrament becomes a reality first on the tongue.[277] With that, a certain restraint entered in:[278] the Melanchthonian doctrine of *usus* is presented in its more thought-out form. Eating [*sumptio*] and *usus* must not be said to coincide, but the *sumptio* validates the *usus* as Christ's own act. That could be the same restraint that drove the insightful Simon Pauli to *terminate* Valentin Schacht when, at the beginning of December, he posed the question about the presence before the use with the unguarded addition: "The use must be added first."

On February 15, in front of an appointed commission, Simon Pauli explained that Saliger taught "absolutely before the use [*absolute ante usum*]," which Saliger disputed.[279] The charge recalls the accusation against Morgenstern in Danzig: "How he then will strongly insist hereafter on the absolute consecration and his 'Do this' [*Conficite*]."[280] Saliger defended himself against the accusation of teaching a consecration without communion, in the Roman manner, but the complaint should *rather have been that he taught a consecration in the*

272 Id., fol. 189b.

273 *Apologia[: Gründlicher Gegenbericht]*, fol. Db, Aaa.

274 Wiggers, op. cit., p. 618.

275 Id., op. cit., pp. 620f.

276 Id., op. cit., p. 622.

277 Id., op. cit., pp. 622f.

278 Compare Morgenstern on Danzig, op. cit., fol. D: "For in the beginning they shamelessly argued that bread and wine could not be a sacrament or be the body and blood before they were received."

279 Wiggers, op. cit., p. 627.

280 *Apologia[: Gründlicher Gegenbericht]*, fol. AaIIIb.

* [Translator's note: The italicized words were handwritten in Hardt's working copy.]

*Communion Mass that is** obviously before the beginning of the communing [*Kommunionen*]. At the clergy's request, at the end of March an opinion from Wigand was demanded in the case. Wigand's answer is, in all essential points, in Saliger's favor. First and foremost, Wigand says that an investigation and an affirmation of the presence "before the reception" is necessary to avoid false doctrine. Otherwise there could be "confused and mistaken Christians." Wigand later asserts that a *de facto* unity prevails between Saliger and his opponents: "For I see that Dr. Simon [Pauli] in particular often explained himself just like this."[281] Wigand hopes, in conclusion, that David Chytraeus, for example, will give full clarity to the problem in [some kind of] document.[282]

Wigand's supposition that Chytraeus would agree with him was unfounded. The letter that Chytraeus writes to Saliger from Vienna on April 18 essentially differs from Wigand. The disputation itself is described as presumptuousness. In fact, in Melanchthonian fashion, Saliger's belief in the presence before the reception is rejected: "Since it is enough for the pious mind to learn from the Words of Institution that the bread that is offered to me by the minister is the true body of Christ, why is it necessary to debate about the bread lying on the paten or about what is left after the reception?"[283]

281 Wiggers, op. cit., p. 635.

282 Id., op. cit., p. 636.

283 [Chytraeus,] *Epistola*, p. 669; compare *Apologia[: Gründlicher Gegenbericht]*, fol. HhIIIa, on these controversies, "at which we bear much disapproval." Compare here Wiggers, op. cit., p. 637; Schröder, op. cit., 3:16; Grass, op. cit., p. 117. Chytraeus's words cited here have been understood as a summation of the controversy around Saliger, which correspond with the Formula of Concord, and after nearly four hundred years they have gained decisive significance in the question of implementing the so-called Arnoldshain Theses; compare above, pp. 29ff., paragraph after n. 105 [Swedish edition, p. 34]. Brunner's signature on the Theses may be said to have meant the necessary Lutheran participation. Without it, the Theses would not have gained the character of being an instrument of reconciliation. [Brunner] abandons any reference to the consecration, which would have made it impossible for the rest of the participants to subscribe. He gives this justification in "Die dogmatische und kirchliche Bedeutung des Ertrages der Abendmahlsgesprächs" (p. 110):

> So as a rationale for this stance one may point to Chytraeus's decision in the Saliger Lord's Supper controversy, where what is "essential," as far as it applies in this context, is expressed well with the following words: *Since it is enough for the pious mind to learn from the Words of Institution that the bread that is shown by the minister is the true body of Christ, what need is there to dispute concerning the bread lying in the paten or about what is left after the reception. . . .* For the comfort and assurance of the guest at the Lord's Supper, there must be clear expression in the doctrine of the Lord's Supper that the presented bread and wine convey to him, without question, the body and blood of Christ. The decision on the present question here relies on *this* passage, not on a particular view of the consecratory function of the Words of Institution.

A Luther letter was sent along.[284]

Chytraeus apparently considers Saliger to be driven by speculative ambition and impious dogmatism: "empty and profane curiosity of cleverness rather than true piety."[285] Saliger is unaccustomed to Melanchthonianism's screening process: "It is enough to be of a pious mind." On April 30, Chytraeus sent the dukes of Mecklenburg a copy of the letter to Saliger. From the cover letter it is clear that Saliger's appearance in Lübeck was what first got Chytraeus involved with the issue of the *usus*.[286] He thereby indicates a distance in regard to Wigand and the rest, for whom this question had long been of very great interest and had been made a subject of doctrinal discussion. At the same time, this unawareness includes taking somewhat of a stand. It is impossible that Chytraeus would have been unfamiliar with the struggle in Danzig, even more so since Danzig appealed to Rostock for an opinion, which was not actually given, however.[287]

Even if it can be assumed that Brunner mistakenly views Chytraeus's words as significant for the Lutheran camp at that time, he has adequately rendered the Melanchthonian view and rightly interpreted Chytraeus, in contrast to Schöne (op. cit., p. 55), who in aiming toward harmony tried to make this valid: that "we must not understand this statement as directed against 'before the reception,' which was taught by Saliger and justified by Wigand; what it indeed indicates is the confession concerning the bread that it is the 'true body of Christ' not first in the moment of reception, but already when the minister distributes it." "Shown" [*exhibetur*] meanwhile in Chytraeus is the act of communion in contrast to "lying on the paten"!

284 When Chytraeus says that Luther's letter explicitly deals with "nothing is a sacrament outside the action" [*nihil est sacramentum extra actionem*], it doubtless had to do with the letter to Wolferinus, which Hachenburg (*Vom Anbeten [des Sacraments]*, fol. EVIIb) already found could be misinterpreted as a rejection of everything having to do with the extent of the *usus*. The Melanchthonian Simon Pauli in Rostock in his book *Methodi* (III, fol. 12, quoted in Gollwitzer, op. cit., p. 139 n. 3) cites the letter to Wolferinus but ends the exposition with Melanchthon's letter on the same matter. This significant conflation [of the two] was not noted by Gollwitzer. Compare above also the interpretation in Danzig, p. 286 n. 238 [Swedish edition, p. 257], and WA's comment (WA Br 10:339) on the identity of the Luther letter forwarded by Chytraeus: "This letter, which, according to Chytraeus, 'fundamentally determined the opinion on the controversy' [O. Krabbe], was certainly ours." Schöne (op. cit., p. 17) views the identity of the letter as unclear.

285 Chytraeus, op. cit., ibid.

286 Chytraeus, op. cit., p. 652. Wiggers does not discuss the letter.

287 *Apologia[: Gründlicher Gegenbericht]*, fol. QIIIb. "But though no objection or answer from Rostock (as far as is known to us) results from this matter, Benedict Morgenstern was hindered and prevented from such as he confesses in his preface, with his writing and reporting to Dr. Wigand." Wigand's intervention thus was to keep Rostock quiet. The Danzig Book, however, appeals to Rostock's statement in another case (op. cit., fol. IiIIa): "The Rostock theologians in their writing thus write to the Christians at Andorff who recently left: *Christ says, Take and eat; this (namely, the received and eaten) bread is My body*"; compare here Hartknoch, op. cit., pp. 702f.; Freytag, op. cit., p. 93.

Chytraeus was informed about the controversy but found it to be outside his theological role. Therefore, he did not handle it, nor did he want to handle it.

In the middle of September 1569, Chytraeus returned to Mecklenburg from Austria. On October 5, the controversy was settled by a ducal edict, commonly called the Recess [*Abschied*], which prohibited all unnecessary debates, among other things, about "how and when and in what way the bread in the Supper is the body of Christ."[288] Various misleading expressions were rejected, mainly with points against Roman errors but also in a different direction, whereby Saliger and Wigand were somewhat mollified, such as [this]: "These expressions (which, however, as we find from the *Acta*, are used by no one in our churches), that the body and blood of Christ are not present in the Supper before the consecrated bread and wine are touched with the lips or taken in the mouth, and that the body of Christ is not in the bread, but in the eating, etc. For Dr. Luther says we do not prescribe to God any 'now' or time, but we are satisfied by simply believing that what surely happens is what God says should happen or should be."[289] The last lines are cited without reference to the source, mentioned above, [namely,] Luther's letter to Karlstadt, the way it is in the German Jena edition, part 4, folio 378.[290] The significance of this shall be examined later. Saliger was

---

Danzig, however, had received wholehearted support from the faculty in Wittenberg (Hartknoch, op. cit., ibid.; Freytag, op. cit., pp. 92f.).

288 Wiggers, op. cit., p. 638.

289 Ibid.

290 The folio reference likewise has to do with the Jena edition 1560–1606, but not the one from 1556, where the section is reproduced (fol. 385a; compare the chart in the index in Walch 24:487). According to this earlier edition, the passage is quoted from the Melanchthonian Wolfgang Peristerus 1577 in his *Apologi*, printed in Schröder (op. cit., 3:258ff.), where the quotation is reproduced (p. 292; compare p. 258, where Peristerus appeals to Luther's mentioned Baptism sermon and there makes the third part in the Sacrament into the "act of eating"). Peristerus, who was deposed from his service in Wismar "on account of various administrative offenses" (Wiggers, op. cit., p. 651), afterward went to Danzig (compare Wigand's letter to Johann Albrecht of Mecklenburg; Schröder, op. cit., 3:214: "Now he is in Danzig, for there he has gotten a smattering of plunder"). Wigand in the same connection calls him "wolf." Schmaltz (*Kirchengeschichte Mecklenburgs*, 2:131) reports the not-unimportant situation that the faculty in Rostock in 1575 announced Peristerus's recommendation as orthodox. Peristerus maintains a very detailed Melanchthonianism, which emerges, among other things, in statements such as (Schröder, op. cit., 3:303): "I reject and condemn all papistic and idolatrous ceremonies. . . . Accordingly we should also suppress and abolish . . . the old papistic ceremonies and the elevation." Peristerus sometimes expresses himself without any reservation so that he has the real presence begin only at the eating (compare Schröder, op. cit., 3:293), which a more refined Melanchthonianism would not write. Peristerus seems alone in the view that speaking the words of distribution is the moment of the presence (ibid.). The only contemporaneous commentary on the Saliger controversy that the Göttingen edition of the Confessions adduces (*BS* 997 n. 4) is an earlier writing by Peristerus!

ordered to refrain from further controversies. The Rostock clergy's representatives at the issuing of the edict—Simon Pauli, Lukas Bacmeister, Gelmerus Memorimontius,[291] and Valentin Schacht—accepted the decree of the dukes.[292] Saliger refused and was deposed.

Several days later, the procedure used against Saliger was attacked by Wismar's pastors, who later stood faithfully at his side. The edict is said to be ambiguous, an assertion that is repeated as the Wismar critique continues: "The *status controversiae* was not clearly and plainly established and explained."[293] This is also the essential theological problem in the controversy.

Schöne, more harshly than others, holds the theory that Saliger is an almost manic quibbler and sees everyone involved as embracing Luther's doctrine of the consecration. He writes: "Here we leave it undecided whether Saliger's reason for refusing to sign is valid (according to Holhüter [Wismar]: ambiguity over the *status controversiae*, no condemnation of the antithesis, ambivalent formulations). Only let this much be said here: The Recess [*Abschied*] contains clear condemnations and, in our opinion, states things very precisely and unambiguously."[294] This assessment is based on not knowing the Danzig Book. Against the background of this and Melanchthonianism's definition of *usus*, the Recess does not give a clear answer at all.[295] The real presence is confessed in the whole *actio*, even before the reception, etc., *all of which is consistent with the Danzig Book.* The difference is that the Recess does not contain any opinion offensive to Lutherans concerning the adoration, *reliqua*, etc. They had avoided Danzig's mistake.

The controversy between the pastors in Rostock and Saliger's remaining adherents, the so-called Beatianers, continued even up to the turn of the century.

291 Memorimontius, in 1578 in Holland, withdrew his subscription (Wiggers, op. cit., pp. 641f.) and was reconciled with Saliger who was likewise exiled to Holland, for which the basis given was "Wigand's censure concerning the Danzig controversy" (Schröder, op. cit., 3:468).

292 This dismissal is one of the first cases in which the authorities through a state document decide a doctrinal question within Lutheranism; compare Schöne, op. cit., p. 18.

293 Wiggers, op. cit., p. 644.

294 Schöne, op. cit., p. 58. On the question of Saliger's belligerence, it ought to be pointed out that Wigand wanted to acquit Saliger of such charges (op. cit., p. 636).

295 Schöne (op. cit., p. 62, note *) writes: "Oddly, Hans Kirsten arrives at the opposite view in his rather meager article and leaves out the experience of the Saliger controversy 'Einige Ergänzungen' (*Lutherische Blätter* 41 [April 1955], p. 29)." In the article in question, Kirsten, who in no way deserves Schöne's aspersion, analyzes the Recess [*Abschied*] and finds that the question about the moment of the consecration is not solved. Kirsten's observation is correct. Kirsten then conveys his observations on the Formula of Concord, in which the Recess is somewhat included. This again is not completely correct, since the Formula of Concord is a document put together by several people. Unequivocal judgment about this cannot be made so easily. Not every co-author of it needs to have understood the Recess in its original meaning. Kirsten's analysis of some points of the text, however, retains its value.

In this ongoing controversy, there is evidence that completely elucidates the correctness of the interpretation given above. It is important to establish personal identity within the group of pastors who handled the Beatianers' controversy during the current decades here.[296] Lukas Bacmeister, who took part in the controversy against Saliger and accepted the ducal edict, examined the Beatianers in 1578 and 1596. Valentin Schacht, who also opposed the schism's originator and signed the Recess [*Abschied*], showed up in 1578 along with Simon Pauli, who had the same experiences, and Saliger's former colleague in congregational service, Joachim Banzow. This year is the first time Johann Holdenhagen appears, who returns in 1587, and then it was appropriate for him to act consciously in harmony with the colleagues who handled the matter earlier along with him and who were still members of the ministerium, whose advocate he was at the negotiations and to whose stance he refers. Pauli died first, in 1591; Schacht, in 1607; Bacmeister, in 1608; and the completely dominant Chytraeus of Rostock in 1600.[297]

The negotiations with the Beatianers had the aim of putting an end to an enduring schism. The Beatianers, as well as the Sperberians in Danzig, refused to accept the means of grace from heretical pastors and even refused church burial by the clergy. In 1587, the city's surgeon, Peter Marretisch, a strict Beatianer, submitted a confession of the Sacrament that was examined, among others, by the aforementioned Holdenhagen. The attempt at reconciliation was unsuccessful, however. Holdenhagen urged Marretisch to change a section in the submitted confession to placate the ministerium. It said,

> *Third*, if I or someone else asked what I held concerning the consecrated bread and wine that the minister had at the altar and was going to distribute to the communicants to eat and drink, then I would have to confess from Christ's words that such consecrated bread and such a consecrated cup, which the minister had at the altar or in his hand and was going to give the communicant to eat, was truly the body and blood of the Lord Christ, even before the communicant touched it with his lips.[298]

The pastor's proposed amendment is presented in Marretisch's version like this:

> But regarding the *third* proposition, they [Holdenhagen and Master Oswaldus Slee], along with me, could not consider it right, for it would stir up the old controversy of Johann Saliger. For if I would battle for (adhere to) the words that I put in my last proposition, and they as my soul's caretakers brought such before the ministerium, the ministerium would become even more severely embittered. But if I would change such unnecessary questions and in them replace the word "held" with "is holding,"

296 Compare here Wiggers, op. cit., pp. 652ff.

297 Compare Goetzius, *Elogia germanorum*, pp. 61ff. (Schacht), and *ADB* (for the others).

298 Wiggers, op. cit., p. 661. The archives for this matter do not include the discussion rediscovered in Schwerin.

> "had" with "has," and the words "was going to distribute" with "is distributing," or totally and completely drop such questions, then they would bring my confession before the ministerium. . . .[299] [300]

When Marretisch refused to make the changes, the pastors presented a quotation from Luther's writings that was to persuade the contentious surgeon:

> And since Master *Slee* also asked me in the fear of God to read carefully page 378, volume 4 of Luther, for there I would find how Luther considered questions such as the ones I am posing to be unnecessary and old-fashioned, then I must dare to speak the truth and confess that the question that I presented to the lords, compared to the question that Karlstadt used on *Luther*, indeed are as far apart as heaven is from earth. For *Karlstadt* asks whether Christ *gave* His body before He spoke the first letter of this statement: *This is My body*. But my question is about what I should think concerning the consecrated bread and cup that the minister has at the altar or in his hand and will give the communicant to eat and drink.[301]

Presumably Marretisch stayed with this confession of his and died without Absolution and the Sacrament, faithfully maintaining Saliger's doctrine.[302] Through his meticulous description of the course of events, he has made a valuable contribution to determining the view prevalent in Rostock. *The letter from Luther to Karlstadt, used by the pastors, is the same that was put in the ducal edict of 1569*. Marretisch is completely correct in rejecting it as being pertinent in the actual question here. This comes out in the description of the letter's position given earlier in this volume. Rostock's pastors again apparently thought they found in the letter that Luther, through the hypothetically assumed distribution of Christ's body before the Verba (which is impossible) and the corresponding remarks about Scholasticism's falsely being bound to the syllables, would have fundamentally rescinded all temporal parameters of the real presence in the Supper as it was celebrated and still is celebrated *in reality*. The desired changes seem to show that in Rostock only the *completed* action is viewed legitimately as *usus*, on which to predicate a presence before the reception. Only in or after the reception is there certainty of the presence, which is why "*was going to distribute*" designates a point of time when the action was not validated as completely subordinate to the Word. Therefore, also the subjunctive forms "*would hold*" and "*had*" are dropped in favor of the indicative forms, which indicates that it does not have to do with theoretical expressions from a standpoint temporally before the completed use, but with an affirmation of the presence contemporaneous

299 Id., op. cit., p. 662.

300 [The Swedish edition numbers footnotes up to 99, then restarts at 1, which this translation lists as 101, 201, etc.]

301 Id., op. cit., p. 663.

302 Id., op. cit., p. 666.

with the reception and assured by it. Thereby one might consider himself to have fulfilled the demand for a nonscholastic, "nontemporal" determination of the presence, which was thought to be found in Luther's letter to Karlstadt, while at the same time not violating the latitude that the *usus* had in the likewise-familiar letter to Wolferinus.[303]

The view of the *usus* depicted here had already been advocated in 1590 by Aegidius Hunnius, the defender of the *Book of Concord* and otherwise stalwart anti-Melanchthonian. Since no one knows whether or not, for example, a fire might possibly disrupt an ongoing Mass between consecration and distribution, according to Hunnius the presence can only be said to exist in and with the reception.[304] The same Melanchthonian interpretation is found in Lutheran orthodoxy's leading figure, Johann Gerhard. According to Gerhard, the elevation ought to be omitted since "Christ did not simply say, 'This is My body.'" ["But, 'Take and eat, this is My body.'"]* Christ is speaking only about the bread that is eaten. The elevation therefore might give occasion to artolatry.[305] Only the Papists teach that "as soon as the words of God were offered, they were true; therefore, they were true even before the action of eating and drinking."[306]

---

303 Compare above, pp. 276ff., paragraph that includes n. 194 [Swedish edition, pp. 228ff.].

304 Quoted from Pieper, op. cit., 3:34 n. 1371: "'Art. S. Loc. de sacramentis,' 1590, pp. 712f."; about him compare *RE*, s.v. "Hunnius, Agidius." — What is said here above about Rostock's definition of *usus* in a certain sense should shed new light on the Uppsala meeting in Sweden in 1593. While an earlier investigation concluded that the leading churchmen in Sweden, who received their education from the faculty in Rostock, therefore maintained a Lutheranism of a milder kind, averse to the Formula of Concord, Cnattingius (in "Nicolaus Bothniensis' teser om Skriften 1584 och Uppsala mötes beslut," pp. 192ff.) demonstrated that the churchmen in question, like Chytraeus himself, stood on the foundation of the Formula of Concord and that thus Swedish Lutheranism at this time could widely be judged as unified. The analysis that is made above demands that the judgment of Cnattingius be somewhat adjusted. What was fostered in Rostock's doctrine of the Sacrament must have differed dogmatically from the view, for example, of the adoration of the Sacrament that Laurentius Petri claimed as that of Swedish Lutheranism. Thus the explanation given for what was fostered in Rostock is the so-called professor-faction's battle against the elevation at the Uppsala meeting. The battle over this and related church usage is a battle between the heritage from Luther, supplied through George of Anhalt and Laurentius Petri, and the heritage from Melanchthon, supplied through Rostock (Chytraeus).

305 * [Translator's note: I have added the bracketed words from Gerhard to complete the thought.]

Gerhard, *Loci theologici*, 4:205.

306 Id., op. cit., p. 166. At the same time it ought to be remembered that Gerhard can still speak about an adoration of Christ in the Sacrament (id., op. cit., 4:168): "Christ must be adored in the Eucharist," and he concludes his chapter on the Supper with Aquinas's [hymn] *Adoro te devote, latens Deitas, qui sub his figuris vere latitas* ["O Godhead hid, devoutly I adore Thee, Who truly art within the forms before me" (translation by E. Caswall)] (id., op. cit., 4:208). But what matters here is only an adoring

Gerhard asserts: "The eucharistic action is of one kind and a definite whole; the essential parts of this action are consecration, distribution, [and] reception consisting of eating and drinking, which are called sacramental acts." Only in the completion of this whole thing does the Sacrament exist: "Therefore, the eucharistic bread is finally the *koinonia* of the body of Christ when it is blessed [and] distributed according to the order and command of Christ."[307] It is completely consistent to say about the Sacrament: "As Christ is present in the Supper illocally, so also He works in the mystery nontemporally [*intemporaliter*] (as I might say it), that is, without measure of time."[308] Thereby Gerhard comes into conflict with the thesis of Chemnitz who very correctly is cited against him by the Roman Catholic Robert Bellarmine: "because Chemnitz says that the body of the Lord is on the altar before the eating."[309] Gerhard solves the problem by ascribing his own "nontemporally" to Chemnitz. Christ's body is indeed present "before the eating," but not so that this presence may be fixed objectively at this point of time. Communing first makes the action into action and creates a complete "formal cause" [*causa formalis*], which justifies the assertion of a presence "before the eating" [*ante manducationem*].

It is hardly correct to see Johann Gerhard and seventeenth-century orthodoxy in his successors as the culmination of the materialization of the Lord's Supper doctrine in contrast to its earlier, more spiritualized form in Luther, as Andrén did.[310] Gerhard, the foremost name of orthodoxy, on the contrary gives

---

contemplation of the objective gifts, which are bestowed in the Sacrament, not a ritual act with the real presence as the direct object; compare [Edward Frederick] Peters, op. cit., p. 470, concerning seventeenth-century orthodoxy: "There is no theologian who says that one is not to worship the flesh of Christ, but all Lutheran theologians investigated insist that Christians are not to direct this worship to the Sacrament"; p. 482: "The seventeenth century, then, puts itself into the Melanchthonian camp rather than on the side of Luther concerning the question of the adoration of the Sacrament"; p. 464: "Nevertheless, at least partly because of this polemical reaction to Rome, the idea of an objective identification of the body with the bread is weak in seventeenth-century theology." Peters shows (p. 465) that even Hülsemann, who otherwise correctly interprets Luther's doctrine on the three modes of presence (compare above, p. 82 n. 27 [Swedish edition, p. 79]) rejects the adoration with a quotation from Gerhard that distinguishes between disallowed sacramental adoration and a proper reverence during the conducting of the Sacrament.

307 Gerhard, op. cit., 4:152.

308 Id., op. cit., 4:153.

309 Bellarmine, *Disputationes* III, p. 993; Gerhard, op. cit., 4:153.

310 Andrén, op. cit., pp. 68, 76, 78. It is given that the [rise of the] seventeenth-century [orthodoxy] did not immediately mean that the older Lutheran view ceased; compare [Edward Frederick] Peters (op. cit., p. 548): "There are still a few theologians in the seventeenth century who agree with Martin Luther that the presence of the body and blood of Christ are to be defined from the time of the Words of consecration until the last elements have been received." There, Peters (p. 565), with all correctness,

expression to the view of the Melanchthonian school to combat the tangibility in time and space that was viewed as Roman Catholic but that in fact existed also in Luther and older Lutheranism.

George of Anhalt and His Successors

Prince George III of Anhalt has already been mentioned several times. Hachenburg[311] and Sperber[312] called upon him. Even for greater and more significant theologians, he was an authority and ambassador of Luther's view on the adoration and *extra usum*. In his exchange of letters with Luther, George liked to touch on those sacramental questions and in one case exacted Luther's clear reply about *extra usum*, the elevation, adoration, and the expression "the bread is the body." In the letter, Luther briefly introduced his answer to George's questions:

> Many might wish a little letter to be written to the Church concerning in what way and how far to understand this statement—that the sacraments are not valid outside their use [*extra usum*], etc.—by which many profane spirits protect their condemned abuses. [Luther answers:] *If it be necessary, let it be done* [*Si opus sit, fiat*]. 24. Also concerning the exhibiting or elevation of the Sacrament, as they call it, whether or not it must be retained or omitted, and whether it may be expedient for this controversy that has arisen concerning this thing to be cured by some short writing. [Luther answers:] *It has been done* [*Factum est*].[313] 25. Concerning these who assert

considers the Wittenberg faculty's statement from 1619 that asserts that the use ceases only after everything within the framework of the Mass is consumed. Andrén (op. cit.) cites this as "this new interpretation"! Andrén in his work refers to Kawerau, "Über die liturgische Gestaltung der 'Konsekration' in der lutherischen Abendmahlsfeier," but Kawerau (op. cit., p. 357) makes it perfectly clear [that he thinks] that Luther is working with "still surviving notions of the Catholic circle of thought" and [that he] thinks that Luther did not draw the conclusions from the rest of his insights. Andrén interprets Luther as independent from these "Catholic" thought patterns. The liturgical material with which Andrén supports his thesis does not seem completely convincing. The so-called Communion cloth, which was held by two church servants (acolytes) under the communicant's chin, becomes for Andrén a sign particular to materialistic orthodoxy—"a testimony that the dominance of the Word was continuing to disappear within evangelical Christianity" (op. cit., p. 78), which regardless of the starting point seems somewhat strongly worded—but Meyer (*Luther und die Messe*, p. 363 n. 67, according to Preuss, *Luther als Kommunikant*, pp. 210f.) thinks that the same [type of] cloth was used in Luther's Wittenberg. Compare Andrén, op. cit., p. 77: "By the thought of grace taking over the role of the thought of forgiveness of sins in the view of the Supper under orthodoxy, the old Communion cloths could again gain a legitimate place within the framework of the Divine Service."

311 Compare above, p. 274ff., text after n. 184 [Swedish edition, p. 248].

312 Compare above, p. 282, text at n. 217 [Swedish edition, p. 254].

313 The intended writing is *Brief Confession concerning the Holy Sacrament* (WA 54:162.31ff. [cf. AE 38:287]).

that the body and blood are exhibited with the bread and wine, yet do not wish to confess expressly that the bread is the body of the Lord, etc. [Luther answers:] *They may be suspect, unless they make a clear confession* [*Suspecti sint, nisi clare confiteantur*]. Concerning the adoration. [Luther answers:] *Let it stand* [*Stet*].[314]

Although the promised writing on *extra usum* did not come to be, George spent a great deal of his ecclesiastical effort in preserving and passing on the heritage from Luther on this and similar points. His contribution is little known, and his influence on a whole generation of Lutheran theologians is completely disregarded in the research.[315]

314 WA Br 11[:245].77ff., no. 4181, Anhang. This juxtaposition of the various points has great interest through the fact that [the expression] "with the bread" [*cum pane*] is said to be suspect. The presentation indicates that this mode of expression stands in particular relation to "outside the use" [*extra usum*], adoration, and elevation. "The bread is the body" [*Panis est corpus*] gives a different solution to these questions. Granted, Ahlberg (op. cit., p. 240) is right that "with the bread" may not be used as a sure proof of Melanchthonianism. The research here cannot be content with tallying prepositions. But in the quotation above, there is a first differentiation of terms, which in some sense anticipates the later controversy on the formulation of the *Variata* of the Augsburg Confession (Ahlberg, op. cit., p. 243).

315 Gollwitzer, who gives an account of even authors of slight significance, has nothing to say about George [of Anhalt]. [Edward Frederick] Peters (despite an array of bibliographica that is hefty on other points) writes about George of Anhalt (p. 159 n. 98) only that he was ordained in Magdeburg in 1524, was Lutheran, and ruled Anhalt. With that, Peters otherwise passes over the fact that George considered his spiritual office not from his canonic consecration in Magdeburg (at age 17!) but from the ordination without apostolic succession performed in Merseburg Cathedral on August 2, 1545, when Luther, though "somewhat weakened because of a stone," performed "the consecration and laying on of hands with all pleasure and with fine exhortations at the altar." That same day George wrote his brother Joachim a letter, signed for the first time: "Georgius presbyter" (compare Westphal, *Zur Erinnerung an Fürst Georg den Gottseligen zu Anhalt*, pp. 52f.). This is an insignificant detail, which in a larger context, however, is not without importance. It shows that George, whose being at home in the medieval concept of the world caused the editors of the WA not a little headache (WA Br 11[:243], no. 4181): "many a thing remained dark to me" (compare, for example, the question on ordination "*per saltum*" [by a single leap, passing over the intermediate steps], [WA Br 11:244].24f., which in WA, no. 8 [see WA Br 11:244], becomes "transition from one pastorate into another [?]"!). [George], so zealous for the sacramental adoration, is not at all an intermediary theologian of the reform-Catholic type. His consecration, which was invalid according to canon law, he defended in a Lutheran way in his writing *De ritu apostolico ordinationis*. Viewed rightly, George was episcopal coadjutor in Merseburg. His ordination certificate is found in CR 5:825, signed by Melanchthon. Compare also George's letter (CR 5:830): "Especially among us there was Dr. Martin Luther by whom we were initiated by the sacred mystery of ordination through the laying on of hands." George's office as coadjutor was exercised, however, *de facto* as the office of bishop (op. cit., pp. 55ff.); compare George, op. cit., p. 14: "Therefore, though we do not wear the episcopal crowns or caps, nevertheless that chosen assembly had been entrusted to us at our coronation. Just as Paul

Like no one else among his contemporaries, George safeguarded Luther's doctrine of the Supper in his writings and in his handling of church questions, as bishop and later as pious territorial leader. His writings[316] include a great wealth of material passed on in connection with excerpts from Luther's writings and Luther's letters to George, all expressed in the conviction that Lutheranism represents the true continuation of the Church catholic. The mystery of the real presence and the adoration of the Sacrament of the Altar are portrayed with glowing colors. Some dogmatically important excerpts could be cited here through the intermediary of Chemnitz, Kirchner, and Selnecker's *History of the Sacramental Controversy*, which, when giving the source, cites George's words and at the same time subscribes to what they say. This form of citation really shows George's influence. George, and along with him the *History of the Sacramental Controversy*, ensures against those who deny the adoration: "We want nothing to do with those who . . . consider the adoration of the venerable Sacrament—yes, of Christ in the Sacrament—as idolatry."[317]

> And though our dear Lord Jesus Christ instituted His holy Supper not for the sake of viewing and adoration, yet that is not forbidden nor excessive nor to be considered idolatrous, but rather proper and right when this holy Supper is celebrated according to the institution of our dear Lord Jesus Christ, so that one may attend it with all devotion and reverence, and one may adore our Lord Jesus Christ, true God and man, in it, who in this venerable Sacrament not only according to His divine omnipotence and in a spiritual way but also bodily, truly, and essentially, yet invisibly, is present as the one who sits at the right hand of divine majesty and is exalted by God and given a name that is above every name, that at the name of Jesus they should bow. . . .[318]

> The eyes see bread and wine; all outward senses witness nothing else, but faith recognizes as truly present the Lord Christ, who offers His very body and blood in this most holy mystery. The same Lord Christ, present under

---

says to the Philippians [in chapter 4]: You are my joy and crown." — George's significance, however, has been noted at any rate; compare Müller, "Beziehungen zwischen den Kurfürsten Joachim I. und II. von Brandenburg und dem Fürsten Georg III von Anhalt in den Jahren 1534–40," pp. 127ff. In the preface to this volume on the four-hundredth anniversary of George's birth, Müller calls George "the actual reformer of the Mark [of Brandenburg]."

316 *Reverendissimi et illustrissimi principis . . . Conciones et scripta.* There is a separate edition of *Die vierdte predigt vom Hochwirdigen Sacrament.*

317 *Histori des Sacramentsstreits*, p. 541; George, *Die Vierdte Predigt vom Hochwirdigen Sacrament*, fol. 11b.

318 *Histori des Sacramentsstreits*; see George, op. cit., fol. 15bf. In the latter, the verb "adore it" [*daselbs anbette*] disappeared, but it is found in the Latin version in *Conciones et scripta*, fol. 249b ("*adoretur*").

the Sacrament, yet invisibly, concealed and hidden, is adored everywhere by the believers, [who adore] not the element of the bread or the outward form.[319]

In 1579, after the publication of the Formula of Concord, Selnecker published an excerpt from George's work, laid out according to the pattern of the Formula of Concord, whereby George posthumously might endorse the new confession. Here, at the end of the Lord's Supper article, in the place that corresponds to the acceptance of the adoration in the Formula of Concord,[320] a defense of the sacramental adoration is cited: "In the Sacrament, however, and in the hearts of the believers, the main thing is not that He is adored in that same place, but that He Himself deals with us and brings help to us. But it does not follow from this, not even that He must be adored in the Sacrament. . . . There are four illustrious sermons of this most illustrious prince for pious people to read."[321] In the section on adiaphora that can be resumed in Christian freedom when necessary, the *elevation* is expressly mentioned. Here Luther's letter to George from 1542 is quoted: "And perhaps one day a time will come that will include reasons for the elevation; then it is free to us and without danger that one

319 *Histori des Sacramentsstreits*, p. 543; George, *Die Vierdte Predigt vom Hochwirdigen Sacrament*, fol. 17b. *Solida ac vera Confessionis Augustanae historia*, p. 481, the Latin edition of *Histori des Sacramentsstreits*, continues: "not the external and visible form, or, as the Scholastics say, the accidence without the subject," which corresponds to George's *Die Vierdte Predigt vom Hochwirdigen Sacrament*: "And as also the Scholastics call the accidence without subject. As when the reverend and learned Dr. Martin also writes about it more extensively in the *Babylonian Captivity*." (But apparently the Latin translation of George's sermon in *Conciones et scripta*, fol. 250B, was the closest model for the *Solida ac vera Confessionis Augustanae historia*.) George's reference to Scholasticism thus goes back to WA 6:509.35f. [cf. AE 36:31f.], where Luther shows how even during the Middle Ages this was true among the people: "They do not adore the accidence, but Christ hidden there"; compare below, pp. 306–7 n. 326, about Laurentius Petri. This traditional Lutheran identification with the Roman Catholic layman's faith in the real presence was repeated in Selnecker, *Ein Gesprech Vom Heiligen Abendmahl*, fol. GIIIaf.: "So there are still many good-hearted people [Papists], who look more to the Word of the Lord Christ than to your [Calvinists'] inane glosses, with which we can better compare ourselves than with your imagination." Later Karl IX of Sweden, then Duke Karl of Södermanland, understood this as a confession of the adoration and commented in the dedication copy that Selnecker unsuspectingly sent to Karl: "more pleasing to publicly idolatrous people than to poor Christians." On the closing words about Calvinism, on "your imagination" Karl, loyal to his Reformed conviction, commented: "worthy of Christians." Karl's handwriting has been identified by H. Jarv, PhD, at the manuscript department of the Royal Library by comparison with Karl's letters.

320 *BS* 1016.4ff. [cf. FC SD VII 126]; but compare here below, p. 310 n. 339.

321 The writing in question was printed together with George, *De ritu apostolico ordinationis*, pp. 39ff., with the title *Reverendissimi et illustrissimi Principis et Domini, Domini Georgij Principis Anhaltini ac vere Episcopi, Sententiae, de controversis quibusdam articulis*, where the above quotation is found, p. 61.

might elevate again."[322] Thus for Selnecker the words of the Formula of Concord

322 Op. cit., p. 81, here cited according to the original WA Br 10[:86].25ff., no. 3762. Selnecker embraced both the Lutheran concept of *usus* and the adoration. Gollwitzer (op. cit., p. 136) makes Selnecker into a Melanchthonian on this point by misunderstanding Selnecker, *Christliche warhafftige Widerlegung*, fol. FIIa, where the text in its context says:

> And then the good rule is taken that there is no Sacrament outside the proper use instituted by God Himself. As when the consecrated bread is not given, received, eaten, and the cup [is not] drunk, there is no Sacrament. We also do not need here the Calvinists' questions, who continually think of starting with us by asking whether or not the pastor at the altar has the body of Christ in his hands when he has the consecrated bread. For these malicious, unbrotherly, sophistic questions need no other answer than only that we do not truncate the action and do not take one thing without the other but retain the whole action, as the Lord Christ instituted it.

Gollwitzer thinks that Selnecker here *rejects* "the question affirmed by the actual Lutherans," but Selnecker in this passage is disputing instead what is really in the Calvinistic question to the "actual" Lutherans: whether the extended concept of *usus* doesn't invalidate "the good rule" about *extra usum*. The answer is "that we do not truncate the action," and thus at the same time are justified in teaching the Lutheran *usus* and in rejecting the Roman *abusus*, which is *extra usum*. Also [Edward Frederick] Peters (op. cit., p. 457) in this respect incorrectly categorizes Selnecker among the Melanchthonians. — Also in a passage that outwardly is unclear in regard to dogmatics, Selnecker reveals his belief in the adoration. He writes (ibid.) that one does well to pray, "Lord Jesus, now in this place, in this church, from this altar, in this congregation, on my sickbed, etc., You feed me with Your true body and quench me with Your precious blood. Have mercy on me, and let me continually be and abide in You." These words from 1576 are obviously an answer to the so-called Torgau Articles, *Kurtz Bekenntnis*, of 1574, which vigorously turns against the adoration and writes (op. cit., fol. HIIa) that the prayer "Lord Jesus Christ, You are truly and bodily present here, have mercy on me" is directed "to the bread." Selnecker thus is speaking in a situation of doctrinal controversy, where the very prayer in question is attacked as adoration. His stance thereby becomes a defense of the adoration. (On Selnecker's stance on *Kurtz Bekenntnis*, compare Heppe, op. cit., 2:440: "The Torgau Articles were exposed by strict Lutheran theologians abroad, as well as by Johann Wigand and Nicolaus Selnecker, for their lack of confessional character"; Ritschl, op. cit., 4:67: "the stance of that Torgau confession, repeatedly criticized by the stricter Lutherans as being rather unclear and uncertain.") One must be aware that the Communion prayer of the medieval Mass is directed to the eucharistic Christ; compare Biel's commentary on "Lord Jesus Christ, Son of the living God," *Canonis misse expositio*, lect. 82 B: "First, nearby, intentionally directing the eyes toward the Sacrament, toward Christ who is truly and really present in the visible forms, he says: [Lord Jesus Christ] . . ."; compare Meyer, *Luther und die Messe*, p. 299. When Luther in the *Formula Missae* (WA 12:213.15ff. [cf. AE 53:29]) mentions this prayer as a Communion prayer ("one will not pray badly"), there is no reason to think that the pastor should look in another direction. No criticism is expressed against Biel's words, well-known to Luther. When the prayer is criticized in *The Abomination of the Secret Mass* (WA 18:34.11f. [cf. AE 36:324]), the criticism has to do not with this point but with justification through faith in contrast to sacrifice; compare WA 18:34.19f. [cf. AE 36:325], on the next prayer ("*Perceptio corporis tui*") ["May the receiving of Thy body . . ."]: "This little prayer might fit, if it

about freedom to resume a practice once laid aside[323] are seen immediately as regarding the elevation.

In another writing by Selnecker, from 1576, George of Anhalt stands side by side with Scripture and the Confessions: "This doctrine is grounded in the prophetic and apostolic Scriptures; in Luther's catechisms, the Augsburg Confession, the Apology, and the Smalcald Articles; and likewise comprised in our writings also explained in the books of the precious hero Prince George of Anhalt, etc., of praiseworthy Christian memory."[324] George now takes the position that the Formula of Concord made claim to, having been completed that same year: [the claim of] completing and summarizing the earlier confessions. In other places, too, Selnecker systematically professed George's authority.[325]

George's influence extended even beyond Germany. In 1562 Laurentius Petri published *On Some Parts of Our Lord Jesus Christ's Supper, regarding Dialog* [*Om någor stycker wårs Herras Jesu Christi nattward anrörandes Dialogus*]. To not a small extent, this is a translation of George's sermon on the adoration of the Sacrament. What Laurentius Petri has, in citing a quotation from Luther and oral tradition about Luther's own practice of the adoration in the Mass, is all

---

were accompanied by this: 'As You spoke to me and commanded me to believe,' so that the Word of God was included."

323 *BS* 1063.5ff.

324 Selnecker, *Christliche warhafftige Widerlegung*, fol. BIVb.

325 Compare here Zeeden, *Martin Luther und die Reformation im Urteil des deutschen Luthertums*, 2:60, which, from Selnecker, *Historica oratio: Vom Leben und Wandels des Ehrwirdigen Herrn und thewren Mannes Gottes D. Martini Lutheri*, fol. 85a, cites among Luther's successors: "Philip, Doctor Pommer [Bugenhagen], Schnepf, Brenz, Prince George of Anhalt . . ." (nine more names follow). George is thus placed here only as number five. In *Necessaria et brevis Repetitio simplicis verae et perspicuae doctrinae de Coena Domini*, Selnecker automatically calls upon "the books of Dr. Luther and the most illustrious and most reverend Prince George of Anhalt." The book is quoted here according to a handwritten copy in Uppsala University Library, bound in volume no. 49.VIII.4.337, together with several printed books, with the inscription "*Selnec. Con: Exegesin.*" For the identification, compare, for example, Gollwitzer, op. cit., p. 100 n. 1, with the citation (= manuscript, fol. 15a, numbering from the first handwritten page; the reference to George is found in fol. 66). In *De ratione methodica*, p. 141, published in *Notatio Nicolai Selnecceri de studio sacrae Theologiae*, Selnecker quotes George, pp. 140–42.

derived from George, who even here is shown to be an especially important link between Luther and the generation of the Formula of Concord.[326]

George's influence extended as far away as what was then Hungary. At the synod in Leutschau [now Levoča, Slovakia] in 1597, the Augsburg Confession was read in German first, and then their own national confession, set up parallel with it. In the exposition of the Augsburg Confession, which was then adopted, writings from Luther and George are set forth as explanation to the article on the Lord's Supper in these confessions:

> Then, as far as the tenth article of each confession, its statements are taken not only from the aforementioned refutatory [*Elenchticis*] writings of Luther (as Philip Melanchthon calls them) but also from the German volume of the most holy, most illustrious Prince and Bishop George of Anhalt, approved and most diligently commended to the churches, with a splendid preface by Dr. Philip Melanchthon, 1555. In this declaration, the heroic prince with incredible zeal approves the doctrine of the Church and of Luther, both concerning the person and concerning the Supper of the Lord. Indeed, in contrast, it condemns Zwinglians and all Sacramentarians,

326 When Laurentius Petri (op. cit., fol. GVIb) quotes Luther's words "If I could see (he said) the Holy Spirit descend from heaven in the likeness of a dove as John the Baptizer saw Him, then I would fall down on my knees, lift up my hands, and say, O Holy Spirit, be merciful to me, etc. Then should I not also do the same at the most worthy Sacrament where Christ Himself is present?" he himself thereby pointed to his source, namely, George, who is alone in this information; [see] George, *Die Vierdte Predigt vom Hochwirdigen Sacrament*, fol. 18B, though Laurentius Petri in fact writes: "as many have heard from his own mouth." Compare besides, for example:

George, op. cit., fol. 18A	**Laurentius Petri, op. cit., fol. GIIIa**
(For indeed even in the papacy there was not the great misunderstanding and opinion that the element of bread and wine would be adored.) But when one also would ask the most uneducated, they indeed would say they adored Christ, whom they believe is truly present there, and [they do] not [adore] a creature.	So that everyone would ask anyone of the older uneducated what he adores in the Sacrament, he would surely answer that he does not adore bread and wine there but Jesus Christ whom he believes to be truly present there.
fol. 19b	
And [one] should not imagine that it is the body and blood of our Lord Jesus Christ only for those who receive it at that time and not for those [others]. For we eat and drink; nevertheless the food and drink is and remains [there] even if others and I do not receive, and watch others receive. . . . Thus it is and remains also the essential true body and blood of Christ, that it is done according to His institution, [and] it behooves me also to regard and honor it as such even if I do not partake at that same time, but it is received worthily by others for salvation or even unworthily for condemnation. For just as I am also there when a little child is baptized, it is indeed truly holy Baptism at which I should stand with all devotion and reverence, even though I myself am not being baptized.	And the opinion should be far from us that some imagine occurs, namely, that it should be called our Lord's body and blood only for those who at that time go to it. For just as food and drink are there as they are and so remain even though I stand and watch others eat and drink, likewise Christ's true body and blood are and remain [present] and therefore ought to be regarded and honored by me even though I do not go to it with others at the same time. Likewise, when I am present where someone is baptized, that it indeed is a true Baptism toward which I should act in a godly way, though I myself am not being baptized then.
fol. 20af.	
It is also not to be allowed that such outward veneration that flows from a pure, believing heart at this holy Sacrament performed according to Christ's institution be rebuked, rejected, resisted, or condemned as idolatry. For as little as those before the Lord's ark and mercy seat in the Old Testament prayed in true faith were idolatrous, and they did not adore the ark, the Lord Himself, who therein there promised to hear, that is how little also those are to be considered as idolatrous who adore in the most worthy Sacrament not the element of bread but the Lord Christ, who is the true mercy seat; [they adore Him] both spiritually and with outward devotional gestures.	Therefore, it is also not to be allowed that such honor and reverence that is done with genuflecting and other such things at the Sacrament when it is performed according to the Lord's institution is vilified, rebuked, rejected, and likewise condemned as idolatry. For they were not considered as idolaters who in the Old Testament fell down and worshiped before the Lord's ark and mercy seat, which were in the tabernacle and the temple; nor did they therefore think that they then were worshiping the ark but the Lord Himself, who there had promised He would hear prayers. How much less should they be considered as idolaters who in the Supper or Sacrament adore not bread or wine but the Lord Christ, the real and true mercy seat?
fol. 20b	**fol. HVb**
And as also is customary when one mentions [the name] Jesus that they, as is reasonable, genuflect. Also when one sings "Gloria Patri" and "And was made man," etc.	One indeed genuflects (as also is right) when the name of Jesus is mentioned. Also when one sings "Gloria Patri," etc.; "the Word became flesh," etc.

as foreigners to the Church of God and heretics, on account of their impious dogmas, and diligently declares that they must be avoided.[327]

Also the next day, there were readings from George's writings, and when the question of the sacramental adoration was raised, "I [that is, Severinus Sculteti (Severin Škultéty)] read a splendid passage from the same German volume by Anhalt concerning internal and external adoration of Christ."[328] Even a generation after his death, George of Anhalt was able to answer these questions and with his "incredible zeal," which made his writings into anthems in honor of the Sacrament, to uphold the heritage from Luther at the threshold of an era that soon would be dominated by Melanchthonianism.[329]

The view of Chemnitz has already been partially heard through quotations from *History of the Sacramental Controversy*, where George's words on the adoration are presented by the north German theologians. Chemnitz himself in his own writings does not quote George. But his view on the adoration is the same as that of George. In his *Repetitio sanae doctrinae* in 1561, Chemnitz has a whole chapter "On the Veneration of the Sacrament."[330] After rejecting the Papists'

327 "Acta conventus Pastorum & aliquot Politicorum è quinque liberis civitatibus superioris Hungariae, Leutschowiae habiti: diebus 24. 25. & 26 Novembris: Anni 1597," in Hutter, *Concordia concors*, p. 372. The situation is not unlike the Uppsala meeting in Sweden with the introduction and explanation of the Augsburg Confession. Even in Uppsala, George played a role through the heritage of Laurentius Petri; compare above, p. 298 n. 304 [Swedish edition, p. 268].

328 Hutter, op. cit., p. 373.

329 In Anhalt, after George's death, the candidates for ordination were required to take an oath on George's writings, but in this case it is a declaration of dynastic loyalty rather than a continuity with George's theology, since Anhalt departed from George's doctrine of the real presence, the adoration, and the omnipresence, and, finally, was pronounced Reformed; compare *RE*, s.v. "George III von Anhalt," and Niemeyer, *Collectio Confessionum*, pp. 615f. The authors of the Formula of Concord could rightly assert their agreement with George when the Anhalt theologians refused to sign the Formula of Concord; compare Hutter, op. cit., p. 197. — Lucas Cranach the Younger in 1565 painted George at Christ's right side at the institution of the Supper in the altarpiece in Dessau's castle chapel. To the right of George sits Luther and to the left of Christ is Melanchthon. The rest of the table guests are other famous theologians, while the members of the princely house of Anhalt take their places in the periphery of the picture; compare here [Thulin,] *Reformation in Europa*, p. 55, where the piece is reproduced (text, p. 54). One of George's nephews who can be seen in the background is supposed to be the prince at whose Baptism, according to Hachenburg's information (id., *Vom anbeten des Sacraments*, fol. GIIIbf.) the discussed Baptism sermon on "the three parts necessary for every sacrament" was preached: "at the infant Baptism of the young lord of Anhalt." WA 37:xliii does not have this information, which also explains why the sermon, published in 1543, was "dedicated to the most illustrious and most praiseworthy princes of Anhalt" (WA 37:xliv).

330 Id., op. cit., pp. 205ff. Gollwitzer (op. cit., p. 139 n. 1) wrongly understands this chapter as expressing merely "prayerful co-implementation of the action."

bread-worship "*extra usum*," he professes Luther's words that the Eucharist is worthy of adoration, [words] that were often repeated by the Gnesio-Lutheran camp.[331] Chemnitz recalls that Ambrose speaks about "having to approach with fear," and [he recalls] Chrysostom's "awe-inspiring mysteries and awe-inspiring chalice [*tremenda mysteria et tremendum calicem*]." Before this terrifyingly holy thing, gestures of adoration spontaneously follow: "When the inward heart indeed thinks thus concerning this Sacrament, and it approaches with this devotion, as it is said, then external gestures follow freely and voluntarily in reverence and veneration for this Sacrament."[332]

In his great *Examination of the Council of Trent* in 1565, as support for the adoration of the Sacrament, which is said to be "outside of controversy" [*extra controversiam*] in relation to the papal church, Chemnitz cites various quotations from the church fathers,[333] for example, the words of Ambrose: "The flesh of Christ, which we indeed adore today in the mysteries";[334] and those of Augustine: "Moreover, no one eats this flesh unless he has first adored it . . . not only would we not be sinning by adoring, but we would sin by not adoring."[335] There is an enlightening difference in regard to the Augustine quotation compared to Brenz, who disputes that this would apply to the eucharistic adoration: "He [Augustine] is not speaking there concerning the Lord's Eucharist, but concerning Christ Himself."[336] Petrus a Soto [Pedro de Soto], Brenz's Roman Catholic opponent, had cited this Augustine quotation in the *Assertio catholicae fidei*, in defense of the thesis that "Christ must indeed be adored in this Sacrament."[337] Chemnitz and Petrus a Soto thus have the same view on the meaning of the quotation, while Brenz refuses to see in it a support for the adoration of the Sacrament, which he rejects. In the essential part of the section, Chemnitz's own formulations counter:

> Therefore, Christ is truly and substantially present in the action of the Lord's Supper as God and man, in divine and human natures, and must be adored in spirit and truth. No one denies this unless he either denies or doubts

331 Compare here Hachenburg, *Wider den jrrthumb der newen zwinglianer*, fol. Da; Morgenstern, op. cit., fol. Kb; Laurentius Petri, op. cit., fol. GIIb (compare the latter, Kjöllerström, op. cit., pp. 81f., 105).

332 Chemnitz, op. cit., p. 211.

333 Id., op. cit., p. 320. In order to support the Lutheran Christology concerning Christ's body being worthy of adoration, Chemnitz inserted the same quotation in his [*De duabus naturis in Christo*], p. 171 [cf. *Two Natures in Christ*, p. 420]. The same quotation is repeated later in the Catalog of Testimonies in the *Book of Concord*; see below, nn. 334–35.

334 PL 16:794 D = *BS* 1118.14f. [cf. Catalog of Testimonies III; *Triglotta* 1126–27].

335 PL 39:1264 = *BS* 1118.35f. [cf. Catalog of Testimonies III; *Triglotta* 1126–27].

336 Brenz, *Apologia Confessionis Wirtenbergensis*, in *Opera* 8:570.

337 Pedro de Soto, *Assertio catholicae fidei*, p. 93, in Brenz, *Opera*, vol. 8.

> the presence of Christ in the Supper along with the Sacramentarians. Nor indeed can the remembrance [*anámnesis*] and proclamation of Christ's death be done in the Supper without that adoration that is done in spirit and truth.[338]

This formulation is, as far as can be determined, the model for the Formula of Concord's statement when it has this rejection: "Also when it is taught[339] that the elements, the visible species or forms of the consecrated bread and wine, should

338 Chemnitz, op. cit., p. 321 [cf. *Examination of the Council of Trent*, 2:279]..

339 It ought to be noted that the initial rejection of the adoration of the outward forms *is not aimed at the Roman Church.* If any such polemic had been intended, it would have been taken up under the three anathemas against Rome (*BS* 1010.11ff. [cf. FC SD VIII 107–110]), where only adoration outside the liturgy is rejected. But that is not done except that "Also, where it is taught that the elements . . . should be adored" is listed as no. 15 among the 16 antitheses in the Solid Declaration (the final part of the Formula of Concord) directed against the Sacramentarians [cf. FC SD VII 126–127]. This does not mean that the adoration of the Sacrament (bread-worship [artolatry]) was a Reformed false doctrine, but indeed *that the Reformed incorrectly attributed this error to the Lutherans, which is why it must be rejected.* Clarity is gained if one considers the final antithesis, no. 16, in the Solid Declaration according to which the above is cited, or even better the parallel presentation in the Epitome (the first part of the Formula of Concord), which here for once is more extensive. No. 15 in the Solid Declaration is taken up as no. 19 here (*BS* 803.6ff. [cf. FC Ep VII 40–42]):

> 19. That the outward visible elements of bread and wine should be adored.
> 20. Likewise, we also entrust to the proper judgment of God all . . . blasphemous questions . . . brought with great offense by the Sacramentarians . . .
> 21. As we hereby completely condemn the Capernaitic eating, . . . which the Sacramentarians against the testimony of their conscience willfully impose upon us beyond all our repeated testimony, and in such a way make our doctrine hated among their hearers.

These statements thus are not directed against Rome or against any existing false doctrine whatsoever, but in fact against the maliciously fabricated accusations of artolatry and Capernaitism made by the Sacramentarians against Lutheranism. It is therefore completely wrong for the Göttingen edition of the Lutheran Confessions in this way to refer here to the Tridentine canons on the veneration of the Sacrament (*BS* 1016 n. 3). Furthermore, when the same edition (*BS* 1016 n. 2) refers to Saliger (compare above, pp. 273–74 n. 181 [Swedish edition, p. 246], which uses Melanchthon's examples of adoration as "examples of 'artolatry' on the Protestant side") and to Carpzov (*Isagoge*, p. 1458), which likewise, in following Melanchthon, rejects all adoration of Christ "(1) with [*cum*] bread and wine; (2) or in [*in*] bread and wine; (3) or through [*per*] bread and wine; (4) or in the presence of [*coram*] bread and wine"—then through this footnote-apparatus the text gets a meaning that is the opposite of what is actually there. The Göttingen edition's procedure is partly that they uncritically took up Frank (op. cit., 3:141). It is certainly true, as shall be presented more precisely above, that even Melanchthonians subscribed to the Formula of Concord and that they had views of exactly the type that Carpzov defines. The text as such, however, does not leave room for an interpretation such as the one in the Göttingen edition. Nor could the Melanchthonians here have read more than a demarcation against the Sacramentarians. On the other hand, Gnesio-Lutherans and Melanchthonians could

be adored; but Christ Himself, true God and man, who is truly and essentially present in the Supper in its true use, should be worshiped in spirit and truth, as well as in all other places, especially when His congregation is gathered—no one will deny this, or else he is an Arian heretic."[340] Chemnitz's defense of the adoration in the *Examination of the Council of Trent* is followed by a careful examination of Trent's wording. In this [the Decrees of the Council of Trent], he finds the statement: "That whole thing that was instituted by the Lord to be consumed must be adored with the ritual of *latria*."[341] Against this, Chemnitz points out that both earthly and heavenly things are found in the Eucharist. If the former should also be adored, artolatry arises. Chemnitz continues: "They indeed also fabricate their transubstantiation so that the substance of the bread is not worshiped at the same time"; that is, in order to avoid the accusation of bread worship, Rome has made up the theory about the change of substance. Under this condition, it is completely correct to say, "The whole thing must be adored." But as transubstantiation meanwhile is "uncertain," it becomes heretical to teach "that the whole thing must be adored." "To avoid idolatry, therefore, this careful distinction must made," Chemnitz writes, and adds, "The adoration must not be directed to the earthly elements of bread and wine, but to Christ as God and man, who in that action instituted and promised His presence as a special means of grace, just as the Israelites adored not wood, not gold, not the cherubim of the ark of the covenant, but only God Himself who had promised His presence there."[342] Note well—it is not a differentiation against an artolatry *practiced* in the

have interpreted the *positive* confession of the adoration in various ways. This shall be reported more precisely above.

340 *BS* 1016.4ff. [cf. FC SD VII 126]. Also the formulation "for he is an Arian heretic" has its paradigm in Chemnitz (op. cit., p. 320 [cf. *Examination of the Council of Trent*, 2:277]): "no one but an Arian denies." But it ought to be noted that Chemnitz's presentation is built on three points: only Arians deny that Christ should be adored; only Nestorians deny that the human nature should be adored; only Sacramentarians deny that Christ should be adored in the Sacrament. Through the Formula of Concord taking up [the expression] "no one but an Arian" on the adoration of the Sacrament, the Formula of Concord became easier for the south German school to accept as orthodox Lutheran in its Christology. [The south Germans] did not consider themselves to be Arian, and they allowed the adoration of Christ *at* the use of the Supper, but not *in* the elements. Through the omission of "no one . . . except with the Sacramentarians . . . denies," the absolute relation of real presence to adoration is no longer emphasized. Through these various minor [instances of] lack of clarity, the misunderstanding is created that would unite Gnesio-Lutherans and Melanchthonians by subscribing to the Formula of Concord.

341 Chemnitz, op. cit., p. 321 [cf. *Examination of the Council of Trent*, 2:279].

342 Ibid. [cf. *Examination of the Council of Trent*, 2:280]. (A similar passage is found in *Repetitio sanae doctrinae*, p. 207.) It continues, among other things, with the words "nor indeed is it held enclosed in them locally." This may not be interpreted as a criticism against the Roman concept of the presence, about which Chemnitz has just as

Roman Church but against a formulation in Trent.[343] In the same examination, Chemnitz expressly defends the correctness of adoring God, without special command, "under external and visible symbols" with an outward act, according to 1 Corinthians 14, falling down in *proskynésis* before holy men, "proclaiming

---

little to say as Luther. On the interpretation of the concept, compare above, pp. 167–68 n. 177 [Swedish edition, p. 154]. The statement *is not attacking Rome* but *rather defending Lutheranism*, which could only be attacked from the Reformed way of creating the local inclusion, which blends the divine and earthly into a new substance.

343 Westphal (op. cit., p. 306) writes: "If someone perhaps wrote or spoke about the adoration of the Sacrament or the Eucharist, must it therefore be presumed that he is adoring the bread?" Page 308:

> When the Sacrament or the Eucharist is called by the more excellent part—indeed, the celestial thing—I think that it is piously called the adoration of the Sacrament or Eucharist instead of calling it the adoration of Christ who is present in the Eucharist. Nevertheless, I would gladly abstain from ambiguous and dangerous ways of speaking, and it would be preferable to avoid them rather than to give occasion or material to risk, contention, and lies.

Unfortunately these wise words about the ambiguity of the terms of the Eucharist were not followed by Chemnitz. This action of thus criticizing Trent's "*totum adorandum*" ["the whole thing must be adored"] on Lutheran presuppositions (the incorrectness of transubstantiation) did not contribute to clarifying Chemnitz's own ambitions and gave rise to an interpretation that did not accord with these. So it happened with the Swedish bishop Petrus Melartopeus, who cites verbatim Chemnitz's stipulations here quoted above, but now as support for a correct procedure regarding the adoration and for abolishing the elevation. In a pastoral letter, Melartopeus writes (*P. Melartopeus' herdabrev till Åbo stifts prästerskap 1595*, p. 198): "The adoration must not be directed to any earthly elements, but to Christ who is God and man, who in that action instituted and promised His presence in a special means of grace." This quotation, in which "any" has simply been inserted and "*et veneratio*" ["and veneration"] has disappeared, can be seen as an evidence of the influence on Swedish church life already made by Cnattingius by this time from Chemnitz's *Examination of the Council of Trent* (Cnattingius, "Nikolaus Botniensis' teser om Skriften 1584 og Uppsala mötes beslut," pp. 161ff.). With regard to content, however, Melartopeus does not connect to Chemnitz. For Melartopeus, the people's demeanor in church at the elevation of the Sacrament is idolatry (*P. Melartopeus' herdabrev till Åbo stifts prästerskap 1595*, p. 196): "The uneducated people, who as soon as the elevation is done, gawk so greatly, thus showing that they are directing their prayer and adoration to the bread and the wine, which they see elevated." This view is very obviously in contrast to how the Lutheran proponents of the adoration defend the adoration of the host as popular piety; compare above, p. 303 n. 319 [Swedish edition, p. 272], put into print in Sweden in Laurentius Petri's words borrowed from George of Anhalt: "So that where someone would ask any one of the older uneducated people what he adores in the Sacrament, he would surely reply that he does not adore the bread and wine there, but Jesus Christ"; compare above, pp. 306–7 n. 326 [Swedish edition, p. 274]. The view of Melartopeus thus is not as closely in agreement with the earlier Swedish reformers as Andrén (op. cit., p. 278) thinks. Nor can Melartopeus be said to teach the eucharistic adoration, as was thought by Hellström (*Elevationsstriden och enighetsförbundet*, p. 88). Hellström at the same time, however, clearly sees (ibid.) the difference between the claim of Melartopeus that the people adore the bread and rejection of this accusation by Laurentius Petri.

that God is indeed in you."[344] Here various Old Testament examples are cited. The adoration that Chemnitz describes allows actual acts of faith to include adoration, in the way that was already described as possible in connection with the presentation of Luther.[345] Chemnitz thereby shows that faith can never really act without adoration toward the eucharistic Christ: "when in our thoughts and uncleanness and wretchedness, with our fervent prayers, we call upon Christ, God and man, whom we believe is truly and substantially present in that act, as He is our Mediator, Propitiator, Advocate, Intercessor, Justifier, and Savior."[346]

Brenz and Andreae

As already mentioned, Brenz in his *Apologia Confessionis* expressly rejects the adoration of the Sacrament. On the Augustine quotation that Petrus a Soto and Chemnitz both found to teach the eucharistic adoration, he comments: "Augustine is not speaking there about the Eucharist."[347] The adoration of God in the brothers is rejected as an impossibility: "We do not bow down on our knees before those men."[348] It also says, "God fills heaven and earth. Can it be therefore that heaven and earth must be adored?"[349] Certainly the adoration of Christ is conceded "always and everywhere, either in heaven or in earth, either in the Eucharist or outside the Eucharist," but this latter concession does not mean the adoration of the Sacrament, but simply that faith's continual adoration, of course, does not cease when receiving the Sacrament. At Communion, this applies: "He does not wish, however, that we honor Him by adoring the bread"; "He calls us away from artolatry [*artolatreia*] and leads us toward worship of Christ [*Christolatreia*]."[350] He rejects genuflecting when one calls out, "Have mercy on me, O God, according to Your great mercy."[351]

344 Chemnitz, op. cit., p. 320 [cf. *Examination of the Council of Trent*, 2:277–78].

345 Compare above, p. 244, paragraph that includes n. 55 [Swedish edition, pp. 222ff.].

346 Chemnitz, op. cit., p. 322 [cf. *Examination of the Council of Trent*, 2:282].

347 Brenz, op. cit., *Opera* 8:570.

348 Id., op. cit., p. 571; compare *P. Melartopeus' herdabrev till Åbo stifts prästerskap 1595*, p. 197: "One must not for that reason forbid the pious."

349 Brenz, ibid.

350 Brenz, op. cit., pp. 571f.

351 Brenz, op. cit., p. 571. On one occasion Brenz introduced the adoration in front of the monstrance, but the reasoning was basically directed against the adoration of the Mass; compare [Edward Frederick] Peters, op. cit., p. 54: "John Brenz seems to object to an adoration within the Mass itself." Consistent with his otherwise Melanchthonian view, in 1562 Brenz explained the question of the *reliqua* of the Sacrament as an adiaphoron. (Concerning Brenz's earlier view, however, see above, p. 110, text around n. 135 [Swedish edition, pp. 103f.].) The early church, which Brenz here finds ideal (Bidembach, *Consilia Theologica*, Decas III, pp. 110f.): "had no definite consistent order but here, as with an adiaphoron, used her permitted freedom, and no one was

[Jacob] Andreae's discussion of the sacramental adoration, in *How Each Christian Should Answer from His Catechism Why He No Longer Goes to Mass* from 1588, bears traces of following the presentation of Brenz, mentioned above. Andreae writes:

> It does not follow therefore, when one says Christ should be adored [and] Christ is in the Sacrament, that therefore one should also adore the Sacrament—as it also does not follow: God is in this or that creature; therefore, one should adore the creature. How much less should it be allowed to fall down before a piece of bread and adore it and to show it divine honor? It would also follow irrefutably that one must adore all peasants who in true faith had received the body and blood of Christ . . . and for whose sake He should be in the bread. . . . So it goes against the institution of Christ, who commanded us to eat the Sacrament and not to adore it.[352]

The adoration of the Sacrament is expressly said to be worse than the idolatry of the heathen. Using the reasoning concerning the purpose of the Sacrament as an answer to the question about the possibility of the adoration may be considered a typical Melanchthonian solution.[353]

Even in 1578, Andreae maintains this opinion of his in a letter to the elector of the Palatinate, in which he defends the then-completed Formula of Concord and Luther, against the elector's complaints that they teach sacramental adoration:

> Thus he [Luther] in no way endorses the papistic adoration or worship of the Sacrament but only teaches how one should go to the venerable Sacrament reverently, which the Holy Scripture also calls adoration, but he does not teach the adoration of the Sacrament in a papistic way. But in the event that this and similar things may be found in Dr. Luther's writings, it is not at all approved in the Book of Concord. . . .[354]

In the context, transubstantiation is specifically rejected, which the elector calls "idolatrous," and he is assured that Melanchthon's authority will not be minimized through the Formula of Concord. Andreae is keen to present the Formula of Concord in the best light to the elector, who clearly shows awe for Luther's solid doctrine of the Sacrament. The defense that Andreae thereby produces shows a certain amount of uncertainty about Luther's actual position. It

---

offended over this." Brenz cites, as an example, that they used the reservation of the Sacrament for the sick, that sometimes they gave the *reliqua* after the Mass to "innocent children." If offense might arise, everything should be completely consumed. In all these points, the congregation has complete freedom including the use of the Communion cloth; compare above, pp. 299–300 n. 310.

352 Printed in Bidembach, op. cit., Decas I, p. 86.

353 Compare CR 2:249: "on account of the man, not on account of the bread"; Gollwitzer, op. cit., p. 65.

354 Printed in Hutter, op. cit., fol. 145b.

is apparent that Andreae thereby also gives the Formula of Concord an interpretation that neither is in accord with the view that the majority of the other co-authors held, nor can it be reconciled with the fact that the document itself omits any rejection of the Roman adoration of the Sacrament in its use.

The *Solida Refutatio* gives a fundamental definition of "adoration in spirit and truth," which excludes the adoration of the Sacrament. "Although indeed God Himself may in reality be divinely [present] in whatever tree or wood, nevertheless He is not adored nor should He be adored for that reason in the tree, but in spirit and truth. So also in this mystery, the Christ who is present with His body is indeed adored, but not in the bread, but in spirit and truth."[355] Here adoration "in the *bread*" becomes the opposite of "in the *spirit*." The spirit becomes the opposite of the physical act, not the [opposite of a] wrong act without the gift of the Spirit.[356] The danger in adoring the Sacrament will no longer be that self-righteousness may make the adoration of the Sacrament into a substitute for receiving it in faith, as Luther thought might happen.[357] The adoration of the Sacrament becomes unspiritual because it is physical and directed toward a physical thing.

Andreae had expressed to the elector of the Palatinate some uncertainty regarding Luther's meaning. The *Solida Refutatio* again wants to correct this. Luther's writing *On the Adoration of the Sacrament* becomes the object of a careful exposition. It is pointed out that Luther found there that the "adoration" essentially in biblical phraseology refers precisely to the physical show of respect that is done identically toward both God and princes. It therefore ought to be distinguished from the actual expression "pray" [*beten, orare*], even if "adore" [*an-beten, ad-orare*, "pray toward"] gives the appearance of meaning "pray" [*bedja*, or "worship"].[358] From this the *Solida Refutatio* draws the following conclusion: "It affirms that the adoration of Christ in the Sacrament is not prayer, but nothing more than reverence that occurs internally in the heart and externally with the whole body, and it affirms that it is neither commanded nor forbidden by Christ."[359] Thus Luther's whole presentation is turned upside down.

355 [Andreae,] *Solida Refutatio*, p. 386.

356 Compare above, p. 277, text around n. 198 [Swedish edition, p. 250], and Brenz, "In evangelium Ioannis," *Opera* 6:199: "Therefore, God is not *flesh*. Or if He is not flesh, how does He seek carnal worshipers? . . . Indeed, even if the Son of God . . . assumed humanity [*hominem*], nevertheless God Himself according to His essence does not have human form, does not have physical eyes, hands, and feet. Then it is understood that God does not judge according to carnal reasoning, nor respect carnal worship, nor to be worshiped, as Paul said, by human hands, nor to be enclosed in one place, as flesh. . . ."

357 Compare above, pp. 242–43, text around n. 47 [Swedish edition, pp. 220f.].

358 [Andreae,] *Solida Refutatio*, p. 667.

359 Op. cit., p. 670.

For Luther it was essential that the outward "adoration" toward the Sacrament should be accompanied by true *internal* adoration: "From this outward adoration you may now mark what Christ calls a true spiritual adoration, namely, a reverence or bowing of the heart, whereby you show and confess from the bottom of your heart that you are His subservient creature."[360] The outward adoration or *proskynésis* before the Sacrament is identical in form with certain courtly gestures, but that certainly does not mean, as the *Solida Refutatio* seems to think, that Luther means that the adoration of the Sacrament is *something less than real adoration*, "nothing more than reverence," *mere* veneration, "since he understands it concerning only external and civil honor that is offered also to men, that is, to kings"![361] Despite the outward similarity, Luther thinks "the distinction is greater than between heaven and earth, for the heart considers God to be God, but the prince to be a man." By definition, the "adoration of the Sacrament" conceded by the *Solida Refutatio* belongs in the fourth objectionable group mentioned by Luther: "The fourth, those who adore Him only outwardly. These last are good for nothing; enough has been said about them."[362]

---

360 WA 11:446.13ff. [cf. AE 36:293].

361 [Andreae,] *Solida Refutatio*, p. 667.

362 WA 11:449.24f. [cf. AE 36:296]. This view of the adoration is identical with Cruciger's proposal to make the adoration into something less than latreia; compare above, p. 98 n. 89 and p. 111 n. 142 [Swedish edition, p. 93]. In accord with Brenz and Andreae is *Iudicium und Bericht M. Georgij Condonij Superintendentis zu Laugingen / gestellet in Anno 1572 uber der Frag: Ob man das Sacrament anbetten soll*, Bidembach, op. cit., Dec. IX, pp. 66f. Here the adoration is allowed only as a conversation of the heart with Christ at Communion. Beyer (*Abendmahl und Messe*, pp. 55f.) writes about the Heidelberg Catechism's anathema on bread worship (1563):

> The Lutheran Supper is not included in this judgment. Apparently in the view of the Heidelberg theologians there was no continuation of the adoration in Lutheranism. [Note 43: In fact this usage of the adoration in the Supper was still retained in Lutheranism and was interpreted as a gesture of thanks for its gifts.] That is the only way to explain their consistently noted criticism of the absence of the adoration, which must not be absent when one takes seriously the bodily presence of Christ in the Sacrament. . . . But when it comes to the implementation of the adoration among the Lutherans, it cannot be said by them that "those who want [to say that] the true Christ is bodily in the bread, but deny that He must be adored in it, rob Christ of His honor."

The Lutheranism that the Heidelberg theologians here had in mind must be the Württemberg-Melanchthonian type. Through the Book of Concord a different Lutheranism came into view and gave rise to a different stance; compare above in the text. The Lutheran adoration existed at this point in time even within the Upper Palatinate; compare Götz, *Die Erste Einführung des Kalvinismus in der Oberpfalz 1559–1576*, p. 10: "Even in the Palatinate, the people had not stopped adoring the Lord's body in the host, [and] some ministers expressly told the people they held in their hands the true and essential body of the Lord."

Even the Reformed view, of course, conceded what was proper in the adoration of Christ in celebrating the Supper, in the sense of an intensified adoration of the heavenly Christ. The so-called Neustadt Admonition [*Admonitio Neostadiensis*], directed against the *Book of Concord* and in turn prompting the *Apology of the Book of Concord*, writes: "But it is a far different thing to adore Christ always and everywhere, particularly moreover in the use of the Lord's Supper, where one is not filled unless he is hungry, that is, that he sincerely desires the Communion of Christ [more] than to adore Him in the bread. This ceremonial adoration, directed to the place of the bread, . . . which undoubtedly is idolatrous. . . ."[363] About the *Book of Concord* it says, "They condemn the adoration of the elements, bread and wine. But they establish the adoration of the Christ in the elements, which the Papists require, which Luther left free, [and] which their associates defended even in published books. And with the bodily presence of Christ sensibly posited in the bread, the honor of adoration cannot be denied to Him in the bread. . . ."[364] This Reformed presentation does greater justice to Luther and to the opinion that the main part of the north German brothers of the Concordia read in the *Book of Concord* than what Andreae and the *Solida Refutatio* may be considered to have done. This way of handling it need not be ascribed to Andreae's diplomatic ingenuity, which otherwise gained him many detractors.[365] There is no indication that the discord was evident to the north and south German participants in Lutheranism's theological work of unity [the *Book of Concord*]. The distance between Württemberg and northern Germany was great, and no regular connection existed between the churches. Only occasionally did there arise a vague sense that the obvious liturgical differences between the richness in the north and the austerity in the south might conceal something.[366] Otherwise unity could easily have been achieved on the statement that says nothing in and of itself, [the statement] that bread and wine should not be adored in the use of the Supper, but rather Christ [should be adored]. The Roman use of the Sacrament *extra usum* could also have been characterized by both sides as idolatry. So, from both sides, one could in good conscience speak about mutual unity.

363 *De libro concordiae . . . Admonitio*, pp. 320f.

364 Ibid.

365 Compare here Heppe, op. cit., 4:256f.

366 Compare Heppe, op. cit., 4:53, Hamburg's statement on the Swabian Concord: "For one hears that the Swabian churches in their ceremonies very much depart from the custom of the Lower Saxons. Also Swabia was very far from these lands, so that one could not interact with the churches there with very active communication"; compare id., p. 51.

The Formula of Concord

The ducal edict, which by church authority decided the controversy about Saliger on the part of Mecklenburg, partially ended up in the Lord's Supper section of the Formula of Concord.[367] The theological sections of the edict are thought to have been authored by Chytraeus, though this cannot be confirmed with complete clarity.[368] Of course, the Rostock faculty under the leadership of Chytraeus could see their own thoughts about *usus* represented in the Formula of Concord's use of the Recess [*Abschied*]. But the section used is very short and says only that the *extra usum* rule makes it so that the Sacrament does not exist in the Roman private Mass. But the Recess being brought to the fore through the long process that culminated in the Formula of Concord would have depended most likely on Chemnitz. The reconciliation, which Chemnitz effected between Lübeck's pastors and the layman Lambert Fredeland on June 30, 1574, with reference to the Recess,[369] occurred at a conference that meant the beginning of Andreae's[370] examination of the so-called Swabian Concord, where the section

---

367 *BS* 1000.27–1001.15.[[FC SD VII 83–85].

368 Frank, op. cit., 3:147 n. 144; compare Wismar theologian Holthüter's records, Wiggers, op. cit., pp. 643f.

369 Schöne, op. cit., pp. 21f. The vastness of the edict's statements comes out in this case. Already in Lübeck's own confession on June 9, 1574, the Recess [*Abschied*] was quoted extensively (compare what is printed in Starck, op. cit., pp. 456f.) in order to encounter a typical Melanchthonian exposition. (This quotation is not identified in Schöne, op. cit., pp. 20, 37f.) The idiosyncrasy of this confession was obscure to Schöne (op. cit., ibid.), just as it once was for Chemnitz, who follows Wigand's trusting attitude toward Rostock, and who in the end presents Lübeck's doctrine so positively to the strict Beatian [Saligerian] Fredeland "that he declared that he did not know that the ministerium taught the way it now presents its doctrine, and apologized" (Schöne, op. cit., pp. 21f.). This whitewashing of Lübeck seems to have become too much even for Lukas Bacmeister; compare Starck, op. cit., p. 285; Schöne, op. cit., p. 22:

> The disclaimers that Fredeland makes in relation to his conviction of how sincere the doctrine of the ministers was do not seem to have been completely unwarranted. Yet [perhaps] Bacmeister himself saw the objective as still [being able to] persuade the assembly [*Convent*] subsequently, not only on account of the type and manner of its polemics against Fredeland but also for this reason, that some had "not spoken before the assembly very correctly and accurately about the three essential parts of the holy Supper and its consecration."

Thus Bacmeister points out that at this point in time Rostock held the third part of the Sacrament to be the command of God [*mandatum Dei*] and not the *actio*. The actual outcome, however, remained the same as earlier, through the consecration being verified by the *sumptio* ["eating"]; compare above, pp. 297–98, paragraph that includes n. 302 [Swedish edition, p. 267].

370 Heppe, op. cit., 4:44ff.; Schöne and Heppe do not put these two facts together.

on *extra usum* was lacking.[371] It seems natural that this coincidence influenced the use of the Recess. In the Swabian-Saxon Concord, which was the result of that elaboration, a section on the consecration was added, where part of the Recess is reprinted.[372] The actual editing of this Concord, which builds on submissions from interested parties, however, was in the hands of the Rostock faculty.[373] Regardless of who inspired the Rostock faculty through their submissions, this is then actually responsible for the appearance of certain parts of the Recess in the confession that after minor changes became the Formula of Concord itself.[374] The Saliger controversy can be used as an answer key in reading the section on the consecration in the new confessional writing that came about in this way. Even the Gnesio-Lutherans were wholeheartedly able to approve the formulations, which nevertheless always leave room for the special thesis of Rostock and the rest of Melanchthonianism: only the action completed through the eating proves the consecration's legitimacy. Compared to the Danzig Book, outwardly it seems that one could chalk up a sure victory on the part of the Gnesio-Lutherans: the consecration effects the presence; "[it] is efficacious through the spoken Word, by virtue of the first institution, yet

371 Compare here the text in Heppe, op. cit., III; Beilage, I, p. 75. (Note! Wrong heading: "Die schwäbisch-sächsische Concordie" should be "schwäbische Concordie"; compare Heppe, op. cit., III, p. IV n. 1.)

372 Compare here the text in Heppe, op. cit., III, Beilagen, pp. 269ff.

373 Heppe, op. cit., 3:50. The whole section on the Supper is ascribed to Chytraeus personally by Montgomery (op. cit., p. 21, with reference to [George J.] Fritschel, *The Formula of Concord: Its Origin and Contents* (Philadelphia[: Lutheran Publication Society], 1916), p. 102. Heppe (op. cit., 3:52) thinks that the chapters on free will and the Supper were completely newly written by the faculty in Rostock and that the *former* of these can be ascribed to Chytraeus. No clear picture of the sequence of events is given in the literature. A completely new research effort is needed here. Ritschel, Frank, and Heppe are too dependent on older literature (Saliger, Seckendorf). It would be desirable if the four-hundredth anniversary of the origin of the Book of Concord (1980) could be celebrated on the basis of a newly written, thoroughly historical examination.

374 Chytraeus viewed these minor changes as personally insulting and for this reason withdrew from the closing negotiations in the Bergen Cloister (Heppe, op. cit., 3:206 n. 2). Chytraeus himself in his displeasure explained that none of his contributions remained, which is an immoderate exaggeration, however (compare Montgomery, op. cit., ibid.). Among the things excised in the Lord's Supper section is an extensive inquiry into the various causes of the Sacrament. It may be said to have formed a framework for Chytraeus's and Rostock's Melanchthonian-philosophical concept of *actio*. Its removal is a reminder that it is impossible to consider the Recess and the Formula of Concord identical. But the removal actually happened not because some Gnesio-Lutheran realized the connection, but it was really only a matter of paring down Chytraeus's somewhat pedantic verbiage.

through His Word, which He then wants to have repeated."[375] Meanwhile, from a Melanchthonian viewpoint, this concession was well balanced through the proviso: "But this blessing by itself, . . . where the whole action . . . is not held . . . , makes no Sacrament."[376] An analysis of a joint document of this kind can go no further. One only knows what the various signers meant by "consecration," "presence," etc., by studying their private writings. The *status controversiae* can be discovered and confirmed in only two ways: either by a direct examination of the term *actio* or indirectly by a dogmatic investigation on the elevation, adoration, and the *reliqua* of the Sacrament. The view of the various signers has been traced in the foregoing, and the differences have been noted. Neither is there any reason here to imagine a compromise. Not even the Wismar theologians, who heavily criticized Rostock and called down God's curse on the city, could state what Rostock's doctrine [actually] was, only what they did *not* want to say.[377] Signing the Formula of Concord on this point, therefore, actually included only the rejection of the Roman doctrine of the *usus* and a very marginal identification of *usus* and *sumptio*: "not only the oral reception."[378]

Already in the Swabian-Saxon Concord there is a reference to Luther in connection with the investigations around *extra usum*: "This rule, first of all, is directed against such papistic misuses, and was stated by Dr. Luther himself, volume 4, Jena edition."[379] In contrast to the other quotations, information about the intended page is missing here. Nor is anything like that included along with the reference in the Formula of Concord.[380] Nor have the various editions of the Book of Concord during the following centuries been able to contribute the more

---

375 *BS* 998.36ff. [cf. FC SD VII 75]. The words "through the spoken Word, by virtue of the first institution" were introduced after a proposal from Prussia (*BS* 998 n. 1). Compare here Bacmeister's words, above, p. 318 n. 369.

376 *BS* 1000.27ff. [cf. FC SD VII 83].

377 Compare Wiggers, op. cit., p. 645. This, of course, does not mean that all the participants working on the Concordia were unaware of the actual differences here. Found among the authors of the Torgau Articles (compare above, pp. 304–5 n. 322) is the first court preacher, Dr. Martin Mirus (compare Heppe, op. cit., 2:430). Two years later, consistent with this, at the convent in Lichtenberg (Heppe, op. cit., 3:91), Mirus attacks Andreas Musculus, one of the authors of the Formula of Concord, for, among other things, "transubstantiation, artolatry." The same Mirus is among the first of the subscribers to the Book of Concord: *Concordia Christliche, Widerholete, einmütige Bekentnijs* (Dresden, 1580), fol. α1. This is one of the cases where some compromise must have been made.

378 *BS* 1001.17f. [cf. FC SD VII 86]. Thus at any rate, some of Peristerus's statements were affected; compare above, p. 294 n. 290.

379 Heppe, op. cit., III, Beilage III, p. 272.

380 *BS* 1001.36 [cf. FC SD VII 87].

precise identification of the reference.[381] The letter to Karlstadt is reproduced in part 4 of the German Jena edition, but though that was used in the controversy against Saliger and cited in the Recess [*Abschied*], it cannot in any way be said to be an explanation of the rule about *extra usum*. The Formula of Concord apparently thought it could invoke Luther for the actual expression "Nothing has the character of a Sacrament outside the use instituted by Christ or outside the instituted action."[382] The only reasonable solution is that the reference has in view the Latin Jena edition, part 4, folio 486bf., where Luther's correspondence with Wolferinus is reproduced with its explicit: "Truly Dr. Philip wrote correctly that there is no Sacrament outside the sacramental action."[383] This is much more credible as the letters were taken up for discussion several times during the earlier controversies.[384] The very different interpretations of Luther's opinion that were offered by this make it completely impossible to deduce any dogmatic position by reference to these letters. Formally confessionalizing the correspondence with Wolferinus thus says nothing about how *extra usum* and the *reliqua* of the Sacrament were understood. All sides could find their views within the framework of the expressions in these letters. It was simply a mutual proposition for all of them that the *reliqua* ought to be consumed. The dogmatic meaning [of this proposition] remained unresolved.[385]

---

381 The statement is missing, among others, in subsequent editions: *Concordia Christliche, Widerholete, einmütige Bekentnijs* (Dresden, 1580), fol. 301a; *Concordia Christliche Widerholete einmütige Bekentnüs* (Tübingen, 1580), fol. 209b; *Concordia Christliche Widerholete, einmütige Bekentnis* (Dresden, 1581), fol. 349b; *Concordia Pia . . .* (Leipzig, 1584), p. 726; *Concordia, Christliche, widerholete, einmütige Bekentnis* (Leipzig, 1622), p. 301; *Concordia Pia . . .* (Leipzig, 1626), p. 750; *Concordia Pia . . .* (Leipzig, 1719), p. 750; *Libri symbolici . . . recensuit Carolus Augustus Hase* (Leipzig, 1846), p. 780; *Die symbolischen Bücher der Evangelisch-Lutherischen Kirche*, ed. J. T. Müller, 3rd ed. (Stuttgart, 1868), p. 666. The Göttingen edition (*BS* 1001 n. 2) refers to WA 30/2:254f., but this reference is obviously incorrect, pointed out also by [Edward Frederick] Peters (op. cit., p. 119). The writing intended with this reference, *Vermahnung an die Geistlichen zu Augsburg*, is found in the German Jena edition, part 5, and does not take up the rule about *extra usum* for theological treatment but only rejects certain misuses in connection with it.

382 *BS* 1001.7f. [cf. FC SD VII 85].

383 *Tomus quartus et idem ultimus omnium Reverendi Patris . . . Mart. Lutheri* (Jena, 1561), fol. 487a.

384 Compare above, p. 293 n. 284 [Swedish edition, p. 263]. Compare also how Wigand in 1585, in summary form on the treatment of *extra usum*, writes (*De sacramentarijsmo*, fol. 212b): "Also Luther in the letter to Wolferinus, Latin volume 4. Truly Philip wrote correctly: There is no Sacrament outside the sacramental action." For Wigand, who was recognized by both parties as an arbitrator in the Saliger controversy, it was thus natural to point out the letter to Wolferinus as constituting Luther's support for the statement about *extra usum*.

385 Compare [Edward Frederick] Peters, op. cit., p. 422: "If one judges from the statements of some of the church orders, however, one may take it for granted that many German

The modern edition of the Lutheran Confessions, as already shown, wants to interpret the various statements about *usus* in light of the view of the Melanchthonian school. A conclusive example of this will be given, along with its consequences within the research and modern doctrinal formation. In the last part of the anathemas in the Solid Declaration against Reformed errors, it says that coarse, physical questions about the Sacrament's heavenly mysteries are rejected.[386] The Epitome, the parallel text to the Solid Declaration, gives a clarifying comment here, when in a similar formulation it continues: "Also then we hereby condemn the Capernaitic eating of the body of Christ, as if one tears His flesh with the teeth."[387] The whole time this has to do with the Reformed accusations against Lutheranism, "brought forward by the Sacramentarians with great offense,"[388] "which the Sacramentarians willfully force upon us ... against the testimony of their conscience."[389] The Göttingen edition cites here as commentary "*Kurtz Bekenntnis 1571 H 1.2*," from which are cited statements that reject the Capernaitic eating but also [reject] any expression about the

Lutherans followed Luther's advice to consume all of the remaining elements. None of the writers under discussion suggest following Melanchthon," that is, to consign the *reliqua* to profane [nonreligious] use. But, for Melanchthon, this was only a dogmatic possibility and not advice to be put into practice. For this reason, which Peters does not notice, Melanchthonianism could very well follow Lutheran practice without embracing Lutheran doctrine.

386 *BS* 1016.16f. [cf. FC SD VII 127].

387 *BS* 803.20f. [cf. FC Ep VII 42].

388 *BS* 803.16f. [cf. FC Ep VII 41].

389 *BS* 803.23ff. [cf. FC Ep VII 42]. Capernaitic eating means that Christ's body, upon being received, would be crushed and subjected to the same conditions that apply to the elements otherwise, from which follows the conclusion: "which is not to be said, for the sake of modesty" (*BS* 803.11f. [cf. FC Ep VII 41]). Luther did not hold such a view, which Gollwitzer (op. cit., p. 205) suggests. Luther's affirmation of Berengar's confession ("to be torn with the teeth of the faithful") is preceded by (WA 26:442.35f. [cf. AE 37:300]) "and yet it always remains true that no one sees, grasps, eats, or chews the body of Christ the way one visibly sees and chews other flesh" (compare above, p. 145 n. 99 [Swedish edition, p. 135]). Gollwitzer also cites the instructions for the doctrinal colloquy in Cassel in 1534, in which the pointed expression of a Capernaitic type is supposed to be included, and he refers to the instructions printed in Enders 10:94. Obviously Gollwitzer did not actually make use of Enders, but the Erlangen edition 55:70, since he overlooks the fact that Enders took out the words, as they are not included in the original (compare WA 30:298), which reprints the text according to the original in Corpus Christi College in Cambridge. — The Colloquy in Worms rejected the thought that Christ's body was united with the wafer even after the eating, with the statement (CR 9:278): "After this use, when the bread is being digested in the stomach, the bread is different"; compare Salig, op. cit., 3:303f. Not only Melanchthon and Brenz but also Jacob Rungius, who was a defender of the adoration (compare above, p. 280, after n. 204 [Swedish edition, pp. 252f.]) subscribed to this statement. In 1559 after the Diet of Augsburg, Andreae polemicized against Roman belief and practice on this particular point; compare Salig, op. cit., 3:422 n. (h).

moment of the presence.[390] Sasse joins this form of commentary and on this point has the Formula of Concord anathematize temporal fixing of the consecration's effect.[391] With reference to the Göttingen edition and Sasse's use of it, both theological faculties at St. Louis and Springfield [now Fort Wayne] in North America, belonging to a modern Lutheran church body [The Lutheran Church—Missouri Synod], cited "*Kurtz Bekenntnis 1571*, a forerunner of the Formula of Concord," as support for rejecting any determinations of the beginning of the presence and for the assertion that the Sacrament's character as means of grace excludes "speculative questions."[392]

But the Göttingen edition's comment is incorrect. The intended writing is not *Kurtze, Christliche und Einfeltige Widerholung der Bekentnis der Kirchen Gottes* from 1571, also called the Dresden *Abschied*, as the formulation seems to indicate. This writing, moreover, within the circles around the Formula of Concord was expressly considered to be heretical.[393] This has to do, instead, with the *Kurtz Bekenntnis und Artickel vom heiligen Abendmahl des Leibes und Bluts Christi* from the year 1574, also called the "Torgau Articles," which coincide with ecclesiastical change in electoral Saxony that same year, when a Calvinist conspiracy was uncovered and a great theological purge was undertaken.[394] Although the Torgau Articles, seen from this viewpoint, were a step toward Lutheran orthodoxy, there is no way they can be seen as forerunners to the Formula of Concord. The Articles dissociate themselves from the omnipresence of Christ's body, the real communication of attributes,[395] and the adoration of the Sacrament.[396] The first two doctrinal points were essential for all who collaborated on the Formula of Concord. The main author [of the Articles] soon had to defend himself against accusations of Calvinism, and men such as Wigand and Selnecker vehemently attacked the Articles.[397] The Torgau Articles do not lend themselves very well as an exposition of the Formula of Concord's own meaning, even less as the Formula of Concord itself comments on this point.

---

390 *BS* 1016 n. 4.

391 Sasse, op. cit., p. 176. Sasse gives an otherwise completely correct picture of the teaching by Luther and Gnesio-Lutheranism on *usus*, adoration, and elevation, but tries to reconcile this with the assertion of a nontemporal presence, which seems dependent on modern perceptions of the early church's view of consecration; compare id., op. cit., pp. 172f.

392 "Brief Studies," pp. 530f.

393 *BS* 841 n. 1.

394 Heppe, op. cit., 2:431; Schmid, *Der Kampf der lutherischen Kirche um Luthers Lehre vom Abendmahl im Reformationszeitalter*, p. 261.

395 *Kurtz Bekenntnis*, fol. EIIa; Ritschl, op. cit., 4:68.

396 *Kurtz Bekenntnis*, fol. HIIa; compare here above, pp. 304–5 n. 322 [Swedish edition, p. 273].

397 Heppe, op. cit., 2:440; Schmid, op. cit., p. 286; Ritschl, op. cit., 4:67.

On the other hand, there is a certain similarity between the *Mecklenburg Edict* of 1569, "how and when and in what way the bread in the Supper is the body of Christ,"[398] and the *Kurtz Bekenntnis* of 1574, "when and how the body of Christ comes to the bread or enters into the bread."[399] [400] The similarity would go back to the Melanchthonian tradition common to both, to both of them being mediated by Paul Eber, who was highly regarded even by Chytraeus, the source for the Recess [*Abschied*],[401] as well as the *Kurtz Bekenntnis*.[402] Thus in the modern text edition of the writing that was to summarize and solve the Lutheran doctrinal controversies, we find an explanation that by its implementation reminds us that it was the Melanchthonian school that would come to bring home the victory when a new century came. With that, older Lutheranism's concrete faith in the Sacrament was sentenced to be rejected as medieval and could no longer be defended or even understood. Its worship practice ceased.[403] The views lying behind this may be presumed to have been relegated to popular piety, there to sleep their hibernation.

398 Wiggers, op. cit., p. 638.

399 *Kurtz Bekenntnis*, fol. HIIa.

400 [The Swedish edition numbers footnotes up to 99, then restarts at 1, which this translation lists as 101, 201, etc.]

401 Chytraeus, *Epistola*, pp. 1007f.: "*praeceptor meus*"; "Concerning the Lord's Supper, I embrace it . . . just as it is stated and defended in the confession of the Wittenberg pastor, Dr. Paul Eber, Wittenberg."

402 *Kurtz Bekenntnis*, fol. Db; Ritschl, op. cit., 4:167 n. 139 (incorrect citation of the folio).

403 On abolishing the elevation, compare Graff, *Geschichte der Auflösung der alten gottesdienstlichen Formen in der evangelischen Kirche Deutschlands*, 1:191f. In Görlitz, for example, the elevation was abolished first in 1689, while elsewhere it could be preserved still into the 1700s.

Bibliography

Aalen, Leiv. "Der Kampf um das Evangelium im Abendmahl: Bezeichnen die Arnoldshainer Thesen einen Friedensschluss?" *Theologische Literaturzeitung* 91, no. 2 (February 1966).

Acta colloquij Montisbellisgartensis. Wittenberg: [Myliandrinis], 1613.

Acta der Disputation zu Flensburg / die Sache des Hochwirdigen Sacraments betreffend / im 1529. Jar / des Donnerstags nach Quasimodo geniti / geschehen. Wittenberg: [Josef Klug], 1529.

Acta et scripta publica ecclesiae Wirtembergicae: recensuit Pfaffius. Tübingen: [Cotta], 1720.

Ahlberg, Bo. *Laurentius Petris nattvardsuppfattning*. Studia theologica lundensia 26. Academic dissertation. Lundg: [Gleerup], 1964.

Althaus, Paul. *Die christliche Wahrheit*. Gütersloh: [C. Bertelsmann], 1952.

———. *Die Theologie Martin Luthers*. Gütersloh: [G. Mohn], 1962. [English translation: *The Theology of Martin Luther*. Translated by Robert C. Schultz. Philadelphia: Fortress, 1966.]

———. "Luthers Abendmahlslehre." *Lutherjahrhuch* 11 (1929).

Andreae, Jacob. *Assertio piae et orthodoxae doctrinae de personali unione, qua respondetur ad primam partem libri Theodori Beze Vezelij* . . . Tübingen: [Morhart], 1565.

———. *De maiestate hominis Christi, eiusque in Eucharistia praesentia* . . . Tübingen: [Morhart], 1565.

———. *Pia, breuis et perspicua expositio controuersiae de duabus naturis in Christo*. Tübingen: [Morhart], 1565.

———. *Repetitio sanae doctrinae reverendissimi in Christo Patris D. D. Martini Lutheri, de persona Christi et de coena Dominica*. Wittenberg: [Crato], 1580.

———. *Solida Refutatio Compilationis Cinglianae et Caluinianae*. Tübingen: [Gruppenbach], [1584].

Andrén, Åke. *Högmässa och nattvärdsgång i reformationstidens svenska kyrkoliv*. Samlingar och studier till Svenska Kyrkans historia 32. Edited by Hilding Pleijel. Stockholm: [Svenska Kyrkans Diakonistyrelses Bokförlag], 1954.

Apologia: Gründlicher Gegenbericht / warhafftige erzelung der Histori des erhabenen und gefürten streits / und Abhandlung der unchristlichen getichten beschwerlichen aufflagen / damit Benedict Morgenstern in seiner vormeinten Widerlegung der Formulae Concordiae oder Notel. Danzig: [Rhode], 1567.

Apologia oder verantwortung des Christlichen Concordien Buchs / In welcher die ware christliche Lehre / so im Concordi Buch verfasset / mit gutem Grunde heiliger Göttlicher Schrifft vertheidiget: Die Verkehrung aber und Calumnien so von unrühigen Leuchten wider gedachtes christlich Buch im Druck aufgesprenget / widerlegt werden. Magdeburg: [Franck], 1584. [English translation: *Apology or Vindication of the Christian Book of Concord.* Translated by James L. Langebartels. Edited by Kevin G. Walker. Chemnitz's Works 10. St. Louis: Concordia Publishing House, 2018].

Arnold, Franz Xaver. *Zur Frage des Naturrechts bei Martin Luther: Ein Beitrag zum Problem der natürlichen Theologie auf reformatorischer Grundlage.* Munich: [Hueber], 1937.

Asendorf, Ulrich. "Zur Frage der *materia coelestis* in der lutherischen Abendmahlslehre." In *Lutherische Abendmahlslehre heute.* [Edited by Hans Wenschkewitz.] Göttingen: [Vandenhoeck & Ruprecht], 1960.

Backes, Ignaz. "Die Christologie des hl. Thomas v. Aquin und die griechischen Kirchenväter." *Forschungen zur Christlichen Literatur- und Dogmengeschichte* 17 (1931).

Bacmeister, Lukas. *Christliche Anleitung wie Ern Johannis Rhuelii . . . Predigt vom Hochwürdigen Nachtmahl des Herrn . . . sey.* Rostock: [Fueß], 1619.

Baier, J. W. *Compendium theologiae.* Edited by C. F. W. Walther. Amended edition. Volume 3. St. Louis: [Concordia Publishing House], 1879.

———. *Compendium Theologiae positivae secundum anni 1694.* Edited by Eduard Preuss. Berlin: [Schlawitz], 1864.

Balthasar, Jacob Henrich von. *Erste Sammlung Einiger zur Pommerischen Kirchen-Historie gehörigen Schriften.* Greiffswald: [Buße], 1723.

Bejerholm, Lars, and Gottfried Hornig. *Wort und Handlung: Untersuchungen zur analytischen Religionsphilosophie.* Gütersloh: [Gütersloher], 1966.

Bellarmine, Robert. *Disputationes* 3. Ingolstadt: [Sartorius], 1605.

Benckert, Heinrich. *Die Stofflichkeit der Abendmahlsgabe: Zum Gespräch über die Arnoldshainer Abendmahlsthesen.* Unio und Confessio 2. Witten: [Luther-Verlag], 1961.

Bergsma, Johannes H. *Die Reform der Messliturgie durch Johannes Bugenhagen (1485–1558).* Hildesheim: [Bernward], 1966.

Beyer, Ulrich. *Abendmahl und Messe: Sinn und Recht der 80. Frage des Heidelberger Katechismus.* Beiträge zur Geschichte und Lehre der reformierten Kirche 19. Neukirchen: [Neukirchener], 1965.

Beyschlag, Friedrich Jacob. *Versuch einer vollständigen Lebens-Beschreibung Joh. Brentii.* Part 1. Hall in Schwaben: [Mayer], 1735.

Bidembach, Felix, ed. *Consilia Theologica.* Frankfurt am Main: [Berner], 1607–14.

Biel, Gabriel. *Canonis misse expositio*. Edited by Heiko A. Oberman and William J. Courtenay. 4 volumes. Veröffentlichungen des Instituts für europäische Geschichte Mainz 31–34. Abteilung abendländische Religionsgeschichte. Wiesbaden: [Steiner], 1963–67.

———. *Epitome et collectorium ex Occamo circa quatuor sententiarum Libros*. Tübingen, 1501. Frankfurt/Main: [Minerva], 1965.

Bindseil, H. E. *Philippi Melanchthonis epistolae*. Halle: [Schwetschke], 1874.

Birch, Bruce T., ed. *The De Sacramento Altaris of William of Ockham*. [Burlington], IA: [Lutheran Library Board], 1930.

Bizer, Ernst. *Fides ex auditu: Eine Untersuchung über die Entdeckung der Gerechtigkeit Gottes durch Martin Luther*. Third expanded edition. Neukirchen: [Neukirchener], 1966.

———. "Glaube und Demut in Luthers Vorlesung über den Römerbrief." In *Luther und Melanchthon: Referate und Berichte des Zweiten Internationalen Kongresses für Lutherforschung, Münster, 8–13 August 1960*. Edited by Vilmos Vajta. Göttingen: [Vandenhoeck & Ruprecht], 1961.

———. "Martin Butzer und der Abendmahlsstreit: Unbekannte und unveröffentlichte Aktenstücke zur Entstehungsgeschichte der Wittenberger Konkordie vom 29. Mai 1536." *Archiv für Reformationsgeschichte* 35–36 (1938–39).

———. *Studien zur Geschichte des Abendmahlsstreits im 16. Jahrhundert*. Beiträge zur Förderung christlicher Theologie 2. Sammlung wissenschaftlicher Monographien 46. Gütersloh: [Bertelsmann], 1940.

Böhner, Philotheus. "A Recent Presentation of Ockham's Philosophy." *Franciscan Studies* 9, no. 4 (1949). (= *Collected Articles on Ockham*. Franciscan Institute Publications Philosophy Series 12. St. Bonaventure: [Franciscan Institute], 1958).

Bonaventura. *Opera omnia*. Florence: Ad Claras Aquas (Quaracchi). 1889.

Bonniwell, William. *A History of the Dominican Liturgy*. New York: [Wagner], 1944.

Brecht, Martin. *Die frühe Theologie des Johannes Brenz*. Beiträge zur historischen Theologie 36. Tübingen: [Mohr], 1966.

Brenz, Johann. *Catechismus piae [!] et utili explicatione illustratus*. s.l., 1555.

———. *De personali unione duarum naturarum in Christo, et ascensu Christi in coelum, ac sessione eius ad dextram Dei patris. Qua vera corporis et sanguinis Christi praesentia in coena explicata est et confirmata*. Tübingen: [Morhart], 1561.

———. *Elenchi paradoxorum . . . a ministris ecclesiae Bremensis*. Bremen: [Wessel], 1585.

———. *Opera*. Volumes 6 and 8. Tübingen: [Gruppenbach], 1584, 1590.

"Brief Studies: The Moment of the Real Presence in the Lord's Supper." *Concordia Theological Monthly* 30 (July 1959).

Brilioth, Yngve. *Nattvarden i evangeliskt gudstjänstliv*. [Second edition.] Stockholm: [Svenska Kyrkans Diakonistyrelses Bokförlag], 1951.

Bring, Ragnar. "On the Lutheran Concept of the Sacrament." In *World Lutheranism of Today: A Tribute to Anders Nygren*. Oxford: [Blackwell], 1950.

Brunner, Peter. "Die dogmatische und kirchliche Bedeutung des Ertrages des Abendmahlsgesprächs." In *Lehrgespräch über das Heilige Abendmahl: Stimmen und Studien zu den Arnoldsheiner Thesen*. Edited by Gottfried Niemeier. Munich: [Kaiser], 1961.

———. *Pro Ecclesia: Gesammelte Aufsätze zur dogmatischen Theologie*. 2 volumes. Berlin and Hamburg: [Lutherisches Verlagshaus], 1962–66.

———. *Zur Lehre vom Gottesdienst der im Namen Jesu versammelten Gemeinde Leiturgia*. Handbuch des evangelischen Gottesdienstes 1. Kassel: [Stauda], 1954. [English translation: *Worship in the Name of Jesus*. Translated by Martin H. Bertram. St. Louis: Concordia Publishing House, 1968, 2003.]

Buescher, Gabriel. *The Eucharistic Teaching of William Ockham*. Franciscan Institute Publications Theology Series 1. St. Bonaventure, NY: [Franciscan Institute], 1950, [1974].

Bugenhagen, Johannes. *Dr. Johannes Bugenhagens Briefwechsel*. Edited by Otto Vogt. Baltische Studien. [Stettin: Saunier,] 1888.

Carpzov, Johann Benedict. *Isagoge in libros . . . symbolicos*. Leipzig: [Wittigau], 1675.

Chemnitz, Martin. *De duabus naturis in Christo*. Frankfurt: [Schumacher], 1690. [English translation: *The Two Natures in Christ*. Translated by J. A. O. Preus. Chemnitz's Works 6. St. Louis: Concordia Publishing House, 1971.]

———. *Enchiridion de praecipuis capitibus doctrinae coelestis*. Leipzig: [Steinmann], 1588. [English translation: *Ministry, Word, and Sacraments: An Enchiridion*. Translated by Luther Poellot. Chemnitz's Works 5. St. Louis: Concordia Publishing House, 2008.]

———. *Examen Concilii Tridentini*. Edited by Eduard Preuss. Berlin: [Schumacher], 1861. [English translation: *The Examination of the Council of Trent*. Translated by Fred Kramer. Chemnitz's Works 1–4. St. Louis: Concordia Publishing House, 1971–86.]

———. *Fundamenta sanae doctrinae de vera et substantiali praesentia, exhibitione et sumptione corporis et sanguinis Domini in coena*. Frankfurt: [Schumacher], 1690.

———. *Repetitio sanae doctrinae de vera praesentia corporis et sanguinis Domini in coena*. Leipzig: [Constantiensis], 1561.

Chytraeus, David. *Epistolae*. Hanover: [Aubrii], 1614.

Cleve, Fredric. *Luthers nattvardslära: Mot bakgrunden av Gabriel Biels uppfattning av nattvard och sakrament*. Acta Academiae Aboensis, Humaniora. Humanistiska Vetenskaper, Socialvetenskaper, Teologi 35. Åbo: [Åbo Akademi], 1968.

Cnattingius, Hans. "Nicolaus Bothniensis' teser om Skriften 1584 och Uppsala mötes beslut." *Kyrkohistorisk Årsskrift* (1937).

Codex Goth. 123. Fols. 425, 429 (microfilm). Staatsbibliothek, Gotha.

Concordia: Christliche Widerholete, einmütige Bekenntnüs. Tübingen: [Gruppenbach], 1580.

Concordia: Christliche widerholete, einmütige Bekentnis. Leipzig, 1622.

Concordia: Christliche Widerholete, einmütige Bekentnüs. Dresden: [Bergen & Stöckel], 1580.

Concordia: Christliche Widerholete, einmütige Bekentnüs. Dresden: [Bergen & Stöckel], 1581.

Concordia Pia. Leipzig: [Deffner], 1584.

Concordia Pia. Leipzig: [Gross], 1626.

Concordia Pia. Leipzig: [Gross], 1719.

Damerau, Rudolf. *Die Abendmahlslehre des Nominalismus insbesondere die des Gabriel Biel.* Studien zu den Grundlagen der Reformation 1. Giessen: [Schmitz, 1964].

De libro concordiae . . . Admonitio. Neustadt: [Harnisch], 1581.

De Waal, Anton. *Die Verklärung auf Thabor in Liturgie und Kunst: Geschichte und Leben.* Frankfurter Zeitgemässe Broschüren, n.s. 31. Hamm (Westf.): [Breer & Thiemann], 1912.

Deferrari, Roy J., and M. Inviolata Barry. *A Lexicon of St. Thomas Aquinas Based on The Summa Theologica and Selected Passages of His Other Works.* Washington, DC: [Catholic University of America Press], 1948–49.

Degering, Hermann, ed. *Luthers Randbemerkungen zu Gabriel Biels Collectorium in quattuor libros sententiarum und zu dessen sacri canonis missae expositio, Lyon, 1514.* Weimar: [Böhlau], 1933.

Dictionnaire de théologie catholique. 15 volumes in 29. Paris, 1909–.

Die symbolischen Bücher der Evangelisch-Lutherischen Kirche. Edited by J. T. Müller. Third edition. Stuttgart: [Liesching], 1868.

Dieckhoff, August Wilhelm. *Die evangelische Abendmahlslehre im Reformationszeitalter.* Göttingen: [Vandenhoeck & Ruprect], 1854.

Diestelmann, Jürgen. "Der Fall Besserer." *Lutherische Blätter* 17, no. 84 (1965).

———. "Die Behandlung der *Reliquiae Sacramenti*: Sanct Athanasius XCIX, Brüdern Rundbrief für Christen Augsburgischen Bekenntnisses." *Theologisches Beiblatt* 14, nos. 39, 44, 52 (Braunschweig).

———. *Konsekration: Luthers Abendmahlsglaube in dogmatisch-liturgischer Sicht.* Luthertum 22. Berlin: [Lutherisches Verlagshaus], 1960.

———. *Luthers Lehre von Konsekration und actio sacramentalis.* Alfershausen, 1969. (Mimeograph.)

Dix, Gregory. *The Shape of Liturgy.* London: [Dacre], 1947.

Dorner, Isaak August. *Entwicklungsgeschichte der Lehre von der Person Christi von den ältesten Zeiten bis auf die Neueste.* Second edition. Berlin: [Schlawitz], 1853–54.

Douglass, E. Jane Dempsey. *Justification in Late Medieval Preaching: A Study of John Geiler of Keisersberg.* Edited by Heiko A. Oberman. Studies in Medieval and Reformation Thought 1. Leiden: [Brill], 1966.

Eber, Paul. *Vom heiligen Sacrament des Leibes und Blutes unseres Herrn Jesu Christi.* Wittenberg: [G. Rhau], 1563.

Eck, Johannes. *Enchiridion locorum communium adversus Lutherum et alios hostes ecclesiae.* Ingolstadt: [Weissenhorn], 1549.

Elert, Werner. *Der christliche Glaube: Grundlinien der lutherischen Dogmatik.* Second edition. Berlin: [Furche], 1941.

———. *Morphologie des Luthertums.* 2 volumes. Munich: [Beck], 1952–53. [English translation: *The Structure of Lutheranism.* Translated by Walter A. Hansen. St. Louis: Concordia Publishing House, 1962.]

———. "Wirkungen der lutherischen Abendmahlslehre in der Geschichte der Weltanschauung." *Allgemeine Evangelisch-Lutherische Kirchenzeitung* 60 (1927).

Enchiridion geistlicher gesenge . . . Wittenberg: [Lufft], 1526.

Enchiridion oder ein handbüchlein . . . Nürnberg: [Hergot], 1525.

Enciclopedia cattolica. Ente per l'Enciclopedia Cattolica e per il Libro Cattolico Città del Vaticano, 1949–54.

Enciclopedia universal ilustrada europeo-americana. Madrid and Barcelona, [1905–]33.

Fagerberg, Holsten. *Die Theologie der lutherischen Bekenntnisschriften von 1529 bis 1537.* Göttingen: [Vandenhoeck & Ruprecht], 1965. [English translation: *A New Look at the Lutheran Confessions.* Translated by Gene J. Lund. St. Louis: Concordia Publishing House, 1972.]

Fendt, Leonhard. *Der lutherische Gottesdienst des 16. Jahrhunderts: Sein Werden und sein Wachsen.* Aus der Welt christlicher Frömmigkeit 5. Munich: [Reinhardt], 1923.

Flacius, Matthias Illyricus. *Omnes libelli Mathiae Fl. Illyrici, hactenus in sacramentaria controversia editi.* [Frankfurt am Main: Braubach], 1567.

Fortescue, Adrian. *The Mass: A Study of the Roman Liturgy.* London: [Longmans, Green & Co.], 1917.

Fortgesetzte sammlung von Alten und Neuen Theologischen Sachen (1745).

Fraenkel, Peter. "Ten Questions concerning Melanchthon, the Fathers and the Eucharist." In *Luther und Melanchthon: Referate und Berichte des Zweiten Internationalen Kongresses für Lutherforschung, Münster, 8–13 August 1960.* Edited by Vilmos Vajta. Göttingen: [Vandenhoeck & Ruprecht], 1961.

Frank, Franz H. R. von. *Die Theologie der Concordienformel.* 4 volumes. Erlangen: [Blaesing], 1858–65.

Freytag, Hermann. "Die Beziehungen Danzigs zu Wittenberg in der Zeit der Reformation." *Zeitschrift des westpreussischen Geschichtsvereins* 38 [Danzig] (1898).

Fricke, Otto. *Die Christologie des Johannes Brenz im Zusammenhang mit der Lehre vom Abendmahl und der Rechtfertigung.* Forschungen zur Geschichte und Lehre des Protestantismus 1.3. Munich: [Kaiser], 1927.

Furberg, Ingemar. *Das Pater Noster in der Messe.* Bibliotheca Theologiae Practicae [21]. Lund: [Gleerup], 1968.

Geistliche Lieder . . . Leipzig, 1539.

Gennrich, Paul-Wilhelm. *Die Christologie Luthers im Abendmahlsstreit 1524–1529.* Königsberg: [Kümmel], 1929.

George III of Anhalt. *De ritu apostolico ordinationis.* Leipzig: [Rhamba], 1579.

———. *Die Vierdte Predigt vom hochwirdigen Sacrament.* Leipzig: [Günther], 1551.

———. *Reverendissimi et illustrissimi principis ac Domini: Domini Georgii Principis Anhaltini . . . Conciones et scripta complectentia summam verae doctrinae.* Wittenberg: [Schwenck], 1570.

———. *Reverendissimi et illustrissimi principis et Domini, Domini Georgij Principis Anhaltini ac vere Episcopi, Sententiae, de controversis quibusdam articulis.* Leipzig, 1579. (Printed together with *De ritu apostolico ordinationis.*)

Gerhard, Johann. *Loci theologici.* Geneva, 1639.

"Geschichte der Elevation bei der Feier des h. Abendmahls, besonders in der Nürnbergischen Kirche." Edited by Georg Ernst Waldau. *Vermischte Beyträge zur Geschichte der stadt Nürnberg* 2, no. 14. Nürnberg, 1787.

Geystlike leder . . . Magdeburg: [Walther], 1534.

Geystlike leder . . . Magdeburg: [Walther], 1543.

Gilson, Etienne, and Philotheus Böhner. *Die Geschichte der christlichen Philosophie.* Paderborn: [Schöningh], 1936–37.

Goetzius, Georg Heinrich. *Elogia germanorum . . . Collectore . . . Goetzio 1–2.* Lübeck, 1708–9.

Gollwitzer, Helmut. *Coena Domini: Die altlutherische Abendmahlslehre in ihrer Auseinandersetzung mit dem Calvinismus, dargestellt an der lutherischen Frühorthodoxie.* Munich: [Kaiser], 1937.

Götz, Johann B. *Die Erste Einführung des Kalvinismus in der Oberpfalz 1559–1576.* Reformationsgeschichtliche Studien und Texte 60. [Münster: Aschendorff], 1933.

Graff, Paul. *Geschichte der Auflösung der alten gottesdienstlichen Formen in der evangelischen Kirche Deutschlands.* Volume 1: *Bis zum Eintritt der Aufklärung und des Rationalismus.* Second edition. Göttingen: [Vandenhoeck & Ruprecht], 1937.

Grane, Leif. *Contra Gabrielem: Luthers Auseinandersetzung mit Gabriel Biel in der Disputatio Contra Scholasticam Theologiam 1517*. Acta Theologica Danica 4. Copenhagen: [Gyldendal], 1962.

———. "Om Luthers anvendelse af den middelalderlige tradition i De captivitate Babylonica." In *Evangelium og sakramente: Studier i Luthers De captivitate Babylonica: Festskrift til K. E. Skydsgaard*. Copenhagen: [Busck], 1962.

Grass, Hans. *Die Abendmahlslehre bei Luther und Calvin: Eine Kritische Untersuchung*. Beiträge zur Förderung christlicher Theologie 2. Sammlung wissenschaftlicher Monographien 47. Gütersloh: [Bertelsmann], 1954.

———. "Die Arnoldshainer Thesen und die lutherische Abendmahlslehre." In *Lehrgespräch über das Heilige Abendmahl: Stimmen und Studien zu den Arnoldshainer Thesen*. Edited by Gottfried Niemeier. Munich: [Kaiser], 1961.

———. "Die Arnoldshainer Thesen und die lutherische Abendmahlslehre." *Neue Zeitschrift für systematische Theologie* 2, no. 1 (1960).

Grillmeier, Alois, and Heinrich Bacht, eds. *Das Konzil von Chalkedon: Geschichte und Gegenwart*. Würzburg: [Echter], 1951.

Grönvik, Lorenz. *Die Taufe in der Theologie Martin Luthers*. Acta Academiae Aboensis A, 36.1. Åbo: [Åbo Akademie], 1968.

Grünwald, Johannes. "Zur Ontologie der Realpräsenz." In *Lutherische Abendmahlslehre heute*. [Edited by Hans Wenschkewitz.] Göttingen: [Vandenhoeck & Ruprecht], 1960.

Gundermann, Iselin. *Untersuchungen zum Gebetbüchlein der Herzogin Dorothea von Preussen*. Wissenschaftliche Abhandlungen der Arbeitsgemeinschaft für Forschung des Landes Nordrhein-Westfalen 36. Cologne: [Westdeutscher Verlag], 1966.

Hachenburg, Johann. *Vom anbeten des Sacraments / dazu vom ubriegen / unnd niderfallen Sacrament im Abendmal des Herrn Christi / Declaration / M. Joannis Hachenburg. Aus den Büchern des Ehr. D. Martini Lutheri seliger gedechtnis / fleissig und rein zusamen getragen*. An den Landgraffen zu Hessen etc. s.1., 1561.

———. *Wider den jrrthumb der newen zwinglianer / nötige unterrichtung /*. Erfurt: [Dolgen], 1557.

Hahn, Fritz. "Faber Stapulensis und Luther." *Zeitschrift für Kirchengeschichte* 57, no. 3–4 (1938).

Hardt, Tom. "Dette är min lekamen. Rec. av Hermann Sasse: *This is my body*, Minneapolis 1959." *Kyrklig Förnyelse* 1, no. 12 (1960).

Harnack, Theodosius. *Luthers Theologie*. 2 volumes. New edition. Munich: [Kaiser], 1927.

Hartknoch, Christophorus. *Preussische Kirchen-Historia*. Frankfurt am Main and Leipzig: [Beckenstein], 1686.

Hartmann, Julius, and Karl Jäger. *Johann Brenz: Nach gedruckten und ungedruckten Quellen*. 2 volumes. Hamburg: [Perthes], 1840–42.

Hartmann, Philipp. *Repertorium Rituum*. Fourteenth edition. Paderborn: [Schöningh], 1940.

Hase, Karl Alfred von. *Herzog Albrecht von Preussen und seine Hofprediger: Eine Königsberger Tragödie aus dem Zeitalter der Reformation*. Leipzig: [Breitkopf & Härtel], 1879.

———. *Libri symbolici [ecclesiae evangelicae sive concordia]*. Leipzig: [Breitkopf & Härtel], 1846.

Hassler, Karin. "Luther och elevationen i nattvardsmässan." *Kyrklig Förnyelse* 1, no. 12 (1960).

Headley, John M. *Luther's View of Church History*. Yale Publications in Religion 6. New Haven: [Yale University Press], 1963.

Heiler, Friedrich. *Urkirche und Ostkirche*. Die Katholische Kirche des Ostens und Westens 1. Munich: [Reinhardt], 1937.

Hellström, Olle. *Elevationsstriden och enighetsförbundet efter Uppsala möte 1593: Några synpunkter på prästerskapets ställning från Uppsala möte till Arboga riksdag*. Kyrkohistorisk Årsskrift 42. Årsg, 1942.

Henry VIII. *Assertio septem sacramentorum adversus Martinum Lutherum, aedita ab invictissimo Angliae o. Franciae rege, & do. Hyberniae Henrico eius nominis octavo*. 1521.

Heppe, Heinrich. *Geschichte des deutschen Protestantismus*. 4 volumes. Marburg: [Elwert], 1852–59.

Herrlinger, Albert. *Die Theologie Melanchthons in ihrer geschichtlichen Entwicklung und im Zusammenhange mit der Lehrgeschichte und Culturbewegung der Reformation*. Gotha: [Perthes], 1879.

Heshusius, Tilemann. *Responsio . . . ad praeiudicium Philippi Melanchthonis de controversia Coenae Domini*. s.l., 1560 (Strassburg).

Hof, Otto. "Taufe und Heilswerk Christi bei Luther." In *Zur Auferbauung des Leibes Christi: Festgabe für Professor Dr. Peter Brunner*. Kassel: [Stauda], 1965.

Hollaz, David. *Examen Theologicum Acroamaticum*. Stockholm and Leipzig, 1725.

Holte, Ragnar. "Luthersk nattvardslära i ljuset av nyare exegetik och patristik." In *Välsignelsens Kalk: Predikningar och Föredrag hållna vid Kyrklig Förnyelses Kyrkodagar kring Nattvarden i Uppsala, 1961*. Edited by Eric Segelberg. Saltsjöbaden, 1962.

Hoogland, Marvin P. *Calvin's Perspective on the Exaltation of Christ in Comparison with the Post-Reformation Doctrine of the Two States*. Akademisch Proefschrift. Kampen: [Kok], 1966.

Huhnke, Hans-Joachim. "An den Oberkirchenrat der Ev.-Luth. Landeskirche Mecklenburgs, Schwerin i. M. den 11 November 1961." *Information der Lutherischen Bruderkreise Deutschlands* 21, no. 25 (January 1962) (mimeograph).

———. "Realpräsenz und Konsekration: Ein Beitrag zu Zentralpunkten lutherischer Abendmahlslehre. Sanct Athanasius. Brüdern Rundbrief Christen

Augsburgischen Bekenntnisses." *Theologisches Beiblatt* 15, no. 31 (June 28, 1964).

Hülsemann, Johann. *Calixtinischer Gewissenswurm*. Leipzig: [Ritz], 1653.

Hunzinger, August Wilhelm. "Luthers Neoplatonismus in der Psalmenvorlesung von 1513 bis 1515." In volume 1 of *Lutherstudien*. Leipzig: [Deichert], 1906.

Hutter, Leonhard. *Concordia concors*. Wittenberg: [Berger], 1614.

Illustrissimi principis . . . Iohannis Friderici Secundi Confutatio . . . Jena: [Rebart], 1559.

Ingebrand, Sven. *Olaus Petris reformatoriska åskådning*. Studia Doctrinae Christianae Upsaliensia I. [Lund: Gleerup,] 1964.

Iserloh, Erwin. *Die Eucharistie in der Darstellung des Johannes Eck: Ein Beitrag zur vortridentinischen Kontroverstheologie über das Messopfer*. Reformationsgeschichtliche Studien und Texte 73/74. Münster: [Aschendorff], 1950.

———. *Gnade und Eucharistie in der philosophischen Theologie des Wilhelm von Ockham: Ihre Bedeutung für die Ursachen der Reformation*. Edited by Joseph Lortz. Veröffentlichungen des Instituts für europäische Geschichte Mainz 8. Abteilung für abendländische Religionsgeschichte. Wiesbaden: [Steiner], 1956.

Jacoby, Hermann. *Die Liturgik der Reformatoren*. Volume 1: *Liturgik Luthers*. Gotha: [Perthes], 1871.

Jannasch, Wilhelm. *Geschichte des lutherischen Gottesdienstes in Lübeck von den Anfängen der Reformation bis zum Ende des Niedersächsischen als Gottesdienstlichesprache*. Gotha: [Klotz], 1928.

Jorissen, Hans. *Die Entfaltung der Transsubstantiationslehre bis zum Beginn der Hochscholastik*. Münsterische Beiträge zur Theologie 28.1. Münster: [Aschendorff], 1965.

Josefson, Ruben. "Luthersk nattvardsuppfattning." In *En bok om kyrkan av svenska teologer*. Lund, 1942.

Junghans, Helmar. *Ockham im Lichte der neueren Forschung*. Arbeiten zur Geschichte und Theologie des Luthertums 21. Berlin: [Lutherisches Verlagshaus], 1968.

Jungmann, Josef Andreas. *Missarum sollemnia: Eine genetische Erklärung der römischen Messe*. 2 volumes. Wien: [Herder], 1948.

Karlstadt, Andreas. *Dialogus oder ein gesprechbüchlein von dem grewlichen unnd abgöttischen missbrauch / des hochwirdigsten sacraments Jesu Christi*. [Basel: Cratander], 1524.

Kattenbusch, F. "Luthers Idee zur Konsubstantiation im Abendmahl." In [*Forschungen zur Kirchengeschichte und zur christlichen Kunst: Johannes Ficker am 12. November 1931 als Festgabe*.] Edited by Walter Elliger. Leipzig: [Dieterich], 1931.

Kawerau, Gustav. "Der Streit über die *Reliquiae Sacramenti* in Eisleben 1543." *Zeitschrift für Kirchengeschichte* 33, [1912].

———. "Ein Beitrag zur Geschichte der lutherischen Lehre von der Konsekration im 16. Jahrhundert." *Zeitschrift für Pastoraltheologie* (1902).

———. *Johann Agricola von Eisleben: Ein Beitrag zur Reformationsgeschichte.* Berlin: [Hertz], 1881.

———. "Über die liturgische Gestaltung der 'Konsekration' in der lutherischen Abendmahlsfeier." *Theologische Studien und Kritiken* 69 (1896).

———. "Zum lutherischen Konsekrationsbegriff." *Zeitschrift für praktische Theologie* 21 (1899).

Kirchner, Timotheus, Nicolaus Selnecker, and Martin Chemnitz. *Histori des Sacramentsstreits.* s.l., 1591.

———. *Solida ac vera confessionis Augustanae historia.* Leipzig: [Deffner], 1585. (= Latin translation of *Histori dess Sacramentsstreits.*)

Kirsten, Hans. "Einige Ergänzungen 'zur lutherischen Lehre von der Konsekration.'" *Lutherische Blätter* 7, no. 41 (1955).

Kjöllerström, Sven. *Striden kring kalvinismen i Sverige under Erik XIV: En kyrkohistorisk studie.* Lunds Universitets Årsskrift 31.5. Lund: [Gleerup], 1935.

Köhler, Walter. *Das Marburger Religionsgespräch: Versuch einer Rekonstruktion.* Schriften des Vereins für Reformationsgeschichte 48.1 (no. 148). Leipzig: Eger & Sievers, 1929.

———. *Zwingli und Luther: Ihr Streit über das Abendmahl nach seinen politischen und religiösen Beziehungen.* Quellen und Forschungen zur Reformationsgeschichte 6–7. Leipzig: Heinsius, 1924; Gütersloh: Bertelsmann, 1953.

Kolde, Theodor. *Analecta lutherana: Briefe und Actenstücke zur Geschichte Luthers: Zugleich ein Supplement zu den bisherigen Sammlungen seines Briefwechsels.* Gotha: [Perthes], 1883.

Koopmans, Jan. *Das altkirchliche Dogma in der Reformation.* Edited by E. Wolf. Beiträge zur evangelischen Theologie 22. Munich: [Kaiser], 1955.

Köstlin, Julius. *Luthers Theologie.* 2 volumes in 1. New edition. Stuttgart: [Steinkopf], 1901. [English translation of earlier edition: *The Theology of Luther in Its Historical Development and Inner Harmony.* 2 volumes. Philadelphia: Lutheran Publication Society, 1897.]

———. *Martin Luther: Sein Leben und seine Schriften.* 2 volumes in 1. New edition. Elberfeld: [Friderichs], 1883. [English translation: *The Life of Martin Luther.* Philadelphia: Lutheran Publication Society, 1883.]

Kötz, Gustav. *Beiträge zur Quellenkunde der Danziger Kirchengeschichte.* Progymnasium zu Neumark Wpr. Beilage zum Bericht über das Schuljahr 1900. Neumark Wpr.: [Koepke], 1901.

———. *Die Danziger Konkordienformel über das Heilige Abendmahl, Notel genannt, und ihre Apologia (1561–1567).* Königsberg: [Jaeger], 1901.

Krauth, Charles P. *The Conservative Reformation and Its Theology: As Represented in the Augsburg Confession, and in the History and Literature of the Evangelical Lutheran Church*. Philadelphia: [Lippincott & Co.], 1871.

Kromayer, Hieronymus. *Theologia positivo-polemica*. 2 volumes. Leipzig, 1707.

Kühne, Gerold. "Die Substanzfrage beim Abendmahl." *Pastoralblätter* 106 (1966) (Stuttgart).

Kurtz Bekenntnis und Artickel vom heiligen Abendmahl. Wittenberg: [Lufft], 1574.

Landgraf, Arthur Michael. *Dogmengeschichte der Frühscholastik* 2/1–3/2. Regensburg: [Friedrich Pustet], 1953–55.

Laurentius Petri. "De quibusdam Articulis, ad Sacramentum coenae dominicae pertinentibus 1566." In *Skrifter och handlingar til uplysning i svenska kyrko och reformations historien*. Utg. av U.v. Troil 3. Uppsala: [Edman], 1791.

———. *Dialogus om then förwandling, som medh messone skedde*. Wittenberg: [Schleich], 1542.

———. *Om någor stycker wårs Herras Jesu Christi nattward anrörandes Dialogus*. Stockholm, 1562.

———. *Refutatio erroris Herbesti de consecratione sacramenti eucharistici*. Hamburg: [Henricus Ginderus], 1588.

———. *Responsio Laurentij Petri Nericij Archiep. Upsal. ad scriptum Dionijsij Beurrei* . . . / Linköpings Stiftsbibliotek, T 235, bl 1 a — 68 (Photocopy.)

Lerle, E. *Die neutestamentliche Raumvorstellung*. Berlin, 1955.

Link, Wilhelm. *Das Ringen Luthers um die Freiheit der Theologie von der Philosophie*. Edited by Ernst Wolf and Manfred Mezger. Second edition. Munich: [Kaiser], 1955.

Liturgia svecanae ecclesiae catholicae et orthodoxae conformis (Johan III's *Red Book*). Stockholm, 1575. Facsimile edition, Malmö, 1953.

Lohse, Bernhard. *Ratio und fides: Eine Untersuchung über die ratio in der Theologie Luthers*. Forschungen zur Kirchen- und Dogmengeschichte 8. Göttingen: [Vandenhoeck & Ruprecht], 1958.

Loofs, Friedrich. *Leitfaden zum Studium der Dogmengeschichte*. Volume 2. Halle (Saale): [Niemeyer], 1953.

Löscher, Valentin Ernst. *Ausführliche Historia Motuum zwischen den Evangelisch-Lutherischen und Reformirten*. Frankfurt and Leipzig: [Gross], [1723].

Luther, Martin. "Luthers Arbeiten an der Übersetzung und Auslegung des Propheten Daniel in den Jahren 1530 und 1541." [Translated] by Otto Albrecht. *Archiv für Reformationsgeschichte* 23 (1926).

Mahlmann, Theodor. *Das neue Dogma der lutherischen Christologie: Problem und Geschichte seiner Begründung*. Gütersloh: [Gütersloher], 1969.

Mansi, Joannes Dominicus, ed. *Sacrorum conciliorum nova et amplissima collectio*. Paris: [Welter], 1901–27.

Massa, Willi. *Die Eucharistiepredigt am Vorabend der Reformation: Eine material-kerygmatische Untersuchung zum Glaubensverständnis von Altarsakrament und Messe am Beginn des 16. Jahrhunderts als Beitrag zur Geschichte der Predigt.* Veröffentlichungen des Missionspriesterseminars St. Augustin, Siegburg 15. [St. Augustin:] Steyler, 1966.

Maurach, Gregor. *Coelum empyreum: Versuch einer Begriffsgeschichte.* Boethius: Texte und Abhandlungen zur Geschichte der exakten Wissenschaften 8. Wiesbaden: [Steiner], 1968.

Maurer, Wilhelm. *Der Junge Melanchthon zwischen Humanismus und Reformation.* Volume 2: *Der Theologe.* Göttingen: [Vandenhoeck & Ruprecht], 1969.

McLelland, Joseph. "Lutheran-Reformed Debate on the Eucharist and Christology." In *Marburg Revisited: A Reexamination of Lutheran and Reformed Traditions.* Edited by Paul C. Empie and James I. McCord. Minneapolis: [Augsburg], 1966.

Meinhold, Peter. *Die Genesisvorlesung Luthers und ihre Herausgeber.* Forschungen zur Kirchen- und Geistesgeschichte 8. Stuttgart: [Kohlhammer], 1936.

———. *Luthers Sprachphilosophie.* Berlin: [Lutherisches Verlagshaus], 1958.

Meister, Karl Severin. *Das katholische deutsche Kirchenlied in seinen Singweisen von den frühesten Zeiten bis gegen Ende des siebzehnten Jahrhunderts.* Auf Grund älterer Handschriften und gedruckter Quellen 1. Freiburg im Breisgau: [Herder], 1862.

Melartopeus, P. *P. Melartopeus' herdabrev till Åbo stifts prästerskap 1595.* Kyrkohistorisk Årsskrift, 1904.

Metzke, Erwin. *Sakrament und Metaphysik: Eine Lutherstudie über das Verhältnis des christlichen Denkens zum leiblich-materiellen.* Lebendige Wissenschafte 9. Edited by D. Hans Friherrn von Campenhausen. Stuttgart: [Kreuz], 1948.

Meyer, Hans Bernhard. "Die Elevation im deutschen Mittelalter und bei Luther." *Zeitschrift für Katholische Theologie* 85 (1963).

———. *Luther und die Messe: Eine liturgiewissenschaftliche Untersuchung über das Verhältnis Luthers zum Messwesen des späten Mittelalters.* Konfessionskundliche und kontroverstheologische Studien 11. Edited by Johann-Adam-Möhler-Institut. Paderborn: [Bonafacius], 1955.

Montgomery, John Warwick. *Chytraeus on Sacrifice: A Reformation Treatise in Biblical Theology. David Chytraeus' "De Sacrificiis" of 1569.* St. Louis: [Concordia Publishing House], 1962.

Morgenstern, Benedict. *Widerlegung der Notel / damit die Sacramentirer zu Dantzig / jhren Irrthumb und Verfolgung / verkleistern und bedecken wollen / und die arme Kirche daselbst / höchlich drucken und beschweren / . . .* Eisleben: [Petri], 1567.

Mücke, H. "Luthers Abendmahlslehre bis 1522 im Zusammenhang mit seiner reformatorischen Entwicklung und mit der Abendmahlslehre dar Scholastik." *Theologische Studien und Kritiken* 3 (1873) (Gotha).

Müller, Nikolaus. "Beziehungen zwischen den Kurfürsten Joachim I. und II. von Brandenburg und dem Fürsten Georg III. vom Anhalt in den Jahren 1534–40." *Jahrbuch für Brandenburgische Kirchengeschichte* [4] (1907).

———. "Zur Geschichte des Gottesdienstes der Domkirche zu Berlin [in den Jahren 1540–1598]." *Jahrbuch für Brandenburgische Kirchengeschichte* [2/3] (1906).

———. [ed.] *Die Wittenberger Bewegung 1521 und 1522.* Second edition. Leipzig: [Heinsius], 1911.

Musculus, Andreas. *Precandi formulae piae et selectae, ex veterum doctorum scriptis purissime congestae, ac in locus 20. orandi, tam pro rebus spiritualibus quam corporalibus, ordine suo digestae.* Stettin: [Eichorn], 1570.

———. *Precationes ex veteribus orthodoxis doctoribus: Ex ecclesiae hymnis et canticis: Ex psalmis denique Dauidis collectae: Et nunc recens recognitae &c actae.* Leipzig, 1592.

———. *Propositiones de vera, reali et substantiale praesentia, Corporis &c Sanguinis Jesu Christi in Sacramento Altaris.* Frankfurt an der Oder: [Eichorn], 1573.

Neuser, Wilhelm H. *Die Abendmahlslehre Melanchthons in ihrer geschichtlichen Entwicklung (1519–1530).* Beiträge zur Geschichte und Lehre der Reformierten Kirche 26 Melanchthon-Studien 2. Neukirchen: [Neukirchener], 1968.

Niemeyer, August Hermann. *Collectio Confessionum.* Leipzig: [Klinkhardt], 1840.

Nilsson, Kjell Ove. *Simul: Das Miteinander von Göttlichem und Menschlichem in Luthers Theologie.* Forschungen zur Kirchen- und Dogmengeschichte 17. Göttingen: [Vandenhoeck & Ruprecht], 1966.

Nordisk teologisk uppslagsbok för kyrka och skola. Volume 2. Lund: [Gleerup], 1955.

Noth, Gottfried. *Grundzüge der Theologie des Martin Chemnitz.* Erlangen: [Gutenberg (Reinhold & Limmert)], 1930.

Nyman, Helge. *Kyrkotjänarens nattvardsgång i lutherskt gudstjänstliv.* Acta Academiae Aboensis. Åbo: [Åbo Akademi], 1955.

Olsson, H. "Den naturliga gudskunskapens problem enligt den senmedeltida nominalismen." *Svensk Teologisk Kvartalskrift* (1950).

Pedersen, E. Thestrup. *Luther som skriftfortolker.* En studie i Luthers skriftsyn, hermeneutik og eksegese 1. Copenhagen: [Nordisk Forlag Anrold Busck], 1959.

Pedersen, Olaf. *Medeltidens världsbild, Astronomi och kultur under medeltiden.* Stockholm: [Wahlström & Widstrand], 1970.

Pelzer, A. "Les 51 articles de Guillaume Occam censurés en Avignon en 1326." *Revue d'histoire ecclésiastique* [18] (1922).

Persson, Per Erik. *Sacra doctrina: En studie till förhållandet mellan ratio och revelatio i Thomas' av Aquino teologi.* Studia theologica lundensia 15. Lund: [Gleerup], 1957.

Peter Lombard. *Libri IV sententiarum*. Studio et cura PP. Collegii S. Bonaventurae in lucem editi. Second edition. Ad Claras Aquas near Florence, 1916.

Peters, Albrecht. *Realpräsenz: Luthers Zeugnis von Christi Gegenwart im Abendmahl*. Arbeiten zur Geschichte und Theologie des Luthertums 5. Berlin: [Lutherisches Verlagshaus], 1960.

———. "Zur Kritik an den Abendmahlsthesen von Amoldshain." *Neue Zeitschrift für systematische Theologie [und Religionsphilosophie]* 2 (1960).

Peters, Edward Frederick. *The Origin and Meaning of the Axiom: "Nothing Has the Character of a Sacrament Outside of the Use," in Sixteenth-Century Lutheran Theology*. ThD thesis, Concordia Seminary, St. Louis, Mo., May 1968. (typewritten-microfilm)

Pieper, Francis. *Christliche Dogmatik*. Volumes 2–3. St. Louis: [Concordia Publishing House], 1917–20. [English translation: *Christian Dogmatics*. Translated by Theodore Engelder et al. St. Louis: Concordia Publishing House, 1951, 1968.]

Planck, [Gottlieb J.]. *Geschichte der Protestantischen Theologie von Luthers Tod bis zu der Einführung der Concordienformel: Geschichte der Entstehung, der Veränderungen und der Bildung unsers protestantischen Lehrbegriffs vom Anfange der Reformation bis zur Einführung der Concordienformel* 4–6. Second edition. Leipzig; [Crusius], 1801.

Prenter, Regin. *Kyrkans tro: Kristen troslära för lekmän*. [Original Danish title: *Kirkens tro: En kristen laere for lægfolk*. Swedish translation by Frithiof Dahlby. Stockholm, 1966. English translation: *The Church's Faith: A Primer of Christian Beliefs*. Translated by Theodor I. Jensen. Philadelphia: Fortress, 1968.]

———. *Skabelse og genløsning: Dogmatik*. Second edition. Copenhagen: [Gad], 1955. [English translation: *Creation and Redemption*. Translated by Theodor I. Jensen. Philadelphia: Fortress, 1967.]

———. *Spiritus Creator: Studier i Luthers theologi*. Copenhagen, 1944. [English translation: *Spiritus Creator*. Translated by John M. Jensen. Philadelphia: Muhlenberg, 1953.]

Pressel, Theodor, ed. *Anecdota Brentiana: Ungedruckte Briefe und Bedenken von Johannes Brenz*. Tübingen: [Heckenhauer], 1868.

Rahner, Karl. "Die Gegenwart Christi im Sakrament des Herrenmahles nach dem katholischen Bekenntnis im Gegenüber zum evangelisch-lutherischen Bekenntnis." In Thomas Sartory, *Die Eucharistie im Verständnis der Konfessionen*. Recklingshausen: [Paulus], 1961.

Religionssachen: Handlung zwischen den theologen und predigern zu Rostock und Herrn J. Saliger 1569. Staatsarchiv Schwerin. (Microfilm).

Rettberg, Fr. W. "Occam und Luther, oder Vergleich ihrer Lehren vom heiligen Abendmahl." *[Theologische] Studien und Kritiken* 12 (1839).

Richter, Aemelius Ludwig. *Die evangelischen Kirchenordnungen des sechszehnten Jahrhunderts*. Weimar: Verlag des Landes-Industriecomptoirs, 1846.

Rietschel, Georg. *Lehrbuch der Liturgik*. 2 volumes. Berlin: [Reuther & Reichard], 1900–1909.

Ritschl, Otto. *Dogmengeschichte des Protestantismus: Grundlagen und Grundzüge der theologischen Gadanken- und Lehrbildung in den protestantischen Kirchen*. 4 volumes. Leipzig: [Hinrichs], 1908; Göttingen: [Vandenhoeck & Ruprecht], 1927.

Rocholl, Rudolf. *Die Realpräsenz: Das Lehrstück von der Gegenwart des Herrn bei den Seinen: Ein Beitrag zur Christologie*. Gütersloh: [Bertelsmann], 1875.

Rungius, Jacob. *Confessio Ecclesiarum Pomeraniae, de vera praesentia: Corporis et Sanguinis Domini nostri Jesu Christi in sacramento Coenae*. [Greifswald: Ferber,] 1582.

Salig, Christian August. *Vollständige Historie der Augsburgischen Confession*. Volume 3. Halle: [Renger], 1735.

Sasse, Hermann. "Das Abendmahl im Neuen Testament." In *Vom Sakrament des Altars: Lutherische Beiträge zur Frage des heiligen Abendmahls*. Edited by Hermann Sasse. Leipzig: [Dörffling & Franke], 1941. [English translation: "The Lord's Supper in the New Testament." In *We Confess Anthology*. Part 2: *The Sacraments*. Translated by Norman Nagel. St. Louis: Concordia Publishing House, 1999.]

———. *This Is My Body: Luther's Contention for the Real Presence in the Sacrament of the Altar*. Minneapolis: [Augsburg], 1959.

———. "Zum Ergebnis des 'Abendmahlsgespräche der Evangelischen Kirche in Deutschland 1947–1957.'" *Lutherische Blätter* 10 (1958).

———. "Zum lutherischen Verständnis der Konsekration." *Briefe an lutherische Pastoren* 26 (July 1952) (mimeograph). [English translation: "The Lutheran Understanding of the Consecration." In *Letters to Lutheran Pastors*. Volume 2. Edited by Matthew C. Harrison. St. Louis: Concordia Publishing House, 2014.]

Schilling, Werner. *Christus unter Brot und Wein: Zur Kritik an den lutherischen Bekenntnissen über das Abendmahl*. Munich: [Claudius], 1960.

Schmaltz, Karl. *Kirchengeschichte Mecklenburgs*. Volume 2. Schwerin: [Bahn], 1936.

Schmid, Heinrich. *Der Kampf der lutherischen Kirche um Luthers Lehre vom Abendmahl im Reformationszeitalter: Im Zusammenhang mit der gesammten Lehrentwicklung dieser Zeit*. Leipzig: [Hinrichs], 1868.

Schöne, Jobst. *Um Christi sakramentale Gegenwart: Der Saligersche Abendmahlsstreit 1568/1569*. Berlin: [Evangelische Verlagsanstalt], 1966.

Schröder, Dieterich. *Kirchen-Historie des Evangelischen Mecklenburgs vom Jahr 1518 bis 1742*. 3 volumes. Rostock: [Müller], 1788–89.

Schwarzenau, Paul. *Der Wandel im theologischen Ansatz bei Melanchthon von 1525–1535*. 1954 (Münster). [Gütersloh: Bertelsmann, 1956].

Seckendorf, Veit Ludwig von. *Historia Lutheranismi*. Leipzig: [Gleditsch], 1694–.

Seeberg, Erich. *Luthers Theologie in ihren Grundzügen*. 2 volumes. Stuttgart: [Kohlhammer], 1937.

Seeberg, Reinhold. *Lehrbuch der Dogmengeschichte*. Volumes 2, 3, 4.1–2. Sixth edition. Stuttgart: [Schwabe], 1960.

Selnecker, Nicolaus. *Christliche warhafftige Widerlegung* (= *Confutatio accusationum*, 1578). Leipzig: [Rambau], 1576.

———. *De ratione methodica: Notatio Nicolai Selneceri De studio sacrae Theologiae*. Leipzig, 1579.

———. *Ein Gesprech vom Heiligen Abendmahl: Geschehen in Lateinischer Sprache / und nu Deutsch verzeichnet*. Leipzig: [Beyer], 1588.

———. *Kurtze Schrifft und Warnung / sich für der Sacramentirer schwarm zu hüten / Auch bericht / wie ein jeder Christ sich in diesen Streit schicken sol / das er sehen könne / wer recht oder unrecht habe*. s.l., 1576.

———. *Necessaria et brevis Repetitio simplicis verae et perspicuae doctrinae de Coena Domini*. Leipzig, 1574. (Quoted from a manuscript copy in Uppsala University Library, bound in volume 49.VIII.4.337 with several printed books, with the inscription "Selnec. Con: Exegesin.")

Solano, Jesús. *Textos eucharisticos primitivos*. 2 volumes. Madrid: [B.A.C.], 1952–54.

Sommerlath, Ernst. "Das Abendmahl bei Luther." In *Vom Sakrament des Altars: Lutherische Beiträge zur Frage des heiligen Abendmahls*. Edited by Hermann Sasse. Leipzig: [Dörffling & Franke], 1941.

Sperber, Erhard. *Christliche und notwendige verantwortung Erhardi Sperbers / wider die grewliche bezichtigung und beschwerliche aufflag der Sacramentirer und Rottengeister zu Dantzig* / . . . Erfurt: [Sachse], 1563.

Spieker, Christian Wilhelm. "Des Johannes Musculus, Pfarrers in der Lebuser Vorstadt zu Frankfurt a.d. Oder, Landesverweisung." *Zeitschrift für die Historische Theologie* 3 (1849).

Starck, Caspar Heinrich. *Lubeca Lutherano-Evangelica, das ist, der Kayserlichen / Freyen / und des Heil. Römischen Reichs Hanse- und Handel-stadt Lübeck Kirchen-Historie*. Hamburg: [Felginer], 1724.

Steinlein, Hermann. "Luthers Anlage zur Bildhaftigkeit." *Lutherjahrbuch* 22 (1940).

Stupperich, Robert von, ed. *Melanchthons Werke in Auswahl*. [*Studienausgabe*.] 4 volumes. Gütersloh: [Gerd Mohn], 1951–65.

Svenska kyrkans bekännelseskrifter. Edited by [Dick] Helander. Uppsala: [Svenska kyrkans diakonistyrelses bokförlag], 1944.

Tappert, Theodore G. "Christology and Lord's Supper in the Perspective of History." In *Marburg Revisited: A Reexamination of Lutheran and Reformed Traditions*. Edited by Paul Empie and James I. McCord. Minneapolis: [Augsburg], 1966.

Thomas à Kempis. *Opera omnia*. Volumen alterum. Freiberg im Breisgau: [Herder], 1904.

Thomas Aquinas. *Die deutsche Thomas-Ausgabe . . . Summa theologica*. Salzburg and Leipzig: [Pustet], 1934–57.

———. *S. Thomas Aquinatis . . . in Evangelia S. Matthaei et S. Joannis commentaria. Tomus secundus. Evangelium secundum Joannem*. Editio IV Taurinensis. Taurini: [Marietti], 1925.

Thulin, Oskar, ed. *Reformation in Europa*. Beratung und Textredaktion Ingetraut Ludolphy. Leipzig: [Kassel], 1967.

Vajta, Vilmos. *Die Theologie des Gottesdienstes bei Luther*. Second revised edition. Göttingen: [Vandenhoeck & Ruprecht], 1954. [English translation: *Luther on Worship: An Interpretation*. Philadelphia: Muhlenberg, 1958.]

Vogelsang, Erich. *Die Anfänge von Luthers Christologie nach der ersten Psalmenvorlesung insbesondere in ihren exegetischen und systematischen Zusammenhängen mit Augustin und der Scholastik dargestellt*. Arbeiten zur Kirchengeschichte 15. [Berlin: de Gruyter,] 1929.

Wagner, James Benjamin. *Ascendit ad coelos: The Doctrine of the Ascension in the Reformed and Lutheran Theology of the Period of Orthodoxy*. Dissertation. Winterthur: [Keller], 1964.

Watterich, Johannes. *Der Konsekrationsmoment im heiligen Abendmahl und seine Geschichte*. Heidelberg: [Winter], 1896.

Westphal, Friedrich. *Zur Erinnerung an Fürst Georg den Gottseligen zu Anhalt*. Schriften des Vereins für Reformationsgeschichte 95. [Leipzig: Brandstetter,] 1907.

Westphal, Joachim. *Apologia confessionis de coena Domini contra corruptelas et calumnias Ioannis Caluini*. Ursellis: [Henricus], 1558.

Wigand, Johann. *De sacramentarijsmo*. Leipzig: [Deffner], 1585.

Wiggers, Julius. "Der Saligersche Abendmahlsstreit." *Zeitschrift für die historische Theologie* [18 (= n.s. 12) (1848)].

Wisløff, Carl Fredrik. *Nattverd og messe: En studie i [Luthers] teologi*. Oslo: [Lutherstiftelsens], 1957.

Zeeden, Ernst Walter. *Martin Luther und die Reformation im Urteil des deutschen Luthertums*. Volume 2: *Dokumente*. Freiburg: [Herder], 1952.